D0335027

HOLOCAUST
A History

ALSO BY DEBÓRAH DWORK AND ROBERT JAN VAN PELT

Auschwitz

ALSO BY DEBÓRAH DWORK

Voices and Views: A History of the Holocaust

Children With A Star: Jewish Youth in Nazi Europe

War is Good for Babies and Other Young Children

ALSO BY ROBERT JAN VAN PELT

The Case for Auschwitz

Architectural Principles in the Age of Historicism

Tempel van de Wereld

HOLOCAUST
A History

Debórah Dwork

&

Robert Jan van Pelt

JOHN MURRAY Albemarle Street, London

© Debórah Dwork and Robert Jan van Pelt 2002

First published by W. W. Norton & Company in the United States of America

First published in Great Britain in 2002
by John Murray (Publishers) Ltd,
50 Albemarle Street, London W1S 4BD

The moral right of the author has been asserted

All rights reserved. No part of this publication may be reproduced in any material form
(including photocopying or storing it in any medium by electronic means and whether or
not transiently or incidentally to some other use of this publication) without the written
permission of the copyright owner, except in accordance with the provisions of the
Copyright, Designs, and Patents Act 1988 or under the terms of a licence issued by the
Copyright Licensing Agency, 90 Tottenham Court Road, London W1T 4LP. Applications
for the copyright owner's written permission to reproduce any part of this publication
should be addressed to the publisher.

A catalogue record for this book is available from the British Library

ISBN 0-7195-5485 3

Printed and bound in Great Britain by
St Edmundsbury Press Ltd,
Bury St Edmunds, Suffolk

This book is dedicated to
the memory of
BERNARD DWORK,
father of Debórah, friend of Robert Jan,
scholar, teacher, confidant,
who served in the U.S. Army during World War II
and asked the right questions all his life

Contents

List of Maps

Acknowledgments

ONE OF THE GREAT pleasures of finishing a book is that it gives authors the opportunity to thank those who helped make the project a product. We could not have garnered the information, collected the photographs, or afforded the costs of this research without the assistance and aid of others.

Our first debt is to the hundreds of women and men who generously, and with great pain, recounted their personal histories and gave us their artifacts from the Holocaust years: letters, diaries, photographs, drawings, ration coupons, identity cards. We are grateful for their time, and for the care they devoted to the enterprise. We do not forget for an instant the searing nature of such recollection, and we thank them for having accepted the burden or, in their words, the "obligation and responsibility." To them we say with Rilke: "Golden thread, you are part of the weaving now."

Individuals and families in every country where Debórah conducted oral histories took on this project with enthusiasm. They wished to see its successful conclusion, and they offered hospitality and help with the practical problems of everyday life away from home. Most important, these friends provided opportunities to meet those whose histories we sought to learn. Our acknowledgments are in alphabetical order by city.

We are delighted to thank Saskia Mazor-van Pelt and Eitan Mazor in Amsterdam for their unstinting hospitality and aid, and Max Arian, Judith Belinfante, Elma Verhey, and David Barnouw for their generous help with introductions and sources. We are deeply obliged to the late Mária Ember for her help in Budapest, which extended in every direction and included her services as a translator from Hungarian into English and from English into Hungarian. We are happily indebted to Esther Fine, a lifelong resident of Cardiff, who welcomed Debórah into her home and her community, and provided all the support services needed to get on with the project. Sylvia and Henry Starkman did the same in Detroit, and we thank them very much. Renate Gruber-Miller and Peter Gruber extended their affectionate arms throughout the whole of Germany, and we could not have managed without them. Chantal and Isabelle Brotherton-Ratcliffe in London took Debórah in as their flatmate month after month, summer after summer, and we are deeply beholden to them. The entire Tolya Barsky-Odette Bérujeau family was involved in Paris, and we thank them all—parents, grandparents, and children—for their energy and cheer. It is a special satisfaction to thank Susan Alice Fischer for her help in Rome, and to the Fiorentino family we are much obliged for their unreserved commitment to this history. It is a pleasure to thank Inga-Brit Aldenby in Stockholm for her graciousness, and her unremitting efforts. Finally, we are sincerely grateful to the Katz-Badian family in Vienna.

This book stands on the shoulders of scholars who preceded us. We enjoyed the benefits of a rich literature in the many areas *Holocaust: A History* traverses: the Holocaust, the Third Reich, World War II, the Great War, the Enlightenment and the French Revolution, the history of the Jews during the middle ages, and of the early Christian Church. We salute our colleagues for their creative and incisive studies, and we urge our readers to avail themselves of the bibliographic information in the notes to each chapter.

We thank our colleagues at Clark and Waterloo. Marion Pritchard and Shelly Tenenbaum were bright rays of sunshine even in the depths of Massachusetts winters, Rick Haldenby lightened Robert Jan's load to enable him to work on this project, and Don McKay's good judgment stood firm throughout.

We are utterly proud of Clark University for taking the lead in rooting serious study of the Holocaust in academia. The first university outside of Israel to establish a full-time, fully endowed chaired professorship in Holocaust History, Clark went on to open a Center for Holocaust and Genocide Studies, established an extensive undergraduate program in this field, and validated its commitment by instituting a Ph.D. program in Holocaust history and genocide studies. This could not have happened—and would not have happened—without the guiding hand of President Richard Traina, and then, upon his retirement, of President John Bassett, as well as Vice President Fred Regan and Provost Roger Kasperson. We specially acknowledge Associate Provost David Angel for his deft direction, vision, equanimity, and for the gift of his time. The genius of this initiative, however, was then-Chair of the Board of Trustees, David Strassler. Astounded to hear in 1993 of the lack of faculty positions in Holocaust history at universities across the country, and the absence of degree programs to train future generations of Holocaust scholars, he determined to put that right. In front, behind, to the side—David Strassler was always there.

David Strassler's generosity of spirit and of pocket was joined by Sidney and Rosalie Rose and Ralph and Shirley Rose, who endowed a chair Debórah came to occupy, as well as by a number of special people who immediately stepped forward to transform an idea into a real Center: Al Tapper, Shirley and Bob Siff, Cathy and Marc Lasry, Hannah and Roman Kent, Steve and Barbara Grossman, Diana Bartley.

This book grew over a number of years, and was supported along the way by many individuals and organizations. We thank the Rose family for the research fund attached to the professorship they endowed, and businessman and philanthropist Robert Weil for his support of this work in Sweden. We hope the anonymous donor who singled out Debórah for support when she was a professor at Yale reads these lines and accepts our thanks and our gratitude. We thank too the Wellcome Trust (London), the American Philosophical Society, American Council of Learned Societies, National Endowment for the Humanities, Guggenheim Foundation, Social Sciences and Humanities Research Council (Canada), and the Woodrow Wilson International Center for Scholars for their generous aid, which helped to defray the cost of travel, tape transcription, research assistance, and salary support.

A study such as *Holocaust: A History* depends upon all kinds of support. We are very appreciative of the many expert librarians and archivists who helped us. It is a great satisfaction to have the opportunity to thank those who transcribed the tapes of the recorded oral histories. Ann Cashion-Sharpe has been (and is still) responsible for the English-language tapes, Gabriella Sommers the Italian, Luc Chauvin and Elizabeth Shelton the French, and Christel van der Eynden the Dutch tapes. The staff at the Center—Susan Eiseman-Levitin, Margaret Hillard, Mikaela Luttrell-Rowland, and Tatyana Macaulay—encouraged this work and sought to give us the time to do it. We thank them for cheering us to the finishing line.

Holocaust has been produced by people who extended themselves beyond all definitions of a "job." Jacques Chazaud's maps clarify complicated geography with grace, and we thank him for working with us once again. We thank, too, copyeditor Ann Adelman for her sympathetic reading of the manuscript, and her astute corrections and suggestions. Julia Druskin and Gina Webster produced a book far more lovely to hold than we ever imagined. And Deirdre O'Dwyer, editorial assistant, facilitated, coordinated, and helped. We are sincerely appreciative and grateful to all.

To our literary agent Anne Borchardt and our editor Ed Barber we offer thanks for instruction and advice. From them we learned many lessons we take with us into the future. Indeed, the Center's first class of Ph.D. students—Beth Cohen, Beth Lilach, and Christine van der Zanden—are already the beneficiaries, secondhand. We thank them, and those who came later, for carrying the field forward. We thank our undergraduates, too; they tested our theories and explanations, and pressed us for greater clarity.

Finally, we thank our parents, aunts, and uncles for nourishing our interest in the past with family stories. Surely they inspire our work: Robert-Jan's great-grandmother, Olga Freiin von Frey und Edler von Galliuff, a Hapsburg loyalist who, reading that the Nazis had burned books in big bonfires, promptly threw all her brown garments into a heap in her garden in Karlovy Vary and set fire to the lot. Or, from the other side of his family, his great-uncle Fritz, a Dutch Jew and a Democrat, who went into hiding an ordinary *mijnheer* and emerged, enraged, to claim his family's centuries-old title of Freiherr von Treuenberg.

DEATH'S GREAT CARNIVAL

F AME DID NOT protect the Hungarian Jewish poet Miklós Radnóti. No longer considered worthy to serve in Hungary's army, Radnóti was drafted into a forced labor battalion in 1940. Thirty-six months earlier, he had been awarded Hungary's highest literary honor, the Baumgarten Prize. Now, he was sent to territory recently annexed from Romania, where he and other men dismantled barbed-wire fortifications. Released after four months of hardship, Radnóti returned to civilian life in Budapest, only to be drafted again into forced labor in 1942. But luck, for a while, stayed with Radnóti. He survived nearly a year and a half of fiercely antisemitic abuse and harsh physical conditions in a forced labor battalion and returned to civilian life once more. It was a short respite.[1]

In the spring of 1944, Hungary caved in to German pressure to deport its Jews. Radnóti's wife, Fanni Gyarmati, went into hiding. His beloved step-mother Ilka Molnar, who had come into his life when he was a small child, and his cherished stepsister Ágica were two of the 36,000 Jews shipped from Nagyvárad to Auschwitz on 24 May. Radnóti was rounded up for forced labor service a third time and sent to the slave labor camp of Heidenau in German-occupied Serbia, close to Bulgaria. Attached to the *Organization Todt,* the Nazi state enterprise responsible for military infrastructural construction, Heidenau supplied men for an army railroad project to connect Belgrade with Bor (Yugoslavia).[2] It was hard labor on short rations. Still, the poet continued to write in a small notebook given to him by a sympathetic Serbian peasant.

The Hungarians evacuated Heidenau in August as Tito's Partisans and Soviet troops approached. The 3,200 inmates were forced-marched back to Hungary, crossing the border on 30 September 1944.[3] There a troop of SS men on horseback took command, and shifted the direction of march toward the Reich. The slaves would work in camps in Germany. Death tightened its grip. Radnóti and his comrades had no food, no water, and no strength to keep the pace set by their masters. A week later, the violinist Miklós Lorsi, bleeding pro-fusely, could no longer stand. Radnóti and a comrade tried to support Lorsi between them, but an SS man would have none of it and shot Lorsi on the spot. Radnóti wrote his epitaph in the small notebook, carefully kept hidden.

I fell beside him; his body turned over,
already taut as a string about to snap.
Shot in the back of the neck. That's how you too will end,
I whispered to myself: just lie quietly,
Patience now flowers into death.
Der springt noch auf, a voice said above me.
On my ear, blood dried, mixed with filth.[4]

Radnóti predicted his fate accurately. A month went by; the SS had moved on, the Fascist Arrow Cross now ran Budapest, and Hungarian guards did the Germans' work. On 8 November, they loaded Radnóti and twenty-one other "stragglers" onto two carts at the rear of the march. At the town of Györ, the carriages and column separated. The guards forced those still on their feet to push on to Germany.

Radnóti and the other men in the carts remained in Györ. Their guards tried to get rid of them by dumping them at a local hospital. But the medical administration refused to accept them. Györ had been *Judenrein* ("cleansed" of Jews) since March, and they wanted no new ones. Why don't you take them somewhere and kill them? someone—it is not clear who—suggested. The guards obliged. They were shot along the Rabca River.

The mass grave was identified nineteen months later, in May 1946. The decomposed bodies were exhumed. Radnóti was recognized by his identity card. His notebook remained intact. He had written his final four poems on the death march. Entitled "Picture Postcards," the last recorded Lorsi's death. "Picture Postcard 1" was written as he and the other slaveworkers set out on the death march from Heidenau. It was a love poem to his wife:

From Bulgaria thick, wild cannon pounding rolls,
It strikes the mountain ridge, then hesitates and falls.
A piled-up blockage of thoughts, animals, carts, and men;
whinnying, the road rears up; the sky runs with its mane.
In this chaos of movement you're in me, permanent,
deep in my conscious you shine, motion forever spent
and mute, like an angel awed by death's great carnival,
or an insect in rotted tree pith, staging its funeral.[5]

The history of a whole continent, an entire civilization, shimmers in the story of Radnóti's life, a shot of silver that throws questions, not answers. Radnóti was a famous, critically acclaimed poet, whose country gloried in its artistic heritage and honored a champion of civil rights as a national hero. Proud of having stood since the late middle ages as a bulwark of Christendom and, from the Enlightenment on, as a bulwark of western civilization against threat from the east, Hungary had long ago emancipated its entire population. With the Nationali-

ties Law of 1868, all Hungarian citizens, of whatever ethnic or religious background, constituted a "single nation, the indivisible, unitary Hungarian nation."
Yet, in the middle of the twentieth century, Hun-
gary denied those civil rights to its Jews, the poet
Radnóti amongst them, and excised them from the
body politic. How did that happen?

How was it possible that Radnóti's government—like other governments across Europe—
abandoned the well-established protections of
property and, by decree, identified its Jewish citizens, forbade them to travel, use a telephone, or listen to a radio; forced them to wear a large yellow
badge, drafted the men as slaveworkers, and exiled
the rest—without indictment, trial, or conviction—to an "unknown destination." How did this
happen in a country that long acknowledged the
principle of habeas corpus and the rule of law?

Why was Radnóti's wife Fanni forced to disappear from public life, and how did she—and thousands of others during the Holocaust years—find
refuge? Why were his stepmother Ilka and stepsis-

*1. Miklós Radnóti and Fanni
Radnóti-Gyarmati, c. 1941.*

ter Ágica rounded up into a hastily formed ghetto in Nagyvárad, loaded onto
trains, and shipped to Auschwitz? And why in the world were they subjected
to a selection that ripped families apart and doomed those considered "useless"
to be killed within hours, and those "capable of work" to slavery until death?

How did the German *Organization Todt,* run by a corps of well-educated
engineers who believed in the power of science and technology to provide happiness and freedom for all, come to demand slave labor battalions to build the
future they envisioned, and to accept that the tracks to that better world would
stretch over the graves of those who had built it? Why did the SS men reject
their national constitution of 1919, which solemnly declared that "all Germans
are equal before the law"; "men and women have the same fundamental rights
and duties"; "all Germans shall enjoy liberty of travel and residence throughout
the whole country"; "personal liberty is inviolable"? Why did they—and millions of other Germans—embrace the Nazi creed that equality, civil rights, and
liberty applied only to "Aryans" and that no Jew in Europe was protected by any
constitution?

What was to be gained by marching debilitated Jews deep into the Reich
during the last months and weeks of the war, when everyone—even the most
ardent Nazi—knew that Germany had lost? And what of the millions of people who witnessed the miserable spectacle of concentration camp slaves? Why
would the civilian administrators of a municipal hospital—recognized since the
Greeks as, literally, a sanctuary—refuse to take in dying Jews?

And why had the Hungarian soldiers who shot Radnóti—and all the men in uniform throughout Europe who killed Jews of both sexes and all ages, nationalities, social classes—why had they abandoned the lessons they learned in their Catholic and Protestant Churches that human beings share a fundamental identity because they all are created in the image and likeness of God? How had they come to abjure the basic Christian idea that love for God must include the love of others: "He who loves God, love also his brother."

These conundrums are marked by paradox. The Christian tradition of the men in uniform (undoubtedly all baptized) that should have enabled them to see Radnóti and his comrades as fellow human beings also provided the anti-Judaism that enabled them to hate and disown their Jewish neighbors. The Hungarian government stripped Radnóti of his rights and drafted him into a slave labor battalion under the aegis of the political concept that should have prevented it: one nation, indivisible. The very reason why post-World War I Germans should have accepted Jews as fellow citizens—their shared suffering in the trenches—in fact prompted the good people of the Weimar Republic to scorn and exclude them. The utopian vision of the *Organization Todt* carried within it the seeds for a dystopian present.

We seek here to untangle the paradoxical developments that led to the murder of Radnóti and between 5 and 6 million other Jews who—in the heart of a civilization that thought itself the zenith of human history—were identified, disenfranchised, marked, imprisoned, and killed, because their existence was seen as a blot on the very civilization to which they had contributed so much.

HOLOCAUST

A History

Chapter One

JEWS, GENTILES, AND GERMANS

ALLIED FORCES liberated the Netherlands in May 1945. Within months, a law by royal decree established policy guidelines for the reunification of Jewish parents with children hidden in Holland during the war. Surviving parents had only a month to return to the Netherlands from wherever in Europe the war's end had found them; their claims would be judged individually, case by case. To prevent disturbing or shocking changes, to maintain a stable environment for the child, all other close relatives were not to know the current address of the child they sought to find. If neither parent claimed a child within thirty days, a newly established board, the War Foster Child Commission (OPK), was formally entrusted with guardianship.[1]

This law was crafted by Gesina van der Molen, a strong-willed, severely Calvinist lawyer, quite active in the resistance. A founder of the underground group *Trouw* ("Faith" or "Loyalty"), van der Molen had worked on two illegal newspapers, *Vrij Nederland (Free Netherlands)* and her own paper, also called *Trouw,* whose target audience was, like her, Orthodox Calvinist. In July 1943 she also became involved in rescuing Jewish children from the Germans. Throughout the war, van der Molen had been an external examiner for student teachers. This job had taken her to a small teachers' training college located right next door to a central deportation point for Jewish children from Amsterdam. When van der Molen saw the youngsters in the adjoining garden, she exclaimed, "I understand why God led me here. I see my task."[2]

By the summer of 1943, few Jewish children were left in Amsterdam to help or hide, so there was not much scope for Gesina van der Molen's considerable energies in that line. A year later, after D-Day, the question of the postwar custody and care of the orphans arose, and she could, and did, take charge. In August 1945, the OPK commission—the official guardianship agency of Jewish children who had survived the war by hiding with gentile foster families—was appointed by the minister of justice with Gesina van der Molen as chair.

To whom did the orphaned Jewish children belong? Dutch (read "Christian") society or the Dutch Jewish community? Should they remain with families that had hidden them during the war, or be placed with Jewish families or in a Jewish orphanage? In an interview published in *Trouw* on 13 June 1945, van der Molen presented her position to the public. She planned to act as the parents would have wanted. "The wish of the parents comes first. This always will be respected. But often this is not known and then we have to act according to probabilities." In other words, "if it can be shown that it is very likely that the parents would have wanted an Orthodox or Zionist education, then the children will be taken to a Jewish family which is both willing and capable of treating the child and raising the child completely as its own. If such a family cannot be found, then we will have to place the child in a Jewish institution. It is different with children about whose parents' wishes nothing is known or of whom it reasonably may be assumed that the parents would not have wanted a Jewish education. If . . . the foster parents would like to keep the child . . . and if, moreover, the child has grown into that family, then we do not want to cut those ties."[3]

Van der Molen's plan, however reasonable in appearance, was fundamentally flawed: the placement of the child depended on someone's (whose?) interpretation (how?) of the wishes of the parents. For van der Molen, these questions were not problems. In an article on "Theft of JEWISH CHILDREN?" in *Trouw* a year later, she wondered whether these children were, after all, so Jewish? "Do these Jewish children really belong to the Jewish community alone? Even if the parents did not have one single tie to Judaism? Even when they felt more Dutch than Jewish? Even when they showed that they were attracted to Christianity?"[4]

Van der Molen asked questions that have haunted and vexed Christians and Christian theology and dogma for sixteen hundred years. At bottom is a basic issue: What is the nature of Jewish identity and the place of Jews in the Christian world? On the one hand, van der Molen acknowledged that Jews did have a place in Dutch society. Orphaned children of Orthodox Jews were to be recognized as Jews and, as such, were to be raised by Jews or in a Jewish institution. At the same time, she also believed in the benefits of conversion, of bringing the children into the national, Christian community. Thus, those orphans whose backgrounds fell short of van der Molen's concept of Jewish orthodoxy were to remain with their wartime Christian "foster" parents, to be raised according to their values. Holland stood at the dawn of a new age; from the ashes of German occupation a new society would rise, with a "true melting together" and no divisions of any sort.[5] Leaving the children in Christian families furthered the project of rebuilding the nation and offered them the opportunity to participate in the national community. The legislation van der Molen proposed, and got enacted by royal decree, expressed the tension between these two world views: one, conservative, that sought to restore the prewar social structure and preserve old boundaries; and the other, radical change (conversion in this case) that, shaped by the idea of evolution and progress, would erase former distinctions.

THESE OPPOSITE WAYS of looking at the world help us understand the position of Jews in European society as Nazism loomed large. The Europe that per-

mitted the Holocaust was not created in 1933. It took centuries to descend so
low, but descend Europe did.

Socially and politically, it all began in the medieval kingdoms that super-
seded the Roman empire. Conservative in structure and outlook, medieval peoples looked backwards in time: what was old had authority; precedent was
honored; what had existed before should continue to exist. They wished to preserve their world precisely as it was, without change or disruption.[6]

The Catholic Church, however, built its authority on the principle of
stability and, at the same time, sought radical change. Like the society which
nourished it for hundreds of years, the Church was a traditional institution. It
relied on tradition, how things had been done in the past, to validate its existence
and practices. Its claim to be the one, true, holy, and universal Church was—
and still is—based on apostolic succession: an unbroken chain that links the
reigning pope to all preceding popes to the apostle Peter ("You are Peter, and
upon this rock I will build my Church," said Jesus, according to the gospel of
Matthew) to Christ, who had entrusted to Peter the keys to the Kingdom of
Heaven.[7] But the Church also sought vigorously to convert Jews and the heathen, and thus was also a formidable force for change. By the middle ages, everyone in Europe but the Jews had converted to Christianity, so the Church's radical
impetus flowed out to a periphery of bloody crusades against, for instance, the
heathen Saracens in the middle east.

The Jews within Christendom sat in an uncomfortable middle. As an agent
of change, the Church sought to convert the Jews, to transform them. As a conservative institution, however, the Church permitted the Jews a place in society.
Jews, after all, were longtime inhabitants; and what existed in the past should
be preserved in the present. Furthermore, Jews held a special place in history
and therefore a particular role. They were the people of the Old Testament;
with them God had made the first covenant (contractual agreement). He had
chosen them to follow his laws and they, in turn, were his chosen people.

According to St. Paul, on the other hand, God had created a new, second
covenant with all humanity through Jesus of Nazareth as Christ the Lord. Jesus
had been anointed ("Christ" in Greek) by God to bring salvation, and thus to
establish the Kingdom of God on earth. This "new covenant," Paul explained
in his second letter to the Corinthians, was "not written in code, but in the
Spirit; for the written code kills, but the Spirit gives life."[8]

Early Christians in the second and third centuries faced a question—how to
interpret the relationship between the old and new covenants, between Jews
and Christians. Radical Christian sects had sprung up, influenced by gnosti-
cism, a belief that true knowledge is available only to select initiates, and that
salvation awaited only those with that knowledge. These groups developed a
theology highlighting their own exclusivity even among Christians, and espousing utter rejection of the Jews. If the old covenant killed and the new covenant
gave life, as St. Paul had claimed, then Jews were agents of the devil.

Main-line Christian theology, destined to shape the conditions of Jewish life in Europe, developed in reaction to these extreme gnostic Christian ideas. Main-line dogma rejected the gnostics' exclusive either/or position and, by contrast, preached a more inclusive and/and position. The old and new covenants were not distinct and separate, but part of one story of salvation, theologians like Irenaeus and Tertullian maintained. While it was true that Christ had initiated a new era, the old one was not totally obsolete: it had been "a shadow of things to come."[9] Furthermore, the Old Testament confirmed the validity of the New Testament. "Behold," Jeremiah had prophesied, "the days are coming, says the Lord, when I will make a new covenant with the house of Israel and the house of Judah, not like the covenant which I made with their fathers. . . ."[10] The existence of the Jews, in short, testified to the history of the covenant, and therefore, as the early fifth-century Church father St. Augustine admonished, they were to be preserved, but preserved in misery.

The Catholic Church held fast to the notion that there was a place for everything and everyone, even the Jews. By the high middle ages this idea was a basic tenet of the dominant theological system of medieval Europe, called scholastic theology, having been developed in the schools—that is, the universities. Scholastic theology did not hold that people had equal positions in society. Indeed, quite the opposite—social divisions and distinctions were respected and strictly maintained. But there was a place, however grand or mean, for everyone. It was precisely in the plenitude in the world, in the articulation of differences, that God's creative power was manifest. No single created thing could bear the imprint of God's image; all were needed to do so. As the great thirteenth-century scholastic theologian, philosopher, and professor at the University of Paris Thomas Aquinas, put it, "There would not be a perfect likeness of God in the universe if all things were of one grade of being. For this reason, then, is there distinction among created things: that by being many, they may receive God's likeness more perfectly than being one."[11]

This idea was given a decidedly political twist by the Italian poet and political philosopher Dante Alighieri. Dante's treatise on monarchy as an institution is a clear articulation of what educated people thought in the middle ages. Human beings existed, he argued, all of mankind existed, to actualize human intellectual potential. "And since that potentiality cannot be fully actualized all at once in any one individual or in any one . . . particular social grouping . . . there must needs be a vast number of individual people in the human race, through which the whole of this potentiality can be actualized."[12] Thus, both medieval theological doctrine and political philosophy supported the proposition that there was a place—not necessarily a good place, but a place—for Jews in the Christian world. Following dogma and theory, the social structure of medieval Europe permitted it in practice.

Medieval Europe was a feudal society. Unlike modern societies, in which a founding constitution clearly defines everyone's rights and privileges, in feudal Europe people were not governed by general rules that pertained equally to everyone. There was no concept of equal rights. To the contrary, medieval Europe abounded with different relationships between individuals or groups: lords and vassals, kings and cities, cities and guilds, guilds and craftsmen. In a society where any group had its particular arrangements with other groups, the Jews could create a niche for their own community.

Throughout the middle ages, European Jewish communities negotiated for rights and privileges with Christian religious and secular officials, seeking to safeguard the autonomy of their community, as well as their religion, culture, and distinctive way of life. Just as Jews were seen by Christian society as separate, "the other," the Jews saw themselves as standing apart, as one people, with a common faith, a national tradition, and a shared hope for future redemption. They were eager both to be marked off from their Christian neighbors and to exclude those neighbors from their community. Far from attempting to integrate into the dominant Christian culture or to assimilate into Christian society, the Jews protected their differences with a network of religious laws and communal rules.[13]

At one and the same time, the Jews formed a closely knit, insular, separate society, and comprised a subgroup of the larger society. Ruled in the first instance by Jewish law and by Jewish officials, the community also fell under secular authority. For example, in the mid-

2. The Frankfurt Ghetto, *1628. Separated from the rest of the city by gates, the ghetto consisted of one street located immediately adjacent to the medieval city walls. The name "Juden Gas[se]" identifies the ghetto street and marks the site of the main synagogue. Engraving by Matthäus Merian the Elder. Reproduced in Helmut Eschwege,* Die Synagoge in der deutschen Geschichte *(Dresden, 1980). Coll. authors.*

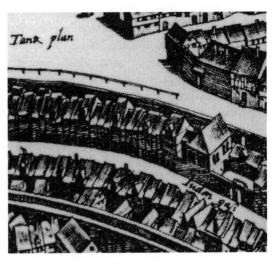

dle ages, people could not simply move to a place and live there. The right to settle within the walls of a city was granted by municipal authorities. These ordinances applied to everyone, but Jews labored under additional layers of complication. The space allocated to them was often severely delimited to a single alley or, at best, a very few streets. In many places, this neighborhood, soon called the "ghetto," was an enclosed area with a gated entrance locked at night and during important Christian festivals, such as the days leading up to and including Easter Sunday. Furthermore, unlike their Christian neighbors, Jews had no right to reside even where they were born unless that privilege was newly granted. The government might expel them at any time—and many governments did. During the plague of the Black Death that ravaged Europe in 1348–49, Jews were expelled "forever" or "for at least two hundred years."[14] But, as they were needed for the economy, ordinances of readmission appeared a year later. They were permitted to return, only on worse terms and with their enclosure more strictly observed. Faced with these conditions, many Jews moved eastward from France and Germany: to Austria, Bohemia, Moravia, Silesia, and on to Poland, where they were offered greater economic opportunities and, they hoped, greater stability.

By the middle of the seventeenth century, half of the world's Jewish population (2 million) lived in central Europe, Poland, and Lithuania, where they were segregated from Christian society by state law and of their own volition. Government ordinances still commonly defined and restricted the Jewish quarter, but even in cities where no legally imposed ghetto existed, Jews tended voluntarily to live near the synagogue, bathhouse, studyhouse, and kosher shops. They spoke Yiddish, and thus had a common language which they used among themselves and did not expect Christians to understand. Earlier laws since 1215 had required Jews to wear distinctive clothes; four hundred years later the conical cap, and the yellow circular cloth patch, the "Jew badge," had disappeared. Still, Jews differed from the rest of the population in their dress and the sidelocks of men and the covered hair of women. For Jews, the Christian world was a place to make a living. Their community lay within Jewish society which, like its Christian counterpart, was conservative and traditional.

The result was an uneasy co-existence, sometimes violent, never equal, but co-existence nevertheless. Looking at the massacre of some 10,000 Jews in the wake of the First Crusade of 1096 to "free" Jerusalem from "infidel" rule; the even more bloody Second Crusade of 1146, when Christians thought it their duty first to kill Jews at home and then to proceed east; the enclosed ghettos; the strict limitations on occupations; and the "Jew badge," it is easy to draw a straight line from traditional Christian anti-Judaism to the annihilatory Nazi racist anti-semitism. Easy, but false. There is no direct line.

The riots, or pogroms, against Jews in the middle ages were given a theological justification—a long-standing and well-rehearsed vocabulary of hatred was used to whip up the masses. But these riots had little religious content.

Rather, Jews and other groups were caught in a political power struggle. In medieval Europe, Jews were commonly under the nominal protection of the king or a local nobleman. To local priests and friars who saw themselves as representing the poor against the privileged, Jews came to symbolize royal power, the elites. Pogroms against the Jewish community that erupted from such tensions were therefore conflicts between religious and secular authorities, with the Jews standing in for the secular power.[15]

Jews were not the only group in medieval Europe that depended on royal protection and thus not the only people to be identified with secular power. All who fell through the social cracks: beggars; lepers; travelers in transit from one city to another; even, from time to time, those whom the Church considered to be heretics such as the Albigensians, a gnostic sect in Aquitaine, were under the protection of the king or another nobleman. Beggars and travelers were individuals, and therefore attracted little attention. But lepers and the Aquitainian Albigensians were communities and, like the Jews, were the victims of intra-community violence. In the Shepherd's Crusade of 1320, which engulfed all of present-day France and northern Spain, lepers were persecuted as viciously as Jews. And despite, or perhaps because of, the protection of the count of Toulouse, the Albigensians became a pawn in a purely political struggle between the Church, the king of France, and a regional lord. The Albigensians were murdered en masse.[16]

In this massacre of the Albigensians lay the first "triumph" of the Inquisition, an arm of the Church established in the thirteenth century to expunge heresy and eliminate heretics. Heretics, Christians who rejected church dogma and therefore the authority of the Church, were a much greater threat than the Jews. The Jews had a covenant with God; they were to be preserved, but pre-

3. Pogrom in the Frankfurt Ghetto, *1614. Engraving by Matthäus Merian the Elder. Reproduced in Helmut Eschwege,* Die Synagoge in der deutschen Geschichte *(Dresden, 1980) Coll. authors.*

served in misery. The heretics, by contrast, had broken the Christian covenant, and were not to be tolerated at all. If the Jews fell victim to sporadic pogroms, those whom the Church deemed heretics—Hussites, Huguenots in France, Calvinists elsewhere, and other Protestants—were hounded by a systematic, powerful, and merciless Inquisition for hundreds of years. It is in the ruthless annihilation of such "heretic" Christian communities that we find a harbinger of the Holocaust.

MEDIEVAL POLITICAL STRUCTURES and power relationships crumbled when assertive central governments arose in the sixteenth and seventeenth centuries. The autonomy enjoyed by cities and local lords was steadily challenged by the kings of Spain, France, England, Russia, and Prussia, seeking to homogenize and thereby modernize their realms. These monarchs instituted universal laws and universal conditions. In surprisingly short order, they established academies (such as the Collège de France) to standardize the language, decreed uniform weights and measures, regularized cartographic conventions, and introduced a national military infrastructure of fortresses and arsenals. The king's guns would be used by the king's soldiers throughout his domain. The early modern period also saw the beginning of national infrastructures for transport and coinage. These ambitious projects ensured royal wealth by creating the conditions for sustained economic growth and consolidated royal power by creating loyal subjects. The principle of individual arrangements no longer applied. Local lords, no longer masters in their own fiefdoms, slid quietly into courtbound aristocrats. Aristocrats and commoners, rich and poor, Catholics and Protestants, were equally accountable to the king.[17]

It was within this social and political context that some men of letters, who came to be known as *les philosophes,* enlightenment philosophers, took the principle of homogenization and universalism to its logical conclusion: social equality. Disgusted by the aristocrats' intrigues, corruption, and overweening privileges, philosophers like Diderot, Voltaire, and Rousseau wanted to build a radically new, classless society based on reason, not tradition.[18]

Where did Jews fit into this new society? Conservative ideas were fading. The fact that Jews were different from Christians, that they were outsiders, mattered little to the philosophes. Indeed, some elements within Jewish tradition appealed to enlightenment thinkers. Ardent advocates of progress through the application of rational thought to social, economic, and political problems, they quite admired the rational ethics of Judaism. But Judaism is much more than a simple system of rational ethics. Like Christianity, Judaism is a religion based on revelation, and the philosophers of the enlightenment were profoundly critical of all beliefs grounded in faith rather than deriving from reason. "Positive religion," as the philosophes called organized religions such as Christianity and Judaism (in contrast to their ideal of "natural religion"), was invented by priests and steeped in superstition. Such religions only fettered free

thinking and thus controlled society. Passionately anti-clerical, the enlightenment philosophers saw all Churches and priests as enemies. Arguing for a political system based on reason, they sought to curb if not nullify the power of the
Church in society. For philosophes such as Voltaire, therefore, the problem with
Jews was not their *differences* from Christians, but what they had *in common:* the
rites and rituals of revealed religion.[19] If Jewish thought had a contribution to
make to an enlightened society, Jewish ways did not. As the French revolution
erupted in 1789, the message was clear: Jews were welcome as individuals to
join the new society that France was to be, but not as members of a traditional
religious community. As Stanislaw de Clermont-Tonnerre, a member of the
National Assembly, put it, "Everything for the Jews as individuals, nothing for
them as a community."[20]

This invitation would have had little impact on the Jewish community had
not many Jews been ready and willing to accept. Influenced by the stirring
Enlightenment movement and the new political structure—strong central
rulers who had altered the power relationships so important to the traditional
Jewish community—Jews, like their gentile neighbors, began to think along
rationalist lines. The *Haskala,* the Jewish Enlightenment, opened new avenues
of study, new possibilities for intellectual engagement. For the first time, the
study of traditional Jewish texts was joined by a pursuit of general knowledge:
science, mathematics, contemporary world affairs, the languages and literature
of the gentile world. These enlightenment Jews increased steadily in numbers
in western and central Europe throughout the second half of the eighteenth
century. They developed radically different ideas from their traditional co-
religionists about scholarship and education, communal organization and leadership, and, ultimately, lifestyle. They wished to establish a new relationship
with the gentile world, to be citizens of the country in which they lived. Emancipation was their goal.[21]

This was not a straightforward proposition, however. Like their Orthodox
brethren, enlightenment Jews were determined to preserve their identity as
Jews. What were to be the terms of the compromise? How could they remain
members of the community of Jews and, simultaneously, become citizens of the
nation? What customs and beliefs were to be retained, and which changed?

The question of emancipation would not have been raised at all if the principle of social equality had not bloomed at the time. Emancipation applied to
the Jews, but the larger issue of social equality applied to everyone. "Liberty,
Equality, Fraternity!" rang through the air during the French revolution in
1789, and has remained the motto of France to this day. It was a succinct formulation of the ideals of the enlightenment philosophers, and indeed many of
their ideas were actualized by the revolution and its aftermath. They envisaged,
and the revolution made possible, the abolition of privileges based on birth, the
creation of government by representation, the institution of a national school
system with a national curriculum. The philosophes had hoped for a society in

which everyone was a citizen of the state, not a subject to the crown, and the revolution removed—in principle if not immediately in fact—barriers to citizenship, including those for Jews.

But if emancipation, citizenship, participation in the body politic, freedom of movement, and entrance into every field of economic activity might be offered to Jews by the enlightened society to which the revolution had given birth, it was also that fiercely anti-religious society that breached the autonomy of the Jewish community, as surely as it curtailed the power of the Church in France. True to its anti-clerical enlightenment principles, the revolution separated the French Church from the Church in Rome. It nationalized Church property, closed monasteries and convents. It also abolished the traditional arrangement accepted for centuries by Christians and Jews that had permitted the Jews to be governed primarily by their own laws and officials.[22]

Inevitably, the revolution opened political discussion of the so-called Jewish Question in the National Assembly of France. That Jews should have freedom of movement and choice of occupation was universally accepted. But what of citizenship? Were the Jews a separate people, a nation unto themselves, or could they be integrated into the new state? In the Assembly debates of December 1789, the conservatives argued that Jews were not a religious sect like other religious sects; they were a nation with laws of its own, according to which it always had acted and wished to continue to act. The radicals disagreed. They envisioned dissolution of Jewish communal structures and, in their place, the establishment of private associations concerned solely with matters of faith.

No decision was taken that December, but two years later, in 1791, the Assembly annulled all legal barriers to citizenship. Gone was the "preservation in misery" policy that had governed Christian-Jewish relations for over a thousand years. Jews might now attain civic integration as Jews. For the politicians of the revolutionary period, religious affiliation was not the issue, and therefore conversion, formerly the only way for a Jew to enter the body politic, was irrelevant. Loyalty to the nation was the new barrier. Could Jews be loyal to France?

This problem lay unresolved during the tumultuous years of, and after, the revolution. The turbulence of the 1790s, however, gave way to the relative political stability of the Napoleonic era (1799–1813) and, perhaps characteristically, Napoleon himself decided to settle the "Jewish Question."[23] He delegated Louis-Mathieu Molé to confront Jewish leaders with the government's concerns. Molé called prominent Jews to a meeting in Paris in July 1806. "His Majesty wants you to be Frenchmen," he declared; "it remains with you to accept such a title and to bear in mind that not to prove worthy of it would be to renounce it."[24] Molé then presented twelve questions dealing with the relationship of the French Jewish community and its laws and customs, to the French nation and civil laws. He also enquired about the ties between French Jews and their co-religionists elsewhere. The Jewish leaders sat silent as Molé spoke, but erupted when asked if they considered France their country and if would they defend it. *"Jusqu' à la mort!"* (To the death!) they exclaimed.²⁵

Emancipation was within the grasp of the Jews of France, but it came only with intracommunal change. According to the "Napoleonic Bargain," Jews ceased to live as they traditionally had done. Abandoning the autonomy of their community, they became "Frenchmen of the Mosaic persuasion." This long-awaited and eagerly sought development was bittersweet. Many Jews who cared about their distinctive identity as Jews saw here a profound dilemma: how both to accept the offer to join the body politic on equal terms and to remain meaningfully Jewish. The terms of this debate have shifted over the past two hundred years, but as every issue of any Jewish newspaper today reflects, it is still current.

Emancipatory movements quickly spread throughout western and central Europe in the wake of the French revolution and Napoleonic conquests. Not even the defeat of Napoleon in May 1814, when the specter of occupation had been dispelled, dimmed its prospect. The fiercest foes of France, those least likely—such as Prussia and Austria—to follow its example, proved willing to offer full emancipation. In this regard, as in many others, the ideals of the philosophes triumphed.

The French revolution thus brought the enlightenment project to fruition. It created the concept of the citizen and a national system of schooling, government by representation, and the abolition of privilege based on birth. It also introduced violence as an instrument of social change. For the first time, a society reinvented itself, and to do so it willfully employed the myriad means of persecution at its disposal. As the great nineteenth-century historian Alexis de Tocqueville explained, the revolution did not seek a change of government, it endeavored to "abolish the old kind of society." To achieve this, "it had to simultaneously attack all the established powers, eliminate old influences, wipe out traditions, transform mores and practices, and in a way empty the human mind of all the ideas on which obedience and respect previously had been based."²⁶ The revolutionaries' means to that end was to murder the royal family and the aristocracy. These elites had long embodied traditional authority and continuity with the past. That link to the past, that authority had to be eradicated: Off with their heads. In the bloodbath known as the Terror, twelve hundred aristocrats went to the guillotine not for what they had done, but for who they were.

Here lay a terrible seed. The revolutionaries had come to believe that a group of people, people of "noble blood," were an obstacle to social and political change. This belief destroyed the last vestiges of the medieval idea that there was a place for everyone. And it opened a horrible prospect: if it was legitimate to execute aristocrats because they stood in the way of social renewal, would it not be legitimate to kill other groups who were seen as impediments to progress?

The Terror, the revolutionaries' decision to kill the king and, subsequently, to annihilate the nobility, introduced a politics based on mass murder. The twentieth century saw much of it. The Terror foreshadows Stalin's murder of the kulaks, whom he perceived as a bulwark against rural collectivization. And it foreshadows Hitler's murder of the Jews, whom he perceived as a barrier to racial utopia. The line from regicide to Judeocide is direct indeed.[27]

THE PHILOSOPHES never anticipated that the enlightened society they envisioned would be introduced by blanket slaughter. They neither advocated nor expected the use of massacre and carnage to effect the radical social changes they sought. This use of violence as an instrument of social change, this introduction of a politics based on mass murder, was an unexpected development. And perhaps Europeans were so shocked by its ferocity and ruthlessness that they did not employ such means again for 150 years.

A second unanticipated development of the French revolution, modern nationalism, blended into European society immediately, however. The revolution introduced the idea of "the people," and defined it in political terms. Once suggested, this notion gathered immense intellectual energy and popular attention throughout the nineteenth century. For the influential French scholar Ernest Renan, the nation was a powerful, spiritual principle incorporating two different factors. "The one is the possession in common of a rich heritage of memories; and the other is the actual agreement, the desire to live together, and the will to continue to make the most of this joint inheritance." For Renan and many others, history was the essence of the nation, and the people inherited that history. It belonged to them, and shaped their view of the present. "To share the glories of the past, and a common will in the present; to have done great deeds together, and the desire to do more—these are the essential conditions of a people's being." The people of a nation were not necessarily of the same race nor did they necessarily speak the same language. To share "a heritage of glory and grief," to have "suffered, rejoiced, and hoped together" and to work together in the present, was "of greater value" than "customs houses and frontiers." "These are the things which are understood, in spite of differences of race and language."[28]

4. The Execution of Louis XVI on the Place de la Concorde, 21 January 1793. Engraving in François Guizot, History of France (Chicago and New York, n.d.) Coll. authors.

Renan's definition depended heavily on a central idea, common to all ideologies of the nation, that nations—and not individuals, classes, or dynasties—are the vehicles of historical destiny. As it enacts its allotted role in history, each nation creates and preserves a moral patrimony which belongs to everyone. This patrimony, or inheritance, consisted of artistic and literary masterpieces, national monuments, institutions, philosophic thought, and political and military history of victories won and defeats endured. Handed down from one generation to the next by public museums and galleries, as well as by the newly created national primary education system, everyone shared the national patrimony. Having it in common created a new social equality. The rich were still rich and the poor still poor, but the spiritual patrimony of the nation belonged equally to both.[29]

Equal too was responsibility for it: national military service for all able-bodied men. Indeed, nationalism proved so seductive that it persuaded millions of peaceful citizens to submit to military service and the terrible risks of war. As a means to mobilize the masses, the nation proved an astonishing triumph. For the great French historian Jules Michelet, nothing provided a more powerful lesson in patriotism than the sight of marching soldiers. When a boy "is just beginning to be a man," Michelet urged his readers, "let his father take him" to

> a great public festival, and there are immense crowds in Paris. He leads him from Notre Dame to the Louvre and the Tuileries and to the Arc de Tri-omphe. From some roof or terrace he shows him the people, the army passing by with its bayonets flashing and glittering, and the tricolored flag.... "Look, my son, look: there is France; there is your native land! All this is like one man—with one soul and one heart. They would all die for a single man, and each one ought also to live and to die for all. Those men passing by, who are armed and now departing, they are going away to fight for us. They are leaving their father and their aged mother who will need them. You will do the same, for you will never forget that your mother is France."[30]

Nationalism always frames a nation's history in mythic terms, and nationalist historians write epic stories in which the aspirations of ordinary people are transfigured into tales of national grandeur. Such histories are fables, of course, presenting historical developments in reverse order. Nowhere is this more transparent than in accounts of the birth of a nation. Royal governments intent upon consolidating power set the foundations of the modern nation. These monarchs demanded a unity of language and imposed a unity of culture. When everyone spoke the same language and shared the same culture, nationalist historians rewrote history, ignoring the dynamic policies that had shaped that nation. Instead, they postulated a mythic beginning at the dawn of time of one original "race," a "people," who spoke one language and had one culture with its own "authentic" traditions and customs. "Their" nation was old, no recent development born of specific political necessity and therefore liable to change, or even to disappear. No, they declared, their nation was an entity from time immemorial, permanent and intransmutable, populated by one people, generation after generation. By the later nineteenth century, nationalist historiography had come to identify "the nation" and "the people" with biological, genetic descent.

Jews had no place in this formulation. Not in 1900 and certainly not in 1800. Popularly perceived in the early nineteenth century as a cohesive, insular community which prayed for a return to their ancestral home in Palestine, they were doubtful candidates for citizenship to nationalist philosophers such as Johann Gottlieb Fichte.[31] "Are you not reminded here of a state within a state?" Fichte asked rhetorically. Arguing against emancipation, he warned his fellow Germans, "Does the obvious idea not occur to you that the Jews constitute a state to which you do not belong, a state that is sounder and stronger than yours? If you grant them civil rights in your states as well, they will trample all your other citizens underfoot."[32]

This was a new kind of anti-Judaism, one couched in political rather than religious terms, and it was taken up with alacrity.[33] Fichte's language may have been extreme, but his argument was echoed by right-wing nationalist historians throughout the nineteenth century. The Jews simply did not belong. They were not part of the nation. Never mind that they had been living in, for example, France or Germany or Italy since Roman times, longer than the tribes that had migrated into those lands in the fifth century and then formed the backbone of the new nations. Nationalist historians either ignored their presence entirely or depicted them as a noxious extranational presence better suited to another equally noxious country. To the nationalist Jules Michelet, France represented the ideal of progress, while England was mired in tradition. According to Michelet, the Jews, with their moneylending, trading, and tradition of finance, were foreign to France and at home in England. "The Jews, whatever be said of them, have a country—the London Stock Exchange; they operate everywhere, but they are rooted in the country of gold. Now that funds of every state are in their hands, what can they love? The land of the status quo—England. What can they hate? The land of progress—France."[34]

If Michelet banished the Jews to England, the German nationalist historian Heinrich von Treitschke banished them to France. In his masterly attempt to write a nationalist history of German unification, the multivolume *History of Germany in the Nineteenth Century,* Treitschke identified the Jews as a corrosive element unsuited to the spiritual German nation, but well suited to radical France. Jews, Treitschke explained, were "chiefly attracted towards the French [nation], not merely from reasonable gratitude, but also from an inner sense of kinship. To a nation [the Jewish nation] which for centuries had ceased to possess a political history, nothing seemed so alien as the historic sense. To the Jews, German veneration for the past appeared ludicrous; but modern France had broken with her history." France was a "raw new state, created, as it were, by pure reason." Thus it was there that Jews "felt more at home."[35]

Progressives who rejected the concept of the nation-state did not know what to make of the Jews either. Nineteenth-century progressives believed in progress. For them the course of history was a continuous move toward improvement, from a society of inequality to a society of equality. They believed that the French revolution had greatly accelerated that development in terms of political equality; they wished to advance the cause of economic equality. And, it seemed to them, the Jews stood in the way.[36]

Jews traditionally had been identified with the world of finance and some Jews, like the Rothschilds, had done extremely well in the new liberal economy of the eighteenth century. For progressive thinkers, then, Jews were not merely "materialistic"; they constituted a positively reactionary historical force. If Jews were to be emancipated they would have to cease to be Jews, and if society were to be emancipated it would have to be free of Jews. In other words, while nationalists saw the Jews as an irritant to be ignored, progressives saw them as a problem to be solved.

One of the first to introduce this idea was not a Christian antisemite, but a Jewish antisemite, Löb Baruch, who trusted to conversion to save him from the traits he despised in the co-religionists of his birth. Known after baptism as Ludwig Börne, he broadcast his contemptuous analysis of Jewish people and Jewish culture to relatives and to the public. The Jews of his native city of Frankfurt valued only three things, "first, money; second, money; third, money,"[37] he wrote to his mother in 1805. Warming to this theme in the years that followed, he expounded at greater length in an essay on *Der ewige Jude (The Eternal Jew)*. Published in 1821, *Der ewige Jude* established the idea that Jews were capitalists, capitalist society was "Jewish," and therefore Judaism was at the root of all the evils of modern life. His concepts and his language were readily accepted. Börne was extremely influential in France as well as Germany, and a new kind of sociological antisemitism became a staple in the language of revolutionaries and reactionaries alike, united in their abhorrence of the new capitalist society.[38]

The young, progressive journalist Karl Marx, a converted Jew like Börne, took these ideas to heart and elaborated upon them.[39] "Let us not seek the secret of the Jew in his religion, but let us seek the secret of religion in the real Jew," he advised his readers in 1843. "What is the profane basis of Judaism? Practical need, self-interest. What is the worldly cult of the Jews? Huckstering. What is his worldly god? Money."[40] If words express concepts—and they do—Marx ensured that "Judaism" connoted capitalism and "Jew" capitalist. And capitalism and capitalists were the very essence of what was wrong with modern society. The problem was that while "politics is in principle superior to the power of money," in actual practice, politics "has become its bondsman." Starting from the baseline position that money was the central tenet of Judaism, Marx quickly jumped to the profoundly deleterious effects of money on society as an institution and on each and every one of its members, thus linking Judaism with destructive power. "Money is the jealous god of Israel, beside which no other god may exist. Money abases all the gods of mankind and changes them into commodities. . . . Money is the alienated essence of man's work and existence; this essence dominates him and he worships it. The god of the Jews has been secularized and become the god of this world." Just in case his readers had missed the connection, Marx hit them over the head by returning to his point of origin: "The bill of exchange is the real god of the Jews."[41] Starting from a single false premise, Marx built a theoretical edifice to explain the conditions of contemporary society. This way of framing the problem that he called the "Jewish Question," adopting the terminology of the antisemitic theologian Bruno Bauer, admitted of but one solution. The Jew in particular, and society in general, could be saved only through the destruction of "Judaism," which for Marx meant both capitalism and Jewish religion and tradition.

Throughout the 1840s progressives such as Karl Marx waited for another revolution that would complete the objectives of the French revolution of 1789. By 1847 conditions seemed ripe: poor harvests and potato blight had destroyed the staple food of Europe. The continent writhed in the grip of famine. Food riots flared in France and Germany. To make matters worse, unemployment rose steadily as craftsmen saw their livelihood threatened or swept away by modern methods of industrial production. At year's end, Marx and his collaborator Friedrich Engels trumpeted the most famous call to arms in history. "Let the ruling classes tremble at a Communistic revolution. The proletarians have nothing to lose but their chains. They have a world to win. WORKING MEN OF ALL COUNTRIES UNITE."[42]

French revolutionaries took to the barricades in February 1848. Demonstrations quickly followed in Germany, demanding freedom of assembly, freedom of the press, and trial by jury. Millions of Germans believed that great things were about to occur. As one revolutionary democrat exulted, "The old world is crumbling, a *new* will rise therefrom; for the lofty goddess Revolution comes rustling on the wings of the storm."[43] This orator of revolution and progress was none other than the composer Richard Wagner. There were only two kinds of people, he proclaimed, those who joined the revolution and those who opposed it. "The one I lead to happiness; over the other grinds my path: for I am Revolution, I am the ever-fashioning Life, I am the only God, to whom each creature testifies, who spans and gives both life and happiness to all that is!"[44]

Wagner's language was not extreme. He was, if not a true reporter, a true spokesman for popular hopes and expectations. But when the smoke cleared, nothing much had changed, and the hopefuls were left frustrated, enraged, and impotent. In Wagner's case, the success of the counterrevolutionaries made him a marked man. Forced into exile, he had plenty of time to ponder what had gone wrong. The revolution had collapsed because the German bourgeoisie had preferred their comfort over community with the people. They had failed to recognize the value of the German nation. Fault lay in a pervasive culture of degeneration. Inspired by Bauer and Marx, Wagner identified "modern Judaistic utilism" as the root of all modern problems. Jews, in short, were a pernicious influence on society.

Wagner elaborated this idea in his essay "Judaism in Music." According to Wagner, the Jew "rules, and will rule, as long as Money remains the power before which all our doings and dealings lose their force."[45] Marx had said as much already in his criticism of capitalist society. What Wagner added was his insistence on the importance of commercialization of the art world as a measure of Jewish power. Claiming that Jews had transformed the suffering of artists for their art into financial profit, Wagner thought it now impossible to create at all. Furthermore, he argued, Jews could not be part of the European community or participate in its culture because they were unable to speak properly the language of their adopted countries. Language was the soul of the nation. Wilhelm Marr, a follower of Wagner, drew the logical conclusion: The Jew could never become German because he would never be able to speak German. Their original tongue was a Semitic language; therefore those who opposed Jews because they defiled and usurped German culture should identify themselves proudly as anti-Semites.[46]

"What is German?" Wagner asked. Culture, not economy, was at the core of German identity, he answered, and the Jew's manipulation of language and art was infinitely more pernicious than his control over money. The Jew had bought the German soul and reduced German *Kultur* (culture) into a sham, a mere image; it destroyed "one of the finest natural dispositions in all the human race."[47]

WAGNER'S IDEAS were echoed by a young Austro-German seditious terrorist imprisoned in a fortress after a failed coup d'état he had led. Recalling his days in prewar Vienna, Adolf Hitler discussed his own discovery of the "Jewish Question" in remarkably similar terms.

> Was there any form of filth or profligacy, particularly in cultural life, without at least one Jew involved in it?
> If you cut even cautiously into such an abscess, you found, like a maggot in a rotting body, often dazzled by the sudden light—a kike.
> What had to be reckoned heavily against the Jews in my eyes was when I became acquainted with their activity in the press, art, literature, and the theatre. All the unctuous reassurances helped little or nothing. It sufficed to look at a billboard, to study the names of them behind the horrible trash they advertised, to make you hard for a long time to come. This was pestilence, spiritual pestilence, worse than the Black Death of olden times, and the people were being infected with it![48]

As we shall see, this was but one of the ideas that Hitler picked up from Wagner and his friends.

Wagner believed that the German nation had been endowed with a rich inner life, one developed in the crucible of the Thirty Years War. The body of the nation had been annihilated, "but the German spirit had passed through";

in the physical ruins, the Germans once again realized they were a nation of the spirit. The grail that had preserved the spirit was music, its keeper Johann Sebastian Bach. Regaining their identity, their unique mission in the world was to proclaim *"that the Beautiful and the Noble came not into the world for sake of profit, nay, not for the sake of even fame and recognition."*[49] Wagner thus saw the new festival theater he built (1876) in the Bavarian town of Bayreuth as the Grail Castle of a new, spiritual Germany. Far from the cosmopolitan theaters operated by Jews, Bayreuth allowed the German nation to regain its sense of self by experiencing the mythic force of its own ancient epic—the *Nibelungen.*

Bayreuth soon became a center for younger Germans who shared Wagner's vision, and a pilgrimage point for foreigners who had come by different paths to similar conclusions. One of them was the French comte de Gobineau.

BORN INTO a family of Bourbon loyalists in 1816, Joseph-Arthur de Gobineau believed throughout his life that the French revolution had been a catastrophe for France. In his view, the upper classes, society's worthiest, had abandoned the state by handing it over to the middle and lower classes. He abhorred and feared the rapid social changes of his time. Such mixing of different groups in the cities of France and the erasure of social divisions must lead to rapid degeneration. A social pessimist, Gobineau obsessed on the idea that history was entirely determined by race. His contemporary Karl Marx might identify class struggle as the engine of social change, and other historians and politicians focused on the struggle between nations, but Gobineau contended that it was the struggle between races.[50]

For Gobineau, the French revolution ideals of equality and the brotherhood of men were both wrong-headed and factually incorrect. Indeed, he was most emphatic about the *inequality* of races. In the tapestry of civilization woven by so many different races, each had its own purpose and function. But one subgroup of the white race, the so-called Aryans, had the most important role.

> Human history is like an immense tapestry. The earth is the frame over which it is stretched. The successive centuries are the tireless weavers. As soon as they are born they immediately seize the shuttle and operate it in the frame, working at it until they die. The broad fabric thus goes on growing beneath their busy fingers. The two most inferior varieties of the human species, the black and yellow races, are the crude foundation, the cotton and the wool, which the secondary families of the white race make supple by adding their silk; while the Aryan group, circling its finer threads through the noble generations, designs on its surface a dazzling masterpiece of arabesques in silver and gold.[51]

Such ideas went beyond the bounds of nationalism. This was racism, and even so ardent a conservative nationalist as Renan called it pernicious nonsense.

"The truth is that no race is pure," Renan declared; Gobineau's premise was "a very grave error."[52] With eerie accuracy, he predicted that, should the count's ideology prevail, "it would spell the ruin of western civilization." In stark contradiction to Gobineau, Renan contended that "apart from anthropological characteristics, there are such things as reason, justice, truth, and beauty, which are the same for all."[53]

There were also, Renan observed, practical problems in applying race to politics. If racial distinctions were based on science, as Gobineau claimed, what would happen when scientific ideas changed? "Should nations then also change together with the [scientific] systems? . . . The patriot would be told: 'You were mistaken: You shed your blood in such-and-such a cause; you thought you were a Celt; no, you are a German.' And then, ten years later, they will come and tell you that you are a Slav."[54]

Nothing daunted, the anti-revolutionary count spun a tale that depicted history as the conflict between strong and weak races. In the history he told, strong races conquered weak ones, but the civilizations they created were undermined by miscegenation. With the admixture of blood between the strong and weak races, the former degenerated and the latter gained power, control, and authority. For Gobineau, the mingling of the races posed a much greater threat than did war.

> The hazard of war cannot destroy the life of a people. At most, it suspends its animation for a time, and in some ways shears it of its outward pomp. So long as the blood and institutions of a nation keep to a sufficient degree the impress of the original race, that nation exists. . . . But if, like the Greeks, and the Romans in the Later Empire, the people has been absolutely drained of its original blood, and the qualities conferred by the blood, then the day of its defeat will be the day of its death. It has used up the time that heaven granted at its birth, for it has completely changed its race, and with its race its nature.[55]

The nineteenth century was an age of general degeneration, Gobineau maintained, a decline rooted in miscegenation, which had begun with the collapse of the strict divisions of medieval society and the introduction of the new nation-state. As a result, civilization had not moved toward social equality, as revolutionaries had claimed, but rapidly descended into mediocrity. Sincerely gloomy, Gobineau believed that all was lost; there was nothing to be done.

Not everyone was quite so glum. Some saw in Gobineau's writings a way to halt the decline, to change course: the preservation of "pure Aryan" blood. If mixing was the problem, strict separation held the solution. The same Austro-German counterrevolutionary who had been inspired by Wagner's writings was enthralled by Gobineau. For Hitler, European civilization was the apex of human development, and it rested on a foundation of "Nordic blood." Well schooled in Gobineau's social theories, Hitler held that so long as the Nordic or "Aryan" group had preserved the purity of its blood, all had been well, but they had "bastardize[d] themselves, or let themselves be bastardized" to dire effect. "Purity of the blood" was key; loss of purity spelled disaster. "Blood mixture and the resultant drop in the racial level is the sole cause of the dying out of old cultures; for men do not perish as a result of lost wars, but by the loss of that force of resistance which is contained only in pure blood," Hitler asserted. "All who are not of good race in this world are chaff."[56] Indeed, the preservation of blood purity was, for Hitler, a holy obligation which he discussed in specifically religious terms. "Blood sin and desecration of the race are the original sin in this world,"[57] he proclaimed. Loss of purity led to racial degeneration, cultural decline, and individual misery. "The lost purity of the blood alone destroys inner happiness forever, plunges man into the abyss for all time, and the consequences can never more be eliminated from body and spirit. Only by examining and comparing all other problems of life in light of this one question shall we see how petty they are by this standard. They are all limited in time—but the question of preserving or not preserving the purity of the blood will endure as long as there are men."[58]

GOBINEAU'S MENTOR, the historian Alexis de Tocqueville, predicted that the count's work would have little impact in France but would find a receptive audience in Germany. It did. Richard Wagner got interested in Gobineau's work in 1876. They met shortly thereafter and quickly became friends. Wagner introduced Gobineau to his circle, and one young man, Ludwig Schemann, identified the count as Germany's new prophet. Creatively interpreting Gobineau's theories for a German public, Schemann postulated that the Aryan soul Gobineau had described lived still in the German nation. Germany must be the last bulwark of culture amidst an increasingly degenerate civilization.

Schemann established the Gobineau Archives and the Gobineau Society in Strasbourg, and became the leader of a small Gobineau cult which successfully influenced public opinion. His doom-and-gloom prophecy of general degeneration resonated with many Germans, matching what they experienced and observed. Oddly, at the close of a century which had witnessed European global conquest, the empire-builders began to suffer from insecurity. Losing the buoyant optimism and self-assured confidence that had engendered a plethora of discoveries and innovations, and the birth of all sorts of organizations and institutions, many Europeans in general, and Germans in particular, worried about national decline. By 1900, Gobineau, with his message of degeneracy, was celebrated in Germany as "the Man of the Time."[59]

Wagner's circle elaborated upon Gobineau's work, concocting the theory that, with their "Aryan blood," Germans would save European civilization. One member, Eugen Kretzer, like Ludwig Schemann, dedicated himself to interpreting Gobineau for the German public. "The superior race is the white race, the ruling family the Aryan family: according to Gobineau the Aryan family has endowed to the Germans, the world-ordering race, to produce the last blossom of world-historical development, and in the future any nation will be vital only if it preserved without mixture Germanic blood in its veins."[60] The time had come, Gobineau's disciples felt, to make a decision. Either the last remains of "Aryan" blood would disappear in a melting pot of races, or "Aryans" had to strive to reverse the process of degeneration; they would renew themselves and become a master nation fit to rule the world. They called, in short, for the emancipation of the "Aryan within." "If we desire to become lords, we must be Aryans," Kretzer maintained. "If we are to be lords, we must become Aryans. We must bring alive and make victorious those kernels of our Aryan inheritance that are within and around us, and we must weed-out, erase, and kill those kernels and the inheritance of the black and yellow factors within us and around us."[61]

The Aryan within: the hero, the man who struggles, the soldier. "Aryanism implies the heroic life, as Beethoven has painted it in the Eroica, not the happiness of the mass, the herd."[62] Heady language indeed, and it did not fall on deaf ears in a society that counted the philosopher Friedrich Nietzsche among its greatest sons. Like many of his contemporaries, Nietzsche mourned that he lived in a time of general collapse. The problem, as he saw it, was Christianity, which had produced a mean culture of mediocrity.[63] Christianity valued the wretched and the weak, and valorized the meek and mild. Nietzsche, by contrast, called for a new man, a proud, powerful man, an *Übermensch* (superman) who would eschew the teachings of Christianity.[64] But if there were *Übermenschen,* there must also be *Untermenschen.* And if Germans, with their "Aryan" blood, were the *Übermenschen,* it did not take the Nazis long to identify Jews as the *Untermenschen.*

Much of the all-too-persuasive nonsense Nazi philosophers would spout as wisdom and Nazi propagandists would pronounce as truth came from Gobineau and selective interpretations of Nietzsche. But neither Gobineau nor Nietzsche were antisemites. To be sure, Gobineau was a racist (which is equally execrable and equally dangerous) and Nietzsche implacably opposed Judaism (he opposed biblical religion in general), but at that point in history, racism and anti-Judaism had not fused into racial antisemitism.

It took Wagner's circle to introduce explicit antisemitism into racist discourse. Identification of the German as the ideal "Aryan" indeed came from his English-born son-in-law, Houston Stewart Chamberlain. While Gobineau believed that history was a struggle between races, Chamberlain simplified the plot in his influential book, *The Foundations of the Nineteenth Century.* For him, history was a struggle between the Aryan or Nordic type and the Jew, the race and the counter-race. And the Jews were in the ascendent. According to Chamberlain, Jews aimed to gain power over gentiles and to dominate the world. They realized, he argued, that purity of their own race held the key to their

5. *Facade of the Oranienburgerstrasse Synagogue in Berlin, completed in 1866. A large building on a prominent site designed in an eclectic style of Romanesque, Moorish, and Mughal themes, this synagogue proudly proclaimed the emancipation of Prussian Jewry. Coll. authors.*

power. Oddly, Chamberlain went on to state a ridiculous proposition: that Jews also sought to befoul other races with their blood. But how could Jews remain pure of blood and yet mix with the blood of other races? Reaching ever deeper, Chamberlain said the plot was simple: "the principal stem remains spotless, not a drop of strange blood comes in," while at the same time "thousands are cut off and employed to infect the Indo-Europeans with Jewish blood." This had been made possible by the emancipation of the Jews, and Chamberlain predicted that in a century or two the Jews would be the only pure race in Europe while "all the rest would be a herd of pseudo-Hebraic mestizos, a people beyond doubt degenerate physically, mentally, and morally."[65]

The old anti-Judaism had oppressed Jews for religious reasons. The new bias came reconfigured into a condemnation of Jews as champions of political radicalism and economic innovation. In the old world a Jew could always cross the line through baptism; now that option evaporated. It mattered not what Jews *believed,* but what they *were.* And this could not be changed.

GERMANY HAD BEEN RACKED by change following the creation of the unified Reich in 1871. The Wagner circle's construct quickly came to organize perceived incongruities and discordances of modern society. "The German" stood for a cookie-cutter concept of traditional, rural values, while "the Jew" stood for modern, urban sophistication. Thus, rural and urban, creativity and imitation, interior vitality and superficial sophistication, authority and democracy, morality and intellect, idealism and materialism, tradition and innovation, loyalty and opportunism, clarity and confusion, health and disease, purity and degeneration, all came down to "German versus Jew."

German paranoia in the late nineteenth century about such a "Jewish threat" was also fed by the rising migration of Jews after 1868 from the east to the west.[66] Fleeing poverty and pogroms, and in search of a better life, some 3 million Russian, Austro-Hungarian, and Romanian Jews left their homelands between 1868 and 1914. Moving west, primarily en route to America, hundreds of thousands passed through Germany, and many Germans feared they might stay. In the popular imagination, this potential inundation spelled disease, economic corruption, and political radicalism. Germany, Heinrich von Treitschke believed, had a "Jewish Problem," these eastern Jews pouring over the border. "Their children and grandchildren will dominate in the future Germany's stock exchanges and newspapers." Convinced that the Jews caused national degeneration wherever they settled, he wondered whether the downfall of German culture could be averted by a violent ejection of the Jews. Deploring the crude character of the antisemitism that had arisen so quickly in Germany, Treitschke nevertheless held that "the instinct of the masses had, in fact, recognized a very serious damage to the life of the new Germany." And he lamented publicly in the utterly respectable *Prussian Annals* of November 1879, "The Jews are our misfortune."[67]

Such opinion from Treitschke, a scholar well known and greatly admired, made antisemitism socially acceptable almost overnight. One contemporary, the historian Theodor Mommsen, noted Treitschke's impact. According to Mommsen, his articles had a "bombshell effect." Worse still: "The muzzle of shame was thus removed from this 'deep and strong movement' [of antisemitism]; and now the waves run high and the foam splashes."[68]

HOWEVER HIGH the waves in Germany, and however far the foam splashed, it was the French who opened the floodgates.[69] In 1894, a captain of the French army named Alfred Dreyfus was arrested. A French secret agent working in the German embassy in Paris had found a letter written by a Frenchman betraying military secrets to the Germans. On the flimsiest of evidence, Dreyfus was identified as the traitor and charged with treason.

The case that unfolded over the next five years, and then with less intensity for another seven, gripped the country. According to contemporary writers such as Marcel Proust, it politicized private dinner parties as greatly as it polarized public discourse.[70] *L'affaire Dreyfus* while *over* Alfred Dreyfus, was not *about* him. There were many issues at stake, and each principal character—the military personnel, the newspaper directors and owners, the politicians—had his own agenda for which the *affaire* provided a suitable battleground. At bottom the central question was an old one—are French Jews like other Frenchmen, or merely a foreign nation living in France, posing as Frenchmen?

"HIGH TREASON. THE JEWISH TRAITOR ALFRED DREYFUS ARRESTED,"[71] wrote Edouard Drumont in the headline of his virulently antisemitic newspaper, *Libre Parole*. Drumont wished to shape antisemitism into an acceptable, mainstream political movement. Calling attention to the influx of eastern European Jews during the past fifteen years, Droumont used menacing slogans like "the Jewish invasion," and broadened his case by demanding "France for the French." For him the Dreyfus *affaire* was a gift: a Jew was a traitor by his very nature. A lot of people agreed. Catholic newspapers took up the antisemitic argument. Jews could not be trusted with national secrets. Monarchists and extreme right-wing nationalists fell right in line.

Dreyfus was tried by court-martial on 19 December 1894. His judges unanimously declared him guilty and sentenced him to life imprisonment in solitary confinement on Devil's Island, a rocky volcanic archipelago off the coast of French Guyana. Apart from his wife and brother, few believed Dreyfus's claim of innocence.

A cry went up. Exclude the Jews! Whether the government would have done that is not clear, for France was quickly embroiled in the next act of the Dreyfus drama. New evidence emerged. A charming liar and cheat, the greatly in debt Major Ferdinand Esterhazy, had written the treasonous letter, not Dreyfus. But the Ministry of War refused to acknowledge error. As it began a cover-up, the public debate grew passionate. A young Jewish writer and critic Bernard Lazare, who had just published a history of antisemitism, took up the cause. He knew why the army had acted, and continued to act, as it did. "It was because [Dreyfus] was a Jew that he was arrested," Lazare declared in a pamphlet, "it was because he was a Jew that he was tried, it was because he was a Jew that he was found guilty, and it is because he is a Jew that the voice of truth and justice is not allowed to speak out on his behalf."[72]

The world-famous novelist Emile Zola saw the situation a bit differently. An ardent supporter of the French Republic, Zola perceived the case against Dreyfus as an attack against republican ideals. A true son of the Enlightenment and an heir to the legacy of 1789, Zola believed that the "Jewish Question" would have been resolved long ago had there been no antisemitism. "Persecution! Really, are you still at that stage!" he upbraided his readers. "Do you cling to that wonderful delusion—doing away with a people by persecuting them! No, no, it's quite the opposite." In language that foreshadowed Gesina van der Molen's call fifty years later for "a true melting together," Zola urged: "Let us embrace the Jews so as to absorb them and blend them into our ranks. . . . Let us put an end to the war between the races by intermingling the races. . . . This will be the great humanitarian and liberating achievement!"[73]

Zola's long-term solution had no impact on the immediate problem. Esterhazy was court-martialed and, after a two-day trial, acquitted upon three minutes of deliberation. Dreyfus's conviction was not reviewed. When Esterhazy was publicly denounced in the press later that year, university students from the Sorbonne took to the streets, demonstrating in support of the major and against Dreyfus. Zola was stunned. "Can young people be anti-Semites?" he asked in shock. "Is that possible? Can it be that their fresh new brains and souls have already been deranged by that idiotic poison?"[74] Zola could not have known that Europe stood at the edge of a century that would produce the most rabid, vicious, and lethal young antisemites in history—Hitler, age forty-four in 1933; Goebbels, age thirty-five; Himmler, thirty-three; Heydrich, twenty-nine. But perhaps he had an inkling as he lamented, "How very sad, how disturbing a prospect for the twentieth century that is about to begin! One hundred years after the Declaration of the Rights of Man, one hundred years after that supreme act of tolerance and emancipation, we are reverting to wars of religion, to the most obnoxious and inane type of fanaticism!" The young, he worried, "will begin the new century by massacring all the Jews, their fellow citizens, because they are of a different race and a different faith!"[75]

Something had to be done. Clearly, military justice did not exist, so Zola organized to have himself tried in the civilian courts. Under the banner headline "J'ACCUSE" (I accuse), Zola published his famous open letter to Félix Faure, the president of France, reminding him of his responsibility to uphold the ideals of justice and specifically accusing eight high-ranking army officers by name. The letter caused a public furor. Antisemites, Catholics, and ultranationalists rioted in thirty towns, attacking Jewish shops and synagogues while crying, "Death to the Jews!" and "Long live the army!" Zola was tried for libel and convicted. But as he had predicted, his trial finally exposed what the army had long known and long covered up: the hand that wrote the notorious letter found in the German embassy in 1894 was indeed that of Esterhazy, not Dreyfus. The tide turned. A year later, in 1899, Dreyfus was pardoned by the president, and in 1906 the verdict reached by the court-martial was revoked.[76]

THE DREYFUS AFFAIR had consumed France for a decade. This country of "liberty, equality, fraternity" had emancipated the Jews before any other in Europe. Now it became starkly clear that even the most liberal political system had not solved the "Jewish Question." Furthermore, Zola's call for total assimilation revealed that the dilemma for Jews and for gentiles posed by emancipation in the nation-state remained unresolved.

A Viennese Jewish journalist named Theodor Herzl had attended the Dreyfus trial in 1894 and witnessed the degrading ceremony in which Dreyfus was stripped of his sword and insignia. If such things could happen in France, Herzl realized, emancipation had failed. Jews must find another solution. "The Edict of the great Revolution had been revoked," Herzl wrote in despair.[77] The Declaration of the Rights of Man was null and void and the ideals of the French revolution had come to nought. And so he suggested what seemed to be the only viable solution in that era of nationalism: the Jews must create their own nation-state. In a private note, the founder of the modern Zionist movement expressed both bitterness and his hope, hope for a Jewish state "where we can have hooked noses, black or red beards, and bow legs, without being despised for it; where we can live at last as free men on our own soil, and where we can die peacefully in our own fatherland." If the Germans had been able to create a united Reich in 1871 out of the "dreams, songs, fantasies, and gold-black bands worn by students," surely Jews, motivated by memories and dreams and the hatred of others, could create their own state in Palestine. "There we can expect the award of

Chapter Two

THE GREAT WAR AND
ITS TERRIBLE OUTCOME

EUROPE SIMMERED on the brink of war throughout the summer of 1914. Germans, Austrians, Russians, French, British, the prospect beckoned to all—war, the proof of the national principle. War was an opportunity to demonstrate the greatness of the nation and to illustrate the unity of the people. War made good on the nationalist promise.

"I know no more parties, I only know Germans," Kaiser Wilhelm proclaimed on 31 July 1914 to more than 300,000 people assembled at the Imperial Palace.[1] Two days later, masses gathered in front of the Feldherrnhalle in Munich to hear the declaration of war. A photograph frames an enthusiastic Adolf Hitler in the crowd. "I fell down on my knees and thanked Heaven from an overflowing heart for granting me the good fortune of being permitted to live at this time. A fight for freedom had begun, mightier than the earth had ever seen,"[2] he remembered a decade later.

Millions across Europe shared Hitler's passion: recruits flocked to arms on both sides, rich and poor, conservative nationalists and liberal universalists, gentiles and Jews. The Austrian Jewish author Stefan Zweig had fiercely criticized nationalism until 1914, when he too was swept away in patriotic fervor.

> In spite of all my hatred and aversion for war, I should not like to have missed the memory of those first days. As never before, thousands and hundreds of thousands felt what they should have felt in peacetime, that they belonged together. A city of two million, a country of nearly fifty million, in that hour felt that they were participating in world history, in a moment which would never recur, and that each one was called upon to cast his infinitesimal self into the glowing mass, there to be purified of all selfishness. All differences of class, rank, and language were swamped at that moment by the rushing feeling of fraternity.... Each individual ... was no longer the isolated person of former times, he had been incorporated into the mass, he was part of the people, and his person, his hitherto unnoticed person, had been given meaning.[3]

Many large factors influenced the outbreak of World War I, but this slaughter of a generation of Europeans was sparked by a minor incident in an out-of-the-way place. The heir to the Austrian throne, Franz Ferdinand, was assassinated by a young Bosnian on 28 June 1914 while the archduke was on an official visit to Sarajevo, the capital of Bosnia-Herzegovina. Bosnia-Herzegovina had been annexed to Austria, and the Bosnian assassin was supported by a group of Serbian nationalists who feared, correctly, that Austria had its eye on Serbia as well.

This was not the cause of the Great War. Political murders were not uncommon at the time, and they did not normally engender wars. And so it was in this case. Austria took its time deciding how to respond. After consultation with Germany, which promised support for belligerent action, Austria delivered an ultimatum to Serbia which that small kingdom could not accept. Tensions mounted and Russia mobilized troops in support of its Slav Serbian brothers. Austria itched to respond. Germany stood by its ally and, aware that France would do likewise by its ally, Russia, the German General Staff decided on a preemptive strike. Germany would defeat the western partner before turning to the enemy in the east. And thus the Reich supported Austria's quarrel with Serbia by declaring war on Russia (1 August) and attacking France by marching through Belgium.

Belgian neutrality had been guaranteed by Britain. Britain too spent some time considering its options. By early August 1914, the decision came down. Britain would join the war. Thus, through incident, calculation, and a great lack of foresight, the European states plunged into war. The war they got, however, was not the war they expected or wanted.

Soldiers on each side marched off singing patriotic songs, firmly believing that they would be home by Christmas. To their horror, they realized in a matter of months that this war, which came to be called the Great War, would not be a brief belligerent encounter marked by decisive battles and limited casualties. To the contrary; it was a long-drawn-out, very bloody affair with mud-bespattered and shell-shocked men spending weeks and months in trenches. By the second year of the war, marked by the so-called great campaigns at the Somme, Verdun, Ypres, and Chemin des Dames, the men at the front understood that war was not an adventure leading to public glory, but a way of life that called for immense personal sacrifice with no end in sight. The battle of Verdun lasted nine months, from February to November 1916. The German supreme command aimed not to capture Verdun but, bleeding the French army to death, to force the Allies to the negotiation table.[4] Peace through carnage. Their plan failed. No armistice came their way, but millions of young men died. At Verdun some 720,000 German and French soldiers lost their lives within meters of each other. Over 1 million German, British, and French men were killed at the Somme; 470,000 German and British at the town of Ypres; and 160,000 German and French at the village of Chemin des Dames. Many more were wounded. Neither side gained, neither side lost. But the earth was soaked in blood.

Sensitive young men of all nations wrote of the slaughter they had seen. To the French veteran Henri Barbusse, "war" had acquired a new meaning. "War is frightful and unnatural weariness, water up the belly, mud and dung and infamous filth. It is befouled faces and tattered flesh, it is the corpses that are no longer like corpses even, floating on the ravenous earth. It is that, that endless monotony of misery, broken by poignant tragedies; it is that, and not the bayonet glittering like silver, nor the bugle's chanticleer call to the sun."[5] A highly decorated German veteran of the western front, Ernst Jünger, agreed. For Jünger, a battlefield was a landscape in which the dead "dissolved into a greenish fishmeat that glowed at night through their torn uniforms."

6. *The trenches, France, 1916. For many soldiers, the desolation of the front shaped an apocalyptic vision of the world. Reproduced in Ernst Jünger,* Das Antlitz des Weltkrieges *(Berlin, 1930). Coll. authors.*

When stepped upon, they left phosphorous tracks. Others had been withered to chalky, stripped down mummies. . . . In the sultry night swollen cadavers would come to spectral life, as hissing gasses escaped from the wounds. Worst of all was the simmering bustle that came from countless worms.[6]

The initial enthusiasm evaporated, but the German experience of national unity survived every blow. "National mobilization," no metaphor for patriotism, pervaded the lives of ordinary people. One-fifth of the German population served in the military, one-third of whom were at the front at any one time. The turnover of soldiers due to death, illness, injury, and capture exploded. On average, the German army lost a third of its men each year. Three-quarters of the wounded subsequently recovered and were reclassified as fit for duty again. Sometimes, men were recalled from the front to work in the hard-pressed war economy. This rotation from battlefront to homefront and back again revealed to women at home how poorly the military campaign was managed. At the same time, soldiers on leave saw the food shortages and the lack of clothes, fuel, and goods caused by the government's economic policy and the Allies' blockade. As each shared the other's misery, support for the government's practices or strategies vanished.[7]

There was indeed little solace to be found on the homefront, where conditions continued to deteriorate. As hundreds of thousands of families lost their male breadwinners, many occupations opened to women for the first time. Now they were not at home to look after their children, who in any case were only intermittently at school. Many schools closed during the war, the buildings requisitioned by the army or cold for lack of fuel, and male teachers conscripted. With mother at work and father at the front, school-age children spent much of each day standing on line with the family ration coupons for food, fuel, and supplies.

The terrible hardships on battlefront and homefront strengthened the experience of national unity. Indeed, it took on a new definition: Germans were a true *Volksgemeinschaft,* a national community independent from the state. Millions felt a sense of great personal investment and sacrifice. As the war stretched on, they came to see themselves as a nation that depended upon the achievements, resilience, and solidarity of ordinary men and women, not on the state.[8]

This schism between people and state, this experience of national unity that transcended the institutions of government and the ordinary understanding of citizenship, found a variety of political expressions during and after the war. One of the more famous was Ernst Jünger's *Essay on Total Mobilization* (1930). According to Jünger, a new Reich had formed, a secret Germany, within the political community of the state. "It is a different Reich, which puts us under obligation,"[9] he explained. This secret Reich was "the source of our feelings, our deeds and thoughts, so vital as no other phenomenon of this world."[10]

The National Socialists appropriated this concept of a secret Reich, the true core of the nation, for their own purposes. Introducing the first issue (April 1934) of the cultural magazine *Das Innere Reich*—an important forum in the Third Reich—the editor asked, "What kind of a Fatherland was this, a Germany for which its poorest and most loyal sons died with such incomparable courage and obedience?"

Was this only an external-political reality, a Fatherland that can only be measured in its economic and military power, in its number of inhabitants or the length of its borders? Let us be honest: many of them did not honor this external Fatherland; many even hated it, like sons hate their stepmother. They were indifferent to its mines, conquests and markets, and its monarchical constitutional forms. . . . But why did they then die willingly and piously, seemingly without recognition? They died for Germany! "Germany"—let us remember how softly that word was spoken by the ordinary person, by the illiterate and the uneducated, by the man who seemed to know so little about it. . . . They felt that this eternal Inner Germany, the "Holy Heart of the Nations," as our poets called it without arrogance, was threatened, and the literate and the illiterate, the educated and the uneducated, the rich and the poor . . . marched arm in arm. To them Germany was the same, and they died for her sake like brothers and equals next to each other.[11]

In the initial rush of enthusiasm and community spirit it appeared that distinctions between German gentile and German Jew had finally become irrelevant. Stefan Zweig's wholehearted support of Austria's cause was shared by masses of Jews in the Austro-Hungarian and German empires. Young Jewish men volunteered for military service and Jewish cultural leaders contributed books and pamphlets espousing the German cause.

This moment of solidarity was all too brief.[12] By late 1914, accusations that Jews were shirking military service began to circulate. Perhaps in terms of percentages the number of Jews in the German army matched their share of the population at large but, the rumors maintained, they had been able to find cozy jobs in orderly rooms and offices. Almost a decade later, Hitler complained that "the [military] offices were filled with Jews. Nearly every clerk was a Jew and nearly every Jew was a clerk. I was amazed at this plethora of warriors of the chosen people and could not help but compare them with their rare representatives at the front."[13]

Bowing to antisemitic agitation, the Prussian War Ministry conducted a statistical investigation in the fall of 1916 of the number of Jews in military service and the number at the front. The undertaking itself confirmed popular prejudices: to have an investigation, something must be amiss. In the end, the so-called Jew count clearly demonstrated that German Jews pulled their weight at the front, but the War Ministry refused to publish these results. Even more rumors flowed. Jewish soldiers were humiliated. The Jewish community was humiliated.[14] The only people who should have been humiliated, the antisemites, were not. Even when the statistics were made available after the war, the antisemites continued to twist the truth. In a lengthy rebuttal of the accusations, a German Jew, Franz Oppenheimer, observed that his arguments were unlikely to impress "the gentlemen of the swastika." They would likely remark: "It doesn't matter: the Jew must burn," he noted wryly. And he concluded, "we would be ignorant of the mentality of those people if they did not interpret my refutation as another example of Jewish insolence."[15]

The Germans' experience of World War I marked a watershed separating German gentiles and German Jews.[16] The issue was not one of statistics alone. The nationalist historian Oswald Spengler spoke for a deep antisemitism when he argued that even if Jews had joined the army en masse, they fell short of sharing the Germans' experience.[17] Since Jews *had* joined the army en masse, Spengler articulated a shift in the argument. To be a Jew meant, per se, an inability to be a German, and therefore to stand outside the national community. If the essence of the nation resided in the "secret Reich," there was no place for the Jews.[18]

Such a fundamental rupture often goes unrecognized and little understood

Sind das Deutsche?

*7. "Are These Germans?"
A staple of antisemitic
propaganda after World
War I, cartoons of men
and women with "typical"
Jewish features mocked
Jews' claims to be part of
the German nation. From
Paul Baumgarten,* Juda:
Wesen und Wirken des
Judenthums *(Leipzig,
1936). Coll. authors.*

at the time. Only in retrospect does clarity emerge. The German Jewish novelist Georg Hermann fled to the Netherlands after Hitler came to power in 1933. In a private document written for his children, he reflected upon the ruthless, state-sponsored persecutions that had forced him into exile. Georg Hermann had been an acculturated Jew in Germany. He had opposed the Zionist ideology and, at least until 1914, sincerely believed that Jews belonged in each of the European states. Indeed, prior to the outbreak of the Great War, he hardly realized he was a Jew at all. "Antisemitism was present," he explained to his children, "irritating as a gnat in a summer evening; but one frightened it away and found it quite pleasant out there, mild and warm. After 1914 this changed sharply."[19]

The war became a multi-step test which Jews were meant to fail. First, Hermann said, Jews were asked how they felt about the war. "Are you fully committed to it, or do you somehow have reservations?" If in favor, "then raise your voice for it. Roaring enthusiasm, if you are a spokesman of the spirit." But ardor was not enough, because the next message was, "Do not forget: this war is a German war and not a Jewish war. You may allow yourself and your children to be shot dead in it, you may destroy your fortune in war loans, you may go hungry—but as a Jew you must allow yourself to be constantly insulted by your superiors in the field and in the barracks. You are a Jew and therefore cowardly, but as Aryans, Germans are *ipso facto* courageous."

The situation grew steadily worse as the war went on. According to Hermann, whatever Jews did was interpreted as morally reprehensible. Gentile Germans rigidly refused to accord Jews respect, let alone approval. "If you became officer, you had elbowed your way up. Even if you were in an engineering battalion and wounded at night in the first trench, you did not participate in the great German experience of the front. If you organized the economy—which would have collapsed after three months if not for the Jews— you were a shirker, but if you as a German manufactured shells on lathes and filled your pockets, or if you raised a dozen pigs as a small farmer, you were a German hero, even if, unfortunately, indispensable and could only manifest your heroism in this manner."[20]

In 1935, Georg Hermann realized that "the avalanche that buried us came into motion as early as August 1914, and no matter how much we voted against it, we were unable to stop it." The next generation, he urged, must not be caught off-guard as his had been. "We could only have stopped it," Hermann declared, "if, from the very beginning . . . we would have adopted the technique of our opponents, and assassinated the leaders of their movements, instead of holding their stirrups, so that they could mount their horses."[21]

But the Jews of Germany did not turn to assassination, not in 1914 or 1918 or even 1933, and their opponents asserted whatever they wished. Rewriting history ten years after the so-called revolution of 1914, Hitler maintained that the war had erupted despite the Jews' underhanded efforts to prevent it, that the Jews had not shared the nation's enthusiasm for the war, and that Jews had not participated in the national awakening. Therefore, both the Jews and the government were to blame. "It would have been the duty of a serious government," he declared, "now that the German worker had found his way back to his nation, to exterminate mercilessly the agitators who were misleading the nation. If the best men were dying at the front, the least we could do was to wipe out the vermin."[22]

THE MORTALITY FIGURES from the Great War were staggering. Every family had a husband, son, uncle, or nephew on the front, and every family was affected by death, injury, or mutilation. In Germany, 2 million of the 13 million men in the army were killed; another 4 million were wounded. Russia lost 1.8 million men, France 1.5 million, Austria-Hungary 1.2 million, Turkey and Britain 800,000 each, and Italy 600,000. In relative numbers, Serbia (38%), Turkey (28%), and Romania (25%) suffered even greater losses.

The greatest atrocity of the war, however—and the least remembered—was the massacre of 1.5 million civilian Armenians. This was not military violence but genocide. The genocide of the Armenians was made possible by two events: the final collapse of the Ottoman Empire in the first decade of the twentieth century and the advent of total war in the second. Ruled by the Turks, the Ottoman Empire had been multi-ethnic and multi-religious; it included Muslim minorities, such as Arabs, and non-Muslim minorities, such as Jews and Christians. Ottoman rulers protected these non-Muslim communities and even granted them a measure of autonomy, but not civil rights. Until the end of the nineteenth century, the Christian communities of Ottoman lands had consisted of Greek Orthodox (including Greeks, Bulgarians, Serbs, Romanians, and some Albanians) and Armenians. With the independence of Greece (1830), and then Romania, Serbia, Montenegro, and Bulgaria, only one Christian autonomous community remained within Turkey without a national state: the Armenians.

A group of nationalists popularly called the "Young Turks" or "Ittihads" had staged a successful coup against Ottoman rule in 1908. Like other European nationalists, they rejected the idea of a multi-ethnic empire and embraced "Pan-Turkism," a violent, nationalistic, and intensely racist vision: Turkey for the Turks. The Ittihad ideologue Tekin Alp was certainly correct when he observed that Pan-Turkism merely kept "pace with the ideas of the age, which for some decades centred round the principle of Nationality." Indeed, with the adoption of Pan-Turkism, the Turks finally had "placed themselves on a level with modern nations."[23]

The Ittihad ideal came within reach in the confusion following the coup. The European powers grabbed whatever they could of the crumbled Ottoman empire, leaving the much-reduced Turkish state only Muslim territory. Austria annexed Bosnia-Herzegovina; Bulgaria and Albania unilaterally declared independence; Italy occupied Libya and Rhodes; Greece annexed Thrace; and Serbia took Kosovo. Greeks living in Smyrna and the Armenians were the only significant non-Muslim minority left. They faced a brutal, systematic policy designed to eliminate non-Turks from the social, cultural, and economic life of the country.

Matters worsened still more when an ultranationalist faction of the Ittihad movement gained control in 1913. According to the Austrian military plenipotentiary in Istanbul, Vice Marshal Joseph Pomiankowski, the new government was determined not to repeat the mistakes of earlier Sultans who, in the Ittihad view, "either ought to have had the conquered people [the Armenians] forcibly embrace Islam, or ought to have exterminated them."[24]

The Great War offered the Turks the opportunity they awaited. When Turkey entered the war in October 1914 on the German and Austrian side, Armenians were identified as the internal enemy. "If you want to know how the war is going," wrote a Turkish newspaper, "all you need to do is to look at the face of an Armenian. If he is smiling, then the Allies are winning; if he is downcast, then the Germans are successful."[25]

Europe in World War I

According to the United States ambassador to Turkey, Henry Morgenthau, rumors of future massacres circulated throughout the fall and winter of 1914. The Armenians responded by trying not to give offense. But what the Armenians *did* was of no consequence. It mattered only who they *were*.

Turkish government officials carefully prepared a plan of action. In a minute

written after conversations with leaders of the Ittihadist Party, Max Scheubner Richter, the German vice consul who also commanded a joint German-Turkish special guerrilla unit, noted that non-Turks either would be forcibly Islamized "or otherwise they ought to be destroyed."

> These gentlemen believe that the time is propitious for the realization of this plan. The first item on this agenda concerns the liquidation of the Armenians. Ittihad will dangle before the eyes of the allies a specter of an alleged revolution prepared by the Armenian Dashnak party. Moreover, local incidents of social unrest and acts of Armenian self-defense will deliberately be provoked and inflated and will be used as pretexts to effect the deportations. Once en route, however, the convoys will be attacked and exterminated by Kurdish and Turkish brigands, and in part by gendarmes, who will be instigated for that purpose by Ittihad.[26]

An Ittihad document dating from late 1914 laid out a ten-step plan of destruction (the British satirically called it "The Ten Commandments"). The Turkish government envisioned the destruction of the entire Armenian community. The instructions were unequivocal. "All action to begin everywhere simultaneously, and thus leave no time for preparation of defensive measures,"[27] read point number nine. Through the use of centralized planning and modern communication systems, all Armenians were to be assaulted. For the Turks, the sole question was: when?

They did not have long to wait. In the spring of 1915, Russian troops invaded Turkish territory following a failed Turkish offensive in the Caucasus. Sensing opportunity, nationalist Armenians established a provisional government in the Russian-occupied area. Here was proof of the "internal enemy" the Turks had long claimed them to be, and Enver Pasha, the Turkish minister of war, did not hesitate to tell Ambassador Morgenthau that "the Cabinet itself ordered the deportations."[28] "Deportations" meant "massacres," as German vice consul Scheubner Richter well knew at the time, and Morgenthau soon learned. The upright and astute Morgenthau was horrified by Turkish cruelty and injustice, and dismayed by the sheer effrontery of government officials. "When the Turkish authorities gave the orders for these deportations, they were merely giving the death warrant to a whole race," he wrote. "They understood this well, and, in their conversations with me, they made no particular attempt to conceal the fact."[29]

City after city, village after village, was emptied of Armenians. Without warning, people were summoned to the marketplace and robbed of their possessions. The young men were separated from the others, led to the outskirts of town, and shot. Women, children, and old people were forced on the road toward the Syrian desert. According to an eyewitness report to Morgenthau, "A guard of gendarmerie accompanied each convoy, ostensibly to guide and protect it. Women, scantily clad, carrying babies in their arms or on their backs, marched side by side with old men hobbling along with their canes."

Point nine had been carried out assiduously; action was taken suddenly and simultaneously, and the Armenians had no time to organize defense measures. Appalled, Morganthau traced their suffering. "From thousands of Armenian cities and villages these despairing caravans now set forth; they filled all the roads leading southward; everywhere, as they moved on, they raised a huge dust, and abandoned débris, chairs, blankets, bedclothes, household utensils, and other impediments, marked the course of the processions." The forced flight became a death march. "When the caravans first started, the individuals bore some resemblance to human beings; in a few hours, however, the dust of the road plastered their faces and clothes, the mud caked their lower members, and the slowly advancing mobs, frequently bent with fatigue and crazed by the brutality of their 'protectors,' resembled some new and animal species."[30] This new species was targeted for murder. Convicts released from prison for the purpose, Turkish peasants and Kurds joined gendarmes in murdering Armenians along the way. Starvation, typhus, dysentery, and cholera took their toll too. One convoy of 18,000 at its beginning arrived at a concentration camp near Aleppo with 150 survivors. This camp was but one of many around the city, each a focal point of human misery and a breeding ground for epidemic disease. Writing in 1918, it was clear to Morgenthau that "the whole history of the human race contains no such horrible episode as this."[31]

Rafael de Nogales, a Venezuelan adventurer and mercenary who rose to become Inspector-General of the Turkish forces in Armenia, was not cut of the same moral cloth as Morgenthau, nor was he a perspicacious observer. But he was an important witness nevertheless; he served Turkey in a senior official capacity. Contemptuous of what he saw as the failure of the Armenian men to fight the Turks (as others would be half a century later of Jews who "went like sheep to the slaughter"), de Nogales asked: "Why, I wonder, instead of whimpering like women, did not those cowards revolt like men and crush their petty escort with a single blow?" He ignored the role of the Turks, and ascribed responsibility to the wrong party, but he had compassion for the Armenian women and children who, he said, "had to pay with their lives for the selfish cowardice of husband and father."[32] And it was their plight he described in some detail.

As I was lunching, I saw through a window of the sub-government house a caravan of several hundred Christian women and children resting in the marketplace. Their sunken cheeks and cavernous eyes bore the stamp of death. Among the women, almost all of whom were young, were some mothers with children, or, rather, childish skeletons, in their arms. One of them was mad. She knelt beside the half putrefied cadaver of a new-born babe. Another woman had fallen to the ground, rigid and lifeless. Her two little girls, believing her asleep, sobbed convulsively as they tried in vain to awaken her. By her side, dying in a scarlet pool, was yet another, beautiful and very young, victim of a soldier of the escort. The velvety eyes of the dying girl, who bore every evidence of refinement, mirrored an immense and indescribable agony. . . .

When the hour struck for departure, one after another of those filthy, ragged skeletons struggled to its feet and, taking its place in that mass of misery that shrieked silently to heaven, tottered off, guarded by a group of bearded gendarmes. Behind them pressed a mob of Kurds and ruffians.[33]

8. *Armenian children dead from starvation, 1915. Photo by Armin T. Wegner. Courtesy Sibyl Stevens.*

When de Nogales reported what he had seen to a Turkish government official, the latter told him confidentially that none of the transports reached their destination in the Syrian desert. "When I inquired why not, he answered with a resigned air, 'Because Allah is great and all-powerful.'"[34]

Perhaps it was Allah; the Turks, for their part, flatly denied responsibility. The murder of 1.5 million unarmed Armenian civilians had not been genocide, or even murder, they claimed, and they launched a propaganda offensive to justify their actions. The Turkish War Office produced material "proving" that the Armenians had been in league with the Allies; that they had planned and prepared an uprising in Istanbul intending to hand over the city to the enemy. In fact, the government claimed, the Armenians had been removed to ensure the "internal and external security of the country." Naturally, "regrettable acts of violence have sometimes been committed, but however regrettable these acts might have been, they were inevitable because of the profound indignation of the Moslem population."[35]

Germany, the only European power that could have influenced Turkey, remained silent and did nothing. Harry Stürmer, a German correspondent in Constantinople for the major newspaper *Kölnische Zeitung,* understood that his government's silence and lack of action amounted to complicity. A veteran of many German military operations, Stürmer was no stranger to the brutality and the misery of war. The murder of the Armenians was not a military action, however, and Stürmer knew the difference and knew that his government knew the difference. "The mixture of cowardice, lack of conscience, and lack of foresight of which our Government has been guilty in Armenian affairs is quite enough to undermine completely the political loyalty of any thinking man who has any regard for humanity and civilisation." The genocide of the Armenians was "the meanest, lowest, the most cynical, most criminal act of race-fanaticism that the history of mankind has to show,"[36] Stürmer lamented. And as far as he was concerned, it embarrassed "every German."[37] He resigned his post and went into voluntary exile in Switzerland.

THE ALLIES vigorously condemned Turkey during the war,[38] and called for the establishment of a separate Armenian state. The defeated Ittihad government promised to do so in the Treaty of Sèvres (1920). But they soon lost power. The war hero General Kemal Atatürk stepped into the chaos reigning throughout the land. Pleased by Atatürk's promise to build a wall against Bolshevik expansion, the Allies conveniently forgot the Turks' atrocities. Forgotten too was the Treaty of Sèvres. Hopes for an Armenian national state vanished. By 1922 the Allies and the Turks had rewritten history, denying that genocide had occurred. "The Armenians were moved from the hospitable regions where they were not welcome and could not actually prosper to the most delightful and fertile parts of Syria," William Colby Chester wrote in *Current History,* a magazine of contemporary affairs published by *The New York Times.* "Those from the mountains were taken into Mesopotamia, where the climate is as benign as in Florida and California, whither New York millionaires journey every year for health and recreation. All this was done at great expense of money and effort."[39]

The Allies' peace treaty with Turkey was renegotiated with Atatürk's government the following year, 1923. The Allies abandoned the Armenians completely. Neither "Armenia" nor "Armenian" appeared in the final wording of the new treaty. For the international community, the "Armenian Question" had been solved. It was left to the brilliant British novelist Virginia Woolf to depict the prevailing attitude through a soliloquy by her character Mrs. Dalloway, the wife of a conservative member of Parliament. "She cared much more for her roses than for the Armenians," Mrs. Dalloway mused to herself. "Hunted out of existence, maimed, frozen, the victims of cruelty and injustice (she had heard Richard say over and over again)—no, she could feel nothing for the Albanians, or was it the Armenians? but she loved her roses (didn't that help the Armenians?)—the only flowers she could bear to see cut."[40]

If Virginia Woolf derided the Allies' indifference, Adolf Hitler took comfort from it. In his talk to senior generals at the Obersalzberg on 22 August 1939, just before the invasion of Poland, Hitler reminded his men that German strength was to be in "quickness and brutality." They should not quail at what they were to do. History always sided with the victor. "Ghenghis Khan had millions of women and children killed by his own will and with a gay heart. History sees only in him a great state builder. What weak Western European civilization thinks about me does not matter. . . . Who still talks nowadays of the extermination of the Armenians?"[41]

THE GENOCIDE of the Armenians was carried out by the Turks under cover of the Great War. The war provided both pretext and context for terrible violence against a civilian population. In central and eastern Europe, where hundreds of thousands of civilians, primarily Jews, were massacred, a different scene unfolded. These deaths were a direct result of wartime conditions and politics, which not only permitted but actually engendered vicious cruelty.

Some 7 million Jews lived in an area that became the eastern front: 1 million in Galicia, which belonged to Austria-Hungary, and 6 million in that part of Russia known as the "Pale of Settlement." This region had belonged to the Polish Kingdom in the seventeenth and eighteenth centuries, and was annexed by Russia when Poland was partitioned in 1772. At that time, the Russians forbade Jews living in the formerly Polish territory to move into Russia proper. The area thus came to be called the Pale of Settlement, "pale" meaning an enclosed area or boundary.

Life had become increasingly difficult for Jews in the Pale during the thirty years preceding the Great War. Agricultural production had stagnated while the population had increased. Ensuing widespread poverty and mass starvation had led to increased communal violence. The same conditions abetted revolutionary movements, which prompted another genre of violence against the Jews. Reasoning that insurrection was very un-Russian, conservatives linked these political movements with the Jews. In a situation of weakening government and fermenting revolution, the Jews proved particularly at risk for traditional anti-Judaism and racist antisemitism. The Kishinev pogrom of 1903 which, like other such massacres in the middle ages, took place at Easter time, started with the "blood libel," the myth that Jews used the blood of Christian children to make matzoh. It left fifty-one Jews dead, ten times as many wounded, seven hundred houses burned, and six hundred shops looted. Another round of pogroms followed after the Japanese destroyed Russia's fleet in the far east. This humiliation of the Russians led to no less than forty-five pogroms which the Russian government made no effort to suppress. The Jews, after all, were a foreign element. They could never be Russian.[42]

The identification of the Jews with the enemy, be it external (the Jews were allies of the Japanese, with whom Russia was at war) or internal (Jews led the revolutionary movement), was firmly forged when the Russian garrison in Port Arthur surrendered to the Japanese and urban disorder gave way to the Revolution of 1905. As far as right-wing political organizations were concerned, Jews were to blame. The government concurred. There was no revolutionary movement in Russia, Minister of the Interior Vyacheslev Pleve claimed, there were only Jews who opposed the government.

Clearly it was the government's responsibility to unmask the enemy. And if popular rage were redirected from the czar to the Jews, all the better. "Do you know, brethren, workmen, and peasants, who is the chief author of all our misfortunes?" asked a public broadside approved by an official censor in February

1906 and produced with a secret printing press set up in the St. Petersburg police headquarters. The answer was both old and new. Jews were the problem, of course. But there was a twist to the story: Jews were involved in an international conspiracy to obtain worldwide power by sowing discontent and confusion under the aegis of liberal reform. "Do you know that the Jews of the whole world, inhabiting Russia, America, Germany, and England, have entered into an alliance and decided to completely ruin Russia." Invoking the greatest popular fears and prejudices, the proclamation went on to claim that the Jews "would then, by means of lies and craft, take away the land from the Russian peasant, make him the slave of the Jew, do away with the priests, and convert the Orthodox churches and monasteries into Jewish stables and pig-sties." In the end, "they will make you work day and night, and pay you just enough to keep you from dying of hunger."[43] The proclamation had the desired immediate effect: 690 pogroms erupted, leaving 3,100 Jewish people dead, 2,000 seriously injured, and 15,000 wounded. It did not have the desired long-term effect, however. The revolutionary movement continued to grow.

Extreme right-wing political organizations then seized on a longer rendition of the conspiracy theory, the so-called *Protocols of the Elders of Zion*. A whole-cloth fabrication, the *Protocols* claimed to be the leaked minutes of a secret meeting of senior Jewish leaders at the first Zionist Congress convened by Theodor Herzl in 1897 in Basel. Indeed, according to the *Protocols,* the Congress itself had been a front for the Jews to discuss their machinations to control the world. First published in installments in the St. Petersburg newspaper, *Znamaya,* from 26 August to 7 September 1903, the *Protocols* appeared in book form two years later and subsequently was reworked by the mystical writer Sergei Nilus, who tied the conspiracy of the Council of Elders to the coming of the Anti-Christ.[44]

Nilus's version deeply impressed Czar Nicholas II, who decorated members of the Russian secret police for their "discovery" of the documents. But when ultraconservative politicians sought government permission to make the *Protocols* the centerpiece of a large-scale antisemitic campaign, Minister of Interior Pyotr Stolypin withheld approval pending an investigation of the origin of the text. The inquiry exposed the *Protocols* as sheer invention. "Drop the *Protocols,*" the czar commanded Stolypin. "One cannot defend a pure cause by dirty methods."[45] The czar, however, did not see that the facts were made public, and the *Protocols* went on to have a long and tragically effective life.

AT THE OUTBREAK of the Great War, the Jews, who spoke Yiddish, were identified by their Russian neighbors as "German"-speaking and thus enemy agents. Stories of treachery circulated in the press. As the German armies advanced into Russia, full-scale accusations of Jewish betrayal abounded. By March 1915 Russian policy called for deportation from one area to another within the Pale. At least 600,000 Jews were expelled from their homes. "Old men, sick women, clasping little children in their arms, carrying bundles with some scanty belongings that they snatched up in haste, fill the silent roads with the sound of their moans and sobs," a Jewish relief committee in Russia reported to its board. "Many are those who succumb on their way; indescribable are the sufferings of those who survive."[46]

A Jewish deputy to the Russian parliament took to the floor of the Duma. "Half a million persons have been doomed to a state of beggary and vagabondage," Deputy Friedman emphasized in a speech delivered in August 1915. The situation was inexcusable and unjustifiable. While Jewish soldiers fought for Russia, their families were treated like enemies. "I saw families of reservists," Friedman declared. "I saw among the exiles wounded soldiers wearing the Cross of St. George. It is said that Jewish soldiers in marching through the Polish cities were forced to witness the expulsion of their wives and children." Friedman's description of the deportations is disconcertingly familiar. "The Jews were loaded in freight cars like cattle. The bills of lading were worded as follows: 'Four hundred and fifty Jews, en route to—' "[47]

To their credit, Duma members of every political persuasion agreed with their colleague. They called on the government to halt the deportations. They were joined by 225 writers who signed a manifesto demanding the "complete union of all the nationalities inhabiting Russia" and the placement "of all citizens upon an equal footing."[48] But the government was not required by the constitution to respond to the Duma and, fearing a diminution of his authority, the czar did not act.

Ironically, in light of subsequent history, it was the Germans who answered the calls for an end to the persecution of the Jews. As the Russian armies retreated, ever larger areas of the Pale came under German military authority. Many German soldiers saw themselves as the liberators of people suppressed by the czar. But they did not know what to do with the east European Jews they now encountered. Prior to the war, few Germans visiting Russian Poland had ventured into the neighborhoods of Warsaw, Lublin, Vilna, or Lemberg. Now German soldiers patrolled these areas and German administrators struggled with an array of epidemics. They were at once sympathetic and confounded by the poverty and misery of a world so close and yet utterly unknown to them. "We had no idea that something like that existed so close to our door," the editor of the respected *South German Monthly* wrote in a special issue of the magazine devoted to the *Ostjuden* (eastern European Jews), and his countrymen agreed.[49]

Apprehension followed in the wake of their surprise. Germans at the front may have been willing to help, but German politicians and public figures were appalled at the prospect of some 2 million Jews in the territory Germany now controlled.[50] With no corner of Europe to call their own, masses of *Ostjuden* would migrate to the Reich. A "Jewish stream of immigration [threatens] to inundate our fatherland like a yellow flood, different but no less dangerous than the Mongolian invasion [of 1241]," one high-ranking bureaucrat, Georg Fritz, warned.[51]

Then too, a glimpse of Jewish ghetto life intensified and gave new meaning to an association long in use by antisemites—Jews as vermin. Earlier reaction to the arrival of *Ostjuden* in Germany had focused on the threat that each individual posed to the collective health of the German nation. Now, ghetto conditions suggested that the whole of Polish Jewry was one large and diseased entity. "Nowhere in Europe can one find such a filthy, narrow-chested people as the proletarian East Jews," journalist Wolfgang Heinze declared in the renowned *Prussian Annals.* In a series of articles he elaborated on the "fusty, filthy, fetid, and infested ghettos" inhabited by Jews with "small, degenerate bodies, narrow shoulders, bent backs, and contorted and awkward movements."[52]

INTEREST in the *Ostjuden* began to wane in Germany in 1917 when no diseased refugee horde swept in. In Russia, the "problem" of the Jews faded, eclipsed by the much more dramatic revolution of February 1917, when politicians of all stripes joined to remove the czar and to introduce government by representation. The Kerensky provisional government was established, which the leader of the Bolshevik Party, Vladimir Lenin, did not hesitate to challenge. Getting rid of the czar was only a first step toward Bolshevik rule. Lenin gladly accepted German support in exchange for his promise to take Russia out of the war after the Bolsheviks came to power. He was nothing if not persistent: the Bolsheviks tried to topple the provisional government in April, June, and July, but to no avail. Their fourth attempt, in October 1917, succeeded. Honoring Lenin's agreement with the Germans, Bolshevik emissaries led by Leon Trotsky crossed the front lines to seek an armistice. The Germans proved tough negotiators, demanding the surrender of all the land Russia had gained in the west since the reign of Peter the Great: Estonia, Latvia, and much of the Pale of Settlement. When Trotsky hesitated, the German army marched in and occupied the territory. Faced with this fait accompli, Trotsky agreed a few weeks later in the Peace of Brest-Litovsk to cede the land.

A consistent and outspoken opponent of antisemitism, which he saw as an instrument of the ruling class to divide and thus control the workers, Lenin insisted upon the abolition of all restrictions on Jews. For their part, many urban proletariat Jews supported the Bolshevik government. Indeed, they appeared to dominate Russia's new senior leadership. Leon Trotsky, Grigory Zinovyev, Lev Kamenev, Yakov Sverdlov, and Maksim Litvinov, notwithstanding their Russian pseudonyms (adopted to hide from the czar's secret police, not to obscure their ethnic identity), were Jews.

This was not lost on the czar's supporters. And as the portrait of "the Jew, Karl Marx" replaced icons of saints, the nobility and the officer class remembered the pamphlets that had instigated pogroms twelve years earlier, pamphlets that had predicted the Jews would ruin Russia, dispossess the peasants, close the churches, and enslave the population. They ignored the fact that Marx's followers also dispossessed Jewish artisans and closed Jewish study-houses and synagogues.

Civil war erupted in 1918. The Bolsheviks, or "Reds," controlled most of European Russia. An amalgam of anti-revolutionaries, the "Whites," controlled areas on the periphery of European Russia and nearly all of Siberia. In the summer of 1918, White forces approached the Bolshevik town of Yekaterinburg, to which the czar and his family had been exiled. Fearing that the Whites would liberate the czar and thus gain a powerful symbol of legitimacy, the Reds murdered the entire royal family. The Whites did capture Yekaterinburg, and in the late czarina's room they found three books: the Bible, Tolstoy's *War and Peace,* and Nilus's edition of the *Protocols of the Elders of Zion.* For the White officers who had arrived too late to save their czar and czarina, the *Protocols* became the czarina's last testament. Her blood had sanctified a text that the czar himself had acknowledged to be a forgery. Bolshevik Jewish leadership and Bolshevik policies seemed to confirm its truth.[53]

Presses in White-held territory printed cheap editions of the *Protocols* with a lurid addendum blaming the Bolshevik revolution on a worldwide Jewish conspiracy, and linking it to the reign of the Anti-Christ. This had little immediate impact because few Jews lived in the areas occupied by White forces. But when German troops evacuated the Ukraine in accordance with the armistice of November 1918, Russia regained 1.6 million Jews who had come under German rule in the Peace of Brest-Litovsk. The Whites moved in, unleashing their rage and frustration on the Ukrainian Jews.[54]

General Anton Ivanovich Deniken commanded the main White force in the Ukraine. This so-called Volunteer Army was staffed by Russian officers and consisted primarily of Cossack troops. Although the Jews well remembered the Cossack massacres of their ancestors in 1648–49, they eagerly awaited the arrival of the Whites in 1918. For the most part artisans and tradesmen, the Ukrainian Jews were not sympathetic to the Bolsheviks; they wanted stability, law, and order. But devastation and death followed in the wake of the Volunteer Army. First they looted Jewish property. After their forces suffered decisive defeats in late 1919, they initiated well-organized and ideologically motivated massacres of the Jews. These murders were the most successful military campaign of the White Russian Volunteer Army; at its conclusion this army had shot, bayoneted, hanged, burned, drowned, and buried alive some 120,000 Jews, or about 8 percent of the Ukrainian Jewish polulation.

An English journalist covering White operations in the Ukraine observed that the Russian officers "held that the whole cataclysm [the revolution] had been engineered by some great and mysterious society of international Jews."[55] Echoing the *Protocols,* these officers trumpeted antisemitism, turning it into the very raison d'être of the White counterrevolution. Defeated by the Reds in the end, White officers escaped to the west, taking their belief that Jews were responsible for Bolshevism with them.

Meanwhile, local nationalists along the Baltic declared independence. They prevailed. With the establishment of the new states of Latvia and Estonia, Balts—ethnic Germans whose medieval ancestors had settled in the area—left their home of seven centuries and "returned" to Germany. One of these refugees was Alfred Rosenberg, later a notorious Nazi ideologue and philosopher. He had met Nilus while he, horrified, watched the revolution unfold in Moscow. Nilus had given him a copy of the *Protocols* and Rosenberg was convinced.[56] His mission was clear: he must warn Germans of the dire dangers posed by both Communists and Jews.

It did not take Rosenberg long to sound the alarm. In February 1919 he published his first article on "The Russian Jewish Revolution." The liberal politics of the nineteenth century based on liberty, equality, and fraternity were nothing more than a subversive sirens' song, Rosenberg claimed. "The fruits of this subversion are apparent today. They are so nakedly apparent that even the most unbiased person . . . must become aware that he has placed his confidence in crafty and glib leaders, who intended, not his good, but the *destruction of all laboriously acquired civilization, all culture.* The proof," he said, was "the Russian revolution." Jews were to blame: they had exploited Russian weariness with the war by promising peace, freedom, and bread.[57]

Rosenberg had found his vocation. Using the *Protocols,* he wrote a long and detailed commentary explaining how the Jewish conspiracy had concentrated for twenty years on destroying Germany and Russia. To achieve this, "these two states were to be set against each other." According to Rosenberg, the Jewish press—powerful, persuasive, and manipulative—had propagated an anti-Russian line in Germany and an anti-German line in Russia; thus Germany and Russia had gone to war. As the Elders of Zion had foreseen with glee, the result had been mutual destruction.[58]

THE *Protocols* met with a receptive audience. For the tired, the frustrated, the bitter, and the disenchanted, they appeared to offer a plausible explanation for the situation Germany was in. And there were many tired, frustrated, bitter, and disenchanted Germans by the time Rosenberg published his edition of the *Protocols* in 1923. The tide of war in the west had veered from near victory in the spring of 1918 to utter catastrophe three months later. The Allies mounted a counteroffensive in July, pushing the German army eastward through Belgium. German morale collapsed. It was clear even to the most ardent nationalists that Germany had lost the war. As the Social Democratic leader Philipp Scheidemann put it to General Erich Ludendorff in a meeting of the War Cabinet, the workingman had come to the conclusion that "an end with horror is better than horror without end."[59]

The German supreme command, however, refused to accept either defeat or the widespread public demand for a cessation of hostilities. Starting with the slaughter of Verdun, German generals had ceased to plan military operations according to objective strategies to achieve political aims. Annihilation of the

9. *Cover of a French edition of the*
Protocols of the Elders of Zion, *1934.*
The representation of the conspiracy as
a poisonous spider or an octopus with a
"typically Jewish" face, strangling a
globe, became popular in the 1920s and
remains so today. Institute of Contem-
porary History and Wiener Library
Limited, courtesy of the United States
Holocaust Memorial Museum Photo
Archives, Washington, DC.

enemy had become an end in itself. They no longer thought in terms of military victory or defeat, but about national survival or perdition. And as the generals' ability to consider the war in military terms disappeared, so did their willingness to accept defeat as the result of their own mistakes, their army's exhaustion, or Allied strength. They were not at fault, they told each other; the Socialists undermined the army, so did the homosexuals and the Jews.[60]

The admirals of the German High Seas Fleet, who had not suffered defeat, shared their field colleagues' warped perspective. At the end of October, the naval command ordered its fleet to attack the British. No tactical advantage lay in this battle; it was a suicidal mission, staged solely to redeem naval honor. Not surprisingly, most of the sailors were more interested in their lives than in the fleet's honor. They mutinied.

The sailors' rebellion triggered other mutinies in the army and revolutionary upheavals at home. All over Germany, north to south, Bolshevik-style "Councils of Soldiers and Workers" were formed to replace existing local government. The monarchy fell on 9 November. Wilhelm II abdicated and left for the Netherlands, where he promptly committed the unforgivable folly of cutting down all the ecologically much needed trees on the estate lent to him in Amerongen and then on the one given him in Doorn. The Dutch were not happy with the royal guest to whom they had offered asylum. Back in Weimar, Philipp Scheidemann and his fellow Social Democrat Friedrich Ebert faced widespread revolutionary agitation in Berlin. Hearing rumors that the Communist Karl Liebknecht intended to proclaim a People's Republic, they quickly declared the birth of the German Republic.[61]

By that time, a delegation led by Scheidemann and Ebert's colleague Matthias Erzberger was already involved in armistice negotiations with the Allies in a railway carriage in the forest near Compiègne. Confronting draconian terms, but mindful of the political chaos at home and fearful of a Bolshevik takeover, Erzberger did the best he could. The Allies quite ignored the Peace Treaty of Brest-Litovsk that Germany had concluded with the Bolsheviks in March 1918. Now they demanded the return of all German-occupied territories in the east as well as in the west. They allowed the Germans but one month to demobilize their army. Erzberger hoped for the best, and signed.

Defeated, hungry, and ill, the soldiers were relieved to have survived and they wanted to go home. For months they had known that the only way to end the slaughter was to end the war. It was a spontaneous demobilization: the soldiers just went home. In Erzberger's words, "The German Army has disappeared." The men returned to pick up the pieces of their interrupted lives, to become husbands, fathers, and sons again, to live in a peacetime world with peacetime work.[62]

They brought with them disappointment and anger. The renowned novelist Thomas Mann tried to explain this feeling to the French public. As a result of the armistice, he said, "the German people suffered a collapse, physical and mental ... as history, doubtless, had never known before." Four years of war had ended in an "unparalleled fall," when "a moral fortress that had long defended itself with clenched teeth ... was left without the slightest power of resistance." In Mann's view, "the demoralization had no limits; it could be seen in the *deep and almost fatal anxiety of a whole nation that despaired of itself,* of its history, of its finest treasures ... for all of it had been morally implicated in a war which, it was declared, for that very reason *must* absolutely be won, and which in fact, with such a weight of ideas behind it, ought not to have been lost."[63] In earlier centuries, before the nationalist idea had been born and nationalist ideology had taken hold, losing a war would not have caused such a crisis. But in early twentieth-century Germany, defeat challenged not just national pride but national *identity*.[64]

"And so it had all been in vain," Adolf Hitler wrote in *Mein Kampf.* "In vain all the sacrifices and privations; in vain the hunger and thirst of months that were often endless; in vain the hours in which, with mortal fear clutching at our hearts, we nevertheless did our duty; and in vain the death of two millions who died." He called on their graves to open "and send the silent mud- and blood-covered heroes back as spirits of vengeance to the homeland which had cheated them with such mockery."[65]

German generals agreed. Unwilling since Verdun to admit military failure, they now openly insisted that revolution on the homefront and not defeat on the battlefield had caused the collapse. Germany would have won, Field Marshal Paul von Hindenburg testified in a Reichstag inquiry, had it not been "for secret intentional mutilation of the fleet and the army." Quoting the English general Sir John Frederick Maurice, Hindenburg declared: "The German army was stabbed in the back."[66]

WHILE THE ARMISTICE dismayed Germans, the Treaty of Versailles enraged them. Dashed were their hopes for an equitable settlement of boundaries throughout Europe following the nation-state principle. The American president Woodrow Wilson had sought acceptance of the idea that a people who share a language, culture, and history are entitled to a state of their own, and of a peace without victors or vanquished. But the French were obdurate. They too had suffered four years of fighting and utter destruction, and it had been on their own soil; they saw no need to be fair to Germany. They used the Versailles Treaty as an instrument of revenge, demanding that Germany give up large territories, acknowledge sole responsibility for the war, and pay the astronomical sum of 269 billion Goldmarks.

If revenge is a dish best eaten cold, the French enjoyed a freezing feast. Some statesmen recognized the viciousness of the terms but none acted to soften them. The Italian prime minister Francesco Saverio Nitti saw the treaty as a continuation by the French of the war against Germany. "Germany asked for peace at a time when, in the name of the United States, which had become a decisive factor of victory, Wilson's solemn pledges assured and guaranteed a perfect equality between victors and vanquished. But, when Germany was no longer in a condition to offer any resistance, the Treaty of Versailles broke all pledges which had been given, and introduced new forms of domination and strife into modern history, by adopting a series of measures which could have no other objects than those of strangling Germany, dismembering her, hampering not only her economic unity, but also her political unity, and depressing all the conditions of her existence."[67]

David Lloyd George, the British prime minister, agreed completely and worried about the consequences. "Injustice, arrogance, displayed in the hour of triumph, will never be forgotten or forgiven," he observed in a document dated 25 March 1919 dealing with "Considerations for the Peace Conference." He predicted that the Allies' decision to grant the newly independent Poles all their territorial demands, including areas with large populations of ethnic Germans, would lead to disaster. He was, he declared, "strongly averse to transferring more Germans from German rule to the rule of some other nation than can possibly be helped." However reasonable the nation-state principle might appear theoretically, the political reality created by its actualization would be ruinous. "I cannot conceive any greater cause for future war than that the German people, who have certainly proved themselves one of the most vigorous and powerful races in the world, should be surrounded by a number of small States, many of them consisting of people who have never previously set up a stable government for themselves, but each of them containing large masses of Germans clamouring for reunion with their native land."[68]

In any case, both Lloyd George and Nitti observed, the Poles' demands contravened the very nation-state principle they claimed to champion. This "new Poland," Nitti noted, was not "the Poland heralded by Wilson—a Poland of undeniably Polish elements—but a Poland including large German and Russian populations, and in which the Polish elements account for scarcely more than half the population."[69] Again Lloyd George concurred, and again he worried. With astonishing prescience, he foretold the future very precisely. "In my judgement," he said, the Poles' proposal "that we should place 2,100,000 Germans under the control of a people which is of a different religion and which has never proved its capacity for stable self-government throughout its history must . . . lead sooner or later to a new war in the East of Europe."[70] And so it did. It did *not* lead to the Holocaust, but it did figure centrally in the opening campaign of World War II, Germany's invasion of Poland in September 1939.

Millions of Germans urged their government to reject the Versailles Treaty. "All over Germany, in every region and every social circle, a storm of anger suddenly ignited over the enormous arrogance of the peace terms," reported a National Socialist diatribe. "But in that hour of destiny it was primarily the Jews who were already prepared to sabotage the will to resist, and who thus broke the united front. In that hour, they attacked the German nation in the back."[71] So powerful were they, the Nazis claimed, that the German delegation at Versailles accepted the crushing conditions for peace.

Once antisemitic nationalists had concocted the Jewish stab-in-the-back argument, they found evidence for this dastardly deed everywhere. In their

German territorial losses, 1918-1919

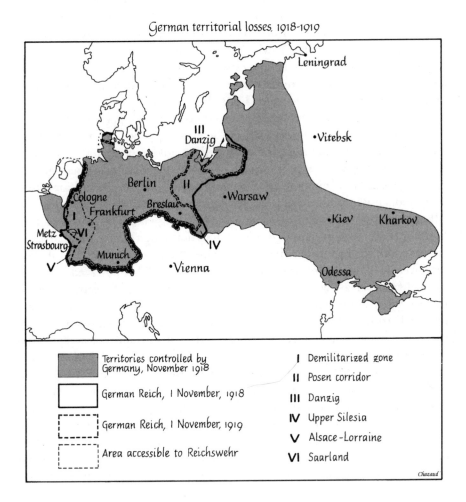

Territories controlled by Germany, November 1918	I Demilitarized zone
German Reich, 1 November, 1918	II Posen corridor
German Reich, 1 November, 1919	III Danzig
	IV Upper Silesia
Area accessible to Reichswehr	V Alsace-Lorraine
	VI Saarland

Chazaud

view, it was the fault of the far too many Jews in the new government that the armistice had been signed. In one particular the antisemites were correct: Jews served in the Council of People's Deputies, the six-member provisional government established after the monarchy fell. Until 1918 Jews had been barred from high government and civil service posts. That two leading positions now were held by Jews (Hugo Haase and Otto Lansberg) constituted a radical change. Furthermore, Jews filled the posts of state secretary in the Ministry of the Interior and in the Ministry of Finance. The prime ministers of Prussia (Paul Hirsch) and of Bavaria (Kurt Eisner) were Jews.[72]

Right-wing nationalists also held Jews responsible for revolutionary agitation and the overthrow of "order." They decried the prominence of Rosa Luxemburg (murdered in 1919) and Paul Levi in the Communist Spartacus movement. And then, just as the Germans were assembling their delegation to negotiate in Versailles in the spring of 1919, the Jews—according to the antisemites—further destabilized the country by instituting the Bavarian Soviet Republic in Munich. Its leaders, the Socialist Ernst Toller, the anarchists Gustav Landauer (murdered in 1919) and Erich Mühsam (murdered, 1934), and the Communists Eugen Leviné, Towia Axelrod, and Max Levien, were unabashedly Jewish.[73] They rejected the suggestion of more timid Munich Jews that, by taking a public role in the Soviet, they would give the antisemites new ammunition. Antisemites, the Jewish radicals declared, should never control the behavior of Jews. Within weeks, free corps units brutally suppressed the Bavarian Soviet Republic, which they called a "Jewish Republic." At least one thousand two hundred supporters of the short-lived government were murdered; corpses lay rotting in the streets for days before being hauled off to mass graves.

No matter how many Jews they killed, or "Jewish" institutions they destroyed, antisemites still believed that Jews held too much power. When the Allies handed the German delegation the crushing take-it-or-leave-it conditions for peace, the antisemites did not fail to notice that Georg Bernhard, the Jewish editor in chief of the liberal daily paper the *Vossische Zeitung,* called on the government to swallow the humiliation and sign.[74] They observed with rancor that Hugo Haase was the first deputy to speak in favor of acceptance of the treaty when it was presented for approval in the Reichstag. And they noted that the Jew Kurt Rosenfeld was the first member of the Prussian legislature to urge the government to acquiesce. What the antisemites would not accept—and Bernhard, Haase, and Rosenfeld saw clearly—was that Germany had no choice. In compliance with the armistice agreement, the Reich had already surrendered its fleet, air force, and heavy weapons. The country simply did not have the military muscle to reject the terms and refuse to sign.

Such practical considerations were of no consequence to a vocal minority of Germans who were too angry to be rational, too intoxicated by nationalist rhetoric to think clearly, and too powerless to act constructively. They believed that the new Weimar Republic had betrayed the nation by signing the treaty. Such a

government could not be "Germany." Losing their trust in the fledgling democratic institutions of the Weimar Republic, many Germans turned to the idea
that the "true Germany" had spurned the treaty and refused to accept the peace.
Their Germany was unconquerable.[75] And so they waited.

Reflecting upon his political development after World War I, Adolf Hitler
explained in *Mein Kampf* that "hatred" had grown in him, "hatred for those
responsible" for the betrayal of the nation. "There is no making pacts with Jews;
there can only be the hard: either—or." Therefore, he said, "I, for my part,
decided to go into politics."[76]

Hitler joined the small Bavarian-based German Workers' Party in September 1919, and soon reorganized it under a new name: the National Socialist German Workers' (Nazi) Party. A number of Balt exiles were early recruits, one of
them Alfred Rosenberg, hard at work on his edition of the *Protocols*. Hitler liked
Rosenberg's tenet of a universal "Judeo-Bolshevik" conspiracy. This notion
charged Jews with using enlightenment ideals—equality of citizens before the
law, freedom of conscience and religion, freedom of the press, compulsory education, universal suffrage, constitutional government, parliamentarianism—as
wedges to dissolve the old bonds that had ensured stability. The chaos they thus
created prepared society for Bolshevism. Hitler admitted to his fellow Nazi
Hermann Rauschning that the *Protocols* might be a forgery but, Rauschning
reported in 1939, "he did not care two straws whether the story was historically
true. If it was not, its intrinsic truth was all the more convincing to him."[77]

The "intrinsic truth" of the *Protocols* blended nicely with racist ingredients
from Gobineau via Houston Stewart Chamberlain and a survival-of-the-fittest
ideology. Humanity was locked in "eternal struggle" for the "preservation and
continuance of the life of a people."[78] Thus, according to Hitler's doctrine, Marx
had been a Jewish sorcerer who sought to destroy national social and political
structures. Bolshevism was the Jews' tool to control the Russian masses. "With
the sure eye of the prophet," Hitler explained, Marx "recognized in the morass
of a slowly decomposing world the most essential poisons, extracted them, and,
like a wizard, prepared them into a concentrated solution for the swifter annihilation of the independent existence of free nations on this earth. And all of this
in the service of his race."[79] This did not augur well, Hitler asserted. Jews threatened the whole world. Hitler prophesied that "if with the help of his Marxist
creed, the Jew is victorious over the other peoples of the world, his crown will
be the funeral wreath of humanity and this planet will, as it did thousands of
years ago, move through the ether devoid of men."[80]

Ferocious measures were required to combat this foe. "In 1918 we paid with
our blood for the fact that in 1914 and 1915 we did not proceed to trample the
head of the Marxist serpent once and for all. If at the beginning of the War and
during the War twelve or fifteen thousand of these Hebrew corrupters of the
people had been held under poison gas, as happened to hundreds of thousands
of our very best German workers in the field, the sacrifice of millions at the

front would not have been in vain."[81] The Germans had fallen short; indeed, they had failed even to recognize the problem. The National Socialist Party would not make that mistake again. Excluding the "Hebrew corrupters" from the body politic was a first step toward protecting the German people. Citizenship, the party demanded, should be restricted to "folk comrades," and only persons "of German blood" could be folk comrades. "No Jew, therefore, can be a folk comrade."[82]

Jews responded in many ways. Some tried logic. Others reminded their fellow citizens of the contributions of Jewish Germans to the nation.[83] Still others, like the Austrian Hugo Bettauer, mocked the Nazis. In his satirical novel *The City Without Jews* (1922), Bettauer painted a picture of what would happen if the antisemites' wish were fulfilled and all the Jews were expelled—in this case from Austria. In his story, the population initially celebrated. The Viennese soon noticed, however, that theaters had gone bankrupt, department stores were in a bad way, and the hotels and health resorts were empty. Vienna had ceased to be a metropolis and was merely "a huge village with a million and a half inhabitants." Worst of all, without the Jews to blame, the Christian Socialist and the National Socialist parties had collapsed. In the end, the expulsion law was revoked and the Jews were welcomed back to Austria.[84]

The City Without Jews sold a quarter of a million copies in its first year, an astronomical figure at the time. The Nazis were not happy. On 19 March 1922 a young party member, the twenty-one-year-old Otto Rothstock, entered Bettauer's office and shot him five times at point-blank range. At his trial, Rothstock justified what he had done as necessary to save German *Kultur* from the menace of Jewish degeneration. Rothstock emerged a popular hero.[85]

IN THE EARLY 1920s, the small National Socialist Party (NSDAP) was only one of many on the extreme right of Germany's political spectrum, and Hitler a little-known, fringe agitator. Within a decade, the NSDAP emerged as a powerful force and Hitler and his ideology were to steer the nation. This meteoric rise was mainly due to the adoption of the political ideas of Italian fascism and to the purely coincidental opportunity provided by the Depression to trumpet the value of NSDAP policies to a disaffected public.

In the 1920s, the Italian political activist Benito Mussolini introduced a radically new form of politics that to many people throughout Europe appeared to offer a viable alternative to democracy. Fascism was no mere regression to premodern forms of government, nor did it advocate maintaining an outmoded and discredited status quo which careened between chaotic and listless. On the contrary: fascism promised Italians a path to eternal youth and future greatness, and it was this that inspired Hitler.[86]

Fascism grew out of the Italians' war experience and their postwar confusion and disappointment. Like the other combatant nations, Italy had been bled white by World War I—four years of combat, 652,000 men dead, 450,000 mutilated, and 1 million wounded. Many Italians felt that they should be rewarded for their suffering and sacrifices. After all, Italy had joined forces with the Allies in 1915 and they had won. Among other territories, they demanded south Tyrol to the west, and Istria, Dalmatia, and Albania all along the Adriatic Sea. Large groups of Italians lived in Istria, and if few resided in Dalmatia, the region nonetheless had a historic connection with Venice. Albania was simply for dessert. Italy's prime minister Francesco Nitti sought to delimit his country's territorial claims. The facts spoke for themselves: there were large numbers of other ethnic peoples in Istria and south Tyrol; one had to look hard for an Italian in Dalmatia, and none was to be found in Albania. Nitti was prepared to press for south Tyrol and Istria for strategic geographic reasons but, he argued, the rest of his countrymen's claims were unreasonable and ill-considered.[87]

Mussolini thought otherwise. "It was in this great historical moment immediately after a victory achieved with untold hardship that our young nation . . . was treacherously deceived," he wrote in his autobiography ten years later.[88] He was equally blunt in 1919, demanding, in the name of those who had fallen, a policy of no compromise. "Fear nothing, glorious spirits! Our task has just begun. No harm shall befall you. We shall defend you. We shall defend the dead and all the dead, even though we put dugouts in the public squares and trenches in the streets of our city," he thundered in the Fascist newspaper *Il Popolo d'Italia (The People of Italy),* of which he was the founder and director.[89]

He meant what he said. A month later, in March 1919, he held the first meeting of those who opposed the peace, the *fasci di combattimento,* the fighting Fascists. They took for their symbol an emblem of the Roman Republic: the *fasces,* the ax which in ancient times had signified authority, with a bound bundle of reeds wrapped around the handle, to illustrate strength in unity. Italy could draw on the greatness of its past to create a magnificent future. This vision attracted the demobilized *arditi,* the Italian shock troops who, in Mussolini's words, "threw themselves into the battle with bombs in their hands, with daggers in their teeth, with a supreme contempt for death, singing their magnificent war hymns."[90] The *arditi,* in turn, influenced Mussolini. He adopted their black-shirt uniform for his movement, and their lust for violent action.

Unlike other political ideologues such as Lenin or Marx, Mussolini had no coherent philosophy. He believed in faith, not reason; in action, not thought. The *arditi* liked that. These "boys in boots," as a contemporary American writer called them, "brought back from the war a passion for action, an indifference to the value of human life other than their own, a contempt for legality and morality and an expert knowledge of firearms."[91] The Fascist program of instinctual action also attracted Italian youths who regretted missing the camaraderie and patriotic fervor of the war. Eager and enthusiastic, these young people were ready for a movement that promised a break with the past and national renewal starting that very day.

The Fascists offered their followers an opportunity for action when the Italian delegation returned from Versailles in June 1919 with little to show for the nation's sacrifices and military successes. Neither Dalmatia, nor Albania, nor the whole of Istria had been ceded to Italy: obviously policies shaped by reason and thought did not deliver the goods. Following the Fascist creed that only action matters, many of Mussolini's followers joined the well-known poet, idealist, and adventurer Gabriele D'Annunzio in capturing the east Istrian city of Fiume. The sheer audacity of this exploit established the ultra-nationalistic and idealist credentials of the Fascist movement. The black shirts' insolence and ferocity certainly frightened many middle-class people, but their emphasis on spiritual values and strict discipline also suggested a safer alternative than communism or anarchism. In contrast to the "Liberty, Equality, Fraternity" of the French Revolution, the Fascists proclaimed the principles of "Responsibility, Hierarchy, and Discipline." And they soon carried the day.

Democratically elected but powerless and lackluster Italian governments limped on until the summer of 1922, when Rome lost control and the country erupted in riots, nationwide strikes of essential services, and economic chaos. Fearful of a Bolshevik uprising, the middle classes turned to the right. For more than two years the Fascists had proved willing and able to beat up left-wing rioters

Europe, territorial changes after 1918

and to quell strikes by force or threat of violence. Stefan Zweig had seen them in action during a general strike in Venice. Although he himself was repelled by their philosophy and tactics, he understood their appeal to others. The central square of Venice, the Piazza San Marco, "looked strikingly deserted," Zweig recalled. Business had come to a standstill.

The shutters of most of the stores were closed, nobody sat at the cafés, only a large number of workers stood under the arcades in small groups, like people waiting for a particular thing to happen. I waited with them and, suddenly, it came. From a side alley a company of young people, in regular formation, approached in rapid march step, confidently singing a song, the words of which were unfamiliar to me—later I knew it be the *Giovinezza* (Youth). They had already passed in their running step, swinging their sticks, before the crowd [of workers], a hundred times greater in numbers, had had time to pounce upon its adversary. This bold and really audacious demonstration on the part of this organized group had happened so quickly that by the time the crowd became aware of the provocation it was too late for them to catch up with their adversaries. Angrily they pressed together and shook their fists, but it was too late. The little storm troop was beyond reach.

Zweig was shocked. "Now, for the first time, I knew that this hazy fascism, until then almost unknown to me, was something real, something well directed, and that it made fanatics of decided, bold young people."[92]

WITH JUST SUCH TACTICS Mussolini conquered Rome. In October 1922 he assembled his black shirts in the capital and, almost before anyone realized what was happening, he had effected a bloodless coup. His March on Rome had been successful, and he assumed the office of prime minister. At thirty-nine, he was the youngest premier in Europe. "Youth is now in the saddle," the infatuated American journalist Clayton Cooper observed in 1923. "The old slow-moving and traditional politicians, more rhetorical than practical, have been replaced by a young and vigorous leadership, intensely patriotic and not without means to enforce their policies."[93] Everything about Italian fascism was young. At the time of the Fascist Party congress in Rome in November 1921, over a quarter of the members were not even twenty-one years old.

In quick succession, the Fascists banned the Communist Party, shut down the Socialist newspapers, established a new Fascist-centered calendar in which the year 1922 became Year I of the Fascist Era, and began to reform and refashion society and the state according to already familiar nationalist notions of popular sovereignty. According to Aúgusto Turati, secretary general of the Fascist Party, Mussolini's Italy was to show a new third way. As a "third force," fascism parted from the liberal democracy that had followed the French Revolution in 1789, and the people's democracy envisioned by the Russian revolution of 1917. "The march on Rome has expressed a new conception of the right of the nation over classes and individuals," Turati explained. The Fascist project was "in contrast with that of the French, which affirms the right of the individual over the nation, and in opposition to that of Russia, which implies the triumph of class over other elements which constitute the nation."[94]

The Fascists talked about "a new order," a society organized according to "the Roman and Italian formula: 'All within the State, and none against the State.'"[95] Each individual became an integral part of the whole. In such a total-itarian state, no real distinction would be drawn between the public and private spheres; everyone was wholly immersed in the new group. Nor did the collective have power. In the Fascist state, the many became the ruling few, and the few became the infallible one: Mussolini. Rejecting the idea of leadership through election, Fascist doctrine proposed an organic model of a leader emerg-ing almost naturally from the nation. "We are all partakers of the divine," a philosopher and apologist of fascism wrote, "but the hero among us is partaker of it in fuller measure than all. . . . The supreme gift of synthesis, intuition, revelation, are denied to us; they belong rightly to the hero and none other."[96] Without such a hero, such a *Duce,* or leader, who, with daring, faith, and mystic intuition, could overcome the confusion of "conflicting ideas, conflicting belief, con-flicting wills," the country would descend into darkness.

FASCISM MARKED a definitive break with earlier forms of modern government and, in the bold way it had come to power, proved an inspiration to many disgruntled vet-erans and impressionable young people at home and abroad. For Hitler and his fellow National Socialists in particular, Mussolini and his Fascist movement provided models to emulate. From them, Hitler learned the value of symbols, slogans, rituals, flags, and uniforms as signs of social acceptance and belonging. He learned too the power of elaborate ceremonies and mass rallies to im-press participants and spectators alike. They demon-strated that the country, arrayed in imposing and disciplined ranks, was no longer in chaos but on the march.[97] Seeing the support Mussolini got from the young, long excluded from the political process, Hitler resolved to reach out to those of the same age in his own country. He adopted Mussolini's language of national

10. Mussolini as Duce. *This image of Mussolini suggests his strength of leadership, and the repeated, radiating word "DU-CE" echoes repeated chants affirming that leadership. The modern design presents the for-ward-looking aspect of Italian fascism. Cover of the catalogue* Mostra della Rivoluzione Fascista *(Rome, 1933). Coll. authors.*

reawakening and rhetoric of a "New Order" which promised to be an alterna-tive to liberal democracy and to communism. The National Socialists also bor-rowed the idea that they belonged to a daring "movement," a historical force that transcended party politics and was destined to resurrect the nation. What mattered was action, not any political program duly established and systemati-cally enacted. What mattered was a guiding myth to energize that action, and the best myth of all was one that identified an opponent, an enemy against whom the masses would rally. Finally, Hitler adopted the Fascist "strong man" con-

11. Hitler as Führer. Unlike Mussolini's claim on leadership, Hitler's understanding of his own destiny as Führer of the German people was imbued with the mysteries of blood and soil. A central symbol of the Nazi mystery was the so-called bloodflag, a swastika banner carried during the failed Putsch that had been soaked in the blood of the fallen and soiled in the mud of the Munich streets. It became the Nazi grail; Hitler established a masslike ceremony in which he transferred the sacrificial power of the fallen of 9 November 1923 to other swastika banners by holding the bloodflag in his right hand and touching other flags with his left. As the power of the one transferred to the other, Hitler also was renewed. Reproduced in Hanns Kerrl, ed., Reichstagung in Nürnberg 1938 (Berlin, 1939). Coll. authors.

cept, a community led by a charismatic leader appointed not by majority vote but by the mysterious workings of destiny. He translated *il Duce,* "the leader," the term by which Mussolini was known, into German: the *Führer,* the leader.[98]

There was one great difference between fascism and Nazism, however. Inspired by the Romans, the Fascists took great pride in their heritage, but they did not want to resurrect the Roman empire. They looked ahead, and sought to create the Man and the Woman of the Future. Anyone, of whatever birth and family background, was welcome to join this project, if he or she were prepared to commit to it wholeheartedly. Fascism, in other words, was like the Roman Catholic Church, open to all who were baptized. And indeed, Jews did join the Fascist Party.[99]

The National Socialists, by contrast, looked backward. The man of the future had existed in the past. To become a man of the future, one had to emancipate the "Aryan" within. The "Aryans," or old Teutons, were no mere examples, paragons from the past, ideals to emulate; they were both past and future. "Non-Aryans" need not apply; they were explicitly excluded.

A year after Mussolini's March on Rome, Hitler attempted his own March on Berlin. The time seemed opportune: in January 1923, French troops had occupied the Rhineland to force Germany into meeting its reparation payments. Industrial and agricultural production declined by a third, exports by two-thirds, and hyperinflation ate away at the last measure of stability. By May, a dollar was worth 54,300 marks, by August 4 million marks, and three months later, 4.2 trillion. Prices doubled in a day, and exchange rates changed by the hour. "A pair of shoe laces cost more than a shoe had once cost, no, more than a fashionable store with two thousand pairs of shoes had cost before; to repair a broken window more than a whole house formerly cost, a book more than a printer's works with a hundred presses," Stefan Zweig recalled.[100] Within a few months, the unit of measure had soared through the thousands to the millions, the billions, and the trillions.

The Communists initiated an armed uprising in Hamburg, while in Bavaria the right-wing General State Commissioner Gustav von Kahr prepared for a "national dictatorship," which in turn led to the formation of anti–"national dictatorship" Communist militia in other states. By November 1923 the (central) Reich and (state) Bavarian governments no longer recognized each other, and the German Reich was on the brink of dissolution.

Hitler and his National Socialists presumed it a propitious moment to stage their "National Revolution," à la Mussolini. Their goal was to topple the Bavarian government, and then to move swiftly on the national government in Berlin.[101] Germany was not Italy, however. Mussolini had been invited: he had a secret invitation from the Italian king Victor Emmanuel III in his pocket when he left Milan for Rome. Hitler had no assurance of either the Bavarian or German authorities' welcome to take over their governments. After a night in one of Munich's beer halls, the Nazis began their own "March" on 9 November— and were stopped a few miles down the road. In the battle that followed, sixteen National Socialists died. Hitler, on the other hand, was convicted of a crime that according to clause 81 of the German penal code carried a sentence of life imprisonment. Praising him as a great German patriot, the court sentenced him to one to five years confinement. Attended by his acolytes in the hotel-like Landsberg fortress, Hitler wrote *Mein Kampf.*

HITLER'S TIMING was wrong in November 1923. The failed Munich Putsch marked the beginning of a seven-year period in which a measure of stability returned to Europe in general and Germany in particular. Within a week, the Weimar government introduced a new currency, the Rentenmark.[102] "When, as if at the sound of a gong, each [trillion] of artificially inflated marks was exchanged for a single new mark, a norm had been created," Stefan Zweig wrote in his autobiography. "And, truly, the muddy tide with all its filth and slime flowed back soon, the bars, the brothels disappeared, conditions became normal again, everybody could now figure clearly how much he had won, how much he had lost."[103] A great number of people had lost, and lost a lot, but at least the unchecked decline seemed at an end. And most Germans had not gone mad or resorted to violence. "The upright little man, the postman and the railroad engineer, the seamstress and the washerwoman, had always, just like other kinds of workers, fulfilled their duties," the novelist and chronicler of German cultural life Hans Ostwald observed with pride. "Doctors had treated the sick, scholars had advanced science, and inventors had developed and realized their ideas. Everyone, no doubt, was visited frequently enough by temptation. But the majority did not succumb, they overcame it."[104]

Germany's situation improved rapidly and significantly. The American-backed Dawes plan went into effect in 1924, mandating an easier schedule of reparation payments. In 1925, Allied troops withdrew from the Rhineland. Germany was admitted into the League of Nations in 1926, and quickly gained the sixth seat on the Permanent Council. In recognition of German reintegration into the international community, the Inter-Allied Military Commission withdrew from German soil (1927), and thus relinquished control over rearmament. In 1928, German industrial production, imports and exports, and real wages surpassed prewar (1913) levels for the first time. Unemployment rates dropped to 6.3 percent that year from 10 percent in 1926.[105]

In such a political and economic climate, the National Socialists floated to the fringe of German public life. They scraped together 2.8 percent of the vote in the Reichstag elections of 1928, while Communists garnered 10.6 percent. The two parties that sought radical change together received fewer than one of every seven votes cast. The great majority of German voters, six out of every seven, supported main-line democratic parties and, by implication, the Weimar Republic. In 1928, there was little future for a party with a radical program.

Chapter Three

NATIONAL SOCIALIST
PROMISE AND PRACTICE

CONTRARY TO POPULAR WISDOM, the Weimar Republic was not doomed to fail. No intrinsic reason foiled its success. Indeed, as we have seen, the German voters in 1928 supported the democratic system upon which the republic was based.

But the Weimar Republic could not catch a break. The government lacked the time to capitalize on its international political successes of the mid-1920s, or to wean the economy from its dependence on American money. Just when things had begun to go well, the New York stock market crashed in November 1929, and Germany faced financial collapse. Funds from America that had propped up the German economy stopped abruptly. American banks called in their short-term loans. The United States government imposed new tariffs, and Germany's European neighbors followed suit. These blows crushed the export-based German economy. Statistics soon reflected the nation's dire condition. German industrial production spiraled down to half its 1928 level; exports dropped 40 percent, and unemployment, which had stood at 2 million in the mid-1920s, shot up to 3 million in 1930, 4.5 million in 1931, 5.6 million in 1932, and 6 million, or 25 percent of the workforce, in January 1933. For many Germans, these figures meant that democracy had failed.[1]

National Socialism appeared to offer a viable alternative, something work-able, like Mussolini's fascism in Italy. A marginal political force during the years of relative prosperity, the Nazis profited from the depression. They claimed to be the party of struggle and change, an attractive notion to young people. Draw-ing on Germany's nineteenth-century youth movement culture, with its skepti-cism of the bourgeois world and its dreams of alternative communities rooted in nature, the Nazis offered young people something that looked like what they wanted. The National Socialists exploited the faith, zeal, and idealism of the youth movement, and appropriated its energy and promise. Young men and women in their twenties and thirties flocked to the party. In 1928, more than two-thirds of Nazi support came from people under forty years old. In cer-tain areas the proportion was even more striking; in the district of Oschatz-Grimma, for example, 84 percent of the Nazi Party members were under forty.

12. Hitler Youth trumpeters. Reproduced in Hanns Kerrl, ed., Reichstagung in Nürnberg *1938 (Berlin, 1939). Coll. authors.*

Less than half of the registered Social Democrats fell into that age group. The Nazi leadership was young as well. In 1930, two-thirds were under forty.[2]

Such youthfulness served the Nazis well. Disappointed in their own generation's choices and failures—the outrageous armistice and the shame of Versailles—a remarkable number of older Germans embraced National Socialism as a source of renewed vigor and hope. Hitler did not belong to the political establishment; his was a fresh face, and his rhetoric and leadership style were new. Old and young alike admired the Nazis' boundless confidence that change was possible and that they were agents of that change. The Nazi political symbolism and rituals—the bold design of the swastika, the uniforms and salutes adopted from the Fascists, the processions copied from the military, the mass rallies lifted from the sports world—all of this offered Germans of many backgrounds a sense of unity, passion, and purpose. No other party had this popular appeal; each attracted but one sector of society.[3]

Using seduction, pressure, and terror, the National Socialists gained adherents. Their system of political symbolism and modern propaganda techniques, as well as a focused program of infiltration, intimidation, and provocation, catapulted them from the political margins to the mainstream. They reached out to everyone—except the Jews. Throughout the wilderness years Hitler had kept his antisemitic course. In 1925, with Nazi popularity nearly ebbed away, he explained that a successful campaign had to be directed against two objectives: a person and a thing. The English had fought against the Kaiser and German militarism; the Nazis were to fight "against the Jew as a person and against Marxism as a thing." In his opinion, "for a people like the German people, it is particularly necessary to indicate one sole enemy, to march against one sole enemy."[4] Both the Jew and Bolshevism were tangible and accessible, clear foci for resentment.

Hitler's antisemitism flowed from a larger ideology of struggle. Struggle, he claimed, was a fact of life. The German people were pitted against the rest of the world, and in such a situation "the stronger, the more able, win, while the less able, the weak, lose."[5] Bismarck, Germany's cool statesman of the nineteenth century, had striven to draw Germany's borders according to principles of strategy, economics, and balanced power relationships. Hitler maintained an ideological stance shorn of practical wisdom and contemptuous of the claims of other states. German national unity was of paramount importance, and Germany's borders were to be expanded to encompass every last person of German or even Germanic descent.

German racial superiority was a basic tenet of National Socialism, and German supremacy was the goal of the unrelenting struggle Hitler preached.[6] His racism proved politically attractive to many of his countrymen; it justified a utopian vision of the unity of all Germanic peoples. Surely here lay an alternative to the limited and limiting concept of the nation as conceived in the wake of the French revolution. "The conception of the nation has become meaningless," Hitler told Hermann Rauschning, a high-ranking Nazi from Danzig. Race transcended national boundaries and race was the core of the German future. "France carried her great revolution beyond her borders with the conception of the nation. With the conception of race, National-Socialism will carry its revolution abroad and re-cast the world."[7]

AT THE END of 1929, Germany's army, concerned about rising unemployment and public restlessness, began to take a serious interest in civilian politics.[8] The charming and clever general Kurt von Schleicher headed the Defense Ministry's Political Bureau. A patient man and a great strategist, von Schleicher assumed responsibility for controlling the fate of the chancellorship. Von Schleicher favored the centrist politician Heinrich Brüning, a Roman Catholic, fiscal conservative, and consistent supporter of military appropriations. The octogenarian president Paul von Hindenburg concurred, and urged the general to secure Brüning's cooperation. Von Schleicher, however, preferred to operate from behind the scenes, and he sent Defense Minister Wilhelm Groener. Walking with Brüning in the Potsdam Woods on 27 December 1929, Groener suggested that it was Brüning's duty as an honorable man to accept Hindenburg's call to form a new government. Brüning was, above all, an honorable man and, at the end of March 1930, he agreed to serve.

Unfortunately, Brüning, although very intelligent, was achingly rigid.[9] Deep in depression, Germany suffered from high and ever-increasing unemployment and from bitter political divisiveness. Brüning's answer to these woes was draconian tax increases and drastic reductions in social welfare services. The Reichstag promptly voted down his budget and he just as promptly dissolved the Reichstag. New elections were set for September 1930.[10]

This gave the Nazis an opportunity. Trumpeting the value of their youthful energy, bold swastika-emblazoned banners, torch-lit pageants, and mesmerizing music, they hammered home their utopian vision of a community of the German *Volk*, with its dystopian underbelly of unmitigated racism. The propaganda campaign worked. Over 80 percent of registered voters went to the polls and, when the count was tabulated, the traditionally strong moderate right had vanished. The Communists did well, winning 77 seats in the Reichstag. The Nazis did better, with 107. Still, Brüning remained in office in September 1930. The National Socialist Party did not come to power.[11]

But Brüning was not only inflexible and unimaginative, he was also unlucky. When he became chancellor in March 1930, 3 million people were unemployed; by December 1931 the figure had nearly doubled. The Depression, which he could not control, took a greater toll each month. And the French and the British, also beyond Brüning's control, stymied his every effort to improve the situation in Germany through diplomacy. Brüning's authority and popularity declined, while civil violence increased. Worker discontent, political terrorism, and bloody street fighting between Nazis and Communists brought the message of frustration and chaos into ordinary people's homes the length and breadth of Germany. It made the promises of the Nazi Party look good.[12]

Brüning's misfortunes were Hitler's keys to power. The Depression was a political—not economic—problem, he told German businessmen at the Industry Club in Düsseldorf in January 1932. The stock market mattered little. At issue was Germany's internal divisions and collapse. The solution was a united body politic that could ease the nation's pain, a body "intolerant of anyone who sins against the nation and its interests, intolerant against anyone who will not acknowledge its vital interests or who opposes them, intolerant and pitiless against anyone who shall attempt once more to destroy or disintegrate this body-politic."[13] Long and tumultuous applause followed. The businessmen believed him and the unemployed did too. Both ends of the economic spectrum flocked to the Nazi banner.

The Nazi slogan, "*Ein Reich, ein Volk, ein Führer*" (One Nation, One People, One Leader), made sense to millions of voters. If Hitler could be a focus of unity for Reich Germans of all social backgrounds and economic interests, he, and perhaps only he, would be able to reestablish Germany's position in Europe, not by restoring the Second Reich, defeated in 1918, but by creating a new, strong Third Reich. The Third Reich would overcome the shame of the Versailles Treaty and prompt German pride by uniting, in one Reich and under one leader, all Germans: the Germans in Germany, in Austria, in Danzig, and in Memel, Poland, and elsewhere.

On the eve of the Reichstag election of 1932 the Nazis were Germany's major political force and their antisemitic rhetoric had become a staple of political discourse. "Nationalism and anti-Semitism dominate the German political picture," the left-wing journalist Carl von Ossietzky noted in despair. "They are the barrel organs of fascism, whose pseudorevolutionary shrieks drown out the softer tremolo of social reaction." The Jewish community appealed to their fellow countrymen not to be taken in. "Why do you tolerate it at all when, in the context of serious political and economic matters, you are presented with such a bogeyman as 'the Jew,' as he appears in the generalizations of the hatemongers?" they asked. "Everywhere you are confronted with 'the Jew.' Wherever he is, he is supposed to dominate you! He is supposed to be responsible for whatever comes up, even the most contradictory things: capitalism and bolshevism, finance capital and marxism. How is this possible?"[14]

Their appeal fell on deaf ears. The Nazis won 230 seats in the 608-deputy Reichstag. They were the largest party, but they still did not control a majority, even with their nominal ally, the German National People's Party. For more than half a year the country boiled in impasse. Hitler repeatedly demanded the chancellorship, but the political leaders of the German National People's Party and other right-wing parties, necessary for a majority coalition, were unwilling to give it to him. With no other candidates for the chancellory, Kurt von Schleicher was forced to take it on, but he could not build a majority either, and he resigned at the end of January 1933. Now it was Hitler's turn, and von Schleicher did not ask the army to stop him.[15]

On 30 January 1933, President von Hindenburg invited Adolf Hitler to assume the chancellorship of a coalition government. According to a deal struck earlier, he would be chancellor and von Hindenburg's lapdog, Franz von Papen, vice chancellor. Von Papen and the other seven gentlemen in the cabinet were confident they could control the oafish chancellor and his two crude cohorts, Interior Minister Wilhelm Frick and Minister without Portfolio Hermann Göring. In their establishment hubris and cynicism, these older gentlemen calculated that they had bought the mass support they had lacked before. Only one right-wing politician, a man who knew Hitler better than anyone else, saw that things would not be so easy. In a letter to his former wartime colleague General von Hindenburg, General Ludendorff, the de facto dictator of Germany from 1916 to 1918 and the figurehead of Hitler's 1923 Putsch, predicted that "this accursed man will cast our Reich into the abyss and bring our nation to inconceivable misery. Future generations will damn you in your grave for what you have done."[16]

History proved Ludendorff right. The men who had given Hitler the chancellory could not control him. And he, for his part, wanted absolute control. He meant to rule by decree, and he needed a two-thirds majority in the Reichstag to do that. New elections were set for 5 March, and the Nazis began a campaign to ensure that the majority of upright German citizens would understand that a fully National Socialist government was the only way to prevent Germany's descent into Bolshevik chaos. The pièce de résistance was the Reichstag fire of 27 February 1933.[17] Organized by Göring and blamed on the Communists, it created such an atmosphere of apprehension that von Hindenburg signed an emergency decree "as a protection against Communist acts of violence endangering the state." No other hurdle lay in the path to dictatorship. The decree permitted "certain restrictions to be imposed on personal freedom, on the right to express a free opinion, the freedom of the press, of association and the right to hold meetings."[18] Large sections of the population welcomed von Hindenburg's decree. A Hamburg schoolteacher openly applauded any and all action to prevent the terror he believed the Communists were about to unleash: "Poison, boiling water, all tools from the most refined to the most primitive, were to be used as weapons. It sounds like a robbers' tale—if it were not Russia that had experienced asiatic methods and orgies of torture that a Germanic mind, even if sick, cannot imagine, and if healthy cannot believe."[19]

In the week between the fire and the election many political opponents were arrested, taken into so-called protective custody, and detained in hastily set up *Schuftzhaftlager,* protective custody camps or, as they were also called, *Konzentrationslager,* concentration camps.[20] Other "enemies of the party," including a number of prominent Jews, went into exile. The philosopher and literary critic Walter Benjamin left Germany for France; the writer Lion Feuchtwanger, who had dared to mock Hitler and the Nazis in his work, fled to Switzerland; Albert Einstein, then on a visit to the United States, wisely chose not to go home.

And still the National Socialists did not win a majority; 288 of the 647 seats went to brownshirts. But with 81 Communist deputies under arrest or in flight, and with the support of Nationalist and Catholic deputies, Hitler attained an effective majority to suspend the constitution.

It took Hitler a mere eighteen days to dispose of the Weimar Republic. So eager were his followers to overthrow democratic structures that they did not wait for orders. Nazis throughout the country spontaneously took over a number of states by pressuring or blackmailing the elected governments to appoint party members to key positions. In Bavaria, the heartland of the Nazi movement, the situation was extreme. Hitler's personal lawyer Hans Frank became the minister of justice for the state of Bavaria; Reichsführer-SS Heinrich Himmler forced his way to the position of chief of police in Munich (the capital of Bavaria); and Reinhard Heydrich, chief of the Nazi Security Service, promptly was appointed head of the Bavarian Political Police. Frank, Himmler, and Heydrich quickly rounded up more than 10,000 Communists and Socialists.

These sweeping changes on the ground were accompanied by symbolic changes in the air. In mid-March, the flag of the republic was lowered and the Nazi banner hoisted high. As one Nazi exulted, "The new flags were raised up the poles, and were greeted with exaltation. Everywhere the old, the rotten, the antiquated gave way; everywhere the new powers achieved ascendancy."[21]

Nazi ascendancy was confirmed in the new Reichstag's first session, which took up only one agenda point: the adoption of the "Enabling Act" (*Gesetz zur Behebung der Not von Volk und Reich* or Law for Removing the Distress of People and Reich), to transfer legislative power to the executive. According to this act, "the laws passed by the Reich government do not have to adhere to the Constitution provided that the institutions of the Reichstag and Reichsrat have no objection."[22] The Social Democratic leader Otto Wels courageously reminded his Reichstag colleagues of the principles of humanism and justice, of freedom and socialism.[23] But the deputies of the German National People's Party, the Center Party, and the smaller parties joined the National Socialists, and when the vote came only the 94 Social Democrats voted against the Enabling Act; all the other 441 deputies voted in favor of it.

Everyone knew that Germany had accepted dictatorship, and most were happy about it—even traditional opponents of the National Socialists such as the Catholics. "As in the August days of 1914, a feeling of national and German emotion has seized our people," the Catholic Teachers' Association rejoiced on

1 April 1933. "We have succeeded in breaking through the un-German spirit which prevailed in the revolution of 1918."[24] The Catholics, who had supported the republic and opposed the National Socialists, should have known better, but they closed their eyes to the fact that they now embraced a dictator. The German Communists who had escaped imprisonment by fleeing to Switzerland were equally—if differently—deluded. They confidently predicted that Hitler's victory would not last. "The rise of the revolutionary tide in Germany will inevitably continue. The resistance of the masses against Fascism will inevitably increase." In fact, Hitler had done communism a service. The Nazi dictatorship "frees the masses from the influence of the Social-Democratic Party and thus accelerates the speed of Germany's march towards the proletarian revolution."[25]

No one paid much attention to the declarations of either the Catholics or the Communists. The Nazis dominated the news on 1 April, with their state-sponsored boycott of all Jewish professionals and of all businesses owned by Jews. Hearing that the American Jewish Congress (contrary to the wishes of the German Jews) planned a worldwide boycott of German goods, Hitler ordered a one-day preemptive strike, thus pacifying his party's virulent and restive anti-semites while not alarming the more pragmatic element that feared radical action perhaps deleterious to the economy.[26]

The Nazi leadership called upon the German people to take defensive action against the Jews, "the guilty ones" who "live in our midst and day after day misuse the right to hospitality, which the German *Volk* has granted them." In the party's view, Jews had been reduced to resident foreigners who could be held hostage to ensure the behavior of the outside world toward Germany. This was pure racism at work: people were held responsible not only for their own deeds but for those of the imagined race-community to which they belonged as well. Just as the Germans belonged to a unified race-organism, so did the Jews. Thus Jews living in Germany were responsible for the actions of Jews abroad. As the Nazi leadership explained to the party faithful, it was "the Jews in our midst" who orchestrated the "campaign of hate and lies against Germany" in the United States. "It would be in their [the German Jews'] power to call the liars in the rest of the world into line. Because they choose not to do so, we will make sure that this crusade of hatred and lies against Germany is no longer directed against the innocent German Volk, but against the responsible agitators them-selves. This smear campaign of boycotting and atrocities must not and shall not injure the German Volk, but rather the Jews themselves—a thousand times more severely."[27]

The proclamation to the German people was very clear:

Men and women of Germany! The people responsible for this mad crime, this base agitation by atrocity-mongering and boycott, are the Jews in Germany. They have asked the brethren of their race abroad to fight against the German people. They have spread lies and calumnies.... Show the Jews that they cannot drag Germany's honour into the mire without being punished for it![28]

The boycott was not an economic success. Many Germans found it inconvenient or financially foolish. Victor Klemperer, a Jewish professor of Romance languages and literature at the Dresden Technical University, took note in his diary of a conversation he had overheard.

> Beside me a soldier of the Reichswehr, a mere boy, and his not very attractive girl. It was the evening before the boycott announcement. Conversation during an Alsbreg advertisement. He: "One really shouldn't go to a Jew to shop." She: "But it's so terribly cheap." He: "Then it's bad and doesn't last." She, reflective, quite matter-of-fact, without the least pathos: "No, really, it's just as good and lasts just as long, really just like in Christian shops—and so much cheaper." He falls silent.[29]

Nevertheless, the boycott was a psychological success. In Bertha Kahn-Rosenthal's memory, "The day it started was the day of the boycott on April 1, 1933." Born in 1922 in the small town of Berfelden in the southern part of Germany, Bertha Rosenthal was eleven years old at the time. Perhaps twenty-five Jewish families lived in her town, and no more than ten Jewish children attended her school in a given year. "The synagogue was in very serious disrepair, but the men went to services and most people kept kosher." The Jewish children went to school with their neighbors on Saturdays; "we had to go to school, that was the law, but we didn't have to write." On Saturday 1 April 1933 Bertha went to school as usual. "In the morning before classes we would all congregate in the *Turnplatz* [gym field] where we played. I remember the boys were on one side and the girls on the other side and we were playing ball. We

13. April 1, 1933. SA men hand out leaflets in front of a Jewish store. One holds a sign identifying the Jewish owners of the store to be "vermin" and "undertakers of German craft" who pay their German employees starvation wages. Reproduced in Gerd Rühle, ed., Das Dritte Reich, Das erste Jahr 1933 (Berlin, 1934). Coll. authors.

were standing there, these four girls, four of us, and no one ever threw the ball to us. That's when we knew. That was it." After school, "we went to my house, and there was a brownshirt walking up and down to make sure nobody would come in. Nobody would have gone in anyway. It was shabbat, and anybody who still dealt with my father [a cattle trader] wouldn't have come on a Saturday." Economically, the boycott had no impact on the Rosenthal family, "but that day of the boycott, April 1, 1933, that was really the watershed. After that, it was as if we weren't there."[30]

Many German Jews, adult and child, shared Bertha Rosenthal's sense of the boycott as a direct attack. Few were prepared for the emotional assault they felt watching their fellow countrymen brand Jewish-owned shops and businesses with large painted Stars of David. Robert Weltsch, a Zionist and editor of the major Jewish newspaper in Germany, the *Jüdische Rundschau,* responded to his community's dismay with a call for pride. Urging his readers to adopt the Shield of David, intended as a mark of shame, as a badge of honor, Weltsch reinterpreted the event: "April 1, 1933 can become the day of Jewish awakening and Jewish rebirth."[31] Weltsch welcomed the fact that all Jews, religiously affiliated with the community or not, indeed even converts to Christianity, were affected. The Nazis had closed the door to assimilation which, Weltsch maintained, was acceptable.

Weltsch was naive. Within weeks, the Jews of Germany were politically and socially disenfranchised, stripped of their rights and privileges as citizens.[32] Taking advantage of SA-initiated violence against Jewish lawyers and Jews in government positions, the Reich government passed its first anti-Jewish measure, the Law for the Restoration of the Regular Civil Service, on 7 April. Paragraph 3, the so-called Aryan Paragraph, ordered the immediate retirement of all civil servants of "non-Aryan origin." A second law passed that day, the Law Concerning the Admission to the Legal Profession, removed Jews from the judiciary. A double-think pattern was set: the authorities officially deplored the street violence against the Jews and, at the same time, passed restrictive laws *against the Jews* to protect them from that violence. The laws were not predicated on the notion that Jews were threatened, however. Rather, these laws posited that the Jews themselves posed a threat to German society. This was cynicism at work: the Jews, posing a threat to the body politic, must nonetheless be protected from the righteous wrath of the public against the danger they posed. For Victor Klemperer, a Jewish convert to Protestantism and a veteran with front-line service, "the pressure I am under is greater than in the war." His country had descended into lawlessness. "In the war I was subject to military law, but subject to law nevertheless; now I am at the mercy of an arbitrary power." It seemed to him that "no beast has fewer rights and is less hounded."[33]

Klemperer had a temporary reprieve; front-line veterans were exempt, and he kept his professorship for a time. Nazi radicals chafed at such temporizing measures. A certain Dr. K. Deutschmann, for instance, declared in the *Völk-*

ischer Beobachter of 25 April that "the fact there were Jews killed in the war and at the front is no particular merit of the Jewish race. After all conscription applied to all of us, and not every Jew was successful in getting out of it. . . . So let us have no false pity, no exceptions with the Jews! Don't get caught by the old nonsense about the 'national' Jewish 'front-line soldier'."[34]

Deutschmann expressed a restlessness common to Nazis throughout Germany. Unwilling to wait for more stringent anti-Jewish laws, they took the initiative and forced the central authorities to act.[35] When local authorities banned Jewish physicians from treating patients in national health insurance clinics and hospitals, the central government hastened to legalize these actions post facto. When local governments barred Jewish children from public schools, the Reich government passed the Law Against the Overcrowding of the German Schools and Universities, which set a 1.5 percent quota on the total number of Jewish students admitted to high schools and universities throughout the country and a maximum of 5 percent for any individual school. The few who managed to surmount these barriers were obliged to carry a special yellow-striped student card and were excluded from student associations. "Aryan" students welcomed the legislation. The ideology of Wagner and his disciples shaped their response. "'When the Jew writes in German, he lies'" a notice posted at the student center at the Technical University in Dresden proclaimed. "'Henceforth he is to be allowed to write only in Hebrew.'" Victor Klemperer, who recorded the announcement in his diary, was sincerely baffled. "The fate of the Hitler Movement will undoubtedly be decided by the Jewish business," he predicted. That was clear. But, he confessed, "I do not understand why they made this point of their program so central. It will sink them. But we will probably go down with them."[36] Like many other Jews in Germany at the time, Klemperer did not take his own observations seriously enough. He did not know how astute he was.

The Reich government needed no prompting by more rabid local au-

14. Over one hundred Jewish trial lawyers lining up in early April 1933 at the Berlin bar association to apply for the right to continue to appear before the Prussian courts. A decree of 31 March 1933 limited the total of Jewish lawyers admitted to the bar to thirty-five. Courtesy Süddeutscher Verlag Bilderdienst, Munich.

thorities to persecute the *Ostjuden,* eastern European Jews. The Law for the Repeal of Naturalization and Recognition of German Citizenship was aimed directly at Jews who had come to Germany from eastern Europe. It revoked the citizenship of everyone who had been naturalized between 9 November 1918 and 30 January 1933.

Ostjuden and German Jews faced more restrictions in the months that followed. In September they were forbidden to own farms; in October from working as newspaper editors. Various exceptions, such as those granted to veterans, prevented full implementation of all the laws, but a clear picture emerged. Jews had been removed from any area of influence over the German national community: government and bureaucracy, health and the judicial system, higher education, culture, and food supply.

The Nazi quest for a pure national community, unpolluted by alien influences and unspoiled by human imperfections, included a campaign against physical impairments as well as a crusade against the Jews. The Führer wished to establish a genetically German, physically flawless people, and to that end the Law for the Prevention of Progeny with Hereditary Diseases passed in July 1933. The mentally handicapped, schizophrenics, manic-depressives, hereditary epileptics, and the blind, deaf, and alcoholic—all were to be sterilized. This edict was followed by the Law Against Dangerous Habitual Criminals, which mandated castration of serious moral offenders. The Nazis estimated that some 400,000 people would be sterilized or castrated as a result of these measures.[37]

THE NEW LAWS and policies were not kept secret from the public. On the contrary: the government publicized its increasingly ferocious and far-reaching antisemitic and racial hygiene policies through the Hitler Youth, schoolbooks, articles, and films. Few Germans objected to this unparalleled disenfranchisement. Never before in the history of western civilization had those who had gained emancipation lost their political and economic rights en masse. Yet the laws were imposed without public outcry.

Perhaps the Germans lacked what they themselves called *Zivilcourage,* civic courage. Perhaps they were indifferent, or greedy for the spoils. George Solmssen, a German Jew on the board of directors of the Deutsche Bank, was shocked by the ease with which his many countrymen who were *not* Nazis accepted anti-Jewish decrees as "self-evident." In a letter of 9 April to the chair of the board, Solmssen emphasized "the total passivity" and "the absence of all feelings of solidarity" among "those who until now worked shoulder to shoulder with Jewish colleagues." He saw an "increasingly more obvious desire to take personal advantage of vacated positions, the hushing up of the disgrace and the shame disastrously inflicted upon people who, although innocent, witness the destruction of their honor and existence from one day to the next." And he concluded, "all of this indicates a situation so hopeless that it would be wrong not to face it squarely without any attempt at prettification."[38]

15. A spread published in a Nazi publication depicting scenes of a concentration camp (left) and an insane asylum (right). The original caption reads: "The National-Socialist state protects the German nation from vermin through its criminal laws, and against the procreation of those of lesser value through its racial legislation." Reproduced in Gerd Rühle, ed., Das Dritte Reich, Das vierte Jahr 1936 *(Berlin, 1937). Coll. authors.*

Solmssen had diagnosed his compatriots accurately. The prevailing response to the disenfranchisement of the mentally ill and the Jews was that it was somehow self-explanatory or self-evident. The concept of inalienable individual rights that, since the Enlightenment, had been central to western society and political systems of governance was abandoned almost without murmur. The eighteenth-century philosophes had proposed the idea that all people were created equal and, therefore, given equal opportunity, all people of all races would do equally well. Their belief in progress—which for them meant a march forward to a society that embraced everyone—was based on the assumption Thomas Jefferson articulated in the American Declaration of Independence: "We hold these truths to be self-evident: that all men are created equal." For the enlightenment philosophers, no essential difference existed between the most civilized and the most primitive nations on earth; the former had been primitive once, and the latter would rise to civilization in the future. At the end of the road, everyone, all peoples, would join in one single humanity.[39]

Enlightenment thinkers perceived political and economic enfranchisement as a forward movement: once achieved, emancipation could not be undone. This was "self-evident" in the eighteenth century, and it is self-evident to us at the beginning of the twenty-first century. It was not, however, self-evident to the

Germans who embraced cultural pessimism in the late nineteenth and early twentieth centuries. They saw contemporary social change as a turn for the worse.[40] They believed their society to be in decline. Rejecting the notion of a single humanity, they seized upon Nietzsche's view of the civilizing process as the victory of a resentful and weak majority over a vital and noble minority. While Nietzsche himself did not call for the deprivation of rights, he did warn against progressive enfranchisement. "The diminution and levelling of European man constitutes our greatest danger, for the sight of him makes us weary.— We can see nothing today that wants to grow greater, we suspect that things will continue to grow down, down, to become thinner, more good-natured, more Chinese, more Christian."[41]

16. *Racial science in the classroom. The original caption reads: "The teacher explains the main characteristics of the Nordic race to his students with the help of the racial table and using a boy of a Nordic type as a model for comparison." Neves Volk, vol. 2 (1934). Coll. authors.*

For many Germans, World War I proved Nietzsche right: the noble, heroic, and disciplined German nation had succumbed to a league of inferior nations. "Universal civilization"—the result of progress—had been the catchword for what the Allies had defended. Against this the Germans posited "*Kultur.*" What it was, nobody really knew. But they were certain about what it was not: it was not democratic, not universally applicable, not the product of progress. The prophet of the new pessimism was the historian Oswald Spengler. European society had disintegrated into "amorphous and dispirited masses of men, scrap material from a great history," he lamented in his best-selling magnum opus, *The Decline of the West.*[42]

The political, social, and economic instability of postwar Europe appeared to verify Spengler's theory of decline. And in 1933 most Germans, from left to right on the political spectrum, agreed that the country was on the brink of collapse, and that therefore the withdrawal of individual rights was an acceptable course of action. It is probable that few imagined the terrible results of this choice. Not even the Jews.

"THE THOUSAND-YEAR history of the German Jews has come to an end," the scholar, Liberal rabbi, and teacher Leo Baeck announced to a meeting of Jewish communal organizations shortly after Hitler had come to power.[43] A small Jewish community lives in Germany at the beginning of the twenty-first century, the majority of them from the east: Ukraine, Romania, Poland, Russia. A small number of Jewish schools operate, and a few Jewish community centers are busy once again. But Leo Baeck was correct. The thousand-year history of which he spoke had come to an end, and what is alive now is growth from a different branch of the tree of Jewish life in Europe.

But at the time, no one, not even Baeck himself, realized how truly he spoke. Indeed, he dreamed of deliverance. "My idea is still this," he mused more than a year later. "I wake up one day and find posters on billboards with the imprint: 'I have taken over executive power—General von . . .' "[44]

European Jews had learned from their history that bad times come and go. Antisemitism was hardly new. Pogroms had raged through Jewish communities in the East just fifteen years earlier following World War I, the Russian revolution, and the reconfiguration of central Europe. Antisemitic legislation had been a staple of civil life in many parts of Europe barely a century earlier. Thus, Jews—in this case, German Jews—had learned both to cope with antisemitism and to battle it as best they could. The primary German Jewish organization responsible for combatting antisemitism was the *Centralverein* (CV) or Central Association of German Citizens of Jewish Faith, to which some 60 percent of Jewish families belonged. Their strategy, and the strategy of many German Jews in 1933, was shaped by historical experience: to hold on and hold out; to press for more and make do with less.[45]

Passionately attached to their homeland and their nation, the 500,000 Jews of Germany in 1933 were baffled and bewildered by the ferocity of National Socialism. The great majority had been born and educated in Germany. They were not at all Orthodox in their religious observance and they lived in big cities. They saw themselves as part of the fabric of German life; they felt they belonged and they believed they belonged. "Germany will remain Germany and no one can rob us of our homeland and of our fatherland,"[46] an editorial in the CV newspaper proclaimed in March 1933. Of course, how German Jews felt made no difference. Thousands upon thousands lost their jobs within weeks and the daily life of virtually every Jew in Germany had altered within half a year.

This dissonance between the German Jews' sense of belonging and their rejection by German government and society gave rise to fear and despair. A record number of Jews committed suicide during Hitler's first year in power. Others, with more options, fled. They were for the most part renowned politicians, professionals, intellectuals, and businessmen who had international contacts to help them leave.[47]

The journalist and novelist Leo Katz was one of some 37,000 Jews who found refuge elsewhere. "We lived in Berlin from 1930 to 1933," his son Friedrich recalled decades later. "During that time, my father wrote for the daily newspaper of the German Communist Party, and as a correspondent for Yiddish newspapers and Soviet Yiddish newspapers. My father's specialty was writing satirical articles, especially about Hitler. In 1933 the Nazis took power. After the Reichstag burned, my father went underground and practically did not live at home any more." But the Nazis had sent someone to spy on his flat. "A few weeks later he came home just to greet my mother and see me and get a few shirts and things. Somebody knocked on the door. It was the police. The policeman began to interview my father." They knew a lot about Leo Katz— Communist, Austrian citizen, and prominent literary figure. "My father did not write under his own name. He wrote under a pseudonym because we were Austrian citizens and could have been expelled as unwanted foreigners if it had been known that the foreigner was writing on German political questions in a German political paper, especially a Communist paper. But the Nazis had an agent in the Communist headquarters who gave them my father's pseudonym, and the police knew about practically every article he had written." Ironically, this interview may well have saved the Katz family. "My father denied everything. And after an hour, the policeman said, 'Look, Mr. Katz, I don't believe one word of what you've said, but I haven't met you. I'm leaving now and I don't know who will come after me. I hope you understand.' So my father took the next train to Paris."

Leo Katz's departure typified the first wave of emigration—men who left seeking safety and with the hope of securing a place for their families. "My mother and I stayed for several months before we went to France to join my father," Friedrich Katz explained. "And I frequently asked my mother, why did you stay? And she said, for two reasons. First, she was working in the Soviet commercial mission, so she thought they would not arrest her. And second, she felt the party might need her to carry out underground work. Which, since we were Jewish, and looking back on it today, I don't think was the most intelligent decision. But my mother really tried for five or six months to carry out underground work."[48]

Between 7 and 8 percent of Germany's Jewish population fled that year. Most Jews remained. They presumed the situation would improve, that the first burst of violence would subside. They could not imagine that conditions would deteriorate, that brutality would become more rampant. As the then twelve-year-old Berliner Ursula Herzberg-Lewinsky put it much later, "The first years, most people, the then-adult people said, 'Oh, this won't last long.' I remember that. I remember that all the adults around me said, 'Oh, well, this won't last long.' Nobody thought that what did happen would happen. They thought it wouldn't last, you see. 'Such a cultured country, a civilized country like Germany.' All the grown-up people around me said that, and I believed it. I didn't question it. But, of course, things got worse and worse and worse."[49]

THE FOUNDATION of the Nazi totalitarian state was solidly in place by 1934. Only one potential challenge remained to Hitler's authority (as Leo Baeck understood and dreamed to see): the army. Under the leadership of Ernst Roehm, the SA (*Sturmabteilung* or Storm Detachment), the armed Nazi toughs charged with conquering the streets for the party, had expanded rapidly. So well organized was the SA that the army leadership began to question its own role in Nazi Germany. Roehm apparently meant to incorporate the regular forces into his brown-shirted legions. And he may well have done, except that Hitler needed the army's goodwill, not to protect the country but to support his political aspirations. Von Hindenburg was failing; Hitler wished to succeed him as president. Only the army could block that move if it chose. To show the generals where he stood (and to get rid of Roehm, who was challenging Hitler's authority a bit too loudly), Hitler organized the murder of the SA leadership. His instrument to do so was the SS (*Schutzstaffel*, or Protection Squad).[50]

Hitler had established an early version of the SS in 1922: the *Strosstrupp Adolf Hitler* (Adolf Hitler Shock Troop) answered to him personally and thus ensured his armed power base. Both the National Socialist Party and the *Strosstrupp* were dissolved after the failed Putsch of 9 November 1923. Shortly after he reorganized the party in 1925, Hitler created a revised *Strosstrupp,* now called the *Schutzstaffeln* (SS, or Protection Squads). The official role of the SS was to provide security for party meetings, which had been an SA function until it too was disbanded in 1923. When the SA was resurrected in 1926, it took over this job. The SS might have faded into obscurity but for the fact that at the 1926 party rally in Weimar, Hitler entrusted the two hundred-strong SS with the Blood Flag, the standard stained with the blood of men shot in the melee of the Putsch. This holy relic was a symbol of those who had fallen, as Hitler wrote in the dedication of *Mein Kampf,* "with loyal faith in the resurrection of their people." These martyrs "must forever recall the wavering and the weak to the fulfillment of his duty, a duty which they themselves in the best faith carried to its final consequence."[51] The Blood Flag thus became the symbol of supreme loyalty to Führer and Fatherland.[52]

Loyalty had long been sanctified in Germany, and was expressed in many ways. Appreciation for loyalty to a cause dovetailed with popular romanticization of the ancient Germanic community and the medieval feudal bond between lord and liege. Germans gloried in their capacity for loyalty to a cause and to a person. According to the historian Karl Lamprecht (1891), loyalty was "the primary source of Germanicism itself." The "ever-recurring German need for closest personal attachment, for complete devotion to each other, perfect community of hopes, efforts and destinies" was "the breath of life of everything good and great."[53] Loyalty was at the core of Richard Wagner's *Nibelungen* opera cycle, and it animated the writings of his son-in-law Houston Stewart Chamberlain. According to Chamberlain, "Germanic loyalty is the girdle that gives immortal beauty to the ephemeral individual, it is the sun without which no knowledge can ripen to wisdom, the charm which alone bestows upon the free individual's passionate action the blessing of permanent achievement."[54]

Hitler's paladin Heinrich Himmler so venerated this particular virtue that Hitler appointed him leader of the SS. Known in party circles as *der treue Heinrich* (the loyal Heinrich), Himmler's appointment was the true beginning of the

SS. With him the SS had found its *Führer*.[55] Himmler immediately set out to portray the SS man as elect precisely because of his loyalty, limiting admission to the "best physically, the most dependable, and the most loyal men in the movement."[56] Outfitted in splendid black uniforms decorated with a silver death's-head insignia, the men appeared formidable indeed. If the SA professed adherence to National Socialist ideals and its institutions, the men of the SS were indoctrinated to owe unconditional loyalty to the person of Adolf Hitler. Their oath of allegiance proved it: *"Meine Ehre heisst Treue"* (My Honor is Loyalty). Loyalty was the center of their universe, and obedience followed.

This triad of loyalty-honor-obedience encouraged the SS to see themselves as independent from the SA, the party, and even from the German state. To provide a new structure and sense of direction in these uncharted waters, Himmler introduced the notion of the SS as an "Order," rather like the Jesuit Order which had selected its members for their intellectual abilities, and the Teutonic Order which had allowed only noblemen to join its ranks. Himmler used race as a dividing line to keep his Black Order "pure."[57] Perfect German ancestry was a prerequisite for admission to the SS. "It remains one of the greatest and most decisive achievements of the *Reichsführer-SS,*" the official SS historian Gunther d' Alquen noted, "that he integrated and clearly applied, with both courage and logical consistency, the theoretical insights of the National Socialist ideology in this field."[58]

An SS man had to look the part too. "I insist on a height of 1.70 meters," Himmler declared. "I personally select a hundred or two a year and insist on photographs which reveal any Slav or Mongolian characteristics."[59] Naturally, those chosen to contribute to the future of the race must produce racially pure children. In his Marriage Order of 31 December 1931, Himmler required potential brides of SS members to be screened carefully; SS men needed his permission to marry. The SS took great pride in the Marriage Order. It affirmed the loyalty of the individual to his leader and proved "the self-confidence of this voluntary community," d' Alquen explained.[60]

During what came to be known as the Night of the Long Knives, the men of the SS unconditionally, loyally, obeyed orders to slaughter their comrades of the SA. Late at night on 30 June 1934, SS troopers snatched SA leaders out of bed and shot them dead. The army collaborated, supplying weapons and transport; regular army units stood by in case of SA resistance. Even after learning that "political enemies" of the Nazi Party had been killed too, including their own General Kurt von Schleicher, the army leadership did not demur. On the contrary: in his Order of the Day to the armed forces on 1 July, Defense Minister General Werner von Blomberg admired Hitler's "soldierly decision and exemplary courage" in destroying "mutineers and traitors."[61]

The SS had proved their loyalty, and emerged as a force of central importance to the new state. At the same time, the massacre helped Hitler consolidate his power in the party; the SA continued to exist, but had been rendered impotent.[62] No one now dared challenge him. For its part, the army was pleased and appeased. When von Hindenburg died a month later, the generals dutifully bowed when Hitler became both chancellor and president. Officers and men who, according to the Enabling Act of 23 March 1933, owed loyalty to the president and not the chancellor, now pledged allegiance to the Führer. On 2 August 1934, every member of the armed services bound himself personally not to "nation and fatherland" as their predecessors had done, but to Adolf Hitler himself.

> I swear by Almighty God this sacred oath; I will render unconditional obedience to Adolf Hitler, the Führer of the German Reich and people, Supreme Commander of the Wehrmacht; as a brave soldier I will at all times be ready to sacrifice my life for this oath.[63]

The German people overwhelmingly (84%) confirmed by plebiscite this union of presidency and chancellorship, and thus repudiated the long tradition of constitutional development in the west. Abandoning, indeed negating, the principle of clearly defined and divided political power, Germans embraced the absolute, indivisible sovereignty of their leader and accepted a government structure in which any restraint upon his will, any attempt to check his directives, was illegal. The precepts of the Enlightenment had no place in Nazi Germany and evidently held little charm for contemporary Germans.

IN 1934 AND 1935, however, German rejection of enlightenment ideals was only part of the story. Contemporary observers also noted a new élan in the country. Many staunch democrats gave Hitler the benefit of the doubt, admiring his program to restore German pride after the humiliation of Versailles. Winston Churchill, a great British nationalist himself, in 1935 commended Hitler for what he had achieved.

> Adolf Hitler was the child of the rage and the grief of a mighty empire and race which had suffered overwhelming defeat in war. He it was who exorcized the spirit of despair from the German spirit by substituting the not less baleful but far less morbid spirit of revenge. When the terrible German armies, which had held half Europe in their grip, recoiled on every front, and sought armistice from those upon whose lands even then they still stood as invaders; when the pride and will-power of the Prussian race broke into surrender and revolution behind the fighting lines; when that Imperial Government, which had been for more than fifty fearful months the terror of almost all nations, collapsed ignominiously, leaving its loyal faithful subjects defenceless and disarmed before the wrath of the sorely-wounded, victorious Allies; then it was that one corporal, a former Austrian house-painter, who set out to regain all.[64]

And Hitler had been successful: by 1935, he had restored Germany's international stature.

Even so, Churchill was uneasy. While Hitler undoubtedly was borne forward by a "passionate love of Germany," he was also pushed by "currents of hatred so intense as to sear the souls of those who swim upon them." It was this hatred, especially of Jews, Churchill believed, which would prove Hitler's undoing.

> The Jews, supposed to have contributed, by a disloyal and pacifist influence, to the collapse of Germany at the end of the Great War, were also deemed to be the main prop of communism and the authors of defeatist doctrines in every form. Therefore, the Jews of Germany, a community numbered by many hundreds of thousands, were to be stripped of all power, driven from every position in public and social life, expelled from the professions, silenced in the Press, and declared a foul and odious race. The twentieth century has witnessed with surprise, not merely the promulgation of these ferocious doctrines, but their enforcement with brutal vigour by the Government and the populace. No past services, no proved patriotism, even wounds sustained in war, could procure immunity for persons whose only crime was that their parents had brought them into the world. Every kind of persecution, grave or petty, upon the world-famous scientists, writers, and composers at the top down to the wretched little Jewish children in the national schools, was practised, was glorified, and is still being practised and glorified.[65]

For Churchill, the fate of the Jews was a warning that, in the end, Hitler's attempt to restore Germany's greatness would come to naught. And history proved Churchill right.

Chapter Four

THE THIRD REICH

F OR MANY GERMANS in the mid-1930s, the apparent success of Nazism—raising Germany out of the mire of economic distress and political chaos—proved Hitler a magnificent leader. All through German history, a popular Nazi book explained, such leaders had emerged to "carry forward a great dream and a deep yearning, with their gaze directed to the far horizon."[1] Hitler was the greatest Führer of all. "Now blazes the Führer's will before Germany. Again a torch illuminates the road leading to the happiness, the struggle, and the victories of the future."[2]

So much for the myth of Hitler, infallible and omnipotent.[3] But how was such a leader to run a modern state? For well over a century, general legislative initiatives had been taken by the leadership, but government bureaucracy had worked out the details and created structures for implementation. In Nazi Germany, however, this division of labor fell away and the normal procedures of government and bureaucracy became increasingly irrelevant. Hitler put forward ideas, concepts, goals. His underlings "worked toward" these ideas through independent initiatives, promoting what they surmised to be their Führer's wishes, and even anticipating them. Ferocious competition raged within party and bureaucracy in the effort to please Hitler and, as the Führer always endorsed the victorious person or faction, he was never embarrassed. As Werner Willikens, a senior civil servant in the Prussian Agricultural Ministry, explained to representatives of the agricultural ministries of the other states, "It is the duty of every single person to attempt, in the spirit of the Führer, to work towards him. Anyone making mistakes will come to notice it soon enough. But the one who works correctly towards the Führer along his lines and towards his aim will in future . . . have the finest reward of one day suddenly attaining the legal confirmation of his work."[4]

Not surprisingly, Nazi policies did not flow from clear concepts and explicit goals; they evolved out of the confused interaction between many separate, mostly inconsistent, and often opposing developments. Early on, pressures arose from all sides: the National Socialist Party pushed revolutionary changes within German society; conservative anti-democrats wished to change nothing. Individuals in high places exploited the chaos to build mini-empires, and all along the Nazi leadership aimed to institute a central dictatorship. By the time of Willikens's speech, the boundaries between the Nazi Party and the state had dissolved completely, and the boundaries between the state and civil society had become very porous indeed. What remained was an institutional jungle in which only rivalry and conflict could be taken for granted. This generated a proliferation of agencies charged with more or less the same responsibility, all eager "to work toward the Führer," all trying to get ahead of the others, all trying to devour the others, if possible. Hitler relished the endemic struggle for power. He believed that it increased efficiency while also forcing compromises or mutual arrangements that he thought stabilized the regime as a whole. As long as ministerial bureaucrats and generals squabbled among themselves, Hitler would be the ultimate arbiter.[5] The system suited him.

ANTISEMITIC measures abounded amidst such bureaucratic chaos and conflict. Ferocity was key to success in the Nazi state hierarchy, and German Jews continuously faced ferocious assaults on many fronts. With the establishment of the Reich Chamber of Culture by Joseph Goebbels, Jews were barred from participation in artistic activities. Everyone involved in the arts—musicians, artists, composers, performers, traders, curators, critics—was required to become a member but, according to Goebbels, the Jew was "unsuited to be a custodian of Germany's cultural wealth."[6]

As per the usual Nazi "salami technique" (discrimination one slice at a time), certain categories of people were exempt at first; later the privileged few were banned as well. By 1935 the Reich Chamber of Culture was *Judenrein* ("cleansed" of Jews). "The custody of German Art shall be in the hands only of suitable and reliable Germans,"[7] proclaimed a letter expelling the formerly exempt. At least on this point, Wagner's dream had come true. He also would have been pleased by the ban on works by Jewish composers such as Mahler, Offenbach, and Schönberg. Jews, dead or alive, were anathema in the German cultural world. The "Jewish" (although a convert to Christianity) conductor Otto Klemperer was hounded out of the concert halls, as were world-renowned soloists like Jascha Heifetz and Vladimir Horowitz.

Jews responded quickly, establishing the Jewish Cultural Association (*Jüdischer Kulturbund*) to provide employment for out-of-work artists and cultural sustenance to Jewish audiences in nearly fifty cities and towns throughout Germany.[8] The *Kulturbund* mounted thousands of presentations before it was shut down in 1941. Art exhibitions, operas, dance performances, plays, concerts, and literary lectures were eagerly attended, despite Gestapo agents in the audience and the possibility of harassment by party faithful in the streets.[9] One of the people who took advantage of these performances was Rudolf Rosenberg. "When I was quite a young boy, I must have been eight or nine, my parents encouraged me very much to go to the opera. I liked it even at that early age. That lasted a few months, then, all of a sudden it seemed to stop." That "stop" had happened in 1933 or 1934, and Rosenberg's surmise, "presumably because it was difficult to get tickets," probably is correct, even though Jews were not officially forbidden from attending "German" cultural events until 1938. "Then, I remember, there came into being a Jewish cultural society. They laid on concerts and poetry readings and all that sort of thing in a disused theater. I remember going to that with my parents. This was the only sort of cultural activity one had in 1936, '37, '38."[10]

The German intellectual world was similarly "cleansed." With the acquiescence and often approval of their gentile colleagues, Jewish schoolteachers and university professors were thrown out of their jobs. Their work, however respected, was no longer mentioned or discussed, and certainly not taught. When the young physicist Werner Heisenberg discussed both Albert Michelson and Albert Einstein, the Nazi Party philosopher Alfred Rosenberg, now in charge of ideological correctness, received a letter from a Berlin high school teacher, a Dr. Rosskothen. "It is scandal enough that the American Jew Michelson and the contemptible Jew Einstein should have received the Nobel Prize from Sweden, a traitor to her race, a prize which the Jewish International cunningly procured for them; but it is even less understandable when a German university professor, who should belong to the National Socialist Movement simply because of his teaching position, stands up for these criminals." Any German who acknowledged the intellectual achievements of Jews was highly suspect. "Should such a man occupy a chair at a German university? In my opinion he should be given the opportunity to make a thorough study of the theories of Jews of the Einstein and Michelson type, and no doubt a concentration camp would be an appropriate spot."[11] Clearly, not only party functionaries approved of concentration camps. It fell to Rosenberg to explain to the high school teacher Dr. Rosskothen why he had not dismissed Heisenberg from his position.

With so many Jewish teachers and professors suddenly unemployed, so many Jewish schoolchildren under siege, and university students banished from class, the Jewish community as well as the Orthodox and Reform movements established schools and organized classes.[12] Lore Gang-Saalheimer's experience was quite typical. When the 1933 law passed, pertaining to "overcrowding" in German schools and universities, Lore Saalheimer was eleven years old and living in Nuremberg. Exempt because her father had fought at Verdun in World War I, she nevertheless felt ostracized. It "began to happen that non-Jewish children would say, 'No, I can't walk home from school with you any more.'" By 1935 she had had enough. "Somehow that seems to have been the year when the consciousness of my Jewishness and the differences, and the fact that I was disadvantaged came home to me." She transferred to the Jewish secondary school and joined the Zionist organization Habonim, as well as a Jewish sports club. She, like many others, began to live a two-layered existence. Externally, "things got worse. . . . Children in the streets used to shout out to me 'Jewish cow.' Or I'd have tickets to Jerusalem thrust in my hand." On another level, however, she was "extremely happy in my Jewish school in Germany. . . . I just loved it."[13]

Lore Saalheimer was not alone in her enjoyment of her school and clubs. It was her personal experience of a larger Jewish cultural renaissance which occurred in Germany between 1933 and 1938 in response to the antisemitism the community confronted. Synagogue attendance grew. The traditional holidays of Passover, Purim, and Chanukah, which celebrated freedom from political oppression, took on a new meaning. In 1933, 60,000 Jewish children aged six to fourteen lived in Germany. In 1932, 14 percent attended Jewish schools; in 1934 the figure rose to 23 percent, by 1936 more than half of the children, 52 percent, attended such schools, and in 1937, a full 60 percent. The number of schools in existence increased too, with the Central Organization of German Jews, the Reform and Orthodox movements, individual Jewish communities, and groups of parents establishing educational institutions.[14]

But what was the community to do with their 58,000 older teenagers and young adults? All children, including Jewish children, were legally obliged to attend school until the age of fourteen. Older adolescents and the college- and university-aged were not compelled to do so, and there was no place to educate them. To meet their needs, youth groups sprouted, seemingly overnight. By 1936 well over half of Jewish young people in Germany belonged to one or another of them. The leaders of the Central Organization of German Jews (forced in 1935 to change its name to the Central Organization of Jews in Germany), which was established in 1933 to represent Jewish interests to the Nazi government, soon realized that despite their most arduous and intensive efforts there was little they could do for the Jews with regard to the authorities. But much could be done within the community. Chaired by Leo Baeck, the Central Organization openly strengthened Jewish communal and cultural life, secretly supported a clandestine Jewish university, and organized schools to teach manual trades and agriculture. These programs were very much in demand by young adults. Unlike their elders, they had no businesses or professions, and clearly saw that the future held little promise for employment. Their only hope was to get out of Germany, and a trade needed elsewhere in the world would improve their prospects for immigration papers. Workshops and schools to train tailors, dressmakers, seamstresses, electricians, locksmiths, blacksmiths, tinsmiths, carpenters, cooks, and so on overflowed with students.[15]

"We have been very lenient with the Jews," Goebbels declared in 1934, about to launch a campaign to obliterate Jews from the civil world and the public arena. "But if they think that therefore they can still be allowed on German stages, offering art to the German people; if they think they can still sneak into editorial offices, writing for German newspapers; if they still strut across the Kurfürstendamm as though nothing had happened, they might take these words as a final warning." So, what was left to them? Using imagery from the medieval ghetto, Goebbels promised: "Jewry can rest assured that we will leave them alone as long as they retire quietly and modestly behind their four walls, as long as they are not provocative, and do not affront the German people with the claim to be treated as equals." Placing responsibility for maintaining the peace squarely on the Jews, Goebbels concluded, "If the Jews do not listen to this warning, they will have themselves to blame for anything that happens to them."[16]

By mid-1935 the Jews of Germany had seen all of the emancipation project undone. Their situation had never been worse. Signs announcing: "Jews not welcome," "No profit for Jews here," "No Jews served," "Jews and dogs not admitted," "The Jews are our misfortune," festooned Germany. Even activities not explicitly forbidden proved inaccessible because "Aryan" Germans conformed to the general philosophy. Theaters refused to sell tickets to Jews, libraries and museums denied admission, shopkeepers turned them away. For Jews, the presumption of innocence, a foundation of civil law, had evaporated. "In any German citizen decency can be presumed," the official Nazi legal periodical explained. But "from Jews as racial enemies the reverse must be expected."[17] As the Berlin rabbi Joachim Prinz realized, the Jews of Germany had become "neighbourless." "Everywhere life depends upon the 'neighbour.' Not necessarily the friend, but the man who is willing to help his neighbour go through life, not to make things difficult for him, to watch his cares and efforts with a friendly eye. That we have lost. The Jews of the big cities do not notice it so keenly, but the Jews of the small towns, those who dwell on the marketplace without a neighbour, whose children go to school each morning with no neighbours' children, it is they who feel the isolation that neighbourlessness means."[18]

Antisemitic action took a sexual turn that summer. To "protect the German nation," the state in 1933 had made it illegal for "the hereditarily ill" and "dangerous habitual criminals" to procreate. Logically, then, the state had the right to protect the nation by prohibiting sexual relations between Germans and Jews. How else could German racial purity be maintained? People—ordinary people and state officials—began to talk openly about a ban on marriages between "Aryan" Germans and Jewish Germans. Action followed. A number of registry offices refused to perform "mixed" marriages, and SA men began to demonstrate outside the houses of such couples. Increasing numbers of Jews were arrested for "race defilement," sexual relations with a gentile partner. A couple pictured in the *Völkischer Beobachter* of 26 July 1935 was paraded through the streets of Hamburg. The woman bore a placard stating: "I am the biggest sow in town and never on the Jew boys frown," while her Jewish partner was forced to carry a placard saying: "Although a Jew boy I never fail to take Goyas [gentile girls] upstairs and tell them the tale."[19] A few days later (31 July), Goebbels's newspaper the *Angriff* focused on the issue.

As a result of the manifest indignation of neighbours at No. 13 Fehlerstrasse, Friedenau, the police of ward 177 had to take into protective custody the Jew race-defiler Urbach who was actually living in a flat at that address with a German girl from Schöneberg. The occupants of neighbouring houses had been forced to witness the infamous conduct of this Jew for eighteen months and more, until their indignation ultimately rose to such a pitch that the police had to take this handsome pair into custody on the charge of arousing public disorder.[20]

One might wonder why it had taken the neighbors eighteen months to reach a state described as "public disorder." Clearly, July 1935 was not January 1934. The situation had changed, and radical Nazis now felt empowered to take ever more violent action.

Party conservatives, antisemites though they were, disliked the SA riffraff and resented their lack of law and order. They wholeheartedly supported anti-semitic measures—but as part of regulated, calculated, thoughtful discrimination. Many Germans, it seemed to them, were not enthusiastic about the visible random violence against Jews; the public actually disliked seeing (and perhaps did not approve of) the harassment, beatings, and destruction of property.

17. "Aryan" woman led through the streets for her long-standing relationship with a Jewish man. The placard reads: "I [illegible] swine have committed race-defilement with the Jew Karl Strauss for years until now [illegible]." Yivo Institute for Jewish Research, courtesy of the United States Holocaust Memorial Museum Photo Archives, Washington, DC.

Furthermore, to men like Hjalmar Schacht, president of the Reichsbank, and General von Blomberg, such disturbances were detrimental to the state. Schacht in particular fretted about economic damage. At a meeting in August with state and party leaders, Schacht emphasized how damaging to the German economy lawless activities had become. If unchecked, he warned, the economic basis of rearmament stood at risk. The government, he concluded, needed to assert its authority, and take leadership on antisemitic policies and practices. Before the Nazi Party rally in Nuremberg on 10 September, Schacht met with Hitler and voiced his concerns.

Hitler had little planned of what to say at the rally, but he had ensured the attendance of the entire Reichstag and diplomatic corps. A huge audience, hundreds of thousands of followers, would be there too. Reich Doctors' Leader Gerhard Wagner's speech on 12 September concerned a forthcoming "Law to Protect German Blood." Hitler seized on that idea. At a special meeting of the Reichstag in Nuremberg on 15 September, he announced that he would propose two laws to establish "a tolerable relation" between Germans and Jews. He then warned that if these laws did not end "Jewish agitation both within Germany and the international sphere," he would be forced to find "a final solution." This was the first mention of "a final solution."[21]

Shortly thereafter the Law for the Protection of German Blood and German Honor prohibited marriages between "Jews and citizens of German or kindred blood" and forbade "sexual relations outside marriages between Jews and nationals of German or kindred blood." To that end, Jews could no longer employ "German women" under the age of forty-five as domestic servants. A second law, the Reich Citizenship Law, limited citizenship to a subject "of German or kindred blood" who shows, through his conduct, "that he is both desirous and fit to serve the German people and Reich faithfully."

In case anyone had any illusions that the previously cherished principles of equality, liberty, and brotherhood had any life left, Dr. Wilhelm Stuckart and Dr. Hans Globke of the Interior Ministry made short shrift of such notions. "National Socialism opposes to the theories of the equality of all men and of the fundamentally unlimited freedom of the individual vis-à-vis the State, the harsh but necessary recognition of the inequality of men and of the differences between them based on the laws of nature," they wrote in their commentary on the Nuremberg Laws. "Inevitably, differences in the rights and duties of the individual derive from the differences in character between races, nations and people."

The sole remaining question was: who was a Jew? The "Aryan Paragraph" of the April 1933 law had labeled anyone with one "non-Aryan" grandparent a "non-Aryan." But a lot of good Germans had "quarter-Jewish" or "half-Jewish" kin: 45 percent of the marriage vows taken by Jews in 1932 had been to non-Jews; in 1933, the figure had risen to 55 percent.[22] Hundreds of thousands of people fell under the broad definition. And what was to be done with converts?

In the end, according to the First Supplementary Decree of the Reich Citizenship Law (November 1935), "a Jew is anyone who is descended from at least three grandparents who are racially full Jews." Judaism, in other words, was in the blood. Even so, complexity lingered. "A Jew is also one who is descended from two full Jewish grandparents, if (a) he belonged to the Jewish religious community at the time this law was issued, or joins the community later, (b) he was married to a Jewish person, at the time the law was issued, or marries one subsequently, (c) he is the offspring of a marriage with a Jew, which was contracted after the Law for the Protection of German Blood and German Honour became effective, (d) he is the offspring of an extramarital relationship with a Jew. . . ."[23]

Joseph Goebbels, the minister for propaganda, felt uneasy. The definition represented a compromise, he wrote in his diary. "Quarter Jews over to us. Half-Jews only in exceptional cases. In the name of God, so that we can have peace. Slickly and unobtrusively launch in the press. Not make too much noise about it."[24] The president of the National Socialist Lawyers' Union, Karl Schmitt, on the other hand, welcomed the new laws. "They penetrate and embrace our whole concept of justice," he exulted in an article in the German jurisprudence journal, the *Deutsche Juristenzeitung* (15 October 1935). "From them will depend in the future the definition of terms like morality, order, decency and public morals. They are the basis of liberty, the kernel of modern German justice. Everything that we as German lawyers do will derive from them, will take from them its meaning and its honor."[25]

Schmitt was closer to the mark. The "mixed-race" or *mischlinge* question attracted little attention. A great number of decrees were promulgated based upon the blood and citizenship laws. Regulations eliminated Jews from the retail trade, banks, industry, building trades, and agricultural businesses. "Aryanization" of the economic sphere.[26]

This purge shone out in daily advertisements in the local newspapers. The *Frankfurter Zeitung* of 6 October, for instance, ran ads featuring the sale of numerous Jewish-owned clothing stores, a tailoring business, a carpet and upholstery enterprise, a drapery concern, a braces and belt factory, and a well-established "Orthopaedic Institution in health resort."[27] Jewish family life of course shifted radically. Ellen Eliel-Wallach was born in Düsseldorf in May 1928. "My father was in the retail trade for wheat, grain, cattlefeed. My mother did not work. We were not very well off, but we were quite well off," she recalled. "Our financial situation deteriorated rapidly. My father was forbidden to go to the exchange, so his trade was completely out. He looked for any means to earn some money, anything. They encountered many difficulties. I think it was in '36, my mother took boxes of oranges and of liquor home and she sold them privately. After school, I had to deliver the oranges to other Jewish families who were in better financial situations than we were." It did not suffice. "My father got some odd jobs. He had to earn money in whatever way was possible.

My mother took in paying guests; they rented one room. But we couldn't make much money out of it."[28] Like many Jewish youngsters, Ellen Eliel-Wallach went to work to supplement the declining family income.

Rudolf Rosenberg was eleven years old and living in Berlin when the Nuremberg Laws took effect. His father was a wholesale tobacconist in a small way; he also had a retail shop. His mother "helped with the business quite actively." His father, Rosenberg recollected, hung on until 1935, then relinquished the retail end and transferred his wholesale trade to the family apartment, on the second floor of a Berlin tenement building. The family slept in one room, used a second for living purposes, and devoted the third to the business. Loyal customers continuing to deal with the Rosenbergs came after dark.[29]

> People used to come and collect their orders of cigarettes and cigars and tobacco, or we went to deliver. I was a delivery boy actually. . . . Shortly after my father transferred the wholesale part of the business up to the flat . . . I started regularly delivering parcels and cigarettes and so on by bike all over the place in Berlin. I had a big rucksack and a sort of carrier on the back of the bike. . . . Not only did I have to deliver parcels of cigarettes, but I also collected money. And I came home with hundreds of marks in my pocket. . . . I went round on my bike every afternoon after I'd done my homework, [from about] four o'clock . . . to say six o'clock in the evening.[30]

Rudolf delivered orders for the family business six afternoons a week, including Saturdays after synagogue. So it went for a year. Then, when he was twelve years old, "suddenly—and it must have hurt them very much—they turned around and said, 'Look, we need your help.' I was old enough at the time to realize this. And that was the end of synagogue going. I had to help in the business on Saturday as well. Because Saturdays (I don't know why) turned out to be one of the busiest days. On Saturday, of course, I did not go to school and therefore I worked full time." Slowly, surely, despite much sacrifice, their small business declined. By the winter of 1937–38 "things had become so difficult— the business was going downhill, people weren't allowed to trade with us—that [our] source of income was swept away from under [our] feet."[31]

In 1936, the well-known left-wing British publisher Victor Gollancz issued *The Yellow Spot: The Extermination of the Jews of Germany,* calling attention to the human horror sweeping across the continent. "A few decades ago," Gollancz observed, "Emile Zola's passionate *J'accuse!* made it possible to stir up world-wide sympathy for the fate of one innocent man—Dreyfus." And he wondered:

> Can the world to-day remain placid confronted by the fate of hundreds of thousands of innocent people in Germany? Is it that the facts are not generally realised, or is it that horrors are now so rife in the world that none is ter-

rible enough to shake us from our acquiescence? No reader of this book can any more escape the facts. But unless they wake us to fight injustice, as a past generation was waked by the voice of Zola, all that we know of civilisation will be in peril of barbarous dissolution.[32]

A point well taken, but not a precise parallel. Zola spoke as a Frenchman to Frenchmen. No one in Germany stood up for the Jews. The workers were silent. The elites were silent.

THE NAZIS' vigorous moves to "solve" the "Jewish Question" spilled over onto some 26,000 Sinti (from the Sindh River in India) and Roma ("human beings" in the Romani language) or, as they were generally called, "Gypsies" (from "Egyptians") living in the Third Reich.[33] Descendants of Indian ethnic groups that had arrived in Europe in the eleventh century with Ottoman armies, the Roma and Sinti roamed in caravans on the margins of western society, making a living as metalworkers, entertainers, and thieves—in many European languages, "gypsy" came to mean "thief."

In Germany, Roma and Sinti stood at the bottom of society, greatly distrusted and constantly harassed by the police.[34] Unlike the Jews, they had not profited from emancipation and, not admitted to civil society, no "Gypsy Question" arose. Insofar as anyone gave any thought to these unwelcome guests from nowhere, they were perceived only as a nuisance—a matter for the police.[35]

When Reichsführer-SS Himmler gained the position of chief of the German police in 1936, the constabulary effectively became subservient to the SS and part of a security infrastructure defined as a *Staatsschutzkorps* (State Protection Corps).[36] The policeman ceased to be merely a "cop"; now a "political soldier," he obtained far-reaching powers to defend the nation against enemies of the state, cleanse

18. Official photograph of the appointment of Reichs-führer-SS Heinrich Himmler by Hermann Göring as Chief of the Gestapo (1934). Thus empowered, Himmler seized police operations nationwide. He formally acquired control over all German police forces in 1936. Reproduced in Gerd Rühle, ed., Das Dritte Reich, Das zweite Jahr 1934 (Berlin, 1935). Coll. authors.

society of parasites, and contribute to the "healthy development of the nation."[37] By decree, police powers were extended in 1938 to arrest people identified as asocials and send them to concentration camps without trial. Asocials included pimps, people with several convictions for brawls and breaking the peace, beggars, "vagabonds at present moving from place to place without work," and "Gypsies and persons travelling in Gypsy fashion who have shown no desire for regular work or have violated the law."[38] "Gypsies" thus became a small but fixed part of the concentration camp population. Those not incarcerated in the SS-run concentration camps were forced to move their caravans into special "Gypsy concentration camps" set up and controlled by the police.[39]

"Gypsies" were assaulted for what they did and for who they were. The Nuremberg Laws, designed "to protect German blood" and limit citizenship to those of "German or related blood," targeted Jews. But Interior Minister Wilhelm Frick made clear through various decrees which followed that these laws also applied to "Gypsies, Negroes and their bastards."[40]

Racial "scientists" studied the problem too. The most prominent "racialist" in the Third Reich, Hans Günther, professor of social anthropology at the University of Jena, wondered why the Sinti and Roma, descendants of Aryans, had fallen so low. The fault lay in miscegenation: Oriental, West-Asiatic and other strains, picked up through their nomadic way of life, had spoilt the "Gypsies'" original purity. Others "studied" the Sinti and Roma too, and with their research the former "Gypsy nuisance" ballooned into a "Gypsy Problem" that had to be solved.[41]

Many offered suggestions. "Gypsies" would never be useful, the chief of police of the rural district of Esslingen wrote to the district magistrate. "For this reason it is necessary that the Gypsy tribe be exterminated by way of sterilization or castration." Articles in popular Nazi magazines trumpeted this solution, and a German medical journal argued that all "Gypsies" should be treated as hereditarily diseased people, incarcerated in concentration camps, and sterilized. "The aim is: merciless elimination of these defective elements of the population."[42] Fortunately for the Roma and Sinti, in 1938 the Nazi leadership was more interested in formulating policies and organizing actions against Jews. Few in number, the "Gypsies" for the time being remained victims of the police, but they did not become the object of political obsession.

The great Nazi cleansing of society also included a group not mentioned in the 1938 list of asocials: all men who engaged in homosexual behavior, whether homosexual, bisexual, or heterosexual.[43] The Nazis were not interested in sexual identity; they cared about sexual practice. For them, homosexual behavior reeked of the degenerate morals of the Weimar Republic, and undermined the nation's need to grow.

No new laws needed to be introduced: article 75 of the penal code of the German Empire, adopted in 1871, sufficed. But what to do with these men once arrested? The Nazis did not think that desire for homosexual sex was passed from father to son, so they did not advocate sterilization. Rather, they pressured the accused men to renounce their sexual desires, marry women, and procreate. To show that they meant business, the police enforced article 75 energetically; some 10,000 men ended up in concentration camps where they were marked with pink triangles so that the guards, kapos, and other inmates would be vigilant that they not fulfill their erotic needs. And again, the German public did not protest. Many approved, and those who did not, stood by and were silent.

FEAR INSPIRED SILENCE. Every German knew of the concentration camps, where there was always room for one more. Complacency encouraged silence. By the time of the 1936 Olympic Games and the 1937 Nuremberg Party Rally, Germany appeared to have left the Depression behind: strength and optimism filled the air. Who could argue with success? Who would be so foolish as to argue with success?

The Nuremberg Rally focused on labor, and contraposed creation and destruction, National Socialism and Bolshevism. In his commencement address, "The Battle Between Creation and Destruction," chief party ideologue Alfred Rosenberg framed the battle between "National Socialism, not only the protector of German history and values . . . but also quite simply the protector of Europe, and Bolshevism, the embodiment of all destructive instincts, all feelings of hatred against great form and great values."[44] The technological triumphs so trumpeted by the Soviets were in fact destructive processes, Rosenberg maintained. The great Soviet engineering projects realized in the Arctic and Siberia rested completely on the back of the Gulag system; 800,000 prisoners worked in brutal conditions on the Trans-Siberian Railway; "in the forced labor camps along the White Sea Canal 300,000 inmates were housed in inhuman conditions. As the year went on they died, and the camps were replenished again and again by new prisoners and exiles consecrated to death."[45]

Rosenberg's catalogue of human suffering preceded a list of the Jews responsible for the Soviet system. He contrasted the Judeo-Bolshevik hell of the Gulag with Hitler's German community—a nation that had rediscovered the blessings of healthy work. German highways and the great works of architecture designed by Albert Speer symbolized "the nation's highest self-respect and the embodiment of a boundless energy to work." The Soviet projects, by contrast, created "under the leadership of Moses Berman, Solomon Firin and their henchmen," proved "that [the Russian] people has regressed to the most wretched slavery."[46] In former years the Nazis had been forced to fight for their goals. By 1937, with the party in power, they now were at liberty to work, Rosenberg concluded happily. The comradeship of arms had metamorphosed into a comradeship of tools.[47]

Rosenberg's address foreshadowed Hitler's keynote speech. Slightly modifying Rosenberg's argument, Hitler divided the world into nations that create culture (*Kulturvolk*) and peoples who cannot. Two forms of art decisively determined a people as a *Kulturvolk*: music and—most especially—architecture. The construction of great and lasting buildings, Hitler declared, was essential to preserve the German *Volk*, for it transformed the masses into a cultural community larger than the work. These grand edifices will "provide the most noble justification for the political might of the German nation," he proclaimed. As powerful witness to a shared past, monumental architecture charged the present generation with a sense of national pride that transcended social and political divisions. "This state ought not be a power without culture, and its force should not be without beauty! The armament of a people is only morally justified if it is the shield and the sword of a higher mission!"[48] He, the Führer, would take direct control of the reconstruction of Germany's major cities. He was Germany's supreme architect.

His words were greeted by a rapturous ovation. This myth—a common past born in the dawn of time now ripened into power and promising a grandeur to come—was both comforting and compelling. The official chronicler of the 1937 Nuremburg Rally spoke for the German masses when he commented that "the greatness of our own time [is] that we do not live day by day, but that we shape our present life in complete harmony with the great tradition of the past and the compelling eternal future of the nation."[49]

The time had now come to keep his promise of "*Ein Reich, Ein Volk, Ein Führer*"; to bring all the Germanic peoples "home" to the Reich by creating a Greater Germany. The first territory to be claimed for that empire was Austria.[50] For almost nine centuries Austria had been united with the rest of Germany, first in the Holy Roman Empire, and then in the German Confederation. When Bismarck unified Germany (1866–71), Austria declined to join the new state; a confederation was one thing, Prussian rule another. The Hapsburgs refused to cowtow to the Hohenzollern.

Many Austrians and Germans believed that the end of World War I might be a propitious time to join their countries, but now the Allies objected. This baffled Stefan Zweig, living in Salzburg. Why were the Austrians refused the right of self-determination granted to Poles, Czechs and Slovaks, and all other peoples of the former empire? "It was the first instance in history, as far as I know, in which a country was saddled with an independence which it exasperatedly resisted," he wrote twenty years later. "A country that did not wish to be, got its orders: You must exist!"[51]

In 1934 Austrian Nazis attempted an *Anschluss* (merger) through a coup d'état, but it failed, mostly because Mussolini would have none of it.[52] He rightly feared Hitler as a neighbor. But Mussolini became increasingly dependent on Hitler, and Austria lost his support. Making the best of a bad situation, Austria's chancellor Kurt von Schuschnigg negotiated a pact with Hitler in July 1936 which recognized Austria's independence, but legalized the Austrian Nazi Party, permitted Nazi rallies, and admitted two thinly disguised Nazis into the Austrian government. A Trojan horse rolled into the country. Undermined by local Nazi activities, Austria descended into chaos; civil order collapsed in 1938 and the government's resolve to defend the republic melted away. Faced with the choice of hostile invasion or Nazi government, Schuschnigg resigned. The new chancellor, Arthur Seyss-Inquart, invited his German brothers to cross the border. On 13 March 1938 the German army marched triumphantly into Vienna, greeted by wildly enthusiastic crowds. Hitler himself arrived the following day to an ecstatic reception. Churchbells pealed as people cheered the Führer's motorcade. George Gedye, the veteran Vienna correspondent for *The Times* of London, was stunned by the "roaring crowds"[53] and the unquenchable thirst of the swaying mob to hear Hitler as he blazed: "the German Reich as it stands today is something no man will ever again break asunder and no man will ever again tear apart."[54]

The following day, even more people spilled into the streets to greet their Führer along his triumphal procession to the political heart of Austria, Heldenplatz (Heroes Square). In Marianne Marco-Braun's memory, "In March 1938, when suddenly Hitler marched in, I say 90 percent—but probably it wasn't 90 percent—of the Austrians stood there and said, 'Heil Hitler!'"[55] Marianne Braun was not so far off in her estimate: a quarter of a million people, over a third of the population of Vienna, participated in the spontaneous, unorchestrated public jubilation.

Popular euphoria for Hitler, National Socialism, and unification with Germany was matched by hatred for and violence against the Jews, surpassing any such open display in Germany to that date.[56] Most

19. Cheering mobs in the Heldenplatz welcome Hitler to Vienna, 14 March 1938. Yad Vashem Photo Archives, courtesy of the United States Holocaust Memorial Museum Photo Archives, Washington, DC.

20. *Hitler Youth force Jewish residents of Vienna to scrub the pavement while their neighbors jeer. Yad Vashem Photo Archives, courtesy of the United States Holocaust Memorial Museum Photo Archives, Washington, DC.*

of Austria's 191,000 Jews lived in Vienna, where they accounted for 10 percent of the population; after Warsaw and Budapest, the Jews of Vienna constituted the third largest Jewish community in Europe. But numbers did not matter. SA men and other Nazis pulled Jewish men and women off the streets, forcing them to clean barrack latrines or scrub the pavement with their bare hands and, sometimes, just for "fun" with their own undergarments or toothbrushes. Robert Kanfer, then eight years old, remembered vividly "these proceedings where women were taken to scrub the street," because his mother was among them.

> From our window you could see the Sobieskiplatz in the 9th district, which is one of these squares where the Austrian nationals had painted their *Kruckenkreuz,* the Austrian cross. They [Nazis] started collecting Jewish women to scrub this off the street. The Nazi family next door, the wife, Mrs. Mihokovic, came to my mother and she said, "Come to our flat, because nobody will look for you at our place." My mother was afraid, and said, "No, I'd rather stay in my own place." Opposite us there was a poor, unmarried woman with two children.... She was standing on the street at that moment and—apparently my mother had left the window open—she said [to the SA], "You forgot Mrs. Kanfer!" So they came and collected her and she went down.
>
> I remember when my mother came back she was crying because she was ashamed of this scrubbing. And the woman next door said, "Mrs. Kanfer, you don't have to be ashamed, you shouldn't be ashamed."[57]

The gleeful participation of people like Mrs. Kanfer's neighbor opposite shocked George Gedye most profoundly. Viennese civility vanished, demonstrating clearly that the Nazi Party had no corner on antisemitic cruelty. This was mass sport.

It is not so much the brutalities of the Austrian Nazis which I have witnessed or verified direct from the victims which blurs the image of the Vienna I thought I knew. It is the heartless, grinning, soberly dressed crowds on the Graben and Kärntnerstrasse, the "Strube's little man" class of Austrian, the fluffy Viennese blondes, fighting one another to get closer to the elevating spectacle of an ashen-faced Jewish surgeon on hands and knees before half-a-dozen young hooligans with swastika armlets and dog-whips, that sticks in my mind. His delicate fingers, which must have made the swift and confident incisions that had saved the lives of many Viennese, held a scrubbing-brush. A storm-trooper was pouring some acid solution over the brush—and his fingers. Another sluiced the pavement from a bucket, taking care to drench the surgeon's striped trousers as he did so. And the Viennese—not uniformed Nazis or a raging mob, but the Viennese "little man" and his wife—just grinned approval at the glorious fun.[58]

Arrests followed hard on the heels of public humiliation. Elisabeth Rosner-Jellinek and her family among thousands of others suffered immediately. On Wednesday, 16 March 1938, two days after Hitler's triumphal entry into Vienna, the Nazis arrested Elisabeth Jellinek's father. A journalist, a Socialist, and a Jew, he had no place in the new Austria. Elisabeth was fourteen years old.

On Friday the 11th or Saturday, my father told my mother that an Austrian industrialist, the owner of a big foodstuffs firm, had offered his private plane to my father, to this censor fellow from the press, and to another person to go to London. I think the third fellow did go, but my father and the censor didn't go. My father, because he didn't know English—so he said—and any-way, who would look after his family? Not only my mother and me, but also his sisters and his brother who were all out of work by that time. Quite against better knowledge (and what he should have known, and I'm sure he did know in his innermost heart), he said he thought it would be okay.

That was on a Sunday, and the Sunday also an uncle of mine from my mother's side who was fairly wealthy offered us money if we wanted to leave Austria. My father had a passport; for his newspaper he had been abroad. But he didn't go.

This went on until Wednesday the 16th. Then an inspector of the police came to our flat. When we came back [from my aunt's place]—we lived on the fourth floor—this man suddenly stepped out from above and identified himself and was very polite, which was unusual. He said, "Would you mind taking leave of your family; I'm afraid I have to arrest you." Well, that was that. My father's friend, the censor, was also arrested.[59]

Mr. Jellinek was sent to a concentration camp right away. He had stayed in Vienna to look after his family; after his arrest he never returned. His wife, who remained in Vienna to do what she could to free her husband, was deported also. Mr. Kanfer, by contrast, was arrested four months after the Anschluss, and released eight months later when his wife could demonstrate that her husband would leave the country within weeks. "I vividly remember—naturally that sort of thing makes an impression on a child—when my father was arrested and taken to a concentration camp. They came to the house. It was July. And he spent four months in Buchenwald and four months in Dachau." Mrs. Kanfer, a "forceful character," took care of her two boys, kept house, and worked to secure the release of her husband. "My mother managed to get him out with a forged visa for some Latin American country which, at the time, you could get with a certain amount of money. With this visa, she managed to get him out under the condition, of course, that he had to leave within four weeks. The whole family chipped in and managed to buy a ticket for Shanghai. He left Vienna in April, 1939 and stayed there [in Shanghai] until 1947. Then there were the three of us left: my mother, my brother, and I."[60]

"We Viennese Jews had the Anschluss to thank for our survival, because things became so bad in Vienna that we realized after six weeks that we had to leave, while in Germany they didn't realize it," Robert Rosner observed decades later.[61] Marianne Braun agreed. "Things rapidly got very bad for the Jews. The Nazis made raids and pulled out men, made them wash floors, all sorts of things. Of course they started closing businesses, or taking over businesses, and putting in their own people, Nazis from Germany. So of course my father, along with many others, realized there wasn't much future for us there." As for fifteen-year-old Marianne herself, "For the first time I couldn't do things I had done before. There were certain places that you couldn't go any more; public places where it was not so safe. So we spent more time in each other's houses, talking about what our parents were doing, which was preparing for emigration."[62]

Braun and Rosner were true reporters. The initial indiscriminate robbery yielded quickly to a systematic and ruthless pressure; on 23 April, Göring issued a decree calling for the registration of all Jewish-owned property in Austria. Jewish lawyers and physicians lost the right to practice, except for a few who looked after Jews. Smaller Jewish communities were liquidated, and their members forced to move to Vienna.

Events moved so rapidly and with such ferocity that the *Times* correspondent George Gedye understood they would be unfathomable to his readers at home. "You will shrug your comfortable shoulders and say 'Bogey tales' when I tell you of women whose husbands had been arrested a week before without any charge, receiving a small parcel from the Viennese postman with a curt intimation—'To pay, 150 Marks, for the cremation of your husband—ashes enclosed from Dachau.'"[63] Trying to convey the attitude of the Austrian Nazis to the Jews, Gedye quoted a remark by Vienna's new Gauleiter, Odilo Globocnik: "The phrase that 'after all the Jews are human beings' will never have the least effect on us."[64]

IF THE GERMANS gave the Austrians the political system they had long desired, the Austrians gave Germans a new benchmark for violent antisemitism. The Nazi government learned a lot from its Vienna experience, and soon brought the lesson home. The excuse for the infamous, nationwide November Pogrom, also called *Kristallnacht* (Crystal Night, or Night of Broken Glass), was Herschel Grynszpan's attempt to assassinate Ernst vom Rath, a diplomat at the German embassy, in Paris on 7 November 1938.

Grynszpan's parents, like thousands of Polish-born Jews in Germany, had become naturalized citizens during the Weimar Republic, only to be stripped of that status by the Nazis in 1933. The Polish government saw the results of the Anschluss and feared the return of newly destitute Jews. On 31 March 1938 they forbade their return to Poland. This alarmed Berlin. If Polish Jews became stateless while residing in Greater Germany, they could not be repatriated to Poland, or for that matter sent anywhere else.[65]

Negotiations opened between Berlin and Warsaw. The Poles did not give in, and in early October the Polish interior minister announced a new ordinance. All Polish citizens abroad must present their passports by 30 October to Polish legations to get a special visa granting them the right to return to Poland. The ordinance did not apply to Polish Jews living in Germany. They were not to receive the visa. The German government reacted immediately. On 26 October Himmler ordered the immediate expulsion of all those affected. As masses of people reached the border, Polish guards held them, sometimes for days, in a no-man's-land between Poland and Germany, kept alive by hastily established Jewish relief groups. Driven to despair by his parents' plight, young Herschel Grynszpan, living in Paris, sought, if not revenge, a public manifestation of outrage and retaliation.

The next day, 8 November, the *Völkischer Beobachter* and other newspapers reported the shooting, and threatened the Jews with reprisals. Attacks began at once on synagogues and Jewish community centers. As ill luck would have it, the Nazi hierarchy was in Munich for the annual commemoration of the 9 November 1923 Putsch, presenting a perfect opportunity for local party bosses assembled in the city to "work towards the Führer." They instructed their organizations at home to destroy synagogues and Jewish-owned businesses; the police would not intervene and those involved would not be arrested.[66]

Lore Gang-Saalheimer lived in Berlin at the time; she was attending a school to acquire skills useful after emigration from Germany. "My parents rang [the next evening] and said 'come home.'"

I travelled home [to Nuremberg on an] express train. . . . I knew enough, I wasn't that stupid that I didn't know something bad had happened. I don't think I realized how bad things were until I got home. My parents were on the platform. My mother was in a sweater and skirt, no makeup, no jewelry, no anything. My father looked awful. . . .

We went home. [There] was an atmosphere of complete gloom and no ornaments, no anything anywhere; the house was in mourning. . . . My par-

ents had had a huge sideboard full of the best china, and [the Nazis] had taken an axe and smashed it, smashed the china. They had had a glass display cabinet with a lot of pretty things in it, and also glasses and so on. [The Nazis] had just taken it and thrown it over. I mean every little tiny last bit of it was broken. . . .

Getting food was difficult. No shops were allowed to serve Jews in Nuremberg at that time, immediately after the 9th of November. . . . I remember my father trying to ring [his toy] factory, and trying to go there, but they wouldn't let him in. He had been dispossessed. [It was like] being struck in the head. The general feeling was one of huddles and talks and whispers, all quietly. The feeling of oppression. It was the first time I think I really felt a feeling of oppression and persecution. . . . This was a quantum step. This was the real thing.[67]

21. Jewish house vandalized during the November Pogrom. Vienna, 10 November 1938. Courtesy Bildarchiv Preussischer Kulturbesitz, Berlin.

Lore Saalheimer's father lost his factory; Hilda Cohen-Rosenthal's father was arrested and sent to a concentration camp. Hilda Rosenthal, ten years old and living in Frankfurt-am-Main, was at home with her family the night the synagogue was burned. "We were together in the room overlooking the town and we saw the tremendous flames of the synagogue burning. That could have been on a Thursday night because I think it was on the following night that they came to take my father to a concentration camp." The Rosenthal family was observant in their religious practice. "And because it was a Friday night [beginning of the Jewish sabbath], there was a tremendous discussion for five or ten minutes: should he carry anything with him? should he take a suitcase of things?"[68]

Alfred Dellheim, from a poorer family than Lore Saalheimer's, nevertheless shared her experience of devastation, and, although not so religious as Hilda Rosenthal, lost his father just the same. Urban and rural, rich and poor, the Jews of Germany suffered the same fate during the November Pogrom. Fred Dellheim's family lived in Mutterstadt; he himself worked in Ludwigshafen with a Czech Jewish company as a printer's apprentice.

> On the 10th of November, somehow I knew, I was told, that in Mutterstadt the synagogue was burning and some houses of Jewish people were demolished. I didn't know what to do. All I wanted was to get home quickly. . . .
> There was a small train going from Mutterstadt to Ludwigshafen. That train had its station in the midst of Mutterstadt. When I arrived there, my mother and my sister, white as I had never seen them before, were standing there. They told me that Father, they [Nazis] had taken him with them, and they didn't know where, and the interior of our house had been completely destroyed.
> We had chickens at home, so we always had twenty or thirty eggs, and they [Nazis] had thrown all the eggs on the ceiling. Everything was smashed to bits and pieces. All the furniture was demolished. Everything that you can demolish was demolished.
> But that wasn't the most important thing. The big question was: what had happened to Father? . . . After about a fortnight we got a card from him, a postcard from the concentration camp Dachau.[69]

In Hilda Rosenthal's memory, her father returned after four weeks; Fred Dellheim's father was incarcerated a bit longer. "At the end of the year, somewhere between Christmas and New Year, I think it was, my father came back from Dachau. He was there for something like six weeks. He had several ribs broken on one side."[70]

WITH THE November Pogrom, the plight of Jews in Germany changed radically. For a long while, many had believed that the Nuremberg Laws conferred stability: Jews would be outcasts, but still tolerated. This myth vanished overnight; literally went up in smoke. The physical demolition of Jewish property, from the destruction of nearly every synagogue to the attacks on Jewish-owned businesses, left no place for Jewish religious or economic life in Germany. The imprisonment of Jewish men in concentration camps left no place for Jews at all. Almost overnight, the myth of an apartheid that would allow the Jews their own life with their own cultural institutions exploded.

The Nazis and their cooperative countrymen made use of the institutions of the modern state and made use of modern means of communication. Their state-sponsored, centrally organized pogrom against property on 9 November culminated in a state-sponsored, centrally organized action against people on 10 November, when 30,000 men were swept out of their homes into concentration camps solely because they were Jews. With their action against *people,* the men and their families (parents, wives, children, siblings), and with their abandonment of the appearance of old-fashioned mob violence, the Germans crossed a significant threshold. It was perhaps a fine line, but a bright one. Clearly, the Nazis no longer felt a political need to hide behind the chimera of wanton mob-driven destruction. Bureaucratic systematized persecution became open policy, insolent, brazen, arrogant, and visible to all. The party leadership knew its country and was correct in its calculations. The elites did not utter a word. The working class did not utter a word. The bourgeoisie shook their heads in dismay, and said nothing. And thus it was not the Nazis alone who crossed the line, but their compatriots too. The Germans crossed a significant threshold.

The pogrom of 9 November 1938 was the end of the beginning; the 10th of November was the beginning of the end. We now know that it was the first step toward Auschwitz, but no one—not even the Nazis—knew it then, and the future was not inevitable. Still, no straight line led to the gas chambers of Birkenau.

Chapter Five

REFUGEES

Jacques Kupfermann's abilities as a painter saved his life. He was born in Vienna in 1930. His parents were from the eastern reaches of Austria-Hungary, which had become Poland, and it was with Polish passports that they had emigrated to the capital city of the former empire. From his early youth it was clear that Jacques had artistic talent and, at hardship to themselves, his parents arranged for him to have lessons. His teacher was an Austrian Nazi.

As happens in human relationships, the teacher's feelings were complicated. In Jacques's memory, she spoke quite frankly to the Kupfermann family as early as 1937. Austria would join Germany, she predicted, and life for the Jews would not be pleasant. She urged Mr. and Mrs. Kupfermann to obtain emigration papers and immigration visas for themselves and for their child. Their Polish passports came under the quota for Poland, which was small and had a long waiting list to be admitted to the United States. With his Austrian passport, Jacques fell under the quota for Austria, proportionally more generous and with fewer applicants on line. By the time of the Anschluss in March 1938, Jacques's parents still had no visas. The situation became desperate and tense. Jacques's teacher told his parents to wait no longer: the boy had talent, he should be spared. Jacques went to relatives in the United States. His parents remained, caught in Europe. Time had run out, and their son never saw them again.

Why couldn't the parents leave Austria and go to the United States with their child? Why were they not free to move about at will? And why weren't the parents admitted into the United States with their son? Wasn't another country prepared to accept them? Why wasn't asylum granted? What options did the Kupfermann family—and millions of other Jews—have to leave Europe after Hitler came to power in 1933?

These questions assume the principles of freedom of movement and asylum, prevalent throughout history, and seriously contravened for the first time by World War I. "There were no permits, no visas" before the Great War, Stefan Zweig explained in the 1930s, "and it always gives me pleasure to astonish the young by telling them that before 1914 I travelled from Europe to India and America without a passport and without ever having seen one."[1]

This changed with World War I when strangers were perceived as a potential national danger. "The humiliations which once had been devised with criminals alone in mind now were imposed upon the traveller, before and during every journey," Zweig continued.[2] Passports with photographs, health certificates, police records, tax statements, foreign exchange certificates, and other documents had to be produced upon demand.

In the postwar period, as Zweig claimed, "human beings were made to feel that they were objects and not subjects, that nothing was their right but everything merely a favour by official grace."[3] But in the premodern world, before the rise of the modern nation-state, official grace had nothing to do with freedom of movement. With no concept of state sovereignty, no precisely defined frontiers, no administrative systems to register individuals and provide them with identity documents, people moved freely between territories.

This common practice known as the *jus communicationis*—the natural right of communication between individuals and peoples—was explained in the founding treatise of international law, *De Indis Noviter Inventis (On the Indians Lately Discovered)*, written in the early 1530s by the Spanish scholastic theologian and legal scholar Francisco de Vitoria (1483–1546). "It was permissible from the beginning of the world (when everything was in common) for any one to set forth and travel wheresoever he would," de Vitoria asserted.[4] The right to move from place to place therefore was firmly enshrined in natural law, and this gave strangers various rights. Thus, de Vitoria concluded, they could not be expelled from their places of sojourn. "To keep certain people out of the city or province as being enemies, or to expel them when they are already there, are acts of war." It was simply "unlawful to banish strangers who have committed no fault."[5]

De Vitoria's work was seminal and, in the centuries that followed, his principles were codified in increasingly comprehensive systems of international law—valid in peace and in war.[6] He did not directly address the issue of asylum, the protection of strangers in one territory who were persecuted in another. However, his injunction that strangers could not be expelled comes close to another central principle of international law: nonrefoulement (from the French *refouler,* "to turn back"), holding that refugees cannot be repatriated. Indeed, so venerable was the practice of asylum that perhaps de Vitoria did not realize it had to be explained explicitly.[7] During his own lifetime, Jews found refuge in a number of Christian countries after their expulsion from Spain in 1492. Later, during the reign of Mary Tudor (1553–58), 23,000 English Protestants fled to Holland, and in the wake of the Revocation in 1685 of the Edict of Nantes, which in 1598 had granted religious liberty to French Protestants, some 2 million Huguenots—for whom the word *réfugiés* was coined—left France to find refuge in Switzerland, Holland, England, Prussia, Denmark, and other Protestant countries. Similarly, the Glorious Revolution in Britain, which brought the Dutch Protestant William III to the throne, forced thousands of English, Irish, and Scottish Catholics to flee to the continent in 1688. These enormous population displacements did not lead to calls to close borders or revoke the principle of asylum.[8]

The development of modern concepts of state sovereignty which granted the state extensive authority to intervene in the lives of its citizens challenged the ancient and early modern customs of free communication and asylum. So did the rise of the nation-state, with its precisely defined frontiers and comprehensive regulations to order the lives of its subjects or citizens. Crossing a border, which had been of no consequence in the premodern age, now became an important act. It transformed a member of a nation-state from a person with rights and obligations into an alien, a migrant, or a refugee—a person subject to different legal treatment.[9]

Nevertheless, throughout the nineteenth century nation-states did not exercise their power to regulate the ingress of foreigners or to delimit the principle of asylum. Despite the explosion of travel with the expansion of the railways and shipping lines, despite mass emigration from Europe primarily to North America, and despite the conscious creation of strong and specific national identities which divided the world into "us" and "them," there were almost no restrictions by any country on the admission, residence, or even employment of foreigners. Passports, visas, and work permits were practically unknown. The principles codified by de Vitoria continued to be accepted, and perhaps explain the relative ease with which western governments accepted the arrival of 2.5 million Russian Jews between 1881 and 1914.

World War I brought an end to sovereign benevolence and unrestricted movement. The United States closed its doors to unimpeded mass immigration. Passports, visas, and residence permits became a matter of course throughout the western world. Individual countries introduced entry restrictions as well as elaborate systems to prohibit or restrict "permissions to work" so as to regulate and protect the local labor market. In most countries, the right to work became a corollary of citizenship. With the creation of government-financed national education systems, and unemployment, health, and old-age benefits for citizens, the gap widened between those with and without rights. If foreigners could merge easily into a new society before the Great War, it was troublesome to do so afterwards. As one observer noted, "it is scarcely an exaggeration to say that the alien in a legal sense is a creature of the post-War world."[10]

This array of restrictions changed the position of the refugee. They permeated his or her existence: more visas, permits, and certificates were required of them than of an ordinary immigrant, yet refugees found such documents far more difficult to obtain. Unlike other aliens, refugees had no home or income and were on the run—*refugees*—people fleeing from danger. Burdensome and costly formalities, irritating to others, became life-threatening obstacles to the refugee.

HOWEVER HARROWING the situation of refugees during the Great War, it was far more so afterwards when some 9 to 10 million people urgently sought asylum just as doors began to close around the world. The greater numbers fleeing much more widespread and systematic persecution than ever before, in a European-wide postwar economy fraught with severe economic difficulties and high unemployment, produced what contemporaries called a crisis.

Who was on the move? In the reconfiguration of Europe, minority groups that had lived in one country fled to another where they were "nationally" attached. People who feared that they would become minorities because the area in which they lived had been ceded to another state also fled to a country where they were "nationally" attached. The numbers were enormous: some 800,000 Germans moved to Germany from areas accorded to Poland; 1.3 million Greeks to Greece from Turkey; 250,000 Bulgarians to Bulgaria from Turkey, Greece, and Romania; 750,000 Turks to Turkey from Bulgaria and Greece; and 400,000 Armenians to the Soviet Republic of Armenia from Turkey. For those so affected, this was a positive aspect of nationalism. These refugees—millions of people—belonged somewhere, and they were relatively well absorbed into their "national homes." Others were admitted to the United States, a self-consciously immigrant society, and there too they were absorbed into the body politic.[11]

A second genre of refugee, however, those who fled genocide (Armenians) or revolution (Russians), posed an intractable problem. Turkish slaughter of the Armenians sent more than 200,000 Armenian refugees surging into Syria and France. After the Russian revolution some 700,000 people fled to Germany, Poland, France, Romania, and, in smaller numbers, elsewhere. In the main, no government agencies came to their assistance. Relief was largely provided by philanthropic organizations which provided food, retraining programs, and a guide through the maze of resettlement bureaucracy.

Only one official agency accepted the refugee problem as a responsibility: the newly established League of Nations. In 1921 the League appointed the famous Polar explorer and Norwegian statesman Fridtjof Nansen as High Commissioner for Russian Refugees. His charge was soon expanded with the addition of Armenians in 1923, and other small national groups in 1926. After Nansen died in 1930, his department continued as the Nansen International Office for Refugees, led by the president of the International Red Cross Committee, Dr. Max Huber.

At first, Nansen's office was to coordinate the work of various organizations to repatriate refugees, like the Belgians who had fled during the war and wished to return to their homes. But for those who had left for political reasons, or because they were persecuted or feared persecution, repatriation was out of the question. One option was fast and mass naturalization for those seeking "national reattachment": Greeks fleeing to Greece, Turks to Turkey, Germans to the German Reich, and the naturalization of all refugees, including Armenians, in Syria and Lebanon who formerly had been citizens of the Ottoman empire.

For most refugees, such naturalization was not an option, and it fell to Nansen's office to help these people in their country of asylum. The League did not provide funds for relief or settlement. Rather, it was the High Commissioner's job to develop infrastructural services such as the International Labor Office to help refugees find employment, and to create and assign a new identity document called the Nansen Passport, which offered some degree of political and legal protection to stateless persons. But it did not grant the things that mattered most: the right of residence, the right to seek employment and, most important of all, nationality. For all its worth, the Nansen Passport did not lift the curse of refugee life: in the system of nation-states, the refugee was a non-person. As Sir John Hope Simpson, who conducted an important survey of the crisis in the late 1930s, put it: "The refugee lacks precisely this indispensable quality of belonging to a nation state; he has a body and soul but not the third attribute of man, a *de facto* nationality." And with "no status of a national . . . he has no 'rights.'"[12]

Options for a refugee narrowed to cumbersome and inflexible naturalization proceedings, involving documents attesting to the refugee's good character, fluency in the language of the host country, and a minimum period of residence—five years in France, Italy, Britain, the Netherlands, and ten in Poland, Lithuania, Yugoslavia, Romania, Bulgaria, Belgium. Naturalization cost money too. The Netherlands required a deposit of up to 1,000 guilders per person, and Britain charged £10 plus the price of a public notice in the newspapers. The Scandinavian countries and Poland demanded evidence that an applicant had adequate means of support.[13]

Once granted, naturalization did not offer unrestricted rights. In France, naturalized physicians had to wait five years to practice medicine, and lawyers marked time for a decade before hanging out a shingle. Far worse, a new legal phenomenon arose during the Great War: denaturalization. The French passed a law allowing the denationalization of French citizens of enemy origin who had retained their original nationality as well. Portugal's government denationalized all citizens born of a German father. Denaturalization laws became even more common after the war. Belgium adopted such legislation in 1922, followed by Italy and France. New citizens, wishing to safeguard their hard-won status, hesitated to support later arrivals. Such aid was politically unpopular, and the recently naturalized were all too vulnerable themselves.

SETTLEMENT in underdeveloped areas might have worked, but although there was much talk, the idea had little political muscle behind it and, after the stock market crash in 1929, no financial support.[14] The sole and very important exception was the Zionist project of Palestine as a land for the Jews. Zionist leaders such as Theodor Herzl had long predicted that a rise in antisemitism would create a massive Jewish refugee problem. At the Zionist Congress of 1900, Max Nordau, Herzl's friend and colleague, compared the Romanian persecution of its Jewish population and the resulting emigration with the expulsion of the Spanish Jews in 1492. Nordau anticipated the eviction of all 270,000 Romanian

Jews.[15] He also believed that Austria would follow suit and expel its 780,000 Galician Jews, which then would inspire Russia to exile its many millions. The only solution for this imminent catastrophe was to create the homeland Herzl had envisioned in *The Jewish State* (1896).[16] Some 80,000 Jews, primarily Zionist pioneers from eastern Europe, heeded Nordau's warning in the prewar years and settled in Ottoman-ruled Palestine.

Immigration to Palestine got a boost during the Great War. Seeking to allay the fears of American Jews about the Allies—which included both Russia and Romania, the two European countries with the worst records of antisemitism— the British foreign secretary Lord Balfour on 2 November 1917 issued a declaration that recognized, in principle, the eventual establishment of a Jewish National Home in Palestine.[17]

A month later, the British general Edmund Allenby entered Jerusalem and his troops soon occupied the entire country. Palestine thus passed from Turkish to British rule. When the League of Nations confirmed British authority in 1922, its Mandate for Palestine included the text of the Balfour Declaration.[18] The establishment of a Jewish "national home" now sat on the League's agenda, and Palestine emerged as a real option for Jewish refugees. Agonizing over the slaughter of his co-religionists in the Ukraine after the war, Max Nordau proposed the immediate transfer of 600,000 Jews to Palestine. Faced with the certain death of up to a third of the refugees due to Palestine's utter lack of infrastructure, resources, or preparation for such a mass movement, the Zionist leadership rejected his plan. Frustrated, Nordau snapped back: It was better for Jews to die in Palestine, contributing to the creation of a Jewish homeland, than to be murdered by antisemites in Europe. He was overruled, but his proposal and his argument reframed the issue of the importance of Palestine as a place of instant asylum.[19]

With no dramatic influx of refugees, the Jewish community in Palestine, known as the *Yishuv* ("settlement"), grew at a measured pace, tripling from some 60,000 to 170,000 in the first decade of British rule. Representing Jewish interests was the Jewish Agency, a semi-autonomous local authority appointed by the World Zionist Organization. It accepted the British government's policy which established the annual number of Jewish immigrants in relation to the ability of the Palestine economy to absorb them. Should greater numbers arrive in the future, capital would be needed; the more people who could pay for themselves, the better. The Jewish Agency would finance those who could not. Thus, those who could bring at least £1,000 sterling (or $5,000, or 15,000 German marks), which was sufficient for one farm or to support the immigration of four families, entered without restrictions.[20] Professionals with £500 and skilled craftsmen needed by the Yishuv with £250 also were admitted without caveat.

The British decided how many Jews could enter; the Jewish Agency determined who they might be. Left-wing Zionist groups, committed to a solid socioeconomic base of farmers and manual laborers, dominated the Yishuv.

They sought strong, young immigrants who had lived as pioneers (*chalutsim*) and had received vocational training and ideological education in agricultural schools before leaving for Palestine. These Jews were to discard their European identity and start anew as Hebrews in the Jewish homeland. In the words of the great Zionist leader David Ben-Gurion (born David Green in Plonsk, Poland), transplanted Jews from the Diaspora to Palestine would not continue Diaspora Jewish life in a new place and a new form. Rather, it meant "taking masses of uprooted, impoverished, sterile Jewish masses, living parasitically off the body of an alien economic body and dependent on others—and introducing them to productive and creative life, implanting them on the land, integrating them into primary production in agriculture, in industry and handicraft—and making them economically independent and self sufficient."[21]

One such pioneer was the Hungarian Zionist—and later novelist and journalist—Arthur Koestler. In 1926, Koestler traveled to Palestine with his immigration certificate, one pound in his pocket, one suitcase, and ready to live a life of heroic poverty. When he arrived in the kibbutz (communal farm) he had agreed to join, he was deeply disappointed. It was a "dismal" and "slumlike" collection of huts surrounded by "dreary vegetable plots" worked by "weary and physically exhausted" people driven only to survive.[22] If Palestine promised a solution to the Jewish refugee problem, it barely sufficed. Conditions were as harsh as they were unfamiliar. Hunger, disease, and on-the-edge maintenance were the realities of Yishuv life. By 1930 this community of unconnected enclaves totaled 4 percent of the area and amounted to only 19 percent of Palestine's population. It soon began to shrink as disenchanted settlers drifted away, Koestler among them. He moved from the kibbutz to Haifa, Tel Aviv, and Jerusalem, and in two years had tired of Palestine. "I was twenty-three and had had my fill of the East—both of Arab romantics and Jewish mystique," he wrote in his autobiography. Among other complaints, Koestler thought that the policy of the Yishuv to adopt Hebrew as its language was mad. Archaic in structure, it could not express twentieth-century thought. Hebrew, in his view, separated the Yishuv from western civilization. "My mind and spirit were longing for Europe, thirsting for Europe, pining for Europe," Koestler admitted.[23] And so he left for France, and he forgot about Zionism.

In the 1920s the project of Palestine clearly was not the solution to the problem of European Jewish refugees, and it certainly was not an option for the millions of non-Jews who sought asylum. European governments, looking at the hordes without a homeland, did not know how to handle or resolve the situation. Longing for order, they relegated responsibility to the police. And the police, true to function, simply drove the refugees out of the country, even if they had no entry papers for anywhere else. As a result, a whole new class of displaced persons shuttled from one country to another with no opportunity to settle in any of them. Joachim Scharf's aunt, who took in Joachim and his sister Monika in 1939, "had settled in Sweden after quite an odyssey. They [his aunt and uncle] had left Germany and actually had no visas for any country. But they went to Denmark; they went to Sweden; they went from Sweden to Finland; from Finland to Estland [Estonia] and Letland [Latvia]. They were pushed off from most places and finally they were permitted, on a displaced persons' visa, to stay in Sweden. Having settled in Sweden, they took on my sister and myself in 1939, a month before the war."[24] Theirs was a most fortunate outcome. The German Jewish philosopher Hannah Arendt, herself a refugee to France in 1933, noted that many thousands of others could find stability only by committing a crime. For "as long as [the refugee's] trial and sentence last, he will be safe from that arbitrary police rule against which there are no lawyers and appeals."[25]

Arendt also observed another result of delegating authority over the refugees to the police: close cooperation between the police forces of many nations. In the 1930s this meant that the police of the very countries Germany would invade just a few years later were on cozy terms with their German counterparts. It seemed to Arendt that "the relations between the Gestapo and the French police were never more cordial than at the time of Léon Blum's popular-front government, which was guided by a decidedly anti-German policy." Did this explain why the Germans "met with so disgracefully little resistance from the police in the countries they occupied," and why they could organize terror so efficiently, assisted by local police forces?[26]

WHEN THE NAZIS came to power in 1933, Europe faced a refugee problem it had not known how to handle since 1918 and that had been exacerbated by the Depression. Rampant unemployment meant that no one wanted immigrants who would take away jobs or add to the welfare rolls. Nevertheless, the 60,000 Germans, some 40,000 of them Jews, who fled immediately found safe havens. Surrounding countries opened their doors even though, due to the Reich Flight Tax, the refugees came with few possessions and little money. The French government, cherishing the ideal of asylum, waived its visa restrictions, and 30,000 German refugees crossed its border. Private charities raised 8 million francs (then $500,000) to support them. The Netherlands and Czechoslovakia also dropped paperwork and admitted 6,000 and 5,000 refugees, respectively. Holland's tiny Jewish community established a *Comité voor Joodsche Vluchtelingen* (Committee for Jewish Refugees), raising as much money as in France.[27] In the middle of the Depression, the committee found employment for most and set up an agricultural training program for younger Jewish refugees.

Perhaps one reason for this sympathy was that the Nazis specially targeted intellectuals. In 1933, some one thousand two hundred Jewish academics lost their university positions. Their mass exodus invited comparison with the flight of Greek scholars from Constantinople after the Turkish conquest in 1452. Here was a direct assault on western civilization itself.[28] Many responded, mounting high-profile efforts to help. Prominent scientists and scholars in England organized the Academic Assistance Council and found posts for 178 academics that first year; similarly, the Emergency Committee for Aid to Displaced German Scholars was founded in the United States; and the *Comité des Savants* (Committee of Scholars) in France.[29]

As 1933 went on, and the first wave of political and intellectual opponents of, or "enemies" of, the regime was followed by succeeding waves of Jews stripped of their ability to earn a living, the problem they posed was raised in the International Labor Office. Philanthropic organizations that had carried the brunt of support for the refugees asked the League of Nations to take action, but the League was reluctant to do so. As the Dutch foreign minister put it when he brought the matter before the League Assembly, "We are faced with the fact that thousands of German subjects have crossed the frontiers of the neighbouring countries and refused to return to their homes for reasons which we are not called upon to judge. For us, therefore, it is a purely technical problem."[30] Refusing to comment on or interfere with Hitler's policies, the League sidestepped the Nansen International Office. A separate body for this "technical problem" was created, and the League appointed the chairman of the board of the American Foreign Policy Association, James G. McDonald, as High Commissioner for Refugees (Jewish and Other) Coming from Germany. Like Nansen before him, McDonald was to coordinate activity between the states confronted with the refugee crisis. And like Nansen, he was not to undertake any direct relief work. But unlike Nansen, McDonald was explicitly forbidden to deal with the refugee problem in a political manner: he was prohibited from intervening directly with the German government because of its hostility toward the League of Nations.[31]

To avoid a German veto, McDonald reported to a separate Governing Body chaired by the British statesman Robert Viscount Cecil of Chelwood, principal draughtsman of the League of Nations Covenant in 1919 and a pillar of the

22. British policemen deport Czech Jews, Croydon airfield, 31 March 1939. Seeking asylum, these refugees had crossed the border into Poland and then flown to Great Britain, only to be denied asylum and sent back to Poland. Courtesy Wide World Photo, New York.

League thereafter. This compromise mollified the Germans but compromised McDonald's authority; he could neither speak nor act with the authority of the League. McDonald's office was treated as a cast-off child of the League and starved for resources. His offices consisted of two small rooms and a staff of six people.

Despite this inauspicious start, McDonald and Lord Cecil believed fervently in the importance of their work. "We are face to face with a great challenge," Lord Cecil admonished the Governing Body, "a challenge to the principles of our civilisation, which have governed the world increasingly for nearly two thousand years. We must either respond to that challenge or, as it seems to me, the civilisation we enjoy will receive a terrible blow from which it may never recover."[32]

HISTORY PROVED Lord Cecil right. In the meantime, during the first year of Hitler's reign, the ancient tradition of asylum held sway. As we have seen, many governments admitted large numbers of German refugees. The entry of German Jews into Palestine, an obvious site for sanctuary, was framed by other considerations and another agenda, however. In 1933, only 20,000 German Jews (4%) belonged to Zionist organizations. Most of them had no interest in emigrating to the cultural desolation of Palestine, inhabited by Arabs and transplanted *Ostjuden,* an arid landscape dotted with spartan communes, a few dingy towns, and Tel Aviv: a provincial, chaotic, and shapeless attempt of a city built on sand. These German Zionists did not even see Zionism as a vehicle to support the *Ostjuden* who did make *aliyah,* or emigrate. German Zionism, a coherent, integrated, and compelling world view, amounted to a kind of ersatz religion for secular Jews.[33] As a result, in 1933 German Jews were marginal in Palestine, comprising only 1 percent of the population.

It was precisely those who had shown little interest in the project of Palestine before who needed asylum now. And they had few friends among those who wrestled with the dilemma between continuing to build the Jewish homeland according to the established long-range vision or abandoning those plans in light of the crisis in Germany. Anticipating pressure to admit large numbers of German Jews, the British government set up a cabinet committee to deal with the problem. The committee did not flinch: The absorption capacity of Palestine's economy determined immigration figures—not politics in Berlin. The Zionist leadership essentially agreed. Speaking before the 18th Zionist Congress in Prague in August 1933, the sociologist and demographer Arthur Ruppin calculated that Palestine could absorb only 100,000 German Jews in the next ten years. "In order that the immigration not flood the existing settlement in Palestine like lava, it must be proportionate to a certain percentage of that settlement,"[34] he declared.

Whatever their attitude toward German Jews, Zionists themselves held a peculiar place in the Nazi world view. Through their filter of racism, National

Socialist leaders looked favorably upon the movement to create a Jewish homeland. "The fundamental idea of the Zionists to organize the Jews as a nation
among nations in their own land is sound and justified, as long as it is not connected with any plan for world domination," the prominent Nazi ideologue
Johann von Leers declared in August 1933.

> If Israel takes up the plough, the hoe and the scythe and is no longer intent
> on making other nations its servants, and wants instead to be a free nation
> among free nations and develop its productive power to the same extent that
> it developed its demonic powers, it will find friends where before it only
> found enemies, and Israel and its neighbors will greet each other across
> freshly-ploughed fields.[35]

Nazis and Zionists agreed that Jews had no place in the Diaspora: Nazis
believed Jews had harmed western civilization; Zionists believed that two thousand years of western civilization's antisemitism was more than enough. The
Nazis wanted the Jews to leave Germany and the Zionists wanted the Jews to
leave Germany.

The Nazis therefore parleyed with the Zionists. The Ha'avara or Transfer
Agreement allowed German Jews the sum required by Britain for unrestricted
entry into Palestine: the equivalent of £1,000 in currency (RM 15,000). It also
permitted transfer of capital in the form of German products or commodities.
Jews sold their possessions in Germany, depositing the marks gained in a German bank. A trust company then spent the money on German cars, building
materials, dyes, pharmaceuticals, and the like, which were shipped to Palestine,
sold for Palestine pounds by another trust company, and given to the settlers.
Thus German Reichsmarks deposited in Germany were changed into Palestine
pounds without straining the foreign currency reserves of the Reichsbank.[36]

Hitler claimed credit for the Ha'avara Agreement. He was a fine fellow
after all.

> In England people assert that their arms are open to welcome all the
> oppressed, especially the Jews who have left Germany. . . . But it would still
> be finer if England did not make her great gesture dependent on the posses-
> sion of 1,000 pounds. England should say: "Anyone may enter" as we unfor-
> tunately have done for 30 years. If we too had declared that no one could
> enter Germany save under the condition of bringing with him 1,000 pounds
> or paying more, then today we should have no Jewish question at all. So we
> wild folk have once more proved ourselves to be better humans, less perhaps
> in external protestations, but at least in our actions![37]

As usual, Hitler got it wrong: Britain required no bankroll to enter the British
islands; £10 were asked to cover the cost of naturalization paperwork.

For a few years the Nazis celebrated this "solution" to the "Jewish Problem."[38] Goebbels's newspaper *Der Angriff* ran twelve articles in the fall of 1934 on a six-month visit to the Yishuv by the chief of the Jewish department of Heydrich's Security Service, SS-Untersturmführer Baron Leopold von Mildenstein. Palestine removed Jews from Europe and actually changed them, he reported. "The soil has reformed him [the Jew] and his kind in a decade," von Mildenstein rejoiced. "This new Jew will be a new people."[39] SS Security chief Reinhard Heydrich, who was to mastermind the genocide of the Jews six years later, agreed in an article for the SS weekly *Das Schwarze Korps* (1935). "The time cannot be far distant when Palestine will again be able to accept its sons who have been lost to it for over a thousand years. Our good wishes together with our official good will go with them."[40]

German Zionists loathed making a deal with the Nazis which implicitly agreed to the liquidation of the German Jewish community, and felt ashamed of the Nazi language in their negotiations. But they saw they had no choice. The Jewish Agency regretted that the agreement broke the boycott against Germany and moved Jews who were not ideal settlers to Palestine, but understood the financial value of the deal for their long-term goals.[41] The number of Jews who wished—and had the financial resources—to benefit from the agreement was limited: between August 1933 and early 1937 only 12,000 German Jews used the Ha'avara Agreement to transfer a proportion of their assets to Palestine. Even so, this influx of money stimulated such an economic growth that the absorptive capacity increased to allow another 20,000 young German Jews without resources to immigrate to Palestine during that period. It also opened up places in Palestine for the besieged Jews in Poland. Thus, during the first five years of Nazi rule, the number of Jews in the Yishuv doubled from 200,000 to 400,000 (or close to 30% of the territory's population of 1.3 million), and the disconnected enclaves grew together. Palestine appeared to be on its way to Jewish statehood.[42]

Permission to emigrate was one thing; adaptation once arrived was another.[43] Among the German Jews who emigrated to Palestine in 1933 was the Zionist writer Arnold Zweig, a friend of the great psychoanalyst Sigmund Freud. Writing to Freud in January 1934, Zweig explained how minor difficulties mounted major obstacles to adjustment. "You will find, dear Father Freud, that I am expatiating too much upon central heating, but these questions of practical life, where the apparatus of civilisation functions only creakingly, are the main problems in this country. We are not yet prepared to give up our standard of living and this country is not yet prepared to satisfy it. And since the Palestinian Jews are rightly proud of what does exist and since we are rightly irritated about what does not, there is much friction on the quiet, especially among the women, much vexation about the immense expense of effort these trifles demand."[44] A year later, Zweig admitted, "I have established quite calmly that I do not belong here. After twenty years of Zionism that is naturally hard to believe."[45] The nation-

23. German Jewish youths living in an agricultural settlement in Palestine read their mail, presumably from family still in the Reich, c. 1938. Central Zionist Archives, courtesy of the United States Holocaust Memorial Museum Photo Archives, Washington, DC.

alism, especially where it concerned Hebrew, depressed him. "People demand here their Hebrew, and I cannot give it to them. I am a German writer and a German European and this fact has certain consequences."[46] Freud counseled him to stay; at least Palestine was safe.[47]

In hindsight, it is easy to be baffled by Zweig's lack of insight and to overlook Freud's prescience. We know that Freud correctly saw that safety was the sole issue, and that Zweig's complaints were trivial. In 1934, however, no one could even imagine what lay ahead. And no one did. Thus, the president of the World Jewish Organization Chaim Weizmann and other Zionist leaders, well tuned to Jewish suffering, continued to favor controlled immigration and to favor young pioneers over bourgeois professionals. For Weizmann the choice came down to the immediate rescue of German Jews or the establishment of a national homeland, the lasting redemption of the Jewish people. Polish Jews fared well under Weizmann's construct: they were ideologically attuned; they were prepared to work in the agricultural settlements; and their position in Poland was even worse than that of the Jews in Germany.[48]

Chaim Weizmann had company in his view that the Jews of Germany were better off than Jews in Poland and had options other than flight. One ally was Nahum Goldmann, a German Jew who had fled to Switzerland in 1933, where he represented the Jewish Agency to the League of Nations. His aim was to fight to secure Jewish rights throughout the world, and to that end he and the well-known American rabbi Stephen S. Wise founded the World Jewish Congress. "There exists in Europe today a Jewish problem of a magnitude and urgency the like of which has not existed in centuries," Goldmann declared in Geneva at the founding conference on 8 August 1936. "One might almost say that it is no longer a fight for minority rights, or for equal rights of citizenship; it has increasingly become a basic issue of physical survival in the most primitive sense of the term."[49] Goldmann rightly observed that "all over Europe, even in the non-totalitarian states, there prevails a mood of resignation, of skepticism, of lethargy in the face of the onslaught of these new power elements and anti-liberal tendencies."[50] Jews all over the world must resist such lassitude and apathy; they must struggle for the restitution of rights in Germany.

Denouncing Nazi policy toward the Jews, Goldmann went on to decry the acquiescence of many German Jews to a new kind of ghetto. History itself forbade the reconstruction of a locked Jewish quarter, he said. "Ways of living which history itself has broken up cannot be put together again. . . . Now, after a century of emancipation, the Jews can either live on as emancipated Jews or else perish as Jews."[51] Jews had to stand firm. "We shall not evacuate our positions, for we have grown into them in the process of history and therefore we have the right to hold them." Neither the Nazis nor any other antisemitic ultra-nationalist regime, such as those in Poland and Romania, should take comfort from Zionism. "If—and I say this because I am a Zionist—we are rebuilding Palestine, we are not doing so because we have given up all hope of ever obtaining equality." There would be no mass exodus of Jews from Europe, for "only with the backing of a strong Diaspora Jewry will the Jews of Palestine be able to bring about that rebirth of Jewish culture for the sake of which we are building the Homeland."[52] In short and "above all, other nations and governments should not be under the delusion that wherever the signal is sounded to deprive the Jews of their rights, world Jewry will be ready to liquidate that Jewish community."[53]

ETHNIC POLES in the newly recreated Poland were as nationalistic and, by the mid-1930s, as antisemitic as their German neighbors.[54] They wanted a Poland for the Poles: a nation-state of one people with a shared language, culture, and history, not a multicultural society. That was very well, but demographics told another story. When Poland's borders had been set in 1921, Ukrainians, Byelorussians, Jews, and Germans accounted for one-third of the population. These minority groups demanded minority rights—autonomy, if not independence. Poland has "bitten off more than it can chew," remarked the German Jewish physician and writer Alfred Döblin during his journey through Poland in 1924.[55] Wilson's idealism had not worked in Poland; it had created only a nation-state with many minorities separated from their own "national communities." In the weakest position of all were the Jews. Unlike the other minority groups, they had no territorial base elsewhere and no large fraternal population next door. And, evidently, the Poles loathed them, as Döblin learned while talking with a young Polish gentleman who had served as an officer during the war. "His hatred of Germans is tied up with fear," Döblin observed. On the other hand, "he expresses pure hatred of the Jews, a hatred intensifying into disgust. One can't do anything to them, he declares. . . . The Pole in my [train] compartment admits that he doesn't even know whether it makes any sense to wipe them out completely, smash them and suck them up." The former officer "spends hours pouring out this hatred, [and] he complains in despair: The Jews

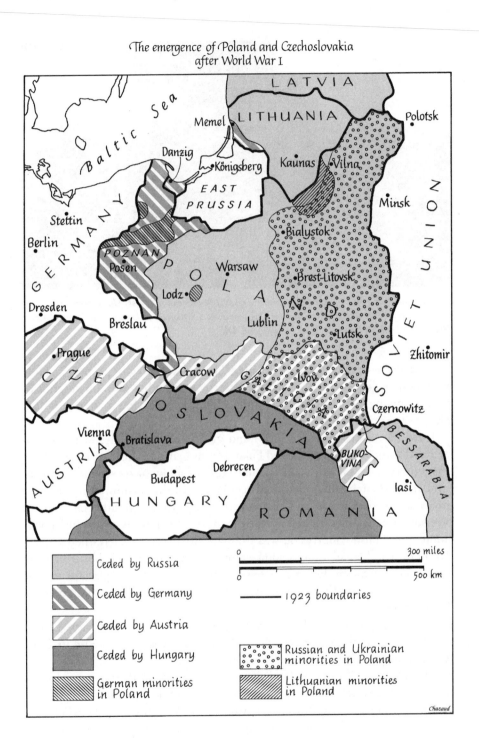

The emergence of Poland and Czechoslovakia
after World War I

Ceded by Russia

Ceded by Germany

Ceded by Austria

Ceded by Hungary

German minorities
in Poland

1923 boundaries

Russian and Ukrainian
minorities in Poland

Lithuanian minorities
in Poland

24. Jews' homes and businesses set on fire during an anti-Jewish riot in Minsk-Mazowiecki, 20 miles east of Warsaw (Poland), 1936. Archiwum Dokumentocji Mechanizney, courtesy of the United States Holocaust Memorial Photo Archives, Washington, DC.

are 'not individual persons in Poland. They're a nation, a people. . . . How wealthy they grow, with our wealth. They're nothing but saprophytes, mushrooms growing from putrescence, fungus living on decaying matter, parasites. They're a race of bacteria.' "[56]

Józef Pilsudski, the much-loved and greatly revered leader of the Polish legions during World War I, ruled Poland from 1926 until his death in 1935. He was conservative and nationalistic, but he did not allow such extreme monocultural and monoreligious voices to direct policy. In the vacuum of his death, a group of anti-democratic and chauvinistic army officers, greatly enamored of Nazism, came to power. Their rhetoric identified the Jews as a "surplus" population. The Polish countryside was dramatically overpopulated, they argued. Part of the rural population should be moved to the cities which, however, were already crowded—by Jews. The Jews would have to leave, perhaps for the island of Madagascar (in the Indian Ocean) or to other places, to make room for the peasants.[57]

Various deportation schemes were adduced. In September 1936 Poland asked the Assembly of the League of Nations for colonies to settle its Jews. Another proposal led to negotiations with the Zionist Revisionist leader Vladimir Jabotinksy, who saw Poland as a vast ghetto, a death trap poised to be sprung on Polish Jewry at any moment.[58] These ideas went nowhere, but the pressure mounted. On 25 November 1936, Chaim Weizmann told the Palestine Royal Commission that Poland's foreign minister, Jozef Beck, had announced a countrywide surplus of 1 million Jews. For Weizmann, catastrophe loomed. The Jews of Romania, Latvia, and Lithuania were also living under a panoply of discriminatory and oppressive measures. Across much of eastern and central Europe, Weizmann saw "a people doomed to be pent up where they are not wanted, and for whom the world is divided into places where they cannot live, and places into which they cannot enter."[59]

By 1937, Poland waged an undeclared war against the Jews, replete with organized pogroms, random acts of street violence, and the institution of "bench ghettos," isolated seating for Jewish students at the universities. A number of professional associations had adopted the Nazis' "Aryan Paragraph," barring Jews from membership. Economic boycotts of Jewish businesses had become common practice, as had destruction of Jewish property and violence against Jews and Christians who did not participate in the antisemitic free-for-all. Polish Jews, poor to begin with, sank into penury. If in the early 1930s 3.0 of the 3.5 million Jews were paupers, 490,000 destitute, and the rest barely able to make a living, within a few years the entire community had gone under.[60] They were as eager to emigrate as their government was to get rid of them. But they had nowhere to go.

ROMANIA TOO had embarked on a new, radical route of antisemitism. Like Poland, Romania found itself a multi-nation-state when its boundaries were set after World War I, and it was just as loathe to accommodate ethnic diversity. Successive Romanian governments hindered the Jews in the newly acquired territories from applying for citizenship, and tried to denaturalize those who already had it. Without citizenship, Jews could not work freely, find a permanent home, or use the public schools, and they were liable for immediate expulsion.[61]

A central figure in Romania's antisemitic movement was Alexander Cuza, professor of economics at Iasi University. Cuza founded the Fascist League of National Christian Defense, which gave birth to the notorious Iron Guard led by Corneliu Zelea Codreanu.[62] An avid reader of the *Protocols of the Elders of Zion* and the writings of Chamberlain, Cuza identified the Jews as a bastard race and the source of national degeneration. His goal was wholesale expulsion, and he was not alone. The poet Octavian Coga was obsessed with what he called the "Jewish invasion" of Romania. He too argued for the deportation of all Jews to French-ruled Madagascar.[63] Whether intellectual leaders such as Cuza and Coga empowered Fascist politicians to pursue violent antisemitism or whether fascism empowered people like Cuza and Coga is not clear, but they clearly abetted each other. The Fascist ideologue Alexandru Razmerita proposed imprisoning the whole Jewish population in concentration camps and working them to death. This plan he saw as more practical than a rival proposal by an Orthodox priest to drown all the Jews in the Black Sea.[64]

Dazzled by the developments in Germany, and facing the rapid rise of Codreanu's Iron Guard, Romania's government was inspired to imitate its Nordic model. The Law for the Protection of National Labor (1934) forced

Density of Jewish settlement
in east-central Europe, 1919

Density of Jewish population

More than 10%

Between 1% and 10%

——— 1923 boundaries

------ 1914 boundaries

0   300 miles

0   500 km

Chazaud

many Jews out of their jobs, and in 1936 a Romanian version of the Nuremberg Laws was introduced, but withdrawn under pressure from the League of Nations. The ruling Liberal Party lost its majority in the general elections of December 1937; Codreanu's Iron Guard won dramatically.[65] Bankrolled by Germany, the Iron Guard had become a formidable political force. This boded ill for the Jews. In a post-election interview with the chief foreign correspondent of the *Daily Herald* (London), Codreanu shrieked: "The Jews, the Jews, they are our curse. They poison our state, our life, our people. They demoralise our nation. They destroy our youth. They are the arch-enemies." And he ranted: "We shall destroy the Jews before they can destroy us." According to Codreanu, "there are three ways to deal with the Jews—assimilation, co-operation and elimination." But: "We do not want the Jews to assimilate with us. We shall never co-operate with them. There remains elimination. That is my solution. I am for eliminating the Jews completely, totally and without exception." They could leave of their own accord, or Romania would throw them out. "The essential thing is that the Jews must go. Every single Jew must leave this country. You ask where they should go? That is not my business. That is a matter for the Jews themselves and for all the nations to decide."[66]

THE NAZIS AGREED with Codreanu. Ever since 1933, their policy had been to "solve" the "Jewish Problem" through emigration. To some extent they had succeeded: by the time they annexed Austria in March 1933, some 120,000 of the 500,000 Jews in Germany had left the Reich. The Anschluss, however, brought Austria's 200,000 Jews into the now Greater Reich. From the Nazi point of view, emigration procedures could not keep up with the "Problem," let alone "solve" it. Something would have to be done to speed up the process.

The mastermind of the new strategy was Adolf Eichmann. Born in the Ruhr in 1906, Eichmann had grown up in Austria, and it was there that he joined the Austrian Nazi Party in 1932. A year later he moved to Germany and enlisted in an Austrian unit of the SS. Eichmann was getting ahead, but his real career began when he joined the head office of Himmler's Security Service (SD) in 1934. There he found a niche in Department II 112 of SS-Untersturmführer von Mildenstein as the SS expert on Zionist matters, which included a trip to Palestine to report on the Jewish colonization project. In 1937, Nazi support for Zionism had waned and the department's focus shifted to "general and fundamental aspects of the Jewish question."[67] When Himmler decided to centralize the management of Jewish emigration procedures (visas, economic arrangements, transfer of capital), Eichmann took charge of the design and implementation of this streamlined "service."[68]

The new system was never set up in Germany itself but, within days of the Anschluss, Eichmann turned up in Vienna to organize the emigration of Jews. His headquarters in a palace stolen from the Rothschild family became the Central Office for Jewish Emigration. As far as Eichmann was concerned, emigration no longer depended upon the initiative of individual Jews. It was an operation supervised by the SD involving officials of the Finance Ministry, the police, the currency control office, and representatives of the Jewish community. He compared his system to a conveyor belt. "The initial application and all the rest of the required papers are put in at one end, and the passport falls off at the other end," he explained rather proudly when interrogated for trial in 1962.

He did not tell the Israeli police captain that the conveyor belt swallowed up the Jews' rights as well as their money, and that the passport they received allowing them to leave was valid for a mere fourteen days. Nor did he explain that the system was financed with money taken from the Jews themselves. What he did report was that his Central Office for Jewish Emigration had forced 50,000 Jews to leave within six months, "a first in the German administrative machine." It made him a star in the Nazi constellation, an attraction for "numerous visitors from various departments in the so-called Old Reich, who came to Vienna for this express purpose." Even his boss, Reinhard Heydrich, "who was then head of the Security Police, came, too."[69]

If for Eichmann the Central Office for Jewish Emigration was a conveyor belt, for Austria's Jews it was a nightmare. "The initial application and all the rest of the required papers are put in on one end," Eichmann boasted airily. But how were those "required papers" to be obtained? The Nazis wanted the Jews to leave. The Jews, humiliated, abused, and terrorized from the first day of the Anschluss, sought to escape. But, as their co-religionists in Germany had learned for five years, emigration—contrary to Codreanu's assertion—was *not* "a matter for the Jews themselves"; it was a desperate search for sponsors abroad, tax clearance forms, entry visas, train tickets, and ship berths.

Elisabeth Rosner-Jellinek and her family were amongst the thousands of Austrian Jews who suffered immediately. Her father was arrested and, from prison, sent to a concentration camp. Elisabeth and her mother had little hope. "My mother would not leave because my father was in concentration camp, and she thought she might do something for him if she remained in Austria. But I should leave. That was decided."[70]

How to obtain a visa? Leaving Austria posed its own difficulties, but without a guarantor no other country would allow her to enter. And who in western Europe or abroad would invite her and guarantee that she would not become a ward of the state? Like many other central European Jews, Elisabeth Jellinek's contacts to enter Britain developed by chance, good luck, and unremitting effort. In the summer of 1937, Elisabeth and her mother went on a cheap vacation to Italy. One day, when a special outing was organized, "my mother and the other girls decided we would all go in so-called Austrian national dress. The girls would all dress up in these dirndl frocks—which only my mother and I did in the end." An English group arrived at the tourist site just as the Jellineks were leaving. "A young man hopped out and asked if he could take a photograph of us because he liked our dresses. So my mother said yes, and it was all very much in a hurry, but we did manage, and we just threw him a paper with our address on it and asked him to send us the photograph."[71]

This little bit of Austrian nationalism, and the pure coincidence of meeting the twenty-five-year-old Arnold Butterworth, "a nice young fellow from Manchester," who was taken with the dirndl costume, assumed great importance a year later. Elisabeth had exchanged a few letters with Butterworth, and after her father's arrest she wrote to him "that things were not so good." She was afraid to be more specific, however, and she did not know how to communicate the gravity of her situation to him. Finally, her opportunity came. "I was very friendly with a [Jewish] girl with a Catholic Hungarian stepmother. Her family decided to move back to Hungary . . . and when she left Vienna I asked her to take a letter with her and post it in Hungary. I really could write then that my father had been arrested, that we were all in danger, and that there was very little possibility to get out of the country, so maybe he could invite me. He answered and said yes, of course, he would see what had to be done and send me the information, the guarantees, and the invitation."[72] With those in hand, Elisabeth was able to leave Austria and enter England.

Emigration plans dominated conversation among Austria's Jews. "We were all talking about emigration and how we can get out," Robert Rosner, then fourteen, recalled. "My father found a cousin, I don't know who, who lived in the States, on a chicken farm somewhere in New Jersey. He wrote. And then we went through telephone directories of New York and looked for Rosners, and wrote letters to all of them."[73] Jews stood on line at embassies, consulates, shipping companies, and government offices, desperate for papers: exit visas, transit visas, receipts for tax payments, clearance forms, ship tickets, train tickets. "You needed a lot of forms," Rosner explained, "you had to go to all sorts of offices. People had to queue up." These formalities led to an unanticipated way for young people to make money. "We kids did this work of queuing up. One had to start at 8:00 in the morning and one had to queue up until 11:00 or 12:00, so an adult would say, 'Would you queue for me?' Sometimes they had to get a form, and then I could get it. But when it came to doing serious business, they had to be there."[74]

The Rosner family, like so many other Jewish families, held out hope of getting away. Robert's sister Paula managed to get the tax clearance form for the family even though their parents owed taxes which they did not have the money to pay. They had moved from the eighth district to the second, and the official in their new district chose not to check (in that pre-computer era) with the office across town. "He said, 'Oh, hell. Nothing is normal. Let's give them no tax debts.'" With the form he gave Paula they were able to obtain an exit visa. But again, a visa for where? "We tried the Palestine office, we tried with families in Palestine."[75] Mr. and Mrs. Rosner, like Jacques Kupfermann's parents, were from what had been the eastern reaches of the former Austro-Hungarian empire when they were born and was by then Romania. "We were thinking, if the situation changed, if we could get to Romania. One uncle of mine tried to leave immediately for Romania, but he didn't succeed. He got sent back. One of my cousins went to Italy and one to Australia. And everyone said, 'we'll try to help you.' We tried Romania. We tried Peru. We thought Peru would be possible."[76] The Rosners, one of the fortunate families, ultimately made their way to Britain.

All the Jews of Austria, like the Jews of Romania, Poland, and Germany, grew desperate to flee. "It just became impossible to live here [in Vienna]," one man put it years later.[77] For all of them, the ubiquitous question was: which country would take them? A common joke circulated in the Jewish community: "What language are you learning?" "The wrong one." They therefore were much heartened on 25 March 1938, when President Franklin Delano Roosevelt announced his intention to call an international conference on the refugee crisis at the French resort town of Evian-les-Bains in July. Their lives were about to be determined by current events over which they had no control and about which they had no voice, but finally the president of the United States had recognized publicly that a solution had to be found.[78]

It was a curious decision for Roosevelt to have taken. Unemployment rates in the United States stood at an all-time high. Politicians and the public feared both immigrant competition for jobs and the financial burden of supporting them. The Great Depression had impoverished millions of families and all but robbed the country of hope and security. Many Americans were isolationists; they wanted nothing to do with Europe and its problems. America must take care of Americans, not resolve European conflicts or open its doors to foreigners. Politicians in Washington read the mood of their constituents at home and advocated a tightly restricted immigration policy.

Then too, the League of Nations already had three agencies to deal with different aspects of the refugee problem: the Nansen Office, the International Labor Office, and the High Commission for Refugees from Germany. Finally, the United States, which had not so far taken European refugees, was hardly in a position to persuade Germany's overburdened neighbors to do more.

We now know that the Evian conference was designed to protect America's image, not to help the Jewish and political refugees of Europe. America had long glowed in its reputation as a refuge for the oppressed. The conference would uphold this principle—if not effect any change in practice. President Roosevelt accordingly issued invitations to twenty-nine countries; to allay fears that the United States would demand great concessions, the invited nations were told that "no country would be expected to receive a greater number of emigrants than is permitted by its existing legislation."[79] All new programs would be financed by private agencies, not public monies. The purpose of the meeting was to facilitate the emigration of "political refugees" (not "Jews") from Germany and Austria.

The conference was a dismal failure and a grave disappointment for Jews frantic to leave Europe. But neither they nor anyone else realized at the time how tragic its results would be. No one was ready to take on the task of finding safe havens for the refugees. And, as everyone refused to act, each country left Evian with tacit international permission to keep its doors closed. In the United States, the State Department saw to it that paperwork became a serious impediment to immigration. Those bureaucrats who devised the forms certainly intended them to keep out refugees. The visa application to be completed by American sponsors of Europeans hoping to enter the United States was a two-sided document over four feet long. In that pre-photocopy machine era, six copies had to be submitted. No reasons were given to explain a rejection. If unsuccessful, the sponsor could do nothing for another six months.

The British, for their part, responding to fierce opposition by Palestinian Arabs to a Jewish National Home and to the entry of Jews who would populate such a state, sealed the escape route to Palestine. The Ha'avara Agreement had worked too well; seeing the Yishuv mushroom moved the Arabs from sullen resignation to violent opposition. Riots in the streets of Jerusalem escalated in April 1936 into a full-scale Arab rebellion. Not certain how to proceed, Britain established the Palestine Royal Commission. A year later the recommendation came down: immigration policy based on economic absorptive capacity alone should be abandoned; "political and psychological factors should be taken into account." Pacification of local Arabs was the order of the day, no matter the consequences to Jews in Europe. The Commission limited the annual immigration of Jews to 12,000 each year for the next five years.

The Nazis—those great Zionists of 1933—were relieved. They too had watched the success of the Ha'avara in dismay. What if a Jewish state actually emerged? In June 1937 the German Foreign Office instructed its embassies that "in view of the anti-German agitation of international Jewry, Germany cannot agree that the formation of a Palestine Jewish state would help the peaceful development of the nations of the world." The SS warned that the creation of a Jewish state in Palestine would lead to "special minority protection to Jews in every country, therefore giving legal protection to the exploitation activity of world Jewry."[80]

Meanwhile negotiations continued about the possible partition of Palestine into two states, one for Arabs and one for Jews. They came to nothing. As for the number of immigrants to be admitted prior to the establishment of such states, in May 1939 the British government issued a White Paper laying out its policy, slashing that figure once again. For each of the next five years, 10,000 Jews would be allowed into Palestine annually. However, given the grave dangers many Jews faced in Europe, an additional 25,000 immigrants would be admitted immediately. That was all.[81]

BY THE TIME of Britain's White Paper, the Jews of Greater Germany had endured the November Pogrom. All of life now held but one aim: to get out and to help those they loved to get out. Rudolf Rosenberg's parents thought that, as Mrs. Rosenberg had been a British citizen until she married, the family would be allowed into Britain, but their situation turned out to be very complicated indeed. According to German law, Mrs. Rosenberg took on her husband's nationality when she married. Mr. Rosenberg, however, was a Romanian national, and therefore both Rudolf and his mother were Romanian citizens.

To make matters worse, Mr. Rosenberg had "deserted from the Romanian army. He came to Berlin with false papers." As his son well understood at the time, "This has a very important bearing on the story of our family, because whilst he was in Berlin until he left in 1938, he managed to get his [Romanian] passport renewed on the basis of his false papers. There was some sort of bribery and corruption involved." A lot of anxiety was involved too. "I do remember—and this is one thing I remember very vividly—that whenever he had to get his passport renewed, whenever the dates came nearer, my father got terribly agitated because he was worried that if he lost his passport, he would lose every chance of leaving Germany because he would be a stateless person."[82]

However difficult the renewal process had been, it became impossible in the fall of 1937. "I remember he came home one evening terribly, terribly depressed, and he said he had to go back to Romania because he had to try to get 'proper papers,' which, of course, again had to be forged. The papers which he had all these years were no longer acceptable to the Romanian embassy in Berlin. They wanted another piece of paper." Mr. Rosenberg had no alternative. Although quite ill at the time, "he just managed to gain enough strength to face this ordeal."

> I remember my mother and I seeing him off at the station. He took all the savings we had, all the ready cash we could lay our hands on. He got to Bucharest and then he set about getting this piece of paper. He literally lived in hiding there because he had to get this piece of paper without it being known to the police. After he'd been away about a fortnight, I remember we got a frantic telegram telling my mother to send more money. How she got the money together, I'll never know, but she got it somehow and she sent him more money.
>
> He came back with a piece of paper that was literally cooked. And when I say "cooked," I mean it was a piece of paper giving him a legal discharge from the Romanian army. This piece of paper had to appear as if it were thirty [sic] years old. So it was literally cooked. My father told me they put it in a stewing pot and boiled it and took it out and dried it on a stove. . . . Anyway, he came back and presented this piece of paper to the Romanian embassy in Berlin and they renewed his passport.[83]

So much for the first, essential step. Rudolf, fourteen and still a minor, eluded the emigration legal web; he went to his mother's English brother in August 1938. "In November there was the famous Kristallnacht, and that gave my parents the final push. When they saw the synagogue burning, they said, 'Right. Now it's really time to go.' They did in fact just lock up the flat, left everything behind. They came to Britain on a return [round-trip] ticket." Luck was with them. Mrs. Rosenberg's parents had their golden wedding anniversary in December 1938, and they were granted an exit visa from Germany to

25. *This float built by the members of the municipal river swim club won first prize in the "Zissel" folk festival in Kassel, Germany. It depicts the departure of the Jews from Kassel. The sign reads: "Isaac, Isidor, Levy and Cohn have become bankrupt, thus receiving their due. They may not swim in the river any more, for they have been expelled to Palestine," c. 1937. Stadtarchiv Nuremberg, courtesy of the United States Holocaust Memorial Museum Photo Archives, Washington, DC.*

celebrate this family occasion. "As far as entering Britain was concerned, my mother could not be refused admittance because of her British birth. And they could not turn my father back because they didn't split up husband and wife."[84]

Lore Gang-Saalheimer, like Rudolf Rosenberg, emigrated to England. She too went to an uncle, who had emigrated from Germany many years before, and she too was joined later by her parents. She, however, did not leave until after the November Pogrom. "I remember my father not being allowed to go to his factory. I remember food being a problem. I remember money being a problem. The other thing I remember is waiting for letters from England. We were waiting for letters from my uncles, from anybody at all from England. There were no letters. It transpired that they thought we might get in trouble if they wrote to us. We felt terribly cut off." Eventually, the Saalheimer family "took up some sort of social life," but the talk was "about emigration, and when and how and what we were going to do, and passports. People had to go to the Gestapo . . . you had to go to various offices and run around. It was that sort of thing that was the preoccupation. Emigration, really I would say, was the whole of one's preoccupation."

No one knew how best to proceed, and everyone was tense. "There were terrible rows. I mean, what I certainly remember were appalling rows: between my mother and my father, between me and my parents, between my aunt and my mother and my father, and between my mother's aunt and my father: rows."

Anxiety increased daily. "Certainly from then on, there was no question that my parents wanted me out, me in particular, me out as quickly as possible, out of Germany as quickly as possible." By the middle of December, Lore Saalheimer's uncle had obtained a student permit for her, which led to a visa and then to England to study. With Lore safely in England, "my uncle gave guarantees for my parents also."[85]

Hilda Cohen-Rosenthal was not so fortunate as Lore Saalheimer or Rudolf Rosenberg. Hilda's father had been arrested during the November Pogrom. "They came and took my father to the concentration camp, and he was away for four weeks. Because he had been in the '14–'18 war, he had won the Iron Cross, and we were told that they released him because of that." The November Pogrom was the divide. "After that, things got frightening." They had to act. "My father and my mother had had a chance, perhaps in the middle of '38, to try and leave Germany. But they, like everybody else even at that time, felt nothing was going to happen. Their family had been there for about five hundred years. They somehow felt as German as the Germans—if not more so. The other thing was that by then my maternal grandfather had died, and my maternal grandmother was living with us. . . . There would be a problem with this old lady and obviously there was no question of leaving her."

Mr. and Mrs. Rosenthal tried to make arrangements for their children. Hilda's seventeen-year-old sister went to work for a Jewish family in England. Her fourteen-year-old brother was caught in Germany. Hilda "came out [of Frankfurt-am-Main] in July of '39 with the children's transport. I remember going to the [central] station with my parents and my brother and this large trunk. . . . We were not a very kissing family . . . and I remember how odd that they all kissed me. . . . I thought I was going on holiday. [The] things I brought out were *khumeshim* [the Five Books of Moses] and *sidurim* [prayer books]. This was the sort of thing my parents gave. What else could they give? [That was] the sort of people they were: the trunk was loaded with . . . special *khumeshim* and special *makhzoyrim* [holiday prayer books], for sending this child of ten out with what they thought was the most important thing in life. . . . There certainly wasn't a scene. Although I wasn't aware that I was going away probably forever, they must have been aware that there was a very strong possibility that they would never see me again. And there was no question; there was no scene and there were no tears."[86]

The kindertransports, special rescue trains organized to send endangered children west to safety (to the Netherlands and England), left from the railway stations of Prague, Vienna, Frankfurt, Berlin, Leipzig, the free city of Danzig, and the Polish city of Zbonszyn in the midst of chaos, tears, and the unending pain of parents left on train platforms. Nearly 10,000 children escaped death in this way.[87] A few years later most of the parents left too, only they went east in boxcars and no one on the platform wept for them.

The usual route from Germany led over the border into the Netherlands, up to the Hook of Holland, across the Channel, to dock at Harwich. Children from Vienna traveled through Germany to the Netherlands via Cologne. Now-adult child refugees remember the preparations and the journey itself quite clearly. "From the moment I knew I was going to go on that transport," Gerda Freistadt-Geiringer recalled of herself at fourteen, "I made myself clothes. I made three or four dresses for myself. I can draw them still. My father went with me to get material in Judengasse; he had friends there. I remember looking through the material in a particular shop in Judengasse. A second time we went to Lichtensteingasse in the ninth district, also to get something, perhaps shoes. But I know we went there. I know I had the time to make three dresses."[88] Robert Rosner, also from Vienna and exactly Gerda's age, got on a transport in April 1939. "I remember I went to Wienerwald, because I wanted to say farewell to those places which were of importance to me. I mean it had always been part of our family life, because my mother went with us on Sundays to the Vienna woods. So I remember I went to Wienerwald. It was something for me. Leaving Vienna was something I felt very deeply."[89]

ASYLUM STILL could be found for youngsters, and desperate parents filled the child transport trains to capacity with their sons and daughters. The November Pogrom had had the effect the Nazis desired: the number of Jews who sought to leave Greater Germany increased dramatically. Some 120,000 left Germany during the winter of 1938–39, almost as many as had left in the previous five years. Estimates anticipated a departure rate of at least 100,000 people per year.[90] Confronted with such a surge, with the prospect of so many adults in need of jobs—in a depressed economy—or public assistance, many nations closed their doors, strengthened their border controls, and refused to simplify or accelerate immigration procedures. Their obdurate refusal to show compassion toward the refugees is well illustrated by the fate of a German passenger liner called the *St. Louis*.[91] Scheduled to carry more than nine hundred Jews to Cuba, the *St. Louis* left Hamburg on 13 May 1939. Most of the refugees (743) had permission to enter the United States, but it would take a number of years before they would be included in the German quota. In need of a safe place to wait their turn, they found that Cuba was willing to host them for the price of $150 per person. At the same time, however, the German government saw in the journey of the *St. Louis* an opportunity for propaganda. German agents in Cuba fanned antisemitic feelings; German newspapers accused the *St. Louis* passengers of having stolen money. Their goal was to portray Jews as criminals and to show the world that no country would accept such people.

The president of Cuba, Frederico Laredo Bru, issued a decree on 5 May, a week before the vessel was due to sail from Hamburg, declaring the *St. Louis* passengers' visas invalid, ostensibly to safeguard Cuban jobs. Aware that the ship might find no safe harbor abroad, the *St. Louis* owners also knew that their passengers must take the chance. Upon arrival in Havana, the unhappy refugees were held aboard ship. The German press was jubilant: it was an international photo opportunity to show that no one wanted Jews.

Cuba's government ordered the *St. Louis* to leave Cuban waters, and on 2 June the ship set sail, steaming up and down between Havana and Miami while

negotiations ensued with the Cuban government. Guarantees and bonds totaling nearly half a million dollars were offered by the Jewish Joint Distribution Committee to ensure the sustenance of the Jews while on Cuban soil awaiting admission into the United States. Cuba rejected the offer. To no avail either were pleas to the United States to admit the refugees immediately. Frantic discussions led nowhere, then stopped.

With no solution in sight, the *St. Louis*'s owners recalled the ship. The German captain, all too clear about what awaited his Jewish passengers in Germany, proposed to run his vessel aground on the English coast, set it on fire, and evacuate those on board. Finally, Belgium, the Netherlands, Great Britain, and France stepped in to accept the refugees, but only temporarily, until their number came up in the United States.

26. Betti Malek, a Belgian Jewish refugee, upon her arrival in London, May 1940. Courtesy Wide World Photo, New York.

Tragically, they were not admitted soon enough. Most of the Jews from the *St. Louis* who waited in Belgium, the Netherlands, and France were caught when Germany occupied those countries. Trapped in the Nazi German murder ring, they perished.

THE JEWS were but one group of refugees in search of asylum in the winter of 1938–39. The end of the Spanish Civil War and the collapse of the Republican government sent hundreds of thousands of Spaniards over the Pyrenees into France. Indeed, during the first two months of 1939, more refugees fled Spain for France than had left Germany since 1933. By early 1939, France harbored some 570,000 refugees, 350,000 of them from Spain and 40,000 from Greater Germany. Overwhelmed by the masses of people crossing the border, the French built a number of refugee internment camps in the foothills of the Pyrenees. At about the same time, the Dutch built Westerbork, an internment camp for German Jewish refugees, in the remote northeast corner of the Netherlands.

Many German Jews who had fled to France ended up in these camps when the French government, standing by its ally Poland, declared war on Germany in September 1939. For the French, the Jews were enemy aliens, even though they were refugees from the Nazi government. Strangers of any stripe were considered dangerous. The Hungarian ex-Communist, ex-Zionist Arthur Koestler had returned to Europe from Palestine six years before. No matter. He was picked up in Paris and deported to the French camp of Le Vernet.

The first impression on approaching it was of a mess of barbed wire and more barbed wire. It ran all around the camp in a three-fold fence and across it in various directions, with trenches running parallel.

The ground was arid; stony and dusty when dry, ankle-deep in mud when it rained, knobbly with frozen clods when it was cold. . . .

The hutments were built of wooden planks, covered with a sort of water-proofed paper. Each hutment housed 200 men. It was 30 yards long and 5 yards wide. Its furnishing consisted of two lower and two upper platforms of planks, each 2 yards wide, running along the two walls and leaving a narrow passage in the middle. The space between the lower and upper platforms was 1 yard, so that those on the lower planks could never stand erect. On each row slept fifty men, feet toward the passage . . . each man disposed of a space 21 inches wide to sleep on. This meant that all five had to sleep on their sides, facing the same way, and if one turned over, all had to turn over.

The boards were covered with a thin layer of straw, and the straw was the sole movable furniture in the hutment. It was, in fact, a barn. There were no windows, only rectangular slabs cut of the wall-planks, which served as shutters. There was no stove during the winter of 1939, no lighting, and there were no blankets. The camp had no refectory for meals, not a single table or stool in the hutments; it didn't provide spoons, or forks to eat with, nor soap to wash with. A fraction of its population could afford to buy those things; the others were reduced to a Stone Age level.[92]

The outbreak of war exacerbated the situation of refugees who had found asylum. Worse: war closed the borders. Refugees could not flee. Emigration and immigration became rescue actions; and what formerly had been legal or at least semi-legal became clandestine and illicit. Ellen Eliel-Wallach, born in Düsseldorf in 1928, moved with her family to Cologne just before the November Pogrom. They hoped to join Ellen's uncle in the Netherlands. "In the beginning of '39 we got passports on the condition that we would be out of Germany by the end of the year. My father had to go to the Gestapo every month, and every month they told him, 'If you are not out of Germany by the end of the year, you will see the concentration camp from the inside.' On the day before Christmas, a foreigner, or a stranger, came to our room, showing me a small photograph of my uncle." The plan was to smuggle the Wallach family into the Netherlands. Holland had not declared war on anybody, had not yet been invaded, and still hoped to maintain a neutral status as it had during World War I; but "you couldn't go officially any more because Dutch people didn't want all these immigrants."

I was dressed, very warmly dressed. It was winter; it was quite cold. By train we went to Gronau. We went out of the train, and there were strangers standing there with two bicycles, one for my father and one for my mother. I went on the stranger's bike because that is where they put me. I didn't see my parents any more. Off they cycled, and I cycled with the strange man. It was Christmas eve and the frontier was not so very well guarded.

We came to a farmhouse, and there was my father. They told us that we were already in the Netherlands, in the middle of nowhere, in the fields. From there we went on. . . . Everybody had a blanket with him or her, but we had to throw the blankets away because it was too obvious to have a blanket with us. So we really arrived in Amsterdam without anything but the clothes we had on. Nothing. The next day came the sister of my aunt and her father, in the same way, with the same cyclists.

I think we went to Amsterdam the day after that. We didn't just go by train, or whatever, because there were police everywhere. Dutch police. And they didn't want to have any foreigners. We were illegal. We had a passport, but not a visa for Holland. A taxi went to Amsterdam to make sure the way was clear. We went in a second taxi.[93]

The war and British and American policy sealed the escape routes. Refugee policy, both national and international, had been a disaster for the Jews.

Chapter Six

GENTILE LIFE UNDER
GERMAN OCCUPATION

FEW JEWS made it onto the admission quota lists and through the endless bureaucratic red tape of exit, transit, and entry visas in time. Flight from the Nazi regime was not a solution to the problems of European Jews and thus, as country after country fell to the German army, the National Socialist solution to the "Jewish Problem" became a European-wide Judeocide. The Wehrmacht, the German army, carried Nazi antisemitic policies to the corners of the continent.

The Germans did not go to war expressly seeking to murder the Jews of Europe. Another agenda fueled their attack on Poland on 1 September 1939. First, they were determined to regain land lost under the Treaty of Versailles. A few prescient observers had understood the meaning of that loss at the time. In 1919, the great sociologist Max Weber predicted that if Germany had to cede large territories in the East, "the world will witness the rise of a German irredentist movement, that will differ in its revolutionary means from the Italian, Serbian, or Irish only insofar as the will of seventy million will stand behind it."[1] The contemporary English historian of Germany, William Harbutt Dawson, warned that the Germans believed "that only another war will restore to them territories which are still just as dear to them as Alsace and Lorraine are said to be to the French. That is a dangerous frame of mind into which to drive a great nation."[2]

To regain their lost lands would not be enough, however. Germans meant to create a physical country that incorporated the ethnic "German nation." This old ambition, born in the bitterness of the Napoleonic Wars, was as powerful as it was venerable. To bolster resistance against the French "cosmopolitan empire," as the Germans called it, they adopted the biblical rhetoric of God's Chosen People. They, the Germans, were the people chosen by God to fulfill His mission; it was their task to protect the "Germanic" from the "non-Germanic."

Speaking for this new patriotism forged in defeat and despair was the eminent Prussian philosopher Johann Gottlieb Fichte. Fichte saw the Jews as "a state within a state." In his call for German nationalism, he exhorted his fellow Christian countrymen to rediscover their German identity. During the French occupation of Berlin, Fichte delivered fourteen lectures called *Addresses to the German Nation*. Arguing that the Germans, unlike other peoples, had remained true to themselves, Fichte importuned the inhabitants of all German states to accept their unique vocation: bond together as the German nation to become "the re-generator and re-creator of the world." "You, of all modern peoples, are the one in whom the seed of perfection most unmistakably lies, and to whom the lead in its development is committed," he declared. If they stood as one, the Germans would become "the most glorious among peoples."[3]

Audiences thrilled to his words and Germans far and wide drifted into megalomania.[4] Here began a century-long campaign to actualize one Reich. Bismarck's unification of German states in 1871 had not included Austria. Hitler corrected that problem with the Anschluss of 1938. The new Greater German Reich now included a total of 72 million Germans; even so, Luxembourg, Lichtenstein, and the free city of Danzig, almost totally German in population, as well as Switzerland (72% German) and Czechoslovakia (23%), all lay outside the Reich Nor did it escape notice that Germans living in other countries added 6 million more.

In total, more than 14 million Germans lived, unfortunately, outside Hitler's Reich, and the Nazis believed they should "come home." The slogan *"Ein Volk, ein Reich, ein Führer"* was not mere words. It was a goal to be achieved either by annexing the areas inhabited by ethnic Germans or by moving the *Volk* to the homeland. At the same time, according to Nazi ideology, Germany was already overcrowded. The Reich must expand. Hitler underlined this view at a meeting convened in the Reich Chancellory on 5 November 1937. His purpose, he told army leaders, was to secure and enlarge the racial community. "It was therefore a question of space," his adjutant Friedrich Hossbach noted in a report of the conference.

> The German racial community comprised over 85 million people and, by reason of their number and the narrow limits of habitable space in Europe, it constituted a tightly packed racial core such as was not to be found in any other country and such as implied the right to a greater living space than in the case of other peoples. If there existed no political result, territorially speaking, corresponding to this German racial core, that was a consequence of centuries of historical development, and in the continuance of these political conditions lay the greatest danger to the preservation of the German race at its present peak. To arrest the decline of Germanism in Austria and Czechoslovakia was as little possible as to maintain the present level in Germany itself. Instead of increase, sterility was setting in. . . . Germany's future was therefore wholly conditional upon solving the need for space.[5]

The quest for *Lebensraum*, "living space," forged together the drive to unify all ethnic Germans under one flag and the determination to right the wrongs of Versailles by reclaiming the lands lost in the east. By the end of the 1930s living space had become, in the words of the German émigré Hans Weigert, "the national obsession of the German people, strong enough to upset, in our day, the balance of the world."[6] He was right. According to the Nazis and their many friends, Germany did not have enough land to bring the population into harmony with the soil. The space the country needed was in the east. "The fate of Germany is rooted in the east. . . . National Socialism has once more turned the face of the whole people clearly and with conviction to the east," a Nazi philosopher of blood and soil, Walther Darré, bubbled.[7] But trouble brewed in the east. "We look on with dumb resignation while formerly purely German cities— Reval [Tallinn], Riga, Warsaw, and so forth—are lost to our folk." Germans had but one choice: "Our people must prepare for the struggle and also for this, that in that battle there can be only one outcome for us: absolute victory! The idea of blood and soil gives us the moral right to take back as much eastern land *as is necessary to achieve harmony between the body of our people and geopolitical space.*"[8]

Germans fretted in particular about the fecundity of their neighbors to the east. The expression of racism in sexual terms was not subtle. "The biological power of the Poles is more than double that of the Germans," a geopolitical "scientist" observed. Therefore, "more than any other area does the German-Polish border region call on the biological defense of the German people as a whole."[9]

The obsession with the German-Polish border, fueled in equal measure by rage and yearning, and justified by geopolitical "scholarship," strengthened the German conviction that Germans and Poles stood against each other, like light and darkness, in an eternal battle between the forces of good and the powers of evil. And if Poles were the champions of darkness, the Soviet state, looming beyond Poland, was hell itself, a menace to all that was civilized, a force of utter destruction, devastation, and ruin.

THE ANSCHLUSS of Austria in March 1938 was Hitler's first move to achieve his foreign policy objectives. It neither restored the lands lost at Versailles nor increased German *Lebensraum,* but it did bring Austria into the Reich. Had Hitler been a Christian missionary, he would have claimed credit for saving Austria's German soul.

Hitler's success fed his audacity. Within half a year he demanded annexation of the German-inhabited border area encircling Czechoslovakia, known as Sudetenland. Like the Austrians, the 3.5 million Sudeten Germans attempted an Anschluss with Germany after World War I, but in their case too the Allies objected. They became a minority in the new, cobbled-together Czecho-Slovakia.[10] In this new state of 14.5 million people, Czechs claimed the majority with 7.5 million, Germans constituted the largest minority (3 million), then Slovaks (2.2 million), Hungarians (700,000), Ruthenians (550,000), and Jews (350,000).

Bohemia and Moravia had been the industrial heart of the Hapsburg empire, and their factories provided the base for prosperity, democratic institutions, and advanced social legislation throughout the 1920s. So long as business prospered Germans and Slovaks tolerated the political predominance of the Czechs, which crept even into the name of the state, changing from Czecho-Slovakia to Czechoslovakia in the 1920s. But with the Depression the Germans remembered their love for the Reich, the Slovaks agitated for autonomy, and the Hungarians and Ruthenians became restless. Inspired by Nazi propaganda and financed from Nazi coffers, Sudeten Germans called for unity with Germany, and in the spring of 1938 Hitler led their chorus.[11] He cast a greedy eye on the Czech lands, dreaming of *Lebensraum* for Germans and of seizing Czech armament works for the Reich.[12] Suddenly the "suffering" of fellow Germans under the Czech yoke became front-page news in the German papers immediately after the Anschluss.

Under the influence of intense Nazi propaganda, with great monetary support from the German government, and on instructions of the Gestapo, the Sudeten-German militia FS (*Freiwilliger Schutzdienst* or Voluntary Defense Service) followed the pattern set by Austrian Nazis a few months earlier and fomented disorder in the Sudeten area. Czech attempts to quell the riots in early September led to German accusations of atrocities. Hitler ordered the mobilization of reservists, and left Berlin for the Party

Europe in the Summer of 1938

Congress in Nuremberg. There he ranted and raged against Czechoslovakia, accusing its government of ruining the Sudeten Germans, subjecting them to "slow but steady extermination. The misery of the Sudeten Germans defies description."[13]

Broadcast over German radio, Hitler's speech triggered a Sudeten-German

Putsch that was quickly suppressed by the Czech army. The government dissolved the Sudeten German party and banned the FS. Hitler threatened to invade, but the Czechs would not back down. In no uncertain terms, they announced their intention to resist. Fearing a European war, British prime minister Neville Chamberlain, French prime minister Edouard Daladier, and Italian Duce Mussolini offered to mediate the crisis. And indeed, the British, French, and Italian leaders met with Hitler in Munich—while Czech president Edvard Beneš was not invited. Hoping for "peace for our time," as Chamberlain put it, the English and French bowed to Hitler's demands. The Sudeten area, with its heavily fortified border, became part of the Greater German Reich. In exchange, Hitler assured everyone that he had no more territorial ambitions.

With the exception of the Czechs, most of the world was relieved. Peace-loving people told themselves that a decent deal had been struck; Sudeten Germans had achieved self-determination. It was not difficult for them to justify the transfer of Sudetenland to Germany. Winston Churchill was one of the few to disagree, condemning the Munich Agreement in an impassioned speech to the House of Commons on 5 October 1938. "The Czechs, left to themselves and told they were going to get no help from the Western Powers, would have been able to make better terms than they got after all this tremendous perturbation; they could hardly have had worse." But the crux of the matter, Churchill predicted, was not that this grave mistake would cause the collapse of Czechoslovakia. The real issue was the resolve of Britain, France, and the other democracies to stand up for their principles. Quoting the Bible, Churchill proclaimed: "Thou art weighed in the balance and found wanting."

> And do not suppose that this is the end. This is only the beginning of the reckoning. This is only the first sip, the first foretaste of a bitter cup which will be proffered to us year by year unless, by a supreme recovery of moral health and martial vigor, we arise again and take our stand for freedom as in the olden time.[14]

Britain and France had undermined the Czechs. Ready to wage war against Germany before Munich, they now lost the courage to hold on to what was left.[15] Resolutely anti-German, President Beneš resigned. So did the rest of the country. The leading liberal daily spoke for many on 4 October 1938: "If we cannot sing with the angels, we shall howl with the wolves." Force, not law, ruled the world; the Czechs would do well to find their place among the powerful. "Let us seek—we have no other choice—accommodation with Germany."[16] The new president Emil Hácha tried to do just that.

The Germans demanded no less. Prague must take orders from Berlin on matters of foreign policy. Czechoslovakia must reduce its army, limit freedom of the press, adjust its economy to suit German needs, and introduce anti-Jewish legislation, Hitler told Czechoslovak foreign minister Frantisek Chvalkovsky on 14 October.

The Jews in Czechoslovakia had watched the situation brewing. Arnost Graumann and his parents lived in Prague and they, like "everybody, tried to get out of the country." By early summer 1938 the atmosphere was so tense that the Graumann family looked for an exit route for eighteen-year-old Arnost. "The only thing I was really good at was swimming," he explained decades later.[17]

> In the last years [of the republic], the national swimming team, picked on time trials, was 100% Jewish, much to the evident fury of the Czech and German [swimming] clubs in the country. The team chosen for the Olympic Games in Berlin (1936) was entirely Jewish, except for one single Czech water polo player. I was one of the two chosen representatives for breast-stroke swimming. In the event, we all refused to go, and were disqualified from official competition for a year, leaving the field open to the Czech swimmers. They won all the events, but never got near to breaking the records we had established.[18]

Arnost belonged to the Prague branch of the Jewish international sports organization Maccabi. "Clubs were either Czech and very antisemitic, or German and even more antisemitic. And in Prague, swimming was the sport of Jewish young people. . . . It hasn't been repeated [except for] Mark Spitz in America."[19]

After the Anschluss with Austria, Jews "pretended that everything was going to be all right."

> It was wishful thinking. The Jewish people who always spoke Czech, they said, "We are not Jews, we are Czech. Everybody knows we are Czech. We were born here. We've got nothing to do with all this Jewish business, we're not all that religious. They won't go after us because we are Czech." The ones who spoke German tried to pretend they were more German than Jewish. . . . They made themselves believe the Germans would perceive them to be Germans. "My father was in the Austro-Hungarian army and he had a decoration for bravery."
>
> But the fact was that everybody knew perfectly well what was going to happen. And one knew, even then, that there were concentration camps. There were already people being killed in the concentration camps. In those days they said, "Shot while escaping." Well, everyone was forever escaping, and there were an awful lot of escapees being shot in the back. One knew. If you heard the speeches, and read the books, and listened to the famous *Horst Wessel Lied*.[20]

Arnost Graumann set out to swim his way to safety. "The plan was that I should somehow or another manage to get an invitation to come to London for a swimming club competition." He trained as if his life depended on it. "And for that purpose I did this special record attempt, the 400 meters breaststroke record attempt, specially convened for my benefit. And I duly broke the record." Impressed, the Maccabi Swimming Club in London invited him to a "swimming gala" scheduled in October at the Goulston Street baths in the East End.[21]

Arnost had no permission to remain in Britain or to work there, but in this invitation lay his ticket out of Prague. "We knew perfectly well what was going on. And I certainly know, absolutely for sure, that when I saw my mother waving me good-bye at the railway station in Prague, that I was convinced that I was never going to see her again."[22] He didn't.

Arnost Graumann's parents, like most Jews in Czechoslovakia, had no way to slip out of the country. Trapped, they remained, subject to increasingly violent antisemitism. After the November Pogrom that year, Hitler became truly possessed by the idea that the Czechs had to deal with its "Jewish Problem" aggressively. The Jews were still poisoning the nation, he harangued Chvalkovsky in January 1939. Chvalkovsky agreed; his government wished to solve its "Jewish Question," but faced many obstacles. Czechoslovakia could not even get rid of its 22,000 Jewish refugees.

> [He] complained bitterly about the British, who had promised so much—for instance, to let 2,000 Jews emigrate to Australia and New Zealand. Today, these 2,000 Jews were still in a concentration camp and the British were not making any arrangements to remove them. . . . He [Chvalkovsky] was wondering where and across what frontiers to help the Jews. He could not dump them on the German frontier, nor on the Polish or Hungarian frontier. At the Hungarian frontier they had been driven back by the military. . . . The Führer pointed to the possibility that interested states might take some spot in the world, put the Jews there, and then say to the Anglo-Saxon states oozing with humanity: "Here they are; either they starve to death or you put your many speeches into practice."[23]

Chvalkovsky met with the German minister of foreign affairs, Joachim von Ribbentrop, who also waxed choleric about the Jews.[24] Clearly, German-Czechoslovak relations were to be determined by Prague's obedience to Berlin on this issue.

After his return to Czechoslovakia, Chvalkovsky shared his uneasiness with the French minister in Prague, Victor Leopold de Lacroix. The latter reported back to French Foreign Minister Georges Bonnet that "what appears to have most impressed him, was the importance which Herr Hitler and Herr von Ribbentrop attached to the Jewish Question—absolutely out of proportion to the importance assigned to the other questions dealt with."

> "Do not imitate the sentimental and leisurely manner in which we ourselves treated this problem," the two statesmen [Hitler and Ribbentrop] are

reported to have said. "Our kindness was nothing but weakness and we regret it. This vermin must be destroyed. The Jews are our sworn enemies, and by the end of the year no Jew will be left in Germany. The French, Americans and the English are not responsible for the difficulties in our relations with Paris, London or Washington. The Jews are responsible. We will give similar advice to Romania, Hungary, etc. Germany will seek to form a bloc of antisemitic states, for she could not adopt a friendly attitude towards states in which the Jews either by their economic activity or as a result of their high positions could exercise any kind of influence."[25]

Chvalkovsky may have been uneasy but, a pragmatic politician, he got his government in line. A few days after the meetings in Berlin, Andor Hencke, the German chargé d'affaires in Prague, informed Ribbentrop that "the cabinet is said to have decided on intensified regulations in the Jewish question."[26] The government forced Jews from civil service, universities, and public hospitals through "voluntary resignations" and "early retirements" from 15 January 1939 on.[27] It also signed its own version of the Ha'avara Agreement with the Jewish Agency in Palestine to solve a now suddenly urgent "Jewish Problem" through emigration.

The Czechoslovaks aproved. In Chechoslovakia, nationality was a matter of language, not "race," and the majority of the 117,000 Jews in the Czech lands spoke German. Virtually all the writers who constitued the "Prague School" in German literature were Jews: Franz Kafka, Max Brod, Felix Weltsch, and so on. The center of German life in Prague, the Neues Deutsches Theater (New German Theater) was run by Jews for Jews.[28] Furthermore, a little over 30 percent of the Czech Jews had claimed German nationality in the 1930 census, while 36 percent opted for Czech and 31 percent Jewish nationality. Popular sentiment held these German-identified Jews responsible for the Sudeten-German claim.[29]

Antisemitic agitation abounded. On 9 February 1939 the British chargé d'affaires J. M. Troutbeck wrote to the British foreign secretary Lord Halifax that "there is a diversity of view among unprejudiced persons as to how far the Czechs are merely alleging German pressure as an excuse for taking action which they themselves desire." The diplomat noted that especially Czechs at the beginning of their career, "particularly in the liberal professions . . . beat the anti-Semitic drum."[30]

Czech efforts to please Berlin—or to suit themselves—made no difference. Within two months of Chvalkovsky's meetings in Berlin, Czechoslovakia ceased to exist. Loss of Sudetenland had destabilized the young republic and the Slovaks moved away from the union to establish an independent state; the Ruthenians joined Hungary. Seizing this unhappy internal situation as an opportunity for Nazi Germany, Hitler moblized his forces and ordered Hacha to Berlin on 14 March 1939. Invasion was imminent, he barked, and Hacha signed a German-drafted declaration stating that "the Czechoslovak President

... confidently placed the fate of the Czech people and country in the hands of the Führer of the German Reich."[31] The German army marched in the next day, imposing a "protectorate" upon the remaining Czech lands of Bohemia and Moravia.[32]

This protectorate was like none other: normally, protectorates "protect" a weak but sovereign state, whereas the Protectorate of Bohemia and Moravia formed "part of the Greater German Reich."[33] Still, the Protectorate had "some sovereign rights conceded to it ... in conformity with the political, military, and economic requirements of the Reich."[34] The German inhabitants of the area received German citizenship; the other inhabitants became "Nationals of the Protectorate of Bohemia and Moravia." Hacha stayed on as "State President," but a German "Reich Protector" was to be the "guardian of German interests."[35]

Intended as a model of what the future might hold for other small nations, the Protectorate offered conditions palatable to the Czechs. In exchange for submission, the Germans preserved Czech institutions and some vestiges of sovereignty. Broken in spirit, the Czechs accepted the deal and adjusted to the situation. Daily life hardly changed; in fact the economic union with Germany improved living standards. With their large armament works, Bohemia and Moravia supplied guns to the Germans and butter to the Czechs.[36]

The Jews got none, of course. Czech Fascists beat Jews up, and Czech businessmen and professionals called on the government to remove Jews from trade and the professions. Prague needed no prodding: 600,000 Czechs had lived in Sudetenland, and many had chosen to move out. All Czech army personnel, nearly all Czech government officials, and many Czech nationalists had fled into Bohemia and Moravia. Lacking a livelihood, they turned to the government to find them jobs. The politicians, for their part, counted on the cash proceeds from expropriation of Jewish property to restructure the national economy. Greed overcame moral principles with ease.[37]

The Germans, however, had no intention of sharing the spoils with the Czechs. They kept the solution of the "Jewish Question" under direct German control, ensuring that all Jewish assets would benefit Germans, not Czechs. They chose to move smoothly, avoiding the violent scenes of Vienna a year earlier.[38] Systematic "Aryanization" began in the summer of 1939, with all Jewish businesses grasped by German hands.

THE BRITISH, in the meantime, reeled from Hitler's about-face since Munich, none more than Neville Chamberlain. He vividly remembered waving the piece of paper that promised "peace for our time," and announcing, to cheering crowds, that he had brought "peace with honour." Now, he recognized clearly that the Czechs were not Germans, and that the Germans should not rule them. Speaking on 17 March in his native city of Birmingham, he lamented the Czechs' fate. "Every man and woman in this country who remembers the fate of the Jews and the political prisoners in Austria must today be filled with distress and foreboding." While the Austrian Anschluss and the severance of the Sudeten area "had shocked and affronted public opinion," Hitler's position in those cases might be justified.

> But the events which have taken place this week in complete disregard of the principles laid down by the German government itself seem to fall into a different category, and they must cause us all to be asking ourselves: "Is this the end of an old adventure, or is it the beginning of a new? Is this the last attack upon a small State, or is it to be followed by others? Is this, in fact, a step in the direction of an attempt to dominate the world by force?"[39]

Uneasiness grew in London and Paris. Unfazed, the German minister of foreign affairs, von Ribbentrop, demanded the return of Danzig to the Reich and the creation of a "corridor," an extraterritorial highway and railway connection between mainland Germany and its detached province of East Prussia, marooned in Poland. Assuming correctly that the Polish government would reject the German proposal, Hitler instructed his generals on 25 March 1939 to prepare plans for invasion. Chamberlain did not know this, but Churchill's call for a "supreme recovery of moral health and martial vigor" echoed in his mind. On 31 March, he rose in the House of Commons to announce that Britain and France "would feel themselves bound at once to lend the Polish Government all support in their power" if Poland were attacked.[40] Unimpressed by the British prime minister's words, Hitler decided on 3 April to begin the Polish campaign on 1 September.

In the meantime, Germany and the Soviet Union made a deal. Never mind that for years Nazi propaganda had depicted Russia as a barbaric state. Their non-aggression pact included a secret agreement to partition Poland between them.[41] By this point, specific reasons for German rage had become irrelevant. As Count Galeazzo Ciano, Mussolini's minister of foreign affairs, observed, they wanted war because they wanted war. "It was at his residence at Fuschl that von Ribbentrop, while we were waiting to be seated at the dinner table, told me of the German decision to set a match to the European powder keg. This he told me in much the same tone that he would have used about an inconsequential administrative detail," Ciano noted in his diary. "'Well, Ribbentrop,' I asked, as we were walking together in the garden, 'what do you want? The Corridor or Danzig?' 'Not that any more,' he said, gazing at me with cold metallic eyes. 'We want war!'"[42]

During the night of Thursday 31 August 1939, SS men dressed in Polish uniforms staged a sham assault on a German radio station in the border city of Gleiwitz. In response to this "Polish attack," five German armies totaling 1.5 million men and 2,000 tanks began to cross the border on 1 September at 5:45 a.m., as the Luftwaffe attacked Polish air bases throughout the country. The Soviet army invaded from the east on the 17th. Warsaw held out heroically under brutally heavy bombardment until the 27th. The next day, the Germans and the Soviets ratified their agreement to split the country; the new border ran along the Bug River.[43]

Most Germans viewed the conquest of Poland as an act of historical justice. They agreed with the sentiment articulated by Nazi Party official Franz Lüdtke: "The standards of our incomparable army fluttered in places where in early times German men had worked the fields, and where in the middle ages German burghers and farmers had built towns and villages."[44] In German eyes, the attack on Poland did it all—it brought ethnic Germans "home to the Reich," it restored German lands lost at Versailles, and it provided *Lebensraum* in the east.

Unfortunately for the Germans, it also pushed England and France to declare war on the Reich. This was not part of Hitler's foreign policy plan, and on 6 October he publicly announced his willingness in the Reichstag to make peace—but not to withdraw from Poland. The Poles, he said, did not deserve to run their own country. "Anyone who travels in that country for two or three weeks will get the proper idea of the classical German term '*Polnische Wirt-schaft,*' meaning a 'Polish state of affairs'!"[45] He would bring order to Poland, he thundered, including the "demarcation of the boundary for the Reich, which will do justice to historical, ethnographical and economic facts."[46] It was Germany's most important task "to establish a new order of ethnographic conditions, that is to say, resettlement of nationalities in such a manner that the process ultimately results in the obtaining of clearer dividing lines than is the case in the present."[47]

Nothing new here. Nazi racism ranked Poles one notch higher than Jews and far below the lordly Germans. The great British playwright George Bernard Shaw saw that racism as reason enough to go into battle. In the fall of 1939 Shaw wrote (but was not permitted to deliver) a radio broadcast:

My quarrel with him [Hitler] is a very plain one. I happen to be what he calls a Nordic. In stature, in colour, in length of head, I am the perfect blond beast whom Mr. Hitler classes as the salt of the earth, divinely destined to rule over all lesser breeds. But I have a friend who happens to be a Jew. His name is Albert Einstein: and he is a far greater human prodigy than Mr. Hitler and myself rolled into one. . . . Well, Adolf Hitler would compel me, the Nordic Shaw, to insult Albert Einstein; to claim moral superiority to him and unlimited power over him, drive him out of his house, exile him, be punished for miscegenation if I allow a relative of mine to marry a relative of his, and finally kill him as part of a general duty to exterminate his race. . . .

Now this is not the sort of thing that sane men can afford to argue with. It is on the face of it pernicious nonsense; and the moment any ruler starts imposing it as a political philosophy on his nation or any other nation by physical force, there is nothing for it but for the sane men to muster their own physical forces and go for him.[48]

Insufficiently alarmed by Hitler's racism but nevertheless bound by treaty to support Poland, neither England nor France responded to Hitler's offer. No matter. The Führer proceeded to annex the west of Poland in an unprecedented act of territorial aggression; for centuries, the annexation of foreign territories had occurred only within the context of peace treaties when a defeated government formally ceded land and inhabitants to the victor. Hitler ignored the Polish government, which had fled first to Romania and then to London. The facts on the ground crystallized the positions of victor and vanquished: annexation had made a peace treaty impossible, but neither Germans nor Poles wished to make such an agreement in any case. The Poles were patriotically committed to resistance, and the Germans were ideologically fixed on subjugation. It was to be a very brutal and most bitter occupation regime.

THE GERMAN REIGN in Poland—and later in each country the Nazi regime occupied—violated every tenet of what was known in international law as "belligerent occupation."[49] Over the centuries, a consensus had emerged that both occupier and occupied should strive to preserve the structures of society and to prevent chaos. The occupying authority was, therefore, to intervene as little as possible in the life of the occupied.[50] In the nineteenth century, wars were short and occupation was a transient phenomenon that interfered minimally in the day-to-day order; peaceful cohabitation between the local population and the occupying army, with little interaction between the two, was assumed. Changes in political status occurred at the peace treaty negotiating table. Furthermore, war was not a conflict between two nations of citizen-combatants. Civilians were civilians and soldiers were soldiers. Indeed, war was seen as a match between governments and their armies, in which civilians were the cheering fans of the fighting teams. "I conduct war with the French soldiers, not with the French citizens," said King William of Prussia on 11 August 1870.[51]

Article 43 of the Hague Land Warfare Convention of 1907 expressed customary international law, and offered guidance to occupation administrations:

> The authority of the legitimate power having in fact passed into the hands of the occupant, the latter shall take all the measures in his power to restore and ensure, as far as possible, public order and [civil life], while respecting, unless absolutely prevented, the laws in force in the country.[52]

What article 43 failed to recognize, however, were the full implications of the nation-state principle: self-determination of a people. By the beginning of the twentieth century, annexation without agreement of the affected population had become unacceptable.[53] Woodrow Wilson was specific on this point. "There shall be no annexations, no contributions, no punitive damages," he proclaimed in his famous speech of 11 February 1918 on the Four Principles of Right and Justice which should be part of the settlement of World War I. "Peoples are not to be handed about from one sovereignty to another by an international conference, or an understanding between rivals and antagonists. National aspirations must be respected; people may now be dominated and governed only by their own consent."[54] Wilson's principles were included in the Covenant of the League of Nations, which abolished the right of conquest in favor of the right to self-determination.

The dismemberment of Czechoslovakia
and Poland, 1938-1939

German annexation of Austria, March 1938	
German annexation from Czechoslovakia, November 1938-March 1939	
German annexation of Memel, Danzig and from Poland, 1939	International boundaries, 1 January 1941
Hungarian annexation from Czechoslovakia, 1938-39	Boundary between German and Soviet spheres of influence
Hungarian annexation from Romania, 1940	Soviet annexation from Romania, 1940
Soviet annexation from Poland, September 1939	Soviet annexation of Baltic countries, 1940
	Lithuanian annexation from Poland, September 1939

0 ____ 300 miles
0 ____ 500 km

Chazaud

NONE OF THIS precedent or law mattered to the Germans in September 1939. In a matter of days, Poles learned that life would not go on as it had done before. They were "frightful material" and the Jews "the most appalling people one can imagine," Hitler told the chief ideologue of the Nazi Party, Alfred Rosenberg, shortly after the invasion. German-occupied Poland would be divided into three parts. The eastern area between the Vistula and the Bug would be reserved "for the whole of Jewry (from the Reich as well) in addition to all other unreliable elements." Hitler wished to Germanize and colonize the western region, Rosenberg wrote in his diary. "This would be a major task for the whole nation: to create a German granary, a strong peasantry, to resettle good Germans from all over the world." The Poles were to be allowed a kind of homeland somewhere in the middle of their former country—at least for the time being.[55] This radical occupation program introduced a level of violence in civil society that harked back to the time of the ancient Assyrians.

The terror was initiated by the *Einsatzgruppen,* the special SS units that followed the army, charged with arresting and murdering political opponents and Jews. They already had been in operation in conjunction with the annexation of Austria and the conquest of the Czech lands. Prior to the invasion in September 1939, six major units with several hundred members each were formed, with one unit attached to each of the five advancing armies, and one unit specially designated for the area around the city of Posen. After Poland had been conquered, the *Einsatzgruppen* terrorized Jews and Polish intellectuals and other prominent leaders of Polish society.[56] Their victims ran into the tens of thousands, and the *Einsatzgruppen* were well on their way toward evolving into what they became after the invasion of the Soviet Union: the mobile arm of the German annihilation machinery.

By the end of October, more than 500 towns and villages had been burned and more than 16,000 Poles summarily executed. In the city of Bydgoszcz an Englishwoman, Miss Baker-Beall, witnessed the Germans' arrival and the town's descent into "a nightmare of horror." In response to the alleged killing of ethnic Germans, the *Einsatzgruppe* began to execute boy scouts, "who were set up in the marketplace against a wall and shot. No reason was given. A devoted priest who rushed to administer the Last Sacrament was shot too."[57]

Then the relocations began. According to the German-Soviet Non-Aggression Pact, Germans in the Soviet part, and White Russians and Ukrainians in the German part, were to be moved to the "right" side of the border by a plenipotentiary of the German government. To his delight, Heinrich Himmler, who coveted this role, was chosen by Hitler. If the Versailles Treaty had established borders to fit national populations, the Nazis created new borders and forcibly moved populations to fit within them. Ethnic Germans were resettled in the annexed territories of western Poland through a state-sponsored program that included the transfer of property, the organized transport of people, temporary housing in the reception area, naturalization, and final settlement.

Reichsführer-SS Heinrich Himmler, *Reichskommissar für die Festigung deutschen Volkstums,* or the plenipotentiary in charge of the "Consolidation of German Nationhood," as the decree of 7 October 1939 described his mission, masterminded all this. The conquest of Poland meant that "the Greater German Reich is able to accept and settle within its space German people, who up to the present had to live in foreign lands, and to arrange the settlement of national groups within its spheres of interest in such a way that better dividing lines between them are attained," the preamble explained. It was the triple task of the Reichsführer-SS to "bring back those German citizens and ethnic Germans abroad who are eligible for a permanent return to the Reich"; to "eliminate the harmful influence of such alien parts of the population as constitute a danger to the Reich and the German community"; and to "create new German colonies by resettlement, and especially by the resettlement of German citizens and ethnic Germans coming back from abroad."[58]

Himmler was pleased. Responsibility for 10 million ethnic Germans increased his power base and strengthened his position in the Nazi hierarchy. Fine use could be made of them—manpower for the *Waffen-SS* (armed SS units), and labor for an increasingly labor-poor Germany. Here too was a valuable source of "racial material" for building the New Europe, a mission the SS, a self-appointed racial elite, wished to lead.

Between 9 October 1939 and 25 March 1941 when the Soviets closed the border according to schedule, Himmler brought 490,640 ethnic Germans from Latvia, Estonia, the Soviet Union, Romania, and Lithuania home to the Reich. Most Germans applauded and cheered. Journalist Hanns Johst was enraptured by a meeting he attended in the government house of Upper Silesia, located in the town of Kattowitz (Katowice). Himmler and the military and civilian authorities in the region talked openly of policies to accommodate the returnees. "It is wonderful to experience how one organizes here calmly and dispassionately the migration of whole nations. Hundreds of thousands of people stream into the Reich, and are settled in the East . . . others are deported . . . and all this occurs while the nation fights the greatest defensive battle for its existence." And he concluded, "At such moments I almost understand the hatred of the Western world for everything German. Nothing was ever so hateful as superiority, as natural superiority, by virtue of the belief in an idea, by virtue of the achievements and by virtue of the results."[59]

Just as Himmler had the power to bring in ethnic Germans, he also had the authority to deport non-German populations from the annexed territories. Indeed, Hitler and his colleagues considered it self-evident that if ethnic Germans must abandon their age-old homes, the Reich certainly had a right to move other people anywhere. It was Himmler's job to oversee the mass expulsion of Poles and Jews to make room for the new ethnic German inhabitants. Within days of his appointment, Himmler began to deport hundreds of thousands of Poles and Jews from that area, dumping them into the newly created "Government General," as the remaining Polish territory was called.[60]

The first major town to be "cleansed" was Gdynia, designated by the German government as a port of arrival for ethnic Germans from Estonia and Latvia. The "returnees" were to be given the homes of the erstwhile Polish population. Two days before the first shipload of ethnic Germans left the Estonian harbor of Tallinn, deportations began in Gdynia.

On October 17, 1939, at 8 a.m. I heard someone knocking at the door of my flat. As my maid was afraid to open, I went to the door myself. I found there two German gendarmes, who roughly told me that in a few hours I had to be ready to travel with my children and everybody in the house. When I said that I had small children, that my husband was a prisoner of war, and that I could not get ready to travel in so short a time, the gendarmes answered that not only must I be ready, but that the flat must be swept, the plates and the dishes washed and the keys left in the cupboards, so that the Ger-

27. *The Matschak family awaits deportation, 1940. This photo comes from a collection of images assembled for Heinrich Himmler recording the success of "ethnic cleansing" in the recently annexed areas of Poland. Courtesy Bundesarchiv, Berlin.*

mans who were to live in my house should have no trouble. In so many words, they further declared that I was to entitled to take with me only one suitcase of not more than fifty kilograms weight and a small handbag with food for a few days.[61]

A three-day journey in bolted cattle cars to the Government General followed. The German authorities on the receiving end dumped the deportees on local town officials and philanthropies. "At Koniecpol or Radom twenty persons are put in one room, sleeping on foul straw which has not been changed for three months," a report to the Polish government-in-exile in London lamented. "As the quarters are not heated, the damp and mildew reach a yard and a half up the walls. They are given food once a day from a cauldron; it consists of potato soup without any fat. Bread for the refugees costs a zloty for a loaf weighing a kilogram (2.25 lbs). At Czestachowa the situation is still worse, for neither bread nor potatoes can be bought." The results were dire. "The poor exiles drop with weakness, and many are seriously ill; dysentery and typhus are spreading. The lack of clothing—for they were deported just as they stood—the lack of bedding and linen leads to many of them freezing to death."[62]

Poles who remained behind were pressed to Germanize. The Nazis were sure that some German blood ran in Polish veins, and they wished to bring it back into the national community. Himmler's Germanization policy was thus two-pronged: to regain both blood and soil. As his aide Ulrich Greifelt explained in May 1940, "the removal of persons of alien race from the annexed Eastern territories is one of the most important aims to be achieved in the German East." At the same time, it was equally important "to regain for Germanism the German blood existing in these districts even in cases where the person concerned is Polonized in language and religion." Therefore it was "an absolute national-political necessity to screen the annexed Eastern territories and later also the General Government for such persons of Teutonic blood in order to make this lost German blood again available to our own people."[63] Some 200,000 Polish children considered of promising "Aryan" character were separated from their parents and sent to Germany for forced Germanization.

Poles in the annexed territories had no rights, and Poles in the Government General fared little better. Dominated in every detail of their daily lives by the German administration that ruled them, they suffered the destruction of the political, social, and intellectual elite of the country. In November 1939 the entire faculty of the ancient and renowned Jagiellonian University in Cracow was arrested and deported to the Sachsenhausen concentration camp. A few months later, the Germans murdered some six thousand intellectuals, senior civil servants, magistrates, lawyers, physicians, and clergymen.[64]

The Germans aimed to eradicate Polish culture, and mass murders were but one means to that end. They took many other less bloody but nevertheless fiercely aggressive measures too. German authorities closed down schools and the press, seized museum collections and archives, carted away monuments to Polish heroes, and renamed cities and towns. This was a systematic effort to deny history, to destroy all national institutions, and to reduce the population to serfdom. Heinrich Himmler, Hitler's loyal paladin, knew precisely what he sought to accomplish:

> The non-German population of the eastern territories must not receive any education higher than that of an elementary school with four forms [grades]. The objective of this elementary school must be to teach: simple arithmetic up to 500 at the most, how to write one's own name, and to teach that it is God's commandment to be obedient to the Germans and to be honest, hard working, and well-behaved. I consider it unnecessary to teach reading.[65]

The Poles were to be a leaderless laboring class. Only their toil permitted them "to participate in [German] eternal cultural deeds and monuments." Himmler's note, endorsed by Hitler but unpublished at the time, would have revealed little the Poles did not already know: they were under attack; they faced extinction as a nation. It was in response to their plight that the Polish Jew Raphael Lemkin, who had escaped first to Sweden and then to the United States, coined the word "genocide," from the Greek word *genos* ("people" or "tribe") and the Latin *cide* ("killing"), in 1942.[66]

Underground networks managed to inform the Polish government-in-exile in London, which publicized these atrocities. They noted again and again that German actions in Poland were "violations of the most elementary principles of human rights as recognized by civilized nations and set down, notably, in the Rules annexed to the Fourth Hague Convention (1907) relating to the rights and obligations of the enemy authority over the occupied territory of the hostile state."[67] Only one conclusion could be drawn: In their occupation of Poland, the Germans had introduced a new concept: "total war."

> This total war, in the full sense of the term, does not end with the occupation of the country. On the contrary, it changes into a merciless war against a peaceable population abandoned without defense to the arbitrary power of the invader. In this monstrous war all means are allowed. They are chosen in advance, methodically and with calculation. Thus the war of races follows and completes the war of armies. We owe this new doctrine of total war, and particularly the conception of the exterminating occupation of the invaded country, to the Third Reich.[68]

This was no exaggeration. Germany's reign of terror left little of prewar Poland intact. Its government, refusing to surrender, had fled to England. Unlike the French, the Danes, or the king of the Belgians, who cooperated with the Germans when the invading armies conquered their country, the Polish government did not collaborate. By the end of the war, several other London-based governments-in-exile had joined Poland's. They became a powerful focus for patriotism and resistance. The Poles and, later, the Norwegians, Dutch, Luxembourgers, Yugoslavs, and Greeks, knew that their statesmen and sovereigns were alive and well, waiting and working to return.

No country suffered so severely as Poland. New persecutions came fast and hard. Everybody knew the constant terror of random violence and mass murders. And the young and able-bodied feared the systematic violence of manhunts for forced labor that began with the use of Polish prisoners of war and increased with dragnets to catch civilians. By May 1940 at least a million Poles—prisoners of war and civilians—worked in the Reich as part of the so-called *Poleneinsatz* (Polish Service). Daily life—going to work, attending school, getting food—became an ordeal.

Most of Poland's farm produce—fruit, vegetables, grain, and livestock—went directly to Germany. Severely rationed to a substandard diet, the Poles were left to starve to death slowly. A black market thrived. It was economically advantageous to farmers to sell their products surreptitiously, and the rest of the population needed the foodstuffs they sold. But the risk for both buyer and seller could not have been greater. There was only one penalty for failure to comply with the occupation regime: death by immediate execution.

GENTILE POLES suffered tremendously under a genocidal occupation. Polish Jews suffered even more. Sadly, the awareness that both were victims did not lessen Polish antisemitism. "The Jews Must Emigrate," demanded an article in *Naród (Nation)*, the organ of the underground Labor Party, on 20 January 1942.

> The events which have been taking place in Poland during the last 30 months have created a situation which makes our consent to the return of the Jews to their privileged positions impossible, unless one wishes to expose our country to upheavals which are liable to endanger our future statehood. To put it bluntly: it is no longer a question of restoring lost political and property rights of the Jews, but a question of leaving our country altogether.[69]

"Our feelings towards Jews have not changed," the prominent resistor Zofia Kossak-Szczucka wrote a few months later. One of the organizers of Zegota, a Polish organization to help Jews, she nevertheless retained her prejudices undiminished. "We still consider them to be political, economic, and ideological enemies of Poland."[70] Yet Kossak-Szczucka did not think that this meant Jews should be abandoned to their fate. For the right-wing underground journal *Szaniec,* Jews were Poland's enemies because they "pin their hopes on the Soviets." In that, "they bet against Poland."[71]

But the Germans went too far for the Poles. Expulsion was one thing, mass murder another. In August 1942, *Wiadomosci Polskie (Polish News)*, the weekly publication of the Home Army—an organization embodying the best in Polish patriotism and the worst of Polish prejudice—described conditions in the Warsaw ghetto, and deportations of men, women, and children in boxcars to an unknown destination. "The tragic scenes are hidden from our eyes by high walls, but incessant gunshots and dreadful rumors give us some idea of the unimaginable horror."

> Germany will be stamped with eternal infamy, since human history, which abounds in horrible and frightening moments, has not yet witnessed a mass murder on such a scale and perpetrated in such a dreadful fashion. Pale by comparison were the Mongol inroads with their enslavements and impalings, the Roman and Turkish galleys, the tortures employed by the Inquisition, the cruelties of the French Revolution. Even the twisted Soviet practices, which reached their peak in the trials of defendants accusing themselves, are dwarfed by Nazi methods used to exterminate millions of Jews.[72]

Most Poles were shocked, in part because they believed, with reason, that the Jews' fate foreshadowed their own. The genocide of the Jews caused "signs of disquiet" among the Poles, the commander of the Home Army wrote on 10 November 1942. They feared that "after the operation is completed the Germans will begin the liquidation of the Poles in the same manner."[73]

THE "RACE" of Poles were to be subjugated; the Danes, by contrast, were to be wooed. To Denmark, Germany offered partnership and collaboration. The Danes, after all, were a "Nordic people," the highest sort of "Aryan." They were also cooperative.

To forestall a British occupation of Norway which would threaten the supply of Swedish iron ore and Finnish nickel ore to Germany, and to ensure its own access to the ocean, the Wehrmacht occupied Denmark in April 1940 on its way north to Norway. The Danes quickly surrendered. King Christian stayed on the throne, national sovereignty went undisturbed, and most aspects of prewar civilian life remained intact for nearly three and a half years. Here was the most lenient form of occupation; a "model protectorate," according to Hitler.[74]

Berlin appointed a plenipotentiary of the German Reich, Cecil von Renthe-Fink, to supervise the Danish government. The Danes accommodated to the situation and established a policy of negotiation intended to avoid the consequences of war. This arrangement, with no basis in international law, was nevertheless accepted by both governments. The Germans interfered very little in Danish society; the Danish army remained intact, and free parliamentary elections were held as late as March 1943. The tiny Danish Nazi Party got scant support from the Germans at first, and then none at all. Most remarkably, Renthe-Fink did not menace the five thousand Danish Jews or one thousand five hundred German Jewish refugees for fear it would "cause paralysis of or serious disturbances in political and economic life."[75] Indeed, when Danish Nazis tried to make their Jewish neighbors into a "Question," they were stopped in their tracks by Professor Hal Koch to whom many Danes looked as a great moral authority, and none other than Renthe-Fink himself who, in turn, was supported by Foreign Minister Ribbentrop. In Denmark, the Germans never even suggested that Jews wear a special mark. The story that King Christian defied such an order is a myth. No order was given.

As the war progressed, gentiles all over Europe suffered from hunger and privation. In Denmark, by contrast, the standard of living actually improved. And while Jews throughout the German-controlled continent were hounded out of civil society, forced into ghettos or transit camps, and transported to murder facilities, Danish Jews continued to live as they had before. Both for the government and the public, the position of the Jews was an important barometer of German-Danish relations. The Germans understood that, and the situation served them well. After all, only 6,500 Jews lived in Denmark. Maintaining the calm status quo ensured an uninterrupted supply of Danish agricultural products to the Reich, small expenditure on German occupation personnel, little call on already strained German resources and, for the military, a comfortable alternative to the deadly eastern front. Clearly, the Germans had much to gain by this arrangement. It suited their racist policies and their practical agenda.

By August 1943, however, the Danes were no longer satisfied with their government's policy of cooperation.[76] They expressed their support of democracy through sabotage, strikes, and mass demonstrations. German authorities responded by declaring a state of emergency and dismantling the Danish armed forces. The policy of negotiation collapsed, and Himmler established a new security apparatus under Higher SS and Police Leader Günther Pancke. The position of the Jews became precarious. But, as we shall see, both the lack of poverty and the maintenance of democratic values during the war years served the Danes well when their Jewish countrymen were threatened in October 1943. The sudden shift of the Jews' status from full members of civil society to a hunted group affronted the Danish population, and they promptly rallied to their neighbors' cause.

ACROSS EUROPE, occupation regimes of varying severity were instituted in the countries that Germany conquered: Poland in 1939, followed in 1940 by Denmark, and then, in order, Norway, the Netherlands, Luxembourg, Belgium, and France. The administration of Poland and Denmark lay at opposite ends of the spectrum: one malignant, the other benign.

The occupation regimes imposed upon Norway and the Netherlands on the one hand, and Belgium and France on the other, also differed greatly. Like their Scandinavian neighbors, the Norwegians were "Nordic" people, and the "Nordic" Dutch had a special place in the Nazi German heart—they were the "little brothers." The Norwegian and Dutch armies, however, fought to protect their nations from occupation.

The Germans believed that the racially valuable Norwegians had a fine future in a German-ruled Europe. Vidkun Quisling, an eager Norwegian National Socialist, declared himself head of the government the very day of the invasion. Few followed him. The problem was that with the exception of Quisling and his cohort, the Norwegians did not realize the great future ahead of them. As the Germans advanced, King Haakon and his government fled to London where they continued the war in exile.

With weak support from the Germans and nearly none from the Norwegians, Quisling wielded little power.[77] Norway's real rulers were Reichskommissar Josef Terboven, army commander Nikolaus von Falkenhorst, and Higher SS and Police Leader Wilhelm Rediess. It was their job to Nazify a recalcitrant population. In the meantime, the Germans demanded a high daily fee to pay for their occupation costs, and they isolated Norway from the imports upon which the country depended. Forced to render the Germans an ever-growing share of their national income—from 25 percent in 1940 to some 40 percent in 1943—the Norwegians suffered increasingly from widespread poverty and near-famine conditions.[78]

If the Germans hoped that misery and privation would prompt the Norwegians to accept their responsibilities as Nordic people in the Nazis' New Order, they were disappointed. But the occupation regime was not entirely unsuccessful: the Norwegian police, under the leadership of Police Minister Jonas Lie, quite saw the point. As Hannah Arendt later observed, the cooperation of indigenous police with their German counterparts was a striking feature of occupation. It was through the Norwegian police that the Germans effectively gained control of the local population. And it was through them that Nazi racist policies were enacted. On 10 January 1942, at the Germans' request, Lie ordered the ominous "J" stamped on identity cards of the approximately one thousand eight hundred Jews living in Norway. A few months later, Jews were required to fill out forms at local police stations, which were used to compile a central register.[79]

The *Blitzkrieg* (whirlwind war or, literally, "lightning war") launched by Germans in Poland, Denmark, and Norway quickly spread to the Low Countries and France. The Dutch, expecting respect for their neutrality as during World War I, were ill-prepared and dismayed by the 10 May invasion. It took the Germans but five days and a new weapon in the arsenal of war—bombing to bits the civilian city of Rotterdam, killing nearly one thousand people of all ages—to force the Dutch to capitulate. The queen and the government fled to England. They brought the Allies important resources: the Dutch navy, a large merchant fleet, and the oil- and rubber-rich Dutch East Indies.

Nazi Germans were frustrated. Scandinavians might be glorious Nordic Vikings, but the Dutch were blood relatives bound to Germany by geography, history, and language. In the German view, the Netherlands was merely an estuary of the Rhine and belonged to Germany; the Low Countries had been an integral part of the Holy Roman Empire until 1648; the Dutch language was really Low German.[80] Perhaps most important was the central role of the Dutch in German history. In fact, the Dutch had started the great "Push to the East," a program of systematic immigration that reached to Estonia and the Ukraine. These pioneers went in the hope of a better life, but the German historians who wrote about them centuries later saw them as missionaries of German culture.[81] By the late nineteenth century, the land they settled was called "the German East," and it became a primary Nazi obsession.

Hitler appointed the Austrian Nazi, Arthur Seyss-Inquart, Reich Commissioner of the Netherlands. He set out on a process of self-Nazification using the Dutch National Socialist movement led by Anton Mussert, meaning to prepare the Dutch for their ultimate reintegration into the Reich.[82] As in Norway, the Germans failed. Most Dutch people did not wish to take a place either in German history or the German future. They wanted to preserve Dutch identity and Dutch values in a Nazi-dominated Europe.

One of those values was tolerance. Since the tiny Dutch Republic's sixteenth-century war with powerful Spain, Holland had been a haven for the oppressed and a foe of tyranny. The Jews of the Iberian Peninsula had fled to Holland when threatened by the Inquisition. And the Dutch took in the French philosopher Descartes when he ran afoul of the French government.

This history, and the myths associated with it, galvanized the Dutch into action when the Germans brutally raided the Jewish quarter of Amsterdam on Saturday and Sunday, 22–23 February 1941. In broad daylight, and before thousands of non-Jews, some 600 German security police sealed off the area, punched, slapped, and beat women and children who got in their way, and marched between 425 and 450 young Jewish men to a central square, where they were forced to run a gauntlet.

Beating the Jews was sport for the Germans; their real business was deportation. Shipped to the stone quarries of Mauthausen, only one of these young men survived the war: Max Nebig of Amsterdam. According to Eugon Kogon, a German journalist who survived Buchenwald, the morning after the Dutch Jews arrived in Mauthausen, fifty "were chased from the bathhouse naked and driven into the electrified fence." The rest were "shunted into the quarry," where they were tortured continuously and clubbed to death. "On the third day the SS opened the so-called 'death gate' and with a fearful barrage of blows drove the Jews across the guard line, the guards on the watchtowers shooting them down in heaps with their machine-guns." The Jews then joined hands and jumped to their death in the pit. "The civilian employees at the Mauthausen quarry requested that these suicides by jumping be stopped, since the fragments of flesh and brains clinging to the rocks afforded too gruesome a sight."[83]

The Dutch did not know what would happen to the young men, but they knew that they had been arrested because they were Jews. This was enough; it was an assault on the Dutch sense of social order, and they expressed their outrage in a strike that started with municipal employees and was joined by the metal and shipyard workers, as well as mass street demonstrations that spread throughout Amsterdam. From Tuesday 25 February through Thursday 27 February 1941, a wave of strikes and civil unrest paralyzed transportation systems and industrial production in the provinces of North Holland and Utrecht. The Germans declared a state of emergency and deployed police and SS troops. The public could not tolerate the German anti-Jewish policies, and the Germans would not tolerate public protest. Force prevailed. The strike was brutally quelled. Strikers and demonstrators were wounded and killed on city streets.[84]

The February strike had revealed German intentions and Dutch powerlessness. Cowed into unenthusiastic tacit compliance, the great majority of Dutch citizens turned to their daily affairs. A few volunteered for the Nazi New Order and, as we shall see, a few resisted it. Most people focused on their immediate concerns, and grudgingly accepted the German presence for the duration.[85]

The Germans recognized sullen acquiescence when they saw it. "The Führer expects the Anglo-American invasion attempt to come in the Netherlands," Propaganda Minister Joseph Goebbels wrote in his diary on 10 September 1943. "We are weakest there, and the population would be most inclined to give the necessary support to such an undertaking. As everybody knows, the Dutch are the most insolent and obstreperous people in the entire West."[86]

Perhaps it was for this reason that the occupation regime maintained a very

visible presence throughout the war. Seyss-Inquart was to rule through the
Dutch civil service, which had not fled for London with the queen and elected
government officials. In an early conversation with German military authorities, these administrative heads of the various ministries told the occupation
authorities that they were prepared to cooperate, but that they had "concern
only about the Jewish Question." They assumed, they said, that the Germans
would respect the Hague Land Warfare Convention, and that they would
administer the Netherlands according to article 43. The Germans, of course,
assured them they would, but by the February strike their actions had belied
their promises.[87]

In principle, Seyss-Inquart answered only to Hitler. In practice, however,
other Nazi officials quickly carved Holland into the jungle that characterized

28. SS weekly Das Schwarze
Korps (26 June 1941) article
entitled "Usefully Employed."
This piece about the Dutch
Jews arrested in February
1941 shows the detainees after
their transfer to Mauthausen.
They are marked by two triangles making a Star of
David, and the letter "N" for
Niederlande, the Nether-
lands. The text reads: "The
pictures on this page are not
the result of years of intensive
collection activity. Nor are
they taken from a display case
of freaks in a wax museum.
They also are not pictures of
Germany's now long-past
housecleaning of Jewish
criminals. These illustrations
merely depict Dutch labor
leaders. Having committed
terrible crimes, they are now
employed in strict working
conditions for the public good,
and this time against their
will. Not too long ago they
must have thought that their
'future business' would be
quite different." Courtesy
Sterling Memorial Library,
Yale University, New Haven.

the German state: each German agency in Holland listened directly to Berlin, and not to Seyss-Inquart. Organized chaos ensued in which Germans acted at best next to each other, and more often against each other. The Dutch did not profit from this situation, but Germans who knew what they wanted from the country did. Göring, through his agents, thoroughly exploited the economic wealth of the country, while Himmler, through his representative, the violent and vicious SS-Brigadeführer Hans Rauter, carried out the Reich's racial policies very effectively indeed. By the end of the war, nearly 80 percent of the 140,000 Jews living in the Netherlands in May 1940 had been killed.

For Dutch gentiles, daily life was not murderous but it was grim. Their diet deteriorated, and by the time of the hunger winter of 1944, many suffered from malnutrition. With little fuel available, public transportation became a memory and heating a luxury. Bicycles were a precious commodity, although rubber tires were not to be found; they—like shoes—were made of wood. Clogs clattered once again on cobblestones. Daily life became a constant struggle to eat, to find clothing, or even cleaning materials. Social life evaporated as ever larger numbers of people spent ever longer hours working, and standing on line in hope of securing basic household necessities.

IF THE NAZI government in Berlin hoped to ease the Norwegians and Dutch into the Greater Germanic realm, they had no such aspirations for Belgium and France. Indeed, they had no real idea what to do with France. Norway and the Netherlands were saddled with a severe civilian occupation regime committed to Nazi ideology; Belgium and France dealt with a military occupation authority whose main focus was the priorities of war. In both cases Jews died. Gentiles in Norway and the Netherlands suffered widespread privation and the loss of national institutions. The Belgians and French suffered equally widespread privation but maintained their national institutions—and with them, a chimera of normality. By 1944, this made little difference, but the road to that end—the experience of the years 1940 through 1943—was not the same in those countries with a government-in-exile and those countries which seemed to have a national authority at home.

The Germans invaded Luxembourg, Belgium, France, and the Netherlands simultaneously. Luxembourg was overrun in a day; Grandduchess Charlotte refused to welcome the invaders and fled to England, but the Germans hardly noticed and simply annexed Luxembourg to the Reich and began a rapid Germanization program. Belgium fought for eighteen days; and when it capitulated the country was physically, morally, and constitutionally in shambles. While the government left for England to continue the war, King Leopold decided that the country had fulfilled its obligation to defend itself, and remained in Belgium with the army. The Belgian government-in-exile denounced Leopold, declaring his action unconstitutional.[88]

The Germans took advantage of the king's presence. Belgium, they believed, would give them little trouble, and they were correct. The military governor of Belgium, General Alexander von Falkenhausen, was no Nazi ideologue. Germany's occupation of Belgium in 1914–18 had been fraught with errors he had no wish to repeat. He knew that many Belgians remembered the German brutality of twenty years before. His German military government would be one of goodwill, he vowed. The military authorities maintained relations with the monarchy and, in that heavily Catholic country, with the Church, while Belgian Fascists were held in check. Belgium was not Poland. The occupation regime in Belgium did not terrorize or plunder the local population. Indeed, the army even helped refugees who had fled in advance of the invading forces to go home.

Von Falkenhausen was well rewarded for his efforts. With king and Church secure, and young men returned to their families, a sense of normality quickly returned. Gentile Belgians made do and knuckled under, with broad participation by the local elites and acceptance by the rest.[89]

Not so the Jews, who lived on the edge. The situation for the Jews was much more precarious, of course. Neither von Falkenhausen nor his military administration was particularly interested in the Jews, but the Nazi agencies that descended on the country in the wake of the occupation were. The SD (*Sicherheitsdienst,* security forces), initially requested by the military authorities because they felt their own security apparatus was insufficient, refused to leave after relative calm had been established. Fully empowered as a police force in 1941, the SD took orders regarding the Jews directly from Berlin.

If the Belgians accommodated, the French collaborated. And if the experience of World War I in Belgium was a negative example to be avoided, the humiliation of Germany by France in 1918 was a constant inspiration to the Nazis for revenge in 1940. Within weeks of the German invasion, both British and French forces had crumpled. In full retreat, the British were evacuated from Dunkirk across the Channel between 27 May and 4 June in an astonishing rescue operation aboard anything that could float. Chaos reigned in an overwhelmed and exhausted France. Its government fled from Paris to Tours, and then to Bordeaux on 10 June.[90] As many as 10 million of the country's 40 million citizens took to the road, seeking to escape the enemy by going south. When the Germans entered Paris on 14 June, they found the city nearly deserted. Perhaps less than a third (800,000) of the normal population (3 million) of the capital saw the swastika replace the *tricolore* on the Hôtel de Ville by midday. "Everyone had taken to the roads," the historian and sociologist Evelyne Sullerot remembered.

> We saw thousands fleeing, unbelievable scenes. All the Belgians, all of northern France had come to the southwest because they never dreamed the Germans would penetrate that far. They had all streamed down. Food was scarce. A tomato was worth a fortune. It is difficult to imagine. People slept outdoors on the beach. The beach was covered with families all in black. The

old women were dressed in black. The peasants came with some of their live-stock, with their carts, their wheelbarrows. The country was thrown into total confusion, like an anthill that had been knocked over.[91]

The French prime minister, Paul Reynaud, dithered. "You take Hitler for another Wilhelm I, the old gentleman who took Alsace-Lorraine from us, and that was all there was to it. But Hitler is Genghis Khan," he warned his cabinet on 10 June.[92] He himself was inclined to flee with the government to French North Africa and remain at war, but he was powerless before the army's reluctance. Realizing that the generals would not carry on, Reynaud resigned on the 16th, and the eighty-four-year-old hero of World War I, Field Marshal Philippe Pétain, succeeded him.

Pétain, who had served as ambassador to Spain until a month earlier, was sympathetic to fascism and had always opposed the war. Speaking on the radio the following day, Pétain assured the public: "I make a gift of myself to France to lessen her misfortune." Despite his Christ-like rhetoric, Pétain lacked divinity. A political reactionary and military defeatist, the aged Pétain had few qualities that would help the French people weather the deeply divisive storms of German occupation.

Urging the soldiers to lay down their arms, Pétain sought an armistice. On 22 June 1940, the victorious Adolf Hitler and his entourage met with the defeated French general Charles Huntziger in the same railway carriage that Field Marshal Ferdinand Foch had used when he dictated the armistice terms to Matthias Erzberger and his colleagues in November 1918. For twenty-two years, the wooden dining car had sat in a museum in Paris. Now Hitler ordered it sent to the spot in the forest of Compiègne which had been the site of German mortification. There French representatives met the Führer, who took Marshal Foch's former seat at the middle of the table.[93]

That was not the sole historical echo in June 1940. Lieutenant General Bogislav von Studnitz demanded that the French military commander of Paris, General Fernand Dentz, return German regimental flags captured in World War I. General Dentz might have been happy to comply, but he had no idea where they were. Of greater moment, the French were allowed to maintain an army of 100,000 men, precisely the figure set for the Germans at Versailles. The insolence with which the French had treated Germany's army in November 1918, demanding total demobilization within a month, was now served back in full: the Reich refused to release the 1.5 million French prisoners of war. Furthermore, any French citizen who continued to fight on the Allies' side was to be considered a *franc-tireur,* a maverick freefighter, who was not entitled to protection under the Geneva Convention. War reparations had been demanded of the Germans twenty years earlier. Now the French were required to pay a crippling 400 million francs per day for the privilege of German occupation, 60 percent of the national income. This burden had grave consequences for nearly everyone throughout the country.

Pétain   Laval

"THAT'S NOT FRANCE!"

29. *Cartoon by David Low,* Evening Standard *(London), 15 July 1940. The Vichy regime had abandoned traditional Bastille Day festivities, the annual celebration in France on 14 July of the fall of the Bastille and the start of the revolution in 1789.*

The French came to the table with little to offer, and they got little from the Germans. But they got just enough to obscure the Nazi government's ultimate goals. The Germans recognized Pétain and his cabinet as the legitimate government of all of France, including its empire. While Pétain's authority in theory extended across the whole of France, in fact the German army occupied the industrial north and west including Paris; the unoccupied "Free Zone" covered the agricultural southern third of the country.

Pétain's government had landed in German-occupied Bordeaux. Finding neither that city nor a return to German-occupied Paris congenial to the image of sovereignty, they removed to the spa town of Vichy, with its many hotels and healthy water. The armistice was signed on 22 June, and when the French government, the senators and deputies, met in Vichy on 10 July they voted overwhelmingly to give full powers to Pétain.

The extent of the German occupying presence was significantly different in France, both north and south, than in the other occupied countries of 1939 and 1940, except Denmark. To most French people the "occupation" initially appeared to be a delimited military phenomenon, not a social, political, and economic stranglehold. The French had a legitimate national government on French soil, duly authorized by elected representatives. The army might be reduced to 100,000 men—but they had an army, and no claim was made on their splendid navy. The Mediterranean coast was left under Vichy control, which permitted the French access to their north African territories. And Marshal Pétain's Vichy government had its own deeply conservative national agenda, the "National Revolution," which it pursued largely unimpeded for several years.

Vichy's policy with regard to Germany, as Pétain unabashedly announced, was collaboration. Hitler stopped off to see the marshal on his way back to Berlin from a meeting with Spain's Fascist leader, Generalissimo Francisco Franco.

Pétain went on the air to report to the French nation: "It is in a spirit of honor and in order to preserve the unity of France—unity which has lasted for ten centuries—within the New European Order which is being built, that I today embark on the path of collaboration." The widely disseminated photograph of Pétain and Hitler in uniform, shaking hands at the railway station of the town of Montoire, portrayed allies, not conqueror and conquered. This view was presented as a realistic policy: it was only reasonable to acknowledge that Germany had won the war and was to shape the New Europe.[94]

This policy also allowed Pétain and his government to abolish parliamentary democracy and replace it with an authoritarian form of government. Gone were the time-honored exalted ideals of *Liberté, Egalité, Fraternité*. The day's new slogan became the prosaic obligations of *Travail, Famille, Patrie* (Work, Family, and Homeland). Adopting a reactionary program of *rénovation française* (National Renovation), the Vichy government promulgated the virtues of loyalty, hierarchy, and obedience, and promised an activist policy to restore old values. The regime eschewed many aspects of social modernization, and rejected all movements and people identified with it. Thus, the nationalism preached by Vichy was firmly anti-Communist and antisemitic. The supporters of Vichy France may have deplored that it had

Europe January 1941

taken Hitler's victory to clean up the prewar mess, but they were relieved that now they could "set things right."

By the second year of German rule, however, it had become clear to many in France that nothing would be set right. They realized that France was, in fact, both defeated and occupied, and that the occupation did not have limited, spe-

cific goals but was a ubiquitous, omnipotent authority. "In 1871 [after the Franco-Prussian War] the Germans occupied only"; Paul Simon, a Parisian, wrote in early 1942, "this time they are interfering in everything. They have installed themselves in the railways, public administration, police forces, banks, insurance companies, press, wireless, films, law and education. They are everywhere, even in the so-called unoccupied zone, and in the colonies. . . . They are . . . suppressing all liberty, even of thought. . . . A regime of tyranny has been set up . . . and every day fresh executions take place."[95]

Both men and women were affected, but not necessarily in identical ways. With 1.5 million Frenchmen interned in Germany, the women left at home had the double burden of working and taking care of their families. Rationing was introduced to ensure equitable distribution of consumer goods, but women waited on long lines for items that either were sold out by the time they got their turn or simply were not to be had. Coupons were needed for almost everything. Bread and meat were rationed by the end of September 1940; other goods followed soon after: foodstuffs, ersatz tobacco and wine, clothes, shoes, detergents and soap, school supplies, household articles made of iron.

Nearly everyone went hungry as the occupation wore on, allotments decreased, availability even of the rationed quantities dwindled, and people became so poor they could not afford the goods they were entitled to get. The war winters were among the coldest on record. The French chopped up furniture to burn, used newspaper to insulate their clothes, shoes, and boots, and refashioned curtains and blankets into garments. Ill-shod, ill-fed, ill-clothed, lacking heating fuel and electricity, most people focused on everyday matters. They had little energy to do much more.

Hitler had appeared to offer France a partnership, a "collaboration," in his New Order; in fact he was interested only in exploitation. He really had no idea where France fit in Nazi Europe. The attack on France had been a rational military action. No plan existed beyond conquest, but one soon emerged—to loot the country of its resources. Allowing the French to maintain their sovereignty and government was a cheap and convenient way to get them to do the dirty work. The French were responsible for delivering the quotas the Germans set for agricultural products, industrial goods, gentiles to work as "volunteer" laborers in Germany, and Jews for deportation "to the east." By late 1942, Berlin realized that matters would run more smoothly if the German military occupied the whole country. Choosing the historical date of 11 November, the German army crossed the demarcation line and occupied Vichy France.

Nothing daunted, Pétain and his government hung on in office, resorting to ever more extreme moves to prove their power and legitimacy. In December Vichy ordered Jews in the southern zone to get their identity cards marked; then the government established the *milice* (French militia) early in the new year. "The vanguard in maintaining order," according to Pétain, the *miliciens* swore an oath of allegiance "to fight against democracy, against Gaullist insurrection, and against Jewish leprosy."[96] At the same time, greater numbers of disaffected, disenchanted, and disgusted French people turned to resistance operations. Armed groups, called *maquis,* grew apace. The *milice* and the *maquis* identified each other as the enemy. By 1944 Philippe Pétain, the hero of Verdun, had left his legacy: France simmered in civil war.

Chapter Seven

THE ASSAULT OF
TOTAL WAR

HITLER HAD ACHIEVED most of his war aims by June 1940. With the Anschluss of Austria, the annexation of Sudetenland, Bohemia and Moravia, Danzig and western Poland, and German-inhabited areas of Belgium and France, 12.5 million Germans had returned to the Reich without leaving their homes; another half million had relocated to German territory. In 1937 the German Reich encompassed 65 million Germans, 65 percent of Germans in Europe; by the end of 1940, the Greater Reich had 78 million Germans, or 78 percent. Then too, the "racially valuable" Norwegians, Danes, and Dutch also were under German control—an additional bonus.

Hitler was riding high; his goals within reach. Life was good. The sight of German troops marching down the Champs-Elysées assuaged the humiliation of Versailles. Only two vexing matters remained: an ally he loathed to the east—the Soviet Union—and a foe he admired to the west—Great Britain. Contrary to expectation and against all odds, Britain had not folded. Neville Chamberlain, with whom he had done satisfactory business in Munich in 1938, had stepped down as prime minister on 10 May 1940. Winston Churchill, cut of another cloth entirely, was now in charge. It was perturbing to have so equal an adversary. Fortunately Churchill was a heavy smoker and a drunk, the teetotaler Führer consoled himself. Surely he either would drop dead or, in an inebriated stupor, err egregiously.

Churchill did smoke heavily and he drank a bottle of whiskey a day. But he did not err egregiously. His vivid historical imagination gave him a moral and intellectual compass to guide him through the turbulence of the moment. A great nationalist, Churchill was proud of Britain's past and hopeful for its future. It seemed to him that a historic moment was upon them. Thus, as Belgium fell and France teetered and Britain's foreign secretary Lord Halifax suggested a negotiated peace with Hitler using Mussolini as mediator, Churchill stood firm.[1] Chamberlain, who had learned that no deal with Hitler endured, supported Churchill. The prime minister took the matter to the House of Commons on 28 May:

DRUNKEN " WELTANSCHAUUNG "

31. Cartoon of Winston Churchill as a drunkard, Der Stürmer, 26 February 1942. The original caption read: "Churchill tries to find luck in drink, but the bottle distorts the view."

30. Cartoon of Winston Churchill as the captain of the ship of state, Daily Mail (London), 20 May 1940.

Meanwhile the house should prepare itself for hard and heavy tidings. I have only to add that nothing which may happen in this battle can in any way relieve us from our duty to defend the world cause to which we have vowed ourselves; nor should it destroy our confidence in our power to make our way, as on former occasions in our history, through disaster and through grief to the ultimate defeat of our enemies.[2]

France fell three weeks later. The British supported their prime minister: they would fight on. Speaking again to the House of Commons, Churchill gave Hitler his country's message:

What General Weygand called the Battle of France is over. I expect that the Battle of Britain is about to begin. Upon this battle depends the survival of Christian civilization. Upon it depends our own British life, and the long continuity of our institutions and our Empire. The whole fury and might of the enemy must very soon be turned on us. Hitler knows that he will have to break us in this Island, or lose the war. . . . Let us therefore brace ourselves to our duties, and so bear ourselves that, if the British Empire and its Commonwealth last for a thousand years, men will still say, "This was their finest hour."[3]

Hitler lost the Battle of Britain waged in the skies that summer. The British had defended themselves; they were not conquered. Clearly the war was going to last longer than he had imagined. Hitler had to prepare for an extended campaign: food from the agriculturally rich Danube basin and oil from the Ploesti fields in Romania would do nicely.

Germany had long seen south-central Europe as its backyard. During World War I, the concept of *Mitteleuropa* (Central Europe), a German-led, self-sufficient commonwealth reaching from the North Sea to Turkey, had taken hold.[4] Germans were to be the leaders, German the common language, and the nationalities of the Danube—Slovakians, Hungarians, Romanians, Bulgarians, Yugoslavs—the junior partners. The time had now come for Hitler to pursue this vision.

WITH THE ANSCHLUSS of Austria, the establishment of the Protectorate of Bohemia and Moravia, and the birth of independent Slovakia, Germany had achieved much in south-central Europe. Slovakia, small and poor, with few natural resources, brought the Reich the military advantages of first-class arms factories and useful territory for launching military operations.[5] The Slovaks and their leaders did not mind serving Germany. They finally had the state they had dreamed of, and it combined nationalism with the Roman Catholic Church. Sovereignity was invested in God, and the separation between church and state disappeared. The Church controlled the state, and at the helm stood Monsignor Josef Tiso. Far from the battlefront until 1944, and out of Allied bomber reach, most Slovaks fared well throughout the war.

Most, but not all: 4 percent of the population—the Jews—stood at risk in this devoutly Roman Catholic satellite state. The 90,000 Jews who remained in Slovakia after Hungary took its bite of territory played an important economic role and dominated the professions.[6] Pandering to Berlin, the Slovak government hurried through a law defining who was a Jew, and then restricted the participation of Jews in the professions to 4 percent. Slovaks applauded, hoping for more: the "Aryanization" of Jewish wealth until it comprised only 4 percent of the national wealth—with the rest going to Slovaks. But the government, facing a paucity of educated Slovaks to take the Jews' places, and preferring Jewish Slovaks to German immigrants, stopped short. Lulled by the sense of being indispensable, the Jews took heart.

They were bitterly disappointed. In 1940 the Fascist Hlinka Guard rattled their chains. Hitler intervened, and Tiso appointed the radical antisemite and National Socialist professor Vojtech Tuka as prime minister. The Germans did not need to tell Tuka to proceed with zeal, and he happily received political advisers from Berlin for militia questions, police questions, propaganda questions, economic questions, and the "Jewish Question." Eichmann's aide SS-Hauptsturmführer Dieter Wisleceny arrived in Bratislava as an adviser to Tuka's government. They soon issued a plethora of decrees and regulations, culminating in the *Codex Judaicus* (Jewish Code) of September 1941. Longer than the Slovak Constitution, written in the spirit of the Nuremberg Laws, the *Codex Judaicus* made the Germans happy, but not the Slovak episcopate. Seeing themselves as the guardians of the Slovak state, the bishops protested adopting a racial principle that failed to recognize conversion. Their stand embarrassed the government; the Slovak president, after all, was a clergyman. But all parties saved face: section 225 ensured that "The President of the Republic shall have the right to exempt individuals [of his choosing] from the provisions of this code."[7] Tiso promised he would use this when appropriate. This satisfied the bishops. No one said anything about the victimization of the Jews.

Political and economic expediency framed more by traditional Roman Catholic anti-Judaism than modern racist antisemitism ruled the Slovak treatment of the Jews. But the presence of Wisleceny boded ill. In the end Berlin, not Bratislava, would determine the fate of Slovakia's Jews.

THE GERMAN-IMPOSED return of the southern part of Slovakia to Hungary was the first instance of German arbitration in the squabbles that had erupted upon the dissolution of the Austro-Hungarian empire in 1918. The postwar attempt to draw political boundaries according to ethnic population concentrations, difficult enough in eastern Europe, had proven impossible in the patchwork of nationalities to the south. Territorial grievances and irredentist movements proliferated, made worse by poverty and depression—and the politics that ensued.[8]

Of all the countries along the Danube, Hungary had lost the most, deprived of 71 percent of its land and 63 percent of its population in postwar settlements. In the unstable situation that followed, a Soviet regime took power in 1919, headed by Béla Kun.[9] The Socialist-Communist leadership was largely Jewish, a fact useful to its opponents. Hungary had fallen to the worldwide Jewish conspiracy, they claimed. Communism meant the rule of the Jew over the Christian. "Anti-Semitic feeling is growing steadily in Budapest (which is not surprising, considering that not only the whole Government, save 2, and 28 out of the 36 ministerial commissioners are Jews, but also a large proportion of the Red officers)," an official at the British Foreign Office commented in 1919 to a colleague attending the Peace Conference in Paris. A British secret agent in Budapest code-named Semjan "and others are convinced that a Pogrom in Budapest in the not very distant future is certain and that it will far out-do Russian records. . . . Personally, I do not think that anything on earth can stop the anti-Semitic movement in Hungary, but sheer massacre at least can be stopped."[10]

Kun's regime lasted 133 days. It was followed by a period of violent and bloody White terror. Officers, soldiers, and students at the core of the movement called for the rebirth of Hungary as a pure Christian nation in which Jews had no place. They preached undiluted racist antisemitism. "The Jew may be christened a thousand times; he never can strip off his Semite race."[11] Thousands of Jews were killed, and the traditionally good relations between gentiles and Jews, largely middle class, assimilated, and (despite the fantasies of the Whites) conservative and patriotic, turned raw.

Into this explosion stepped the anti-Communist, Russophobic Admiral

Miklós Horthy.[12] A highly decorated World War I officer, Horthy would later (February 1920) become "Regent" of the Kingdom of Hungary and block attempts by the Hapsburg family to regain the vacant throne. But that had not yet happened when he partnered with Prime Minister István Bethlen in November 1919 to wrest control from the rabid right. Like the Whites, Horthy was a self-declared antisemite. But he and Bethlen were also pragmatic: they

The dismemberment of Hungary after World War I

Areas lost by Austria	
Areas lost by Hungary	
Areas lost by Germany	
Areas lost by Russia	
Area lost by Bulgaria	
Hungarians in ceded Hungarian territories	

0 — 300 miles
0 — 500 km

——— International boundaries 1914
- - - - Internal border between Austria and Hungary

CS   Lost to Czechoslovakia

PO   Lost to Poland

RO   Lost to Romania

YU   Lost to Yugoslavia

AU   Lost to Austria

IT   Lost to Italy

Chazaud

believed that Hungary's hope for economic revival lay with its Jewish middle class, so terrorized by the White Guards. Traditional rather than revolutionary antisemites, Horthy and Bethlen credited the Elders of Zion conspiracy, and at the same time enjoyed the company of Jews, played bridge with them, and trusted their judgment about the economy. At any rate, they were determined to restore public order.[13] "I am against all kinds of shrill anti-Semitism," Bethlen announced in his inaugural speech as prime minister. "Equality before the law is guaranteed by the nation and cannot be interfered with. I admit that there is currently a Jewish Question in the country, but its solution lies in our becoming economically independent of them. This is also in their own interest, because as soon as they are no longer indispensable, harmony will be reestablished."[14]

A kingdom without a king ruled by an admiral without a navy fared surprisingly well for at least fifteen years.[15] White Guard leaders went underground politically, where they organized secret societies soldered together by extreme nationalism, anti-Bolshevism, and antisemitism. When the Nazis came to power in 1933, the Whites stood ready to join up and were rewarded with generous support. One large glitch marred this cozy bond: the Hungarians were not "Aryans" and did not wish to be; they were Turanians. As the refrain of a popular song from the time put it, "No, we are not Aryans. We are not Aryans, no!"[16]

"Aryan" or Turanian, in the 1930s the secret societies grew into the Fascist Arrow Cross movement. Led by an army officer named Ferenc Szálasi who modeled himself on Hitler, and supported by army officers, many of them ethnic Germans, the new party adopted a green-shirt uniform and a swastika-like cross composed of four arrows. And as it gained strength, the Jews withdrew from Hungary's political and intellectual life. Their continued existence was bought at the price of silence. "We are . . . condemned to subsistence at the periphery of the intellectual life of our age. We must observe fasting, political fasting . . ." the Hungarian Jewish writer Aladár Komlós lamented.[17]

Depression-driven poverty made matters worse. In early 1937 the conservative newspaper *Uj Magyarsag* went after the Jews. It published a long list of statistics to portray the Jews' stranglehold on the Hungarian economy: of the country's twenty largest industrial enterprises, 70 percent of the board members were Jews; 84.3 percent of taxpayers with incomes over 100,000 pengö were Jews, and 85.6 percent of those with incomes between 30,000 and 100,000 pengö.[18] In response, by then former prime minister Bethlen argued in parliament that the government should assist Christian Hungarians in establishing businesses and, concurrently, stamp out antisemitic agitation. Instead of solving the problem, Bethlen said, Jew-baiting only produced unrest.

Horthy and Bethlen's policy of pragmatic antisemitism and equally pragmatic protectionism became harder to maintain as Hungary became ever more dependent on Germany as its primary trading partner, and Arrow Cross membership grew to three-quarters of a million and its support swelled to a quarter of the nation. Hungary was geographically vulnerable too: the Anschluss of Austria meant a common border with the new Greater Germany. On 5 March 1938, Prime Minister Kálmán Darányi called for the Christian share of the economy and cultural life to be more proportionate to their numbers. "Such a solution," he explained, "would be in the interests of the Jews themselves, for anti-Semitism and the propagation of extremist and intolerant movements would thus be greatly lessened."[19]

Many Jews were prepared to accept economic restrictions had they guaranteed an end to harassment. They were all too aware of what was happening just over the border in Austria, where their co-religionists were suffering terribly. The fate of Austria's Jews was no abstraction: twenty years earlier the men had served the same Austro-Hungarian emperor-king and had sheltered in the same trenches. It seemed to Hungarian Jews that the Law for the More Efficient Protection of the Social and Economic Balance (May 1938) was preferable to the murderous antisemitism on the streets of Vienna. The Hungarian law defined Jews as people of the Jewish confession, who were converted to Judaism after 1919, or who were born later to Jewish parents. The bill limited participation of Jews in the economy to 20 percent.

But what would come next? the Jews worried. Their fears were justified. A second law, Concerning the Restriction of the Participation of the Jews in Public and Economic Life, soon came before the Hungarian parliament. Explicitly echoing German anti-Jewish legislation, the new bill adopted racist antisemitism, redefining Jews who had converted to Christianity after 1 August 1919 as Jews and thus transforming 100,000 confessional Christians into legal Jews. It also decreased the participation of Jews in the economy to a mere 6 percent. The Jews protested. "Let the battlefields of the war for independence, the marshes of Volhynia, and the Karst rocks speak out on behalf of justice for us; in the trenches no one asked who was of which religion."[20]

Horthy, a proud antisemite but also a man with a strong code of honor, opposed the legislation and it failed. He made his position clear in a letter dated 14 October 1940 to Hungary's new prime minister, Count Pál Teleki. "As regards the Jewish problem, I have been an anti-Semite through all my life.... I have considered it intolerable that here in Hungary every factory, bank, large fortune, business, theatre, press, commercial enterprise, etc., should be in the hands of Jews, and that the Jews should be the image reflected of Hungary, especially abroad." Yet, he said,

> I can't look with indifference at inhumanity, senseless humiliations, when we still need [the Jews]. In addition, I consider for example the Arrow-Cross men to be by far more dangerous and worthless for my country than I do the Jew. The latter is tied to this country from interest, and is more faithful to his adopted country than the Arrow-Cross men, who, like the Iron Guard [in Romania]. with their muddled brains, want to play the country into the hands of the Germans.[21]

Horthy may not have wanted "to play the country into the hands of the Germans," but he certainly was willing to allow Hungary to profit from German aggression. After the Munich Agreement of 1938, Hungary got the southern part of Slovakia with its more than 700,000 Magyars and 78,000 Jews. In March 1939 the country expanded again with the addition of Ruthenia, which gave Hungary another 550,000 people, including 72,000 Yiddish-speaking Jews, as well as a common border with its ally Poland.

That border lasted for a mere six months. In September 1939 Hungary refused to help Germany in its conquest of Poland, opening its frontier to retreating Polish soldiers.[22] When the USSR annexed Polish territory next to Hungary's new province of Ruthenia, the Hungarian-Polish border became a Hungarian-Soviet border. The shadow cast by the Soviet Union nudged Hungary closer to Germany, and gave Horthy an opportunity to ask for the return of Transylvania,

32. *Admiral Horthy, on horseback, enters Czechoslovak territories annexed by Hungary, November 1938. Yad Vashem Photo Archives, courtesy of the United States Holocaust Memorial Museum Photo Archives, Washington, DC.*

which had been lost after World War I. "Our historic task has always been to cover Europe against the East," Horthy argued in a letter to Hitler. "Without the possession of the Carpathians we are unable to come up to this task. For this reason the possession of this ridge is of vital importance. Transylvania is the only natural fortress of Europe, and it would be to the advantage of Germany if this country were in trustworthy hands. Sooner or later Germany and Russia will have to settle accounts."[23] Hitler quite saw Horthy's point, and he forced Romania to give the northern part of Transylvania to Hungary.

Such largess brought Hungary into the Tripartite Pact composed of Germany, Italy, and Japan. Now formally allied to Germany, Hungary moved closer to its Nazi partner and the Arrow Cross became a formidable force in the country. Emboldened, they fulminated in parliament that the Jews "should be removed from the country and from the face of the earth."[24]

While this clearly did not bode well for the Jews, Horthy's government continued to steer a course between institutional antisemitism and the violence of German racist antisemitism so visible in Austria and Poland. Thus, as the prime minister explained, socially, "we have to prevent large scale intermixing between Jews and non-Jews." Financially, "we must not allow the keys of the country's economy to be left in the hands of the Jews, half-Jews, or their strawmen."[25] And the government began to draft its own set of Nuremberg laws— but it was in no hurry to introduce them to parliament.

Never mind. Hungary's greed got the best of it. In 1941 Horthy let Germany use Hungarian territory to launch an attack on Yugoslavia, and got a piece of the conquered country in return. Having accepted so much since 1939 from its bellicose ally, Hungary joined Germany in June 1941 and, reluctantly, declared war on the Soviet Union. Pushed by the Arrow Cross, the government declared war on the western Allies in December.

The position of the Jews deteriorated sharply. A new law "Concerning the Protection of the Race" forbade marriages between Jews and non-Jews. It defined Jews solely according to "blood lines"—anyone with two Jewish grand-parents was a Jew. Miklós Kállay, a member of parliament, refused to support the bill. The prime minister, recently returned from discussions with Hitler and Ribbentrop, rebuked him. "He said to me in a sharp tone: 'You are playing irre-sponsibly with the existence of the country. I know the situation and I felt the pressure. Don't you see that this is the only country in the whole German sphere of interest where there are no German soldiers? Your resistance will only invoke the brutal intervention of the Germans.' "[26]

Horthy committed upward of a quarter of a million men to the war against the Soviet Union. Jewish men—like the poet Miklós Radnóti—were not allowed to serve. Drafted into forced labor battalions for "unreliable" ele-ments, they were attached to the army and used for especially dangerous work. Of the 130,000 Jewish men up to the age of sixty inducted into these battalions, some 40,000 were killed. What Horthy wanted most was to maintain control of domestic affairs; to that end, he declined to accept the Nazi German program against the Jews. In this, he was supported by his son István Horthy and by Miklós Kállay, who had condemned the Hungarians' Nuremberg bill in 1941 and who became prime minister in 1942. So greatly did Horthy depend upon his son that he elevated him to the rank of vice-regent.

None of this pleased the Germans, who found the Hungarians slack and positively abhorred István Horthy. "The eldest son of Horthy has been desig-nated as his [father's] deputy by acclamation of the Hungarian House of Repre-sentatives," Goebbels complained in his diary on 20 February 1942.

> This is a piece of first rate political skulduggery. But we are keeping hands off. . . . Horthy's son is a pronounced Jew-lover, and Anglophile to the bones, and a man without any profound education and without broad polit-ical comprehension; in short, a personality with whom, if he were Regent of Hungary, we would have some difficulties to iron out. But this isn't the time to bother about such delicate questions. When in need the devil will eat flies, and in wartime we will stand even for an objectionable deputy regent of Hungary. After all, we must have something left to do after the war![27]

Kállay made no secret of his position on the "Jewish Question" and, as far as the Germans were concerned, he was probably even worse than Horthy junior.

The Germans never flagged in their effort to coopt Hungary into the "Final Solution" of the "Jewish Problem." In Berlin, Martin Luther of the Reich Foreign Office told Hungarian ambassador Döme Sztójay on 2 October that the Hungarians should proceed apace. They should exclude Jews from the cultural and economic life of the country, force them to wear an identifying mark, and deport them to the east. According to Luther, Sztójay did not respond with alacrity.

> From former conversations with the prime minister he [Sztójay] knows that Kállay is especially interested in knowing whether after their deportation to the east the Jews are provided with means of livelihood. There are rumors in this regard which he, Sztójay, does not believe, of course, but which nevertheless worry the prime minister . . . I answered that all deported Jews, including, of course, the Hungarian Jews, will be employed in building roads in the East and later will be brought together in a reservation. This answer calmed him visibly, and he observed that such information will have a specifically calming and encouraging effect on the prime minister.[28]

It did not. Kállay steadfastly refused to deport Hungary's Jews. "I must contradict those people who can see no other problem in this country except the Jewish problem," he declared in a speech on 22 October 1942. "Our country has many problems beside which the Jewish problem pales into insignificance. Those who can see Hungary only through such spectacles are degraded men who must be eliminated from our community."[29] The Arrow Cross, in other words, not the Jews, ought to "be eliminated."

Kállay and Horthy had bobbed and swerved their way diplomatically for well over a year, but when the Hungarian army crumpled under the Soviet offensive in January 1943, they knew what they had to do: extricate Hungary from Germany's grasp. But Berlin waxed avid for greater control over its reluctant allies.

Horthy was summoned in April to Klessheim Castle near Salzburg to meet with Hitler, who importuned him once again. Popular contemporary accounts held that Horthy told Hitler, "They may be lousy Jews, but they are our lousy Jews." Perhaps. Horthy readily acknowledged a "Jewish Problem," but Hungary would handle it. Hungary had adopted anti-Jewish laws as early as 1920, and in the two decades since, "Hungary follows unswervingly her course to bring about a solution to the Jewish question, which she considers an internal affair of the country, by her own methods." Just like "other problems of universal importance, the various sovereign states will have to find the most appropriate methods of solving these problems themselves."[30] Horthy did not know what more he could do; "he could not after all kill them." Hitler disagreed. "Jews had to be treated like tuberculosis germs which could infect a healthy body. . . . Nations which could not defend themselves against the Jews perished."[31]

Still, Horthy was not persuaded. "The Jewish question is being solved least satisfactorily by the Hungarians," Goebbels wrote in his diary on 8 May 1943.

The Hungarian state is permeated with Jews, and the Führer did not succeed during his talk with Horthy in convincing the latter of the necessity of more stringent measures. Horthy himself . . . will continue to resist every effort to tackle the Jewish problem aggressively. He gave a number of humanitarian counterarguments which of course don't apply at all to this situation. You just cannot talk humanitarianism when dealing with Jews.[32]

The Jews of Hungary remained part of the body politic. Elsewhere in Europe millions of Jews already had been slaughtered. In Hungary, they suffered from social death—economic marginalization and rejection from the cultural life of the nation—but they were not marked, they were not isolated in ghettos, and they were not murdered. Hungarian Jews thought they would survive by fading into obscurity and through Horthy's protection. Foreign observers disagreed. Lewis Namier, a historian who worked at the Jewish Agency in London, expressed his apprehensions to an official at the British Foreign Office about the future of Hungarian Jewry. The Jewish Agency, Namier explained, was "most seriously concerned at the possible consequences to the 800,000 Jews, who now enjoy comparative security, of any premature desertion of Germany by the Hungarian Government. The Jews here [in Britain] . . . feel that Germany could not possibly tolerate Hungarian defection, and as long as the German army was in position to do so would answer such a move by the Hungarian Government by a German occupation of the country, the result of which would be extermination of the last important body of Jewry left in Europe."[33]

Namier was correct. The end came when Hungary, choosing the lesser of two evils, sought to surrender to the Soviets in March 1944. The Germans took charge of the Hungarian government and the Jews faced an abyss. Hitler blamed the Jews. "The Jews, who control everything in Hungary, and individual reactionary or partly Jewish and corrupt elements of the Hungarian aristocracy have brought the Hungarian people, who were well disposed towards us, into this situation," he wrote in his order to the army to commence the invasion.[34] For Horthy, it was a moment of decision. He would not go into exile, like the king of Norway, queen of Holland, government of Poland, or Grandduchess Charlotte of Luxembourg. He was an admiral, he explained to Kállay. "The captain cannot leave his ship; he must remain on the bridge to the last." And, after expressing his concern for the Hungarian men to be dragged to the "Russian shambles," he asked his prime minister: "Who will defend the Jews or our refugees if I leave my post?"[35] But Horthy could not protect them. For the Jews, the sudden presence of the German legation, SS, and police meant utter devastation and loss.

HUNGARY DRIFTED into Germany's orbit because the Reich was its central trade partner. Germany then increased Hungary's landmass, seducing the government into alliance. Romania too had important trade relations with Germany, which needed the oil from Romania's rich Ploesti fields. Romania also hoped that Germany would help it hold on to the land gained at the end of World War I. Thus, in both Hungary and Romania, economic dependency and territorial ambitions opened the door to German influence.

Romania, like Hungary, did not commit to the Axis immediately, but there too the antisemitic right gained great popular support, and a home-grown Fascist movement, the Iron Guard, grew powerful in domestic politics. In late 1937, after the Iron Guard's dramatic electoral success, it appeared that its leader, the violently antisemitic Codreanu, was poised to establish a Fascist dictatorship. Now threatened from the right, King Carol appointed a new prime minister, the equally antisemitic, but monarchist, poet Coga. Coga's deputy was the academic Cuza, who boasted of being "the father of modern antisemitism," and who regarded Hitler as merely an able exponent of his tenets.[36]

Coga aimed "to eliminate 500,000 Jews from Roumanian life and citizenship and to expatriate them," he explained in the *Daily Herald* on 10 January 1938. "My first measure will be to declare that we cannot take responsibility for retaining this people in our state life."[37] Ten days later, Coga described the Jews as alien settlers who ought to be expelled. These statements prepared the public for a royal decree of 22 January, which demanded massive documentary proof of citizenship from all Jews living within Romania's borders. This was an impossible task in document-poor Romania. Panic ensued: Jewish businesses closed, capital fled abroad, the value of Romanian stocks in foreign markets plummeted, and Romanian commerce came to a virtual standstill. The economic crisis prompted King Carol to dismiss Coga, who left shouting, "Israel has triumphed."[38]

The Coga-Cuza government had lasted only three weeks, but the damage it wrought would last for years. A new government cobbled together by the Orthodox primate patriarch Miron Christea professed equal rights for all, but it did not repeal the royal decree. In eighteen months, 225,223 Jews were denationalized, 38.1 percent of the Jewish population. One antisemitic bill after another flew through parliament, reducing Romania's Jews to the penury of German Jews. Social death soon followed, and racist antisemitism gained currency. In August 1940, King Carol II signed a decree which forbade marriages between Jews and Romanians "with Rumanian blood."[39]

These policies were rooted in domestic Romanian antisemitism, but their adoption was quickened by international affairs. Throughout the 1930s, the League of Nations, which guaranteed minorities' rights, had weakened and finally disintegrated. With that, no one, no institution, could stop the antisemitic juggernaut. Jews stood exposed to the whims of an increasingly oppressive government. Pressured by the Reich, Romania signed a trade agreement with Germany in March 1939. And after Poland had been routed, a second trade agreement put Romania's oil industry, the fifth largest in the world, at the disposal of Germany. Moreover, Romania's agricultural production would be diverted to industrial crops such as flax, cotton, oil seed, and fodder, all desperately needed by the Reich.[40]

Then came the fall of France in June 1940. Romanians were devastated; it was a defining moment politically and morally, the British novelist Olivia Manning living in Bucharest noted. "For Bucharest, the fall of France was the fall of civilisation," she observed in *The Balkan Trilogy*. "France was the ideal for all of those who struggled against their peasant origin. All culture, art and fashion, liberal opinion and concepts of freedom were believed to come from France." Manning sensed the prevailing mood in the city.

> With France lost, there would be no stay or force against savagery. Except for a handful of natural fascists, no one really believed in the New Order. The truth was evident even to those invested in Germany: the victory of Nazi Germany would be the victory of darkness. Cut off from Western Europe, Rumania would be open to persecution, bigotry, cruelty, superstition and tyranny.[41]

Vultures moved in. Emboldened by the collapse of Romania's western ally, the Soviet Union demanded the return of Bessarabia and northern Bukovina. Romania turned to Germany for help, but Hitler had made a deal with Stalin and was more interested in pleasing the Soviet Union than in aiding Romania. Bulgaria then demanded the return of southern Dobrudja, lost in 1919. Again, Germany instructed Romania to yield. Finally, Hungary came to pick at the carcass. It wanted Transylvania. Romania bridled, and the two nations grew bellicose.[42] Hitler, needing regional stability to maintain the stream of Romanian oil, intervened via a telegram to King Carol telling him he "could well cede a little something to Hungary and Bulgaria,"[43] and called upon Ribbentrop and Ciano to arbitrate the dispute. Ciano saw the Führer on 28 August. According to Ciano's diary entry, Hitler told him the only thing that mattered was "that peace be preserved there, and that Rumanian oil continue to flow into his reservoirs."[44] Ribbentrop and Ciano met in Vienna the next day, and in the so-called Vienna Arbitration gave half of Transylvania to Hungary. "Ceremony of the signature at the Belvedere," Ciano noted in his diary on 30 August 1940. "The Hungarians can't contain their joy when they see the map. Then we hear a loud thud. It was [Romania's foreign minister] Manoilescu, who fainted on the table. Doctors, massage, camphorated oil. Finally he comes to, but shows the shock very much."[45]

Ironically, the loss of so much territory relieved Romania's "Jewish Problem." Forfeiting Bessarabia and northern Bukovina, Romania also lost 275,000 primarily Russian- or Yiddish-speaking Jews never integrated into Romanian society. With the transfer of northern Transylvania, almost 150,000 Jews became Hungary's "problem." The territorial losses, however, also destabilized an already rickety political situation. General Ion Antonescu, who called himself *conducator* (leader), threw out King Carol II, who had kept the Iron Guard in check. Carol abdicated in favor of his nineteen-year-old son, Mihai I. General Antonescu—pro-British by conviction, pro-German from necessity, and antisemitic to the core—brought the Iron Guard into the government.[46]

Territorial changes in the Danube basin, 1938-1941

Despite his distrust of the Iron Guard's revolutionary Fascist program, he agreed that the remaining 300,000 Jews from Old Romania should be eliminated. Antonescu introduced a second wave of antisemitic legislation intended to "Romanianize" the country by expelling Jews from schools, universities, and the professions, remove them from commerce, and expropriate Jewish-owned agricultural properties and businesses.

With powerful internal support for the Nazi agenda, and no external ally to counter German pressure, Romania joined the Axis in the autumn of 1940. German troops entered the country in preparation for the coming attack on the Soviet Union across Romania's border. One would have thought this a good thing for the Iron Guard, but Hitler needed political stability in Romania and an effective Romanian army. The Iron Guard was as troublesome as the SA had been in 1934. With German approval, Antonescu suppressed the Iron Guard in a bloody action in January 1941 and established a military dictatorship. Then Hitler got what he wanted: On 22 June 1941, the Romanian army joined the German assault on the USSR.

Antonescu got what he wanted too. When Romania captured Odessa, the Germans returned northern Bukovina and Bessarabia and threw in Transnistria as well. For Romanians, the price in human life was high and got progressively higher as troop numbers grew on the eastern front. For Jews in the acquired territories, it was equally deadly.

BULGARIA, like its neighbors along the Danube, had territorial grievances. It had lost Macedonia, Thrace, and southern Dobrudja, and it wanted them back. Furthermore, as an ally of the Central Powers during the Great War, Bulgaria had ended up on the losing side and was saddled with an enormous reparations debt of 2.25 billion gold francs. Truncated and frustrated, Bulgaria looked to improve its situation.

Again like its neighbors, Bulgaria lay within Germany's trade orbit. By 1939 the Reich accounted for 70 percent of Bulgaria's foreign trade. But the Bulgarians did not have happy memories of the Germans, who had treated them like a colony during World War I. Nor did the German antisemitic legislation since 1933 resonate in Bulgaria, which did not believe it had a "Jewish Problem." Its Jewish community of 50,000 in a country of 6 million was quite small and, unlike Hungary, Jews hardly figured in academic, professional, or economic life. Antisemitism, in short, was virtually nonexistent.[47]

However, Germany's rearrangement of Europe piqued King Boris III, the real (not titular) head of state, who wished to regain territories lost by his father. If land was to be had, why shouldn't Bulgaria get some of it? In February 1940 King Boris appointed an ardent admirer of Germany, Professor Bogdan Filov, as prime minister. For minister of the interior, Filov turned to Peter Gabrovski, a fellow Germanophile and the leader of the Ratnik Fascist organization. By the summer of 1940 Germany had become popular in Bulgaria. And Bulgaria was rewarded for its applause when Germany told Romania to give the Bulgarians southern Dobrudja. Pro-Axis sentiment warmed. As Britain's ambassador in Sofia observed, "Many waverers who had not yet committed themselves to the German side were swept into the vortex of pro-German enthusiasm."[48]

There was a price to be paid, of course: the introduction of antisemitic legislation. This was Hitler's measure of loyalty, the coin of his realm. Romania passed such laws in the autumn of 1940, and Bulgaria's Interior Minister Gabrovski followed suit with a proposed Law for the Defense of the Nation, which was adopted and signed by Boris III. "I delayed and I didn't want to do it," he told a confidant. "But now that they have it in Romania, Hungary and even France, I decided it was better that we did it, instead of having it imposed upon us."[49] Deputy Speaker Dimiter Peshev, who supported the bill, admitted in his diary that he only did so to pay lip service to Germany. "The interest of [our] policy with Germany, policy from which we expected the achievements of basic national and political goals, could justify certain temporary restrictive measures against the Jews, if they could help that policy. Nobody, though, agreed or admitted that these measures could be permanent, or that they would take the dimensions and form applied by the Germans."[50]

This shield philosophy ("I did it to avoid worse") and the realpolitik of antisemitism ("Let us pass such measures temporarily to achieve our aims, but with no intention of full enactment") thrived during World War II, and always with bloody results. Remarkably, few Bulgarians accepted the bill or its rationale. The law is "unnecessary, harmful, and opposed to our principles of right and justice," the Bulgarian Lawyers Association declared in an open letter to parliament. "A Law that would enslave a part of the Bulgarian citizens will remain a black page in our new history,"[51] wrote twenty-one Bulgarian writers and poets in a letter to the prime minister. The Bulgarian Orthodox Church, through its bishops, warned that while nations have the right to defend themselves, "in this justified effort they shouldn't admit injustice and violence against others."[52] The law stood, but it clearly lacked popular support.

The Germans, however, knew how persuasive greed could be. Hitler offered King Boris what the Bulgarians had long desired: access to the Aegean. Bulgaria joined the Tripartite Pact on 1 March 1941, and German troops moved into the country. By allowing the German army a base for the invasion of Greece and Yugoslavia, Bulgarians received all the territories they ever had believed were theirs. With the addition of Thrace and Macedonia, even anti-German Bulgarians were ecstatic. "We were all intoxicated by the idea that for the first time in history we would get our just due, which we had demanded in vain for so long," one anti-German reflected. "All of us, from the most extreme nationalist to the Communists, were satisfied over the successes which Hitler's New Order in the Balkans had brought."[53]

Lucky Bulgaria. It achieved all of its territorial goals before Operation Barbarossa, leaving Germany little leverage to force Bulgarians into action against

Russia. Withstanding a lot of German pressure, Bulgaria never became a full partner in the Axis, nor did it send troops into areas beyond what it considered "Greater Bulgaria." This augured well for the Jews in Old Bulgaria. Alas, the 15,000 Jews in the annexed territories of Thrace and Macedonia were not afforded the same protection—indeed, they were not protected at all.[54]

IF BULGARIA was lucky and reasonably content, Yugoslavia was the soul of misfortune and internal discontents. Created at the end of World War I as the Kingdom of Serbs, Croats, and Slovenes, the new country took in the kingdoms of Serbia and Montenegro; the former Hapsburg territories of Slovenia and Croatia; and Bosnia-Herzegovina with its turbulent nineteenth-century history of nationalism—claimed by Serbia, but occupied (1878) and then annexed (1908) by Austria Hungary—which had led to the incident that triggered World War I.

That war—the Great War—had resolved nothing. Serbs and Montenegrans were Greek Orthodox and had fought on the Allied side. Slovenes and Croats, Roman Catholic, had joined the Central Powers. Each area had its own legal, educational, and political traditions. To complicate matters, Bosnia-Herzegovina and the Serbian province of Kosovo had a large Muslim minority population, and neighboring states near and far (Germany, Hungary, Romania, Turkey, Bulgaria, Italy) laid claim to their respective ethnic peoples living in every one of these areas.[55]

Frustrated by a decade's futile effort to integrate his polyglot state, King Alexander gave up on democracy in 1928 and established a royal dictatorship. He changed the name of the country to Yugoslavia to emphasize the unity of the population, and he introduced a pro-Yugoslavian nationalism and anti-regional chauvinism program. In response, the Croat nationalist Ante Pavelić founded an underground organization, the *Ustashe* ("Rebellion"), which preached Croat independence, and used terrorism to achieve that goal. It was a basic tenet of the Ustashe creed that no accommodation was possible between Croats and Serbs.[56]

King Alexander was murdered by a member of the Ustashe in 1934. Still, the country carried on under the prince regent, Paul. Then, as elsewhere on the continent, German aggression exerted great influence on the domestic situation well before the country itself was occupied. With the Anschluss of Austria, Germany drew nearer: it now had a common boundary with Yugoslavia. And with the Munich Agreement of 1938 and the division of Czechoslovakia, Croat separatists brazenly demanded the autonomy the Slovaks had gained. In this, they turned to Germany to help them.[57]

When war broke out in 1939, the Yugoslav government tried in vain to follow a policy of neutrality. But no one in the country was neutral, and everyone had different sympathies. The Serbs were Anglophile; the Croats admired Germany; many Montenegrins looked to Italy for support; and Macedonians to Bulgaria. None of it mattered. Germany was closing in. By the end of 1940, all of Yugoslavia's neighbors—except Greece, which was at war with Italy—were formally or informally part of the Axis.

In early 1941, Germany pressured Yugoslavia to join too. Mussolini's attack on Greece (28 October 1940) had been no *Blitzkrieg*. Aided by the British, the Greek army had repulsed the Italians. Mussolini needed Hitler's help, and Hitler wanted to launch his Greek operations from Yugoslavia. Choosing between the Axis or an invasion, the Yugoslav government joined the Tripartite Pact. Pro-British Serbian nationalists immediately revolted and took control of the country on 27 March 1941. The prince regent was exiled, and his nephew installed as King Peter II.[58]

Hitler exploded at this intolerable affront and ordered an attack. "The military Putsch in Yugoslavia has changed the political situation in the Balkans. Even if Yugoslavia at first should give declarations of loyalty, she must be considered as a foe and therefore be destroyed as quickly as possible."[59] Hitler meant every word. "Operation Punishment" began on 6 April 1941 with the bombing of Belgrade, which had been declared an open city and thus was undefended. Invaded by both Germany and Italy, the Yugoslav army capitulated on 17 April. Yugoslavia was no more. The Germans carved it up and served a piece each to Italy, Hungary, and Bulgaria.[60]

The eager Croatian nationalist Ante Pavelić had not waited for the surrender of his country; he had proclaimed the "Independent State of Croatia" a week earlier. What Pavelić meant by "independence" he explained to German foreign minister Ribbentrop's trusted troubleshooter for southeast Europe, Anton Veesenmeyer. Pavelić had only two wishes, Veesenmeyer reported to Berlin: first to obtain German recognition of Croatia; and second, an opportunity to thank Hitler in person and promise him "to live and die for the Führer."[61] Rewarding such sycophancy, Germany allowed the new "Independent State of Croatia" to take Bosnia and Herzegovina. But Pavelić was not to be master in his own house: Axis powers divided the new "state" into two occupation zones, one under Italian and the other under German authority.[62]

Ustashe ideology prevailed, however, and it demanded a nation-state. Some 2 million of the 6.3 million inhabitants of Independent Croatia were Serb, and they were targeted for systematic and ruthless elimination. The preferred method was conversion to Catholicism and absorption into the Croat community, or expulsion, but murder was acceptable. Other minorities, particularly the 40,000 Jews and 30,000 "Gypsies," were to be erased too, but conversion was not an option offered to them. A reign of terror ensued, led by the infamous Croat interior minister Andrija Artuković, well known for his slogan, "If you can't kill Serbs or Jews, you are an enemy of the state." The Ustashe stripped Serbs of their legal rights, their livelihood, and their property. They forced 200,000 to 300,000 to convert, expelled thousands more, and slaughtered some 350,000 Serb civilians of all ages.[63]

Vast numbers of Serbs fled to German-occupied Serbia, or into the mountains, where they created a resistance movement against the Ustashe and the Germans. But the Yugoslav Partisan movement was as divided as the country. Led by Colonel Draža Mihajlović, the Chetniks (from *ceta,* a group of men engaged in guerrilla warfare) were organized by royalist officers and soldiers. The Yugoslav government-in-exile in London recognized the Chetniks as the Yugoslav Army in the Homeland. The Chetniks, like the government-in-exile, were chauvinist Serbian nationalists; anti-Croatian and anti-Muslim. They were also undisciplined, poorly coordinated, and totally lacking in a vision for the national future. Remembering the massive Serb losses in World War I—20 percent of the population—Mihajlović's main goal was to save Serb lives. Intimidated by the Germans' policy to murder 100 Serb hostages for every German assassinated, and to kill 50 hostages for every German wounded, and appalled by the loss of more than 20,000 Serb hostages hanged or shot within half a year, Mihajlović sought to avoid engagement with the enemy.[64] This cozy arrangement between Mihajlović and the Germans did not deprive Germans of hostages, it merely changed the pool from which they were drawn. In October 1941 the German chief of civil administration in Serbia, Staatsrat Harald Turner, instructed local Wehrmacht commanders to avail themselves of "all Jewish men and all male Gypsies." This policy did not bring the Germans the territorial control they sought, but it had a collateral effect they found useful. "In the interests of pacification, the Gypsy question has been fully liquidated. Serbia is the only country in which the Jewish question and the Gypsy question has been solved,"[65] Turner reported to Berlin in 1942.

Turner was not exactly right: many Jews, Roma, and Sinti—as well as large numbers of Serbs—had joined the other main Partisan force, led by the Croat Josip Broz, known as Tito. Tito's group was Communist, and derived much benefit from the party's twenty years of experience as an underground, illegal organization. Unlike the Chetniks, Tito's Partisans turned no faction away, and envisioned a federal model to solve the country's ethnic tensions. Well organized, with able political and military leaders and good contacts with other left-wing groups, the Communists appealed to many sectors of Yugoslav society, especially young people. Tito's Partisans inspired confidence. Controlling ever-widening areas, they set up a government apparatus of their own that offered a much-needed sense of security. Nor was Tito in the least deterred by the Germans' reprisal policy. He captured the yearnings, aspirations, and imagination of the Yugoslav people; by 1944 some 800,000 men and women had joined his movement of armed resistance.[66]

Mihajlović tried to establish control over the Communist Partisans. But Tito refused to come in under the Chetnik umbrella. Desperate for power, the Chetniks requested help first from the Italians and then from the Germans. Initially opportunistic collaborators, they quickly became Axis auxiliaries, and the tensions between the two resistance organizations burst into full-scale hostilities which engulfed the country in a bloody civil war. Chetniks fought Tito's Partisans; the Partisans fought the Germans and Ustashis; and the Ustashe fought everyone but ethnic Croats and Germans.

The prominent Italian Fascist writer Curzio Malaparte visited occupied

Croatia as a correspondent for the *Corriere della Sera*. Introduced to Ante Pavelić, he was invited to call on the *Poglavnik* (leader), as Pavelić styled himself, with Raffaelle Casertano, the Italian ambassador. The war had escalated by that point. "The partisan bands had pushed by night into the very suburbs of Zagreb, but the loyal *ustashis* of Pavelić would soon quash those tiresome guerrillas," Malaparte predicted. Pavelić commented upon the situation, and his role.

> "The Croatian people," said Ante Pavelič, "wish to be ruled with goodness and justice. I am here to provide them."
> While he spoke, I gazed at the wicker basket on the Poglavnik's desk. The lid was raised and the basket seemed to be filled with mussels, or shelled oysters—as they are occasionally displayed in the windows of Fortnum and Mason in Piccadilly in London. Casertano looked at me and winked, "Would you like a nice oyster stew?"
> "Are they Dalmatian oysters?" I asked the Poglavnik.
> Ante Pavelič removed the lid from the basket and revealed the mussels, that slimy and jelly-mass, and smiling, with that tired good-natured smile of his, "It is a present from my loyal *ustashis*. Forty pounds of human eyes."[67]

In the end, Yugoslavia paid a staggering price for German occupation and the internal strife that it unleashed. Of the 14 million Yugoslavs alive in 1940, 1.5 million were dead by 1945, some 11 percent of the population. This casualty rate was second only to Poland. But in Poland, half the victims were Jews and they were killed by the Germans. In Yugoslavia, the Jews accounted for but 3 percent of the victims. Thus, while the Germans certainly murdered hundreds of thousands of Yugoslavs, that unhappy nation participated in its own decimation.

HITLER INVADED Greece the same day as Yugoslavia, and had far greater success than his ally, Mussolini. Envy overcame *il Duce*. After patronizing Hitler in the 1920s, Mussolini had watched Germany devour great chunks of central Europe in 1938 and early 1939. Why couldn't Italy conquer as well?[68] In April 1939, he ordered the army to invade Albania, which was overrun in a day and annexed immediately. Satisfying enough; but then Mussolini sat on the sidelines when Hitler moved against Poland. A traditional agricultural society, Italy had a crippling lack of raw materials, a weak scientific and technological base, and a small class of entrepreneurs with no access to capital. Fascists could bellow with the best of them, but Italy simply did not have the resources necessary for war. The Germans asked the Italians what they needed and, as Mussolini's son-in-law Count Ciano admitted in his diary, "It's enough to kill a bull—if a bull could read." He continued, "I remain alone with the Duce and we prepare a message to Hitler. We explain to him why it is that our needs are so vast, and we

33. Ustashi soldiers pose with the severed head of their victim, 1942. Muzej Revolucije Naradnosti Jugoslavije, courtesy of the United States Holocaust Memorial Museum Photo Archives, Washington, DC.

conclude by saying that Italy absolutely cannot enter the war without such provisions." Hitler replied that he would "annihilate Poland and beat France and Britain without help."[69]

When Germany conquered Denmark and Norway, Mussolini fumed. "It is humiliating to remain with our hands folded while others write history," he complained to his son-in-law. "To make a people great it is necessary to send them into battle even if you have to kick them in the pants. That is what I shall do." Still, Mussolini restrained himself: he declared war on France and Britain only after the former had fallen and the latter had been pushed off the continent. Those countries were not in Italy's orbit anyway, but Romania was. And when Germany marched on Bucharest, Mussolini grew indignant. "Hitler always faces me with a *fait accompli*," he seethed. "This time I am going to pay him back in his own coin. He will find out from the papers that I have occupied Greece. In this way the equilibrium will be re-established."[70]

Nothing of the sort occurred, but Hitler did learn of Italy's Greek adventure in a way most suited to annoy him. On the train to Berlin from a disastrous meeting with Franco (who had refused to join the Axis) and a useless meeting with Pétain at Montoire, Hitler heard that Mussolini was about to invade Greece, and ordered the engineer to change direction and head for Florence. Three hours north of the city, news reached him that the invasion had started. Hitler was furious. "Never will the Italians be able to do much against the Greeks in the Balkans during the autumn rains and winter snows," Ribbentrop recalled him to have said. Mussolini did not let him talk about it. For seven hours Hitler was shuttled about the tourist sites: lunch at Palazzo Medici, a concert at Palazzo Pitti, and a museum tour through the Palazzo Vecchio.

The *Duce* may have outflanked Hitler diplomatically, but the Italian army needed German muscle. Its invasion quickly turned into a retreat that left the Greeks with half of Albania. For twenty years Italy's Fascists had declared that there was only one true test of a man or a nation: war. And Mussolini had lost his war. His alternatives, as Winston Churchill explained in a radio broadcast to the Italian people on 23 December 1940, were to stand up alone to the Greeks and the British, or "to call in Attila over the Brenner Pass with his hordes of ravenous soldiery and his gangs of Gestapo policemen to occupy, hold down, and protect the Italian people, for whom he and his Nazi followers cherish the most bitter and outspoken contempt that is on record between races."[71]

Mussolini chose Attila, and the Führer invaded on 6 April 1941. By the end of the month, the Greek government had abandoned the mainland for Crete, Athens stood occupied, and resistance had collapsed. General Georgios Tsolakoglu, commander of the Western Macedonian Army, became prime minister of a collaborationist regime controlled by the German and Italian plenipotentiaries. The Italians, whom the Greeks despised, occupied most of their country, and the Germans, whom the Greeks loathed, held Athens and Salonika with its strategically important hinterland. Bulgaria got Thrace.

Germany plundered Greece ruthlessly and systematically of its foodstuffs and raw materials. Such expropriation led to a rapid collapse of the Greek economy. Factories closed for lack of raw materials, or because their equipment and stock were shipped to Germany. Public transport came to a halt.[72]

Food grew scarce. By the end of 1941, the Greeks lived on a mere one-third of the minimum daily nutritional requirement and the country sank into famine. People simply collapsed and died in the streets, the corpses left there until municipal carts made their collection rounds. Starvation affected morale and mood. "We are all quick to anger," one man observed in his diary. "I feel faint when I'm in a crowd. I want to hit whoever is in front of me." "Nothing has any importance today except the question of food—or rather hunger," a young Athenian lawyer lamented. Some 100,000 people died of starvation in the famine of 1941–42. This, the Greeks believed, revealed a deliberate German policy of genocide. "Greeks . . . accuse [the Germans] of destroying food rather than letting the Greeks have it," a Swiss woman who left Salonika in December 1941 reported, "they are convinced that hunger is the Germans' 'secret weapon' and that this is being systematically used against them for the purpose of their deliberate extermination." It was, she felt, "a logical appraisal of German behavior in Greece since the invasion of Russia."[73] Logical, but not correct. The Germans simply did not care what happened to the Greeks. They took whatever was useful to keep the Reich going on the warfront and the homefront. If occupied populations died of starvation, exposure, and infectious diseases, it could not be helped. The needs of the *Herrenvolk* were what mattered.

IF THE GERMANS' policy in Greece was bloody but pragmatic, their policy in Russia was fueled by violent racism. It was in the Soviet Union, not Greece, that the Germans used famine as a genocidal weapon. For Hitler, the German-Soviet Pact of 1939 was merely a temporary expedient. On Sunday, 22 June 1941, the Wehrmacht surprised its neighbor and ally with Operation Barbarossa, an all-out offensive.[74] Here was a different war. The subjugation of Poland was meant to right the wrongs of Versailles. The attack on Russia was a geopolitical assault to conquer *Lebensraum* in the East, and an ideological crusade to destroy the Judeo-Bolshevik conspiracy to rule the world.[75] As German troops sped toward the heart of Russia enjoying victory after stunning victory, Franz Lüdtke, the National Socialist historian of the German East, wrote a book distributed to soldiers portraying the war as a European-German-National Socialism vs. Asian-Jewish-Bolshevik conflict. "As these lines are written we witness the final confrontation in the European East," he told the men. "All the destructive forces of the space stretching east of our nation's soul into Asia have gathered in the crucible of Bolshevism, from which a wind of destruction blows. Under the command of the Führer, Germany has become the savior not only of German culture but of all of Western culture." Operation Barbarossa was a death struggle between good and evil, the forces of light against the forces of darkness, the *Übermensch* versus the *Untermensch*. "German National Socialism and Jewish Bolshevism could not coexist. One had to yield."[76]

This was no mere propaganda for army privates. It expressed an ideology that had shaped decisions about the Russian campaign months before the invasion, and it embodied the position of Germany's political and military leadership.[77] "Clash of two ideologies," General Franz Halder explained in his diary after he and other generals had met with Hitler on 30 March 1941. "Communism is an enormous danger for our future. We must forget the idea of comradeship between soldiers. . . . This is a war of extermination."[78]

Nazi leaders and the German high command planned carefully for military contingencies and for

Europe
January 1943

economic exploitation of the territory they aimed to gain. But they deliberately made no arrangements for administration of the conquered land. They meant to eliminate every vestige of the Soviet state structure. There would be no districts, no provinces, no republics—and no rights, no form of autonomy, and no personal freedom. Every Soviet would be completely at the mercy of German authorities.

German soldiers would be fed at the expense of Russia. The army calculated rather precisely that implementation of this policy would kill 30 million people.[79] This was not cold-blooded exploitation, as in Greece. This was genocide. As Göring remarked to Ciano, "This year between twenty and thirty million persons will die in Russia of hunger. Perhaps it is well that it should be so, for certain nations must be decimated."[80]

Germans had expected a short campaign, and at first their *Blitzkrieg* technique promised just that. The Wehrmacht, with the *Einsatzgruppen* right behind, overran much of the Ukraine, Byelorussia, Lithuania, Latvia, and Estonia in just three weeks. By the beginning of September, German troops camped at the gates of Leningrad. But Hitler had lost valuable time in Yugoslavia and Greece. And the Soviet Union was a huge country, and Stalin a formidable foe. Stalin's scorched-earth policy made it impossible for the Wehrmacht to live off the land and the October autumn rains wreaked havoc with the Germans' supply lines. The rutted roads of August became mud-traps for German quartermaster trucks by November. Exhausted and plagued with infrastructure problems, the German army failed to reach Moscow before the winter frost set in. The Soviets, meanwhile, had raised new troops, and there the Russian front line from Leningrad to Rostov-on-Don stood firm in the winter of 1941.

Even so, a tremendous amount of territory and a great number of people came under German rule. The Baltic states and Byelorussia were put together in what the Germans called *Reichskommissariat Ostland* (Reich East Lands Administration). The western Ukraine, which had been Polish before 1939, now was added to the General Government, while the rest of the Ukraine became *Reichskommissariat Ukraine* (Reich Ukraine Administration). The area to the east of Ostland and Ukraine was placed under military government, and Bessarabia and northern Bukovina were returned to Romania, which also received Transnistria.[81]

In the first six months of Operation Barbarossa, Germany captured two-fifths of the Soviet civilian population and 3 million Soviet soldiers. In its conduct of the Soviet campaign, Germany simply ignored the Geneva conventions and longstanding international custom. Denied prisoner of war status, some 2 million Soviet soldiers were murdered in their first year of captivity: 600,000 killed outright, and the rest dead from exposure to the weather, starvation, and disease.[82] The army made its position clear: "the special situation of the Eastern campaign . . . demands special measures." Gone were "the regulations and orders concerning prisoners-of-war" which were based "solely on military objectives"; now "a political objective must be attained, which is to protect the German nation from Bolshevik inciters."[83]

The Soviet people soon learned the fate of their captured sons, husbands, and brothers, and they learned that German brutality did not stop at the battlefield. Following the model established in Poland and copied elsewhere in occupied Europe, Soviet civilians were terrorized with dragnet operations for the

Russeneinsatz (Russian Service). Between 1942 and 1944, 2.8 million Russian civilian women and men were deported for forced labor in German mines, the armaments industry, agriculture, and for railroad maintenance. These were forced, not slave, laborers: they received a tiny pittance of a wage. But they were not allowed to use public facilities or participate in public or social life in any way; sexual contact with a German was punishable by death.[84]

As German hopes faded for a quick victory in Russia and the Reich mobilized all its resources to carry on, the dragnets increased. In 1942, 2.6 million foreign civilians and 1.5 million prisoners of war were working in Germany; in 1944, the numbers had risen to 5.3 million foreign civilians and 1.8 million POWs. The largest group was Soviet (2.8 million), followed by Poles (1.7) and French (1.3). By that time, nearly one of every four workers in Germany was a forced laborer. It was the greatest use of such labor since the abolition of slavery in America.[85]

These workers lived in 20,000 miserable camps across the Reich. The slave labor camps were run according to Nazi racist ideology: nationals of western countries were paid better, got rations that kept them alive, and their working conditions were no worse than those of German workers. The *Untermensch* of the east got watery turnip soup three times a day and a tiny ration of bread. They toiled long hours with little rest under unsafe and unhygienic conditions. Infectious disease, especially tuberculosis, ran wild.

With famine rampant at home, their young men dying in battle and in POW compounds, and mass deportations to slave labor camps a common occurrence, more Soviets turned to armed resistance.[86] By now, German policy toward partisans was well established. The Germans fought them ruthlessly, using unarmed civilians as pawns. That did not stop the partisans. They carried on their fight against the German enemy, with no consideration for the needs or safety of the local population. As in Yugoslavia, the German reprisal policy was one hundred Russians dead for every soldier shot. Collective punishment was the rule. Villages near partisan attacks were burned, all the men killed, and the women and children left to fend for themselves without food or shelter, or to be murdered by the SS. "It must be borne in mind, whatever the cir-

34. Two destitute war orphans, Ukraine, 1942. Photo H. Hoeffke. Courtesy Bildarchiv Preussischer Kulturbesitz, Berlin.

cumstances, that the collapse of Germany in 1918, the subsequent sufferings of the German people, and the fight against National Socialism which cost the blood of innumerable supporters of the Movement, were caused primarily by Bolshevik influence," the German high command reminded the soldiers.[87]

GERMAN RULE in the Soviet Union was ferocious, and the various nationalities in this area—Russians, Ukrainians, Belorussians, Lithuanians, Latvians,
and Estonians—suffered terribly. The local peoples were at the mercy of the
Germans, as were the Jews. The Jews in the German-occupied part of the Soviet
Union, unlike their co-religionists in Bulgaria, Hungary, or even Romania and
Slovakia, had no recourse to local officials who might have had a bit of sympathy. For protection, they could only look to their gentile neighbors—and many
of these were antisemites.

Most of the area under German occupation had belonged to the czarist Pale
of Settlement, densely populated by Jews and permeated with popular antisemitism. Home to pogroms before World War I and massacres by the White
Armies during the Civil War, the Pale was transfigured under Soviet rule. The
Communists destroyed Jewish communal organizations and restructured the
economy, pushing Jews out of trades and crafts and into industry. Thus Soviets
had solved the czar's "Jewish Problem" through forced assimilation. Antisemitism was dead as a political issue; indeed it was a crime against the state. Yet
popular, spontaneous antisemitism, driven underground, did not diminish. The
peasants claimed that Jews were to blame for the devastation of the Ukraine by
the Moscow-engineered famine in the early 1930s, and the repressive measures
thereafter.

Lithuanians and Latvians nourished their own special rage against the Jews,
who had benefited by the annexation of those countries by the Soviet Union in
1940. Immediately after the German invasion in June 1941, Lithuanian nationalists hoping to gain an independent state if they showed sufficient vigor in solving their "Jewish Problem," intellectuals and former military and government
officials who had lost their positions under Soviet rule, and opportunists hungry for Jewish property, all began to massacre Jews wherever they could find
them.[88] Pleasantly surprised, the Germans reported back to Berlin that "the attitude of the Lithuanian population is friendly towards the German so far."

> They help the German soldiers, the police officials, and the other organiza-
> tions already functioning in this area as much as possible. Their cooperation
> consists chiefly in looking for and turning over Lithuanian Communists, dis-
> persed Red Army soldiers, and Jews. After the retreat of the Red Army, the
> population of Kaunas [Kovno] killed about 2,500 Jews during a spontaneous
> uprising. In addition, a rather large number of Jews was shot by Auxiliary
> Police Service.[89]

The Latvians, however, disappointed their invaders at first. "Unlike the
Lithuanians who have an active attitude, the Latvians are hesitatingly organiz-
ing and forming a front against the Jews."[90] The occupation regime blitzed the
Latvians with propaganda. The Jews were blamed for Latvian suffering under
Soviet rule. The Germans exhumed mass graves of Latvians killed by Soviet

secret police and pointed their fingers at the Jews. And then the occupiers opened the purse wide and urged Latvians to loot Jewish property—and keep it.[91] With so much prodding, the Latvians got their act together. "Self-cleansing operations" had been late in starting, the Germans observed, but by August all Latvian towns had now seen "pogroms, destruction of synagogues, and liquidation of Jews and Communists."[92]

The Ukrainians who inhabited the southern part of Soviet-annexed Poland and the Soviet Republic of Ukraine proved a frustration. "In the first hours after the Bolshevik withdrawal, the Ukrainian population displayed commendable activity against the Jews,"[93] an intelligence officer noted. The Ukrainians "hate the Jews from the depths of their soul," another added. "But they will not expend the energy, given their present mood, to proceed towards the total destruction of the remaining Jews."[94] How baffling. The Ukrainians hated the Jews and approved German measures against them. Nevertheless, "almost nowhere could the population be induced to take active steps against the Jews."[95] The complaint persisted. By the end of October, the Germans had given up on the Ukrainians. Despite all efforts, "[Ukrainians are] still indifferent to such an extent that often we Germans simply do not understand."[96]

Lacking a strong nationalist movement to start with, and having no expectations for a German-sponsored independent state, the Belorussians had no special reason to show devotion to the German cause and no political motivation to go after the Jews. Indeed, the Belorussians never became really enthusiastic about doing so. They simply were unable, German intelligence claimed, "to take the initiative in regard to the treatment of the Jews."[97]

By the end of 1941, Lithuanian, Latvian, and Ukrainian expectations of independence, or even autonomy, had not materialized. The peasants, who had hoped that a thorough land reform would reverse Soviet collectivization, were disappointed also. The Germans, whom they had greeted so happily, shocked and dismayed them. And so they focused on daily survival, on holding out. So did the rest of the Soviet Union. The Muscovites and Leningraders prevailed; neither city fell that crucial winter of 1941–42. Stalemated by the Soviets, the German army in the summer of 1942 tried to go south to the Caucasus and Stalingrad. But the six months that a Russian winter had bought for Stalin proved enough. Stiff Soviet resistance forged into a powerful offensive. Slowly but surely, the Russian army pushed the Germans out of the Soviet Union. By the summer of 1943, the German advance had become a full-scale retreat. And as the eastern front crumbled, Italy collapsed as an ally.

ITALY'S RELATIONS with Nazi Germany had always been tangled. Italian fascism had inspired Nazism in the 1920s, but fascism, unlike Nazism, was not inherently racist or antisemitic.[98] The question of the Jews, so central to National Socialism, was rarely discussed in Italy—and then only to assert that no "Jewish Problem" existed.[99]

A year before Hitler came to power, the well-known German Jewish writer Emil Ludwig published a series of interviews with the *Duce*. Translated by the Italian government into twelve languages, *Talks with Mussolini* became an authorized biography. Mussolini was not reticent about his views on race. "I shall never believe that the degree of purity of race can be biologically proved. It is odd that the prophets of the so-called nobility of the German race were none of them Germans. ... National Pride needs no delirium of race," he told Ludwig. When asked specifically about antisemitism, Mussolini replied, "we have none in Italy," and went on to say, "Jewish Italians have always been good citizens and fought bravely as soldiers. They occupy eminent positions in universities, banks, and the army. Quite a number are generals."[100]

In Italy, antisemitism was not encouraged by the monarchy, the Catholic Church, or the Fascist Party. Jews were welcomed into the party, and they held prominent positions in state government. So strong was Mussolini's position on this matter, and so confident was he in his relations with the junior Hitler, that he instructed the Italian ambassador in Berlin to protest the Führer's treatment of Germany's Jews.

In the mid-1930s Italy and Germany grew closer, a poor augury for the Italian Jews. Germany supported Italy when it suffered inter-

The war aims of a Greater Germanic Reich

national isolation after its invasion and conquest of Abyssinia and, in 1937, both
nations went to Franco's aid in the Spanish Civil War. Despite their declaration
of mutual loyalty with the Pact of Steel in May 1939, however, Italy did not join
Germany in the attack on Poland, and indeed remained neutral until June 1940.
By this point, Germany clearly had emerged as the senior partner and Mussolini

tried to right that balance with an ill-fated invasion of Egypt in September 1940, followed by his equally disastrous adventure in Greece a month later. In both cases, the Italians were about to lose to the British when the Germans intervened. By the end of 1940, Italy depended on Germany to conduct war. In exchange for labor and foodstuffs, it received German fuel and raw materials.

The increased political and military dependency between 1937 and 1940 brought an antisemitic program in its wake. Ludwig's *Talks with Mussolini* was withdrawn from circulation in the summer of 1938 and the *Manifesto della razza* (*Race Manifesto*), written with Mussolini's blessing, was published instead.[101] In part, the *Manifesto* was meant to justify Italy's racism in staking out an African empire: the pragmatic value of racism. But Mussolini also needed to maintain Hitler's goodwill: the strategic value of racism. "Jews do not belong to the Italian race," the authors of the *Manifesto* averred. "The Jews represent the only population that can never be assimilated in Italy, because they are constituted of non-European racial elements, absolutely different from the elements that gave origin to the Italians."[102]

35. Propaganda photo of Mussolini (left) and Hitler (right) illustrating their comradeship, as echoed in the sculpture by Josef Thorak, Berlin, 1938.

Pope Pius XI, leader of the largest organization in the world to hold as a tenet of its faith the equality of all souls, responded immediately, publicly decrying the *Manifesto* as a "disgraceful imitation" of Hitler's mythology.[103] King Victor Emmanuel was equally aghast but, too timid for confrontation, made his remarks privately. "It passes my comprehension how a great man like him can import these racial fashions from Berlin into Italy. Yet he must understand that if he falls into the German rut, he will range himself against the Church, the bourgeoisie, and the army high command."[104]

Mussolini proceeded nevertheless, and evidently with gusto. A series of decrees on 1 and 2 September flowed forth relating to foreign-born Jews living in Italy; one of them excluded all persons of the "Jewish race" from teaching positions in the state schools. Jews also were banned from all scientific, literary, and artistic bodies. On 6 October 1942, the Fascist Grand Council resolved that Italians were forbidden to marry Jews, and Jews were forbidden to own more than 50 hectares (123 acres) of land, to direct enterprises with more than one hundred employees, or to serve in the armed forces.

Italian Catholics were shocked and Italian Jews were stunned. Then, both began to adapt. Years later, Laura Fermi, the Jewish wife of physicist Enrico Fermi, remembered a harsh irony—an invitation had arrived from Columbia University; although well protected by Fermi's world-famous status, the couple decided it was time to emigrate; Fermi accepted. One day in November, the Fermis went shopping to convert their savings into expensive items they were permitted to take abroad: a fur coat, watches. They returned home in the late afternoon and turned on the news.

> Hard, emphatic, pitiless, the commentator's voice read the second set of racial laws. The laws issued that day limited the activities and civil status of the Jews. Their children were excluded from public schools, Jewish teachers were dismissed. Jewish lawyers, physicians, and other professionals could practice for Jewish clients only. Many Jewish firms were dissolved. "Aryan" servants were not allowed to work for Jews or to live in their homes. Jews were to be deprived of full citizenship rights, and their passports would be withdrawn.[105]

The telephone rang a few minutes later. It was Stockholm calling. Enrico Fermi had just been awarded the Nobel Prize for physics in honor of his discovery of "new radioactive substances belonging to the entire race of elements. . . ." It was a new twist on the concept of race for the Fermis that day.

Laura Fermi's position was unique, of course: no other Italian Jew was married to an Italian Nobel laureate at the time. The situation of fifteen-year-old Mariella Milano-Piperno was much more typical. Her parents tried to "sweeten the pill" of Mussolini's fascism, she explained decades later, but after passage in November 1938 of the racial laws which excluded her from school she felt "marginalized." That was, she said, the heart of the matter. "The day that we could not return to school, I remember that I was ashamed before my companions, to tell them: I cannot come because I am a Jewish girl." And then the questions came. "Why? What did I do not to be allowed to go to school?"[106]

Like other Italian Jewish families, the Pipernos had two choices: send their children to a Catholic school with its Catholic rituals, or to a non-denominational private school designed for remedial students who had to repeat a year, having failed in the public schools. Rome—and many other cities in Italy—had a Jewish primary school (grades one through five), but there was little in the way of Jewish secondary education. To meet that need, a number of Jewish communities organized schools for their young people; they were taught by the very teachers and professors dismissed by the same racial laws.[107]

Mariella Piperno's family considered the matter carefully. They wished Mariella and her sister to live as normal a life as possible and to continue to go

to school with Catholic Italian children. Furthermore, the children's grandmother, who was rather elderly at the time, "remembered all that the Jews had
suffered in the ghetto [of Rome] when it was closed [until 1870], and she
remembered with terror that fact of being enclosed all together." She urged her
granddaughters, "'Now that we have obtained liberty, why don't you profit by
it, revel in it! Why must you enclose yourselves once again?'" For two months
Mariella Piperno attended a non-denominational private school, but the education she received was so poor that she soon enrolled in the Jewish high school.[108]

By all accounts La Scuola Ebraica di Roma, like its counterparts elsewhere,
was an extraordinary institution. It provided three courses: an academic high
school, a technical institute, and a teachers' training school, and functioned for
five academic years, from 1938 through 1943. According to Italian law it was
accredited by the state, and its principal, a state employee, was an "Aryan."

When we went to the Jewish School, Mariella Piperno explained, "we asked:
'Who are we? What does it mean to be Jews?'" They, who had been assimilated
before and lived among Catholics all their lives, now were on the outside. What
to make of that? They faced these questions when they were together at the
Jewish School and in doing so they learned that Judaism was not a religion
alone. "This was the great discovery of the Jewish School: when we began to
understand that to be Jewish was not only to be of the Jewish religion. A Jewish culture existed, a Jewish civilization existed, that, in other words, all that is
meant by Judaism existed. And this was very important. In my opinion, the
Jewish School was like the opening of a book for us, and we began to read in
this book which had been completely closed to us before."[109] Many of their professors were renowned; Emma Castelnuovo taught mathematics, for instance,
and Monferrini history and philosophy. These last subjects they had to relearn
completely, having previously been taught according to Fascist ideology.

Many Italian Catholics were disgusted by the Provisions for the Defense of
the Italian Race, as the legislation of 17 November 1938 was called, among them
Victor Emmanuel III. "I found the Duce in a state of indignation against the
King," Ciano reported on 28 November. "Three times in the course of their
conversation this morning the King said to him that he feels an 'infinite pity for
the Jews.'... The Duce said that there are 20,000 spineless people in Italy who
are moved by the fate of the Jews. The King replied that he is one of them."[110]

Il Duce had underestimated the number of "spineless people." Italy was not
Germany. The antisemitic legislation was not popular and, enacted in a country where people laughed at the government, the severity of the policy was mit-
igated by the practice of Italian life. As we shall see, the fury of persecution held
off until the German invasion five years later.

MUSSOLINI REMAINED tied to Hitler for the rest of his short life, but in fact,
Italian fascism soon saw the beginning of the end. Muddling in Africa, defeated
in Greece, fascism lost the popular support that had brought it to power in 1922.

To save the regime—not the country—Mussolini allowed Italy to become Germany's "vassal," as Churchill put it in a broadcast in April 1941.[111] Whatever shred of enthusiasm the Italians still had for war in 1942 froze in the snows of Russia and evaporated in the north African deserts. Agents of the royal family approached the Allies about a possible armistice in December 1942, but no deal was possible with Mussolini still in power, and he wasn't going anywhere.

War, the basic principle of his political philosophy, proved his undoing. Italian troops suffered disastrous losses in early 1943. Italian civilians endured heavy Allied bomber attacks. In March, some 100,000 workers struck in Turin to express their disgust with the war and the regime. "All participate, Fascists and anti-Fascists," the chief of police observed. Still, Mussolini hung on until Sicily was invaded by Allied forces that summer. Dismissed by the Fascist Grand Council, the *Duce* was arrested on July 25 and interned. Three days later, the Fascist Party itself was dissolved.

Hitler was not persuaded by Mussolini's successor Marshal Pietro Badoglio's promise to continue the war and to maintain the Rome-Berlin Axis. In fact, as Goebbels confided to his diary (27 July), events in Italy posed a threat to the Nazi regime.

> It is quite obvious that the German people are uneasy and deeply distressed because we can't tell them anything at present about the background of the Italian crisis. What are we to tell them anyway? We can't say, much less write, what we think personally. Anything we can write will fail to explain the Italian crisis to our people. We must therefore be satisfied for the present with publishing the momentous news without telling the people that the question at issue in Rome is not only Mussolini's resignation but a very profound organic and ideological crisis of Fascism, perhaps even its liquidation. Knowledge of these events might conceivably encourage some subversive elements here in Germany to think that they could put over the same thing here that Badoglio and his henchmen accomplished in Rome.[112]

As Hitler suspected, Badoglio began to negotiate secretly with the Allies. An armistice was signed on 3 September 1943 and made public on 9 September when Allied troops landed on the mainland at Salerno. Furious but not surprised, Hitler ordered the sixteen German divisions stationed in Italy to disarm Italian troops and occupy the country, and he annexed a chunk of the country to the Reich. Mussolini was liberated in a daring raid by the Germans, and allowed to set up a born-again Fascist government, the Republica Sociale Italiana, headquartered in the resort town of Salò on Lake Garda, less than ten miles from the new Italian-German border. There the *Duce* lived, in the words of Goebbels, "a life of make-believe and struts around in a heroic pose that has no place in the world of realities."[113]

Mussolini, once held in awe by Hitler, was now held in contempt. "The

Führer now realizes that Italy never was a power, is no power today, and won't be a power in the future," Goebbels wrote. "Italy has abdicated as a people and as a nation."[114] The Italian Social Republic was nothing more than a facade for an occupation regime bathed in disdain. Demobilized Italian soldiers were sent by the hundreds of thousands to the Reich, where they were treated as enemy forced laborers. Italian civilians suffered the terror, hunger, dearth of goods, and loss of freedom common throughout the German-occupied continent: That was Hitler's New Europe.[115]

With Germans in the north and the Allies in the south, Italy became a battleground. A partisan movement called the *resistenza armata* (armed resistance movement) sprang into life in German-occupied areas, made up of soldiers seeking to escape German captivity, young people on the run from Mussolini's new army, villagers, factory workers, Communists and conservatives, Catholics and secular citizens—some 200,000 in total. More passionate about fighting against the Fascists and the Germans than they had been about fighting as Fascists for the government, the partisans took to the mountains in Emilia, the Piedmont, and the Veneto. "Beaten, abandoned, betrayed, they still knew, on their own, how to find the proper path of revolt—alone, without propaganda, in a rush of faith," admired Davido Lajolo, a Fascist officer who had fought in Spain.[116]

The Germans retaliated—as always—with bloody reprisals against the civilian population. But Italian partisans—as others elsewhere—continued their attacks, to aid and abet the Allied advance. As the Allies mounted the boot of Italy, from Salerno (September '43) to Naples (October) to the German-held north: Rome (June '44), Florence (August), and, finally, Bologna (April '45), the land was laid waste by fighting, and 15 percent of Italy's Jews were murdered.

ITALY HAD MANAGED a separate peace with the Allies in 1943 before the Germans invaded. Hungary, another reluctant German ally, failed to pull that off a year later. By that point, everyone knew that Germany would be defeated. But when? Hitler would not surrender. Horthy, by contrast, very much wished to lay down arms and sue for peace; he had only wanted territory. Correctly interpreting the refusal of Horthy's government to deport the Jews as a sign of disengagement from the Reich and rapprochement with the Allies, Hitler forced Horthy to accept a German shadow government. Hitler "objected to the fact that Hungary has not yet introduced the steps necessary to settle the Jewish question. We are accused, therefore, of the crime of not having carried out Hitler's wishes, and I am charged with not having permitted the Jews to be massacred," Horthy reported to the Crown Council after his command visit to the Führer in March 1944.[117] German tanks rolled into Budapest five months later.

In total, some 265 million people fell under occupation of the Greater Reich during World War II. Few of them believed that Germany would so thoroughly violate international law. They had the experience of history: France had been occupied by Germany in 1870–71. Both France and Belgium lived under German rule during World War I. In neither case had the occupations been violent. Why should 1939 and 1940 be any different? Many among the political and social elites, the judiciary and civil bureaucracy, at first sincerely believed it was their job to accommodate the occupying power.

Such placid assumptions quickly disappeared. Although the Germans did not know what their National Socialist "New Order" was to be, they were very clear that they wanted absolute authority. Violating article 43 of the Hague Convention, they assumed plenary legislative powers. "If someone asks today, what do you think of the New Europe, we have to answer that we don't know," Goebbels admitted to German journalists on 5 April 1940. "Let us first have power, then people will see, and we will see too, what we can make of it."[118]

What Germany made of it was the greatest catastrophe in the history of western civilization.

Chapter Eight

JEWISH LIFE UNDER
GERMAN OCCUPATION

"IT WAS A FRIDAY; September 1, 1939," Sara Grossman-Weil, a twenty-year-old at the time, recalled nearly half a century later. "The Germans invaded Poland and came into Lodz. I did not comprehend it, and I couldn't believe that there is actually a war going on."[1]

"I had a choice," she continued. She was supposed to start her studies at the Hebrew University in Jerusalem.

> I could have gone to Palestine; I could have left because I had all the papers. It wasn't that difficult a decision for me. I knew I wouldn't go because I didn't want to go; I didn't want to leave my family. . . .
>
> There was a panic and a tremendous worry in everyone's home: what will happen to each and every one of us? And above everything else, the worry was about the men. The Germans, as soon as they came into Lodz, they had all the cooperation of the Germans who lived in Lodz. By this time every little German boy who was seven or ten years old had his Jew at whom he wanted to point his finger. He had a Jewish family that he accused of being the enemy of this German state. Walking in the street was extremely dangerous, but there we had to walk because people were still going to work. And young men and women, but especially men, were taken off the street and never came back. This was in the very beginning of the invasion.[2]

The first weeks were filled by chaos and upheaval. In Sara Weil's family—three adult sons, a daughter, and parents—as in Jewish and gentile families across Poland, the young men left for Warsaw. Everyone hoped to defend the capital and, if possible, to repel the Germans. They did not succeed. Despite their heroic attempts, the army capitulated in less than three weeks. "Our men came home. Needless to say how delighted we were that they all came home, all in one piece. . . . We settled down, but just for a very short time."[3]

When the German occupying authority took charge in Lodz, daily life fell apart. "There was a scarcity of food, and we began to look and buy food on the black market already. The money was devalued, and in order to get some food

you needed much, much more money than before the occupation." Such hard-
ships affected all Poles. Jews, however, were singled out for abuse—both by the
Germans and by their Polish neighbors. And this too commenced immediately.
"Jews were beaten up on the street. From the roofs, from the cellars, from any
hiding place that was discovered or known to the Germans or to the Poles, the
Jews were taken. Most of them never came back. This was in October."[4]

From one day to the next, Jews were subjected to an ever more brutal reign
of random terror. Germans assaulted and besieged them, in private and in public. It was common for Germans to pound on the doors of apartments and
homes, and drag away the inhabitants for no discernable reason. "This knocking at the door always stays with me."

I was with my mother when three Germans came in. *"Ist hier ein Jude? Ist
hier ein Jude?* Who lives here? Who lives here?" So we told them: my
mother, my father, and I. "Where is your father?" "My father is out." My
father was upstairs [in a separate room on the third floor] *davening* [praying].
My father put on his prayer shawl every morning and he was saying his
prayers. But we knew how dangerous it was downstairs since many of our
neighbors had been taken. He was praying upstairs. The men ran up the
stairs. They knocked at every apartment.

My father was upstairs praying for whatever he prayed for. And whom-
ever he prayed to maybe listened to him at this time. They were running up
the stairs, knocking at every door, dragging out the people to make sure
there are no men there. And I was going after them. As we were approaching the studio room where my father was, I was telling them this place is
vacant. The Polish family has moved away. No one is there. They didn't
believe me. They kept on knocking, and we knew that my father knew he's
not to open the door. No matter what. This going up, the three flights, and
not knowing what would happen was enough to get a heart attack, no matter how young I was. Until they began to walk down, I had my heart in my
mouth. It was a terrible, horrifying experience for me. It took me days to
come back to myself. And this is how we had to hide my father.[5]

Lodz was in that part of Poland annexed to the Reich, and thus the Jews of
that city came under the direct authority of the local Gauleiter, Arthur Greiser.
The Germans' goal, since 1933, had been to evict the Jews. Now, along with
land they considered theirs, they had gained Jews they did not want. Not knowing what to do with the Jews, they decided to isolate them in a confined area, to
facilitate their future movement. The establishment of the ghetto was ordered
by the Lodz chief of police, SS-Brigadeführer Johannes Schäfer, on 8 February
1940. He chose Baluty, the poorest neighborhood located on the periphery of
the city.

36. Sarah Grossman-Weil, age twenty, 1939. Coll. authors.

We were told that we had to leave for the ghetto. Whoever could, procrastinated, because what it meant is to leave our house, our businesses; to leave everything that is familiar and everything that was ours. We had to leave and move to the ghetto. "To move" meant to leave all the possessions except for personal items. And everyone was trying to put it off. But slowly, people were moving. If they could, they put table and chairs on a wagon and transported it. Or a cabinet, or whatever they could. . . . People were putting off the move, but slowly you could see a movement from the city to the ghetto.

Finally, we moved to the ghetto. We moved to one room on the ground floor, just a stove, no water, very, very primitive. If I remember correctly, the roof was covered with straw. And we lived there in that hut that never before was considered living quarters.[6]

Time is relative: Sara Weil remembered the process as slow. In fact, it took less than three months; by Schäfer's order the Jewish quarter in Lodz was closed on 30 April.

For the Jews of conquered Europe, German edicts and orders assailed them like a storm that beat them senselessly. Overpowered and overwhelmed, with vanishingly few options for asylum and scant means of escape, the Jews of German-occupied Europe coped, managing each day at a time. This was true of young adults like Sara Weil, and it was the hallmark of children like Mira Teeman. "I was born in Poland, in Lodz," she recalled from the safety of Stockholm over fifty years later.[7]

When the war broke out, I was thirteen. I went to school. I had one brother. His name was Stephan. As far as I know, he disappeared in Auschwitz. At that time, he was about sixteen years old. So we were four, my parents and the two children. I think, as far as I can understand, that we were quite wealthy. We had a nursemaid until the war, and a cook, and a woman who came to wash. We had a house in the city with a garden. I went to a private school, so did my brother. Everything changed at once in September '39.[8]

Mira Teeman's world collapsed. "For me, the war began on the 1st of September, '39." Stability became a memory. "One day in October when I came from the school, there was a red paper on the door to our house. It was *beschlagnahmt* [appropriated]. The Germans had taken the house. When I came in, my mother was trying to pack the things together." Her mother thought she could take their possessions, but "a German officer came in and he said, 'What do you think? You have to take out all this.'" Only personal things were allowed. "We had to leave the house in twenty-four hours. It was so early, October '39, and we didn't know where to go."[9]

Mira Teeman's family went to an aunt; ten people lived in three rooms.

However cramped the situation, it got worse. On 10 March 1940, her fourteenth birthday, they moved to the ghetto. "It was very hard. We had an apartment of two rooms and a kitchen"—for fifteen people. "Not only were the conditions awful, but also the pressure with it which came from the authorities of the ghetto, the ghetto police, and from the Germans. They [the Germans] came into the ghetto and marched on the streets. They beat people up, and they were shooting, and they were screaming."[10]

And still the storm continued. Mira Teeman's father became ill with pleurisy and tuberculosis in 1941. He died eight months later, in the spring of 1942. "For my mother it was—she couldn't live without him. They met when she was thirteen and he was a year older. When he died he was forty-eight, and she died a year after. Then we were alone."[11]

THE GERMANS, by contrast, had power and control. They decided what to do and chose when to do it. The conditions of Jewish life—although not, as we shall see, the internal richness of it—were shaped by the Germans' ideology and their orders. And the removal of the Jews into ghettos was only a part of their policy of resettlement and their philosophy of racism.

German antisemitism mushroomed with the conquest of Poland. In Germany, Jews had been largely invisible—except for the *Ostjuden* (east European Jews). And Poland was full of *Ostjuden* made destitute by antisemitic measures passed after the death of President Pilsudski in 1935. Every city had slums of impoverished, emaciated, and unhealthy masses of Jews. The Germans were appalled. In 1933, 500,000 Jews lived in the German Reich; after the Polish campaign, 2.3 million Jews fell under direct German rule. It was as if six years of work to resolve the Jewish Question through emigration had been in vain.

Antisemitic propaganda combined with anti-Polish sentiment. How well the Nazi propaganda had done its work can be seen in the attitudes of German soldiers. "I do not understand how this kind of people is biologically capable of remaining alive," a soldier in Lublin wrote in his diary on 11 November 1939. "Every morning a large contingent of laborers of younger Jews, aged between 20 and 30, passes by our platoon: each one of them looks from their eyes with galloping consumption. Figures that can elsewhere only be seen in hospitals walk around by thousands. . . . Added to the biological corruption is the filth, which cannot be described."[12]

That soldier spoke for many Germans in the fall of 1939—Polish Jewry was lice-ridden, diseased, and degenerate. The popular magazine the *Illustrierter Beobachter,* for instance, ran an article on what the editors considered to be the most important ritual of Polish Jewry: the daily search for lice.[13] The wretched conditions of eastern Jewry provided the Germans with the empirical evidence to "prove" their antisemitic ideology. The ghettos were "the breeding ground of World Jewry" and the breeding ground for "the spread of typhus."[14] Typhus, "louse-fever" in German (*fleck-fieber*), was renamed Jew-fever (*Judenfieber*).

For the Germans, the problem was clear. So was the solution: incarcerate the

Jews in a segregated "quarantine" area. Even before the ghetto walls went up in Warsaw, the chairman of the German-imposed, newly created Jewish Council, Adam Czerniakow, reported in his diary (18 November 1939): "The community ordered to place at its border signs stating *Achtung: Seuchengefahr Eintritt verboten* [Danger: Epidemics—Entry Prohibited]."[15] But as Eduard Könekamp of the German Foreign Institute reported from Poland in December that year to his colleagues in Stuttgart, the "Jewish Problem" in Poland was not to be solved with placards. "The extermination of these subhumans lies in the interests of the whole world," Könekamp stated flatly. "This extermination is one of the most difficult problems," he added. "We will not get by with executions," he warned. "And we cannot allow the shooting of women and children."[16]

IN TIME, the Germans overcame such delicacy of feeling, but meanwhile they considered a series of "solutions" to the "Jewish Problem." At first, emigration appeared to be the answer, and it was a policy pursued most vigorously in the Reich and post-Anschluss Austria. After the Polish campaign, the Germans turned to territorial "solutions"—mass resettlements of ethnic Germans, Poles, and Jews. Hitler unfolded his vision to the party ideologue, Alfred Rosenberg, in September 1939. Poland was to be divided into three segments. The eastern area between the Vistula and Bug rivers was reserved "for the whole of Jewry (from the Reich as well) as well as all other unreliable elements." The western part was to be Germanized and colonized. "This would be a major task for the whole nation: to create a German granary, a strong peasantry, to resettle good Germans from all over the world." In the middle, the Poles were allowed some kind of homeland. "The future would show whether after a few decades the cordon of settlement would have to be pushed further forward."[17]

The new Jewish "homeland" between the Vistula and the Bug was the initiative of Adolf Eichmann, a member of Heydrich's Reich Security Main Office. In 1939, Eichmann headed the Central Office for Jewish Emigration for the Protectorate of Bohemia and Moravia. He had gained quite a reputation in post-Anschluss Vienna, overseeing the emigration of 150,000 Austrian Jews in one year. After German occupation of the Czech lands, he was moved to Prague, where he did less well because by then Czech Jews found it almost impossible to get visas.

Fearing failure, Eichmann looked for another solution. In late September he found a new "home" for Czech Jewry: the region around the town of Nisko in Poland's Lublin district. Eichmann and his immediate superior, Franz Stahlecker, visited the area. "We saw an enormous territory," Eichmann recalled in 1960, "river, villages, markets, small towns, and we said to ourselves: This is perfect, why not resettle the Poles, seeing that there's so much resettling being done in any case, and then move Jews into this big territory." Eichmann believed that a reservation for Jews "would take care of one point of the party program: solution of the Jewish problem."

Eichmann explained his plan to Heydrich, who told Himmler, who told Hitler. They all must have agreed that Eichmann's proposal had a territorial logic: from west to east, the newly conquered territories would be settled by Germans, Poles, and Jews. Eichmann got approval to proceed and, a few weeks later, was promoted to head of Subsection IV (Gestapo)-B (Sects)-4 (Jews) of the Reich Security Main Office in Berlin.[18]

The Germans shrugged at a high mortality for Jews deported to the Lublin area. Eduard Könekamp of the German Foreign Institute, for instance, noted with relief and satisfaction that 450 of 1,000 Jews in a transport from Lublin had died en route.[19] As to survivors, District Governor Friedrich Schmidt told Deputy General Governor Arthur Seyss-Inquart that the marshy character of the reservation would result in the "considerable decimation of the Jews."[20]

LEBENSRAUM FOR THE CONQUERED

37. Cartoon by David Low, Evening Standard *(London), 20 January 1940. The drawing refers to the deportation of Jews to the Nisko reservation.*

These plans were not secret. Journalists in Britain and America wrote about them in major papers. According to *The Times* of London (24 October), the German plan to create "a Jewish State" in the Lublin area was a "remarkable example of political cynicism." "To thrust 3 million Jews, relatively few of whom are agriculturists, into the Lublin region and to force them to settle there would doom them to famine. That, perhaps, is the intention."[21] The American writer Oswald Garrison Villard agreed. "What may prove to be the final act of the incredibly brutal and cruel tragedy which Adolf Hitler has inflicted on the Jews in his power is now going on," Villard wrote in the December issue of the *Spectator.* Almost 2 million Jews were to be brought to the 3,000-square-mile area. "This mass-migration by force has been begun now, in the dead of winter, and in a manner that cannot be interpreted as anything else than a determination to create, not a Jewish state, but a most horrible concentration camp, which can certainly become nothing else than a habitation of death." No preparations had been made in advance of the deportees' arrival. "If they cannot find shelter in the deserted homes of the evacuated Polish peasantry, why, they can freeze to death, or build new homes, without means, without materials, without tools, without anything."[22]

None of this criticism daunted the Germans. They were daunted, however, by practical difficulties, the sheer mechanics of moving so many people—which grew even more cumbersome when Heydrich included the Sinti and Roma living in the Greater German Reich. Furthermore, the Wehrmacht saw security dangers in an influx of Jews so close to the Soviet border.[23] By the spring of 1940

Eichmann's project collapsed. Scandalized by such ineptitude, German authorities in the Government General had convinced Göring, who was responsible for Jewish policy, to cancel it. A total of 95,000 Jews had been moved to Nisko. Many had died. None of the surviving deportees was allowed to return.

The "problem" remained. Germans wished to be rid of Jews in the German East, but where to send them? After the Nisko fiasco, ghettoization, which had been instituted in annexed Poland, seemed the least problematical course. "I received today the Skizze des Sperrgebietes Warschau [sketch of closed-off area of Warsaw]. A ghetto in spite of everything," Adam Czerniakow wrote with a heavy heart in his diary on 10 May 1940.[24] But even this policy was on again, off again. Less than two months later, Governor General Hans Frank issued instructions "to abandon all ghetto construction plans in view of the Führer's plan to send the Jews to Madagascar after the war."[25]

The fall of France had spawned a new plan: Heydrich and the German Foreign Office formulated the so-called Madagascar option, which envisioned the wholesale deportation of European Jewry to the island of Madagascar, a French colony of 241,000 square miles and 4 million inhabitants, set in the Indian Ocean. Alfred Rosenberg had proposed such a scheme to the party faithful in January 1939. Recanting his former enthusiasm for a Jewish state in Palestine, Rosenberg suggested that a reservation would be a better solution.

> Jewry is striving today for a Jewish state in Palestine. Not in order to offer a home to Jews all over the world, however, but for other reasons: world Jewry has to have a little miniature state in order to send extraterritorial ministers and representatives to all countries of the world and through them to promote its lust for domination. But above all they wanted a center of Jewry; a Jewish state where Jewish swindlers from all over the world, hunted by the police of other countries, can be sheltered, provided with new passports and then sent to other parts of the world. It is hoped that the friends of the Jews in the world, especially the Western democracies who dispose over so much space on all continents, will allot the Jews a territory outside of Palestine, *not in order to establish a Jewish state, however, but a Jewish reservation.*[26]

A German Foreign Office circular printed Rosenberg's proposal with the formal statement: "That is the program of German foreign policy on the Jewish question."[27] Now that France had capitulated, Rosenberg's solution appeared within reach. The Germans simply assumed that Madagascar would be ceded to them and the transport could be worked out.[28] The problem of the more than 3 million Jews in areas under German rule could no longer be solved through enigration, Heydrich told an official of the German Foreign Office. A "territorial final solution" was necessary.[29] Madagascar fit the bill.

News of the Madagascar project reached Adam Czerniakow on 1 July. Adam Gerhard Mende, chief of the Jewish Section of the Gestapo in Warsaw, had informed him that the war would be over in a month; then the Jews of Warsaw "would all leave for Madagascar,"[30] the chairman of the Jewish Council of Warsaw confided to his diary. "In this way the Zionist dream is to come true," he added laconically.

If Czerniakow did not elaborate, Governor General Hans Frank certainly did. Speaking of the future of the Lublin territory, he assured his compatriots that the Government General soon would be Jew-free. "As soon as international transport allows for the possibility to remove the Jews [laughter], the Jews will be deported piece by piece, man by man, woman by woman, young woman by young woman. I assume that I will not have to feel sorry for you about this [renewed laughter]."[31] Reinhard Heydrich, whose job it was to organize mass resettlements, supported the Madagascar option too. Of course, the Germans "must eliminate" the Jews. "Biological extermination, however, is undignified for the German people as a civilized nation. Thus after the victory we will impose the condition on the enemy powers that the holds of their ships be used to transport the Jews along with their belongings to Madagascar or elsewhere."[32]

38. A propaganda vehicle to "sell" fake one-way tickets for Madagascar to Jews. The man next to the truck wears a mock Freemasons' hat marked with a Jewish star and carries a bag labeled "Devisen" (hard currency). The advertisement on the van reads: "Special Train for Jews Going to Madagascar, but no Return." Stadtarchiv Nuremberg, courtesy of the United States Holocaust Memorial Museum Photo Archives, Washington, DC.

The Madagascar plan showed that the Nazis had learned how to think big about the "Jewish Problem." In 1933, they trumpeted Germany's mission to get rid of all Jews in the Reich. In the late thirty's, their scope widened to the Greater Reich. Now that, in mid-1940, they ruled so much of Europe, it was their job to free the whole continent from the "scourge" of the Jews: ship them to Magacascar. But the plan came to naught. France did not cede the island, and the war did not end. Göring's Luftwaffe failed to subjugate England; there was no negotiated peace, and that was the end of that.

The Germans remained interested in a territorial solution, however, and Hitler's decision in December 1940 to attack the Soviet Union in the spring promised new possibilities. Nevertheless, during the months of planning for Operation Barbarossa, Nazi leaders thought more about what they would force the Jews to do than where they would be forced to live. No one developed a detailed plan for a Jewish reservation in the soon-to-be-conquered land, but there was a lot of discussion about the use of Jews as slave laborers to drain the

Pripet marshes in eastern Poland and to develop the northeast of European Russia.

Putting Jews to work had been a high priority for the Germans since their invasion of Poland in 1939. One of Hans Frank's first decrees as Governor General subjected all Jews aged fourteen to sixty-one to forced labor. German newspapers carried many gleeful and profusely illustrated articles about the new measures. The weekly *Illustrierter Beobachter,* for example, ran an article on 12 October with a photograph of Jewish men carrying bricks under the headline: "The Jews Must Work!"[33] "It gives us particular pleasure to use the beloved gentlemen of Abraham's seed for carrying straw and setting up camps," one Dr. Emil Strodthoff wrote in the *Völkischer Beobachter* of 28 November. "We simply went through the streets, collecting them, and whoever, despite a friendly request, thought he had no time, was soon taught better."[34]

The press in neutral countries followed the story. "Untold thousands of Jews, who in former times belonged to the professions, are now compelled by the German authorities to do other kinds of work, such as building roads, clearing forests, etc.," the Zürich *Die Tat* reported in its issue of 1 January 1940.

> In the district of Lublin, where as is known most of the Jews live, they now have begun to call upon Jews for reclamation work. Spread over wide areas, they are at work on the regulation of streams and rivers, building dikes and draining swamps. In the Lublin district, from 12,000 to 14,000 Jews were rounded up for this kind of work. They have been allocated to forty-five work centers. They live in thirty-four camps. Within the next few weeks other districts will follow the example of Lublin and, as the *Warschauer Zeitung* reports, the remaining Jews will be employed in this and similar work.[35]

Paradoxical as it may have seemed to some, Jewish forced labor was to make good a German promise to repair Polish roads, straighten the riverbanks, and dig new canals.

The particularly sadistic SS-Brigadeführer Odilo Globocnik had created the first comprehensive scheme of Jewish slave labor, and it was he who took the next step, linking deportation with slave labor. He proposed to move all of the Jews, as a slave labor force, to areas in need of development. Globocnik's proposal met with favor. On 20 March 1941 Eichmann told representatives of the Propaganda Ministry that the Führer had assigned "the task of planning the final evacuation of the Jews" to Heydrich, who had done his work and submitted a scheme two months previously.[36]

There is little documentation about this aspect of Nazi policy. What is clear is that the invasion of the East led to speculation about what to do with the 40,000 square miles of Pripet marshes and the usefulness of the Jews in this regard. In a conversation with Hansjulius Schepers, the director of regional planning in Cracow, on 19 July 1941, Hans Frank noted that "in its present state, this region has minimal value, but with a thoroughly implemented program of drainage and cultivation, considerable value can without doubt be extracted from this region." Frank had peat as well as a potential of 5 million acres of arable land in mind, and he had no doubt as to who would do the work. "I believe it is possible to engage certain population elements (especially Jewish ones) in a productive activity serving the Reich. You are well aware that in this regard I cannot complain of shortages of labor."[37] As late as 25 October 1941, well after mass murder had become practice, Hitler mentioned the marshes in a conversation with Himmler and Heydrich. "From the rostrum of the Reichstag I prophesied to Jewry that, in the event of war's proving inevitable, the Jew would disappear from Europe. That race of criminals has on its conscience the two million dead of the First World War, and now already hundreds of thousands more. Let nobody tell me that all the same we can't park them in the marshy parts of Russia! Who's worrying about our troops?"[38] Nazi cogitations about Jewish relocation are important to note, not because the schemes came to pass, but as a way into Nazi thinking. Long after the Nazis dropped the idea of Madagascar and marshes, the language of these notions still circulated as a synonym for "final solution through resettlement."

The Nisko plan did affect some 95,000 Jews; the Madagascar and Pripet Marsh plans never got off the drawing board. But while the schemes themselves evaporated, the time consumed by their planning greatly affected Jews in German-controlled Europe. With relocation an option, the Jews were in limbo and the Germans did not resolve to murder Jews en masse. To be sure: hundreds of thousands of Jews were killed during this time. But the process of annihilation we call the Holocaust had not yet begun. These attempts at a territorial solution reveal that the Germans themselves did not know in 1939 or even 1940 what they would do in 1941. What ultimately happened did not occur due to some slippery slope, or an inexorable series of events. History is not fated; it is enacted step by step, person by person, moment by moment.

WHEN WE THINK about the Holocaust, the machinery of death and the death-dealers loom large. They occupy center stage, while the daily lives of Jews—their hopes and fears, plans and worries—slip onto the margin. "The Jews" all too often are seen as a mass of living dead until they were in fact dead. This distortion of the entire period especially warps our view of the period from September 1939 until the summer of 1941. At no time were the Jews simply sitting in a ghetto or in hiding waiting to be deported and murdered. Life went on at home, in hiding, and in ghettos until the moment of death or, far less frequently, liberation. During the early period, however, when the Germans had not yet decided upon their policy of total annihilation, the Jews had a slightly greater scope for action.

Life was of course hard and grew harder. How to continue to earn a living, how to carry on within German regulations that radically restricted their activities? Jewish physicians, for example, could no longer treat gentile patients, and Jewish patients could no longer be treated by gentile physicians: Jewish physicians therefore tried to earn a living by treating Jewish patients. Similarly, when public schools barred both Jewish teachers and Jewish children, Jewish schools sprang up, staffed by Jewish teachers and attended by Jewish children. Some people who had owned businesses and shops tried to get by with Jewish clientele; others defied the regulations and continued to trade—clandestinely and at great risk—with those gentile customers brave enough to deal with Jews.

Jewish children suffered less from the economic sanctions than their parents did. Certainly, families had less money, but daily life went on. Families remained intact. Food and clothing, immediate activities and future plans, were not threatened in obvious ways. Then the insular childhood world was shattered by a second wave of antisemitic legislation designed to segregate Jews from the rest of the population. Now unwelcome in public places, they could not go to the movies or ice cream parlors; they could not play in parks or swim in municipal pools.

The sudden, shocking introduction of school segregation was the first of the legalized social abuses aimed at Jewish children. It was neither the last nor the worst. On the contrary, it was but the beginning of the road to social death. The external marking with the Star of David was another step. Transportation became problematic. Bicycles were appropriated; only the last car of the metro or trolley could be used; travel was allowed just at certain hours of the day; and then it was prohibited entirely. Their world continued to shrink: curfews, no visits between Jews and gentiles. Jewish friends dwindled—deported or disappeared. Jewish life narrowed to home, garden, and courtyards. And yet they had their homes, gardens, and courtyards until, like Sara Grossman-Weil or Mira Teeman, they faced the moment of departure—go into hiding, escape as a refugee, to the ghetto, deportation. Now the Jews were beyond social segregation from the world they had known; they were physically isolated from it.[39]

RELATIVELY FEW Jews anywhere in Europe either escaped or went into hiding during the war. In the east, the vast majority lost their rights immediately, were soon marked with the star, and then jammed into ghettos. Within weeks of occupying Poland, the Germans severed Jews from the body politic by setting up a *Judenrat* or Council of Jewish Elders in every community. These "Jewish Councils" were composed of prominent Jewish men designated by the Germans to carry out their orders, and to deal with the myriad problems of a community under duress. The Councils oversaw housing allocations, food distribution, hygiene services, medical care, and youth services; they established and maintained orphanages, hospitals, and apprenticeship schools, often the only education the Germans permitted Jewish children. Created to "govern" the Jews, these German-imposed *Judenräte* had many responsibilities and great authority within the community but no power outside it and no leverage at all with the Nazis.[40] As the National Socialist writer Hermann Erich Seifert explained in his book on Polish Jewry, "The individual Jew does not exist for the German authorities in occupied territory." The Germans dealt with the Council of Elders, and "there is no discussion of or argument against the German orders."[41]

Separation of the Jews from the Polish body politic was followed by segregation.[42] Throughout German-annexed and German-occupied Poland, decrees in the fall of 1939 ordered all Jews in some places, and all Jews over the age of twelve in others, to wear the Star of David mark. "Thursday, November 16. Lodz. We are returning to the Middle Ages," fifteen-year-old Dawid Sierakowiak wrote in his diary. "The yellow patch once again becomes part of Jewish dress. Today an order was announced that all Jews, no matter what age or sex, have to wear a band of 'Jewish yellow,' 10 centimeters wide, on their right arm, just below the armpit." On 12 December, Dawid reported: "I read an order changing the Jewish yellow armbands to yellow 10-centimeter 'Stars of David' (*Davidstern*) that must be worn on the right chest and on the back of the right shoulder." The import of the decree was not lost on him. "The barbarity proceeds. They will soon order us to smear tar on our noses and wear shorts." Each antisemitic decree carried multiple hardships. In this case, it meant humiliation, danger, cost, and more tasks to be done. "New work in the evening: ripping off the armbands and sewing on the new decorations."[43]

For Halina Nelken in Cracow, the same age as Dawid Sierakowiak but from a more assimilated family, the mark raised questions about Jewish identity and Jewish appearance. "8 December 1939. The Germans have issued a most hideous ordinance," Halina wrote in her diary. "From now on, all Jews have to wear a white band with a blue Star of David on the right arm." Halina understood that this was a subversion of the Jewish symbol of the Shield of David. "David was the greatest king of the Jews, and the Star of Zion was once a sign of triumph—today it is to be a sign of contempt." Under these circumstances, she found it difficult to focus on the studies she and a group of girls had undertaken clandestinely after the Germans had closed their school.

And how could anyone concentrate on Newton's law of gravity? One of the girls in our group, Anka, said she is ashamed, that she is never going to wear this armband, that she does not look Jewish. I also do not look Jewish, for according to the German definition in their newspaper, *Stürmer,* racially pure Jews have scraggly black hair, long, hooked noses, and flat feet. There is nothing black about me except—in [her brother] Felek's opinion—my character, but even if this were true, character doesn't show on the surface, so to the eye I'm not in the least like a Jew. However, I'll probably wear the armband. If everyone has to, everyone must.

We talked about it at home. Mama fried potato pancakes for supper. Papa said . . . the Germans are the ones who should be ashamed of the armband, and not us. He's going to wear the Star of David with pride. At this, Mama smiled a bit ironically. "Since when did you become such a devoted Jew?" But Papa was not joking. "If being of Jewish origin is a sentence of death, I will die as a Jew. I do not want a different fate from the rest of my people."

He got up and left the room. Shivers went down my spine. Mama also felt uneasy. We cleared the table in silence and I wanted to sit down to my homework. But how could I concentrate on Newton's laws of gravity in the face of German laws?[44]

Emanuel Nelken, a well-to-do banker in Cracow and an assimilated Polish patriot, went to synagogue on Rosh Hashanah and Yom Kippur. Chaim Kaplan, by contrast, was deeply imbued with Jewish tradition and learning. As a Jewish educator in Warsaw, religious observance permeated his daily existence. Yet the two men faced the armband order in a very similar spirit.

November 30, 1939

Today two harsh decrees reached us. First, the "Star of David" decree— just like the one in Cracow, except that in Cracow the authorities announced the decree in advance, about two weeks before it became effective, and the leaders of the community had the time to prepare the Zionist symbols, whereas in Warsaw, or rather in the Warsaw district, the decree was published on November 30 to become effective on December 1. Most likely this was done on purpose, in order to catch many Jews in the act of sabotage. . . .

In any event, the conqueror is turning us into Jews whether we like it or not. . . . The Nazis have marked us with the Jewish national colors, which are our pride. In this sense we have been set apart from the Jews of Lodz, the city which has been annexed to the Reich. The "yellow badge" of medieval days has been stuck to them, but as for me, I shall wear my badge with personal satisfaction.[45]

An armband might be worn with pride, but segregation in a closed ghetto was literally unbelievable until that moment came. Less than a fortnight before the Jewish quarter of Warsaw became a closed ghetto, Kaplan, an astute and intelligent observer of current events, could not imagine such a transformation. Nearly six months earlier, in May 1940, thick walls separating the designated Jewish area from the rest of the city had been thrown up at the Germans' command and the Jewish community's expense. Gentiles living in the Jewish quarter had moved out and Jews living in now forbidden areas had moved into allocated streets. And the example of Lodz, where a closed ghetto had been established in the spring, was very much on his mind. Yet Kaplan did not believe that Warsaw would suffer the same fate. "A Jewish ghetto in the traditional sense is impossible; certainly a closed ghetto is inconceivable," he wrote in his diary on 2 November 1940.

Many churches and government buildings are in the heart of the ghetto. They cannot be eliminated, they fulfill necessary functions. Besides that, it is impossible to cut off the trolley routes going from one end of the city to the other through the ghetto. For hundreds of years the great metropolis was built on general civil foundations, and the basis of race was entirely foreign to it. Neighborhoods and backyards of people of different faiths were next to each other, and in spite of all religious and moral differences between them, mutual trade and dealings developed which brought benefits to all. To differentiate citizens of one country according to race, and to erect partitions between them, is a sick pathological idea. From its inception to its execution, it may be considered a symptom of insanity.[46]

Just two days later Kaplan noted: "The face of Warsaw has changed so that no one who knows it would recognize it. People from outside do not enter now, but if a miracle were to take place and one of its inhabitants who fled returned to the city, he would say, 'Can this be Warsaw?' "[47]

GHETTO POLICY, so sudden and wrenching to Jews, had long been on German drawing boards. At a meeting called by Göring after the 1938 November Pogrom, he had broached the idea. Reinhard Heydrich had opposed it, fearing that ghettos would become a nest for Jewish criminals and a source of epidemics. A year later, Heydrich had come around, calling for segregation of the Jews of Warsaw.[48] This time, Warsaw's local military leader vetoed the plan; instead, he designated the traditional Jewish quarter a *Seuchengebiet* (Epidemic Zone) and off-limits to Germans. Nothing more was done at that time because the German leadership fully expected Warsaw's Jews to be shipped to the Nisko reservation. Indeed, the succession of plans for territorial solutions and the creation and longevity of closed ghettos were intimately interrelated.[49]

When Eichmann conceived the Nisko project, he had not calculated how to get the Jews there. It quickly became clear, however, that he would need holding pens where Jews from smaller communities could be assembled before transport en masse to the east. The large industrial city of Lodz would do nicely. To control and confine the Nisko-bound Jews, the Lodz chief of police ordered the creation of a ghetto in February 1940. Incarcerating more than 160,000 people, it was closed on 30 April.

At the same time, the Nisko plan prevented the establishment of a ghetto in Warsaw. On 8 March, the decision was taken anew not to close the Warsaw ghetto, "as the General Government is considering the idea of declaring the Lublin district a collection point for all Jews in the General Government."[50] Lodz, of course, was in the annexed territories, the area to be "cleansed" of Jews, while Warsaw was in the General Government, the area that would receive Jews if Nisko did not prove workable.

Göring halted all further deportations to the Nisko area on 24 March 1940. Lacking anywhere to dump their Jews, the German authorities in Warsaw now began to plan for a local ghetto. Three days later (27 March) they ordered the Jewish Council to build a seven-foot-high *Seuchenmauer* (epidemic wall) around the Jewish quarter to prevent the spread of epidemics to the gentile population. As the chairman of the Jewish Council, Adam Czerniakow, noted in his diary on 13 April, "we are to pay for the walls."[51]

Initially, the walls were intended to be temporary. The victory over France later that spring and the chance of a negotiated peace with Great Britain had breathed life into the idea of a Jewish reservation in Madagascar. But while Nazi leaders ruminated, Hitler decided to invade the Soviet Union. Over a million German soldiers would mass in the General Government to spring into Operation Barbarossa, the largest offensive in history. As fears of epidemics rose, ghettoization of the Jews emerged as a military necessity.

Of course, German troops might have been protected by improving the living conditions of the Jews. Such a thought was beyond the mental horizon of German planners. By the beginning of September 1940, German public health officials insisted that in Jewish neighborhoods lay the potential for a massive typhus epidemic. They urged the Governor General to follow the example of Lodz.[52] Frank took their advice, separating gentile and Jewish populations. "The German Army and population must be protected at all costs from the immune bacillus-carrier of the plagues—the Jew," he decreed.[53]

The Germans moved rapidly throughout Warsaw district. "Suddenly we see ourselves penned in on all sides," Chaim Kaplan wrote in his diary on 17 November, a mere fifteen days after the idea of a "closed ghetto" seemed "inconceivable." "We are segregated and separated from the world and the fullness thereof, driven out of the society of the human race."[54]

The Jews of Cracow suffered the same fate the following spring, and for them too it felt just as sudden, just as great a rupture. "Bad news arrives suddenly and in quick succession," Halina Nelken wrote in her diary on 5 March 1941. "Today, finally, the rule about the creation of the ghetto in Podgórze. Bewildered as I am, I feel empty." A month later the ghetto was sealed. "I cannot even imagine living within the limits of the ghetto, within its few congested little streets without any green space. Just the thought of it chokes me," she lamented.[55]

WHILE HIGH-LEVEL German bureaucrats continued to imagine shipping the Jews to Madagascar, and working them as slaves on the Pripet marshes, Jews in the closed ghettos of German-annexed and German-occupied Poland adapted as best they could. As the Orthodox Jewish scholar Hillel Seidman, chief archivist of the Warsaw ghetto, noted in his private diary, some managed and others didn't.

From the beginning, two distinct types emerged in the Ghetto. There were yesterday's men who recalled their previous importance and lived on their memories. They long for the past when life was more or less normal and dream of a more pleasant future. But they have as little as possible to do with the present. Currently they are desultory in outlook and behavior and wield little influence.

Then there are the up-and-coming men of today. Though they have little past experience, they have become quickly acclimatized to the bewildering change of fortunes. Now they wield the upper hand.[56]

In the ghetto, Seidman observed, people's essential attributes crystallized:

Those who were small-minded before have become even more petty; those who were already evil have inevitably become worse. Many have become selfish and extremely sensitive to every possible need. They are so terrified of death that the smallest matter—even a single slice of bread—is magnified into a question of life and death.[57]

Most ghetto inmates, whatever their personality traits, tried to understand their existence by viewing it within a continuum of Jewish history. Enforced ghetto life was not without precedent. Not until the 1800s were Jews allowed to live beyond the ghetto of Frankfurt; Rome's ghetto opened in 1870. Cities like Vilna, where there never had been a walled ghetto or locked gates, had historic Jewish quarters, traditional neighborhoods. Thus, the inhabitants of east European ghettos were connected to the history of the place in which they now were compelled to live. These streets, synagogues, and markets had grown over centuries to meet the Jewish community's needs; they now suggested that life could go on. Such optimism ran through the hundreds of thousands of refugee Jews evicted from their home towns all over Poland.[58] Forced to flee to large cities, they arrived dazed and destitute, but to a place in one way or another familiar. The concept of a ghetto had a past in Jewish memory and the ghettos themselves had a Jewish past. It was logical that, initially, there was hope for a Jewish future.

"There's been the growth of a strong sense of historical consciousness recently," the forty-year-old intellectual and community worker Emmanuel Ringelblum jotted down for his clandestine collection of notes about the Warsaw ghetto on 8 November 1940. Ringelblum was in a position to know; he had developed a cadre of people to report on the situation of the Jews, and he collated the information thus obtained. "We tie in fact after fact from our daily experience with the events of history. We are returning to the Middle Ages.— Spoke to a Jewish scholar. The Jews created another world for themselves in the past, living in it forgot the troubles around them, allowed no one from the outside to come in."[59]

For Jews to cling to such an illusion suited the Germans. In March 1941 Alfred Rosenberg's Frankfurt-based Institute for Research into the Jewish

Question held a conference where the prominent Nazi specialist on east European Jewry, Peter-Heinz Sepharim, laid out the differences. "The ghetto of the middle ages was in essence a community voluntarily living together, in addition to which it by no means excluded business contacts between Jews and non-Jews," he explained to his colleagues. The ghettos established in Poland, by contrast, were "a forced measure." Furthermore, "if it makes sense," the inhabitants of the new ghettos should have no "contact or possibility of contact with non-Jews."[60] The goal for the Germans, in other words, was to segregate and isolate the Jews while they proceeded to invade the Soviet Union without fear of contagion; in the long term they could decide what to do with this "scourge of humanity." The goal for the Jews was to understand the incomprehensible—what the Germans wanted of them—and to find a way to go forward with life each day.

Going forward meant earning enough to eat. It was as simple and as stark as that: starvation was staved off by a slice of stale bread, a bowl of thin soup, a potato bought with money laboriously earned. In October 1939 Chaim Kaplan reported that "tens of thousands of people are left without a source of livelihood"; fourteen months later all social classes were affected. "Professional people, deprived of their occupations, are in part sitting idle. . . . Artisans are idle because there is no one to give them shoes to mend or clothes to sew." While they lived on "two or three zloty a day," there were "thousands and tens of thousands who live on charity and eat at the soup kitchens. The latter number a hundred thousand each day."[61]

One employer grew apace: the *Judenrat*. With so many responsibilities for the welfare of the Jews and so many demands from the Germans, Jewish Councils became big bureaucracies.[62] "The ghetto state needs civil servants," Kaplan noted, "and it employs thousands." The term "ghetto state" was barely an exaggeration: the population of many ghettos equalled that of a small city. The *Judenräte* established scores of specialized offices and divisions, mimicking a municipality—a Registration Office, Records Office, Firefighting Division, Rent Office, Tax Office, Welfare Division, and Health Division, all staffed by people who had lost their jobs with the German antisemitic measures. As Kaplan noted, "There were the Jewish policemen with their rubber clubs (they were not given arms). . . . At all events, four thousand Jewish youths who were eliminated from their former jobs were given these new 'posts of honor,'" Then too, "the post office employs several hundred people." And finally, "the administrative work within the *Judenrat* itself also engages thousands of people. Their salary is small and is never paid on time, but at least they have a foothold."[63]

A foothold also was gained by those employed in ghetto workshops producing goods for the Germans.[64] No one believed that the Germans intended to murder everyone. The Jewish Councils thus adopted a strategy of compliance with their conquerors in order to save their people. The Germans encouraged this, giving Jewish leaders to understand that Jewish labor was essential to the

Reich. *Arbeit macht frei*: Work will set you free. These words, first emblazoned on the gates of Dachau and later taken up in Auschwitz, acquired new meaning in the ghetto. The Jews had to make themselves indispensable; salvation lay in work. Jacob Gens, the Elder of Vilna ghetto, and Mordechai Chaim Rumkowski, the Elder of the Lodz ghetto, transformed their communities into urban work camps. To a lesser extent, others did too. A job making products for the Germans came to be seen as a sinecure. And while the Germans were considering territorial "solutions" to the Jewish "problem," this perception was not inaccurate.

"Rysiek Podlaski sent his brother to me with a note urging me to go immediately to the tailor workshop where his father is the manager," Dawid Sierakowiak wrote in his diary on 10 April 1941. "I will be able to earn a few marks there. I went right away, and, indeed, I got a job from Podlaski for a few days as a 2-mark laborer." An extra benefit: "Every day I will get an additional dinner (for 20 pf. [pfennigs])." Dawid connected work and food repeatedly. "Since a lot of matzoth was left [after Passover], Rumkowski decided to give an extra treat to workers and clerks in the administration. He gave each worker a package of matzoth for the nominal price of 3 RM, 25 pf. Father received one package at his workplace, and I received one in mine . . . considering our hunger, it's simply wonderful." Three weeks later he exulted, "The most important thing is that . . . Mom has received a job as peeler in a communal kitchen. She works fourteen to fifteen hours a day, and her salary is supposed to be 20 to 25 RM a month. The main advantage is that she will receive the workers' two substantial soups a day for free. So at least Mom won't starve; at home we also will be better off."[65]

Ghetto conditions altered prewar work norms. Smuggling, previously illegal and unrespectable, remained illegal but became heroic. Smuggling was a necessary fact of the ghetto world. At one point Adam Czerniakow estimated that smuggling accounted for 80 percent of the food available in the ghetto.[66] Abraham Lewin, formerly a teacher at a private, Zionist-oriented Jewish girls' school, recorded the smuggling activities of adults and children in the ghetto at regular intervals in his diary. "I live by the wall that divides the ghetto from Przejazd Street. A gap has appeared in the wall through which someone could quite easily crawl, or which is wide enough for a sack with 100 kg of potatoes or corn or other foodstuffs. The smuggling goes on without a break from dawn at half past five until nine in the evening," he wrote in May 1942. Lewin fully understood the danger. "What they must go through, those who spend all day busy at the wall, these smugglers." But it was through them that "flour, potatoes, milk, butter, meat and other produce are brought into the ghetto."[67] A month later, he lamented the death of yet another two smugglers. The day after they "had fallen victim . . . the smuggling on Nowolipie and Przejazd Street was halted, almost as if in mourning for the memory of the smugglers from the smuggling groups who had died." The next day, however, "regardless of the appalling campaign of terror against the smugglers, and in spite of the large number of victims that have fallen in the last few days, the smuggling was going again at full throttle, as if nothing had happened. This shows that under the present conditions smuggling is life's imperative."[68]

Abraham Lewin practiced his own "illegal" activity. In Warsaw, as in the whole Government General, German authorities barred Jewish children from Polish schools and banned Jewish schools under the pretext that they would serve as a breeding ground for infectious disease. Elementary education continued to be prohibited in the ghetto until September 1941 and secondary schooling was never reinstated.[69] Teaching, like smuggling, was forbidden by the Reich. Prior to the Germans' antisemitic regulations, Lewin had taught Hebrew, Biblical Studies, and Jewish Studies at the Yehudia School. He and the rest of the Yehudia staff began clandestine classes after the ghetto was established. In its own way, teaching, like smuggling, was essential to ghetto life.

The efforts of the Yehudia staff were not unique. All over the ghetto, students and teachers met secretly to continue the process of education. To go to school, to persevere with one's studies, was an essential activity that embodied the principle of normality: life would go on, a future lay beyond this madness. Many children longed to learn, and many adults wished to continue to teach. In her diary-memoir *Winter in the Morning,* Janina Bauman, then fourteen, explained that she and a group of her friends in the Warsaw ghetto contacted teachers they knew and set up classes. Her ten-year-old sister Sophie also joined a study group. In the early spring of 1941 Janina Bauman's uncle, with whom she, her mother, and sister lived, contracted typhus. Everyone in the flat was forced to remain indoors during the weeks of quarantine. When he recovered and she was allowed to return to school, she was overjoyed.

> *16 April 1941, evening*
> Freedom, freedom at last! Everything was fun today, even sitting on this awful settee in Ala's room, squeezed between Zula and Hanka. Even the maths. I've missed quite a lot, by the way, but Hanka says she'll help me make it up in no time. They all seemed extremely pleased when I appeared out of the blue. Renata was so surprised that she kissed me, forgetting all sanitary precautions. Nina said she had rather expected me to die from typhus, the silly cow.
>
> Lots of news. . . . Irena wanted to join our group, but eight is enough, said the girls, and flatly turned her down. So she asked the teachers to let her join the boys. They didn't mind and the boys were delighted, at least she says so. They are nine all together now. Could be nice to meet them—same teachers, same problems.[70]

Important as education was to the young people, it was equally essential to the teachers, who had no other way to earn a living and faced fast-approaching

39. Geography lesson in the Lodz ghetto, c. 1941. The boy points out Haifa on a map of Palestine. Institute of Contemporary History and Wiener Library Ltd., courtesy of the United States Holocaust Memorial Museum Photo Archives, Washington, DC. Damaged original photo.

penury. "The unemployed Jewish teachers have found a way to partially save themselves from starving. They got together and organized small groups of children who come to the teacher's home to be taught for two or three hours. Hundreds of teachers support themselves in this fashion," Chaim Kaplan confided to his diary on 14 December 1939. He recognized the irregularity. "It is possible that the ban against study also applies to such small groups, and if questions were asked they would have to be stopped. But no one asks questions. The matter is done quietly, underhandedly. There is no other solution."[71]

Radom, like Warsaw, was in the Government General. A ghetto was instituted in that city early in 1940, and soon a school functioned there, held in three rooms of a former religious school and welcoming three shifts of children each day.[72] Not nearly enough. Most young people carried on their education in private—and even that was prohibited. The nine-year-old Hanna Kent-Sztarkman took informal lessons for a brief period, but they were important to her. Hanna, her mother, and older brother Heniek were refugees in Radom; they had fled from Lodz. "Since the Germans decided to divide Poland into a protectorate [the Government General], and part include in the Reich, and our city, Lodz, was supposed to be part of the Reich, my parents felt that perhaps life in the protectorate would be easier," she explained decades later. "The town where my mother had lived, and where my grandmother and my aunt lived, Radom, was part of the protectorate, so we decided that we'd slowly move there. Well, Heniek left first, then my mother and I; it was in December 1939. My father and my sister were supposed to follow as soon as they sold whatever they could."[73] In the end, father and daughter did not manage to leave Lodz before the ghetto was closed, and their attempts to escape didn't succeed; the two parts of the family never reunited.

Hanna Sztarkman's mother and brother went to work in Radom; Hanna, at nine, stayed home. "I did not go to school," she recalled. "I read any book that I could get a hold of, but of course, we didn't have a library." Fortunately, friends from Lodz also landed in Radom. "There were four daughters . . . one of [them] and my sister had graduated from gymnasium [academic high school] together. The youngest, who was a couple of years older than I am, took me and another girl and she would teach us a little bit of mathematics and things, while you could. Later on, even this couldn't work out. You just didn't. I read a lot, that was just about it." This was a terrible loss to her. It was much more than simply a way of passing the time. "Living is hoping, and I kept hoping that somehow something will happen and the war will end. One just had to be strong enough to wait and I took each day the way it came. . . . What worried me was: will I ever be able to catch up with my education? It is funny, but this is what I was talking to Heniek about—will I ever be able to catch up with my education! In such a horrible situation; yet I tried to keep some normalcy, to look forward to something."[74]

Lodz ghetto, in annexed Poland, managed a marginally normal school system under the *Judenrat*. Inevitably, however, the harshness of ghetto life overwhelmed the students. At first Mira Teeman attended school after her family's forced move into the ghetto. "Our king, Rumkowski, opened a high school. Maybe it was just a year or so that I went to that school. But at that time, my father was very ill. I couldn't stay. How could I try to study Latin or Hebrew or something when my mind was occupied with my father's dying? I couldn't."[75] Ghetto conditions squeezed out childhood occupations. As Esther Geizhals-Zucker recalled, "Then my schooling stopped in the ghetto. I had no more school because I had to work in order to get a ration card in order to get food. And there was no room for school."[76]

Lithuania, under Russian control since 1939, was quickly occupied when the Germans attacked the Soviet Union in June 1941. By that time the Jewish community of Kovno was the eighth largest in German-occupied eastern Europe, and Vilna had twice as many Jews (55,000 in 1931) as Kovno (27,200 in 1934). In both cities, a ghetto area was quickly established. On 10 July 1941 the suburb of Slobodka across the river from Kovno was designated; it was an impoverished area, and had little real estate anyone wanted. Jews were marked with the star, front and back, and five days later were expelled from the city and ordered into the ghetto. All schools were closed in the ghetto. In December 1941, two elementary schools were reopened at the initiative of the teachers, only to be closed again by the authorities in the winter months of 1942, this time because of a shortage of firewood to heat the classrooms; then in April they opened again, only to be forbidden again in the summer.[77]

None of this made any difference to one Mrs. Segal and the children she taught. "March 21, 1943," the Zionist lawyer Avraham Golub, now deputy secretary to the new Jewish Council, wrote in his diary. Mrs. Segal "pays no heed to the bans and prohibitions. Although the Jewish school has been officially closed on orders from the Germans, this order has yet to reach this courageous and distinguished educator. Every day, children gather in her own small room, where she teaches them the alphabet, to say 'Shalom' in Hebrew, and to sing Hebrew songs. She implants in their hearts a love for the Jewish people and a longing for their homeland—the land of Israel."[78]

The redoubtable Mrs. Segal was completely devoted to her kindergartners in Kovno. "Today is Purim," Avraham Golub wrote in his diary. "Hitler has promised that there will be no more Purim festivities for the

40. Children exercise in the kindergarten established by Ita Rozencwajc in Warsaw ghetto, 1941. Ita Diamont, courtesy of the United States Holocaust Memorial Museum Photo Archives, Washington, DC. Damaged original photo.

Jews. I do not know whether his other predictions will come true, but this one is yet to be fulfilled." And he continued:

> Here in the ghetto we are celebrating Purim in a new style. None other than our children, our Mosheles and Shlomeles, give lie to Hitler's predictions by celebrating Purim with all their innocence and enthusiasm.
>
> The children—pupils of the pioneer of National Hebrew education in the ghetto, Mrs. Segal—have been preparing the Purim festivities for many weeks. They have been learning the Purim songs, the dances, the games. . . . Who is going to play the part of Mordechai, Haman, Queen Esther and Vashti? The children have been telling their parents all about their Purim preparations, and the parents—if there are any parents left alive—let themselves be drawn in by the festive atmosphere.
>
> The distinguished educator Mrs. Segal has been involved in these preparations more than anybody else. After all, these are her children, the children of her kindergarten, whom she has been looking after since the first day of the Ghetto.[79]

While younger children went to kindergartens and elementary education classes, older youths in Kovno as elsewhere attended classes and clandestine study groups. In Kovno, a number of teachers attached to ORT, the philanthropic Organization for Rehabilitation and Training, managed to run a vocational school. The tools for the school were smuggled in by the instructors as well as by Jewish slave laborers who lived in the ghetto but worked at German labor sites outside the walls. This was accomplished despite searches at the ghetto gates and the danger to their own lives and the lives of their families. The number of students grew steadily. This school too was closed in August 1942, but in the autumn the Council convinced German authorities that the vocational school was needed to develop the ghetto industry, and it was reopened.[80]

Tamarah Lazerson was thirteen years old when the Germans occupied Kovno in 1941. She was past elementary school age, and the opening of schools at that level did not help her. Just about one year later, on 21 September 1942, she wrote in her diary, "My old wound has reopened. The school year has begun. I am deeply pained that another year will go to waste. But what can I do?" And two months later: "A long time had passed since I have read a book. It's terribly hard to obtain them now. To add to our troubles, the electricity has been cut off. My room is dark and unheated. Nothing to do but to crawl into bed. At seven o'clock and sometimes even earlier, I crawl into bed. Memories overwhelm me and there's no way to shake them off."[81]

By April of the following year, Tamarah was at the vocational school. "I am now working in a trade school and am very pleased. The lectures are interesting. We take notes diligently and then study them at home. I cannot recognize myself, for I am now preparing for life in Eretz Yisrael [the Land of Israel]. Today I handed in quite a long essay for our wall newspaper. I ended it with the slogan: 'Eretz Yisrael awaits us!' I am happy!" The school became an anchor for Tamarah, validating her daily existence. 20 May 1943: "At long last I have found an aim in life. I am no longer forlorn—an individual without a homeland and a people. No! I have found an aim: to struggle, to study, to devote my strength to advance the well-being of my people and my homeland. I am proud of it."[82]

Fourteen-year-old Yitskhok Rudashevski in Vilna shared her sentiments exactly. He too felt lost without the opportunity for education. To go to school provided a structure for normality; its absence meant a void and dead end. On 19 September 1942, fifteen months after Vilna fell to the German army (24 June 1941) and a year after the institution of the ghetto (6 September 1941), Rudashevski admitted his despair in his diary. "It is cold and sad. When in the world will we get back to our studies? When I used to go to my lessons, I knew how to divide the days, and the days would fly, and now they drag by for me grayly and sadly. Oh, how dreary and sad it is to sit locked up in a ghetto." A few weeks later (5 October), classes began and he was delighted. "Finally I have lived to see the day. Today we go to school. The day passed quite differently. Lessons, subjects. . . . There is a happy spirit in school. . . . My own life is shaping up in quite a different way! We waste less time, the day is divided and flies by very quickly. . . . Yes, that is how it should be in the ghetto, the day should fly by and we should not waste time."[83]

MANY GHETTO communities carried on a rich cultural and intellectual life in the face of persecution. As the Jewish Councils well realized, Jewish musicians, actors, poets, and writers who had lost their jobs when the war began needed employment. Special culture departments were organized, and negotiations ensued with the German authorities for permission to mount performances, public lectures, and exhibits. "We are asking for permission to have concerts in order to provide jobs for the musicians," Czerniakow noted in his diary on 1 August 1940. He was successful. "A benefit concert in 'Melody Palace' took place in support of the Child[ren]'s Month fund," he reported over a year later.[84]

By decree, only music by non-Aryans was to be played. "One dare not play Aryan music, and only the music of those Jews who were Aryans by adoption [conversion], i.e., Mendelssohn, Calmann, Bizet, and Meyerbeer," Emmanuel Ringelblum explained in February 1941.[85] But cultural expression was not so easily curbed. For Chaim Kaplan, it was a question of segregation. The Jews were socially, politically, and physically segregated from the rest of the world, but they continued to claim a cultural and intellectual connection with civilization beyond the ghetto walls until that too became life-threatening.

April 30, 1942 . . .
The process of discrimination between Jews and other peoples intensifies daily. It is now forbidden to a Jew to drink at the fountains of Aryan wisdom and culture. In order to implement this prohibition fully, the Commissar of the ghetto, Auerswald, published an order which, on pain of all kinds of harsh penalties, strictly forbids the ghetto cafés and theaters to use any literary, art, or musical work produced or composed by an Aryan. As a matter of fact, this prohibition has been in existence for a while, but it was honored in the breach more than in the practice. Now the Nazis have begun to enforce it rigorously.[86]

Czerniakow was more laconic: "At noon a concert . . . Jewish compositions were played and sung. The audience was full. A very good performance."[87]

Both observers were correct. German insistence upon the "racial purity" of musical material was another manifestation of segregation. Nevertheless, ghetto artists played what the rules allowed, drawing large and appreciative

41. Kovno ghetto orchestra. Left to right: *conductor Michael Hofmekler, a boy named Yankale, Boris Stupel, an unknown man, and* (standing) *concertmaster Alexander Stupel, c. 1943.* Photo George Kadish. Michael Hofmekler, courtesy of the United States Holocaust Memorial Museum Photo Archives, Washington, DC.

audiences. Occasionally they managed to mock the German's rule. "Jewish music, which has been banned from Aryan coffee-houses and from the radio, is becoming again a bond between Jews and Christians," Ringelblum wrote in his private notebook in June 1942.

> The other day I heard of one such place of contact between the Ghetto and the Aryan side. At 3 o'clock every Sunday a Jewish symphony orchestra meets at the street crossing of Panska and Zhelazna and they play next to the barbed wire fence which divides the Ghetto from the other side. Hundreds and hundreds of Aryans listen to the music; they go away after each half-hour, leaving the place free for a new crowd of Poles who come to listen to the forbidden music. A Polish policeman collects money from the listeners and gives [the zlotys] to a Jewish policeman, who in turn hands them over to the orchestra. This way it goes on all through the afternoon and until the curfew hour, new crowds of Christians coming again and again to listen to Jewish music.[88]

Christians could not patronize theater performances and literary evenings, which were extremely popular too, as were evening entertainment "clubs." According to Ringelblum, in April 1941 "there are sixty-one night spots in the Warsaw Ghetto."[89]

The vibrant cultural life of the Jews of Warsaw was to be found in many of the long-term ghettos in the German-occupied or annexed east. "Today the ghetto was like a proper city. There was a charity concert in the large hall of the orphanage," Halina Nelken wrote of Cracow on 22 June 1941, the day the Germans invaded the Soviet Union.[90] And in Lodz, as one of the contributors to the clandestine *Chronicle* reported, the deportation of Jews from the west into the ghetto added luster.

> By the second half of November [1941] the House of Culture began to organize concert performances in which the newcomers took part. From the very beginning these concerts have been a great attraction for music lovers. It is worth mentioning that one result of the resettling of new people here is that the ghetto has acquired an array of talented performers—pianists and singers. The piano performances by maestro [Leopold] Birkenfeld of Vienna deserve special mention. Each of Birkenfeld's concerts is truly a feast for the ghetto's music lovers.[91]

Despite hunger, disease, random acts of violence, and planned deportations, the Jews continued to create and produce beauty. Birkenfeld was deported on 14 May 1942; almost immediately another entry noted that "there was a concert performed by the symphony orchestra ... Beethoven's works (excerpts from *Egmont*) were on the program. Miss [Bronislawa] Rotsztat, the favorite of the ghetto audiences, enchanted the public with her beautiful violin performance."[92] The symphony orchestra played, on average, ten concerts a month in 1941 and four each month in 1942. Vilna too had a symphony orchestra. Some political leaders criticized this form of popular forgetting; too audacious, they said; too unmindful of the ghetto's desperate plight. "Theatrical Performances Should Not be Held in Cemeteries," one leaflet proclaimed. But even a harsh critic recognized the value of the yearning for a cultural life. "And yet life is stronger than anything else. The pulse of life begins to beat again in the Vilna ghetto," he wrote. "The concerts, which were at first boycotted, have been accepted by the public; the halls are full. Literary evenings are crowded, and the hall cannot accommodate the throngs who turn out."[93]

At the same time, the ghetto inmates' daily ordeal was nearly impossible. They were isolated in a sphere where the rules changed capriciously every day. No one knew what tomorrow might bring. Cut off from the rest of the world, everyone hungered for news.

> With everybody continually hoping and praying for salvation, the Ghetto provides a fertile breeding ground for the "news broadcasts." . . . People remain hungry for news. Whoever they meet, they ask, *"Vos herts zech?*— What's new?" and not merely as a matter of habit. They genuinely want to know of any developments—particularly good news. One Jew even pleaded, "Let it be untrue, but let it at least be good!" In response to the constant, insatiable demand for news, there has sprung up in the Ghetto a whole distribution network—manufacturers, wholesalers, and retailers—of new stories. There are those who listen to the BBC on clandestine radios or hear reports from non-Jewish acquaintances. Some have become adept at reading between the lines, while others have authoritative sources.
>
> But ghetto cynics retell a story of one inveterate supplier of news stories who was feeling a bit low. When asked the inevitable *"Vos herts zech?"* he replied angrily, "I can't be bothered, make up some story yourself!"[94]

They had little information about the world, and the world had little information about the ghetto. Whatever the Germans chose to tell was a lie. On 19 May 1942 Germans were filming the ghetto, Abraham Lewin recorded in his dairy. They selected people who still looked respectable, brought them to a restaurant, seated them at tables, and ordered meat, fish, liqueurs, and pastries served—at the expense of the Jewish community. "The Jews ate, and the Germans filmed," Lewin wrote. "It is not hard to imagine the motivation behind this. Let the world see the kind of paradise the Jews are living in."[95] On camera and off camera: life continued in the face of death. For the moment.

EARLIER IN this chapter, we pointed out that when one thinks about the Holocaust, the machinery of death and its perpetrators loom large. Similarly, when one thinks about "the Jews" during the Holocaust, it is the Jews of eastern Europe who occupy the center stage, while their co-religionists of central and western Europe are marginalized. This is a distortion of the history of a continentwide genocide; the assault on Jews west of the Oder and the Danube is as important to our understanding of this era as is the onslaught against Jews to the east. Numerically, the communities in the east were far larger, but the suffering of and actions against the smaller western communities were no less important. The extirpation of the one thousand two hundred Jews of Norway from civil society is as great an offense against western civilization as is the extirpation from the body politic of the 3 million Jews of Poland.

While the Germans pondered "territorial solutions" to the "Jewish Problem," the Jews in the west—especially German Jews who had lived under the Nazi regime since 1933—were in limbo, as were the Jews in the east. Poland's Jews were eventually segregated in ghettos surrounded by thick walls as in Warsaw or barbed wire as in Lodz; German Jewry's "limbo status" was invisible, but no less effective for that. As we have seen, the Jews of Germany were relentlessly isolated politically, economically, and socially. By 1938 the Nazi government sought to erase the past; the memory or recognition of former achievements by Jews. A decree of July 1938, for example, ordered that "insofar as this has not yet happened, all streets or parts of streets named after Jews or half-Jews are to be renamed immediately. The old street signs are to be removed at the same time as the new ones are erected."[96]

The November Pogrom of 1938 was a turning point in this process, and it was so understood at the time by German Jews and gentiles alike. For both, it was the end of the beginning; no one knew what the end would be, but everyone recognized a fundamental change. Göring, as plenipotentiary of the Four Year Plan, immediately passed a decree to eliminate Jews from the German economy by 1 January 1939.[97] That same day the Jews were fined RM 100 million, soon increased to 20 percent of Jewish capital, for the "hostile attitude of Jewry against the German people and Reich."[98]

The robbery was not limited to financial assets. In February 1939 Jews were obliged to hand in their valuables: gold, platinum, silver, jewels, artworks, carpets, and so on, keeping only their own wedding band, that of a deceased spouse, one silver watch, and one setting of silver cutlery for personal use.[99] Pawnbrokers acted as agents for the state in this theft. A report written by the overseer of the Dortmundt municipal pawnbrokers complained of the amount of work involved, especially as Jews had waited until the last moment to turn in their possessions. From 23 March to the 31st, when all valuables had to be surrendered, the pawnbrokers had had to work from eight o'clock in the morning until eleven o'clock at night, with only short breaks for lunch and dinner. Nevertheless, the overseer concluded, their work had been necessary. "When in future years a researcher, who only knows about Jews from hearsay, will investigate the papers in the municipal archive in Dortmundt, he will gain the knowledge that also the German municipal pawnbrokers contributed their small part to the Solution of the Jewish Question in Germany."[100]

Jews had only one place in the economy: as forced laborers. With the invasion of Poland in September 1939 and the enlistment of German men in the armed forces, the use of Jewish forced labor mushroomed. Jews were called upon to do the most difficult, exhausting, and dirty jobs in factories, and they received none of the benefits (paid state vacation days, insurance, additional rations) accorded to "Aryans." Nor, often, did their employers provide them with tools to do the assigned work. Jewish forced laborers became a fixture in ammunition works and on street paving and snow removal crews, and cleaning work was also commonly assigned. The Jewish workers came from all strata of society, and as some 83 percent of young Jews under the age of twenty-five had emigrated, leaving two-thirds of the community past middle age, the laborers were also rather elderly. In 1939 the cleaning crew of the toilets of arriving trains at the Lehrter station in Berlin consisted of a former high school teacher, a former owner of a factory, and a painter. They were not given the supplies they needed to do the job.[101]

Jews had no right to a pension, and they received the lowest wages; a normal hourly wage was RM 0.90, while a Jewish forced laborer would earn as little as RM 0.16. Jews were guarded at the worksite: they arrived together under guard, worked in close formation, were not allowed to speak or move about, and left as they came. Hilma Geffen-Ludomer, one of some 10,000 teenagers and young adults remaining in Germany, remembered the end of her school career and the summons for factory work. "When you were fourteen and up, you were to go to the factory for the war effort. I had finished one year in the commercial school, and we had just started the second year, and we were all taken and sent to the factory," she explained. "I worked for Deutsche Telefon Werke, DeTeWe. . . . We were in a separate room; we had a foreman, a non-Jew, a real Nazi; and a woman who was a foreman who was rather nice. And then we were all thrown together, widowed women, younger women like me, kids like me from fourteen and up (I was fifteen). I think we were about twenty-five or thirty. We had absolutely no contact with the other factory workers. We were totally separated. And we had this guy sitting there, this Nazi, looking at us, and the woman who trained us."[102]

Many women were affected even more adversely than the men. First, they did ten hours of forced labor; then, returning home, they were faced with their usual household chores, made nearly impossible by a lack of foodstuffs to cook with and cleaning agents to wash with. Perhaps the situation was most hopeless for young Jews. Denied education or jobs with any meaning, they had no future.

Paid less than everyone else and taxed more, the Jews of Germany sank ever deeper into penury. Whatever money was left could be spent on fewer and fewer items. On 1 December 1939, just three months after the war began, the

Agricultural Ministry determined that Jews would not be allowed to purchase special food allocations. Victor Klemperer, the Jewish professor of Romance languages and literature who taught at the Dresden Technical University, was a convert to Christianity and was married to a Christian woman. He described his visit to the Jewish Community House in Dresden "beside the burned-down and leveled synagogue" to pay yet another tax imposed on the Jews alone. "The coupons for gingerbread and chocolate were being cut from the food ration cards." And, he added, "clothing cards had to be surrendered as well: Jews receive clothing only on special application to the Community."[103] From that point on, Jews were forbidden to buy clothing, shoes, or shoe leather. Growing children's sole source of "new" garments was used clothing from communal supplies or people fortunate enough to emigrate.

As the months passed, new orders carried more restrictions—fewer meat, fruit, and butter coupons, and none for legumes, cocoa, or rice. Jews were banned from buying unrationed foods, such as chicken, fish, and smoked meats.[104] Restricted shopping hours, usually late in the afternoon after "Aryan" customers had emptied the shelves, meant that nothing remained to buy when they were permitted to shop.

With little money and even less available for purchase, Jews and those whom (like Klemperer) the Nazis labeled Jews leaned ever more heavily on gentile friends or relations. And gentiles were ever more fearful. On Christmas eve 1939, a former student brought Klemperer food: two veal scallops, an egg, some honey, a bar of chocolate, and a few other things. "We were both deeply moved," Klemperer wrote in his diary. "These extraordinary times. These are presents one gives a professor! It is an expression of courage and a profession of opposition." A year later, the same former student sent a much smaller package, with a couple of gingerbreads and apples, a little pearl barley, some blancmange powder, and an unsigned holiday card.[105] By Christmastime 1941, the Germans had given up on a "territorial solution" to the "Jewish Problem," and the Jews of Germany had been marked with a star. The former student sent nothing.

By that time, too, Jews were not allowed to purchase soap or shaving cream. The purpose of this order was stated explicitly: "by means of this men will be marked as Jews by their beards."[106] As in the east, the Germans transformed Jews into the caricatures the Nazis had depicted from the beginning. In the winter of 1941–42 Jews were forced to surrender their warm clothes, especially woolens and furs which were to go to the army. Dressed in old garments, unable to wash properly, men unshaven, the Jews became the shabby and apparently depraved underclass German propaganda had described for the better part of a decade. This was no small matter in the Third Reich: asocials were automatically imprisoned in concentration camps. If a Jew defied the regulations, she or he was deported or killed just the same. The forty-eight-year-old Margarethe Frank was arrested in Rheydt on 7 February 1942 because she was wearing a fur collar and muff. The Gestapo head office recommended imprisonment in the

Ravensbrück concentration camp: she had "sabotaged the measures of the state to ensure the military readiness of the Wehrmacht."[107] Margarethe Frank was not deported to Ravensbrück; on 22 April she was sent to the village of Izbica in Lublin district, a waiting room for the Belzec extermination camp.

THE DECREES that robbed Jews of their possessions and locked them out of the economy were accompanied by decrees designed to ensure their isolation from society. Immediately after the November Pogrom they were banned from theaters, cinemas, concerts, or exhibitions.[108] The next month they were forced to sell their cars and forbidden to use the dining or sleeping cars in trains. All hotels and restaurants used by party members were off-limits.[109]

As the years passed, Jews were isolated from each other too. The myth of a separate Jewish sphere, which had led to a cultural and spiritual renaissance among German Jews, exploded. The government closed Jewish publishing houses and bookshops.[110] Jewish organizations, so critical in community life before, were shut down as well. The introduction of a curfew made human contact even more difficult. In May 1940, Jews were not allowed out from nine in the evening until five the next morning. In October the period was lengthened from 8:00 p.m. until 6:00 a.m. "New intensification of Jewish harassment," Victor Klemperer wrote on 20 December. "After eight o'clock confined in the apartment itself. Visiting other residents in the house, spending time in the entrance hall or on the stairs, is prohibited."[111]

If the November Pogrom in 1938 was a hinge moment, so was the period in the late summer and early fall of 1941 when the Germans abandoned the idea of a "territorial solution" to the "Jewish Problem." "The 'Jewish star,' black on yellow cloth, at the center in Hebrew-like lettering 'Jew,' to be worn on the left breast, large as the palm of a hand, issued to us yesterday for 10 pfennigs, to be worn from tomorrow," Klemperer recorded in his diary on 18 September 1941. And then, with infinite sadness and severe understatement, "Today we were outside together in daylight for the last time."[112]

Life's boundaries continued to shrink. Typewriters, bicycles, and cameras were requisitioned in November. Information about the outside world diminished or ceased when they were forbidden newspapers or magazines in February 1942. And friendships with non-Jews were outlawed in April; visits were prohibited.

At the same time as contact and communication with the gentile world was cut, so were the boundaries of personal privacy. Jews had no right to reach out, nor had they any right to private space. On very short notice, they were forced to move to so-called Jew houses, in which one family was crammed into a single room. The well-known poet and writer Gertrud Kolmar decided to remain in Germany when her brother and sisters emigrated; their seventy-eight-year-old father could not leave, and he needed someone to look after him. Forced to sell the family house, father and daughter moved into a four-room apartment in Berlin. Kolmar was called up for forced labor in an ammunition factory in 1941, and she and her father were compelled to take in more and more lodgers. "Since my bed is in the dining area, I actually have no refuge any more, no space to myself," she wrote to her sister.[113]

Jews were forced to invade the private space of other Jews, but the Gestapo crossed the threshold to torment their victims and to enjoy and enrich themselves. Segregation did not bring safety for the Jews, who were constantly subject to the random violence of house searches. "I should like, for once, to lay down the timetable of an ordinary day," Klemperer, frustrated, confided to his diary in August 1942.

> On waking up: Will "they" come today? (There are days that are dangerous and days that are not—e.g., Friday is very dangerous, then "they" presume that purchases already have been made for Sunday.) While washing, showering, shaving: Where to put the soap if "they" come now. Then breakfast: taking everything out of its hiding place, carrying it back to its hiding place. Then doing without a cigar; fear while smoking a pipe [filled with blackberry leaves], for which one doesn't go to prison but does earn blows. Doing without a newspaper. Then the postwoman ringing the bell. Is it the postwoman, or is it "them"? And *what* will the postwoman bring? Then my hours of work. A diary can be fatal; book from the lending library earns blows, manuscripts are torn up. Every few minutes a car goes past. Is it "them"? To the window every time, the kitchen window is at the front, the workroom at the back. Someone or other will certainly ring the doorbell at least once in the morning, at least once in the afternoon. Is it "them"? Then shopping. One suspects "them" in every car, on every bicycle, in every pedestrian. (I have been abused often enough.) It occurs to me that I have just now been carrying my briefcase under my left arm—perhaps the star was concealed, perhaps someone has denounced me. . . . Then I have to call on someone. Question on the way there: Will I be caught up in a house search when I get there? Question on the way home: Have "they" been to our house meanwhile, or are "they" there even now? Agony, when a car stops close by. Is it "them"?[114]

THE MISERY the Nazis had imposed over a number of years upon the Jews of Germany was introduced within a matter of months in Belgium, the Netherlands, and Luxembourg.[115] But if in the Low Countries the anti-Jewish measures were a German initiative—weakly resisted, it is true, but every step German-imposed nevertheless—in France, the French themselves took the initiative. No one was more stunned by this than the Jews living in France. German Jews lived in a country in which antisemitism was built into the state legal system; it was official policy. The Jews of Poland lived in a country with a long history of deep antisemitism. The Germans would not have tolerated any interference by the Poles in their antisemitic program, of course, but the Jews did not expect much from gentile Poles in the way of protection. The Jews in France, by contrast, both native-born and refugee, believed that French authorities would seek to safeguard them. France was the country of the Rights of Man, of asylum, of *liberté, egalité, fraternité.* Those were the founding principles of the state. Jews who had fled to France from the Nazi regime elsewhere in Europe trusted in the national promise of protection. They were utterly betrayed.[116]

Refugees were the first target of the Vichy French government. More than expendable, the Pétain regime longed to be rid of them. French reactionaries had felt threatened in the 1930s by the political experiment of the Popular Front government led by a Jew, Léon Blum, and by the new popular mass culture, which they also attributed to the pernicious influence of the Jews. They wanted to turn back the clock, to regain old and apparently lost values that centered on family and a narrow concept of national unity. One way to protect traditional French culture and values would be to pass the French equivalent to the Nuremberg Laws. "What we want to say is that a giant step will have been taken toward justice and national security when the Jewish people are considered a foreign people," an editorial in the right-wing newspaper *Je suis partout* proclaimed in April 1938.[117] Such sentiments were socially acceptable. Prime Minister Edouard Daladier did not hesitate to appoint Jean Giraudoux, author of a book that spoke of the "invasion" of France by "hundreds of thousands of Ashkenazis" (East European Jews), to the Commissariat of Public Information.[118]

After the November Pogrom in 1938 and the final collapse of the Spanish Republican government early in 1939, the number of people seeking asylum swelled, raising the antisemitic and anti-refugee rhetoric to a new pitch. The declaration of war in 1939 and the swift defeat of France in 1940 proved to arch conservatives that their contentions were correct. Blum's Popular Front had indeed undone France. In the hysteria and bitterness that followed, the refugees were the first to be blamed for the debacle and the first to be victimized. As Arthur Koestler, interned in one of the hastily erected internment camps for Spanish refugees, put it, "A few years ago we had been called the martyrs of Fascist barbarism, pioneers in the fight for civilization, defenders of liberty, and what not; the press and statesmen of the West had made rather a fuss about us, probably to drown the voice of their own bad conscience. Now we had become the scum of the earth."[119]

With German hegemony in the north and Pétain's government in the south, reactionaries could pursue their xenophobic and antisemitic agenda. They acted not at the behest of the Germans, but to advance their vision of France. Within weeks, Vichy authorities interned all Jewish refugees from Germany and Austria. Foreign Jews who had volunteered to fight in the French army were stripped of their military status and incarcerated in labor camps. A significant number were shipped to the Sahara as slave laborers on the Trans-Sahara Railway.

The Germans in Paris had no interest in rounding up Jews at that point; they wished to prevent those who had fled to the south from returning to their homes. Vichy France proved a fine dumping ground; Germans expelled three thousand Jews from Alsace (now annexed to the Reich) to Vichy in the summer of 1940. The operation worked so well that, with ultimate transit to Madagascar in mind, Berlin deported 6,504 German Jews from Baden and the Palatinate to Lyon in sealed trains. A German Foreign Office "Report on the Deportation of Jews of German Nationality to Southern France" of 30 October 1940 described the action. "According to the Gauleiters' orders, 'all persons of Jewish race' must be deported 'in so far as they are fit to travel,' without regard to age or sex." This included veterans, "even men who had participated in the World War of 1914–1918 on the German side as front soldiers and, in some cases, as officers of the old Wehrmacht," as well as the elderly: "The old people's homes in Mannheim, Karlsruhe, Ludwigshafen etc. were evacuated." The army participated in this action. "Wehrmacht vehicles were made available to transport people from remote places to the assembly points." The Jews were given little time to prepare, "a quarter of an hour to two hours depending on the locality." And the ruthless haste provided an excuse for depradation. "Since in many cases the emigration did not take place according to the rules, i.e. without having fulfilled the legal provisions, e.g. payment of the Reich emigration [lit. 'flight'] tax, the property has been impounded."

The transports, the Foreign Office official continued, "have arrived in concentration camps in the south of France at the foot of the Pyrenees after a journey of several days. Since there is a shortage of food and suitable accommodation for the deportees, who consist mainly of old men and women, it is believed here that the French government is intending to send them on to Madagascar as soon as the sea routes have been reopened."[120]

The "suitable accommodation" for these Jews—never sent to Madagascar but, ultimately, to Auschwitz—was a camp in Gurs in the foothills of the Pyrenees. Built as an internment center for Spanish Civil War refugees, Gurs had become an internment center for German Jewish refugees in September 1939. After the arrival of the Jews from Alsace in the summer of 1940, the Vichy government ordered provincial prefects (governors) to intern all foreign Jews. So many people had been stripped of their French citizenship by Pétain's government that "foreign Jews" meant some 50 percent of the Jews living in France.

Like Le Vernet, where Koestler had been interned in 1939, Gurs, Agde, Rivesaltes, Argelès, Les Milles, and the other French camps were crude, miserable places. The normal habits of everyday existence—to eat, drink, relieve oneself, wash one's clothes, and clean oneself—became complicated and enervating undertakings. Women and children were separated from their menfolk. Marie Claus-Grindel was seven and a half years old when her mother, two younger sisters (aged five and four), and she were deported in September 1940 to the transit camp of Agde. Earlier that year they had fled to the small town of La Châtre in the south of France from their home in Strasbourg. The mayor of La Châtre ordered them and all the other refugee Jews to be sent away to a camp. Like other camps, Agde had been built for Spanish refugees. According to a report by Secours Suisse (Swiss Aid) dated 20 November 1940, the camp population was 3,060, 70 of them children.[121] Marie Grindel and her sisters were among them. "It was a camp with no water. Only once a day water trucks came to bring water and we had to queue for hours to have a little bit of water." To go to the toi-let was hazardous and frightening. It was a type of trench latrine; the platform stood a meter high and one reached it by ladder. No walls surrounded the pit; the excrement was fully visible. "One thing which shocked me a lot at the time: it was the toilets. I had [to mount with] a ladder; it was very high, about a meter, with big holes [in the platform], and I could see all the feces below. I was so afraid to fall into it. This is one of the most horrible things, the fear of falling into that shit."[122]

42. Lina Wachtheimer walks through the mud in the Gurs transit camp. Museum of Jewish Heritage, New York, courtesy of the United States Holocaust Memorial Museum, Washington DC.

Washing oneself and one's clothes also posed a problem. According to a report on camp conditions in France (May 1941), in Rivesaltes "the wash basins are too small, the wash houses cannot be cleaned, and at Rivesaltes they are not always provided with drainage pipes." Filth, of course, abounded and "infection with lice was endemic everywhere."[123]

All went hungry, as the May 1941 report detailed.

> Famine rages in the camps, its sinister precursory symptoms already have marked the inmates by the dozens; for six months a considerable part of the population . . . has suffered cruelly from a malnutrition which is only imper-fectly explained by the figure of 800 calories (instead of the essential 1,500 calories—while normal life demands 2,000 to 2,500 calories) and has paid a heavy toll in disease and death. . . .
>
> We assert, after an exhaustive investigation, that the daily ration that con-tains ever smaller quantities of fat, sugar, and albumen does not reach 500 calories per person per day. We contend that, if this situation continues (and in all likelihood it will become worse), the number of survivors will be but a small percentage. . . .
>
> It is a question of life or death.[124]

Despite these harsh conditions, in the transit camps of France (and elsewhere in western and central Europe) as in the ghettos of the east, education remained of great importance to children; a symbol of normal life and a sign of hope for the future. Deportations from the upper Rhineland stretched the population of Gurs to about 13,200, of whom (as the German Jewish population was quite elderly by then) only 400 were children. Of the 250 school-aged youngsters, "200 are divided amongst the four women's blocks, I, K, L, and M," an anonymous social worker reported. Barracks were grouped together into blocks and each block was surrounded by barbed wire. At Gurs one such block contained twenty-two to twenty-four barracks, or twelve to fifteen hundred people. "The rest are in the men's blocks, D, E, G. The I, K, L, and M blocks have their own individual schools. The communal school of the three others will begin one day soon." Taught by teachers from Baden, the curriculum followed that of a normal school: "French, English, arithmetic, geography, religion, (grammar), the natural sciences, gymnastics and the manual skills."[125]

Nor did cultural activities cease in the transit camps. In France, unlike anywhere else in Europe, social workers from various philanthropic organizations (such as OSE; the American Friends' Service Committee; the Unitarian Service; CIMADE; Service Social d'Aide aux Emigrants; and Secours Suisse) were permitted to live in the camps on a voluntary basis to help as best they could. According to Elisabeth Hirsch, a social worker at Gurs, the camp "was very well organized, from the social [i.e., cultural] point of view, by the inmates themselves. That was in '41. [There were] physicians, musicians, nurses; really very competent people who organized lectures and concerts. There was the rabbi who did commentaries on the Torah—really remarkable things."[126] Ruth Lambert, the OSE resident social worker at Gurs, agreed. In a letter written in 1944 summarizing her stay in the camp, she noted: Fritz "Brunner [the violinist, and his accompanist, the pianist] Leval and their concerts, every Sunday from 10:30 AM until noon for fifteen months. Painting exhibits, handicrafts. Plays, the famous revues of Nathan-Leval, numerous artists of all sorts and marvelous caricaturists!"[127] The program for a Christmas concert in 1940 featured Gounod's "Ave Maria," the overture from Mozart's *Marriage of Figaro,* a Puccini duet from *La Bohème,* and "Frére Jacques," "Daughter of Zion," and a children's chorus.[128]

Jews in the transit camps, like their co-religionists in ghettos in the east, struggled to go on living. They did not know what awaited them, but they understood their plight was dire. "Take my child," many mothers implored Vivette Samuel, an OSE voluntary intern at Rivesaltes. "Everyone presents her 'case' as the most urgent. Mme G . . . enters my office with her four children: Henri, Jacques, Frieda, and Léon." Madame G. had heard about the OSE social workers, and she had come in the hope of obtaining the release of her children. "All her energy was focused on this new goal: to get her children away, to give them a chance to leave the filth, the vermin, and the crowding. 'So that they may live, if our end is to die.'"[129]

What Madame G. did not know was that life outside the barbed wire was not safe either. In July 1940, a Vichy government commission reviewed all naturalizations since 1927, looking to strip "undesirables" of their French citizenship. The following month, legal restraints against hatemongering in the press were quashed. Most ominous, the Pétain regime passed its own *Statut des juifs* in October, defining Jewishness and excluding those so labeled from the upper echelons of the civil service, the officer corps and the ranks of non-commissioned officers, and from professions that influenced public opinion: teaching, the press, radio, film, and theater.[130]

These moves jibed with Himmler's security police in Paris. The Jewish affairs bureau of the local Gestapo office was headed by SS-Hauptsturmführer Theodor Dannecker, an ideologically committed antisemite who answered directly to Adolf Eichmann at the Reich Security Main Office in Berlin. Dannecker convened the representatives of various German agencies for a meeting in Paris on 3 February 1941 to discuss the removal of all Jews from Europe. It was the first of a series of weekly meetings on the subject.

At Dannecker's suggestion, Vichy authorities created a special department for Jewish affairs, the Commissariat Général aux Questions Juives (CGQJ) in March. The CGQJ was headed by another convinced antisemite, but also an anti-German French nationalist, Xavier Vallat. Vallat saw himself as a surgeon called upon to save France. To do so, he must use a scalpel. "France was stricken with a Jewish brain fever of which she almost died," he claimed.[131] Clearly, the "disease" had to be cut away. Some 25,000 established and culturally assimilated families could remain, but the rest of the Jews in France would have to go. Where that might be, Vallat neither knew nor cared. "It will be the victor's business, if he intends to organize a durable peace, to find the means, worldwide if possible, European in any case, to settle the wandering Jew."

Vallat established a new and even more stringent *Statut des juifs* (2 June 1941), and he ordered a census of all Jews in the unoccupied zone. Prefects had been granted the power to intern foreign Jews in October 1940. Now they could intern any Jew suspected of having violated the *Statut des juifs,* or any the prefect simply wished to punish for another reason. Thus the French Jews lost civil protection. They also were stripped of business and property; without prodding by the Germans, Vichy passed a series of measures to "Aryanize" Jewish property.

Sometimes a step ahead of the Germans, and always nimbly adopting their suggestions,

43. Distribution of Star of David patch to Jews at a Paris police station, June 1942. Bibliothèque Historique de la Ville de Paris, courtesy of the United States Holocaust Memorial Museum Photo Archives, Washington, DC.

Pétain and his ministers collaborated fully in Hitler's antisemitic program for the New Europe. Only one boundary did Vichy refuse to cross. Despite the urging of General Otto von Stülpnagel, head of the military government in the occupied zone, French authorities refused to mark Jews with a star. Measures removing the Jews from public life were sufficient, Prime Minister Admiral François Darlan told the Germans. The star would "profoundly shock public opinion which would see these measures as mere harassment without any real utility either for the future of the country or for the security of the occupation troops."[132] If the Germans insisted upon it, he warned, French people would begin to see the Jews as martyrs.

The occupation authorities introduced the star in the northern zone without the cooperation of Vichy in June 1942. And, as Darlan had predicted, it was this measure that finally seemed to generate public nausea. In the country that had formulated the rights of man, to be forcibly marked was seen as an offense against human dignity. Jews were fellow citizens. Their persecution measured the defeat of the French nation and reflected their own sense of helplessness. "Ces pauvres gens" (Those poor people), Odette Bérujeau, visibly pained, recalled fifty years later. A young Catholic widow with four small children to raise in wartime Paris, she lived near the predominantly Jewish neighborhood of the rue des Rosiers, and remembered the sight of the starred Jews vividly. "It was horrible, just to see it was horrible—and I did not even know what would come." What Madame Bérujeau also remembered was her impotence: "And what could I do?"[133]

Darlan had been correct. The star that spotlighted the Jews also cast its glare on the atrocities committed against them. Most French people may have felt as helpless as Odette Bérujeau, but helplessness did not mean complicity. Vichy could no longer count on tacit popular support for antisemitic measures. Initiative now fell to the Germans. They were prepared. The trains began to roll east in July.

Chapter Nine

IN THE SHADOW
OF DEATH

WESTERN EUROPEAN JEWS faced death when the Germans opened the box-cars and pulled them out onto the unloading ramps of Sobibór, Treblinka, and Auschwitz. Jews in the ghettos of eastern Europe faced death every day. No Jew in the west starved to death or died of infectious disease arising from murderous overcrowding in the cities' Jewish quarters. Not so the east. All the smuggling and the concerts and the clandestine classes could not long relieve the misery of the ghetto. Every Jewish person faced hunger, disease, and a constant threat of deportation. Physical conditions in the ghetto led to death. German policy led to death. In Warsaw, for example, 30 percent of the city's population squeezed into 2.5 percent of its area. Refugees from smaller cities and towns in the Warsaw district swelled the ghetto population to 450,000 in 1941, or 110,000 people per square kilometer and over nine persons per room.[1] A mere 4 percent of the city streets fell within the Jewish quarter (73 out of 1,800), and most did not run their entire length; a piece was in the ghetto and the remainder was on the "other side." Food was as unequally allocated as land: daily rations allowed the Germans came to 2,613 calories, 699 to gentile Poles, and 184 for Jews.[2] An American Jewish philanthropic organization, the Joint Distribution Committee, reported at the end of 1940 that 1.25 million people, or 57 percent of the Jewish population in Nazi-occupied Poland (the Government General and the areas annexed to the Reich), needed social assistance.[3] And this was just the beginning.

Other ghettos of the German-occupied east suffered just as deeply. Hanna Kent-Sztarkman, her eighteen-year-old brother Heniek, and their mother arrived in Radom without family savings or possessions. As Heniek explained, "We found ourselves without means very, very quickly." He and his mother realized how important it was, especially for people such as they who lacked money or connections, to find employment. "The main work in the ghetto was to work for the *Altestenrat* [Jewish Council], so I got some meaningless clerical job in the health department," Heniek recalled. It was January 1940. "Eventually I was transferred to another department which had to do with the allocation of provisions."[4]

While Heniek's job was useful, Mrs. Sztarkman's position was far more valuable: it provided food. She worked in an SS military camp which eventually had some eighty Jewish slave skilled laborers attached to it. "One of the fellows who worked there told [my mother] that they were looking for somebody [to cook for the Jewish workers]. None of the ladies of Radom, at this stage of the game, were forced to take such a position, because they were local while we were already uprooted. So [my mother] was more inclined to take such a job than they were at this stage." It was thanks to this that the family did not starve. "She brought, usually hidden on her body, lentils or potatoes or beans. We lived on that, together with the normal rations which were almost non-existent, just a few decagrams of bread."[5]

44. Heniek Sztarkman, age twenty, 1941. Coll. authors.

Day by day, week by week, month by month, the situation worsened, conditions deteriorated, and the atmosphere tensed. They were, as Heniek said, "dancing on the rim of the volcano."[6] One could not live long on the official ration. "I remember walking on the street and seeing those youths swollen with hunger," Hanna recalled. "People were starving. We were among the lucky few that we were not starving from hunger because of my mother's work, and my brother was working. There was always some food, there was no starvation for us. But you could see swollen children lying on the streets. It became such an everyday thing."[7]

In Radom, as in the streets of Warsaw, Vilna, Lodz, and elsewhere, starving children begged for bread, and then grew too weak to beg at all. In a starkly visible way, these children indexed the misery of the community. Philanthropic organizations and Jewish Councils strove to cope with destitute and orphaned children, but the needs overwhelmed their meager resources. Refugee shelters, orphanages, day centers, and house committee grass-roots efforts could not support their clients, and so many more remained outside the institutional network. According to Adolf Berman, the director of CENTOS (the National Society for the Care of Orphans), "of the over 400,000 Jews living within the [Warsaw] ghetto walls, approximately 100,000 were children below the age of 15. At least 75 percent of these children were in need of assistance and welfare." Enormous effort and energy focused on this disaster, but "it soon became evident that . . . it was not possible to render aid to the thousands of children who had recently become orphans as a result of the terrible mortality rate (from starvation and plague [i.e., typhus]) or even to alleviate the distress of the 'street urchins' and children of the refugees. It was impossible to assist the large numbers of other children who were in urgent need."[8]

"Two little boys are begging in the street next to our gate," Janina Bauman wrote in her diary on 18 April 1941.

I see them every time I go out. Or they might be girls, I don't know. Their heads are shaven, clothes in rags, frightfully emaciated tiny faces bring to mind birds rather than human beings. Their huge black eyes, though, are human; so full of sadness. . . . The younger one may be five or six, the older ten perhaps. They don't move, they don't speak. The little one sits on the pavement, the bigger one just stands there with his claw of a hand stretched out.[9]

"The most painful" sight for Emmanuel Ringelblum "was the begging of three- and four-year old children."[10] Chaim Kaplan agreed. "In the gutters, amidst the refuse, one can see almost naked and barefoot little children wailing pitifully," he wrote in his diary on 4 January 1942.[11] "Children's bodies and crying serve as a persistent background for the ghetto," Ringelblum lamented.[12] They were present day and night.

A special class of beggars consists of those who beg after nine o'clock at night. . . . They walk out right into the middle of the street, begging for bread. Most of them are children. In the surrounding silence of the night, the cries of the hungry beggar children are terribly insistent. . . . These beggars are completely unconcerned about curfews. . . . They are afraid of nothing and of no one. It's a common thing for beggar children like these to die on the sidewalk at night. I was told about one such horrible scene that took place in front of Muranowska Street where a six-year-old beggar boy lay gasping all night, too weak to roll over to the piece of bread that had been thrown down to him from the balcony.[13]

Hunger and famine haunted ghetto life, for everyone. As Sara Grossman-Weil explained half a century later:

Children were brought into the [Lodz] ghetto who couldn't walk for lack of nourishment. They just couldn't walk. This is how rampant hunger was. This is what malnutrition did to us. We were always on the look-out for some food, for some crumbs. You wouldn't dare to leave a crumb on the table. You would put anything into your mouth.

I don't think anything hurts as much as hunger. You become wild. You're not responsible for what you say and what you

45. Destitute orphans, Warsaw ghetto. Photo Joe. J. Heydecker.

do. You become an animal in the full meaning of the word. You prey on others. You will steal. This is what hunger does to us. It dehumanizes you. You're not a human being any more.

Slowly, slowly the Germans were achieving their goal. I think they let us suffer from hunger, not because there was not enough food, but because this was their method of demoralizing us, of degrading us, of torturing us. These were their methods, and they implemented these methods scrupulously.

Therefore we had very many, many deaths daily. Very many sick people for whom there was no medication, no help, no remedy. We just stayed there, and laid there, and the end was coming.

I never knew that nutrition, that food, not only is important to satisfy your hunger, but what it does to your physique. It impairs your walking, movements, sight, hearing. Every sense is not so sharp or acute as it should be. This was what was happening in the ghetto. . . .

We were so suppressed, we were so dehumanized, we were so under-the-boot, so obsessed with satisfying this terrible hunger that nothing else mattered really. There was no other topic of conversation—if there was any conversation. There was no socializing to speak of. Other than that there was nothing to live for, just some dim hope that maybe the tomorrow will be better than the today.[14]

Disease followed in the wake of starvation, and death followed disease. Hunger was so prevalent that physicians in the Warsaw ghetto studied clinical and biochemical aspects of starvation, smuggling out their findings to be published after the war.[15]

In the early 1930s, 8 percent of all deaths among Warsaw's Jews was due to tuberculosis; by 1941 the figure had soared to 33.7 percent. In Lodz, tuberculosis accounted for over half of all illness from infectious diseases during the entire duration of the ghetto (1940–44).[16] The Jews well knew this danger, and its close association with hunger. "Friday, May 16 [1941]. Lodz. I have been examined by a doctor at school. She was terrified at how thin I am," Dawid Sierakowiak confided to his diary. "She immediately gave me a referral for X rays. Perhaps I will now be able to get a double portion of soup in school." He feared falling ill. "The checkup has left me frightened and worried. Lung disease is the latest hit in ghetto fashion; it sweeps people away as much as dysentery and typhus. As for the food, it's worse and worse everywhere."[17]

With its dramatic symptoms of a vivid skin rash, high fever, delirium, and rapid weakening, typhus was even more alarming. Again, German brutality was to blame—overcrowding, lack of running water and flush toilets, soap and other cleaning agents, food, and clean clothes. Body lice, which transmit typhus, thrived in such filth. "The poor are terribly lousy. They don't have half a cake of soap among them, live in fearful conditions, crowded, filthy," Emmanuel Ringelblum noted in June 1941. "The nurses of the TOZ—Society for the Protection of the Health of Jews—found complete nests of lice under the bandages of the poor." Within a few months, typhus struck indiscriminately. "Next to hunger, typhus is the question that is most generally absorbing for the Jewish populace. It has become the burning question of the hour. The graph line of typhus cases keeps climbing. For example, now, the middle of August, there are some six or seven thousand patients in [private] apartments, and about nine hundred in hospitals." Indeed, by this time, Ringelblum recorded the common belief that typhus was "particularly dangerous for the so-called 'better class of people.'" According to Ringelblum, the professional class did "everything to avoid lice. Some of them smear oil and naphtha on their bodies, others carry [vials of] foul-smelling sabidilla around with them to drive off the lice. But the lice are omnipresent."[18]

Winter promised greater hardships. "The doctors are fearful that next winter every fifth person—and some maintain that the figure will be as high as every other person—will be sick with typhus. All the disinfection techniques are to no avail."[19] Ringelblum's apprehensions proved correct. "This is our third winter under the Nazi regime and our second within the ghetto," Chaim Kaplan wrote in his diary on 10 November 1941. "Contagious diseases and especially typhus continue to take their toll. There is not a family which has not lost one or even several of its members."[20]

When the Polish patriot Jan Kozielowski (better known by his underground name Jan Karski) smuggled himself into the ghetto in the fall of 1942 to obtain firsthand knowledge about the destruction of Polish Jewry, he was overwhelmed. Determined to pass this information to the west, Karski courted danger constantly. But after witnessing two Hitler Youth boys casually murder an ordinary Jew on a ghetto street, he fled. "It is hard to explain why I ran," Karski reflected. "There was no occasion for speed and, if anything, our haste could have aroused suspicion. But I ran, I think, simply to get a breath of clean air and a drink of water. Everything there seemed polluted by death, the stench of rotting corpses, filth and decay." Disease was so present as to be almost palpable. "I was careful to avoid touching a wall or a human being. I would have refused a drink of water in that city of death if I had been dying of thirst. I believe I even held my breath as much as I could in order to breathe in less of the contaminated air."[21]

The Germans had triumphed: they had transformed the ghetto into what they had said it was all along, a breeding ground for disease—typhus, in particular. As an instruction manual for SS men explained,

The German East was for centuries the German people's space of destiny. It will remain so for the following centuries. The *ethnic mosaic* of the East demands a *new arrangement,* which is historically, morally and ethically totally justified.

With the *new ordering of the space of the East* there is not only the *German-Polish problem* and that caused by other ethnic minorities, but also the *Solution to the Jewish Problem* as such. . . . **Europe's East became the launching pad and reserve of Jewry. Because from there new hordes of Jews descended again and again on the world. . . .**

The problem of *fighting epidemics* in the East stands in close connection with the solution to the Jewish Problem. Epidemics have always been more frequent and stronger in eastern Europe than in other areas of the continent. ... The *Ghettos* were the places from which these originated. The comprehensive fight against epidemics, including inoculation and sanitary measures, had to be initiated in the East to gain control over this curse.[22]

Ghettos such as these provided the perfect dumping ground for "Gypsies" too. Not knowing where else to unload them, the Germans alighted on this "solution." With Himmler's approval, 4,996 Austrian Roma and Sinti were sent to Lodz ghetto in November 1941.[23] They were incarcerated in a few houses with no furniture and little sanitation, separated from the ghetto by a barbed-wire fence. Food came from the Jewish Council.[24] Mortality was high: on 1 December, the chroniclers of the Lodz ghetto noted that 213 "Gypsies" already had died. "The overwhelming majority of the bodies removed from the camp were those of children."[25] Separated from the Jews while alive, the Roma and Sinti were also buried in their own plot in the Jewish cemetery. Typhus broke out in the "Gypsy" section in December and raged uncontrolled until the Germans decided to end the epidemic with a mortal blow. "For the last ten days the 'Gypsies' have been taken away in trucks," the *Chronicle* recorded. "The camp, which is practically deserted now, will no doubt be entirely eliminated by the end of this week. Apparently, its elimination was dictated by necessity, since there was a danger that the typhus would spread."[26] Sanitation through murder: they had been taken to a killing center in the nearby village of Chelmno.

The *Chronicle* did not report what the Lodz Jews thought of the Roma and Sinti, but Emmanuel Ringelblum confided his dismay to his diary when they were deported to the Warsaw ghetto. "We are being afflicted now with a new blight—the Gypsies," he wrote on 17 June 1942.

How will we put up with them nobody knows. They wear white armbands with a red "Z" printed on them, standing for Gypsies [in German, *Zigeuner*], or as the Poles say, "zlodzieje" [Polish for "thieves"]. ... Perhaps the Herrenvolk do it simply for aesthetic reasons. They cannot abide the faces of dirty beggars. ... It is also possible that they wish to toss into the Ghetto everything that is characteristically dirty, shabby, bizarre, of which one ought to be frightened and which anyway has to be destroyed. That was the reason for throwing Gypsies first into the Lodz Ghetto, and then to Chelmno and finally gassing them there.

Meanwhile 240 families were brought to 5 Pokorna Street. People are afraid of them. They will rob, steal, break window panes and pinch bread out of shop windows. They will not quietly starve to death as Jews do.[27]

Chaim Kaplan looked at the forced cohabitation of Jews and "Gypsies" with more equanimity. It was "an excellent match," he observed on 18 June.

Just as the Jew is a wanderer, so is the Gypsy, and the main thing is that the Nuremberg Laws fall on both of them, and marriage between them and "Aryans" is forbidden. For all these reasons the two can dwell together. The impure can't defile the impure.[28]

The marriage was not to last. That same day Adam Czerniakow noted drily, "It is reported that the Gypsies are to be deported from the ghetto. Thus I will not be an emperor of the Ethiopians anymore."[29] Perhaps, as in Lodz, fear of disease prompted the Germans to strike once again. Certainly they dreaded the typhus that the conditions they imposed engendered.

Walled ghettos were a "sanitary measure," Hans Frank explained to Curzio Malaparte, the correspondent for Italy's *Corriere della Sera,* assigned in 1941 to report on his country's army on the eastern front. An adventurer, journalist, novelist, publisher, politician, musician, and actor, Malaparte had been prominent in the Fascist movement in the 1920s. Disillusioned with Mussolini in the 1930s, he was exiled for a year to the Lipari Islands. Upon his release, Malaparte joined *Corriere della Sera.* As he traveled in this official capacity he filed articles, kept a diary, and wrote *Kaputt,* the book that would make him famous after the war.

The events described in *Kaputt* were sketched in his diary and, when they involved Hans Frank, in the

Die Ghettos, die Seuchenherde Polens; Stadtplan von Warschau mit Einzeichnung der verseuchten Bezirke. Im Ghetto liegt Seuchenherd neben Seuchenherd. Um eine Verschleppung der Seuchen zu vermeiden, wird für die nichtjüdische Bevölkerung der Zutritt zu den verseuchten Gebieten verboten

Starrend vor Ungeziefer und Schmutz, erfüllt mit Gezeter und Gestank, das ist das Ghetto

46. *A German propaganda book about the occupation of Poland shows the Warsaw ghetto as a breeding ground of infectious diseases. The caption reads: "The ghettos are the source of epidemics in Poland. A map of Warsaw with indications of the infected areas. In the ghetto, one source of epidemics is next to another. To avoid the spread of epidemics, the non-Jewish population has been forbidden to enter the infected areas." The lower caption reads: "Bristling with vermin and filth, filled to the brim with screaming and stench: that is the ghetto." H. Gauweiler,* Deutsches Vorfeld im Osten *(Cracow, 1941). Coll. authors.*

Governor General's diary as well. Thus, for example, Frank noted that he had
"tea because of the reception of 'the Italian chief editor' Malaparte" when the
journalist arrived in Cracow on 23 January 1942.³⁰ Malaparte went on to dinner
that evening with Otto Gustav Wächter, the governor of Cracow. The next day,
Malaparte, Frank's senior aide in charge of press affairs Emil Gassner, Frank
and his wife Brigitte, and Mrs. Wächter traveled to Warsaw, although not
together. No matter. After Malaparte visited the ghetto in the morning—pruri-
ence? pure interest? compassion?—he met up with the rest of the company for
lunch at the Belvedere Palace. Ludwig Fischer, the governor of Warsaw, joined
them. Hearing that Malaparte had walked through the ghetto, Brigitte Frank
remarked that the Jewish quarter was very dirty, "*so schmutzig.*" "Jews like to
live like that," said Emil Gassner, laughing.

Malaparte reconstructed the conversation in *Kaputt.* No German would tolerate living under such conditions, Frank announced.

> "A German would not be able to live under such conditions," said Wächter.
> "The German people are a civilized people," I said.
> "*Ja, natürlich,*" said Fischer.
> "It must be admitted that it is not altogether the fault of the Jews," said
> Frank. "The space in which they are herded is rather small for a population
> of that size. But, basically, the Jews like to live in filth. Filth is their natural
> habitat. Perhaps it is because they are all sick, and the sick, as a last resort,
> tend to take refuge in filth. It is sad that they die like rats."

The conversation continued, turning to the slower than expected decline of the
ghetto population.

> "The Jews persist in having children," I said. "It is all the fault of the chil-
> dren."
> "*Ach, die kinder!*—Ah, the children!" said Frau Brigitte Frank.
> "*Ja, so schmutzig*—Yes, so dirty," said Frau Fischer.
> "Ah, did you notice the children in the ghetto?" asked Frank. "They are
> horrible! They are dirty and diseased; they are covered with scabs and prey
> for vermin; they would be pitiful if they were not so loathsome. They look
> like skeletons. The child death rate is very high in the ghettos. What's the
> children's death rate in the Warsaw ghetto?" he asked, turning to Governor
> Fischer.
> "Fifty-four percent," replied Fischer.
> "The Jews are a diseased race, in full decay," said Frank. "They are all
> degenerates. They do not know how to rear children or how to care for
> them, as we do in Germany."
> "Germany is a country with a high *Kultur,*" I said.
> "*Ja, natürlich,* in child hygiene Germany leads the world," said Frank.³¹

The dinner-table talk that night foretold acts to come. The Germans indeed wished Jews to die faster in the ghettos of eastern Europe. Whenever the authorities believed a ghetto population was too large, they staged dragnet operations, or *razzias,* without warning, and shipped off the unlucky souls to an "unknown destination." And when the Germans finally abandoned the idea of a "territorial solution" to "the Jewish Problem" in the late summer to early fall of 1941, they emptied the ghettos one by one. Shoved into a central square, Jews were marched to a train siding, and deported to a killing installation or slave labor concentration camp.

Kovno's ghetto was formed in July 1941 and sealed on 15 August. Ten weeks later, on Saturday 25 October, SS-Oberscharführer Helmut Rauca, the Gestapo official in charge of Kovno's Jewish affairs, "accompanied by a high-ranking Gestapo officer," entered "the offices of the [Jewish] Council." As Avraham Golub recorded immediately after the events had taken place, "Rauca did not waste time. He opened with a major pronouncement: it is imperative to increase the size of the Jewish labor force in view of its importance for the German war effort—an illusion to the indispensability of Jewish labor to the Germans." He intended, he said, to increase the food rations for the workers and their families; thus they had to be separated from ghetto inmates who were not part of the labor force. "To carry out this operation a roll call would take place. The Council was to issue an order in which all the Ghetto inmates, without exception, and irrespective of sex and age, were called to Demokratu Square on October 28 at 6 A.M. on the dot. In the square they should line up by families and the workplace of the family head. When leaving for the roll call they were to leave their apartments, closets, and drawers open. Anybody found after 6 A.M. in his home would be shot on the spot."[32]

A fearful Council complied and posted the announcement in Yiddish and German. "No one in the Ghetto closed an eye on the night of October 27." Some prayed, others mourned. People threw big parties to eat all the food and drink all the liquor they had. This might be their last feast. Why leave anything for the Germans? Some ghetto inhabitants who thought they qualified as "workers" sought to adopt orphans in order to protect them through their own job papers; single women or widows looked to attach themselves to "husband" laborers.[33]

Tuesday morning, October 28, was rainy . . .
Many families stepped along slowly, holding hands. They all made their way in the same direction—to Demokratu Square. It was a procession of mourners grieving over themselves. . . .
A deathlike silence pervaded this procession tens of thousands strong. Every person dragged himself along, absorbed in his own thoughts, pondering his own fate and the fate of his family whose lives hung by a thread.

Thirty thousand lonely people, forgotten by God and by man, delivered to the whim of tyrants whose hands had already spilled the blood of many Jews.

All of them, especially heads of families, had equipped themselves with some sort of document, even a certificate of being employed by one of the ghetto institutions, or a high school graduation diploma, or a German university diploma. . . .

The Ghetto inmates were lined up in columns according to the workplace of the family heads. . . .

The square was surrounded by machine-gun emplacements. Rauca positioned himself on top of a little mound from which he could watch the great crowd. . . . Then he signaled with the baton he held in his hand and ordered. . . . "Forward!" The selection had begun. . . .

At first, nobody knew which was the "good" side. Many therefore rejoiced at finding themselves on the right. . . .

Those who tried to pass over from the right to the left, in order to join their families, or because they guessed—correctly, as it turned out—that that was the "good" side, immediately felt the pain of blows dealt by the hands and rifle butts of the policemen and the partisans, who brutally drove them back. . . .[34]

The selection went on all day and into the night. At its end, 10,000 people were sealed into a small area. The following morning "the assault was so unexpected and so brutal that the wretched inmates did not have a single moment to grasp what was going on." They were force-marched on a uphill road that "led Jews in one direction alone—to a place from which no one returned."[35] And no one did. The ghetto population had numbered 30,022 people in August; some 2,500 had been killed in two *Aktionen* on 26 September and 4 October. Now 10,000 were murdered; about 17,000 Jews remained in the Kovno ghetto.

Adam Czerniakow, Elder of the Warsaw ghetto, faced the same dilemma: Should he comply with a German order that promised work for all, but separated elderly parents from adult sons, small children from their parents? On 22 July 1942, the Germans demanded Czerniakow's signature on a deportation order for resettlement to the east. It was nearly a year after the Kovno *Aktion,* and Czerniakow had few illusions left. The Germans continued to insist that "resettlement" meant agricultural work, but Czerniakow was not deceived. He understood that all of his effort as head of the *Judenrat* had been mere manipulation, a convenience for the Germans.

If the Elder of the Kovno ghetto, Elkhanan Elkes, finally had been persuaded by Rauca that the roll call was "a purely administrative matter" and that "no evil intentions lurked behind it,"[36] Czerniakow, ten months later, realized that what he was asked to do was the very essence of evil. It was nothing less than participation in a selection for murder, nothing less than collaboration in the Germans' arrogation to themselves of the right to decide who would live and who was to die. Children were on the list of people to be "resettled." Czerniakow knew that "resettled" meant "murdered," and he would not sign. He preferred to kill himself rather than to collude in the murder of children. He committed suicide the following day. "I am powerless . . . I can no longer bear all this," his note explained.[37]

Other *Judenrat* chairmen reasoned differently. Both Jacob Gens of Vilna and Chaim Rumkowski of Lodz had transformed their ghetto communities into urban work camps. They believed that survival of at least part of the population would be achieved through productivity; since the ghetto Jews were merely a labor force, those unable to work were at risk for deportation: the aged, the ill, infants and children.[38]

Who should be protected—and who sacrificed? Gens made his decision. "We shall not give the children, they are our future. We shall not give young women. . . . We shall not give [our workers], for we need them here ourselves."[39] He chose instead the elderly and ill. On 17 July 1942 an *Aktion* was carried out in Vilna; its target was one hundred aged or chronically ill people. Gens defended his course, claiming that "he had rejected a German demand to seize children, but that he had to obey their order to transfer the old and ill who were unable to look after themselves."[40]

We saw that Esther Geizhals-Zucker left school early in 1942. She had just turned twelve and went to work as a garment presser. A position in the ghetto factories meant soup at noon and a chance to avoid deportation. "I had to go to work in order to maintain my ration card. [I] did something horrible. We had irons, and the irons we were working on weren't electric so we used to burn coal in it. And I used to have to burn the coal in the iron so it would make the iron hot. I remember getting horrible headaches from the fumes of the coal. I used to get terrible headaches, but I had to do it."[41]

Within a few months the choice Esther Zucker had made became a matter of ghetto policy. Everyone had to work. So important was it to give an impression of the ghetto as a work camp that when German authorities visited the ghetto on 4 June, no children, old, weak, or ill people were to be seen on the streets. "In a word, the ghetto seemed to be a labor camp where idle people are not . . . on the streets during the day," the *Chronicle* reported. "The populace knows and understands that this is not an ordinary inspection but concerns something larger, more important—the question of its very existence. The result of today's inspection is still unknown, but a positive impression could be read on the visitors' faces."[42]

Resettlement rumors circulated constantly that summer. According to the official lists, 70,000 of the approximately 100,000 ghetto inhabitants were employed in mid-1942. This meant that nearly every family had one "idle" person; all feared the loss of their loved ones. "The rumors about a resumption of resettlement that began to circulate through the ghetto on Saturday afternoon

47. *Children in the Lodz ghetto are taught to sew in order to integrate them into the labor force, and thus protect them from deportation to an annihilation camp, c. 1942. Photo Mendel Grossman. Beit Lohamei Haghettaot, courtesy of the United States Holocaust Memorial Museum Photo Archives, Washington, DC. Damaged original photo.*

[20 June], causing widespread anxiety, were probably caused by the Chairman's [Rumkowski's] demand that he be presented with a list of the number of children over the age of 10 who . . . have been given jobs. . . . A second rumor sprang up at once in connection with the Chairman's having supposedly ordered that children between the ages of 8 and 10 . . . be employed."[43] While these stories were denied by the *Judenrat*, a "drive to employ children over the age of 10" began, and by 2 July was "making vigorous progress." Still the uneasiness persisted, and for good reason. What of those under ten? "Rumors are circulating among the populace that the Chairman is also attempting to find employment for younger children as well—those from 8 years old and up."[44]

Ghetto authorities continued to deny the rumors and, at the same time, worked hectically to place children ten years and older. It was an enormous undertaking. Youngsters had to be trained to do skilled work, and places in workshops had to be secured. By 20 July, 13,000 children labored "in various Community workshops as apprentices," but an apprentice did not have the status of a skilled worker. A two-month intensive course pushed as many children into the ranks of the skilled laborers as quickly as possible.[45] Still, rumors persisted and, in the end, they proved correct. The employed were not marked for the 5–12 September "resettlement" action; only children under the age of ten and adults over sixty-five were to be deported.

"In his speech of September 4, 1942," the *Chronicle* reported, "the Chairman announced that, by order of the [German] authorities, about 25,000 Jews under the age of 10 and over 65 must be resettled out of the ghetto. . . . It was said that had this action encountered any difficulties or resistance, the German authorities would have stepped in."[46] Rumkowski asked the assembled crowd, "Should we comply and do it, or should we leave it for others to do?" But he had resolved his dilemma. "We all, myself and my closest associates, have come to the conclusion that despite the horrible responsibility, we have to accept the evil order. I have to perform this bloody operation myself; I simply must cut off the limbs to save the body! I have to take away the children, because otherwise others will also be taken, God forbid."[47]

Sara Grossman-Weil witnessed the action against the children.

In 1942, there was a general *sperre,* an important selection. We were warned
not to go out from our homes. Should we be found in the street, we'll be shot
without questions. It was in the morning when this was proclaimed.

They were going from street to street, from house to house, not one, not
two, not three, but a group of SS men, with dogs, and calling for the population of a given building to come out. When they came to our building, we
all walked out. . . .

We all lined up in our backyard, the men, the women, the young, and the
elderly. Some people were taken away; many of us went back to our rooms,
to our homes.

All the children were taken away. We had to line them up, since there was
such a cadre of the SS men. They had enough SS men to go into every room
to see whether there is anyone hiding or anyone left behind. We had all the
children out, twelve, thirteen, ten years old, eight years old. The children
were taken away; thrown, literally thrown, onto the wagon. And when the
mother objected, either she was taken with them, or shot. Or they tore the
child away from her and let her go. And all the children, small children, little ones, five-, six-, four-, seven-year-old ones were thrown, literally thrown,
into this wagon. The cries were reaching the sky, but there was no help,
there was no one to turn to, to plead your case, to beg.[48]

As a community, Jews in the ghettos of Nazi Europe were utterly powerless,
unable even to shield their own children from mortal harm. Nor could they
defend the elderly or the ill. Sara Grossman-Weil knew that this dragnet
included those over sixty-five as well as those under ten. She had married
Menek Grossman while living in the ghetto and they were very much in love,
but when the *Aktion* started she did not worry about her husband. At that particular moment, her mother happened to be with her brother Meyer in one area
of the ghetto, her father was alone in quite another, and she in yet a third.

I was thinking of my father, who was far away, who was all alone. I knew
that if he's there [alone], he's doomed; if no one will hide my father, we'll
have no more of my father alive. I took to the street, and I ran through the
cellars, and each time I had to come out to the street, I looked to the left and
to the right, and in front of me, and I leapt and went further, and again into
a house. And this is how I got through [the ghetto] safely, miraculously,
wondering how I did it. But I did get through to my parents' house. It was
a distance—actually, it was far away—how I ever did it, I don't know how.
I didn't think, "What am I doing?" or how I am exposing myself. I just felt
I must do it, because I couldn't live with myself if I wouldn't have done it.
So I ran from one place to another, hiding, looking, until I got there.

When I opened the door, my father said, "Sarale, if there is an afterworld,
you will have it." My father was a very religious man, and knowing how

irreligious I was at the time, it was something for him to say to me. He knew how I lost my belief, because very often I would say to him, in Yiddish, "Where is your God? Where is he? Tell me, show me, prove it to me." And my father would say, "Sarale, don't ask me such questions." He did not have the answer, so he did not want me to ask the question.

I took my father and I hid him—where, how, I don't know. I waited, and when the selection of the entire ghetto was over, I returned home.

When I came home, this was the first time, and I think the last time, I saw my husband so enraged. "Why did you do it? How could you do it? Why didn't you tell me! I was going out of my mind not knowing where you were!" I said to him, "I had to do it. You wouldn't have let me do it, but I *had* to do it. And here I am." At first he couldn't forgive me because I had caused so much anguish; he had such worries; he had such trepidations. He didn't know what happened to me. So it took a long time until he forgave me. But I had rescued my father, and this is what was important to me.[49]

Deportations went forward: Kovno in October 1941, Vilna and Warsaw in July 1942, Lodz that September, and in the many other ghettos of the German-occupied east. Those, like Dawid Sierakowiak, who remained in the ghettos, the "lucky" ones dodging deportation for the moment, endured biting pain and excruciating sorrow. Dawid's sick mother lay in the ghetto hospital at the time of the September *Aktion*. Her family could not help her. Dawid adored her and, with good reason, worried about her ceaselessly. "[S]uddenly, as though I divide, I find myself in her mind and body. The hour of her deportation is coming closer, and there's no help from anywhere." Knowing what was to come, he mourned the departure of his mother before he heard the final news. "[T]he greatest rainfall can't wash away a completely broken heart, and nothing will fill up the eternal emptiness in the soul, brain, mind, and heart that is created by the loss of one's most loved person."[50]

Everyone suffered, everyone grieved. "Eclipse of the sun, universal blackness. My Luba was taken away during a blockade on 30 Gesia Street," Abraham Lewin wrote on the twenty-second "day of the slaughter of the Jews of Warsaw." Language failed him. "I have no words to describe my desolation. . . . Terror and blackness. And over all this disaster hangs my own private anguish."[51] No one, Hillel Seidman observed, could comprehend the events that befell the community. On 8 December 1942, he hosted a meeting of "men of many disciplines, great *rabbanim* and intellectuals who view the world from different perspectives."

In normal times [they] are brilliant thinkers and profound speakers, yet now they cannot find the right words to categorize the catastrophe we are living through nor discover any hint of it in our history. . . . Any attempted comparison with a historical precedent seems absurd, without relevance. Is the

Armenian genocide comparable to what we are suffering? The *churban* [destruction] of both Temples, the Spanish expulsion, the massacres perpetrated by the Crusaders or the Cossacks, or any of the other tragedies throughout our long history soaked with the tears of centuries, all appear dwarfed in comparison with our present calamity—it has a unique dimension all of its own.[52]

Atrocities and a living insanity permeated ghetto life under German occupation. Jews were shot at random as they went about their daily business; people dropped dead of hunger on the streets. Murderous orders, murderous conditions, shootings, killings. The only option for the survivors of each day's assaults was to cope, to manage. And so they carried on. Other than suicide, for most people there were no choices. "We went on with our daily lives after this selection. And we found ourselves without the people who were with us yesterday." It was not a question of the "will to live" or some strategy for survival, Sara Grossman-Weil explained. It wasn't even hope. "We didn't have so much hope, but we also didn't think what will happen to us tomorrow. There was no room or place or even the strength or the will to think about it."[53]

Many Jews, including Halina Nelken, were baffled by their neighbors—and their own—ability to continue with the daily business of life. "It is incomprehensible that after the tragic shock of *Aussiedlung* [deportation from Cracow ghetto], and in such a relatively short time, life in the ghetto is returning to its normal routine. In a single moment our world is turned upside down, and the next day we brush our teeth, eat breakfast, go to work, and perform a thousand daily activities."[54] Józef Zelkowicz, one of the chroniclers of the Lodz ghetto, observed the same phenomenon. "It would seem that the events of recent days would have immersed the entire population of the ghetto in mourning for a long time to come, and yet, right after the incidents, and even during the resettlement action, the populace was obsessed with daily concerns—getting bread, rations, and so forth—and often went from immediate personal tragedy right back into daily life."[55] The same was true in Warsaw. "Everybody has suffered their individual trauma and loss, yet they continue their habitual search for food and shelter; hoping to live for another day," Hillel Seidman noted. "Most survivors pay no attention at all and continue to function blindly as if nothing has happened. We seem to live in a separate existence—that which existed before the war. Those who did not personally witness the actual slaughter of their precious family (and most of us have not actually seen their murder) behave as if their relatives are still alive."[56]

For Zelkowicz, as for Nelken and Seidman, it was "beyond comprehension" that "after losing those nearest to them, people talk constantly about rations, potatoes, soup, etc.!" He wondered if this was "some sort of numbing of the nerves . . . or a symptom of an illness that manifests itself in atrophied emotional reactions?"[57] Seidman ascribed it to "a retreat from the bitter truth into a world of make-believe and delusion. For us, fantasy substitutes for reality, while reality recedes into fantasy. We exist uneasily between two conflicting worlds."[58]

We now know that both Zelkowicz and Seidman were correct: survivors were not indifferent to their losses; rather, they cared so very much that they could not absorb such pain in all its entirety. And basic, elemental hunger did indeed drive them to carry on each day. Food—the want of food, the search for food—was an inescapable imperative. In the midst of the *Aktion* Abraham Lewin reported "the terrible hunger: bread, 88 zloty, potatoes, 30" followed by "In a building on Lezno Street, where 150 people used to live, there are now 30 left. Of these eight were killed yesterday." Devastation came in many forms: food prices, head counts. "Hunger forces us to beg, to ask for a little food. Even in such terrible hours as these a hungry person wants to still the hunger."[59]

According to the chroniclers of the Lodz ghetto, food supplies had an enormous influence on morale. "Saturday, May 8, 1943. . . . The ghetto is in a vastly better mood. The continuing potato deliveries are still the main topic of the day." With food, survival was possible. "Stomachs are full, hunger pains have subsided, and, after a long period of starvation, people have begun to recover gradually and to gain some weight. A better psychological state of mind has come with physical recovery. There are sparks of hope in people's eyes."[60]

But more than merely the habit of living, the grip of routine, or the need to eat was at work. The ghetto inhabitants did not confine their life-affirming activities to the search for food and work. In Cracow, as Halina Nelken observed, "even the weekly charity concerts at the orphanage have resumed."[61] In Lodz, musical concerts recommenced after a two-month hiatus. Speaking to the audience on 14 November, Rumkowski addressed "the ghetto's current problems, chiefly the placing of homeless children and the food situation." The following day, the authors of the *Chronicle* noted, "the Chairman has definitely resolved that regular performances [will] again be given . . . as before the last resettlement."[62] That week there were "three evening revue performances" and a concert. In Kovno, the *Aktion* of 28 October 1941 had been unleashed before the Jews in the ghetto had even had the opportunity to organize cultural activities, yet there also planning for an orchestra began a few months later.[63]

It was in Kovno too that the vocational school became a center for cultural life in the ghetto. There were literary readings and lectures about literature. A choir of one hundred singers was established, as well as a lending library and a drama circle. In July 1943 the students produced a show augmenting an exhibition of artworks produced by the children, and *The Kabbalists,* a play by the famous Yiddish writer I. L. Peretz, was performed. After each *Aktion,* the remaining teachers and students resumed their classes. Indeed, the school existed, albeit in a camouflaged state, until the final liquidation of the ghetto (by then formally a concentration camp) in July 1944. The children appreciated it, wanted it, longed for it.[64]

Young Jews throughout the German-ruled east looked for relief from the misery of the ghetto and ways of coping with the suffering they endured each day. Vilna's youth club network was very important to young people like Yitskhok Rudashevski. "Finally, the club too was opened," he wrote in his diary on 5 Monday 1942. Two days later, he remarked, "Life has become a little more interesting. The club work has begun. We have groups for literature, natural science. After leaving class at 7:30 I go immediately to the club. It is gay there, we have a good time." Yitskhok and his companions became completely engrossed with the club activities. "The days pass quickly," he observed. "[W]e enjoy ourselves a little. . . . Our youth works and does not perish." The projects were an antidote to misery. "It is cold outside, it is cold at home, so you want to run to the club where you do not feel anything. . . . With such activity you do not feel the cold."[65]

The Zionist youth organizations, popular before the war and still functioning in the ghettos, offered camaraderie and hope. Mania Salinger-Tenenbaum, for instance, joined the Masada organization in Radom when she was fourteen years old and in her first year of gymnasium. "Masada was my second home. . . . I mean, from school, I went straight to Masada. I just came home to sleep. Saturday I was in Masada. Sunday I was in Masada. So it was Masada that was my whole social and political life during my high school years." This closeness, this intensity and special warmth continued after the war had begun and throughout the time of the ghetto or Radom. "I was in a group of eight people. It was *our* group. . . . So my friendships of before the war and during the war were very strong."[66]

JEWISH YOUNG PEOPLE, indeed most Jews, were very strong too, but a relentless German death machine was stronger. The 2 to 3 million Jews and the small groups of Roma and Sinti in the long-term ghettos of eastern Europe would have succumbed eventually to the lethal conditions of their daily lives. In Warsaw, 84,896 people or 18 percent of the average population died between September 1939 and August 1942; in Lodz, 43,743 people or 34.7 percent died between May 1940 and July 1944. Any stability of the physical environment of the Jewish quarter with its streets, synagogues, and markets had been a chimera. From its inception to its liquidation, the ghetto had proved a slow extermination center. But "slow" was not fast enough. Each ghetto came, in time, to its "final liquidation."

In Warsaw, many young women and men began to realize in the spring of 1942 that there was no way out; everyone was marked for murder.[67] The massive German *Aktionen* throughout the ghetto in July, August, and September proved these forebodings to be true. All their struggles to survive day by day had come to naught: parents, wives, husbands, brothers, sisters, children, had been snatched up and deported. Those who remained in the ghetto were, for the most part, able-bodied, bereft, and desperate. They had no one and nothing left to lose. Armed resistance at least offered revenge, even if it did not promise survival. By the time the Germans mounted their "final *Aktion*" to clear Warsaw of Jews in April 1943, these young people were determined to act.

Their numbers were not large. Some 500 combatants belonged to the Jewish Fighting Organization (ZOB), approximately 250 to the Jewish Fighting Union (ZZW), and an unspecified number to small, unaffiliated groups. They had few weapons and little ammunition. Untrained in military matters and emaciated from years of starvation rations, they defied 2,054 German soldiers and 36 officers with armored vehicles, tanks, cannons, flamethrowers, and machine guns. Holding out for over a month, Jewish resistance fighters had the satisfaction of inflicting losses and forcing the Germans to reckon with them as combatants prepared to kill.[68]

The Polish underground Home Army—pound, patriotic, and deeply prejudiced against Jews—marveled at the ghetto revolt. The Germans' "crime of well-organized and planned murder of European Jewry in its entirety on a scale unprecedented in the modern history of the world" was "facilitated," the Home Army bulletin claimed, "by the lack of active resistance of Jews dragged like cattle to be slaughtered." Not any longer.

A week ago, the second act of the beastly extermination of Jews in Poland unfolded. The Germans proceeded to deport the 40,000 Jews who still remained in Warsaw. The ghetto answered with armed resistance. The Jewish Combat Organization waged an unequal battle. With weak forces, lacking weapons and ammunition, deprived of water, blinded by smoke and fire, the Jewish fighters defended streets and single houses. They retreated step by step, in dead silence, pressed not only by their enemy armed with modern weapons, but also flushed out by fires in densely built houses. Their victory would be a weakening of the invaders' forces; their victory would be to enable some of the ghetto inmates to escape; their ultimate victory will be death, weapons in hand. . . .

The defense of the Warsaw ghetto dealt a serious blow to the remnants of the prestige of Nazi Germany. It is the will of the *Zeitgeist* that the same Germans who with utter contempt sought to cross out the Jewish people from the register of living nations, provided them with the opportunity of glorious struggle, thus adding the gruesome item of an entire nation to the long list of their crimes. The entire German nation will answer for this before the tribunal of humankind, for it has been carrying out the crimes conceived in its leaders' minds with obedience and premeditation.[69]

The Warsaw ghetto uprising is one instance of one form of resistance by Jews. There were armed revolts elsewhere, even in the death camps of Birkenau, Sobibór, and Treblinka. And there were other kinds of resistance, the development of rescue operations, and cultural and spiritual initiatives to bind the community together, to hold fast to Jewish history, ethics, and customs. But the Warsaw ghetto uprising was unique in scope and scale, degree of aggression and assertiveness.

The Germans quelled the uprising and went on to liquidate the ghettos of Kovno in June, Bedzin and Bialystok in August, and Tarnow, Przemysl, and Vilna in September. Lodz, an exception, continued as a work camp until the summer of 1944. By that time, nearly all the Jews of eastern Europe had been killed. With the Soviet army approaching, the Germans became frantic to finish their task and Lodz ghetto fell victim to their frenzy.

Pushed by the Germans, on Friday 16 June 1944, the Elder of the Jews of Lodz, Mordechai Chaim Rumkowski, issued a proclamation calling for "voluntary registration for labor outside the ghettos." Voluntary registration was quickly succeeded by compulsory deportation. For four weeks pressure rose on workshop managers; they were required to compile lists of people not essential to production. The first transport of six hundred people was to leave on Wednesday 21 June, but "because the requisitioned freight cars will not be available it was rescheduled for the 23rd," the ghetto chroniclers recorded. A pall fell. "Twenty-five transports have been announced. Everyone knows that the situation is serious, that the existence of the ghetto is in jeopardy. . . . Nearly every ghetto dweller is affected this time. Everyone is losing a relative, a friend, a roommate, a colleague." During the next three weeks some people volunteered, enticed by the prospect of leaving the misery of the ghetto or by the purchase price of their own bodies as a substitute for another on the list: "three loaves of bread, a half kilogram of margarine, one pound of sugar." Many more sought desperately to avoid the fate doled out to them and cajoled those in power to delete their names. Others neither volunteered nor hid; they went when ordered to do so. In all, 7,196 people were deported from Lodz to the death camp in Chelmno. Then, on 15 July, "toward noon, the Eldest was instructed to halt the resettlement." According to the authors of the *Chronicle,* "Never has the ghetto been so happy . . . People embraced in the streets, kissed in the workshops and departments: 'The resettlement's over!' "[70]

As the authors observed, "no one gave a second thought to whether this was only a brief interruption of or a final halt to the transports."[71] It was merely a respite. On Wednesday 2 August 1944 the final deportation order, signed by Rumkowski, was posted on the walls of the ghetto. Sara Grossman-Weil, age twenty-five when she was deported from Lodz, left with her husband Manny, his brother, wife, and two children, and her mother and father-in-law.

We were talking about *Übersiedlung;* transports will be going out from the ghetto to a very large place which will be established as a tremendous workshop, because the Third Reich needed our work. We will be organized in such a way, we were told; the work has to be very efficient, and since we are skilled, we will do fine. The families will keep together, and we will work

for the Third Reich. . . . "It's just a question of *Übersiedlung,*" of transport-
ing us from one place to another. And we believed it. I believed it. I am sure
Manny believed it, and so did his family. And so did my family. . . .

People were going, people were leaving. . . . Suddenly we heard rumors
that they were put in a concentration camp. We didn't have any details, but
evidently someone came back, or escaped, or heard that it's not as they are
promising. But since we didn't have anything to go by, or to hold on to, and
we did not have any choice, we did go too.

We went with the [tailoring] workshop which was managed by my
brother-in-law. We did not go with my workshop or with Manny's because
we wanted to prolong it. We wanted to put off leaving the ghetto because we
did not want to separate from the family. . . .

I was in a dilemma. Should we stay, or should I go with the Grossmans?
. . . I didn't know what to do. I wanted to go with my husband and I wanted
to stay with my parents. I was torn. I was angered. I didn't want to make the
decision.[72]

Sara Grossman-Weil's decision laid out the boundaries of the choices available to her. Family had held her center for nearly five years of ghetto life, to keep
her family together. In the ghetto "we were still in our homes. Whether it was
a room two by two or twenty by two, we were in our homes and with the family."[73] This principle had kept her in Poland when she could have gone to Palestine in the summer of 1939 and, later, had deterred her from letting friends help
her to pass as a gentile on the "Aryan" side. Now she faced another choice: to
part from her parents and brothers, or her husband and in-laws. For Sara
Grossman-Weil, the deportation order spelled the end of what she might
achieve, maintain, or manage. She left on a transport with her husband,
mother- and father-in-law, brother-in-law, his wife Esther, their adolescent
adopted daughter Regina, and their little girl, Mirka. They were herded to the
train station and ordered onto the cattle cars.

Chapter Ten

TOWARD THE
"FINAL SOLUTION"

In 1933, Nazi rabid antisemitism went public. Some had predicted that power would moderate the National Socialists' vitriol, but holding the reins of state had quite the opposite effect. "There will be a time when the Jewish question will be radically solved in the whole world because humanity cannot find any other way," the insolent editor of the scurrilous *Stürmer* and Gauleiter for Franconia, Julius Streicher, bellowed to people massed before Nuremberg's main synagogue in August 1938. Inciting the crowd to destroy the building, he assured them their goals were just. "We want to vigilantly ensure that German blood and German soul remain pure because, if the Jew gains power once again in Germany, then the German nation is doomed forever." The mob had a job to do. "You workers of the city of Nuremberg, who were once slaves of the Jews and who are now joyfully assisting in the construction of the new Reich of Adolf Hitler, I am now giving you a historical order: Begin!"[1]

The November Pogrom took care of the synagogue problem throughout most of Germany and, in ever more violent terms, the Nazis moved from Jewish property to Jewish people. "We are about to bring the Jewish question to its totalitarian solution. The program is clear," the SS bi-weekly, *Das Schwarze Korps,* announced on 24 November. "Complete elimination, absolute separation!" This meant "much more" than "merely the elimination of the Jews from German economic life." After all, "no German can any longer be expected to dwell under the same roof with Jews."

> Jews therefore must be driven from our houses and residences and lodged in streets and blocks where they are among themselves and have as little contact with Germans as possible. They must be branded with marks of identification. . . .
>
> In such complete isolation this tribe of parasites will . . . sink into criminality, obeying their inherent, blood-conditioned bent. . . .
>
> At such a stage of development we would be faced with the harsh necessity of rooting out the Jewish underworld in the same manner in which our state, founded on law, extirpates criminals: with fire and sword. The

result would be the actual and final end of Jewry in Germany, its absolute annihilation.[2]

Das Schwarze Korps focused on the Jews of Germany, but Adolf Hitler attacked international Jewry, which he blamed for Germany's sufferings since World War I. In a speech delivered before the 885 deputies of the "Greater German Reichstag" to commemorate the sixth anniversary of his reign, Hitler ridiculed the Jews who sought to flee Germany and taunted the rest of the world for its unwillingness to accept these would-be refugees. "Should not the outside world be most grateful to us for setting free these glorious bearers of culture and placing them at its disposal?"[3] Hitler followed mockery with threats.

> And there is yet one more topic on which I would like to speak on this day, perhaps not only memorable for us Germans: I have been a prophet very often in my lifetime, and this earned me mostly ridicule. In the time of my struggle for power, it was primarily the Jewish people who mocked my prophecy that, one day, I would assume leadership of this Germany, of this State, and of the entire Volk, and that I would press for a resolution of the Jewish question, among many other problems. The resounding laughter of the Jews in Germany then may well be stuck in their throats today, I suspect.
>
> Once again I will be a prophet: should international Jewry of finance succeed, both within and beyond Europe, in plunging mankind into yet another world war, then the result will not be a Bolshevization of the earth and the victory of Jewry, but the annihilation of the Jewish race in Europe.[4]

Mass murder was Hitler's subject: Judeocide. But while words are powerful because they persuade, the Nazis' language of destruction was not a program for murder. To transform their general idea into a concrete plan other factors had to come into play: an unsettled, changeable political bureaucracy; the violence of war; and a far-reaching government apparatus.

HITLER DEALT with ideas, aims, goals. Precise instructions were superfluous. His underlings "worked towards" these ideas, taking independent initiatives to promote what they surmised the Führer's wishes to be, even to anticipate them. This led to ferocious competition within the party. Hitler always endorsed the victorious person or faction and thus was never embarrassed. Ferocity drove the Nazi state hierarchy and policies emerged out of an institutional jungle of rivalry and conflict. Programs, laws, decrees, regulations, written and even specific oral directives were simply not needed. Broad authorization sufficed.

One general goal was the Führer's wish to cleanse Germany of the incurably ill. This neo-Darwinian idea flowered in the late nineteenth century with the support of the influential biologist Ernst Haeckel. Ignoring Charles Darwin's injunction that civil society could not and should not be interpreted in terms of "selection" and "struggle for existence," Haeckel insisted that if natural selection did not kill degenerates, human beings should step in.[5] Such crackpot thinking at first found little acceptance. But the carnage of the Great War, revolution, economic depression, and inflation led a few prominent lawyers and physicians to reconsider public policy toward the insane, incurably ill, and totally invalid.

In 1920 a short, very readable volume, *The Destruction of Life Unworthy of Life,* was published; it contained two essays, one by the legal scholar Karl Binding and the other by the neuropathologist Alfred Hoche. The war, they said, had wasted "the most valuable and self-sufficient lives full of energy and vigor." Binding compared it to the massive energy spent to sustain "worthless lives" in asylums.[6] In conclusion, Hoche confidently predicted that "a new period will come which, on the basis of a higher morality, will cease continually implementing the demands of an exaggerated concept of humanity and an exaggerated view of the value of human life at great cost."[7]

Hitler embraced these ideas, and elaborated upon them in *Mein Kampf.* The state must be ruthless with regard to the unfit. "It is a half-measure to let incurably sick people steadily contaminate the remaining healthy ones," he asserted. "This is in keeping with the humanitarianism which, to avoid hurting one individual, lets a hundred others perish. The demand that defective people be prevented from propagating equally defective offspring is a demand of the clearest reason and if systematically executed represents the most humane act of mankind."[8]

As usual, Hitler meant what he said. As we have seen, within months of coming to power, he decreed the Law for the Prevention of Progeny with Hereditary Diseases and the Law Against Dangerous Habitual Criminals. Initial estimates suggested that these two laws would lead to the sterilization or castration of some 400,000 people, but these measures did not go far enough for Hitler. Marriage itself was to be regulated: the Law to Preserve the Hereditary Soundness of the German People forbade the marriage of people diagnosed as having a dangerous contagious disease, a mental disorder, or various hereditary diseases. It was passed in 1935.[9]

These new laws and policies were quite public. And as schoolbooks, articles, and films rallied Germans behind far-reaching racial hygiene policies, segments of the party moved to ever more violent positions. In 1937 *Das Schwarze Korps* spoke out in favor of killing the unfit in an article entitled "Concerning the Topic of Euthanasia." Responding to a letter from a reader who demanded a law permitting the killing of all "idiotic" children if the parents agreed, the editors wrote approvingly, "Nature would let this unfit creature starve to death. We may be more humane and give it a painless mercy-death. That is the only appropriate humanitarian act in such cases, and it is one hundred times more noble, decent and humane than that cowardice that hides behind humanitarian babble and loads the poor creature with the burden of existence, and the family and the national community with the burden of care."[10]

The SS was ahead of the medical community only in that its members were prepared to print what physicians believed. Indeed, discussions about killing the "unworthy" had already begun among doctors, but Hitler had expressed the opinion that a euthanasia program would have to wait for war, when the German people would be forced to face the significance of individual lives. No specific action was taken; yet his acolytes looked for a way to "work toward the Führer." Reischsleiter Philipp Bouhler soon saw his chance.

Bouhler headed the Nazi office that handled Hitler's private business, including personal appeals to the Führer. In late 1938 an increasing number of letters arrived from family members of mentally handicapped people requesting the "mercy-death" of their loved ones. Realizing that the euthanasia issue could promote his Chancellory of the Führer, as his office was called, the ambitious Bouhler gave Hitler the entreaty of a certain Herr Kauer from Leipzig. Kauer's child had been born blind, appeared idiotic, and lacked one leg and part of an arm. At Bouhler's suggestion, Hitler instructed his personal physician, Dr. Karl Brandt, to examine the child and, if the father's description was correct, to kill the youngster. Brandt obeyed. Hitler liked playing God, and he authorized Bouhler and Brandt to treat similar cases in the same way. Bouhler happily obliged, pleased to control a sensitive operation close to Hitler's heart.[11]

No law was passed, no written, formal order sent to Bouhler by the Führer. But he had been given the nod, and he and Brandt founded the Reich Committee for the Scientific Registration of Serious Hereditarily and Congenitally Based Illnesses, run by bureaucrats from his chancellory and the Reich Interior Ministry as well as physicians supportive of radical racial hygiene measures. That same month (August), the Reich Interior Ministry decreed that midwives and physicians had to report all newborns and children up to the age of three with various conditions to the Reich Committee. Investigators on the committee examined the information submitted and authorized the murder of "positive" cases in special *Kinderfachabteilingen* (Pediatric Departments) established in thirty asylums. The willingness to kill now moved from the printed page to the act itself. Five thousand children were murdered. The language of destruction had become a program of murder, although no law had been passed, no written, formal order given.[12]

Well satisfied, Hitler instructed Bouhler to organize the murder of adults "unfit for life." Bouhler, again, was happy to oblige. His deputy, Viktor Brack, volunteered to find the best means of execution. After consultation with Albert Widmann, chief of the Chemical Department of the Criminal Technical Institute of the Criminal Police (Kripo), and an expert in carbon monoxide poisoning, Brack recommended bottled carbon monoxide produced by BASF.[13] Bouhler, in the meantime, busily secured the cooperation of physicians, technical experts, and the police. In mid-October, he also gained an informal authorization—but not a law, decree, or order—from Hitler himself, written on the Führer's personal notepaper. Backdated to 1 September 1939, the day Germany had invaded Poland, the document explained that "*Reichsleiter* Bouhler and Dr. med. Brandt are charged with responsibility to extend the powers of specific doctors in such a way that, after the most careful assessment of their condition, those suffering from illnesses deemed to be incurable may be granted a mercy death."[14]

Widmann conducted the first experimental gassing at an unused prison in the town of Brandenburg on 4 January 1940.[15] Christian Wirth, a police officer from Stuttgart, built the gas chamber, installed the gas cylinders, and designed the fake showers. Between eighteen and twenty patients were brought to an anteroom, undressed, and led into the gas chamber. The door was locked. Dr. Widmann then turned the valve in the presence of, among others, Dr. Karl Brandt, Dr. Irmfried Eberl, the physician in charge of the Brandenburg asylum, and Christian Wirth. The patients died within minutes. Their bodies were cremated in two mobile incinerators brought in for the occasion.[16]

The operation, code-named T4 for the headquarters at Tiergartenstrasse 4, began a few weeks later with the gassing of a busload of inmates sent to the Grafeneck asylum west of Ulm. Brandenburg went on line in February, then Hartheim (near Linz) and Sonnenstein (near Dresden) in May, Bernburg (south of Magdeburg) in September, and Hadamar (north of Frankfurt) in January 1941.[17] Procedures never varied. Institutions profiled patients to the Reich Committee where three doctors assessed each file. Those judged "positive" were placed on a transport list which was sent to the asylum. The patients went in buses with darkened windows to one of the six killing centers. Stripped naked upon arrival, they waited while a physician checked their files. "Someone then stamped them," a stoker in the crematorium at Hartheim recalled. "An orderly had to stamp them individually on the shoulder or the chest with a consecutive number. The number was approximately 3–4 cm in size. Those people who had gold teeth or a gold bridge were marked with a cross on their backs. After this procedure, the people were led into a nearby room and photographed."[18] They were then led into the gas chamber and killed. An hour and a half later, the fans went on, and stokers moved the corpses to the mortuary.

A victim's family received a letter saying that their relative had been transferred to a new asylum, fallen ill, and that "all attempts by the doctors to keep the patient alive were unfortunately unsuccessful." After the usual condolences, the letter stated that "in accordance with police instructions we were obliged to cremate the corpse immediately. This measure is designed to protect the country from the spread of infectious diseases which represent a serious threat in wartime and we must strictly abide by it."[19]

Inmates from asylums in East and West Prussia and the Wartheland were not brought to a T4 death chamber. They were gassed in a truck operated by a *Sonderkommando,* or Special Squad, headed by SS-Hauptsturmführer Herbert Lange. Stationed in Posen, Lange drove to an asylum, presented a list of names to the staff, and loaded inmates into the airtight cargo area of a large Kaiser's Coffee truck. After leaving the grounds of the asylum, the driver opened the valves of the carbon monoxide cylinders stored in his truck cabin and connected to the cargo area, and killed his passengers.[20]

Its supporters judged operation T4 an unqualified success. In 1939 Bracht had estimated that 65,000 to 75,000 asylum inmates were candidates for death. When Hitler stopped the program on 24 August 1941, the T4 officials congratulated themselves that "70,273 persons have been disinfected."[21] They took pride as well in the money they had saved the Reich. Assuming a life expectancy of ten years, and an average daily cost of RM 3.50 per patient, they calculated that the program had saved the German people RM 885,439,800.[22] Their report did not mention that, on termination of the operation, its personnel had been offered jobs in the east. Nor did it mention that while the 70,273 victims amounted to one in five of all institutionalized patients, that figure included all of the Jewish inmates. Their papers had not been given even a cursory glance.[23]

Although T4 officially had closed, its technology went forward. In the spring of 1941 Himmler had contacted Bouhler: could the T4 program be extended to concentration camps? Bouhler was happy to please. Code-named 14f13 (14f referred to the Inspectorate of Concentration Camps, and 13 to "the special treatment of sick and frail prisoners"), the new program organized roving teams of T4 physicians which visited the camps ferreting out the mentally ill, chronically sick, and invalid prisoners. Jewish prisoners who fell into these categories were immediately selected for "treatment" in Sonnenstein, Hartheim, or Bernburg. Gentile prisoners' papers went to the headquarters at Tiergartenstrasse 4, where a final decision was taken.[24]

Very quickly, the 14f13 program became the Nazi way to label dissenting political views as "mental deficiency." And Jewish inmates soon became invisible as individuals; they were seen as a group and diagnosed collectively. In a letter from one of the participants in operation 14f13, Dr. Friedrich Mennecke, to his wife, the good doctor described his work in Buchenwald, and the pleasures of the SS mess hall.

> At noon we stopped for lunch and ate in the officers' mess (1st class! Boiled beef, red cabbage, boiled potatoes, apple compote—All for RM 1.50!, no coupons). . . . At 1.30 pm we began examining again, but then Ribbentrop's speech came on which we listened to. He said a lot of good things, did you hear the speech too? Then we examined again until about 4 o'clock, I did 105 patients, Müller 78 patients, so the first batch came to 183 forms completed. The second portion consisting of 1,200 Jews, who were not "examined," but for whom it was enough to take the reason for arrest (often very extensive!) from the records and to put that down on the forms. Therefore it is purely notational work, which will certainly occupy until Monday, perhaps longer. Out of this second portion of Jews we did: me 17, Müller 15. On the dot of 5 pm I "threw in the towel" and went to supper: a cold platter of cervelat sausage (9 big slices), butter, bread, coffee! Cost RM 0.80 without coupons![25]

What a bargain.

GERMANY INVADED Yugoslavia and Greece in April 1941 and the Soviet Union in June. Its rhetoric of destruction soared into the apocalyptic. Infected by the experience of total war and by the demonization of Bolsheviks as the absolute enemy, Germans saw the spring of 1941 as a truly historic moment.

They were told to do so. Minister of Propaganda Josef Goebbels orchestrated an extensive publicity campaign. The invasion of Russia, he proclaimed, was a conflict between the whole of Europe (most of which was occupied by that time) and Asia. "With unique singleness of purpose [Europe] is rising, as it were, against the suppressor of all human culture and civilization. The hour of the birth of the new Europe has arrived without pressure or compulsion from Germany," he boomed.[26] Called "The Veil Drops," Goebbels's campaign depicted Soviet society as a "gigantic system of cheats and exploiters." There was no doubt who was responsible for the pitiful hovels, lice-ridden homes, neglected roads, and filthy villages. "By means of their diabolical system of bolshevism, the Jews have cast the people of the Soviet Union into this unspeakable condition of deepest misery."[27] The Russians were in the clutches of Judeo-Bolshevism, and it was the mission of the European/German *Mensch* to slay the Asiatic/Soviet *Untermensch*.

Goebbels chose his themes with precision. Many analysts traced Germany's defeat in World War I to severe food shortages that crushed morale on the homefront. The Nazis were therefore convinced that keeping Germans well fed was key to their success. Propaganda was important, but bacon, butter, and beans were essential to bind Germany into a Reich of One People with One Führer. Any means to that end was justified. In this mortal combat, Germans needed the food and their foes could starve to death.

Herbert Backe headed up the Ministry of Food and Agriculture. Relentless and without remorse, Backe traveled to each occupied country as it fell to organize the plunder of food. Despite the vast territories under German control during the winter of 1940–41, supplies at home had been scarcer than expected and rations decreased. By the late spring of 1941 meat allotments were so meager that the German public had become restless. The regime was not delivering. As war with the Soviet Union approached, Backe's aides calculated that tens of millions of Russians would have to die in order to safeguard German meat rations. German food would not go east to the invading army; rather, German soldiers would be fed at the expense of the local population.

Backe worked closely with the military personnel of the Economic Defense Staff, East, organized by Göring to coordinate economic aspects of the war against the Soviet Union. Backe provided the expertise on food supplies, and on 23 May, a month before the invasion, the Economic Defense Staff published its policy on this matter. "Many tens of millions of people will become superfluous," the staff (which included representatives of Göring's Four Year Plan, ministries involved with the economy, and the army) decided. "Efforts to save the population from starving to death by bringing in surplus food from the black-soil region [of Russia] can be made only at the expense of feeding Europe. They undermine Germany's ability to hold out in the war and to withstand the blockade of Germany and Europe. There must be absolute clarity on this point."

Approved by "the highest authorities" (i.e., Hitler, Göring, and Himmler), thousands of these directives were distributed to military and economic leaders at all levels. And thousands of ordinary civil servants and army officers with long careers before 1933 accepted the genocidal policy. The instructions called for genocide on the grounds of economy and geopolitics—Slavs must die so that Germans will live—rather than due to a specific racial ideology—Slavs must die because they are Slavs—but this was genocide just the same. The siege of Leningrad, an effort to starve the city to death, and the deaths by starvation of millions of Soviet civilians and POWs, were rooted in these directives.

Backe looked to the east to become the bread basket of the New Europe, and he contended that "a true granary" was characterized by "low density of settlement."[28] This fit the Nazi vision of an agrarian utopia in the east: a landscape dotted with prosperous farms and attractive small towns, where a new generation of Germans could be raised in the harmony of blood and soil. There the ideal of the master race would be realized, and the aristocracy of the New Order reared.

A number of planning agencies competed for control of this massive Nazi-utopian project. All put forward grandiose plans. Geography professor Konrad Meyer led the way. As the Wehrmacht won victory after victory, Meyer developed a great master plan, the *Generalplan Ost* (General Plan, East), to organize the occupied east according to Nazi ideology.[29] The east was territory to be wiped clean and redeveloped. Millions of Germans would emigrate east. Through settlement, the conquered areas would become German and remain German. A year later, in 1942, a Dr. Erhard Wetzel calculated the "price" of Meyer's plan. Among other costs was the deportation of some 41 to 51 million people, which included 80 to 85 percent of all Poles. Where these people would go was not specified. It was tacitly understood that they would be killed.[30]

It is important to underline the significance of Meyer's *Generalplan*. Mass murder was no longer the province of the military, the police, or others trained to kill; nor was it under the jurisdiction of perverted madmen obsessed with sadistic cruelty. These programs to rid Germany of those "unfit to live," to murder those millions of "superfluous" non-Germans, were formulated by proud professionals, by workaday civil servants. They looked to translate ideas into action—to identify, separate, isolate, deport, and kill—in a surefooted, thorough, and fiscally responsible manner.

The Holocaust involved an entire bureaucracy, an efficient machinery of state that was rooted in the ideals and practices of the Prussian enlightenment. Frederick the Great's bureaucracy had been "a unique administration: cheap, clean, conscious of duty and happy to take responsibility," the National Socialist educational philosopher Dietrich Klagges explained approvingly.[31] The

Nazis wanted no less. Civil servants agreed. It mattered not that two hundred years had passed since Frederick the Great had instituted his civil service; its values and habits of bureaucracy were very much alive. Like their administrative ancestors, the bureaucrats of Nazi Germany reveled in being small cogs in a great machine. Every program needed many different people, each with his own set of skills, and each responsible for a discrete part. Technical competence, not moral responsibility, was valued by bureaucrat and administrator alike. No one valued asking questions: "Why are we doing this? Why *should* we do this?" And no one asked them.[32]

THIS BLINKERED attitude served the Nazis well when they embarked upon the "Final Solution" to the "Jewish Problem." By then they also had the example of the murder of the Romanian Jews by their Romanian countrymen. The Germans were convinced they could do it better. They were right.

The invasion of the Soviet Union proved a turning point in the Holocaust. Remarkably, the first victims were not Russian Jews, but Romanian Jews. And the murderers were not Germans, but Romanians. For Romanians, the war—and especially the Soviet campaign which had everyone's attention—provided a cover to unleash their own "Final Solution." No need for German racist anti-semitism. They had their own brand. Like earlier Cossack pogroms, the Romanian massacres were explosions of extreme violence, viciousness, and perverted sadism. And as in the Armenian genocide, the Romanians, like the Turks, organized forced death marches to locations where the few survivors died of disease and starvation. Unlike the Germans, neither the Turks nor the Romanians had the destruction machinery to guarantee the systematic murder of every last targeted person.

The home-grown Fascist Iron Guard drove Romanian Judeocide. "The Jews are to blame! The Jews have insulted the Rumanian army," the Iron Guard trumpeted when Romania lost territories to Hungary, Bulgaria, and the Soviet Union after the fall of France in 1940.[33] In revenge for this national humiliation, retreating Romanian army units tortured and massacred Jews in the town of Dorohoi and elsewhere. The 16th Infantry Regiment commanded by Major Valeriu Carp attacked with particular relish, cutting off fingers and tongues and raping the women before shooting everyone.[34]

The Iron Guard was rewarded for its savagery by General Ion Antonescu, who came to power and brought its leaders into the government. But Antonescu was shrewd. When Romania joined the Axis and sent troops against the Soviet Union, the Guard—vitriolic, but a destabilizing influence—was kicked out. The Guard left devastation in its wake. For three days (21–23 January 1941), the Guard pillaged and sacked the Jewish quarter of Bucharest, destroying seven large synagogues and murdering hundreds. Mutilated corpses littered the city morgue and bodies hung like cattle carcasses in the municipal slaughterhouse. Smeared with blood, a girl of five hung from a hook by her feet like a calf.[35]

48. A Bucharest synagogue in ruins after an Iron Guard-instigated pogrom, January 1941. YIVO Institute for Jewish Research, courtesy of the United States Holocaust Memorial Museum Photo Archives, Washington, DC. Damaged original photo.

The Iron Guard had lost its place in government, but not among the people. Its stronghold was Iasi, a city on the border of Old Romania and Bessarabia, a territory surrendered to the Soviet Union in 1940. The hometown of Cuza and starting point for Codreanu's political career, Iasi was a Guard stronghold. It also served as a launching site for the attack on Russia in 1941. Romanian troops took heavy casualties in that invasion, and the combination of Guard activity and this military humiliation triggered a massacre of local Jews. Completely Romanian in origin and execution, it was the first mass murder of Jews in the Soviet campaign.[36]

"It was a brilliant morning; the air, cleansed and freshened by the storm of the previous night, glistened on everything like a transparent varnish. I went to the window and looked down Lapusneanu Street," the Italian war correspondent Malaparte wrote, describing the day after the pogrom. "Scattered about in the street were human forms lying in awkward positions. The gutters were strewn with dead bodies, heaped one upon another. Several hundred corpses were dumped in the center of the churchyard." And there were still more to take away. "Squads of Jews, watched over by policemen and soldiers armed with tommy guns, were at work moving the bodies to one side, clearing the middle of the road and piling the corpses up along the walls so they would not block traffic. German and Romanian trucks loaded with corpses kept going by."

Nauseated, Malaparte withdrew. Then he heard people laughing.

I forced myself to go back to the window. The road was crowded with people—squads of soldiers and policemen, groups of men and women, and bands of gypsies with their hair in long ringlets were gaily and noisily chattering with one another, as they despoiled the corpses, lifting them, rolling them over, turning them on their sides to draw off their coats, their trousers and their underclothes; feet were rammed against dead bellies to help pull of the shoes; people came running to share in the loot; others made off with arms piled high with clothing. It was a gay bustle, a merry occasion, a feast and a marketplace all in one. The dead twisted into cruel postures were left naked.[37]

This was too much for Malaparte. He confronted the crowd. "One of them looked at me in amazement, picked up some suits and two or three pairs of shoes from a pile of clothing on the ground and pushed them toward me saying, 'Don't get angry, *Domnule Capitan,* there's enough for everybody.'"[38]

Romanian deputy prime minister Mihai Antonescu made no secret of the fact that the reconquest of Bessarabia and northern Bukovina was an opportunity to "solve" the "Jewish Problem."[39] "We are in the most favorable and broadly opportune moment in history for total ethnic purification, for a revision of national life, and for purging our race of all those elements which are foreign to its soul, which have grown like mistletoes and darken our future," he told the officials assigned to those territories, on 3 July 1941. "The campaign for ethnic purification will be developed by driving out all the Jews and isolating them in labor camps and in places where they can no longer exert their destructive influence," he continued. "If there comes a need in order to complete the work of ethnic purification, the provincial governments will also advise us on measures for enforced emigration of the Jewish population."[40]

49. *The Iasi massacre. To the left are corpses; to the right, Jews who will be packed into a death train to Calarasi, 29 June 1941. Serviciul Roman de Informatii, courtesy of the United States Holocaust Memorial Museum Photo Archives, Washington, DC. Original photo is blurred.*

If Mihai Antonescu envisioned forced emigration, the syphilitic chief of state Ion Antonescu (no kin) was prepared for bloodier measures. "If it is needed, shoot all of them with machine guns," he declared in a cabinet meeting of 8 July. What posterity would think was of no consequence. "It makes no difference to me that we will go down in history as barbarians. The Roman Empire performed a series of acts of barbarism according to our present standards, and nevertheless it was the most magnificent of political establishments. There has not existed a more favorable moment in our history."[41]

Evidently, the population agreed. They slaughtered the primarily Yiddish-speaking Jews of reconquered Bessarabia and Bukovina who had not integrated into Romanian society in the interwar years, and forced the survivors into ghettos. Transnistria was new territory for Romania and an excellent dumping ground.[42] Romanian authorities began to deport from "Old Romania" Jews they considered Communist sympathizers, as well as masses of Jews from the recently established ghettos. In 1942, they also included some 25,000 Roma and

Sinti—the first step toward "solving" Romania's "Gypsy Problem," which had suddenly become political dynamite. Once Romanians accepted massive deportations as a fine way to achieve an ethnically homogeneous state, they found no reason to spare the "Gypsies."[43] Locked into camps and ghettos of bombed-out houses, stables, barns, and pigsties, the Jews felled trees, paved roads, and dug peat for their masters. Many tens of thousands died from starvation, cold, and disease.[44] One survivor was Ghizela Herscovici, taken to the Dniester River in November 1941. Pregnant and fearful for herself and her unborn child, she confided to her diary:

> The officers order us into barges that are waiting for us. We leave our country, Romania.
>
> My father fought valiantly at Marasesti in World War I between 1916 and 1918. He was wounded and received decorations by His Majesty King Ferdinand I. The soldiers take away his decorations with the humiliating remark, "From whom did you steal these decorations?"
>
> It is almost sunset. Afraid and exhausted we reach Moghilev. New soldiers direct us to a Lager. Dirt and ruins all around us. We lie down on a cold, wet cement floor. Naked, barefoot, shivering children beg for a piece of bread. We try to find a little corner, a better place to rest after so long a voyage. What a painful journey. One cannot find the proper words to describe it, nor enough ink or paper to record our thoughts, our feelings and our misery.[45]

The Romanian army, now well into the Ukraine, viciously attacked Ukrainian Jews as well. Humiliated anew by the loss of 19,000 soldiers in the campaign to conquer Odessa, the men again turned their frustrated fury on the Jews.[46]

50. *The deportation of Romanian Jews to Transnistria, July 1941. Courtesy Bundesarchiv, Berlin.*

They rounded Jews up in the streets and shot some five thousand immediately. They then forced some 20,000, primarily children and women, into four large warehouses. Soldiers ripped holes in the warehouse walls and machine-gunned the crowd. A second lieutenant in the 23d Infantry regiment, one Alexa Neacsu, testified after the war that some still lived after a day and night of shooting.

> Observing that by machine gun fire alone they could not succeed in killing all those who were inside, those who were in charge of this operation and who were visibly worn out and worried went into another conference and resorted to spattering the warehouses with kerosene for lighting and gasoline and setting them afire. When the fire broke out, some of those who were still inside the warehouses and who were only slightly wounded or unscathed tried to escape by jumping out of windows or to get out over the roof. The soldiers had a general order to the effect that if anyone should come out they should be shot. . . . Those who appeared were naked, because they had torn off their clothes, which had caught fire. Some of the women threw children out of the windows.[47]

51. Before an execution: a Romanian officer stands on the backs of (presumably) Jewish men crouched in a ditch, summer 1941. Dokumentationsarchiv des Österreichischen Widerstandes, courtesy of the United States Holocaust Memorial Museum Photo Archives, Washington, DC.

The soldiers set fire to three of the warehouses. They shelled the fourth.

The Romanians incarcerated the remaining 70,000 Ukrainian Jews in the ghetto of Slobodka. Many of these survivors did not live long. Slobodka became a departure point for deadly marches to the murderous camps of Domanievka, Bogdanovska, and Akmicetca, all of them commanded by Colonel Modest Isopescu, who ordered the massacre of the 48,000 inmates of Bogdanovska a few days before Christmas 1941. Following the Odessa model, his men packed stables and barns with Jews and set them ablaze. When there were no more barns to burn, for three days on end, Jews were pushed to the edge of a cliff and shot.

As a holiday treat, Isopescu entertained visitors from Bucharest with the spectacle. Isopescu's soldiers repeated their "success" in Dumanosca, where they killed the 18,000 inmates.[48] But the colonel had something special in mind for the four thousand Jews in Akmicetca. They were left to starve to death. Every few days, Isopescu visited the camp to check on their progress and to photograph the dying inmates.[49]

This was an orgy of cruelty. Observers could not understand what was happening. The American envoy in Bucharest, Franklin Mott Gunther, was baffled. Then he realized with horror that Antonescu meant it when he said: this was the most "favorable moment in our history" to "solve" Romania's "Jewish Problem."[50]

> During this time of sanguine conflict, when mounting lists of Rumanian dead, wounded and missing have become a relative commonplace, when accounts of terror and ruthlessness resound throughout Europe, it may be felt that the prosecution of a program of extermination of the Jews, by shootings here and massacres there, not to mention mass deportations and general spoliation, will draw less attention from the public opinion than in normal time. However that may be, it is becoming more and more evident that the Rumanians, obviously with the moral support of the Germans, are utilizing the present period for handling the Jewish problem in their own way. I have it on good authority that Marshal Antonescu has stated to, or within the hearing of the Spanish Minister (who is particularly interested in the problem because of the Spanish Jews in Rumania) that "this is wartime, and a good time to settle the Jewish problem once and for all."[51]

Opportunism, however, cuts many ways. As Axis fortunes waned, the Romanians lost their appetite for pogroms. "Germany has lost the war," Antonescu reportedly muttered in October 1942.[52] By the time of the battle of Stalingrad in December, Romania's two armies on the eastern front had crumbled. Antonescu had bet on the wrong horse. It was time to cultivate the Allies. Perhaps assistance to the Jews would win postwar sympathy. After all, Romania simply had sought revenge on the Jews who had betrayed the motherland (the Jews of Bessarabia and Bukovina) and Jews to whom Romania had no obligation (the Ukrainian Jews of Transnistria). True, that came to a total of 250,000 dead "Israelites," but most Jews of Old Romania had merely suffered antisemitic legislation—except, of course, those murdered by the Iron Guard, and those thought to be Communist sympathizers or foes of the state, and those deported for a hundred other "reasons" or for no reason at all. Still, Romania controlled the fate of over 350,000 Jews. They could be allowed to emigrate, Antonescu calculated—for a price.

And that is precisely what he did. On 12 December 1942 Manfred Freiherr von Killinger, the German ambassador in Bucharest, reported to the German

Foreign Office in Berlin that Antonescu had ordered the emigration of 75,000 to 80,000 Jews to Palestine and Syria at a prince's ransom of 200,000 lei per person. The German Foreign Office objected, but to no avail. Smaller groups followed, headed for Palestine.[53] Romania became a transit way for open and clandestine emigration from Slovakia, Hungary, northern Transylvania, and Poland. By May 1943 Antonescu was prepared to permit the emigration of Transnistrian Jewish survivors of the Romanian atrocities, if the Red Cross organized ships.[54] Commercial and tactical as ever, the Romanian government had shifted ground considerably.

It had already done so in relation to the Roma and Sinti. The first deportation of 25,000 of the 260,000-strong community to Transnistria in spring 1942 had been the last. Sinti and Roma, unlike Jews, had been drafted into the Romanian army. Home on leave, they discovered their families had been deported. Many had gone to Transnistria to free their relatives. Then too, most of the Sinti and Roma had not been incarcerated in closed ghettos, and roamed the countryside in search of food and firewood—to the dismay of the 125,000 ethnic Germans living in Transnistria. Too embarrassing for the military and too complicated for the government, the "Gypsy" deportation program was dropped.[55]

Antonescu flaunted his barbarism. Himmler claimed to be the most civilized of men. Indeed, everything Himmler and his men did, they did in the name of civilization. That was Himmler's great aim—a finer civilization—and toward that goal he schemed and plotted and waited for his moment. When Hitler decided to invade Russia, Himmler anticipated that he would oversee German settlement there. He prepared his men to subjugate the Russian lands ruthlessly, and he waited for the appointment he felt was due him. But Hitler did not extend Himmler's authority as Reich Commissioner for the Consolidation of the German Nation to include Russia. Perhaps to preserve the balance of power between Himmler and Göring, Hitler turned instead to Alfred Rosenberg, the Balt who had been his mentor in Russian affairs twenty years earlier and who had become politically irrelevant by 1941. Rosenberg and Hitler met on 2 April and Hitler promised his old mentor an appointment as "political adviser in a decisive capacity." A few weeks later, the Führer directed Rosenberg to establish a department to deal with Eastern Questions. Himmler was confident that Rosenberg would not know what to do with the Jews. All talk, no action. That would never satisfy Hitler. Himmler bided his time.

In July 1941, with German troops deep inside Russia, Himmler saw his chance. To show Hitler that he was still ready to be chosen, he readied Meyer's first General Plan for the East in territories which were not under his jurisdiction, but where his men provided the police force. Lublin district lay halfway between the annexed territories Himmler already controlled and the Russian lands he coveted. His trusted friend Odilo Globocnik was the Higher SS and

Police Leader in Lublin. Himmler visited Globocnik, urging him to enlarge the existing SS enterprises, which depended on Jewish forced labor, and directing him to establish a 50,000-inmate concentration camp in Majdanek, a suburb of Lublin. That would take care of the manpower problem.

While Himmler set up his chips in Lublin, Heydrich took care of politics in Berlin. This entailed a visit to Göring. In 1941 Göring was officially responsible for "Jewish Affairs," but in 1939 he had entrusted the emigration or expulsion of all German Jews to Heydrich. The conquest of Russia had opened up space for a new Jewish reservation. Heydrich rightly assumed that a simple extension of the powers given to him in 1939 could strengthen Himmler's case for territorial powers in the east. At the end of July he drafted a letter for Göring to sign authorizing him, Heydrich, to take charge of a Final Solution of the Jewish Question in Europe. Heydrich visited Göring on 31 July. Göring signed the letter.

Himmler now had his opportunity to show Hitler that while Rosenberg might envision a future of ghettos and labor battalions for the Jews, he meant business. Immediately, the *Einsatzgruppen* began to massacre Jewish men, women, and children. They were on their way toward the genocide of all Russian Jews.[56]

Only the army could have restrained Himmler's killing, and the army stepped aside.[57] The generals had other problems. Their plans had been dashed. By the beginning of August, German generals had to admit an error: they had underestimated Soviet resilience and efficiency, the sheer size of the theater of operations, and the difficulties caused by poor roads. The German offensive was running weeks behind schedule. If the Red Army survived for two months, the campaign would fail and Germany would sink into a permanent two-front war. In a situation of escalating frustration and rage, the army left the *Einsatzgruppen* to its work.[58]

Here was born the myth of the "clean" German army. The Wehrmacht took no responsibility for failing to control the front and to curb Himmler's forces. On the contrary: army officers lamented the *Einsatzgruppen*'s actions as if powerless, as if the killing units were monstrous—but totally independent. In truth the army merely turned a blind eye, tacit permission which over time matured into active and systematic collaboration. "We were confronted by a scene that was so abominable and cruel that we were utterly shattered and horrified," Major Karl Rösler wrote to General Rudolf Schniewindt about a massacre he had witnessed near Zhitomir at the end of July.

> The earth had been dug out and was piled up to one side of it. This pile of earth and the wall of the pit were stained red by streams of blood. The pit itself was filled with innumerable human bodies of all types, both male and female. . . . Behind the piles of earth dug from it stood a squad of [Himmler's] police under the command of a police officer. There were traces of blood on their uniforms. In a wide circle around the pit stood scores of sol-

diers from the troop detachments stationed there, some of them in bathing trunks, watching the proceedings. There were also an equal number of civilians, including women and children. By going up very close to the pit I saw something that to this day I can never forget. Among the bodies in the pit lay an old man with a white beard, who still had a small walking-stick hanging over his left arm. It was clear that the old man was still alive as he was panting for breath and so I asked one of the policemen to kill him once and for all, to which he replied in a jocular fashion, "I've already shot him seven times in the belly, don't worry, he'll snuff it soon enough."[59]

If Rösler was revolted, clearly the soldiers and civilians were not. For them, this was entertainment. For Berlin, it was a matter of statistics. Every corpse counted. The Nazis excelled at the bookkeeping of murder. The *Einsatzgruppen* and German police officials sent regular dispatches listing their achievements. On 1 December 1941 SS-Standartenführer Karl Jäger reported on the activities of *Einsatzkommando 3* in Lithuania from 2 July to 1 December.[60] First, he identified the victims as "Jews," "Jewesses," and a few "Comm. Officials," "Russ. Comm.," and "Lith. Comm." By page two, however, he categorized more explicitly: on 15 and 16 August his men killed "3,200 Jews, Jewesses and J. Children, 5 Lith. Comm., 1 Pole, 1 partisan." From that day on, children became a significant line item. On the third page, a massacre on 23 August accounted for "1,312 Jews, 4,602 Jewesses, 1,609 Jewish children" in Panevezyes. Russian and Lithuanian Communists disappeared from his bookkeeping; now whole Jewish communities are targeted. The massacres become genocide.

By 1 December Jäger's men had killed 133,346 people.[61] "Today I can confirm that our objective, to solve the Jewish problem for Lithuania, has been achieved by EK 3," he declared proudly. No easy feat.

52. Einsatzgruppe *at work. 1941. Dokumentationsarchiv des Österreichischen Widerstandes, courtesy of the United States Holocaust Memorial Museum Photo Archives, Washington, DC.*

The decision to clear each district of Jews systematically required a thorough preparation of each individual action and a reconnaissance of the prevailing conditions in the district concerned. The Jews had to be assembled at one or several places. Depending on the number of Jews a place for the graves had to be found and then the graves dug. The distance from the assembly point to the graves was on average 4 to 5 km. The Jews were transported in detachments of 500 to the execution area, with a distance of at least 2 km between them.[62]

Notwithstanding this well-organized and streamlined system, "the acutely stressful nature of the work" could not be overlooked. These *Aktionen* were terrible for the men, Jäger suggested.

Frayed nerves led to insubordination, drunkenness, and mental breakdowns. Himmler and Heydrich had to find, and quickly, a less personal way to murder masses of people. The T4 program worked. Gas chambers were useful, but stationary installations, like those in Hadamar, Hartheim, and the other asylums did not meet the roving *Einsatzgruppen's* needs. The T4 program had also used vans transformed into mobile gas chambers. But its gas cylinders were bulky, heavy, and expensive.

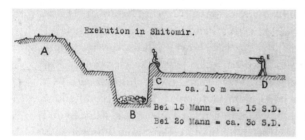

53. *Sketch made by a member of an* Einsatzgruppe *to illustrate the shooting procedure followed in Zhitomir. A key provided with the drawing reads: "A = railway embankment as bullet catcher; B = trench; C = the victims (not bound, not blindfolded, in groups of 5–20 persons) had to kneel down and face the railroad; C–D = a distance of c. 10 meters; E = Security Service execution commando, 1 commander, 2 officers, and 15 to 30 men [young men]." Courtesy Schweizerische Bundesarchiv, Berne.*

Heydrich turned to Dr. Widmann of the Criminal Technical Institute of the Criminal Police. Not long before, Widmann and his supervisor Dr. Walter Hess had chatted, as they rode on the Berlin underground, about their boss Artur Nebe's close brush with death. Drunk after a party, Nebe had fallen asleep in his garage with the car engine still running.[63] If exhaust gases could almost kill the head of the Criminal Police, they certainly could kill Jews.

Heydrich instructed the head of Department IID (Technical Affairs) of the Reich Security Main Office, SS-Obersturmbannführer Walter Rauff, to develop and construct a new type of gas van. The SS worked quickly. New killing vans first arrived in December 1941, but they never became popular. They often got stuck and broke down. Then too, the people locked in the cargo area died from suffocation instead of poisoning. This didn't trouble the *Einsatzgruppen*—until they opened the doors to unload corpses and found horribly distorted faces, and masses of bodies covered with urine, excrement, and menstrual blood. The vans proved even more nerve-wracking than the shootings.[64]

Himmler and Heydrich went back into conclave. Meanwhile, as the campaign in Russia rolled on, selected letters from the front were published at home. The government wanted the German people to know, through a controlled medium, what their young men faced on the eastern front. "A chapter in itself is the fact that presently the Jewish question is being solved with imposing thoroughness amid enthusiastic cheers of the native population," wrote a certain lance corporal Heinrich Sachs. "As the Führer put it in one of his speeches shortly before the outbreak of war: 'Should Jewry succeed in inciting the European nations to a senseless war, this will mean the end of this race in Europe!' The Jew ought to have known that the Führer is accustomed to take his word seriously, and now he has to bear the consequences. They are inexorably hard but necessary if ultimately quiet and peace are to reign among nations."[65] Germany's people got the message. Judeocide became public knowledge.[66]

THE GERMANS targeted Russian Jewry for annihilation in the summer of 1941. Polish Jews were next. Step had followed step; way had led to way. In 1933 getting rid of the German Jews had been seen as a sufficient "solution" to the "Jewish Problem." By the summer of 1941 the Germans had broadened their horizons to include all Jews. In eight years, the powerful men of Berlin had grown ever more confident and cocksure. They controlled Europe. The earlier territorial solution had naturally included all Jews in any "solution." It followed that genocide would include all Jews as well.

"This winter there is a danger that not all the Jews can be fed anymore," SS-Sturmbannführer Rolf-Heinz Höppner wrote to Eichmann about the Lodz ghetto. "One should weigh honestly, if the most humane solution might not be to finish off those of the Jews who are not employable by means of some quick-working device. At any rate, that would be more pleasant than to let them starve to death."[67]

Höppner had gas vans in mind. In the event, winter conditions did not prompt the Germans to bring in these mobile killing installations. Himmler sent 20,000 German and Czech Jews to Lodz. Arthur Greiser, the Gauleiter or provincial governor, panicked. The ghetto was already overcrowded. What was he going to do with so many additional Jews? Appalled, he instructed the local Higher SS and Police Leader, Wilhelm Koppe, to do something. Koppe did not fail him. He remembered Herbert Lange's T4 gas vans and dispatched Lange's *Sonderkommando* to the village of Chelmno, known to the Germans as Kulmhof. Koppe and Lange decided that between 100 and 150 Jews at a time were to be taken by truck to a country house in Kulmhof surrounded by a high fence. "The loaded lorries entered the camp grounds and stopped before the house, where the new-comers were addressed by a representative of the *Sonderkommando,* who told them that they were going to work in the East, and promised them fair treatment, and good food," Judge Wladyslaw Bednarz explained in his 1945 report.

> He also told them that first they must take a bath and deliver their clothes to be disinfected. From the court-yard they were sent inside the house, to a heated room on the first floor, where they undressed. They then came downstairs to a corridor, on the walls of which were inscriptions: "to the doctor" or "to the bath"; the latter with an arrow pointing to the front door. When they had gone out they were told that they were going in a closed car to the bath-house.
>
> Before the door of the country house stood a large lorry with a door in the rear, so placed that it could be entered directly with the help of a ladder.
>
> The time assigned for loading it was very short, gendarmes standing in the corridor and driving the wretched victims into the car as quickly as possible with shouts and blows.
>
> When the whole of one batch had been forced into the car, the door was banged and the engine started, poisoning with its exhaust those who were locked inside. The process was usually complete in 4 or 5 minutes, and then the lorry was driven to Rzuchow wood about 4 km (2.5 miles) away, where the corpses were unloaded and burnt.[68]

By the time the gas vans had left the country house, a second truckload of Jews arrived, unaware of what had happened to the earlier group. Unlike the later camps in Belzec, Sobibór, Treblinka, and Auschwitz, where most people guessed that something was terribly wrong when they disembarked from the trains, those brought to Kulmhof did not realize German perfidy until they saw the gas van—and then it was too late. For the Germans, Kulmhof was a great success: there they killed some 150,000 Jews between 8 December 1941 and 9 April 1943. Just two survived: Simon Srebnik and Mordechaï Podchlebnik.

WHILE POLISH JEWS were murdered in Chelmno, German Jews were deported to Poland and the occupied east. Stripped of everything—German nationality, all assets and rights—through a series of administrative measures and secret ordinances, they were shipped to ghettos in Riga and Minsk.[69] "It was observed that some of the [German] Jews [transported to Minsk] had a totally mistaken picture about their future," an intelligence officer reported to Berlin. "They imagined, for example, that they are pioneers and will be used to colonize the East."[70] As in Lodz, the Germans killed local Jews to make room for the arrivals from the Reich.

By now, late 1941, the Germans and their allies were slaughtering Jews throughout the east. The Wehrmacht was fully involved. It had moved far beyond facilitating the *Einsatzgruppen* and participating in the murder of Jews as "partisans." Now the army operated on its own initiative. On the order of

Lieutenant General Walter Braemer, army commander in Ostland, a police reserve battalion attached to his forces massacred the inhabitants of the Smilovic, Koidanavo, and Slutsk ghettos.[71]

The perpetrators knew what to do on the ground. But they were not quite clear about policy. The "Brown Portfolio," the official guidelines for treatment of the Jews, did not mention genocide.[72] Nor were the perpetrators totally comfortable murdering German Jews. As Wilhelm Kube, the General Commissioner for White Russia, explained to his superior Heinrich Lohse, Reich Commissioner of Ostland, "I am certainly tough and prepared to do my bit towards the solution of the Jewish question, but people from our own cultural sphere are rather different from the brutalised hordes living here."[73]

Lohse, a civilian Nazi, sympathized. He had intervened in the execution of some Jews two months earlier. When the SS complained to his supervisor in Berlin, Lohse protested that he had not been given clear instructions. "I have forbidden the indiscriminate executions of Jews in Lepaya because they were not carried out in a justifiable manner," he declared. And then he asked, is "your inquiry . . . a directive to liquidate all Jews in the east. Is this to take place without regard to age and sex and their usefulness to the economy? . . . So far I have not been able to find such a directive either in the regulations regarding the Jewish question in the 'Brown Portfolio' or in other decrees."[74] It took the political department of the Ministry of the Eastern Territories over a month to respond. "The Jewish question has probably been clarified by now through verbal discussions. Economic considerations are to be regarded as fundamentally irrelevant in the settlement of the problem."[75]

Lohse had written on 15 November; the reply was dated 18 December. During those fateful five weeks, Japan attacked the American fleet in Pearl Harbor, the United States declared war on Japan, and Hitler declared war on the United States. The European War had become a World War. Hitler responded immediately in a speech to the Gauleiters on 12 December. "As it concerns the Jewish Question, the Führer is resolved to make a clean sweep," Goebbels recorded in his diary. "He had warned the Jews that if they again unleashed a world war, they would be destroyed. That has been no empty threat." Paraphrasing Hitler, Goebbels continued, "The world war has arrived, and the destruction of Jewry must follow. This matter is to be considered without any sentimentality. It is not for us to have pity on the Jews, but on the German people. If the German people once again has sacrificed 160,000 men in the eastern campaign, then those who caused this bloody conflict must pay for it with their lives."[76]

Profoundly antisemitic, Hitler believed the myth of the immensely powerful Jew. He had trusted the American Jews to keep their government out of the war in order to protect their co-religionists in Germany. Now that Germany was at war with the United States, he had no use for the German Jews. No need to store them in Lodz and Minsk; they were expendable.

Still, Lohse's question remained unanswered. What *was* the government policy with regard to the Jews, and who was responsible for formulating and implementing it? By the end of November many individuals and agencies had taken the initiative to kill Jews. Koppe had set up his own extermination installation in Kulmhof. Rosenberg's Ministry for the Occupied Eastern Territories was negotiating with unemployed T4 specialists to bring their expertise to Riga and Minsk. And the Wehrmacht was busy too.

If Himmler was sure of anything, it was that *he* wanted to be in charge, and not some local Gauleiters, Reichskommissars, or—far worse for the political future of the SS—Wehrmacht generals. He saw himself as Hitler's most loyal vassal, and he understood that his Führer was determined to annihilate the Jews. Himmler wished above all else to "work toward the Führer." Then too, his vision of a German East was close to his heart. He took seriously his mission of forging a *Volk* of physically perfect and genetically German people entitled to the *Lebensraum* of the east. But how to manage it? He knew that Hitler would not formally appoint him Reich Commissioner for the Final Solution of the Jewish Question. Indeed, the Führer regretted the written authorization he had given Bouhler and Brack to begin the euthanasia program. Himmler had to gain official authorization another way. Göring's letter expanding Heydrich's authority to "carry out all necessary preparations with regard to organizational, substantive, and financial viewpoints for a total solution of the Jewish Question in the German sphere of influence in Europe"[77] was the best Himmler could do. He would use it to establish his authority.

54. *Reinhard Heydrich, 1935. Reproduced in Gerd Rühle, ed., Das Dritte Reich, Das vierte Jahr 1936 (Berlin, 1937). Coll. authors.*

To that end, Heydrich invited top bureaucrats—but not Hitler's powerful inner circle—to a meeting in the Berlin Interpol Office at 56 Am grossen Wannsee on 9 December. The object, he said, was to secure "a uniform view among the relevant central agencies of the further tasks concerned with the remaining work on this final solution." This conference was specially urgent because "from 10 October onwards the Jews have been evacuated from Reich territory, including the Protectorate, to the East in a continuous series of transports."[78] Heydrich attached a copy of Göring's letter to each invitation.

Hans Frank immediately dispatched his deputy, Dr. Bühler, to Berlin for preliminary discussions with Heydrich. Upon Bühler's return, Governor General Frank called a special session of his administrators. Senior officials from each of the five districts of the General Government (Cracow, Lublin, Radom, Warsaw, and Galicia) and SS and police officers chatted about the terrible food situation in the General Government and a typhus epidemic, for which they blamed the Jews. Finally, Frank spoke. He stunned everyone happily discussing the execution of groups of Jews by pronouncing a death sentence over Polish Jewry as a whole. "The Jews must be finished one way or the other." Warning against compassion, which only Germans deserved, Frank announced that "a major Jewish emigration will begin."

But what will happen to the Jews? Do you imagine that they will be settled in the Ostland in villages? . . . Gentlemen, I must ask you to arm yourselves against any feelings of compassion. We must exterminate the Jews wherever we find them and wherever it is possible to do so in order to maintain the whole structure of the Reich here. . . . The General Government must be just as free of Jews as the Reich is. Where and how that occurs is a matter for the agencies which we must establish and deploy here and I will inform you of how they will work in good time.[79]

The Governor General urged his subordinates to keep their eyes on the prize: "this territory of the General Government will be the next part of Europe that will be subjected to a process of thorough Germanization. We will build the great Reich highways which will cover this land. Along these Reich highways we will build German settlement villages."[80] Frank achieved his purpose. Everyone urged Bühler, their representative at the Wannsee conference, to request that the General Government be the first territory cleansed of Jews.

Himmler, meanwhile, looked forward to the conference, which had been postponed to 20 January 1942 because Japan had bombed Pearl Harbor on 7 December 1941 and opened a new theater of war. The meeting at Wannsee promised to bring him everything he wanted: authority over the Final Solution to the Jewish Question and complete control over Jews as a slave labor force. Dreaming of the future, he asked chief of SS construction Hans Kammler for a building program that would realize his vision of a Germanized East. Boldly, Kammler proposed an 80-billion-mark construction project. Himmler presumed that SS companies like DEST (the Deutsche Erd- und Steinwerke, or German Earth and Stone Works), which he had founded years before, would supply him with stone, brick, chalk, and cement. He also counted on a special arrangement with the Hermann-Göring-Werke for steel. Lumber would come from the Russian forests. But he needed labor to produce the materials and for construction.[81]

A paradoxical situation developed in the SS empire. For Heydrich, chief of the Reich Security Main Office, the Jews were a nuisance to be deported. For Kammler, chief of SS Construction, Jews who could work were a valuable resource. The conflict troubled Himmler. There was no place for Jews in his German utopia, but he could not build it without them. These apparently mutually exclusive demands were resolved at the Wannsee conference.

Heydrich chaired the meeting, opening with a reference to Göring's letter. He then proceeded to his central objective. "Primary responsibility for the handling of the Final Solution of the Jewish Question . . . is to lie centrally, regardless of geographic boundaries, with the *Reichsführer-SS* and Chief of the German Police' [i.e., Himmler]," he claimed flatly.[82] No one protested. Heydrich wrapped up the conference in ninety minutes. Too few Jews had emigrated between 1933 and 1939, and 11 million remained in Europe. "In the course of the Final Solution, the Jews are now to be suitably assigned as labor in the East," he announced. "In big labor gangs, with the sexes separated, Jews capable of work will be brought to these areas, employed in roadbuilding, in which task a large part will undoubtedly disappear through natural diminution. The remnant that may eventually remain ... will have to be appropriately dealt with."[83]

Heydrich had prevailed, vindicating Himmler's trust. Bühler prevailed too. He did not betray his fellow administrators in Cracow, Warsaw, Lublin, Radom, and Galicia. As the Wannsee conference drew to a close, he took the floor to request that the Final Solution begin as quickly as possible in the General Government. Almost as an afterthought, he added, "Of the approximately 2.5 million Jews here in question, the majority are unfit for work."[84]

The gentleman at the Wannsee conference did not discuss the fate of the 800,000 to 1 million Roma and Sinti in Europe. Officials of the Reichskommissariat Ostland and Rosenberg's ministry discussed the issue throughout 1942 and most of 1943. Finally Himmler intervened, and the Ministry for the Occupied Eastern Territories decided in November 1943 to treat sedentary Roma and Sinti like the local population, while "itinerating Gypsies and *Zigeuner-Mischlinge* ... are to be assigned the same status as Jews and are to be put in concentration camps."[85]

The "Final Solution of the Jewish Problem," January 1942

For most Roma and Sinti in Nazi Europe, to be assigned the same status as Jews did not necessarily mean to be treated the same.[86] With no strong ideology to shape the action against the Roma and Sinti, with no sustained propaganda effort to keep focus and maintain public attention, lacking the motivation of greed to fuel participation by broad layers of the population, and no interest on

Hitler's part, the *Porramous* ("Devouring") of the "Gypsies" flagged just when the genocide of the Jews turned in a full Holocaust or *Shoah* ("Ruin").

The Nazis never wavered about the Jews. Only the fate of the "half- and quarter-Jews" hovered over the Wannsee conference table. State Secretary of the Interior Wilhelm Stuckart argued that deportation and killing of *Mischlinge* would create difficulties because of their ties with "Aryan" Germans, and the participants agreed to postpone this decision until the Reich had won the war. But for "full Jews"—no delay. Hitler spoke in the Berlin sports arena ten days later. "It is clear to us that this war can end only with the extermination of the Germanic people or the disappearance of Jewry from Europe," he announced to a wildly enthusiastic crowd. Consciously substituting his speech of 30 January 1939 with that of the first day of the war, the Führer continued, "On September 1, I already stated in the German Reichstag, and I avoid rash prophecies, that this war will not turn out the way the Jews imagine it, that is, with the extermination of the European-Aryan peoples, but that the result of this war will be the destruction of Jewry. For the first time, now, the old Jewish law will be applied—eye for eye, tooth for tooth!"[87]

And what of the Madagascar plan? Franz Rademacher of the Jewish Department in the Foreign Office wrote to his colleague Harald Bielfeld of the Africa and Colonial Affairs Department on 10 February 1942. "The war against the Soviet Union has offered the possibility of putting other territories at our disposal for the final solution," Rademacher assured Bielfeld. "Therefore the Führer has decided that the Jews shall not be deported to Madagascar but to the east. As a result it is no longer necessary that Madagascar be taken into consideration for the final solution."[88]

Chapter Eleven

HOLOCAUST

As the German leadership sorted out the bureaucratic details of the "Final Solution," the Italian journalist Curzio Malaparte visited Warsaw, toured the ghetto, and lunched with Governor General and Mrs. Hans Frank and other high-ranking German officials. Still stunned by the Iasi massacre, Malaparte described this mass murder of seven thousand Jews.

"Quite a respectable figure," said Frank, "but it was not a decent way to do it; it is not necessary to do it that way."

"No, that's not the way to do it," said Fischer, the Governor of Warsaw, shaking his head in disapproval.

"Not a civilized way," Wächter, the Governor of Cracow and one of Dolfuss' murderers, said in a disgusted tone.

"The Romanians are not a civilized people," said Frank contemptuously.

"*Ja, es hat kein Kultur*—Yes, they have no culture," said Fischer shaking his head.

"Though my heart is not as soft as yours," said Frank, "I share and I understand your horror at the Jassy massacres. As a man, a German, and as Governor-General of Poland I disapprove of pogroms."

"Very kind of you," I answered with a bow.

"Germany is a country that has a higher civilization and abominates barbaric methods," said Frank gazing around him with an expression of sincere indignation.

"*Natürlich*," the others chorused.

"Germany," said Wächter, "is called upon to carry out a great civilizing mission in the East."[1]

The Germans had quite a different way of doing things. They were not Romanians, and they did not behave like Romanians.

"We Germans are guided by reason and method and not by bestial instincts; we always act scientifically. When necessary, but only when absolutely necessary," repeated Frank stressing each syllable and glaring at me as if to imprint his words on my brow. "We used surgeons as our models, never butchers. Have you perchance even seen a massacre of Jews in the streets of a German city?" he went on. "You never have, have you? You might have witnessed some demonstrations by students, some harmless rowdy boyish pranks. Yet, within a short time, not a single Jew will be left in Germany."

"All a method of organization," said Fischer."[2]

And, truly, few Jews soon remained in Germany, a triumph of "organization." How to "solve" the "Jewish Problem" in a civilized manner, that was the question; how to kill in a surgical style? How to be "decent" murderers?

The SS leadership, well aware that they must steer the Judeocide, feared that their men might kill for pleasure rather than on orders. "I have spoken to the Reichsführer-SS [Himmler] about this important matter," an SS judge wrote to the head office of the SS court system on 26 October 1942. "Deciding whether and how to punish men for shooting Jews who have not been ordered or authorized to do so," the court must consider "the motive for this action."

(1) Execution for pure political motives shall result in no punishment, unless punishment is necessary for the purpose of maintaining order. . . .
(2) Men acting out of self-seeking, sadistic or sexual motives should be punished by a court of law and, where applicable, on charges of murder or manslaughter.[3]

SS-Untersturmführer Max Täubner did not belong to an *Einsatzgruppe* created specifically to kill Jews. Nevertheless, he and his unit organized a private crusade. Täubner photographed these actions and showed the pictures to his wife and friends. Tried and convicted, the SS court found that the murders Täubner had initiated had "degenerated into vicious excesses."[4] His actions had created "extremely difficult moral conflicts" for his men. One such man, a certain Heinrich Hesse, testified that he "was glad" he had been "able to shoot" a "beautiful [Jewish] woman . . . so that she did not fall into the hands of the Untersturmführer." And he added: "But please don't take that to mean that I enjoyed it."[5]

Cases like Täubner's comforted SS leaders: it allowed them to see themselves as decent fellows. To murder masses of people imposed an enormous burden, Himmler reminded SS leaders in Posen (4 October 1943). "Most of you must know what it means to see a hundred corpses lie side by side, or five hundred, or a thousand. To have stuck this out and—excepting cases of human weakness—to have kept our integrity, that is what has made us hard. In our history, this is an unwritten and never-to-be-written page of glory." Such difficult work, but they had managed. "We have carried out this heaviest of our tasks in a spirit of love for our people. And our inward being, our soul, our character has not suffered injury from it."[6]

How had Himmler managed it? His evil genius inspired a centralized program of management and developed the extermination structure of Chelmno into a sophisticated annihilation camp. Eichmann's Subsection IV (Gestapo)-B (Sects)-4 (Jews) of the Reich Security Main Office in Berlin took over. No more local initiatives. The murder machinery would run with the assembly-line efficiency he was so proud of.[7] Many arms of the Nazi state participated in this process—and it lead to a new entity in the history of the western world: the extermination camp. Isolated from a curious public or a prying journalist, these camps offered several advantages. They spared the *Einsatzgruppen* the ordeal of shooting masses of people at close range. Mass incineration took care of the corpse problem. Then too, these camps provided an ideal opportunity to collect, sort, and send victims' possessions to the Reich. No free-for-all as in Iasi. And no corruption of the SS from theft.

Himmler charged his old friend in Lublin, SS and Police Leader Odilo Globocnik, with building these camps. Viktor Brack, former head of T4, was only too happy to help. He had trained personnel and tried and true methods to offer. Globocnik accepted with alacrity. "I placed some of my men at the disposal of Brigadeführer Globocnik," Brack wrote to Himmler. "Following a further request from him, I have transferred additional personnel. Brigadeführer Globocnik took the opportunity of expressing the opinion that the whole Jewish action should be carried out as quickly as possible to avoid the danger of one day finding ourselves stuck in the middle of it in the event of difficulties forcing us to halt the action."[8]

"The whole Jewish action" was indeed "carried out as quickly as possible." Belzec was the first of three annihilation sites which came to be called the Operation Reinhard camps, in memory of Reinhard Heydrich, assassinated by the Czech underground in June 1942. All three—Belzec, Sobibór, and Treblinka—were designed with the help of T4 personnel, situated close to railway lines, built rather quickly and very cheaply.[9] The Germans learned as they went. They employed Polish laborers to build Belzec; Jewish slaves were used for Sobibór and Treblinka. Two civilian contracting firms moved along the construction of Treblinka with labor rounded up in the nearby Warsaw ghetto. Nails, cables, even wallpaper came from the ransacked ghetto too.

The first camp to use stationary gas installations, Belzec opened for business in March 1942. The system was sordidly simple. A train of "resettlement workers" arrived and the deportees were hauled out and forced to surrender their possessions in an orderly fashion. They were told they had arrived at a transit camp en route to the east. They took off their clothes in an undressing station and walked naked along an S-shaped path bordered by high barbed-wire fences covered in ivy. Entering gas chambers disguised as showers, they were killed in fifteen to thirty minutes by carbon monoxide poisoning. The corpses were burned in open-pit fires.[10]

As the diary of the German non-commissioned officer Wilhelm Cornides makes clear, the mass murders at Belzec were no clandestine operation. On his way to Chelm, Cornides stopped in the Galician town of Rawa Ruska on 30 August. Strolling through the streets the next day, he "saw a transport train run into the station," as he noted in his journal. Barbed wire zigzagged across the train windows; the doors were shut.

> On the roof and running boards sat guards with rifles. One could see from a distance that the cars were jammed full of people. I turned and walked along the whole train: it consisted of 38 cattle cars and one passenger car. In each of the cars there were at least 60 Jews . . . the youngest were surely not more than two years old. As soon as the train halted, the Jews attempted to pass out bottles in order to get water. The train, however, was surrounded by SS guards, so that no one could come near. At that moment a train arrived from the direction of Jaroslav; the travelers streamed toward the exit without bothering about the transport . . . I talked to a policeman on duty at the railway station. Upon my question as to where the Jews actually came from, he answered: "Those are probably the last ones from Lvov. That has been going on now for 5 weeks uninterruptedly. In Jaroslav they let remain only 8, no one knows why." I asked: "How far are they going?" Then he said: "To Belzec." "And then?" "Poison." I asked: "Gas?" He shrugged his shoulders. Then he said only: "At the beginning they always shot them, I believe."[11]

Later that afternoon Cornides counted the cars of an empty transport traveling in the opposite direction: fifty-six wagons.

Cornides continued his journey to Chelm, boarding a train at 4:40 that afternoon. The sight he had seen a few hours earlier alerted him to what might come. Punctiliously, he recorded the time of his diary entries. "In my compartment I spoke with a railway policeman's wife who is currently visiting her husband here," he recorded less than an hour later (5:30). He learned a lot from her. The transports, she told him, passed through daily, sometimes with German Jews as well as *Ostjuden*. Cornides and his fellow passenger were joined by the railway policeman who served as the train escort. "'Do the Jews know then what is happening with them?' Cornides asked the other two. The woman answered: 'Those who come from far won't know anything, but here in the vicinity they know already. They attempt to run away then, if they notice that someone is coming for them. So, for example, most recently in Cholm where 3 were shot on the way through the city.' 'In the railway documents these trains run under the name of resettlement transports,' remarked the railway policeman. Then he said that after Heydrich was murdered, several transports with Czechs passed through. Camp Belzec is supposed to be located right on the railway line and the woman promised to show it to me when we pass it." She did.

6:20 p.m.

We passed camp Belzec. Before then, we traveled for some time through a tall pine forest. When the woman called, "Now it comes," one could see a high hedge of fir trees. A strong sweetish odor could be made out distinctly. "But they are stinking already," says the woman. "Oh nonsense, that is only the gas," the railway policeman said laughing. Meanwhile—we had gone on about 200 yards—the sweetish odor was transformed into a strong smell of something burning. "That is from the crematory," says the policeman. A short distance farther the fence stopped. In front of it, one could see a guard house with an SS post. A double track led into the camp. One track branched off from the main line, the other ran over a turntable from the camp to a row of sheds about 250 yards away. . . . SS guards, rifle under the arm, stood by. One of the sheds was open; one could distinctly see that it was filled with bundles of clothes to the ceiling. As we went on, I looked back one more time. The fence was too high to see anything at all. The woman says that sometimes, while going by, one can see smoke rising from the camp, but I could notice nothing of the sort.[12]

Upon arrival in Chelm, his destination that day, Cornides struck up a conversation with a policeman. The Ukrainian guards who worked in the camp, the man told him, came into town to sell the loot they stole from the Jewish victims: gold, watches, and other things. But how were the Jews actually killed? Cornides wanted to know. "They are told that they must get rid of their lice, and then they must take off their clothes, and then they come into a room, where first off they get a hot blast of air which is already mixed with a small dose of gas. That is enough to make them unconscious. The rest comes after. And then they are burnt immediately."[13]

The Chelm policeman was well informed although not an eyewitness. There were few personal witnesses, of course. Few who entered Belzec ever left. Upon occasion, however, there was the rare visitor. One was Kurt Gerstein. A German Protestant who had enlisted in the SS in March 1941, Gerstein used his position to gather information about the genocide of the Jews in the hope of informing the outside world. Early in 1942 Gerstein was appointed head of the Disinfection Services of the *Waffen-SS*. He specialized in disinfection apparatus and the purification of drinking water for soldiers. He also was considered an expert on prussic acid and toxic gases. It was for this reason that Gerstein was chosen to go to Belzec; the camp authorities and their superiors hoped he could suggest cleaner and quicker alternatives to their carbon monoxide poisoning system.[14]

Gerstein was not told where he was going. The Central Security Office simply ordered him to obtain a hundred kilograms of the gas which had proved so effective in Auschwitz, Zyklon B (prussic acid), and to transport it to a place known to his driver. When he arrived at Belzec, he was given a tour of the facilities and asked to perfect the function of the gas chambers. He noted that a "small special station with two platforms was set up against a yellow sand hill, immediately to the north of the Lublin-Lvov railway. . . . Alongside the station was a large hut marked 'Cloak Room' with a wicket inside marked 'Valuables.'

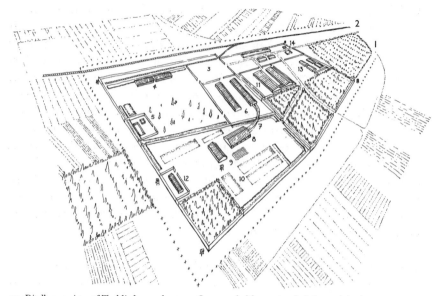

55. Bird's-eye view of Treblinka, early 1943. Surrounded by antitank defenses (1), the camp was connected by a railway spur (2) to the main line. At the station (3) were barracks to sort the goods brought by the deportees (4) and a sham hospital where those who might interrupt the smooth operation of the killing process were shot (5). Most of the deportees were brought immediately to the undressing barracks (6), and from there, via the so-called funnel (7) to the gas chambers (8). The corpses were burned on "roasts" (9) and the ashes buried in former mass graves (10), exhumed by 1943 in favor of cremation. Earth walls screened this part of Treblinka from the rest of the camp. The Jewish slaveworkers in the reception area of the camp lived in barracks (11) close to the undressing barracks (6); those who worked at the killing center were quartered close to the gas chambers (12). The SS and Ukrainian guards had their own livingquarters (13) near the official entrance to the camp (14). Reconstruction by Marc Downing. Coll. authors.

Further on, a hall, designated 'Hairdresser,' containing about a hundred chairs. Then came a passage about 150 yards long, open to the wind and flanked on both sides with barbed wire and notices saying: 'To the Baths and Inhalation Room.'" This path led to "a building of the bathhouse type; left and right, large pots of geraniums and other flowers. On the roof, a copper Star of David. The building was labeled: 'Heckenholt Foundation.'"[15]

Gerstein witnessed the entire process of murder from the arrival of the train to the mass burial of its six thousand passengers. "The train drew in, 200 Ukrainians detailed for the task tore open the doors and, laying about them with their leather whips, drove the Jews out of the cars. Instructions boomed from a loudspeaker, ordering them to remove all clothing, artificial limbs, and spectacles. Using small pieces of string handed out by a little Jewish boy, they were to tie their shoes together. All valuables and money were to be handed in at the valuables counter, but no voucher or receipt was given. Women and young girls were to have their hair cut off in the hairdresser's hut (an S.S.-Unterführer on duty told me: 'That's to make something special for U-boat crews')."[16] The plun-

der of the Jews, begun when they were still at home, had reached its penulti-
mate stage. Only the gold in their teeth remained. It was extracted after their
death. In nine months, from March to December 1942, some 550,000 Jews were
gassed to death and burned in the open pits of Belzec. They came from the districts of Galicia, Cracow, and Lublin, where Jews had lived for centuries. The
bureaucrats were more than half a million people closer to their ideal of a *Judenrein* Government General.[17]

Sobibór was built more quickly than Belzec and was more efficient. Open-
pit burning and a system of grate fires destroyed the bodies. Claiming victims
from Lublin district (in which it was located) as well as Minsk, Slovakia, the
Netherlands, and France, Sobibór was in operation from April to June 1942 and
again from October 1942 until a breakout on 14 October 1943. Some three hundred inmates fled to the nearby forest, but they did not find sanctuary. Only
thirty or so were alive at the end of the war.[18]

The acme of the killing centers was Treblinka. Technological improvements
in the murder system made it the most effective assembly line for death among
the Operation Reinhard camps. Located 120 kilometers northeast of Warsaw,
Treblinka started to function in July 1942. As in Sobibór and Belzec, gas chambers were used to kill people by carbon monoxide poisoning. The Germans
maximized this potential with thirteen gas chambers by the end. The victims
were buried in mass graves. Later, camp personnel ordered slaveworkers to
open the pits and burn the bodies. Despite a breakout of some 150–200 men (of
whom 60–70 survived), Treblinka was in operation from July 1942 to October
1943. This enormous death machine devoured at least 750,000 people, people
from near and far: Warsaw, Radom, Bialystok, and Lublin districts as well as
Germany, Macedonia, Thrace, and the transit camp of Theresienstadt. By the
time the Germans closed Treblinka, they had killed most of Europe's Jews.[19]
And they valued the possessions robbed from the Operation Reinhard victims
at the three annihilation sites at RM 178,745,960 and 59 pfennigs.[20]

The Germans constructed Belzec, Sobibór, and Treblinka solely to murder
Jews. Auschwitz and Majdanek, built for other purposes, were transformed into
killing sites.[21] Auschwitz went into operation in May 1940 as a concentration
camp for Polish resisters and intellectuals. As German needs changed, the camp
acquired new functions. When the Germans decided to locate the Kattowitz
Gestapo Summary Court, chaired by Dr. Rudolf Mildner, in Auschwitz, the
camp became an execution site for "outsiders" who were never registered there.
Polish resisters from all over eastern Upper Silesia were brought to Auschwitz
to be interrogated, convicted, and killed.

Mildner's court convened in block 11. Initially, the resisters were executed in
the courtyard between blocks 10 and 11. It soon became clear, however, that it
would be more efficient to bring the condemned to the crematorium and kill
them in the mortuary. "The walls were stained with blood, and in the background there lay the corpses of those already shot," Pery Broad, one of the SS

men employed in the camp's own Gestapo office, wrote after the war. "A wide stream of blood was flowing towards the drain in the middle of the hall. The victims were obliged to step quite close to the corpses and formed a line. Their feet were stained with blood; they stood in puddles of it. . . . The right-hand man of the camp leader, *SS-Hauptscharführer* Palitzsch, did the shooting. He killed one person after another with a practised shot in the back of the neck."[22] The stench was so foul that in the summer of 1941 the chief of the Political Department, Grabner, prevailed on the head of the camp building office, August Schlachter, to install a more sophisticated ventilation system that not only extracted the air he found sickening, but brought in a fresh supply from the outside.[23] The corpses were burned in the incineration room next door.

The use of concentration camps as execution grounds for "undesirables" who were not registered inmates acquired particular urgency when Germany attacked the Soviet Union. Hitler was obsessed by the "stab in the back" of World War I, and he assured his admirers that it would not be repeated. The soldiers at the eastern front did not have to worry. "I've ordered Himmler," Hitler confided to his inner clique, "in the event of there some day being reason to fear troubles back at home, to liquidate everything he finds in the concentration camps. Thus at a stroke the revolution would be deprived of its leaders."[24] Hitler expanded on this idea on at least one other occasion: not only all the camp inmates but rioters, opposition leaders, and Soviet prisoners of war should be killed also if a "stab in the back" were attempted.[25]

Himmler, anticipating Hitler's wishes, did not wait for trouble. The Soviet POWs were the first to be targeted, and Heydrich was already busy with that problem. But where were they going to be killed? Auschwitz was a good choice. Himmler controlled 15 square miles around the camp: he could do anything he pleased there.

The feared stab in the back, a revolution at home in Germany, never materialized, but the use of concentration camps to annihilate "outsiders" whose very existence threatened the state took root. A few hundred Soviet POWs arrived in Auschwitz on 18 July. They were locked into block 11. As no extermination facility existed, liquidation followed the established pattern. "They were shot in the gravel pits . . . or in the courtyard of Block 11," the commandant of the camp Rudolf Höss recalled after the war.[26] Camp physicians then began to experiment with more clinical methods of murder. Prisoners were injected with phenol, gasoline perhydrol, ether, and other substances, and after a number of trials, phenol injections into the heart were found to be the most efficient.[27] But the camp authorities were not satisfied. They wanted to kill thousands upon thousands of people, and phenol injections were too labor-intensive. Also too personal. One-on-one contact between murderer and victim lowered the killers' spirits.

The T4 program gas chambers seemed a good solution, but the carbon monoxide chambers would not do: the piping was too complex and the gas too expensive.[28] The Auschwitz personnel knew a lot about hydrocyanide. They had overseen the construction of delousing installations that summer, and they understood the lethal potential of Zyklon B. Höss instructed Lagerführer Karl Fritsch to carry out a pilot experiment. Fritsch obliged with a transport of Soviet POWs whom he took to block 11 and locked into a basement cell. Fritsch threw Zyklon B crystals into the room and all the men died.[29]

Encouraged, Fritsch conducted the first mass execution with Zyklon B on 3 September 1941. Wojciech Barz, an inmate who worked as a nurse, recalled that a few months after the beginning of the war against the Soviet Union he was ordered to bring very ill inmates into the underground cells of block 11.

> They were locked into these cells. Around 10 in the evening we heard that the SS drove a large group of people to that place. We heard screaming in Russian, orders of the SS, and the sound of beating. In the middle of the night three days later, we nurses were ordered to go to Block 11. We had to clear the corpses from the basements cells. We saw that a large group of Russian prisoners simply had been gassed in those cells together with the sick inmates who we had brought there. The image we saw when we opened the cell doors was that of an over-packed suitcase. The corpses fell towards us. I estimate that some 60 corpses were pushed together in a small cell. It was so packed that they could not fall over when they died, but remained standing.[30]

Still not good enough, the Germans thought. Some prisoners survived, the procedure took too long, the corpses had to be moved to the crematorium on the other side of the camp, and it took two days to air out the building. In short, the basement of block 11 was not an ideal gas chamber. At the same time, these first exercises proved how easy it was to convert any space into a Zyklon B gas chamber. Unlike the carbon monoxide gas chamber, with its system of pipes and perforated vents and its cumbersome gas cylinders, the hydrocyanide chamber required only a small porthole, perhaps in the roof, through which to drop the Zyklon B crystals.

Fritsch remembered that the morgue attached to the crematorium had a flat roof. Why not make one or more openings in it? A month earlier, the morgue had been equipped with a new and powerful ventilation system, ready-made for poisonous gas.

Fritsch's men punched three square portholes through the morgue roof and covered them with tight-fitting wooden lids,[31] then murdered nine hundred Soviets on 16 September.[32] "The entire transport fit exactly in the room," Höss recalled. "The doors were closed and the gas poured in through the opening in the roof. How long the process lasted, I don't know, but for quite some time sounds could be heard. As the gas was thrown in some of them yelled 'Gas!' and a tremendous screaming and shoving started toward both doors, but the doors were able to withstand all the force." A few hours later the fans were turned on and the doors opened. "I really didn't waste any thoughts about the killing of the Russian prisoners of war," Höss confessed in 1946. "It was ordered; I had to carry it out. But I must admit openly that the gassings had a calming effect on me, since in the near future the mass annihilation of the Jews was to begin."[33]

Far from stressful, mass murder had become "calming." A *Judenrein* Europe was at hand. And it could be achieved nearly anonymously. Romanians had faced the Jews they killed. So had the *Einsatzgruppen*. In Auschwitz-Birkenau, anonymity ruled. The moment of death disappeared behind locked doors. So did the corpses. In Auschwitz-Birkenau, unlike the Operation Reinhard camps, gas chambers and crematoria worked in tandem. Slave laborers burned bodies in the building where they had been killed. As far as the Germans and their co-workers were concerned, people walked down a flight of steps into a basement . . . and smoke billowed from the chimney. With so little direct contact between killer and victim, who could be held responsible? Everyone had an out; every-one could say that what he did was not so important. And everyone did say it. Indeed, many claimed, like the physicians at the railroad siding selecting who was to live and who to die, that they did their best to grant a stay of execution. Thus, they had it both ways. They rejoiced in their participation in the great Nazi project to annihilate the Jews. And at the same time, they held on to a shred of the old moral system. They were not responsible. Indeed, they had saved as many as possible.[34]

IN THE SPRING of 1942 the Germans evidently made an important decision. Annihilation of the Jews had gone well in the east. Western Europe's Jews must now be dealt with. But how? Perhaps someone suggested an Operation Rein-hard camp in Belgium or an Auschwitz in France, but if so the idea got nowhere. Western Europe's Jews would be sent east.[35]

This created the new logistical difficulty of moving many Jews over long dis-tances. In the Soviet Union, *Einsatzgruppen* killed Jews on the spot. There was no need to collect and ship people to extermination centers. In Poland, ghettos served as storage pens. The distances to the camps were short and the authori-ties coordinated their activities. The situation was more complicated in the west where there were no closed ghettos and Jews had long been integrated into soci-ety. Local sensibilities might be offended. Cattle cars in the central train station would not do. So the Germans sent Jews by third-class rail to an isolated tran-sit camp within the country—and from thence east. Thus, all except the—by then—rather routine initial deportation was screened from public view. No direct connection existed between the capital cities of western Europe and the new necropoli in the east.

The transit camps served another function as well. The often-competing agencies involved in the "Final Solution" shared a common policy of Judeocide, but each had its own agenda, priorities, and schedule. A *razzia* in Paris, for

56. Dutch Jews await a deportation train to Westerbork, Amsterdam, 1942. Courtesy Nederlands Instituut voor Oorlogsdocumentatie, Amsterdam.

example, was not always coordinated properly with the maximum "legal" dispossession of Jewish property, the military's demand that week on the railways, or the current extermination capacity in the death camps. Germans used the transit camps as holding pens for Jews until the gas chambers of Sobibór or Birkenau could accommodate them and empty railway cars could move them. Thus, they maximized the efficiency of the murder machinery.

Depredation marked each step of the way. Money and property missed earlier was exacted as payment for the privilege to remain in the camp. Jews with marginally valid passports from neutral countries were identified and separated, perhaps to be of future political value as hostages. From time to time, people with highly specialized skills (like diamond cutting) were set aside.

Finally, the transit camps furnished the Germans with an implicit subterfuge: these were permanent settlements, they suggested. In one case, the implicit was explicit. "The Führer Gives the Jews a Town," proclaimed a Nazi propaganda film about the most famous transit camp, Theresienstadt in Czechoslovakia. The Germans' perversions notwithstanding, transit camps were not stable, merry communities but temporary wretched stopovers on the way east. Indeed, many of the people photographed by the Germans had been deported and killed by the time the film was shown.

Terezín, or as the Germans called it, Theresienstadt, had been built as a fortified garrison town by the Austrian emperor Joseph II and named in honor of his mother, Maria Theresa. Over a century and a half later Reinhard Heydrich transformed it into a transit camp. By his order of February 1942, the small walled city not far from Prague was evacuated and a "Jewish settlement" or "old people's ghetto" officially was established. Originally intended as a place for elderly Jews unfit for "hard labor," Terezín helped to perpetuate the myth of Jewish resettlement in Poland. To obviate embarrassing questions, highly decorated or severely disabled war veterans also were eligible for Theresien-stadt, as were a certain number of very well known Jews.[36] Terezín, however, was hardly a settlement or a ghetto. As the statistics clearly show, it was simply another transit center. Of the 141,162 Jews registered in Theresienstadt, 88,202 subsequently were deported east; 276 were handed over to the Gestapo and disappeared; 33,456 died; 1,623 were released to neutral countries (1,200 to Switzerland and 423 to Sweden) in 1945; 31 were let go; 764 escaped; and 16,832 remained, which included 22 unregistered children born there.[37]

Oddly enough, the purely theoretical role of Terezín as a stable community affected inmates, too. Despite constant threat of deportation, lack of food and hygiene, and omnipresent disease, the Jews created an intellectual and cultural life for adults and children. Ellen Eliel-Wallach remembered that a few days after she and her parents arrived in Theresienstadt, they happened to meet "Max, the brother of my (future) aunt [whom they already knew]. He was from Würtzburg. He said, 'Even in Würtzburg I didn't see such a good performance of *Tosca*.' I said, this man is mad! I think this man must be mad!" Ellen was fif-teen years old at the time. Born in Düsseldorf, she and her family had emigrated illegally to the Netherlands and had lived in Amsterdam, Haarlem, and Arn-hem. In December 1942, the family was deported to the Dutch transit camp of Westerbork, where they remained until September 1943, when they were shipped to Bergen-Belsen in Germany, and then, in January 1944, to There-sienstadt. "He [Max] was talking about an opera performance! . . . He said it seriously. He was a cultured man, I realized that. Yet I hadn't had any experi-ence with opera by that time. I thought he must be mad!" For her what was bizarre was that he was not insane, that "operas *were* performed in Theresien-stadt." While the deportation trains continued to be filled with a thousand peo-ple at a time, "there was some culture, the possibility of culture. But later on, all those people, all those cultured people were taken to Auschwitz anyhow."[38]

The Germans did not permit musical performances to enrich the inmates' lives. Rather, this display of culture suited their propaganda program. In order to show off Terezín as a functioning, unexceptional city with a stable population and a normal civic life, starting in the summer of 1943 a coffeehouse, bank, post office, and even a petty crimes court were opened. Stores sold goods robbed from the newly arriving inmates. (Sometimes people repurchased their own posses-sions.)[39] The Germans allowed the Jews to establish a cultural department, and music, art, and theater became part of the life of Terezín. The artistic activity in this antechamber to Auschwitz was quite wonderful. Art and music in par-ticular flourished. There were five cabaret groups, several small orchestras, a "municipal" orchestra of thirty-five musicians, and a jazz band. A number of operas were produced, including Smetana's *Bartered Bride,* Mozart's *Bastien and Bastienne,* and Krasa's *Brundibar.* One man founded a puppet theater; lectures, poetry recitations, literature readings, and art exhibitions were warmly sup-ported by the inmates.

The backbone of transit camp life, however, was work, not culture; deportation, not opera. Ellen Eliel-Wallach "got a [new] assignment for work" in the summer of 1944. "It is very painful for me," she admitted decades later.

I think I liked to do that work. I worked with babies who were separated from their mothers. I think they had to work. Some girls took care of the babies. We schlepped with warm water to bathe them and to do everything possible to make life as comfortable as possible. All those babies later went to Auschwitz. But, of course, yes, while you were doing that you did not think of it, you just did your duty, you took care of the children as well as possible.[40]

Ellen did not know about Auschwitz then. She only knew that these little babies were taken away. "Later, when I came to Auschwitz, I realized. I had got a special apron, a kind of an apron; my mother took the apron home [after the war]. The apron I wore was still there, but not the babies."[41]

Ellen Wallach, the babies, their mothers, indeed nearly all inmates left the transit camps in cattle cars bound for the east. From occupied France, the Netherlands, Belgium, and Terezín in Czechoslovakia, they were locked up and shipped out. The rhythm of departing trains became the pulse of transit camp life. In some camps deportation trains ran irregularly, depending on the *razzia* (dragnet) activity in the surrounding area for victims. In Westerbork, a camp with a consistently large population, the train left on a weekly basis. Every Tuesday the camp commandant filled it with those who could no longer obtain the much-coveted postponement. For Irene Butter-Hasenberg, as for the other Westerbork inmates, this weekly cycle was a nightmare. "The trauma of seeing

57. The cast and backdrop of Johann Krasa's Brundibar, Theresienstadt, 1944. The image is a still from the Nazi propaganda movie known since the war as The Führer Gives a Town to the Jews, shot in Theresienstadt in 1944. Reproduced in Anna D. Dutlinger, ed., Arts, Music and Education as Strategies for Survival: Theresienstadt 1941–45 (New York, 2001).

your people go every week even if you weren't going" was horrendous. "You might be glad [to be spared], but you were still suffering." It became "the overwhelming impression of life in Westerbork; it revolved around the railroad track."[42] The journalist Philip Mechanicus shared Irene Hasenberg's feelings, and he confided his excruciating relief to his diary when, by a miracle, no train was scheduled one week.

> Tuesday, August 3rd [1943]: No transport this morning. Peace and quiet. The world seems kind and merciful. Children thank God that their parents have escaped the executioner for another week and parents thank Heaven because their children are safe for the time being. Every week means one more week and every week may be the last. Perhaps the war will not be over quite as soon as we hoped, but the regime in Germany may collapse just like the regime in Italy and then, at any rate, the persecution of the Jews will be over. Every week now represents a double or treble gain.[43]

Ultimately, no one was spared. As late as 17 October 1944, Terezín inmate Helga Pollack told her father in despair, "On a slip of paper a person's destiny is decided."[44] Friends had been claimed for transport the day before, and others were scheduled to go the day after. Ellen Wallach's father was deported from Terezín on 28 September. Her turn came two weeks later. "My mother by that time was assigned luckily to a kind of war industry with mica [so she was protected]. . . . On October 12 I went on transport without my mother. My mother asked me, 'Shall I join you out of my own free will?' Then I took one of the gravest decisions I ever had to take. I said, 'No; in this time you do not do anything out of your own free will. You stay here. I'll go by myself.' Then I went on the train."[45]

TRANSIT CAMPS may have screened the truth of deportation, but they could not disguise neighborhood *razzias* or the evictions of families from their own apartments. The Jew-hunters openly pursued their quarry in the full light of day. Success lay in catching their prey and intimidating everyone else. They scored on both counts. "The deportation of the Jews was carried out in all areas of Baden and the Palatinate smoothly and without incident," Heydrich reported to the Foreign Office on 29 October 1940 about the forced removal to the French Unoccupied Zone. "The occurrence of the action itself was hardly noticed by the population."[46]

Whether the Baden and Palatinate Germans "hardly noticed" or, like Madame Bérujeau who saw the *razzias* in the rue des Rosiers, felt helpless is unclear. Some witnesses, convinced antisemites, either approved or did not care when Jewish civilians of all ages and both sexes were forcibly removed. Most people, however, simply did not know what to do. "I think more people did not act because they did not know how to begin," the Dutch resister Marion

Pritchard-van Binsbergen observed half a century later.[47] The Berlin novelist and journalist Ruth Andreas-Friedrich noted that bafflement in her private diary. Heavily involved in rescue activities, she worried about many Jews, including her former dentist and his wife. Finally, she called on their neighbors. "I understand they're sensible."

> Tuesday, February 16, 1943
> A friendly lady opens the door.
>   "I beg your pardon, could you tell me if Mrs. Jakob is at home?"
> She shakes her head, and bursts into tears.
>   "Will she . . . will she be back today?"
>   . . . "She won't be back. She won't be back ever," she says sobbing.
>   "Tell me," I ask softly. "Possibly we can do something, help somehow."
>   "Help? When the Gestapo has stormed the house like a fortification—burst open locks and sawed through steel bolts? I ask you, who's to help—who *can* help in a case like that?"[48]

Fiercely committed to resistance, Ruth Andreas-Friedrich tried to understand what stopped others. Was it because "this horror is so inconceivable that imagination rebels at grasping it as reality"? Or cowardice? A primitive instinct for self-preservation?[49] Her Nazi countrymen and their allies did not ask themselves these questions. What was important was that they could act with impunity. No one in occupied Europe, no group would stop the deportation trains.

They were not so sure about the free world, however. Nor were they absolutely brazen about the "Final Solution." As the Germans moved from "territorial solutions" to mass murder, they became the first deniers of the Holocaust they were perpetrating. They sensed that most people would tolerate

58. Departure from the transit camp of Westerbork to Auschwitz, 1944. Courtesy Nederlands Instituut voor Oorlogsdocumentatie, Amsterdam.

the forced deportation of Jews from their homes, neighborhoods, even from Europe. But would they countenance genocide?

A language of denial sprang up in the midst of murder. The leadership took pride in their annihilation program. But they did not wish to trumpet details. Addressing an audience of SS leaders in Posen in October 1943, Himmler noted with satisfaction that "the annihilation of the Jewish people" had been surrounded by a "tactful" silence. "In our history, this is an unwritten and never-to-be-written page of glory."[50] He and his colleagues certainly did their best to keep it "unwritten." They coded the terms of destruction. "Resettlement" and "evacuation of the Jews" meant deportation to death camps; "special action," "special measures" meant killing; "Final Solution" meant Judeocide; and "east" or "further east" meant killing centers. Ordered to keep silent, even the Auschwitz architects and engineers rarely referred directly to gassing or to gas chambers.

Words carry concepts, and silence can obfuscate anything, even genocide. The murk that surrounded so many millions of murders allowed the free world—far from the deportations and killings—and even some in occupied Europe to say: I *see* nothing; I *hear* nothing; I really *know* nothing, a reasonable doubt. World War I atrocity propaganda had been largely discredited. Perhaps history was repeating itself?

With gruesome irony, the most notorious story to frighten the British public back in 1917 concerned a German *Kadeververwerkungsanstalt* (corpse exploitation establishment), operated behind the front lines by the *DAVG—Deutsche Abfall-Verwertungs Geselschafft* (German Offal Utilization Company, Inc.). Printed in *The Times* on 17 April 1917, no one doubted its veracity at the time.

> The factory is invisible from the railway. It is placed deep in forest country, with a specially thick growth of trees about it. Live wires surround it. A special double track leads to it. The works are about 700 ft. long and 110 ft. broad, and the railway runs completely round them. In the north-west corner of the works the discharge of the trains takes place.
>
> The trains arrive full of bare bodies, which are unloaded by workers who live at the works. The men wear oilskin overalls and masks with mica eyepieces. They are equipped with long hooked poles, and push the bundles of bodies to an endless chain, which picks them with big hooks, attached at intervals of 2 ft. The bodies are transported on this endless chain into a long, narrow compartment, where they pass through a bath which disinfects them. They then go through a drying chamber, and finally are automatically carried into a digester or great cauldron, in which they are dropped by an apparatus which detaches them from the chain. In the digester they remain from six to eight hours, and are treated by steam, which breaks them up while they are slowly stirred by the machinery.
>
> From this treatment result several products. The fats are broken up into stearine, a form of tallow, and oils, which require to be redistilled before they can be used. The process of distillation is carried out by boiling the oil with carbonate of soda, and some of the by-products resulting from this are used by German soap makers.[51]

This completely fabricated atrocity story prompted widespread skepticism after it was discredited in 1928. Few British people wished to be fooled once

again. Indeed, most people in the late 1930s and 1940s debunked everything
that did not fit their customary, liberal view of the civilized western world.
Thus, German Jewish refugees met with utter disbelief when they described
Nazi violence. When the former director of the Jewish hospital in Breslau, Dr.
Ludwig Gutmann, told his acquaintance the philosopher Professor F. A. Lindemann about the November Pogrom, the latter "somewhat sneeringly interrupted me, saying 'You must not tell me atrocity legends.' "[52] And Lindemann
was a staunch anti-Nazi.

Americans were no more credulous. During the war they judged most
reports of German atrocities as exaggerations at best. When the Polish government-in-exile published a long report on Nazi terror in German-occupied
Poland (1940), one American editorial warned its readers that twenty years earlier "a great many of the atrocity stories which were so well attested and so
strenuously told, so indignantly believed and so commonly repeated, were
found to be absolute fakes."[53] *Time* mockingly called news from Poland "the
'atrocity' story of the week."[54]

But news from Poland only grew worse. The Polish underground staked
their hopes on an eyewitness. Surely the Allies would believe the decorated soldier Jan Kozielewski, known by his underground name Jan Karski. Disguised
as a Latvian policeman, Karski had been to Belzec. He saw the murder of a
whole transport of Jews.[55]

Clandestinely and under cover, Karski made his way to London. His first
stop was the Polish government-in-exile. A part of his detailed account was
published in the *Polish Fortnightly Review* on 1 December 1942. The Germans
had deported seven thousand people a day from the Warsaw ghetto since 24
July, readers learned. Those too ill to travel were killed on the spot or at the Jewish cemetery. The rest were loaded onto trains.

> The deportees were carried off to three execution camps, at Treblinka, Bel-
> zec and Sobibor. Here the trains were unloaded, the condemned were
> stripped naked and then killed, probably by poison gas or electrocution. For
> the purpose of burying the bodies a great bulldozer has been taken to Tre-
> blinka, and this machine works without stopping. The stench of the decom-
> posing bodies has nauseated all the peasants for three miles around and
> forced them to flight. In addition to Treblinka, there are also camps at Belzec
> and Sobibor. It has not been possible to ascertain whether any of those who
> have been carried off have been left alive. We have information only of
> extermination.[56]

The Polish government-in-exile repeated this information in a special note to
each of the Allies. Desperate for the free world to respond, Karski sought meetings with any power willing to see him.

There was now sufficient evidence to conclude that "large-scale massacres of
Jews were taking place in Poland," the British foreign secretary told the War

Cabinet on 14 December 1942. Jews from German-occupied nations were transported to Poland, he added, "and it might well be that these transfers were being made with a view to wholesale extermination."[57] World War I fables were World War II facts. The British issued a Declaration on behalf of eleven Allied governments and the French National Committee in the House of Commons on 17 December. The Germans "are now carrying into effect Hitler's oft-repeated intention to exterminate the Jewish people in Europe."

> From all the occupied countries Jews are being transported in conditions of appalling horror and brutality to Eastern Europe. In Poland, which has been made the principal Nazi slaughterhouse, the ghettos established by the German invader are being systematically emptied of all Jews except a few highly skilled workers required for war industries. None of those taken away are ever heard of again. The able-bodied are slowly worked to death in labour camps. The infirm are left to die of exposure and starvation or are deliberately massacred in mass executions. The number of victims of these bloody cruelties is reckoned in many hundreds of thousands of entirely innocent men, women and children.[58]

The estimate was low: 3.5 to 4 million Jews had been killed by then.

British radio reports of annihilation of Jews enraged Goebbels. Speaking to colleagues at the Ministry of Propaganda, he described the "alleged anti-Jewish atrocities in the East" as a "delicate" subject. The best strategy "of getting away from the embarrassing subject of the Jews," he fumed, was to raise "a general hullabaloo about atrocities. . . . This general hullabaloo will then eventually result in this subject disappearing from the agenda."[59]

Goebbels could have spared himself the aggravation. The Allies acknowledged Judeocide, but they did not want it on their agenda. American and British citizens supported the war against Hitler, not a war to save Jews. Still, to their credit, Allied governments specifically identified the Jews as victims of ruthless and brazen mass murder. The Pope could not quite speak the word "Jew." In his Christmas speech of 1942 he remembered the "hundreds of thousands who, without personal guilt, sometimes for no other reason but on account of their nationality or descent, were doomed to death or exposed to a progressive deterioration of their condition."[60] Mussolini contemptuously—and correctly—dismissed the Holy Father's broadcast as "a speech of platitudes which might better be made by the parish priest of Predappio," his native village.[61]

Nobody had accurate figures. Not even the Nazis knew precisely how many Jews they had killed. Eager to quantify his results—and what more remained to do—Himmler commissioned Richard Korherr, chief statistician of the SS, to compile a progress report. Here was a statistician's nightmare, Korherr, a civilian and a staunch Nazi, complained. Jews constituted a race and "the classification of the race presupposes many years of training and a knowledge of genealogy," he sniffed. "Jewish statistics have never been compiled on the basis of race but rather on the basis of religion."[62]

Korherr managed despite these difficulties. He estimated how many Jews had lived in the Greater Reich, other territories and countries, and the Russian territories, and duly noted the number "evacuated." He was not too subtle, however. The 1,449,692 Polish Jews "evacuated" had been subjected to "special treatment."[63]

Everyone knew that "special treatment" was a code word for murder. So while Himmler liked the numbers, he objected to Korherr's language. The statistician quickly amended his text to "passed through the camp." Pleased, Himmler asked for a summary for Hitler. Korherr gladly obliged. In 1937, there were 17 million Jews in the world, of whom 10.3 million (60%) lived in Europe, he explained. But the "figures indicate that the Jewish population of Europe has already been reduced by *4 million,*" he reassured the Führer. Indeed, "if one take[s] into account the Jewish emigration" and other factors, "then the reduction of the Jewish population of Europe from 1937 to the beginning of 1943 could be estimated at 4 1/2 million." Happily, "on the European continent (after Russia with c. 4 million) only Hungary (750,000), Rumania (302,000) and possibly France have large Jewish populations."[64] "*Altogether,*" Korherr concluded cheerfully, "*European Jewry must have been reduced by almost 1/2 since 1933, that is to say, during the first decade of the development of power of National Socialism.* Again half, that is a quarter of the total Jewish population of 1937, has fled to other continents."[65] Korherr carefully underlined this passage. He did Himmler proud.

WHILE THE FÜHRER celebrated his annihilation program, his armies failed at Stalingrad. Throughout the following year, 1943, the Wehrmacht waged a defensive war against the Soviets. Thanks to the Red Army, 500,000 Russian Jews never saw a German soldier. But for two-thirds of the nearly 2 million in occupied areas, the turning point in the war on the eastern front had come too late. The great annihilation operations on the way east in 1942 had left fewer Jews to kill as the Germans retreated west in 1943.

Unable to carry their "Final Solution" to Russia's remaining Jews, and aware that the tide of war had changed, the Germans turned their guns on Europe's last large Jewish community still in reach. Socially ostracized, economically and culturally marginalized, Hungary's Jews were nevertheless alive. Hitler's unwilling partner, the Regent Horthy, had not taken the final step. Such foot-dragging was unacceptable to the Germans. Furthermore, according to the German Foreign Office specialist on Hungary, Edmund Veesenmayer, the Jews controlled Budapest. Were it not for them, the Hungarians would be stouter allies. "The key to the defeatist mentality of competent circles in Hungary and the extensive sabotage of the common war objectives," he warned in April 1943, "should be sought chiefly in Hungarian Jewry."[66]

For the Germans, 1943 began badly and got worse. Perhaps if Hungary were brought in line, the situation might improve. "The Jew is our Enemy No. 1," Veesenmayer emphasized in his report of December that year. "These 1.1 million Jews are all saboteurs as far as the Reich is concerned, and there are at least as many—if not twice as many—Hungarians who are henchmen of the Jews, auxiliary troops and camouflage, helping them to realize a fantastically large-scale plan of sabotage and spying."[67]

Hungary must give up its Jews. The Germans effectively took charge of the government in March 1944, with the help of the Arrow Cross and without a military occupation. Hitler forced Horthy to dismiss the obstinate prime minister Kállay and to accept the supine antisemite Szótay, who had always toed the German line. Horthy also got Veesenmayer. Officially the German ambassador, in fact Veesenmayer controlled the government. And how Szótay handled the "Jewish Question" was the litmus test of the prime minister's ability. A host of German officials, including Eichmann and his men, arrived in Budapest to organize depredation and deportation.[68]

They planned to use able-bodied Jews as slaves, and they wanted to move fast. The Reich's labor shortage had become so acute that in April 1944 Hitler instructed Himmler to grab 100,000 Jewish slaveworkers from Hungary immedi-

The "Final Solution of the Jewish Problem," January 1943

Extermination camps equiped with gas chambers

C Chelmno   S Sobibór   A Auschwitz
T Treblinka   B Belzec   M Majdanek

ately. Jews unable to work were to be murdered. As the Germans had closed down the death camps built solely and specifically to kill—Chelmno, Sobibór, Belzec, and Treblinka—in 1943, only Auschwitz remained. It had become a gigantic death factory since the first gassings in 1942. Equipped by 1944 with four crematoria boasting eight gas chambers and forty-six ovens, the murder

Areas under direct German rule

Areas under German influence

Areas with anti-Jewish legislation

Areas where Jews were subject to the Final Solution...

mainly through deportation, massacres, or ghettoization

mainly through deportation

mainly through massacres

Traditional area of Jewish settlement

machinery could "process" 4,416 corpses a day. Auschwitz would function as the gateway. Jewish slaves would be shipped to concentration camps attached to industrial plants. The rest would be killed in the crematoria of Birkenau.[69]

By spring of 1944, the Germans expected most arrivals at Auschwitz to prove useless for German industry. The crematoria were overhauled and train lines extended into the camp. Rudi Vrba, a Jewish inmate of Auschwitz from Slovakia, heard from his countryman Filip Müller about the crematoria repairs. Müller, young and able-bodied, was one of the very few survivors of the early Slovakian transports. Now he was a *Sonderkommando* worker, and he had no illusions. Neither did Vrba. "The Nazis, we estimated, were preparing to kill at least a million people," he recalled. "For a while we wondered in which country they would find so many Jews left; but gradually, as the clues filtered through us, we realised who were destined to break all records. It was the Hungarians whom most of us had thought were reasonably safe."

Vrba understood "that we in Auschwitz, perhaps the most isolated spot in Europe, learned a great secret that was known only to the Nazi elite in Berlin."[70] When he heard the SS joke about all the Hungarian salami they soon would eat, he decided to try to escape. "For almost two years I had thought of escape, first selfishly because I wanted my freedom; then in a more objective way because I wanted to tell the world what was happening in Auschwitz," he explained years later. He knew his chances were slim at best. "But now I had an imperative reason. It was no longer a question of reporting a crime, but of preventing one; of warning the Hungarians."[71]

Rudi Vrba and his friend Alfred Wetzler plotted, planned, and miraculously smuggled themselves out of Auschwitz on 10 April 1944. They fled to Slovakia, where the Jewish underground recorded their observations and experiences. The Vrba-Wetzler report reached Switzerland in June. Copies circulated by the middle of the month. The Allies had known Auschwitz-Birkenau was a labor

59. Crematorium 3, Auschwitz-Birkenau, 1943. A vast incineration room with fifteen ovens took up most of the main floor of the building. A large undressing room and the gas chamber were located underground. Courtesy Auschwitz-Birkenau State Museum in Oswiecim, Oswiecim.

camp. The report presented a very different picture, as Richard Lichtheim, the senior Jewish Agency representative in Geneva, clarified. "Large-scale killings [are] carried out in the labour camp of B[irkenau] itself with all the scientific apparatus needed for this purpose, i.e. in specially constructed buildings with gas-chambers and crematoriums."[72]

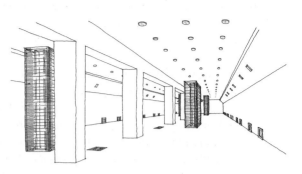

60. Reconstruction of the underground gas chamber of crematorium 3. This gas chamber, like the gas chamber of crematorium 2, was a morgue adapted to genocidal use. After the killing, cyanide gas was removed quickly by a double ventilation system in the walls of the original morgue. The killing agent was introduced through four hollow wire-mesh columns connected to four trap doors in the flat roof of the gas chamber. These columns had a movable pan at the bottom. SS men opened the trap doors, and threw grains of Zyklon B into the pan at the bottom of the wire-mesh columns. Warmed by the body heat, the grains released cyanide gas that filled the chamber. After fifteen minutes, when everyone was dead, the SS men lifted up the pan with the still degassing Zyklon B and emptied it outside, where it continued to degas for hours. The ventilation system was turned on when the Zyklon B was removed, In thirty minutes it was safe for the men of the Sonderkommando to enter. They removed the bodies for incineration in the fifteen ovens on the main floor. Drawing by Marc Downing. Coll. authors.

These revelations slowly made their way from in-trays to out-trays in government offices throughout the free world. Meanwhile, the Germans hastily dispatched trainloads of Hungarian Jews each day. Old hands at this by now, they knew what to do and how to do it: register, mark, segregate, deport. And steal whatever they could. The experience they had gained throughout occupied Europe was brought to bear in Hungary. In April 1944 they tackled the liquidation of a large Jewish community with ease. And they moved quickly, before Hungary collapsed or the Red Army arrived. The deportation of Hungary's Jews was a critical test. It marked the success or failure of their great gift to Europe, the Final Solution of the Jewish Problem.

The new Hungarian government opened the hunting season on Jews on 29 March. The Jews were to be marked "in the interest of national defense and public security," the minister of the interior announced.[73] Eichmann took over from there. Within days, his office issued a series of decrees which Hungarians adopted with alacrity. Jews were not to leave their homes. Jews would establish a Jewish Council.[74] Then the Germans and their now eager Hungarian allies proceeded to rid the country of Jews, first from the periphery and then from the capital. "The Royal Hungarian Government will soon have the country purged of Jews," crowed László Baky, rabid Fascist and antisemite, and new undersecretary in the Ministry of the Interior. "I order the purge to be carried out by regions. As a result of the purge the Jewry—irrespective of sex or age—is to be transported to assigned concentration camps. In towns or large villages a part of the Jews are later to be accommodated in Jewish buildings or ghettos, assigned to them by the police authorities."[75]

Veesenmayer cabled the good news to Berlin on 23 April:

On April 16 began the confining of Jews to ghettos in the Carpathian area. 150,000 Jews already disposed of. Action probably finished end of next week. Approximately 300,000 Jews concerned. Following it, same action planned and prepared in Transylvania and further border-counties in the direction of Rumania. Additional 250,000 to 300,000 Jews to be seized. After that come the counties bordering on Serbia and Croatia. Lastly ghettoization of the central part of the country, terminating with that of Budapest.

Arrangements for transport started and expect conveying 3,000 Jews per day, beginning May 15, mostly from the Carpathian area. If transport technique allows, later simultaneous removal from other ghettos. Place of destination: Auschwitz.[76]

Veesenmayer omitted one detail: Jews were to be stripped of all possessions and their valuables transferred to the Hungarian national bank.

Hungarian gendarmes ousted Mária Ezner, then thirteen years old, her eight-year-old sister, and their mother from their home in Abádszalók on the Hungarian plain on 16 May 1944. Mária's father had been arrested on 20 April, in honor of Hitler's birthday. "We could hire a peasant cart, and on those peasant carts we could go. We had to pay ourselves. And we could bring for every person a bed, for every person a chair, and one table for the family." The gendarmes harried along the Jews of Abádszalók until they reached the larger town of Kunhegyes, seven miles to the south. There they were incarcerated in a ghetto in the "Gypsy" area of town, not in a traditional Jewish quarter. "Gypsies in Hungary had their own streets," Mária Ezner explained decades later. "Gypsies weren't in the village among the inhabitants; there were gypsy streets. Like in the middle ages, there were Jewish streets. . . . The ghetto was [guarded] by Hungarian gendarmes. No Germans."[77]

A month of hunger followed, then an abrupt order to leave in two hours' time. "My mother, with two little children, what could she pack? She was so nervous, because this was the second step. She couldn't know what we should bring with us. It was not important, what we could bring. We had to give it up anyway. But they did not know, and they thought it was very important to pack so carefully."[78] And then the brutal process of depredation began.

We were taken to a great empty field, and everybody had to sit with his baggage, and the gendarmes came to see what we had with us. And then we heard the first things. They took our toothbrushes from us. And my mother stood and said, "Toothbrushes we shouldn't bring?"

And the gendarme said, "You won't need it. You won't need it."

It was the first time. We couldn't understand it.

The wedding ring was pulled off, and my mother said, "In the regulations it said that we could have it."

It was in the regulations, also, that we could have a hundred pengö for each person, and that was taken too.

And my mother said, "But it said in the regulations: one hundred . . ."

But the gendarme said, "You won't need it any more."

We stood there, in this empty field, every family with its baggage. We stood there on the empty field, and my mother's handbag was taken. And she cried out, "Our papers, our personal papers!"

And then the gendarme opened her handbag and ripped our personal papers, and the text was, "You won't need it any more."

And then we were beaten. A little house stood at the end of this field. We didn't understand. We didn't take notice of it. Then we heard names being called of people who had to go to this house. In this house sat several civilian men. They were "detectives," and they asked us where we had hidden our gold, silver, porcelain, and whatever. And who were our Christian friends to whom we had given our valuables. My mother was beaten on the soles of her feet with rubber truncheons; afterwards she could not walk. . . . I was slapped on my face and asked, because I was old enough, I must have helped hide the valuables. I remember this well.

It made me so hot, and I thought, "I hate you, I hate you." Only one thing: "I hate you." And I didn't give an answer. I was strong in my hatred.

Then they sent me to a midwife. That was miserable. The midwives examined women and young girls, maybe they had something in their vaginas, a gold ring or so. I had never seen such a table or such a chair. My mother had to lie on it and she was examined. Then I was examined, and my mother cried, "Take care! She is a child!" And I don't know what I thought of those women.

We left, and my mother went with her arm around my shoulders. She said that we should send my little sister away from us, and she should say that she doesn't know her name, so that she wouldn't be beaten. And we sent her away, but she didn't understand why, and she wanted to stay with us because she understood that something very bad was happening and it was natural that she wanted to be with her nearest persons in the world. I whispered, "Go away, go away, go away!" . . .

It was the 16th of June 1944. It was a very hot day. On the great Hungarian plain it can get as hot as thirty to forty degrees [86–104°F].]. We were on the plain, and each one of us had on his winter coat. In our family our mother said, and in every family the mothers said, "Take your winter coat. We do not know where we will be brought, and your winter coat is very important." So we had our winter coats and we didn't dare take them off. It was forty degrees, and the whole day we sat by our little things that they allowed us to bring. We sat all day and names were called of men and women to be beaten.[79]

Late in the evening, the Jews of Kunhegyes were ordered into the train wagons. They did not know their destination until they arrived at the sugar-processing plant on the outskirts of Szolnok. Jews from the entire region were collected there, and for nearly a fortnight the factory teemed with 4,666 people. There were no toilets, no drinking water, and nothing to eat. There was no room in the factory itself for such crowds, so many (the Ezner family among them) remained in the yard. "It began to rain, and my mother said, 'If a God exists, it is with them.' We sat down in the mud and it rained and it rained."

In Szolnok too the gendarmes searched "the rich Jews" for valuables. As in Kunhegyes, lists were drawn up and names called. In the factory the Ezners were reunited with the children's grandmother and she, a sixty-four-year-old woman, was "investigated" by the Hungarian "detectives." "She was beaten and at the end thrown out through the door. We found her lying with her face in the mud. She didn't know us any more."[80]

The Hungarians deported their prisoners in the Szolnok sugar-processing plant during the last days of June 1944. One transport went to Auschwitz, the other to Strasshof, not far from Vienna. Rumors had gone round the factory, and Mária's mother took them seriously. She heard that the appointed Elder of the Jews had compiled lists for the transports. She went to him, seeking to get her family on the train for Austria and not Poland.

> I said it was the same and she shouldn't take a step. I was a fatalist at that time. I am now. But if she wouldn't have taken that step, I wouldn't sit here. ... She went to the Elder of our community and she said she had heard about a list to Austria, and if it were possible she would like to go to Austria; she speaks German, the children speak German.
>
> The old man told her that this list was for the prominent people in the Jewish community, and we were only three-day's-Jews, we were not leaders. My father wasn't a religious man, and we were not prominent in this Jewish community.
>
> My mother said she had heard that the list was also for Jews who paid high taxes, and could he deny that we were paying a great tax in Abádszalók?
>
> This old man said, "Na, good; but not the grandmother."...
>
> We didn't know if [we were really on] the transport for Austria or for Poland, and we didn't know the difference. My mother thought Poland would be worse; the temperature was harder and the Poles antisemites. In Austria would be a better climate. Maybe, if we worked we could survive.[81]

András Garzó's father faced the same dilemma as Mária's mother when his family was to be deported from Debrecen. There too transports went to Austria and to Poland; the first two went to Strasshof and the third and last to Auschwitz. Again, parents had no way to judge their choices. They had been evicted from their homes, robbed, beaten, and abused. But they had not yet experienced murder. Rumors abounded, but such tales were literally incredible, not to be believed.

It is thus not surprising that while in Debrecen one could get on the list for Austria, András Garzó's father chose not to do so. "The first transport may have been organized on the basis of who wanted to go," the son remembered. "My family was not very clever. We wanted to remain. We hoped maybe something would happen." They did not believe that the Soviet army would liberate Debrecen (which is in the east of Hungary) in time, or even that the Soviets would advance so near that the deportations would cease. András's father simply thought it best for them to stay where they were as long as possible. "He wanted to remain in Debrecen. My mother's family went, and only we, my father's family, remained for the last transport. He had no real hopes. He just thought that we shouldn't move. 'Let us remain. Let us remain here.'"[82] It was a reasonable decision, as valid and logical as that taken by Mária Ezner's mother. But for Mária, "the sugar factory was the worst."[83] For András, much worse was yet to come.[84]

The first transport of Hungarian Jews, one thousand eight hundred people, arrived in Auschwitz on 29 April and pulled over the new spur through the gate into Birkenau. By the end of June, in just two months, half of Hungary's Jewry—381,661 souls—had come there. One of them was Alexander Ehrmann from the town of Királyhelmec. His transport pulled into Birkenau at night.

We arrived around one o'clock in the morning in an area with lights, flood-lights and stench. We saw flames, tall chimneys. We still did not want to accept that it was Auschwitz. We preferred to think we didn't know than to acknowledge, yes, we are there. The train stopped. Outside we heard all kinds of noises, stench, language, commands we didn't understand. It was in German but we didn't know what it meant. Dogs barked. The doors flung open and we saw strange uniformed men in striped clothes. They started to yell at us in the Yiddish of Polish Jews: "*Schnell, Raus!*" We started to ask them, "Where are we?" They answered, "*Raus, raus, raus!*" Sentries and their dogs were there, and they yelled at us also. "*Macht schnell!*"

We got out and they told us to get in formations of five, and to leave all the luggage there. We asked one of the guys, "Tell me, tell me, where are we going?" "*Dort, geht,*" and he pointed towards the flames. We had to move on. . . .

It started to get daylight and we moved on to an area where there was barbed wire on both sides. We walked down an alley, a sentry so often spaced out. We kept on moving, we were prodded to move faster. We were told, "You will be coming to an area where you will be given a bath and change clothes and you'll be told what to do." We were walking, and beyond the barbed wire fences there were piles of rubble and branches, pine tree branches and rubble burning, slowly burning. We're walking by, and the sentries kept on screaming. "*Lauf! lauf!*" and I heard a baby crying. The baby was crying somewhere in the distance and I couldn't stop and look. We moved, and it smelled, a horrible stench. I knew that things in the fire were moving, there were babies in the fire.[85]

Of the total number of incoming Jews between the summer of 1942 and the fall of 1944, between 10 and 30 percent were found fit to work for the German war effort. Most of these were dispatched to Bergen-Belsen, Buchenwald, Dachau, Gross-Rosen, Mauthausen, Neuengamme, Ravensbrück, Sachsenhausen, and 378 other camps in Himmler's empire. Alex Ehrmann and his brother were sent to Warsaw, and set to work in the ruins of the now empty ghetto "tearing down the walls" and "salvaging the bricks."[86]

The rest were killed. Frenetic gassing and burning continued through July 1944. One-third of the total number of people murdered at Auschwitz were killed in two months. Or, to put it differently: Auschwitz had been in operation for thirty-two months. In that period, March 1942 to November 1944, between 1 million and 1.1 million people were killed, on an average of 32,000 to 34,000 a month. During the Hungarian Action the Germans, with dispatch and efficiency, increased that average five- to six-fold, murdering 400,000.

IF THE OUTSIDE WORLD did not "know" what was happening, a lot of information was available. Vrba and Wetzler had done their work well. Whether others would act in consequence was not clear. At the request of Jewish Agency representative Richard Lichtheim, the British Legation in Geneva cabled the Foreign Office in London. Signed by the British minister in Berne and written by Lichtheim, the telegram of 27 June described the disaster explicitly.

Received fresh reports from Hungary stating that nearly one half total of 800,000 Jews in Hungary have already been deported at a rate of 10,000 to 12,000 per diem. Most of these transports are sent to the death camp at Birkenau near Oswiecim in Upper Silesia where in the course of the last year over 1,500,000 Jews from all over Europe have been killed. We have detailed reports about the numbers and methods employed. The four crematoriums in Birkenau have a capacity for gassing and burning 60,000 per diem.[87]

A week later the Foreign Office received an eight-page summary of the Vrba-Wetzler report from another source: Hubert Ripka, acting Czechoslovak minister of foreign affairs, who had obtained it from the Czechoslovak representative in Geneva.[88]

Washington too was well informed. On 24 June Dr. Gerhart Riegner of the World Jewish Congress in Geneva gave the representative of the War Refugee Board in Berne, Roswell D. McClelland, a summary of the report. That same

61. Arrival of Hungarian Jews in Auschwitz-Birkenau, 1944. Courtesy Yad Vashem, Jerusalem.

day McClelland telegraphed the most salient points to Washington. Uneasy about the reliability of the entire report and concerned that transmitting such information could jeopardize his career, McClelland sought assurances before cabling the eight-page summary. Finally convinced the information was true—but still anxious about his future employment—he sent the telegram on 6 July. It addressed a core issue: the role of Auschwitz in the Holocaust.

> Jews who were brought to A[uschwitz] toward end of 1941 were for most part Polish political prisoners and killed by various methods as such. Not until spring of 1942 were transports of Jews en masse sent to B[irkenau] (constructed principally for them) to be exterminated on purely racial grounds.[89]

Prior to Vrba and Wetzler's escape, 145,500 people had been admitted to the camp and registered as inmates. Most deportees did not get that reprieve.

> As first large transports of Jews began to arrive in spring of 1942 process was to admit about 10% of more ablebodied men and 5% of women into B. This selection was made by Gestapo political commission at unloading of trains. Balance including elderly people, women with small children, those ill or otherwise unsuited for work and abandoned children were taken directly to Birkenwald [sic] in trucks and gassed.[90]

McClelland's telegram concluded with a terrifying statistic.

> Authors set number of Jews gassed and burned in B between April 1942 and April 1944 at from 1.5 to 1.75 million about half of them Poles the others (in thousands followed by country of origin) 150 France, 100 Holland, 60 Ger-

many, 50 Lithuania, 50 Belgium, 50 Yugoslavia, Italy and Norway, together 30, Slovakia, 30; Bohemia, Moravia and Austria together 300 from various camps for foreign Jews in Poland.[91]

The New York Times moved faster than McClelland. It had run three stories about Auschwitz before Washington got the Vrba-Wetzler summary. At increasing length and with growing horror, the *Times* correspondent in Geneva wrote about "1,715,000 Jews Said to Have Been Put to Death by the Germans Up to April 15." There was, the author insisted, "incontrovertible confirmation of the facts."[92]

Horthy was in a quandary. A true antisemite who never endorsed genocide, and a passionate Hungarian nationalist, he was embarrassed by the news. He realized Germany had lost the war and Hungary could go down with it. Seeking to save some shred of pride, he gathered his courage. He, who had been summoned by Hitler before, now summoned Veesenmayer to the Royal Palace. Eichmann had to reduce his staff, Horthy ordered. The Germans had violated Hungary's sovereignty. "He said he was in a very difficult position feeling like a puppet, not master of his own country," Veesenmayer reported to Berlin. "In connection with the Jewish question he mentioned that telegrams were pouring in on him by the day from home and abroad."[93]

Veesenmayer protested. The Regent's "name had been inseparable from the idea of the champion fighting against Jews and Bolshevism," he flattered Horthy. "All we [Germans] do is to help him realizing his former ideals."[94] Horthy was not persuaded. He would not budge.

The Germans and their Hungarian antisemitic friends had concentrated one thousand six hundred gendarmes in Budapest, the last zone in Hungary to be "cleansed." They intended to arrest all the Jews in a single day. Fearing these gendarmes would be used to mount a German-initiated Arrow Cross coup against him, Horthy ordered them back to the provinces. This prevented the overthrow of the Regent's government and denied Germans the police force they needed to catch the Budapest Jews. Horthy also fired Baky, the main deportation apologist and champion. Within days, the Hungarian government assured ambassadors of neutral countries that the *Aktionen* would cease.[95]

Hitler was livid. On his orders Ribbentrop instructed Veesenmayer to tell Horthy that Hitler *demanded* a continuation of actions against the Jews. There was nothing subtle about his message. "The Führer expects that the Hungarian Government will take measures against the Budapest Jewry without any further delay." He would not tolerate anything "that could or would weaken their fighting spirit or that could possibly stab the fighting soldiers in the back."[96]

But Hungary's interests now clashed with Germany's. And the Hungarian government wanted an end to the deportations. What did this mean for Jews in Budapest? Neither free nor, for the moment, sent to the trains, 260,000 people subsisted day by day. Like German Jews just three years before, they eked out

an existence in "yellow star" houses throughout the city, forbidden to enter public parks or gardens, and permitted to shop only when the shelves were bare.
Danger loomed on every street corner. Constantly in fear of the Germans
and the equally bloodthirsty Arrow Cross, for the moment, Budapest's Jews
survived.

Chapter Twelve

FROM WHENCE WOULD HELP COME?

Desperate Jews besieged the Swedish legation in Budapest in March 1944. Sweden was neutral; perhaps its representatives could offer asylum. Legally, the legation was supposed to protect only Swedes and the citizens of other countries represented by Sweden. But as one of the legation members, Per Anger, explained years later, "Something had to be done, and quickly. Every day the situation of the Jews worsened."[1]

The diplomats went to work. First, they issued provisional passports. These were simple travel documents, legitimately given to people with relatives or business connections in Sweden. As this passport did not provide legal protection, the legation negotiated with the Hungarian authorities to strengthen its status. They were successful: Jews with provisional passports would be treated as if they were Swedish citizens. They were exempt from wearing the yellow Star of David.

Provisional passports, however, could not be issued to masses of people. An entirely new document was therefore created, certifying that Swedish relatives had applied for Swedish citizenship on behalf of the Jewish person in question. Validated with the minister's signature, stamps, and seal, it was respected by the Hungarians and Germans charged with rounding up Jews.

As this was happening, information about the murder of the Jews, the role of Auschwitz, and the Hungarian Action circulated on both sides of the Atlantic. The War Refugee Board (WRB), a new American organization, was seriously concerned.[2] The WRB had been established by President Roosevelt a few months earlier, in January 1994, in response to a report initially entitled "On the Acquiescence of This Government in the Murder of the Jews" by Secretary of the Treasury Henry Morgenthau, Jr., whose father had witnessed the Armenian genocide. Now the WRB wanted to act quickly on behalf of the Jews. The WRB representative in Stockholm approached the Swedish Foreign Office. The Swedish legation in Budapest also turned to the Foreign Office at home. They needed personnel. There was too much work to be done and too few people to do it.

Raoul Wallenberg, a thirty-two-year-old businessman and a member of a prominent family of Swedish financiers, took the job.3 Appointed secretary of the Swedish legation in Budapest, he was supported by both Stockholm and the WRB. Wallenberg arrived in Budapest in July 1944, just when Horthy halted the deportations. For hundreds of thousands of Hungarian Jews the order came too late. But the Jews of Budapest remained. And who knew when the trains might roll again? There was no time to lose.

In the following months, Wallenberg proved to be courageous, clever, passionately committed, and tireless. He inspired hundreds of people to cooperate in creating a rescue organization. Taking ideas that had been tried before, he pushed them farther and created "protective passports." These new identification papers in the Swedish national colors of blue and yellow carried the Swedish three-crown symbol and were signed by Minister Carl Ivan Danielsson, head of the legation. Explaining that the holder was under the protection of the legation until emigration could be arranged, the passport claimed security for the bearer.

Wallenberg established a special department to fabricate the protective passports. His staff quickly grew to some four hundred people, primarily Jews, who were themselves exempt from wearing the star and, in theory, protected against deportation. With their help, the legation issued some 15,000 to 20,000 passports. No longer concerned solely with Hungarian Jews who had a family or business connection with Sweden, Wallenberg and his colleagues offered protection to everyone they could.

The uneasy limbo came to an abrupt end when the Arrow Cross took power in October. Deportations resumed. Violence and murder exploded on the streets of Budapest and on the banks of the Danube. In some cases, the protective passports did not deter the Germans and their Hungarian allies. Wallenberg organized checkpoints on the major roads out of Budapest and at the border station to demand the release of Jews who had been picked up even though they held these papers. It is said, too, that Wallenberg's staff at these checkpoints, people brave enough to confront the German authorities directly, dared to pass out passports hurriedly, secretly, right there on the spot.

The Swedish legation was but one of the foreign legations in Budapest attempting to save Jews. The Swiss, Spanish, and Portuguese were heavily involved in these activities, as was the papal nuncio, Angelo Rotta.4 It was 1944. The Swiss, Spanish, Portuguese, and Swedes knew that Germany had lost the war. But this fact did not mean that Hungarian Jews were less at risk. Not at all. They were slaughtered as mercilessly as their co-religionists elsewhere. Nor did it protect their rescuers. The inevitable fall of Nazism did, however, give Europe's governments an impetus to support rescue actions.

To a great extent, they succeeded. Andrew Nagy and his mother, for example, did not fare too badly until the Arrow Cross coup. As the dragnet descended upon them, Nagy and his mother, like the other Jews of Budapest, anxiously sought a way to escape. Their apartment house had been marked with a yellow

62. *Jewish women caught in an Arrow Cross dragnet operation in Budapest, October 1944. Courtesy Bundesarchiv, Berlin.*

star. One day they surely would be delivered to the depot. Through her husband's brother-in-law, Mrs. Nagy obtained a Swiss protection pass. Andrew remembered that "I, who was barely over twelve, forged my name on to my mother's Swiss pass. I took an old, beaten-up typewriter from my father's office and typed 'und Sohn' [and son] onto the pass. Clearly it was a different type, it wasn't very sophisticated, but at least the 'und Sohn' appeared so now I was also protected with the Swiss pass."

Shortly thereafter the neutral powers established protected houses hoping to provide greater security. "The Wallenberg Swedish houses, the Swiss houses, even some Vatican houses started [to operate]. Since we had Swiss passes . . . we went to a Swiss house. . . . I vaguely remember that the Swiss house we moved into had something like twenty people to a room. We stayed there for about a day, a day and a half. My mother realized that our apartment house was declared Swedish and . . . we could just as well live in our own apartment. So we went back to the Swedish house. . . . We moved back to our own apartment and spent the rest of the war, the other two and a half months, in our apartment." Luck played its part too. People in "a Swedish house within a block of where we lived [were] taken on Christmas Eve (I think) to the Danube to be machine-gunned into the Danube. So certainly living in a Swedish house did not guarantee safety." But in the Nagys' case, "it saved our lives."[5]

Wallenberg had the support of his government and the WRB. He had diplomatic immunity, determination, and a good deal of luck. It was not a great hand, but with it he and his collaborators protected 70,000 Jews until the Red Army arrived in January 1945.

PARADOXICALLY, their success shines a bright light on the failure of the free world to rescue victims sooner. After the Nazis came to power in 1933—well before the war or the Holocaust—many politicians understood that "rescue"

63. *Hungarian Jews rescued by Raoul Wallenberg from deportation are escorted back to the Budapest ghetto, 28 November 1944. Photo taken clandestinely by Thomas Veres, a colleague of Wallenberg. Thomas Veres, courtesy of the United States Holocaust Memorial Museum Photo Archives, Washington, DC.*

meant "refugees." The League of Nations recognized the new dimension of the refugee crisis and created the High Commission for Refugees (Jewish and Other) Coming from Germany. An American, James McDonald, was appointed High Commissioner, and to satisfy the Germans, McDonald reported to a separate Governing Body chaired by the British statesman Viscount Cecil of Chelwood. McDonald and Lord Cecil were adamant about the importance of their work. We face, Lord Cecil said, "a challenge to the principles of our civilisation."[6]

Today, we may think that Lord Cecil spoke of the humanitarian problem of Jewish refugees from Nazi Germany. In fact, they were just the tip of the refugee iceberg. Pro-Nazi army officers who took power in Poland after Pilsudski's death proclaimed that the solution to their country's problems was the wholesale deportation of the Jewish population. In September 1936 Poland asked the League of Nations to provide colonies for its Jews. This proposal went nowhere, but pressure mounted. Looking at the plight of the Jews in central and eastern Europe, the Zionist leader Chaim Weizmann saw "a people doomed to be pent up where they are not wanted, and for whom the world is divided into places where they cannot live, and places into which they cannot enter."⁷ But for Weizmann, as for Cecil, the critical problem was not Nazi Germany. It was Poland. "The German tragedy," he continued, "is in size much smaller than the Polish; it is of manageable proportions, and, moreover, the German Jews are stronger, economically stronger; they can resist the onslaught much better than the Polish Jews, who have been ground down now for almost a century."⁸

Looking back, we find these words almost unbelievable. But Weizmann could not know what was to come and at the time, amazingly enough, he was correct. In 1936, Polish Jews suffered more grievously at the hands of the Polish government than German Jews at the hands of the Nazis. And, as we have seen, in 1937–38 Romanian Jews endured greater hardships at the hands of the Romanian government than German Jews under the Nazis. With the benefit of hindsight, we know the Germans will invade Poland in September 1939, and that Romania will kowtow. But in 1938, each of these states was sovereign and independent. We think about Jews escaping Nazi Germans. Politicians in 1938 saw Jews seeking asylum from Germany, yes. From Austria too. But, in far greater numbers, from Poland and Romania. Looking to the future, they did not imagine a Holocaust. They envisioned an immense refugee flood.

"The whole of Eastern Jewry is in an insecure position, and both in Poland and in Roumania at different times government spokesmen have suggested that measures will be adopted to induce emigration as a contribution to the solution to the problems raised," explained a 1938 report on the refugee crisis written for the Royal Institute of International Affairs in London.

> Other governments, embarrassed by problems arising from their Jewish minorities, have seen Germany adopt, with little apparent injury to herself and without effective opposition from other states, a policy of victimization that has already led to the emigration of one quarter of her total Jewish population. They have seen the success and impunity with which Germany has carried through a persecution of Jews which has included the substantial confiscation of their property and of their employment. . . . The temptation to these other governments to follow the German example is obvious. If the policy pursued within Germany and later within Austria is taken as a precedent, other countries may . . . adopt a similar policy and . . . begin to convert the domestic problem into an international problem of refugees.⁹

The western world, in short, not only faced the problem of Nazi Germany and Austria, but a flood of 5 million Jewish refugees from the east. This was "a form of blackmail" to which the west would not succumb.

> The refugee problem is . . . too urgent both in its existing form and still more in its potential form to allow postponement of action. . . . Such action must be radical and preventive. . . . The immediate need is to prevent any further

movement of European Jewry from becoming a refugee movement. . . . As a preliminary measure it may be necessary, harsh though it is, to close frontiers, as was done in the case of the threatened emigration from Roumania and has been done in the case of Austria.[10]

The international community must make it crystal clear that it "will not submit to that form of blackmail which other refugee movements would constitute."[11] Defiance and determination were key. The British Foreign Office adopted this view. So did the United States and Canada.

Britain, Canada, and America decided to get tough with Poland, Romania, and Germany. They set out to use political and financial carrots and sticks to force these tyrannical states to allow their citizens to live in peace. Why should the oppressed be forced to move? Why not move the oppressive regimes? Once the British Foreign Office identified the refugees as a form of blackmail, there was no persuading them otherwise. Standing up to Hitler, or to the Poles or Romanians, meant forcing them to keep their Jews. This principle governed the attitude and shaped the actions of people who could have made a difference to vast numbers of European Jews.[12]

However appropriate or inappropriate that position may have been before the Holocaust, it was utter nonsense in the face of mass murder. Rescue became a matter of life or death after the Germans invaded the Soviet Union and unleashed their furious genocidal assault. At the Wannsee conference six months later, they calculated they had another 11 million Jews to kill.

Tragically, by the time the Allies understood that the Germans were sys-

64. Cartoon by David Low, Evening Standard (London), 9 November 1938.

tematically, eagerly, and energetically obliterating the Jews from the face of Europe, they had established principles to guide their joint conduct of the war. And each of these axioms obstructed rescue efforts. First, the British blockaded the continent after the fall of France. They believed it would destroy German morale and hamper the Reich's access to essential raw materials. This strategy had worked in the Great War. Surely, the British reasoned, it would work now: the blockade was not to be lifted under any circumstances. In this case, experience was not a good predictor. The German homefront did not collapse. But the blockade did destroy any chance to trade Jews for goods or for cash.[13]

If Churchill was unyielding about the blockade, he was absolutely adamant that there were to be no negotiations with the Germans that might be construed as possibly leading to a separate peace or a negotiated peace. For Churchill, this was not a war about opposing national interests. This was a fight between good and evil. "I expect that the Battle of Britain is about to begin," he warned his countrymen in June 1940. "Upon this battle depends the survival of Christian civilization. . . . If we can stand up to him [Hitler], all Europe may be free and the life of the world may move forward into broad, sunlit uplands. But if we fail, then the whole world, including the United States, including all that we have known and cared for, will sink into the abyss of a new Dark Age made more sinister, and perhaps more protracted, by the lights of perverted science."[14] Only unconditional surrender of the enemy could end such a conflict. On joining the war in December 1941, the United States concurred wholeheartedly. "Total victory" was their aim.

An important pragmatic reason lay behind the "no negotiation" policy. To win the war, the Allies had to cooperate closely. It was crucial to raise mutual trust and minimize mutual suspicion. No easy matter. Stalin, always paranoid, was obsessively so by 1941. He remembered the Allies' support of the Whites against the Reds during the Russian Civil War; more recently, they had sympathized with the Finns when the Soviets attacked that small country in November 1939. The Allies, for their part, were still reeling from the Ribbentrop-Molotov Non-Aggression Pact of 1939. Each side suspected the other secretly wished to conclude a separate peace with their common enemy. Thus, no negotiations of any kind were permitted—including negotiations about Jews in German clutches.[15]

Finally, the Allies decided not to help the Germans and their collaborators achieve a *"Judenrein"* Europe by removing the Jews for them. Despite much evidence of mass murder, they held fast to the old policy of standing firm against "blackmail." In February 1943, the Romanian government offered to transfer 70,000 Jews to the Allies, suggesting they go to Palestine. Britain's Foreign Office rejected the offer outright. It feared an avalanche of Jews from the Axis countries. The British also worried about raising the ire of antisemitic political movements at home. The Arabs almost certainly would complain as well, so Palestine was out of the question. It occurred to no one to accept the Jews and raise troops among the able-bodied young men—even though Britain certainly could have used the military manpower. Blinkered by their prejudices, neither the Foreign Office nor the State Department was particularly sympathetic to the plight of the Jews. Indeed, the State Department was blatantly and unforgivably antisemitic. As a leader of that pack, Assistant Secretary of State Breckinridge Long, wrote in March 1943, saving Jews "would take the burden and the curse off Hitler."[16] Long's contribution to State Department policy and practice was unremitting obstruction to rescue in any form, including letting in the legal quota of immigrants.

The Allies wished only to win the war. Whatever thought they gave to the Jews lay within that context. "The blunt truth is that the whole complex of human problems raised by the present German domination of Europe . . . can only be dealt with completely by an Allied victory, and any step calculated to prejudice this is not in the interest of the Jews in Europe,"[17] Britain's Foreign Office smugly telegraphed its embassy in Washington. Confidential policy was soon announced in public. "The only real remedy for the consistent Nazi policy of racial and religious persecution lies in an Allied victory; every resource must be bent towards this supreme object," Deputy Prime Minister Clement Attlee responded to a question in the House of Commons on 19 January 1943.[18] "Salvation Through Victory" might have been the slogan of the day—had the Allies thought about Jews long enough to formulate one. The logic of this position escaped the prominent Jewish publisher Victor Gollancz, who had issued *The Yellow Spot* some years before. A man of letters, he took to the press to present another, and he hoped more persuasive, perspective. "I shall be told that 'the best way to save these people is to win the war.' Of course: but what chance is there of winning it in time to save them? There are practical things that might be done *now,* though very soon it may be too late."[19] Gollancz's efforts were to no avail.

The Warsaw Jews who met with Jan Karski before he smuggled himself into Britain understood what he would face. They told Karski that some 1.8 million Polish Jews already had been murdered; the 1.2 million still alive would soon be killed. They pleaded with Karski to propose radical schemes to the Allies in order to save them. "It is an unprecedented situation in history and can be dealt with only by unprecedented methods," they urged. "Let the Allied governments, wherever their hand can reach, in America, England, and Africa, begin public executions of Germans, any they can get hold of. That is what we demand." Appalled, Karski answered that such a proposal would horrify even those sympathetic to the Jews. "We do not dream of its being fulfilled," they explained, "but nevertheless we demand it. We demand it so people will know how we feel about what is being done to us, how helpless we are, how desperate our plight is, how little we stand to gain from an Allied victory as things are now."[20]

The Jews asked to be bought out with money, or materiél, or in exchange for

German nationals in the west. Karski reminded them that such a deal would strengthen the Germans militarily. "'That's just it. That's what we're up against. Everybody tells us, "This is contrary to the strategy of this war," but strategy can be changed, strategy can be adjusted. Let's adjust it to include the rescue of a fraction of the unhappy Jewish people.'"[21] But the Allies were not prepared either to consider extreme measures or to adapt their conduct of the war to rescue Jews.

Nevertheless, public clamor for rescue initiatives prompted the Bermuda Conference of April 1943.[22] Evian conferees in 1938 did not know what lay ahead. Delegates to the Bermuda Conference came armed with a horrible knowledge—and yet did nothing. Worse, they strove to discredit advocates for rescue. Rescue proposals jeopardized national security, the conferees in Bermuda claimed. Were the rescue activists committed to winning the war? To question the policy of rescue through victory, Harold W. Dobbs, president of Princeton University and a member of the American contingent, declared, "would not only be foolish, it would be criminal."[23]

65. Jan Karski. Courtesy of the Jewish Foundation for the Righteous, New York.

While Bermuda delegates dithered, the Warsaw ghetto went up in flames. As 1,000 emaciated ghetto inhabitants, untrained in military matters, defiantly resisted 2,054 German soldiers and 36 officers, the Bermuda Conference shut the matter away. Richard Law, one of the British participants at Bermuda, remarked twenty years later, "We said the results of the conference were confidential, but in fact there were no results that I can recall."[24] "If 6,000,000 cattle had been slaughtered, there would have been more interest,"[25] an American Jew who pleaded for rescue operations observed. In despair, Shmul Zygielboim, the sole Jewish member of the Polish government-in-exile in London, committed suicide.

HELP DID NOT come from the politicians. Nor did it come from the Catholic or Protestant Churches, or any—but one—of the regular civilian armies at the front and throughout occupied Europe. Perhaps because they had other dominating interests, perhaps because their own antisemitic factions bred quiescence, perhaps because they simply were too inflexible to respond promptly to an unfolding tragedy, institutions—the government, the church, the army—failed the Jews of Europe. But across Europe, a few from each of these institutions did not.

Iza Sznejerson and Viktor Erlich were young, active, politically astute, and very much in love when Germany invaded Poland in 1939. Viktor's father Henryk "was on the Germans' black list. He was a council member in Warsaw and a socialist," Iza explained much later. Henryk Erlich was a leader of the Jewish Labor Party, the Bund. "So the whole family decided to leave at that time. Viktor called me up and said, 'Come with us.'" But Iza would not leave her father. "I told him, 'I have a better chance to see you again if I stay in Warsaw than to see my father if I leave.' I said, 'My father is fifty-two and you are twenty-five.'"[26]

The Erlich family, like thousands of other Polish Jews, fled east. They got as far as Bialystok, on the Russian side of the Molotov-Ribbentrop line, when the occupying Soviet army arrived. Henryk Erlich, a former Russian citizen from St. Petersburg who had fled with his wife Sophie in 1918 because they were Socialists and Jewish nationalists and not Communists, feared the NKVD would recognize his name. Not wanting to endanger the rest of the family, he urged them to go on without him. Henryk Erlich was right. He was promptly arrested, but his family did make it to Vilna. "When his father was arrested and they were in Vilna, Viktor sent for me through the underground," Iza recalled. "I thought, not totally without reason, that the whole family was so impractical that they really needed someone practical like me."[27] They did not yet know that Henryk Erlich had committed suicide.[28]

Iza Sznejerson secretly crossed from German-occupied Poland into Soviet-occupied Poland and then into Lithuania. "I left Warsaw in mid-December and I came to Viktor on January 1. So it must have taken two weeks."[29] At the time, Lithuania seemed safe. In neither German nor Russian hands, it was an independent country. But the calm was short-lived. The Soviet Union annexed Lithuania in stages from June through August 1940, and refugee Jews found themselves imperiled once again. The Soviets did not want them and return to German-occupied Poland was unthinkable. They were trapped.

Among those caught were a few Dutch Jews who approached Jan Zwartendijk, the honorary Dutch consul in Kaunas (Lithuania). The Netherlands was occupied by that time, but perhaps he could help them get to a Dutch colony in the Caribbean, Curaçao or Surinam. Zwartendijk checked with the Dutch ambassador in Riga (Latvia), L. P. J. de Decker. No visa was required to enter the islands. This welcome news swept through the refugee community. With an official final destination, they could obtain exit visas from Russian-occupied Lithuania, transit visas across the Soviet Union, ferry from Vladivostok to Tsuruga in Japan, and on to a city. Harbored in Kobe, Tokyo, or Yokohama, they would figure out what to do next. As Iza Erlich-Sznejerson put it, "Our idea was that we would go to Japan. We had never even heard of Curaçao; we didn't know where it was. We didn't know that it existed. The idea was that we would try to get out and . . . Curaçao allowed us to get Japanese transit visas."[30]

The travel permit process worked in reverse. First, one must secure a final destination. With de Decker's approval from Riga, Zwartendijk went to work issuing official signed and sealed statements to the effect that "For Curaçao, no visa is required." Now, would the Japanese consul issue transit visas? In 1936, Japan had signed the Anti-Comintern Pact with Germany and afterward drew ever closer to the Axis. Furthermore, Japan had strained relations with the Soviet Union. There was no reason for the consulate to help Jews and every reason to avoid involvement.

Japan's consul in Kaunas, Chiune Sugihara, thought differently.[31] He was himself persona non grata in the Soviet Union, and he knew about the Gulag. He also knew what was happening to Jews in Poland. Hundreds of desperate, distraught people gathered outside his office every day, pleading for help. According to his wife, he cabled Tokyo three times asking permission to grant the transit visas. His requests were denied.[32] Realizing that he might well suffer consequences, he nevertheless decided to issue visas—thousands of visas, each good for a whole family.

With a final destination and a Japanese transit visa in hand, the refugees got exit visas from Lithuania and transit visas through the Soviet Union. Such a system suited the Russians—they charged the Jews fat fares for their Trans-Siberian Railroad and ferry tickets. Iza Sznejerson and her new husband Viktor, his mother, brother, and sister-in-law were just five of thousands of Jews Chiune Sugihara helped to save. "That's how I got out," she recalled. "The police were looking for us, as the family of Henryk Erlich, in Vilna, so we went to Kaunas. That was one of those crazy stories: that the police were looking for us in one town and we were getting a visa in another."[33]

Curaçao was just smoke-and-mirrors. No one went there. Sugihara saw other sites on refugee documents: Shanghai, the United States, Palestine, Latin America. Some were authentic, others forgeries. But as the days passed and the Soviet-imposed deadline for closing the consulate drew nearer, he didn't even look at that part of the application. He simply signed and stamped Japanese transit visas steadily until the moment of his departure. And then, people say, he threw blank stamped forms from his train window.[34]

Chiune Sugihara, Jan Zwartendijk, and L. P. J. de Decker were not alone among government officials involved in rescue efforts. Aristedes de Sousa Mendes, the Portuguese consul general in Bordeaux, issued thousands of visas until the government in Lisbon realized what he was doing and swiftly recalled him (24 June 1940).[35] Like the Axis diplomat Sugihara, de Sousa Mendes, consul for a neutral (albeit Fascist) nation, had no reason to get involved and acted quite against his government's orders. Both stood to lose a career, and both did. Insubordination was taken seriously. Sugihara was dismissed after the war, de Sousa Mendes upon his return to Lisbon.

Sugihara operated in Soviet-controlled Kaunas in 1940 and de Sousa Mendes in war-torn Bordeaux the same year. Reich Plenipotentiary Werner Best chose to act in German-occupied Denmark in September 1943. The rescue of the Danish Jews is a story that can be told from many perspectives. From the person who heard of the planned *Aktion* first: Rabbi Marcus Melchior spread the word about impending deportation to his congregants at the morning service on 29 September. He urged them to leave the synagogue immediately and to alert others.

That evening Rosh Hashanah would begin. Many families had plans to gather; the "mouth-radio" would work well. From the Danish resistance: Preben Munch Nielson and his resistance group quickly began to hide Jews in homes near the shore and throughout October ferried some one thousand four hundred people in small boats carrying up to twelve at a time across the water to Sweden. Or the story could be told by Jews who were saved, or by Swedes who welcomed them. Each rendition of this new Exodus tale, however, begins with leaked information about the approaching *razzia*. And Werner Best passed that news.

The Reich Security Main Office in Berlin had long pressed German occupation authorities in Denmark to get on with the antisemitic program. Just as long, Plenipotentiary Best had resisted. Best had happily deported Jews from France but, in his new office in Denmark, he couldn't quite see the point. He wanted good working relations with the Danes and they surely would balk at visible, harsh discriminatory measures. In any case, there were only seven to eight thousand Jews in the country; they could be dealt with later. So long as the Danes collaborated and his reign was successful, Best cared little about Berlin's plans for a *Judenrein* New Order in Denmark.

Best's sinecure was threatened when the Danes finally rejected collaborationist politics in August 1943. Faced with popular unrest, the Germans declared martial law and Denmark's government resigned. Best's control was slipping. Perhaps to improve his standing with Berlin, he sent a telegram on 8 September asking the Reich Security Main Office to deport the Jews under the pretext of the emergency situation. Hitler approved the plan. The *Aktion* was set to begin on 2 October.

Best's stock in Berlin rose once again. But his ultimate aim was to stay in power in Copenhagen. He could not discredit the Danes who still were willing to work with him. And so Best foiled the deportation plan. He leaked the date to his aide Georg Duckwitz and he sent Duckwitz to Sweden to make sure Jews would be permitted to land. The Swedish government broadcast its willingness to admit the Jews. A pastoral letter from Sweden's bishops, demanding the liberty of "our Jewish brothers and sisters," was read from church pulpits across the country that Sunday, 3 October. The Danish coast guard and police worked with the resistance. The German navy did not intervene.

Best even tried to rein in the Gestapo and military police, forbidding them to enter Jewish homes by force. Even so, the rescuers faced a well-trained force, dedicated to deporting Jews, and exodus became serious business: perilous and frightening, undertaken at mortal risk under cover of darkness. But the rescuers prevailed. Close to seven thousand Jews were ferried to safety in October. The Gestapo never lost its zeal for catching Jews, but it had to do so without support so plentiful elsewhere. On the contrary: the police, the Church, and the people of Denmark defied them. Housewives, fishermen, students, professional people and working people, Danes low and high, came together to rescue their

Jewish neighbors. The Gestapo's effectiveness plummeted. From Denmark, they shipped some 6 percent of the Jewish population, 477 people, to Theresienstadt.[36] And what of Best? He maintained his position in Denmark until the end of the war.

If Plenipotentiary Best sought to preserve his own well-being, Reichsführer-SS Heinrich Himmler sought to preserve Germany. Himmler had fought for control over the "Final Solution." He believed all the Nazi myths about Jews—that they controlled a worldwide network, that they possessed unlimited riches. Surely this wealth and power could accrue to Germany. "I have asked the Führer about releasing Jews in return for foreign currency," Himmler wrote in December 1942, as the Wehrmacht's *Blitzkrieg* ended at Stalingrad. "He gave me full authority to approve such cases that really bring in considerable foreign currency from abroad."[37] The SS promptly established a camp near the northwest German villages of Bergen and Belsen in anticipation of such deals.

The military stalemate with Russia deteriorated into possible defeat. Himmler could not imagine it but, dreading the prospect of a Germany in Soviet hands, he toyed with making a separate peace with the West. This idea grew as Russia routed the Germans on the eastern front and pushed their way west. It was time to make a deal, and he would use the Jews as his entrée. On Himmler's instructions, Eichmann's aide in Budapest, Dieter Wisleceny, opened discussions with the Hungarian Jewish relief and rescue committee (*Va'adat Ezrah Vehatzalah,* or *Vaada*). Formed in January 1943 to aid Jews who had fled to Hungary, its leaders saw that the entire community was now at mortal risk. Rezsö Kasztner, executive vice president of the Vaada, negotiated on the Jews' behalf. He was joined by Joel Brand, who had experience with the underground rescue of Jews from Poland.[38]

Convinced of an international Jewish conspiracy and confident that Kasztner was dealing directly with the London and Washington leaders of this network, the Nazis struck a first deal as a gesture of good faith. They accepted Vaada's plan to purchase one thousand six hundred Jews for 6.5 million pengö, at that time some 4 million Reichsmarks or $1,600,000. These Jews were to be allowed to emigrate to Palestine. Vaada's first priority was to rescue children, but the Germans objected. A complicated list was then drawn up composed of all kinds of Jews: Zionists, orphans, Orthodox, and so on. People from the formerly Romanian city of Cluj, now Hungary's Koloszvár, were specially favored. Kasztner came from Cluj; his father-in-law still lived there—as did nearly a quarter of the people listed, the Czitrom family among them. The Czitroms were chosen because "my father was one of the more eminent people of the Jewish community, having done things in the social work field," surmised his son Gabor Czitrom.[39]

The Germans shipped the Cluj group to Budapest, where they were housed in the Jewish school for the deaf and dumb. "We spent about a month in Budapest with various rumors: we're not going; we're going. They must have changed so many times."[40] In July, after hundreds of thousands of Jews were delivered to Auschwitz, this group, which had grown to 1,685 people, was sent by train to Bergen-Belsen.

There they sat while negotiations continued. Months passed. "I personally, physically, began somewhat to wear away. I had dysentery and I had some frozen spots on my hands that would not heal." It was December. "One day the word came through that we are now supposed to pack." A privileged group, they still had a few of their own possessions. The train—a passenger train—crept through the south of Germany. "One evening we just stopped at Lindau, which is on the border of Switzerland, on Lake Bodensee. All of Germany was in a blackout. On our train it was cold and we were half-frozen. Then on the other track came a Swiss train. Beautiful carriages. Lights. After a few hours we just got off the German train and boarded the Swiss train. Heated. Illuminated. The train started and we set off to St. Gallen. . . . It was luxury. It was another planet."[41]

Shortly after Wisliceny, Kasztner, and Brand began to discuss ransom exchange, Himmler initiated a much more important negotiation. He had given the Jews reason to hope. He had shown goodwill. Wisliceny would carry on with Kasztner. Now it was time to get to the real deal. Himmler wanted to establish a point of contact with the western Allies. The Vaada could do that, he thought. And if he offered Jews to London and Washington, they would open their door to him and close it on the Russians. Eichmann, acting on Himmler's direct orders, proposed to release 1 million Jews in exchange for a long shopping list which included 10,000 winterized trucks to be used against the Soviets on the eastern front. As packed cattle cars left Hungary bound for Auschwitz, Joel Brand and another man, Bundy Grosz, set out for Istanbul, where they were to contact the western Allies.[42]

Himmler, however, had got it all wrong, failing to appreciate the Allied resolve against a separate peace and vastly inflating the importance of Jews to the West. Neither Washington nor London was all that keen on the release of a million Jews. It would create tremendous problems for them. Where would the Jews go? Palestine was still out of the question. And what about Allied military and civilian internees? Wouldn't there be a public outcry to release them? Deceived by his own fantasy, Himmler could not comprehend that the western Allies would care more about their military alliance with the Soviet Union than the murder of the Jews.[43]

The British suspected Grosz was a double agent working for the Germans, and they nabbed Brand and Grosz in Istanbul. The two men were shuttled off to Cairo, where they stewed in solitary confinement for some months. The leadership in Budapest waited for a response to the German proposal. Whatever Himmler's motivations, it was a real offer. Every day, packed trains rolled away to Auschwitz. Surely the West would do something to stop them. Surely the Allies would parley. But the Jews had it wrong too. There would be no deal. Salvation through victory.

Still, business was business. As Germans and Jews waited, and as the Germans went on deporting Jews and the Jewish community dwindled, Himmler made a deal here, a deal there. Factories in and around Vienna needed labor. For a price, a certain number of Jews would go there instead of Auschwitz. María Ezner's mother fought to secure a place for her family on those transports; András Garzó's father did not. Mrs. Ezner and Dr. Garzó did not know what Kasztner had learned: that conditions would be less harsh in Strasshof than in Auschwitz. In the end, of the 21,000 Jews deported to Strasshof from Hungary, approximately 75 percent survived, including children. Of the 435,000 Hungarian Jews deported to Auschwitz in two months of 1944, 400,000 were murdered immediately.[44] When those two parents made their decisions, however, they had no way to know what their choices meant. But Kasztner had more information than they, and he mobilized all the resources at Vaada's disposal to pay the price Himmler demanded for those trains to go to Strasshof.

AT DIFFERENT TIMES and in various circumstances, compassion, calculation, and greed drove a number of individual officials to defy orders or to ignore fundamental tenets of their regime to save Jews. The entire Italian army in Italian-occupied Croatia, Greece, and France, by contrast, flouted the Germans.[45] Italians were unhappy with their alliance with Germany. They found their Teuton partners overbearing and barbaric. Disgusted with the war, most Italians hoped for an Allied victory.

On the map, however, the Italians profited from German aggression. Their partners had given them Dalmatia, once ruled by Venice, plus large occupation zones in Yugoslavia and Greece and a small part of France. As far as the Germans were concerned, the Italian army, useless as a fighting force, would do as an occupation power. A correct assumption, but not in the way anticipated.

Italian officers heard of Croat atrocities from Serbs and Jews fleeing from the new anti-Serb, antisemitic Croatian state into the Italian zone. The violence escalated when civil war erupted in Croatia. All at once, the Italian officers discovered their army's mission. They were there to save civilization. They had been entrusted with a noble task and a moral duty. Emphasizing the importance of "their word of honor," the Italians formulated their occupation policies accordingly.

Jews swarmed into the Italian-annexed areas of former Yugoslavia in 1942. The local governor wanted to throw them back. But Italy's commanding general, Mario Roatta, would not hear of it. "We have guaranteed them a certain protection and have resisted Croatian pressure to deport them to a concentration camp," he wrote the governor. "It is my opinion that if Jews who have fled to annexed Dalmatia were to be consigned to the Croatians, they would be interned at Jasenovac with the well-known consequences."[46] The Foreign Ministry in Rome agreed. The Jews could not be expelled "for obvious reasons of political prestige and humanity."[47]

Early in 1943, after the fall of Tripoli, Italy's Fascist dream of empire evaporated. Germany stepped up its pressure on the Italians to relinquish their refugee Jews. Stalingrad had fallen too, and Italy faced an uncertain future. Roatta was recalled from Croatia and given a command at home; General Mario Robotti assumed his post. Ciano was relieved of the Foreign Ministry and appointed ambassador to the Vatican; Mussolini himself took over as foreign minister. It was an opportune moment for the German foreign minister to visit *il Duce* and press him on the "Jewish Question."

Robotti met with Mussolini shortly thereafter. "'Minister Ribbentrop, who has been in Rome for three days, has been pressing me in every way to secure at any price the expulsion of the Yugoslav Jews,' Mussolini complained to Robotti. 'I tried to put him off, but he insisted. To get rid of him, I was forced to agree.'" Robotti protested vigorously and, perhaps to get rid of him, Mussolini concluded, "'O.K., O.K., I was forced to give my consent to extradition, but you can produce all the excuses you want so that not even one Jew will be extradited. Say that we simply have no boats available to transport them by sea and that transport by land is impossible.'"[48]

Throughout the months that followed, the Italian army protected refugees in its jurisdiction.[49] A number of Jews and Serbs had just been transferred to the Dalmatian island of Arbe when Mussolini was overthrown in July 1943. Still the army did not abandon them. With the surrender of the Badoglio government in September, the Italian military laid down its arms, and Arbe fell to the Germans and their Croatian allies. Nearly all of the 3,500 Jewish inmates of the Arbe internment camp rushed to join Tito's Partisans; only 204 elderly and ill people remained to be captured by the Germans and sent to Auschwitz. Children too young to fight were taken in by families in Partisan-controlled areas. Jews, like other combatants, died in the next year and a half of war, but the Italian army had given them the opportunity to fight. And because of the Italian occupation army's policies, 3,000 of the 3,500 Jewish refugees to the Italian zone of Yugoslavia survived as a group, while thousands more slipped over the border into Italy, helped tacitly by local army commanders who did not stop them.[50]

As it had been in Yugoslavia, so it went in Italian-occupied Greece and France. By the time Germany gave Italy administration over eight departments in France at the end of 1942, Vichy had been deporting Jews for months. The Italians would have none if it. "The Italians are extremely lax in the treatment of the Jews,"[51] Goebbels grumbled to his diary on 13 December 1942. The Italians, for their part, thought the Germans completely irrational on this issue. "In spite of all the disasters that have struck the Germans, they continue to insist that all the Jews occupied by us be consigned to them," the head of the Department of Occupied Territories in the Italian Foreign Ministry wrote the day Stalingrad fell. "They confirm that by the end of 1943 there will not be a single Jew alive in Europe. Evidently they want to involve us in the brutality of their policies."[52]

This was a German venture in which the Italians wanted no part. Italy might have a second-rate army, but Italians were not Huns. The Germans' policy was "irreconcilable with the dignity of the Italian army."[53] Constantly humiliated by their German allies, the Italians took solace in their civilization and their humanity. And they were right. Their army, unique among the Axis forces, protected the Jews in its domain.

ARMIES ARE NOT typically considered agents of civilization. In the western world, the Churches—Catholic and Protestant—have that role. They are the institutions charged with carrying traditional values into the future. They have but one job: to be the public conscience, the voice of morality, the defender of righteousness, the face of humanity. In all these tasks, the Churches failed utterly and abysmally during the Nazi years. They did not speak on behalf of the Jews. Nor did they remind Christians that it was morally and ethically wrong to rob Jews through "Aryanization," to mark, to segregate, to deport, to kill. The Churches, in short, fell deafeningly silent.

There is a difference, however, between what the French call *la grande église,* or the Church hierarchy, and *la petite église,* local religious organizations or individuals. Throughout Europe, many nuns, priests, ministers, and prelates acted independently. They spoke out against the evil they witnessed and they engaged in all kinds of clandestine rescue activities. A few, like Monsignor Jules-Gérard Saliège—the elderly, partly paralyzed, very popular archbishop of Toulouse—were high-ranking religious authorities. Saliège did not wait for instructions or permission from Rome to make his position clear. Had he done so, he never would have uttered a word. On his own initiative, Saliège publicly decried antisemitism and condemned racism and racial programs from the beginning of the occupation. Appalled by the deportation *Aktionen* sweeping through France in the summer of 1942, Saliège took to all the pulpits in his diocese through a pastoral letter. Despite the local prefect's efforts to prevent it, his missive was read out in every parish on 23 August. "There is a Christian morality, there is a human morality, that imposes obligations and recognizes rights," the archbishop admonished the faithful that Sunday morning.

> That children, women, men, fathers and mothers, should be treated like a vile herd; that family members should be separated from each other and deported to an unknown destination—it has fallen to our times to witness such a sad sight. . . .
>
> Here in our diocese, terribly moving scenes have taken place in the camps of Noé and Récebédou. Jews are men, Jews are women. Foreigners are men, foreigners are women. It is forbidden to harm them, to harm these men, to harm these women, to harm these fathers and mothers of families. They are part of the human race; they are our brothers like all others. A Christian may not forget this.[54]

With this letter, Saliège uttered the first public criticism of Vichy's and Germany's racist policies by an important religious figure since 1940. Three other bishops in the "free zone" made similar statements in the following weeks. Each acted independently of Rome and of each other. Their thirty-one French bishop colleagues said nothing.[55]

If few in high positions resisted racist antisemitic policies or engaged in rescue efforts, many more subordinate figures were energetically committed to all kinds of initiatives. In the summer of 1942, Margaret Ascher-Frydman, her mother, and younger sister lived in the Warsaw ghetto. "My mother learned that there were some children in the [Family of Mary] convent, and asked a woman, a friend, a wife of a lawyer whom my father knew and who was very religious, whether she could ask the sisters to take me. And they took us [the two girls] on the 9th of September. . . . We came to the convent, the sisters were there, and the [Mother] Superior said yes; she accepted us."[56] The Congregation of Franciscan Sisters of the Family of Mary was active throughout Poland, hiding several hundred Jewish children in their homes.[57] It was not unique; perhaps two-thirds of the seventy-four female religious communities in Poland took in Jews, adults and children alike.[58]

Nowhere is the discrepancy between *la grande église* and *la petite église* more obvious than in Rome. While the silence of Pope Pius XII glares bright as the canonical example of tacit collusion and collaboration,[59] a number of monasteries and convents offered refuge after a sudden *razzia* in Rome's ancient ghetto.[60] German troops had marched into the city five weeks earlier, and Rome appeared if not calm, at least stable. This illusion was shattered violently on 16 October 1943. Over a quarter (1,259) of the neighborhood inhabitants were scooped up; ultimately 1,007 were deported.[61]

The dragnet shocked the escapees into action. "The morning of October 16, at dawn, the lawyer Pasquali Lasagni, who was a dear friend of my father . . . telephoned us," Emma Fiorentino-Alatri recalled. He lived in Largo Argentina, adjacent to the ghetto, and he said, " 'Alatri, Alatri! Flee! Flee! They are entering all the Jews' houses and taking them away!' " The Alatri family left the house; the mother and two daughters went one way and the father another. "That day we went out, it was raining, and we left just like that, dressed as we were, without stockings, in sandals, under the rain all day long."[62]

But where to go? Those with contacts and money found refuge more easily. "We approached all the convents on Via Nomentana, but as we did not have a letter of recommendation, all of them answered. 'It is not possible.' . . . I remember as if it were a nightmare that long Via Nomentana that never ends, full of convents, full of gates, full of doorbells that rang."[63]

They found nothing that day. Later, Emma Alatri's aunts gave up their spots at Notre Dame de Sion for the two girls and their mother. "We entered the convent toward the end of October and left at the end of January. During that period my aunts returned, they joined us there. There were many Jews there.

To be honest, they said they had been accepted without a letter of recommen-dation—while we had not been so successful. We stayed until the end of Janu-ary, the beginning of February, and then we could not manage it any more. It cost too much, and no one knew how long the situation would continue. So we left and went to family friends, two sisters on the Via Po. . . . We stayed there until the 4th of June, Liberation Day."[64]

While some, like the Alatri family, could not afford the constant expense, for most money was not the problem. Some convents and monasteries asked only basic maintenance costs or charged nothing. Sergio Tagliacozzo and his two older brothers entered the Collegio Nazareno in the autumn of 1943. In his view, "the problem was not financial or economic. The problem was simply to find a hiding place." The Tagliacozzo brothers lived in the Nazarene school for seven months. "The priests knew that we were Jews, but they did not say any-thing about it to us. They treated us normally, like the other boarding school students. We did not have any problems of any kind. Another one of our cousins was with us, and two or three other boys we knew were Jews, but they did not say anything to us about that."[65]

Protestants on the local level were as active as Catholics, just as the Protes-tant leadership—with similar notable exceptions—was as inert. Grass-roots religious organizations of many denominations often worked together. Late in August 1942, some one thousand two hundred Jews in Lyon were arrested in a sudden dragnet operation and sent to the Venissieux internment camp.[66] "I managed to slip into the camp by calling myself a social welfare representative," Georges Garel explained. Within months he would become a central figure in the venerable Jewish philanthropic organization, l'Oeuvre de Secours aux Enfants (OSE), now dedicated to aid and rescue. But in August 1942, Garel was an engineer working in Lyon. He had come to Venissieux that night to help the OSE social workers in the camp: Elisabeth Hirsch, Hélène Lévy, and Lily Taget. L'abbé Alexandre Glasberg, director of the interconfessional philan-thropic group Les Amitiés Chrétiennes, was in Venissieux too, as was Made-leine Barot, the general secretary of the Protestant Comité Inter-Mouvements Auprès des Evacués (CIMADE).

The camp was in a state of terrible confusion; orders and counterorders shot back and forth. "After midnight we learned that children under sixteen years old could remain in France," Garel recollected. "Many of the wretched moth-ers of these children managed themselves admirably. Giving up their children forever, they left with dignity. Other mothers were crazed and nearly lost their minds. A father that same night opened his veins and his blood splashed the cheeks of the child clasped to his chest. A mother threw herself from the win-dow crying, 'I will not give up my child.'"[67]

Lily Garel-Taget remembered that night as "shocking, hallucinatory . . . it was truly a nightmare." Twenty years old, she had begun to work at the Lyon OSE office that year, partly as a secretary and partly as a social worker. "We were there night and day, it was truly haunting. I went for OSE. . . . It was there that my [future] husband [Georges Garel] began to help and, with abbé Glasberg, who was extraordinary, was able to release the first children from the camp. . . . Abbé Glasberg managed to falsify files; it was really he who managed to get the children out of the camp. The one who was able to do the most, I think, was abbé Glasberg. I saw it."[68]

Adults of French nationality were to be released as well. The question was: who was French and who was not? And precisely how old was each child? "Abbé Glasberg changed the files, pulling out some papers and replacing others." Lily Taget was very conflicted. She came "from a lawyer's family, in other words a family in which the law was the law. I had arrived in a nightmare world where people had to decide who was French and who was not, who could leave the camp and who could not. . . . I had the feeling, 'How can these people judge?' On the other hand, I saw abbé Glasberg, who did absolutely illegal things which just astounded me. I realized little by little that it had to be done, but it was not my upbringing."[69]

"We entered the camp and we obtained [permission] on principle to release children up to sixteen years old," recalled Elisabeth Hirsch. "I was there all night. It was horrible to do that work. There were parents who wished to give up their children, and others who did not want to do so. It was terrible that night, to choose the people to save—that was awful, it was dreadful. Imagine that mass of people whom you know will be deported, just to get out so few: 108 children, that was nothing [in comparison with] the thousands of people who were to be deported."[70] Jews, Catholics, and Protestants worked together, albeit to little avail: in addition to the 108 children, only 60 adults were released. Most of them had less than twenty-four hours of freedom. "During the second night, about 80 people who had been released after screening the previous night were retaken by the police and then deported."[71]

Rescuers had far more success in Le Chambon-sur-Lignon. A small Huguenot village in southern France, Le Chambon shines amid the sad story of civilian complicity and collaboration in the Judeocide. The Chambonnais had a long memory and a basic principle. They remembered oppression under the Catholic rule of Louis XIV, and they believed that all men, being brothers, should be offered refuge.[72] Resistance groups throughout France brought Jews, especially children, to Le Chambon. A few thousand Jewish adults and children came to Le Chambon and stayed throughout the war or were passed over the border to Switzerland. Many were harbored by individual families; others lived in seven group homes supported by a range of philanthropic organizations, including the Society of Friends, the American Congregationalists, and CIMADE, as well as national governments, most notably Switzerland and Sweden. Naomi Lévi lived in "L'Abric," a home run by le Secours Suisse aux Enfants (Swiss Relief for Children).[73]

Naomi had been born in Belgium in 1929 to Polish parents who subsequently divorced. By 1932 Naomi and her mother were living in Paris with her mother's second husband, a naturalized Frenchman. With this second marriage her mother had obtained French nationality, and when the war came to France in 1940, Naomi was the only family member who still had a Polish passport. Foreign Jews were at first targeted more than Jews with French citizenship. Naomi Lévi's parents sent her away, they hoped to safety. "One day I was accompanied to the train station, a tag was put on me, and I left with other children. It was a very long trip, very complicated. One moment that little train, and then you arrive at Chambon. Officially, I left for two months; in reality I stayed for three years.... That village of Chambon is a truly, truly extraordinary village."[74] As Cirlène Liberman-Zinger, who was eight when she began to live at L'Abric, put it, "I have nothing but happy memories of Chambon." She went on to explain, "For me, Chambon was not the war; I did not have to hide there.... It was not something gloomy for me. There were painful times in Marseilles, in Paris, but once I arrived in Chambon it was over. I was no longer afraid."[75]

Her confidence was well placed. Le Chambon succeeded where Rome failed. A small, poor Protestant parish, inspired by a deeply principled pastor, managed what the universal Catholic Church, led by a highly politicized Pope, did not even begin to undertake: to save Jews needing asylum. The population of Le Chambon doubled during the war years. Rome would not have had to aim so high.

Chapter Thirteen

RESCUE

"RESCUE" MEANT "FLIGHT" during the first two years of the war. Efforts to save Jews focused on getting them out of Nazi Europe. In late 1941, the Germans launched the Holocaust, mass murder of all Jews in their reach. Concurrently, America entered the war and escape routes were sealed. "To rescue" took on a new meaning: "to hide." Some Jews crossed the Alps into Switzerland illicitly, or the Pyrenees to reach Spain, or fled east to Asiatic Russia. But for most Jews trapped in the deadly net of Nazism, the only way out was to disappear.

Faced with *razzias,* deportations, and horrifying rumors about "unknown destinations" to which Jews were shipped, a number of organizations across Europe took on hiding work as part of their resistance activities, or reshaped previously legal functions into "illegal" systems to help those in need. Scouting associations, university student clubs, charitable organizations, and the apparatus of political parties, especially the Communist Party, developed rescue networks, running risks at every turn. When Georges Garel agreed in early 1943 to an OSE request to "organize a clandestine network in the southern zone in France for children of trapped Jewish families," he met with Monsignor Saliège. "Monsignor Saliège advised me not to create a new philanthropic organization but to work within the framework of the Catholic or other charitable organizations which already existed." Armed with a note of introduction from the archbishop, Garel contacted public, private, religious, and non-sectarian organizations. The network grew rapidly until it covered nearly the entire southern zone. In each department or diocese a philanthropic society or institution took in children. Among many others these included Catholic (such as the Conferences de St. Vincent de Paul) and Protestant (CIMADE; the Conseil Protestant de la Jeunesse) charities, and official (le Secours National, for instance) and private (Mouvement Populaire des Familles) groups.[1]

The *réseau Garel* (Garel network) was a major step for OSE as it moved toward "illicit" work: saving Jewish lives was, of course, an illegal activity in France by then. Founded by Jewish physicians in Russia in 1912, the Oeuvre de Secours aux Enfants et de Protection de la Santé des Populations Juives was a charitable preventive health care organization. When the war began, OSE supported three hundred refugee children, primarily from Germany and Austria, in special children's homes, *maisons d'enfants*. Children and staff in the Parisian *maisons d'enfants* joined the mass exodus south. OSE then split along geographic lines. OSE-Sud continued legally; OSE-Nord, operating under the conditions of occupation, engaged in clandestine activities, primarily smuggling central and eastern European Jewish children across the demarcation line into the free zone. After the ferocious roundup of the Vel d'Hiv, the organization in the north worked feverishly to hide as many people as possible.[2]

OSE staff in the "free zone" (like everyone else) believed that a French government would deal more kindly with its Jewish citizens and refugees than would the German invaders. The August 1942 dragnets proved otherwise. OSE began underground operations. The legal structure of children's homes and health care centers remained intact, but they also served as a screen for the organization of secret border crossings, for laboratories to produce false identity papers, and to hide those in imminent danger of arrest. The German occupation of Vichy in November 1942 meant that resources had to go to clandestine activities. In January 1943 the OSE directorate asked Georges Garel to develop a *réseau* or network to hide the children in OSE's *maisons d'enfants*.[3]

Garel went to work. He and his associates divided children into two groups. Those who could "pass" as gentiles got false identity cards or birth certificates and doctored food and clothing ration cards, and were dispersed in "Aryan" milieus where they were not known. This group remained under the direct surveillance of Georges Garel. The other children, those who for cultural, religious, or linguistic reasons could not "pass," were cared for by "Circuit B," run by a young woman named Andrée Salomon. They lived at home with their own families or, using their own names, with other families. When OSE went underground completely in February 1944, the children were smuggled over the French border, primarily into Switzerland but occasionally into Spain. By that point, these neighboring countries had changed their policy toward refugees. Jews who, eluding German and Vichy controls, slipped across the frontier were permitted to stay.[4]

The children of the *réseau Garel* remained in France. He and his OSE collaborators found organizations and institutions willing to take the youngsters. At the same time, they prepared these children for their new lives, teaching them their new names and family histories, and providing them with false documentation and ration coupons. The children were then passed to the receiver agencies, which in turn either kept them (in group homes, orphanages, convents, or boarding schools) or matched them with foster families.

By summer's end of 1943 Garel's *réseau* sheltered one thousand five hundred children and its infrastructure was extensive. The clothing department purchased ready-made items or sewed them from scratch. The documents staff turned out a stream of identity and ration cards, birth and baptismal certificates. They obtained false papers in a number of ways. Initially, they altered authentic ones. Later, they cajoled forms out of sympathetic mayors' offices or bought them on the black market. As the need increased, counterfeit documents got printed on underground presses. A transport division stood ready to move children quickly when the need arose.[5]

The *réseau Garel* and Salomon's Circuit B were part of OSE, and they were run by Jews for Jews. Other networks were created by gentiles sharing a common cause. Motivations varied, but goals were identical: to aid and assist Jews through the Nazi years. Zofia Kossak-Szczucka, for instance, was a well-known novelist and president of a conservative Catholic social organization, the Front for Reborn Poland; she joined the democrat Wanda Krahelska-Filipowiczowa to found the Council for Aid to Jews, known by the cryptonym Zegota. Within months, representatives of all the political parties of the Delegatura (official body delegated to represent the Polish government-in-exile on Polish soil) joined this new initiative.

As in France, Jews whose accent or appearance clearly identified them were spirited into hiding. Jews who looked like Catholic Poles and who spoke Polish without a trace of Yiddish needed housing and false documents in order to live openly, passing as Poles. Such a "normal" life was at least as dangerous as life in hiding, but it offered independence. With the required identification—the *Kennkarte*—and a good biographical story, a Jew could obtain an *Arbeitskarte*—employment card—for work and ration cards for shopping. To get a *Kennkarte*, however, one needed a birth certificate. In Poland, most births and deaths were registered by priests. Sympathetic clergy passed hundreds of totally legal birth certificates to Zegota and then destroyed the death certificates. Zegota matched, as well as they could, the sex and age of the deceased with a live Jew. This supply was augmented by fictitious birth certificates, forged birth certificates, and forged *Kennkarten*. Many Poles needed false papers—the resistance, the underground army, Jews. Document production flourished. Some were skillfully done, others were crude. And some cost a lot of money, while others were given free of charge. Jews escaping to the "Aryan" side rose dramatically with the ghetto uprising in April 1943; Zegota used all its political contacts to obtain some 50,000 forged *Kennkarten*.[6]

Irena Sendlerowa was a particularly good choice to oversee the Council's Children's Bureau. In 1939, Sendlerowa worked in the Social Welfare Department of Warsaw's Municipal Administration. From the beginning of the occupation, she used her position to create a network to provide financial and material assistance to Jews. She continued after the ghetto was enclosed. Sendlerowa obtained documents for herself and her close colleague Irena Schultz which allowed them to enter the Jewish quarter, and she established contact with Eva Rechtman who, on the other side of the wall, organized a secret network of women employed by the Jewish charitable organization CENTOS.

Faced with the mass deportations from Warsaw in 1942, Sendlerowa and Schultz determined to smuggle children out of the ghetto and hide them on the

"Aryan" side. Some families in the city were willing to take the children, but how to spirit them out of the ghetto? According to Irena Sendlerowa, Schultz specialized in this. "The children were usually brought out of the ghetto through the underground corridors of the public courts building and through the tram depot in Muranow district," then to their adoptive families or to orphanages and convents.[7] By the end of 1943, in addition to those in private homes, the Children's Bureau had found berths for six hundred youngsters in public and ecclesiastical institutions. Over time, some 2,500 children were registered by the Warsaw branch of the Council.[8]

66. Irena Sendlerowa.
Courtesy of the Jewish
Foundation for the
Righteous, New York.

Underground groups throughout Europe simply sprang up, created by people who felt the need to act. They were local, grass-roots endeavors. The Dutch N.V. group (*Naamloze Venootschap,* or Nameless Limited Company) was one of these marvelous—but tragically too few—clandestine networks. It began with a conversation between Gerard and Jacob Musch and Marianne Marco-Braun. The Brauns had moved to Amsterdam from Vienna in 1938. Marianne was fifteen at the time. There, the family took the unusual step of conversion to the Dutch Reformed Church. In May 1942 "we had to wear the star," she recalled. "And with the star, of course, on Sundays we went to church." Soon thereafter, Marianne and her brother Leo "were called up to go to Germany for work. . . . This is when the brothers Jacob and Gerard Musch came to us. We knew them, but not all that well. They came up one day and they said to us, 'Are you going? What's happening?' I said, 'Well, what can we do?' They said, 'We could possibly find you some addresses to hide.'"

Here was "a totally new idea" for Marianne and her family. Initially her parents opposed it. "I remember my father said, 'This won't be possible; they can hide you, but for how long? They [the Germans] will find you in the end.' So we sat, and we didn't know what to do. [Gerard and Jacob] came back the next day and they said they had an address for us, for my brother and for me. I said, 'But we can't go without our parents. What about our parents?' They felt it was more important to take us, being young. I couldn't take that. I said, 'No, we can't go unless you find something also for my parents.' So they went away again and a couple of days later they came back and said they had found an address for my parents, too."[9]

Thus, Jacob (or Jaap) and Gerard Musch created an underground network more or less by happenstance. Like so many others who took up this work, they had few Jewish friends. But when the Brauns were in danger and needed help, they organized assistance. Gerard Musch recruited his friend, Dick Groenewegen van Wijk and, after placing the Braun family, the three young men worked to rescue Jewish children. They chose children because the Musch brothers and Groenewegen were themselves young and felt less able to deal effectively or authoritatively with older people. Also children, being less of the world, would be easier to hide.

They faced two major practical problems: finding homes for the children, and making contact with those who needed to be hidden. In an uneasy start, they went to the northern province of Friesland, hoping to secure places of refuge, but lacking connections, they came away empty-handed. Undaunted, they journeyed to the southern province of Limburg and there, in the mining town of Heerlen, they found a Protestant minister named Gerard Pontier. As the population of Limburg was overwhelmingly Catholic, the Protestant community was tightly knit. Domine Pontier and his congregants knew one another intimately.

Pastor Pontier led the Musches and Groenewegen to the Vermeer family in nearby Brunssum. Truus Grootendorst-Vermeer still remembers the day Jaap Musch came to the door to speak with her parents. Suddenly, half her family was involved—her mother and father, her brother Piet, and very soon Truus herself, who gave up her job to do this work full time. "My parents couldn't afford to do without my salary then. (I gave them everything and got pocket money!) So for them and for me it was a big step. . . . I thought, here these bloody Germans are doing something against innocent people, and that put my back up. . . . Yes, I liked my office job, but I liked the people more."[10]

At that time, Truus Vermeer had a friend, one day to be her husband, named Cor Grootendorst. She sent a message to Cor asking him to come to Limburg, there was work to do. "And that's how I became number six!" Cor recalled.

CG: Our work was in the first place finding addresses. Going to families (and you almost felt like a salesman), knocking on doors through introductions. We didn't go blindly from house to house. We had to know that the people were safe, and there was a reasonable chance that they might be willing to help. [The introductions came] mostly through the clergy.
TV: My mother, because of her big family, was very well known to and had a good name with a Catholic priest. So we also went to a priest and we got addresses from him as well.
CG: It worked like a snowball virtually. You get one address and even if it's a yes or no, there always would be a person against the Germans. Whether the answer was, "I don't dare to," or for some reason "I can't," the stock question was, "Do you know anyone else who might be willing?" And they gave you two or three addresses. It's like a chain. So it was not too difficult to find potential addresses of people who might help you.[11]

Leaving the Vermeer family and Cor to find willing families, Jaap and Gerard Musch and Dick Groenewegen returned to Amsterdam to get children. In the summer of 1942 the situation for Holland's Jews had become desperate. Jews trapped in daily roundups were marched or driven to a central deportation

67. Jewish children in the Vermeer family's garden, 1943. Courtesy of the Jewish Historical Museum, Amsterdam.

point, first the Central Office for Jewish Emigration, and after mid-October, to a theater, the Hollandsche Schouwburg. There the Germans processed the captive Jews for removal from Amsterdam to the transit camp of Westerbork.

The Germans packed enormous crowds in the theater; often more than one thousand five hundred people plus their allowed luggage. People were held there for days, sometimes weeks. There was no room to sleep, the hygienic conditions were abominable, and the noise unbearable—even for the jailers. To reduce their own discomfort, the Germans decided to send children under twelve across the street to a *crèche,* a child care center, requisitioned as an annex to the Schouwburg. The director of the crèche, Henriette Rodriquez-Pimentel, and the young Jewish women who assisted her were determined to smuggle the children out of the crèche and pass them toward safe addresses. As every person, adult or child, who entered the Schouwburg was registered by an employee of the Jewish Council (which was controlled by the Germans, of course), Pimentel needed a way to destroy the children's records. This task was undertaken by Walter Süskind and Felix Halverstad, who concocted all sorts of ruses to rifle the records. Thus a number of children simply disappeared from the files of the bureaucracy, ceasing officially to exist. No one would be held responsible for them. Pimentel and her assistants could now pass them to resistance workers to be hidden.[12]

Jaap and Gerard Musch and Dick Groenewegen knew about the crèche but not about its underground traffic. Nor did they have connections with Jews who had not yet been arrested. Probably through Piet Meerburg, a leader of an Amsterdam student operation devoted to the same cause,[13] they were given the name of Joop Woortman, alias Theo de Bruin. De Bruin was the sort of person who knew almost everybody in the city, "a real Amsterdammer"; he was also a serious and dedicated resister. Because of his huge social network, which included many Amsterdam Jews, de Bruin had been approached early in the occupation for help with false identity cards, ration coupons, and, finally, hiding places. This work became increasingly consuming, and by the time he met the Musch brothers, he and his wife Semmy were at it full time.

Semmy Woortman-Glasoog's recollection of the initial meeting was that "the boys came to our house."

> We had a meeting, we talked, but the boys didn't know too much because they were very young. But Jaap was a serious man and Theo was, on this point, also very serious. And we talked about what we could do and how it would take shape. I listened and I told them, "You have to realize that if you are going to do what you are talking about, then your life after this is a gift. If you don't want that, you shouldn't go on." And they all said, yes, they wanted to do it. I think the younger boys didn't realize exactly what they did. But Jaap, he knew what he did, he knew; and Theo knew very well, and I knew.[14]

Their plan delegated responsibility link by link. No group told another how they proceeded or named contacts. Theo de Bruin (and to some extent Semmy also) handled the crèche and Jewish families not yet taken to the Schouwburg. According to Rebecca van Delft, who had worked with him, de Bruin was a man of "almost improbable courage and boldness" who did

68. Joop Woortman, alias Theo de Bruin. Courtesy of the Jewish Historical Museum, Amsterdam.

things others considered impossible, including "simply picking up [children] during a razzia in the street."[15] Sometimes he sent Jaap, Dick, or Gerard to collect crèche children from the agreed delivery point, or he gave them the address of a Jewish family with a child to be hidden. But in general it was he who did that part of the rescue work. The three young men got the children in Amsterdam from Theo and Semmy and, with a few young women who had joined the organization, brought them to Limburg.

Rebecca van Delft was the first woman courier. Years later she remembered her "introduction" to the Musch brothers by her schoolfriend, Marianne Braun. "One day in summertime, as I remember, July 1942, at our door came Gerard Musch—an unknown young person, who told me that he came as a friend of Marianne Braun, and if he could have a personal talk with me. It all seemed mysterious to me." The question was, "would I be ready to accompany Jewish children by train from Amsterdam to Heerlen (in the province of Limburg, in the south of Holland) where better could be found homes for them [to] hide, in order to save them out of the hands of the Germans. Of course I was willing to do such a thing: it was just a natural thing to do." Rebecca was eighteen or nineteen at the time, and living at home with her parents. "I don't remember [asking them] for their permission: it was evident that I should do such a thing." In fact, she explained, the work only could have been done by women. "For young men it was very dangerous to do such a thing by train, because the German soldiers always asked young men to show their identification cards: young men should be working in factories in Germany. But young women they would not so easily suspect—and indeed, during the time I did the job I was never stopped by a German soldier."[16]

Rebecca told another schoolfriend, Jooske Koppen-de Neve, about the underground network and put her in touch with Gerard and Jaap. Jooske was happy to assist. After Marianne had been barred from their school, Jooske visited her in the Jewish quarter. "I don't remember exactly where or how that looked. I only remember that I entered that ghetto and then things hit me. I was very confused. It was so horrible that I was very determined to do something about that, as far as for me it could be possible. I was completely *bouleversée,* absolutely turned around. It made me sick, physically sick: the realization of driving together human beings, like cattle; the humiliating facet of it, and being oneself human as well. To be, yes, to be witness of such a thing—that I couldn't digest."

The introduction of the yellow star prompted Jooske to act. "From that moment on I felt *responsible* for her. . . . Things changed that horrible day when I saw Marianne and her brother Leo with a star on their clothes. That was a *horrible* experience. . . . We had heard of it by then, of course. But then you saw, suddenly, the dividing of people; how malicious it was. Yes, I can still feel that now—the fury that such things are possible."[17]

By midsummer of 1942 the "railroad" was in good working order. Theo de Bruin found children and passed them to Gerard, Jaap, Dick, Rebecca, and Jooske. The women traveled alone with the children, or in the company of a man, posing as a married couple. They brought the youngsters to foster homes in Heerlen arranged by the Vermeer family and Cor Grootendorst. In the autumn, de Bruin began to receive children from the crèche as well. With the parents' permission, Süskind and Halverstad destroyed children's registration records, and Pimentel and her assistants smuggled the youths out of the child care center.

Easier said than done. The children may not have existed on paper, but they were real children and the crèche was guarded by Germans. The young women assistants were not under arrest, however. Free to go in and out of the building, they carried small infants out in their backpacks, stuffing pacifiers or bottles in their mouths, and praying that the babies would not cry. Articles commonly used and therefore above suspicion became conveyances: potato sacks, food crates, valises. Older children went other ways. Accompanied by one or two of the staff, toddlers and older children were allowed out of the building, on walks. Sometimes a few of the unregistered children took part and, at a specified point, were whisked away by an underground worker.

Finally, Pimentel gained the cooperation of a school next door—a small teacher's training college called the Hervormde Kweekschool. Seen from the street the two buildings were not connected—an alley ran between them—but despite appearances, their back gardens joined. "The head of the school, Professor van Hulst, saw in the garden that there were a lot of Jewish children and, well, he was good (we call it good or not good) so he tried to help," a young Jewish woman who worked in the crèche recalled. "We could bring the children from the garden of the crèche to the garden of the *kweekschool* and the students and other 'illegal' people came to the *kweekschool* and took them out [by the two side streets,] the Plantage Parklaan and the Plantage Kerklaan."[18] The entrances to the college were not guarded, and thus controls were avoided completely.

One of the couriers was a social work student, Marion Pritchard-van Binsbergen. Every day, on her way to the university she passed a small children's home. One day in 1942 she was frozen by the sight of Germans "taking the children out to a truck. The children didn't move very fast. They were crying and they were upset. The Germans just picked them up by an arm, or a leg, or by their hair, and threw them in the truck. I was sitting on my bike watching this. I knew this street as long as I'd been around. It was like—it was like a murder enacted in the next room right now. It's so shocking, you are immobilized. Two women came down the street from the other end and tried to stop them, and they threw the women on the truck too. And I sat on my bike, watching and doing nothing. Total overwhelming rage. I don't think I was ever as enraged as that in my life before."[19]

It was the last time Marion van Binsbergen "did nothing." She did not belong to a network. Like the vast majority of people involved in rescue, she worked on her own. Helped by many others, and aiding others in turn, Marion van Binsbergen responded to the problems that arose day by day. "There was always work to be done. The people I knew and the people who knew me called on me, but it wasn't organized. Sometimes I was called twice in a day, sometimes weeks would go by without anything special being asked."[20]

Aged twenty-two and, like all rescuers at the time, untrained in clandestine work, Marion van Binsbergen was a passionately committed—and very successful—rescuer. She brought food, clothes, and papers to people in need. She sought out hiding places and escorted the hunted to safe havens. And she took on special missions. Once, for example, "an old friend of mine, a friend since we were born, called me and said she was supposed to deliver a 'package' to the north of Holland the next day, and she's running a fever, and she can't do it, and will I? I said yes. She told me where to pick it up: behind the crèche. I knew what the crèche was. I knew what the function of the Hollandsche Schouwberg was. But I didn't know that this rescue operation was going on."

Marion went by streetcar to the Plantage Kerklaan. She was not quite sure what the "package" would be. "I figured it was something illegal or something secret. And I thought it might be a child, but I didn't think about it. It could have been a number of other things too." So she was not too surprised when "somebody came out and gave me a practically newborn baby girl. I was standing on the sidewalk and somebody gave me the baby." Marion took the first tram to the central station. The train journey north "took all day because the Germans took all our equipment." In German-occupied Holland, there were "no new tires, no new bicycles, no new baby carriages." It took a long time to get anywhere, which made every move arduous and frustrating. And, as Marion explained, "being constantly cold and hungry was debilitating." In this case, the trip took "hours and hours and hours."

> I had been told that I would be met at the station by a man. There was indeed a man, and he told me I was expected, but the people I was supposed to go to weren't around any more. They had been arrested.
>
> He clearly felt he had done his duty by telling me that I had just better get back on another train and go back to Amsterdam. I was tired and cold and hungry, and sick and tired of this poor baby. I had been given a bottle for it, but that was long gone by then. The baby was fussy, and I just wanted to drop it and leave.
>
> This man said I could come to his house with him and rest for a little while. Maybe his wife could find some milk for the baby before we went on our way.
>
> We went to a modest house at the end of the street that runs through the village. We went inside and it was warm. I sat down on a chair and fell asleep. When I woke up, the woman was changing and feeding the baby— and telling her own children that I was a sinner. I had this baby out of wedlock. My punishment was that I would never be allowed to see the baby again.
>
> As he walked me back to the station, the husband apologized for saying these terrible things about me. (In those days, a girl didn't do such things.) But I understood that when the people in the village would ask the children, "Where did this baby come from?" they would give a perfectly (in the context of those times) acceptable explanation.[21]

Marion responded to the many immediate calls for assistance and, at the same time, she hid three Jewish children and their father. Family friends, Miek and Piet Rutgers van der Loeff, asked if she could find a place for their friend Freddie Polak and his children aged four, two, and newborn. "I couldn't find any place that would take a man plus three children. So then Miek arranged for me to live in the servants' quarters of his mother-in-law's house." It was a nice house at 3 Patrijslaan, "a dirt road out in the middle of nowhere" near the village of Huizen. From the fall of 1942 to the fall of 1943, "I went as often as possible on weekends. When I finished the School of Social Work in November of '43, I moved in twenty-four hours a day and took over." There was a lot to do: caring for the children, cleaning them, obtaining food. She was the only one

who could move about and, as food got scarcer, Marion ranged ever farther
afield.

Danger lurked constantly. Miek and Piet had prepared a hiding place under
the floorboards in case of raids. It was large enough for a desk, and Freddie,
who was writing his doctoral dissertation, worked on it there. "The Germans
had to come in a motorized vehicle. There was
enough time so that we would hear the engine,
and by the time they found the house and opened
the gate and figured out which was the front door
and which was the back door, we could hide. We
could do it in thirty seconds. We practiced a lot."[22]

One night three Germans and a Dutch policeman, who was also an NSBer [Dutch Nazi]
came. I had managed to get everyone into the
hiding place, but I didn't have the time, or take
the time, to give Erica, the baby, her sleeping
powder. It was usual for Nazis who had been
and hadn't found the people they were after to
come back after an hour, and then they would
find them. We knew that, but Erica started to
cry, and I took the children out. Freddie was in
the middle of a chapter or something, and he
decided to stay.

69. *Marion Pritchard-van Binsbergen,
with Erica. Courtesy of the Jewish Foundation for the Righteous, New York.*

I put Lex and Tom back to bed and Erica in her crib. Maybe half an hour
later, the Dutchman came back by himself. I hadn't locked the door and I
hadn't put the hiding place back together. I don't remember if he said
anything, but I knew that if I didn't do something he'd definitely find the
kids. . . .

He came in. By this time I was standing between the stove and the head
of the bed. There was a bookshelf above the bed, and the gun Miek had
given me—and I hadn't thought about at all, and I don't remember him
teaching me how to use—was behind the books on the bookshelf. I grabbed
it and shot him.

I don't know if Lex heard the commotion and noise and got [my friend]
Karel, or if Karel heard the shot, but there he was. (Karel, by that time, was
in the garden house of Mr. and Mrs. de Wette next door.) Karel walked to
the village—which was a very dangerous thing to do; it was after curfew—
to talk to the baker, who had a wooden cart and horse to deliver his bread.
Before he returned, the two of them made arrangements with the local
undertaker who agreed to put the body in the coffin with another body and
bury it the next day. It was a big family funeral. I never learned whether the
family minded.

I wish there had been another way. But I have thought about it for fifty years, and I still do not know what that might be. I wasn't going to let him take the children. And so I shot him.[23]

By the end of the war, Marion van Binsbergen said, she had "killed, stolen, lied, everything. I had broken every one of the Ten Commandments, except maybe the first." Still, she did not see her work as part of the "real Resistance." She, like most rescuers, says she did what had to be done. "I didn't think about it. I just did it."

Jews were at least as active in rescue operations as gentiles. Many, like the OSE staff, worked to hide Jews at greater risk. Others were as vulnerable as the people they sought to save. Marion had found the place for Karel Poons, a gay Jewish ballet dancer, in the de Wettes' garden house of the villa next door to hers. He dyed his hair and passed as a gentile. And he too was involved in rescue activities. In July 1944, Karel and Marion were asked to rescue a two-year-old girl who was being held under guard at a physician's house in another village. The Gestapo hoped to get more out of their interrogation of her parents if they knew she was in danger. "Karel insisted on coming with me. I didn't want him to. I could have been in trouble if our plan hadn't worked. But there was absolutely no doubt about the fact that he would have been in serious trouble. He was Jewish. He was gay. He was hiding from the Nazis, and he was now going to kidnap the child the Nazis wanted."

Their plan worked. Karel chatted to the guard at the front door while Marion went in the back where she found the child upstairs, with the doctor's wife and their children. The doctor's wife tried to stop Marion, but "I gave her a good shove. I picked up the little girl, ran downstairs and put her on the back of my bike." Karel kept on talking to the guard as Marion pedaled away.[24]

A number of Jews, in short, sought to save other Jews. More important, perhaps, every Jew who went into hiding or passed as gentile was completely involved in rescue. If one steps back and broadens the lens through which we look at hiding operations, Jews emerge as engaged actors. They were not, and did not behave like, the vermin, bacilli, or numbered pieces the Germans took them to be. From the decision to disappear or to pass, every step was a conscious act. It is true that no Jew survived the Holocaust in hiding without the help of gentiles—and sometimes literally hundreds of gentiles over the course of the years. It is equally true that every Jew actively participated in the process. It was hard work to disappear, to live as if one had vanished from the face of the earth and yet still stay alive. And it was hard work to pass.

Within their ever-constricting sphere in Nazi Europe, Jews struggled to maintain a semblance of independence, a vestige of normality. To go into hiding meant voluntarily to surrender whatever remained of this normality and independence, to accept the severance of all ties with society, with the few friends who remained and, most often, with one's own family. To decide to hide in many cases entailed consenting to life for an indeterminate period in an extraordinarily punitive prison cell, a cell in which one's heart continued to beat, but one was invisible to the eyes, ears, and nose of the world.

A Jew in hiding had to live silently in the shadows. It was too dangerous to go near the window; noise attracted attention. When visitors called on the host family, the hider became still as a corpse. Danger and its friends fear and anxiety were constant companions. A raid could happen at any moment. And what then? A lightning move into a tiny space behind a false wall in a wardrobe or closet, or under the stairs or the floorboards, or in the attic or cellar, leaving no trace of existence. Lives were at stake: the police who had just broken in must find no clue that someone was hiding.

To hide meant to accept dependence on others for food, clothing, medicine, news, safety. Quite often, hider and host did not know each other. A Jew who wished to hide could not choose. One went to people who, with whatever motivation, were willing take one in. Sara Spier was separated from her sister, brother, and parents, and hidden by people who had no sympathy for her former life or her interests.

> The people who hid me were farm laborers. . . . So I came into a totally different milieu where there was no education and a different religion. I felt the difference very forcefully but of course I didn't say anything. I realized they were people who hid me and I couldn't say I didn't like their way of life. For example, they didn't read books. They were always knitting, or doing some embroidery, or busy in the kitchen, or busy in the garden, or doing something. But reading was something luxurious. They accepted that I had my schoolbooks, but when I would ask for some book to read, they said you can do something more useful.[25]

Even so, the host family was kind. No malice lay in their refusal to get books for Sara Spier. Indeed, it might have been dangerous for them suddenly to use the lending library. But Sara Spier, like all Jews in hiding, had no rights. Nor was she entitled to personal preferences. One had to be grateful, because the hosts risked their lives on one's behalf. The official penalty for harboring a Jew was deportation in the west and execution in the east. "The life of a Pole who is hiding a Jew is not an easy one," Emmanuel Ringelblum observed in Warsaw. "Money undoubtedly plays an important role in the hiding of Jews. There are poor families who base their subsistence on the funds paid daily by the Jews to their Aryan landlords. But is there enough money in the world to make up for the constant fear of exposure, fear of the neighbours, the porter and the manager of the block of flats, etc.?"[26] The host's tasks were endless; there were constant daily troubles to resolve, persistent hardships to overcome.

Most people who offered refuge proved steadfast and loyal, doing what they believed to be correct. Observing gentiles who sheltered Jews in the Warsaw area, Ringelblum admired, for example, the M. "family tradition of humanitarianism and tolerance." Mr. W., by contrast, was a patriot. He "was dedicated to the cause of independence for which he daily risked his life." For him, saving Jews was a form of patriotism. "It is the duty of every Pole, a civic duty, to hide Jews. 'Look after them like the apple of your eye.'"[27]

70. *Alexander Roslan was one of the Catholic Poles who put their family's life in jeopardy when he chose to take in three Jewish boys. One of the brothers died of illness; these two survived. Warsaw. Courtesy of the Jewish Foundation for the Righteous, New York.*

More than a half century later, rescuers do not think it extraordinary that they behaved as they did or that they should be specially honored. In fact, of course, their stance was exceptional. Their wonderful deeds should be admired and their probity and rectitude esteemed.

Alas, not all hosts were so estimable. Physical and sexual abuse, facts of daily life in normal times, did not disappear during the Holocaust. In the very unequal power relationship of the hiding situation, abuse might easily occur, leaving the victim few options. "I found [Esther] another place because she was being sexually abused by the oldest boy in the family in the house where she was," Marion van Binsbergen recalled. "The person who told me was the boy's sister." Esther had not said a word. "He had scared the hell out of her. If she told, he was going to hand her over to the Nazis. That was the threat a lot of them used."[28]

More common than actual abuse was the unspoken, and possibly even unconscious, idea of the hiding Jew as a slave. In the hiding situation, a Jew had no intrinsic self-worth. This proved a corrosive to normal morality. The boundaries between two separate integral persons blurred: they were not equal human beings. One was the master and the other the servant. "Slowly, I don't even know how it happened . . . but ultimately and eventually, I became sort of a Cinderella," explained a woman who was hidden with her cousin Gabbie on a professor's farm in Poland.

In other words, I was working from four o'clock in the morning when I would get up to say my prayers and do whatever, and then prepare the feed for the horses who were going out into the fields about six. I had to feed them early so that they would eat for a couple of hours before they went out. I had to clean them down. I remember when we got there, there was a groom who worked in the stables, but later on, there was no more money or food or whatever, so there was no groom. . . . And we took care of the pigs and the cows, and we started working in the fields, planting. All of this was a gradual sort of thing. . . . There was work that was being done during the winter and there was work that was being done in the spring. And as time went, it became more and more work. [It was] really heavy work: baking bread, making the dough, polishing the floors, etc. . . .

Aside from the harshness which life eventually became, there was little food. For everyone. But, you know how it is, if you are the power you find ways to hide bread. . . . Very quickly I found out that nobody was going to look after me but me. And Gabbie was very hungry. So [I was] looking after him. [And I worked.] I worked with the Professor, with the bees, grafting trees, transplanting seedlings. I worked in the kitchen. I worked a lot. I worked in the fields and I worked in the stables and I shoveled out manure. I milked the cows and [sometimes] I took the cows into the pasture. But if there was other work to be done, I did it. I polished floors. Everybody worked. But it was like I was more capable.[29]

A life in hiding "was all of a sudden a way of life without life [without living]," as one man put it.[30] Every act of daily life took on weight—to go to the toilet, to wash, to stem the flow of menstrual blood. Moishe Kobylanski and his family hid in the countryside near Gruszwica, their village in the Ukraine. From the end of 1942 until May or June of 1943 they lived in the straw loft of a pigsty.

Bathroom facilities were excellent. You just went over there in the other end and you bundled everything up in straw. And when I went after food I took it with me and I went crazy to find a place to dump it. The urine was easy. It was in a bottle and as soon as I walked out I dumped it. That was no problem. The fecal matter was a problem. I went where they had cattle manure, I found a place, and I tried to hide it there. But how does human excrement fit in with cattle manure? No good either. It was always a problem because I might leave evidence after myself.[31]

If caught, a Jewish male like Moishe Kobylanski was easily identified by his circumcised penis; on the continent, only Jews were circumcised at that time. Women and older girls had their own biological difficulties. "Menstruating was absolutely harrowing," Herta Montrose-Heymans recalled. "In those days, you had little pads that had to be washed. The [elderly] landlady couldn't hang them on the line, could she? The neighbors knew there was no young person living there."

The Heymans family had moved from Germany to the Netherlands to escape persecution, but the Germans caught up with them. In 1942 they were forced to go underground. In the winter of 1943 Herta moved to an address where she spent the rest of the war years. She, her grandfather, and another elderly man lived with an older couple in a "tiny little working class house" in Enschede, in the east of the Netherlands. The essential problem was to leave no evidence of one's presence, to live without trace of existence. In Herta Heymans's case, for example, not only was it impossible to dry her menstrual pads on the outside clothesline, it was also out of the question to hang out her grandfather's shirts. "Nobody was supposed to know that we were there," she emphasized. "We couldn't hang two shirts out when there was only one man living there." They did not go out, and inside "we whispered, we never spoke up really. It became second nature."[32]

A single slip of the tongue might "burn" the situation. During the bloody Budapest spring of 1944, Paul Sved and his mother obtained false papers and new identities. "I had to swot up [study] laboriously, not only my new name . . . but a new birth date, new name for my mother, new name for my father, had to swot up things like 'Hail Mary' and the Lord's Prayer. All of this was drummed into me relentlessly for reasons I didn't quite understand." Mrs. Sved rented rooms in an area of Budapest forbidden to Jews, and she and her son went "to lodge with a family in our own room with false papers. She had sewn the yellow star on (I remember it very, very clearly) with just a few threads, hers and mine . . . and suitcase and all, [we] walked out of the house with the yellow star. We started to walk down the boulevard and whoosh! My mother whipped off the two yellow stars." They lived in the room Mrs. Sved had taken for a day or two until "stupidly, I said to my mother as she put my overcoat on, 'Where is my star?' I immediately realized what I had said, and I just said, 'Sta-.'" Unluckily, however, "there was a big, fat boy there of age twelve or thirteen who heard that and immediately reported it to his mother. And the mother immediately told us to leave."[33] Under the circumstances, they were lucky: the landlady didn't call the police. But Mrs. Sved's careful plans had collapsed in an instant. Now she had to start all over again.

RESCUE, IN SHORT, was a complex affair in an unprecedented situation. No one—neither Jews nor gentiles—had prior experience in clandestine operations. And everyone faced what had never occurred or existed before. Who, in Nazi Europe, could comprehend that millions of ordinary civilians were being murdered? And who in the free world could envision a *razzia* or life in ghetto— let alone the fate the Germans had in store for their victims? Even as information became available through smuggled reports and photographs, few people could absorb it as knowledge. The limits of the imagination worked for the Germans and their allies during the Holocaust.

Those who could make the imaginative leap understood the barrier. They stormed the barricades of their fellow citizens' minds, but to little avail. "Will you wash your hands of all this?" Victor Gollancz cried. "It can only be because you do not use your imagination." He tried to drive the point home. "Does a little child in Warsaw suffer less and, God forgive us, *fear* less than a child in London, or Leeds, or whatever your town or village may be?"[34]

Arthur Koestler—the Hungarian Jewish refugee who had gone to Palestine, left for France, and ended up in Britain—frequently expressed his bitter frustration with Allied unwillingness to believe the news that trickled in from Europe. "The trouble with being a contemporary in times like this," Koestler told his radio listening public, "is that reality beats the imagination every step. . . . For an educated Englishman it is almost easier to imagine conditions of life under King Canute on this island than conditions of life in, say, contemporary Poland."[35] Nevertheless, Koestler persevered, in print, on the air, and in public. "I have been lecturing now for three years to the troops, and their attitude is the same. They don't believe in concentration camps, they don't believe in the starved children of Greece, in the shot hostages of France, in the mass-graves of Poland; they have never heard of Lidice, Treblinka, or Belzec; you can convince them for an hour, then they shake themselves, their mental self-defence begins to work and in a week the shrug of incredulity has returned like a reflex temporarily weakened by the shock." Americans were no easier to convince. "The other day I met one of the best-known American journalists," he wrote in a *New York Times Magazine* article. "He told me that in the course of some recent public opinion survey nine out of ten average American citizens, when asked whether they believed that the Nazis commit atrocities, answered that it was all propaganda lies, and that they didn't believe a word of it."

Rescuers in Europe despaired. "Tidings of the massacre of the Jews have gone all over the world," Ruth Andreas-Friedrich raged in her diary in February 1944. "Did a single soul lose his appetite for breakfast?" Not even Jewish relatives in safe locations were moved to act.

When we described the distress of one German Jewish woman in burning colors to her Swedish nephew, who lives a comfortable life in Stockholm, far from the horrors of war and Nazi misery, and implored him to strain every nerve to get her out, he answered, "The obligation you ask of me would mean supporting my aunt to the end of the war—specifically, about three hundred crowns a month. Taxes have risen 150 percent, the cost of living 100 percent. After deducting all fixed expenses, I have a tiny fraction left out of my twelve hundred crowns' salary every month. I am faced with the task of supporting five of us on about a hundred and fifty crowns a month. It would be irresponsible of me to make a commitment that I simply could not keep; when the guarantee of twenty-five hundred crowns that Heinz put at my disposal for his mother was gone, I would simply have to put my aunt on the street."

He won't have to put her out on the street; the SS has taken the job off his hands.[36]

Finally, a lack of will compounded the lack of imagination. If everyone, or the majority, or even a significant number of those who *knew*—who saw the viciousness, heard the screams, smelled the burning flesh, read the confirmed but still confidential reports—had taken to rescue work, far more Jews would have been saved. They did not. And so the Allies' strategy of rescue through victory was a self-fulfilling policy.

Some half million Jews in the Soviet Union and 330,000 in England survived because the Germans never got to them. The Soviet and British armies did not collapse. Their resistance protected the neutrality of Portugal, Spain, Ireland, Switzerland, Sweden, and the Vatican, which meant that their 39,000 Jews remained out of the Germans' reach also. Finally, Allied victory saved the 50,000 Jews of Germany's allies Finland and Bulgaria, which had not yet capitulated to German pressure to surrender them. In total, some 10 percent (900,000 people) of those condemned to death never got caught in the German net. At the same time, 80 percent of the 7.5 to 8 million Jews in Nazi Europe were dead by May 1945. Had the Allies not been victorious then, or had their victory come later, the 20 percent who had survived until May 1945 and the Jews the Germans had not yet reached would have been murdered too. Thus, having made it impossible to rescue Jews because such operations would interfere with the "salvation with victory" policy, victory was indeed the salvation for those still alive.

However numerous the heroic hiding operations were, there were far too few of them. And not enough of the actions attempted were, in the end, successful. Rescue was a rare activity. But it *was* undertaken and it is a part of the historical legacy of the Holocaust. Indeed, just because it was rare does not diminish its importance. On the contrary: efforts to save Jews, whether by an individual, a group, or through negotiation, are models of what was possible under German occupation. Knowing how difficult life was for both gentiles and Jews throughout Nazi Europe, and how very efficiently the machinery of death and the murderers operated, it is astonishing that rescue activities were undertaken at all. These endeavors clearly illuminate how people transcended the hardships they endured each day and organized help for others and for themselves. Despite the terror of the German rule, it was possible to circumvent difficulties and negotiate obstacles. Not everyone stood by silently. Not everyone participated in genocide. Other forms of behavior were practicable and feasible.

The history of the Holocaust is a story of utter perdition and ruin. It poses an existential question mark to the very notion of "western civilization." What do such words mean? What, in light of the Holocaust, is the definition of the word "civilization"? And why are the rescuers significant?

When God decided to destroy the city of Sodom because sin and injustice ruled, Abraham reminded God that the righteous would fall with the wicked. Perhaps, Abraham suggested, there were as many as fifty righteous people in Sodom. God agreed with Abraham: the city would be saved if he found fifty such souls. Abraham had won the point. And so he haggled. If God would spare the city for the sake of fifty, why not forty? Or thirty? Or twenty? Or ten? And there the bargain was struck.

Ten righteous people were not to be found. Sodom was destroyed, unlamented to this day. During the Holocaust, by contrast, hundreds of thousands of righteous came forward throughout German Europe. There is no silver lining to the Holocaust. One cannot say, "It was the most lethal, most geographically comprehensive genocide in the history of western civilization *but* the rescuers were heroes." What one can say, however, is: "The Holocaust was the most lethal, most geographically comprehensive genocide in the history of western civilization, *and* the rescuers were heroes." At the same time. And thus the legacy of Mr. W., and the M. family, and Georges Garel, and Marion van Binsbergen is hope.

Chapter Fourteen

THE CONCENTRATION CAMP WORLD

FEW JEWS EVER had an opportunity to benefit from rescue operations which, in any case, were small and far between. The vast majority died in ghettos and transit camps of starvation, exposure, disease, or vicious cruelty (circa 1 million people); or were killed by *Einsatzgruppen* (between 1 and 1.5 million); or murdered in the three Operation Reinhard camps (between 1.5 and 2 million). In total, this accounted for at least 4 million lives. Belzec, Sobibór, and Treblinka, set up in 1942, were closed down at the end of 1943. Only then did the concentration camp system established when the Nazis came to power in 1933 become fully integrated into the plan for genocide.[1]

Initially, the Nazis established concentration camps to incarcerate Communists, Socialists, asocials, or others who did not fit into the national community. Their primary purpose was to "teach" these Germans what they needed to know to return to society.[2] Jews, by definition, could never belong to the national community. Political and social "reeducation" was wasted on them. The many Jews among these political prisoners were therefore treated worse and assigned to the most difficult and dangerous labor details.[3] Buchenwald, for example, was opened in 1937. The first Jews arrived in the spring of 1938. They—unlike the gentiles—were crammed into a bare cattle barn, fed minuscule rations, and forced to work up to sixteen hours a day in the limestone quarry. The men who survived this daily assault stood on the *Appellplatz* (roll-call field) deep into the night, forced to sing antisemitic songs.

> For centuries we have deceived the people,
> no swindle was too large or too bad for us.
> We have lied, cheated, and swindled
> whether it was with the mark or the crown.
> Now the paradise has come to a sudden end;
> gone is the filth and all the swindling.
> Now must our crooked dealer's hands
> be used for the first time in honest work.
> We are the Cohens, the Isaacs, the Wolfensteins,

known everywhere for our ugly mugs.
If there's a race that is still more base,
then it is surely related to us.
Now the Germans have finally seen through us
and put us securely behind barbed wire.
We deceivers of the people have long feared
what has suddenly come true overnight.
Now our crooked Jewish noses mourn;
in vain is hate and discord sown.
Now there is no more stealing,
no feasting and no debauchery.
It is too late; it is forever too late.[4]

All but twenty Jews in that first transport were dead within months. These men had not been imprisoned because they were Jews, but in the camp, as Jews, they were singled out for murderous treatment.

This policy changed with the 1938 November Pogrom. The Germans did not know what to do with the masses of Jewish men they had arrested, and the camps seemed a good solution. That night, transports holding more than 30,000 Jews began to roll. But the camps were already packed to capacity.[5] In any case, the Nazis did not want to keep the Jews. They wanted to terrorize them. While Germans on the streets rioted against their Jewish neighbors with a viciousness never seen in the nation's history, the SS in the camps reached a new pitch of brutality in the short history of the camps. "Even the road from the train station to the camp [Buchenwald] was a form of torture without equal," two Jewish survivors reported immediately after the war. "Because people were arrested without regard to their age, one could see seventy- to eighty-year-old men next to ten-year-old children. Those who fell behind were shot down along this death road. Those who survived were forced to drag the blood-soaked corpses along with them into the camp." The guards "beat every new arrival with iron bars, whips etc. So that virtually every incoming Jew had contusions or wounds on the head. Many weaker men were trampled to death in the throng."

No language has the words to describe the scenes that then took place in roll call square. Before everyone's eyes the SS men plundered in the most shameless fashion those who had been beaten to the ground, murdered, or trampled to death, stealing watches, rings, money, and other objects of value out of their pockets. . . . As a result of the horrible experiences of these first nights, which were repeated again and again until the camp was overflowing with inmates, about seventy Jews went insane. They lay in chains on the cement floor of wooden barracks that had previously served as a washhouse. In groups of four they were gradually taken to the cellblock, where [SS-Hauptscharführer Martin] Sommer beat them to death.[6]

The camps served the Nazis well. They proved a way to extort money and property from wealthy Jews, rob every inmate of personal valuables, and pressure all Jews to leave the country. Prisoners, the Nazi leadership declared, would be released when their families had exit visas and immigration papers in hand. Jewish women flooded consular and government offices in search of required documents. If ever the inmates returned to Germany, they would be confined to camp for life, Heydrich warned on 31 January 1939. Few needed his admonition.

The SS expanded the concentration camp system when World War II began. The *Nacht und Nebel* (Night and Fog) decree of December 1941 permitted them to incarcerate *suspected* resisters in the occupied territories. At the same time, knowing the camps were there subdued the millions of east European forced laborers sent to Germany. The invasion of the Soviet Union changed the composition of the camp population dramatically. In late 1941, three-quarters of the inmates were German. A year later, they accounted for barely a third.

As the Nazis developed their "Final Solution" to the "Jewish Question," they maintained many types of camps. Three emerged as central to Jewish policy: concentration camps; forced labor camps; and the Operation Reinhard camps.[7] By the end of 1943, the Operation Reinhard annihilation centers had closed down. The SS sent the Jewish concentration and slave labor camp inmates to Auschwitz and Majdanek. Unique in the concentration camp world, Auschwitz and Majdanek were the only two camps with a large and ever-growing Jewish population. They were also the only two camps incorporated into the annihilation program and it was to Auschwitz that Jews who had survived until 1944 were sent. And it was there they would be killed. The SS ordered large crematoria with gas chambers. They were manned by a special group of prisoners, the *Sonderkommandos*. They hauled out the bodies from the gas chambers, removed the dental gold, searched the corpses for hidden valuables, cut the dead women's hair, carted the bodies to the ovens, and incinerated them. To refuse this horrifying work meant immediate death. In any case, theirs was only a temporary stay of execution. The *Sonderkommando* men knew too much; every few months a new team was selected. Its first task was to "process" its predecessors.[8]

Salmen Gradowski and his family were deported with all the Jews from the town of Luna in Poland in November 1942 to the transit camp of Kielbasin near Grodno. From Kielbasin they were shipped to Auschwitz in January 1943; Gradowski was thirty-three years old. Late in 1943, he managed to obtain writing materials with which, secretly and at great risk, he wrote an 81-page journal describing his experiences during the past year.[9]

The Jews of Kielbasin knew about Treblinka, he explained. So tension mounted on the deportation train as it approached the vicinity.

The sadness grew with every kilometre and with every kilometre the emptiness became greater. What happened? Here we are approaching the ill-famed station of Treblinka, so tragic for the Jews, where, according to information which had filtered through to us, the majority of Poles and Jews from abroad were swallowed up and wiped out.[10]

The train passed two Polish women who silently ran their fingers across their throats. Then the transport stopped.

Two thousand five hundred persons held their breaths. Teeth were chattering with fright and hearts were beating like mad. This great human mass, bathed in deadly sweat, is awaiting the coming minutes. Each second is an eternity, each second—a step nearer to death. All have grown numb. . . . The whistle awakened them from their torpor. The train wrenched itself free of death and continued on its route. Mothers are kissing their children, husbands are kissing their wives. Tears of joy are shed, all have wakened to live and have heaved sighs of relief. A fresh surge of hopeful thoughts has mastered everyone.[11]

The joy faded as hunger and thirst grew. Finally, they arrived at Auschwitz. They had not heard of it. It was January 1943; rumors had not reached them. Passing through selection on the *Judenrampe,* their hope vanished. "The thought of staying together with the family, this opiate, which had kept up their spirits on the journey, has all at once stopped to act," Gradowski observed. An able-bodied man, he was admitted into the camp. "We came dressed like men and we left in wet rags. In these clothes we look like criminals or like confirmed lunatics. All without caps, bare-headed. One wearing shoes, another slippers, mostly not of a pair and of much too large a size. The clothes too tight or too loose."[12]

They were tattooed. "Everyone got his number. From that moment on you have lost your 'self' and have become transformed into a number. You are no longer what you were before, but a worthless, moving number." Gradowski understood that he had arrived "in a camp of death." Jews did "not come here to live but to die, sooner or later. There is no room for life here." The men were assigned bunks. "They are beds of boards, each for five, six numbers jointly. We are told to climb into them, to push in so far that only the head should be seen." Desperate for information about loved ones, they questioned the "old-timers." "But what does this man tell us! What does he have to say!? The heart trembles. It makes our hair stand on end. 'Those, who drove away in lorries, were led to death at once and those who went on foot also went to meet death—for some after a longer time of torture, for others after a shorter time.'"[13]

Salmen Gradowski learned to live like an inmate.

A loud sound of a bell wakened everybody. All newcomers are quickly driven outside. We have to do exercises before the roll-call. It is rather dark in the open and wet snow is falling. There is commotion in the camp, the

71. Auschwitz-Birkenau, 1943. The wooden barracks were standard army stables for forty-eight horses. When built in Auschwitz-Birkenau in 1942, the official maximum capacity of each of these stables was set at four hundred inmates. At times, occupancy was double that. These barracks were not insulated, had no floors, no sanitary facilities, and almost no heating. Courtesy Auschwitz-Birkenau State Museum in Oswiecim, Oswiecim.

numbers leave the barracks to attend the roll-call. The cold is penetrating. One feels it through one's camp clothes. Bare feet soon begin to bother us. Shouts are heard, "Fall into lines! Dress the ranks!" . . .

At almost each block, beside the men standing in line, bodies of three, four persons are lying. These are the victims of the night that have not lived to see the day. Even yesterday they were standing numbers at the roll-call and today they lie, lifeless and motionless. Life is not important at the roll-call. Numbers are important. Numbers tally.[14]

Permitted to live for the moment, the "numbers" were assigned to work details. There was plenty for slaves to do in Auschwitz. Gradowski was assigned to the worst of the camp evils: the *Sonderkommando*. Others worked for civilian concerns. Himmler and the huge conglomerate IG Farben had contracted to use Jews to construct a new synthetic rubber plant in nearby Monowitz. Jews were also needed in the mines in Jawiszowice and to support the Bata shoe factory. Indeed, as the labor shortage became more acute, the SS created satellite camps in the vicinity to service all kinds of factories. Five more camps opened in 1943 and nineteen in 1944. The SS—which certainly had many categories of prisoners under their control—expanded this system in the Reich and throughout occupied Europe. Hitler's decision in April 1944 to permit the SS to send Jewish prisoners to camps throughout Europe meant that Jews who passed the selection in Auschwitz fanned out across the continent.[15]

In total, from spring 1942 through summer 1944, 1.1 million Jews were deported to Auschwitz; 865,000 were killed on arrival. They got as far as the *Judenrampe* or the ramp at Birkenau, but they never entered the camp and they never got a number. The Germans selected only some 240,000 Jews for slave labor. It was they who entered the camp and all but some 30,000, called *Durchgangsjuden* (transit Jews), were tattooed. About 110,000 of the numbered remained in Auschwitz where 100,000 of them died. The rest (100,000 "numbered" and 30,000 without tattoo) were sent on; some within days, others months or even years later. Sara Grossman-Weil was among them.

72. *Mirka Grossman, 1941. Coll. authors.*

Lodz ghetto was liquidated, workshop by workshop, in August 1944. "Factory workers will travel with their families," Rumkowski's final proclamation read. Sara Grossman-Weil left with her husband's family. They were herded to the train station and ordered onto the cattle cars. "You couldn't throw a pin in, one was sitting on top of the other, with the bundles. We were in this cattle car, this wagon, and we were riding, riding, riding. There was no end to it. And the little one asked, in Polish, 'Daddy, isn't it better that today it's a bad day, but tomorrow it will be better?' She was five years old. And her father said, 'Today doesn't matter, tomorrow will be much better.'"[16]

Tomorrow proved him wrong. The train with the survivors of the Lodz ghetto passed by Kattowitz and Myslowitz, and crossed the Vistula at Neu-Berun, arriving at the station of Auschwitz, where the train turned into a spur and stopped. When the sun began to set, the train backed onto another spur, through a gate, and entered the enormous compound of Birkenau. The bolted doors were opened. Sara Grossman, her relatives, and the rest of the people on the train were hauled out and told to form two columns, one of men, and one of women and children.

I was standing there not knowing what's going on, overwhelmed with the amount of people around us, not believing that they threw us all out from these wagons in the manner they did. How they pushed and shoved and screamed. And these SS men with the dogs in front of us. I lost sight of what was going on. It was crazy. And I was standing with my mother-in-law and my sister-in-law with her little girl, when someone approached us, and said, "Give this child to the grandmother." And my sister-in-law gave the child to my mother-in-law. They went to the left, and we went to the right.[17]

Sara and the other women selected for work entered the camp.

After a while when the entire transport was formed in a line of five, I think it was five, we began to march. There was a young woman who came forth and some others, Jewish women, who began to march with us. They were in the forefront and we followed them. They took us from the platform into Auschwitz, into the camp. As we were marching, I saw columns of women marching on the other side in the opposite direction who were half naked, shaven heads, stretching out their arms. "Food, food. Give me your bread!" Screaming, shouting. I was overwhelmed. I thought that I found myself in an asylum, in a madhouse, in a place with only crazy people. These people were marching in the opposite direction, whether they were crazy I don't know, but to me these were columns of crazy people.[18]

The women arrived at the delousing station. They were registered, shaved of all body hair, showered, and handed rags and wooden shoes.[19]

From there they gathered us again in columns in the rags with the same look that the people who I had seen an hour ago in the columns marching in the opposite direction. We had the same look, except we weren't shouting. We looked like crazy people just as the rest of them. We were led to a lavatory where we had to take care of our needs, and from there we went to a barrack, which was the house where we will be staying. In this barrack we were given a bunk. The size of the bunk is approximately the size of not quite a twin bed, I would say considerably smaller. And on this bunk bed, five people had to find their home, their sleeping quarters. And this was our new home.[20]

Sara quickly learned what happened to Jews in Auschwitz. "The kapos, the Jewish women who were minding us, enlightened us. The ten days I was there, all I heard was, 'You will never get out from here alive.'" For Sara, her sister-in-law Esther, and her niece Regina, Auschwitz was "hell." But they were not there long. "[We] stayed there ten days, and then we were shipped out to Bergen-Belsen. Bergen-Belsen at this time was paradise for me. It was a big open space." They were in a newly opened section, the Tent Camp. "Just straw thrown on the ground, these were our quarters. But we were getting more food than in Auschwitz, and we had freedom without these constant kapos around us." From Bergen-Belsen "we were sent to an *Arbeitslager.* Ninety of us were selected and we were sent to Unterlüss," eighteen miles northeast of Celle. "I was all the time with Regina and Esther."[21]

Unterlüss was indeed a work camp. The appell whistle blew at four-thirty in the morning, "this loud whistle you could hear five hundred miles away." The women ran out of the barracks into the yard and formed into groups. "Each group took off for a given destination. We were contracted by people who needed our labor. In other words, it was private enterprise that hired the

73. *Hungarian Jewish women after their admittance into Auschwitz-Birkenau and delousing in one of the so-called Saunas, summer 1944. Most of these women would be shipped on as slave laborers to other camps. Courtesy Yad Vashem, Jerusalem.*

inmates. And Unterlüss was able to supply the manpower. We were the manpower. So by five we were off to our place of work." Sara felled trees in the nearby forest, she hauled bricks, she cleared away rubble. "There was also a special unit sent to a munitions factory. At one time they selected me to join it, and for several days I was going there." She could not tolerate this work. "We were working with sulphur. The air, the bread we were given as a ration at work, my mouth, eyes, hands, fingers, everything turned yellow. I was sick with the smell, with the air I was breathing. And I decided one evening when we were marching back to our quarters from this camp, that no matter what happens to me, I am not going any more. [The kapo] can just kill me. It wouldn't be so terrible." The kapo never learned who had slipped out of her group. Sara was not beaten to death. Other women had been before, and still more would be. But she was not identified and, escaping the munitions factory and the kapo, she stole into her cousin Bronia's unit, with her sister-in-law Esther and niece Regina, "cutting trees, cleaning rubble, delivering bricks to construction sites"—as before. "It was a very thin line. It was really a brush with—not with death—but a brush with destiny."[22]

The SS gained thousands of slave laborers in the summer and fall of 1944.[23] In addition to the Hungarian and Lodz Jews shipped to Auschwitz, Himmler's empire took over Riga and Kovno ghettos and the camp at Vaivara (near

Tallinn) from the Reich Commissioner for Ostland. The inmates were pushed west to Stutthof (close to the former free city of Danzig) in advance of the approaching Soviet army.[24] From there, prisoners were sent to *Arbeitslagers* all over Germany. Still the slaveholdings increased with inmates from the Gestapo prison in Warsaw and the labor camp at Plaszow, near Cracow. In August, Himmler was master of more than half a million prisoners; the count on 15 January 1945 topped 700,000. By that time, there were more than 650 satellite camps attached to factories and other production sites. Germans, who had once figured so prominently in the concentration camp population, now accounted for only 8 percent of all inmates. Jews, by contrast, initially a marginal presence, were perhaps a quarter of the entire camp population.

With so many slaves at hand, the Germans did not care how long anyone lasted. There was always someone else to take the dead person's space. Replacements were shipped out of Auschwitz continuously. Alex Ehrmann and his brother, deported from Hungary at the end of April 1944, were in Auschwitz for only four or five days before "they put us on a train." They did not know their destination until "we arrived in a station, Praha. Somehow I remembered from geography that Praha meant Warsaw. . . . So again we start marching [through] streets lined on both sides with sentries and dogs. '*Lauf! Lauf!*' and we walked to the Warsaw ghetto." The Germans had established a camp in the ghetto. "We were told we would be working there; we'd be tearing down the walls and buildings, and salvaging material."

Alex and his brother were in the demolition and salvage camp for about three months. In July, the Soviets drew so close to the city that the Germans evacuated the *Lager.*

In the wee hours of the morning, they ordered us out. Finally, around ten-thirty or so we started marching. There was one road open from Warsaw towards Lodz going northwest. On that highway we started marching. We marched all day and we stopped on a field at night. We camped out to sleep. We were accompanied by the SS. They had horse-drawn wagons. Some supplies were on the wagons, and dogs. We were told when we camped that everyone must lie down. Anyone who lifts his head or sits up will be shot without warning.

We slept through that one night. In the morning we got up, started marching again. No food, only the extra rations we had got [in Warsaw]. The soles of my shoes were gone. On the march I had no shoes any more. . . . As people got tired, they fell behind. Pretty soon, word got around that someone was shot in the back. He sat down, and they shot him. So: Go. Don't stop. Just go. As much as it may hurt, as tired as you may be, just keep going. They shoot people who sit down. . . . There were people helping other people, putting their arm around them and dragging them as they marched. But there were casualties. . . .

74. *Selection at Auschwitz-Birkenau, summer 1944. Courtesy Yad Vashem, Jerusalem.*

We were marching already the third or fourth day without food and without water. Even in the field there was nothing left. . . . We were marching for about a week. We were lucky—no rain. At the end of the week it started to rain heavily. And we just couldn't walk; couldn't march. Finally, we were ordered into a remote barn on a farm. No food, no produce we could even steal. We were on that farm for about two and a half days. The rains stopped. We were soaked. They ordered us out into formation and we started to march again. We marched into a railroad yard and they put us on a train. Ninety people in a car sitting in each other's lap. No food. The next day . . . no food. One day, [maybe] the third day, we got salted canned meat. No bread, no water. We ate it, we were going mad from thirst. People started to drink their urine. . . .

Sitting on our wet blankets chafed our seats. When we got off in Dachau six days later, pieces of raw flesh tore off our backsides.[25]

From Dachau, Alex and his brother were marched to the satellite camp of Mühldorf, where the Germans were using slave labor to build an underground aircraft factory.

The main work was cement mixing. . . . I told them I was an electrician, hoping to get into the electrician commando. . . . [After a few days] I was grabbed and put into a cement detail. . . . By then we'd found out that people were falling like flies from the cement; it settled in their lungs. Nobody lasted more than two, three weeks in that commando. They just dried up, visibly dried up as it settled on their lungs. Whether they contracted tuberculosis, or it had the effect of tuberculosis, in any case their noses started running, they developed gangrene in their feet, infection set in. Literally, there were some people falling off the gangplank with their bag of cement, and falling dead. There was a death wagon especially to haul away people who died at work. . . .

We were getting into the fall, and weather started to be a factor also. . . . And lice, we had a *lot* of lice by then. . . . We had typhus already.[26]

The Germans established many slave labor camps to build underground factories. Hanna Kent-Sztarkman's brother Heniek was sent to Vaihingen when the SS military camp in Radom where he and their mother worked was disbanded in the summer of 1944. The Russians were closing in. Transferred first to the SS camp on Szkolna Street, Heniek, Hanna, their mother, and all the remaining Radom Jews were force-marched out of town. "We thought we would be taken somewhere outside of the city where mass executions would be conducted." They were not. They continued to march. "Whenever somebody sat down on the side, couldn't go on any more, they shot them right on the spot."[27]

Marched to Tomaszów, the Radom Jews were pushed into an "empty, tremendous factory hall. This was truly something out of Dante's *Inferno*. All those people were sick and hungry. Dysentery. There was absolutely no place to attend to it, so wherever people were, they just did it. You can imagine this horrible stench and filth. At this point, all civilities, all decorum, went by the wayside." They were locked in the factory hall for two days. "There was no food, absolutely no food. But one wasn't aware of it, one was so obsessed with the idea of what is in store for us? Where are they taking us? If they meant to kill us, they would have done it already. They wouldn't have to drag us so far."[28] What the Radom Jews could not imagine was that they would be dragged even farther—and killed just the same. But first, those who could work would give their labor to the Reich.

The Jews were marched to the railroad and loaded into closed cattle cars. "This is the point where the men were separated from the women. This is the last time I saw my mother." The train rolled into Auschwitz at dawn. "In a charged atmosphere of the SS men cracking the whips and shouting, '*Raus, Juden!*' and driving them on with the butts of the guns," the Jews were pulled out of the train. "Everything took place in an atmosphere of shouting and shots and occasionally a shot is fired and a body falls down—just to create this atmosphere of fear and apprehension and compliance. . . . Prompted by gun butts and kicks, we're unloading quickly and lining up right on the siding in front of the car. 'Strip your clothes. Naked. Completely.'" The selection was done right there. "The SS officer started going through the ranks, looking at us and directing us, 'Left, right; left, right.'"[29]

Heniek passed. "Again among blows and kicks," the lucky ones were forced back onto the same train. Two days later, "we come to an empty camp, barracks only surrounded by barbed wire, and it's empty, completely empty. It's in Württemberg, in southwestern Germany. The name of the place is Vaihingen. It's on the River Ens. The name of the camp was Wiesengrundlager, which means meadowland. But don't be deceived by this bucolic, sylvan designation."[30] No matter how many people were brought in, the population remained static. Hunger, disease, and abuse mowed down the inmates.

Food was always a problem. Always. You were constantly hungry. Later on, as conditions became worse towards the end, there were sometimes periods of three days when there was no food to be had at all. But the purpose of the camp was to build an underground factory. Apparently, they wanted to protect the industry from bombing by the Allies. There was a quarry in those hills, and the idea was to chisel and blast out a hole and build the factory in the rocky ground.

I was assigned to that quarry commando. I went out there for a few weeks and I knew that this was my end. They gave you a pick and you had to swing it all the time in that rock. I [arrived] in good physical condition. I became a skeleton. . . .

Each [guard] carried a whip. Slow down in your swinging on the pick, you felt the whip right on your back. . . . People who sat down or slowed down were pushed off the ledge by the guards as a lesson to the others. . . . I realized I would never last there. I would never last.[31]

Jews had suffered and died for six years, but the Nazis had ensured that their torments remained largely invisible to the German population. It was an unspoken contract concluded in the aftermath of the November Pogrom: the government would not confront the population with their "solution" to the "Jewish Question," and the German people would pretend to themselves and to the officials that they knew nothing. What happened to the Jews was "the government's" business, not theirs. But when Hitler decided to repopulate the *Judenrein* Reich with Jewish slaveworkers in concentration camps throughout Germany serving factories and other production sites, the bargain was broken. German civilians throughout the country saw the slave laborers. If Jews were increasingly invisible from 1933 until 1941, and then had vanished, they were very present from mid-1944 until V-E Day. "Whenever we were marching to this quarry and coming back—" Heniek Sztarkman began:

So here we are: Hundreds and hundreds of zombies, sunken faces, shaven heads, those wooden clogs, walking, looking down, dragging our feet through one of the most picturesque parts of Germany. This was truly one of the most attractive places I have ever seen in my life. All the charm and *Gemütlichkeit* [coziness] of the German countryside was there.

We got to this picturesque town. And, mind you, who was left now? Who was left now in Germany? The old men, the women of all ages, the children. So we were marching through, surrounded by those SS with the machine guns, the pistols at the ready, and those dogs on both sides of us, sometimes snapping at our heels when the guard felt like having some fun. You'd assume that you'd see in those eyes something, some compassion, some fleeting impression of, "Oh, those poor wretches." Something which I would feel—I don't know—for a contemptible murderer who was about to be executed: "Poor wretch!" Some empathy.

I don't recall ever seeing anything but cold hostility. And those are those charming *Frauleins,* those nice *Hausfraus,* and those great *Burgers.* And in their expressions, all I have seen was: "This vermin. This abominable vermin."[32]

Jews were sent to slave labor camps attached to a whole spectrum of enterprises. Helga Kinsky-Pollack was deported from Theresienstadt to Auschwitz. Four days later she was sent on to a sub-camp of Flossenbürg in Oederan (near Chemnitz), where she worked in an ammunition factory. "Soon, of course, [the food] was less and less and less because they didn't have anything in Germany. Then we started losing weight. . . . I lost a lot of weight."[33] Ellen Eliel-Wallach, like Helga Pollack, also was deported from Theresienstadt to Auschwitz. She too was there for just a few days before she went on transport to a sub-camp of Mauthausen in Lenzing, near Linz, in Austria. She was placed in an artificial wool factory. "It was awful work. We were bending over this sulphur dioxide which smells awful. The other people, the non-Jewish prisoners got milk for it, but we did not." The inmates got little of anything else to eat either. "We were fed very badly and very, very little. We had terrible hunger; absolutely awful. I remember a terrible, terrible hunger. It was the autumn and winter of 1944–1945. We were hungry all the time."[34]

Slave labor was needed to maintain productivity, to build new factories in locations shielded from bombings, to clear up debris caused by bombs, and to build new shelters for bombed-out Germans. Mira Teeman was deported to Auschwitz when Lodz ghetto was liquidated in the summer of 1944. "I have dreadful memories of Auschwitz, but at the same time they are not so clear because, thank God, I stayed only twelve days. This was my great luck." Then she too was sent to Germany. "After three days without water and without food, we came to Hamburg. They put us in an old warehouse on the waterfront."[35]

The Germans had established the camp on the Dessauer quay in Hamburg harbor in July; one thousand Czech Jewish women from Auschwitz had preceded Mira, who was one of five hundred Polish Jewish women brought in at the end of August and the beginning of September.

It was in the fall and it was raining. It was very windy. We had to go out to
work in the city, different places, to clean up the ruins. . . . Then, when the
first snow came, we had to go out and clear the streets of snow—in that dress
I got in Auschwitz. It was freezing and wet. One night, when we came [back
to camp], I felt I had a high fever, and I thought, "This is my last night." . . .
But in the morning, the fever was gone. I have seen this many times during
the war: you have extra strength when you know it is not possible to do
otherwise. You cannot be sick now. You are not sick. In the morning I went
together with the others to work.[36]

From the Hamburg harbor warehouses Mira Teeman was sent to a new
camp nearby. Opened on 13 September 1944, the Sasel camp slaves served two
firms. Kowal & Bruns manufactured precast concrete building elements. Wayss
& Freytag was involved in emergency housing and cleanup operations.[37] "We
had to get up every morning, I think it was five o'clock. Then they gave us
bread." The ration got smaller as the weeks went by. "And some kind of warm
water. With this we were supposed to work all day." They marched from the
Sasel Poppenbüttel camp, "four, five kilometers to get to the subway, and we
went through a village with many very beautiful houses, typical German
houses. Women were standing in the windows looking at us. Therefore I say it
is a lie that they didn't know anything, because they could see us twice a day,
coming and going."[38]

The Germans were building small houses for people from the railways who
were, as they said *ausgebombt* [bombed out]. We were building those houses.
What we had to do was to deliver different, ready-made parts of the building; prefabricated elements. I must say, I thought they were very clever,
because construction went very quickly like that. The elements we delivered
were very heavy and we had no gloves. They made our hands bloody. That
was one problem. Then, we had to dig ditches for electricity and for water.
It should be maybe 50 centimeters deep. Then we had to build a road to the
construction site, a macadam road. There was a kind of a kapo, a civilian,
who was directing the roadwork. He was like an animal, sadistic, and dreadful to look at. He told me that, instead of a horse, I should drag the roller to
make the road flat. I couldn't move it. I couldn't. So he shouted at me that I
was as lazy as all Jews are. This was the work we were doing.[39]

The women from Sasel were sent "to different places with very different
kinds of work." For some time, Mira Teeman worked in a sand pit. "At first I
couldn't do it because the shovels were very big, and I couldn't lift it. But after
a while, you get a kind of technique. You can do it, because you never kept the
shovel in the air."[40]

"At the end of March we were told that we would be evacuated to another camp." They marched out. "Again, we were loaded on a train. . . . This time we were sitting in ordinary cars. I don't know if everyone was sitting in ordinary cars, but my friends and I were. There were too many of us to sit down, but still, there were windows and we could look out. I think we were on the train for two or three days, going back and forth, back and forth, because the English were bombing the lines. We wondered, 'Why do they [the Germans] bother? Why?' We came to Bergen-Belsen, of course. We didn't know what Bergen-Belsen was."[41]

WHY THE GERMANS bothered is still a mystery today. What is clear is that they were determined to evacuate the inmates before the Allies arrived.[42] They no longer believed the prisoners would function as slaves. Nor were they interested in keeping the prisoners alive. On the contrary. As the SS moved inmates from camp to camp, the institutions still within German-controlled territory became massively overcrowded. The SS infrastructure cracked. Food—little of it as there was—arrived irregularly. Hordes of terribly ill human beings over-whelmed the minimal hygiene systems. The whole camp kingdom became a death trap. Still worse, when Himmler stopped gassings in Auschwitz in November 1944, the SS created "dying camps." Sick or weak inmates were sim-ply dumped there and left to die. A part of Ravensbrück was set aside for that purpose, as was the small camp in Buchenwald. Nearly all the inmates of the dying camps were Jews, not murdered by gas or bullet but by starvation and dis-ease. The most infamous was Bergen-Belsen. Established in 1943 as a transit camp for Jews who might be exchanged for interned Germans, in late 1944 Bergen-Belsen became a wasteyard for Jews marched in from the east.[43]

Hanna Kent-Sztarkman and her mother were two of the many Auschwitz inmates saved from gassing by Himmler's decree. At the very end of October 1944, Mrs. Sztarkman was selected. Hanna did not want to be parted from her mother. "I said, 'I want to go with my mother.' So Mengele said, 'All right, let her go with her mother.' . . . I assumed that if I went with my mother I would go to my death. I didn't *know* anything, but I assumed that. But I wanted to be with my mother."[44] While they were awaiting their turn to be gassed, the pol-icy changed. A few weeks later, on November 26, Himmler commanded the camp administration in Auschwitz to destroy the gas chambers and crematoria. The Soviet army approached. It was time to evacuate Auschwitz.

Hanna and her mother survived the evacuation to Bergen-Belsen. But life in camp was always tenuous. One day the Ukrainian guards decided to have a bit of sport. One stood on each side of the toilet barrack "and they started yelling for us to get out: '*Raus! Raus! Raus!*' As the women ran out, each of them tried to kick them. . . . It was their game. . . . I was fast. My mother wasn't so fast and they kicked her in her groin. She went down." Mrs. Sztarkman became very weak. She no longer could stand for the long Appells. There were barracks for people in her condition, and in she went. "Every night twenty or thirty people died. In the morning the commando would go in and check: who lived, who died. And they dragged those dead people out. They were not burning corpses any more because they didn't have time, so they just left them in front of the barracks. There were piles and piles of dead people. You walked by next to mountains of dead people."45

Through family connections, Hanna got her mother moved into the hospital barracks. "She had a bed by the window—she and another woman." Hanna went to her mother every day, trying desperately to keep her alive by bartering a portion of her bread for whatever the older woman fancied: sugar or onions or whatever.

One day I came by her bed at the window and she didn't recognize me. Her eyes were still open, she was breathing, but she couldn't see me. Of course, I had seen a lot of dead people, but I didn't see people in the process of dying. The death that I had seen was already final. But I'd never seen a normal person die. I ran into the hospital and I tried to give her some coffee and she couldn't swallow any more. That was February 1945. When the nurse came in, she threw me out of the room. She took my mother out of the bed and I never saw my mother again. I assume she was one of those dead people in the pile I was passing by each day, and eventually she was buried in a common grave. . . .

At that point I was completely alone. . . . I was just existing like this. [I was walking around] . . . seeing mountains of dead people and I knew that my mother was lying among them, and yet I walked around, eating and sort of living, if you call it living.46

Heniek Sztarkman was spared Bergen-Belsen and the other dying camps because he was dying in Vaihingen. "Luck," as he said, had "smiled my way" before he had come to his end at the quarry. He was picked by a certain Herr Koch of the *Organization Todt* to clean up the supplies warehouse. "He gave me a broom, and he said, 'Clean it up.' I did that. Very happy to be inside, not under the eye of the SS guards, and I took my time as long as I possibly could. Then he said to me, 'When you're done, go behind there and sit down,' inside the warehouse behind some lumber. I approached this rather apprehensively because I didn't know his intentions. But I did as he said. [At the end of the day] he said, 'I'll call you again tomorrow.'" Herr Koch was true to his word. Saved from the quarry, the cold, and the SS, Heniek's real problems were lack of food and lots of lice. Typhus was rampant in the camp. "There was a special burial detail that did nothing else but cart bodies from the camp to the burial site."47

In the spring, "I too came down with typhus." He was afraid of the isolation barrack, and even more fearful of the consequences of not standing through Appell. "So I reported to the isolation barrack."

I was lying there with no one so much as to give me a little water. Lo and behold—this is the beginning of April—the French army that was part of Patton's army attacks. There is a rapid breakthrough on the front. The Germans start evacuating. So they line up all the able-bodied people to march out. . . . We [in the isolation barrack] were sure that they would kill us before going out; that this would be part of the evacuation. Whether they decided not to do it, or they didn't have enough time, I don't know. But they left the camp with horrible shouts, on foot, marching out.

About twelve hundred people marched out. My understanding is, and I am not sure about this, that fewer than three hundred survived. For some insane reason those dregs were dragged like some sort of treasure chest throughout all Germany all the way into Bavaria. Of all the things they had to salvage—to keep onto—to hang on to—this pathetic bunch of broken-down Jews. It's just insanity. I guess they had to fulfill their historical mission.[48]

The French army and the Germans' haste spared Heniek that ordeal. He survived. Alex Ehrmann and his brother also were saved by typhus. In February 1945 "the soup got more watery and smaller portions of bread." Nothing else. "Health conditions deteriorated rapidly. More and more deaths. There were empty barracks already [from deaths]." Around the time of Passover, Alex contracted spotted typhus. "There was a barbed wire fence that par-titioned off part of the camp." That was "the sick area." His brother, who worked in the kitchen, looked after him as best he could. "He kept me alive." Alex was delirious most of the time. "One evening, somebody was shaking me. I woke up. One of my friends was saying, 'They're calling your name.' 'Who?' The Oberscharführer. I didn't know if it was good or bad. . . . I can hardly walk. Outside of the gate in the main camp, my brother is there, thank-ing the officer." He had gained permission to put Alexander in the revier or infirmary block. "The next morning a train pulled into the railroad track adja-cent to the barbed wire fence. They took the whole camp away, not one person left, over three thousand people." The revier block was untouched. "So I, in effect, was saved by my brother and by the SS officer."[49] And by the Allies, who arrived before he died.

Sara Grossman-Weil had been in Bergen-Belsen in August 1944 before she was sent to Unterlüss. When production in the satellite camp came to an end, when "the German machinery broke down, and the Germans, after liquidating the camps, were fleeing, we were brought to Bergen-Belsen again." It was the end of March 1945. "Within those months, the Bergen-Belsen we left and the Bergen-Belsen we found when we returned was not to be recognized. This Bergen-Belsen was hell. If there is a stronger word for hell, that is it." Sara was put in a barrack with hundreds of other women. "On the outside were hun-dreds of women dying of thirst, thirst, and thirst again."

It was a sight that is beyond any description or understanding or imagination. You cannot, because when you see the pictures of the dead bodies, you just see pictures. You don't see the bodies, the eyes that talk to you and beg you for water. You don't see the mouths quietly trying to say something and not being able to utter a word. You see and you feel as I did, the agony of these people for whom death would be a blessing. They are just dying and can't die.[50]

75. Bergen-Belsen, April 1945. Courtesy of the United States Holocaust Memorial Museum Photo Archives, Washington, DC.

All around the camp were mounds of bodies. Sara was ordered to move corpses to a large pit. "I looked in disbelief. I couldn't see what I am seeing. I couldn't believe that thousands of bodies are there. The kapo went away for a minute or so to another mound where other women were picking up bodies. I simply ran away. I didn't think what will happen. I just couldn't do it. I didn't want to do it. I ran, which was very, very daring. You don't run away when you are in a concentration camp. You do what you are told. I ran away."

These mounds that you see on some of the pictures that are being shown about the Holocaust, they were real people. They were living, breathing, eating, feeling, thinking people, thousands upon thousands of them. Mothers and daughters and children. These pictures are real. And I saw it, I smelled it, I touched them. They were very, very real. This was Bergen-Belsen in March and the beginning of April in 1945.[51]

Sara, her sister-in-law Esther, and her niece Regina survived. "April 15 is my birthday, and this is when we were liberated. Suddenly, we heard planes were coming, cars with English soldiers were coming, and everywhere, wherever you turned, 'We will be free! We will be free! The English are here!' . . . It was a very beautiful April day. The sun was shining and we felt free. But we were hungry, and broken in body and spirit."[52]

WITH THE LIBERATION of Bergen-Belsen by British troops, and Ohrdruf, Buchenwald, and Dachau by the Americans, large numbers of western observers confronted the horrors of the camps for the first time.[53] Photographs of mountains of emaciated corpses and starved inmates filled the newspapers as reporters transmitted horrified firsthand accounts on the airwaves. "I picked my way over corpse after corpse in the gloom until I heard one voice," Richard Dimbleby reported from Bergen-Belsen for the BBC on 19 April. "I found a girl, she was a living skeleton, impossible to gauge her age for she had practically no hair left, and her face was only a yellow parchment sheet with two holes in it for eyes. She was stretching out her stick of an arm and gasping something, it was 'English, English, medicine, medicine,' and she was trying to cry but she hadn't enough strength. And beyond her down the passage and in the hut there were the convulsive movements of dying people too weak to raise themselves from the floor."[54]

For the British and Americans, the camps proved that the war effort had been justified. Soldiers had not died in vain. Churchill had proclaimed that Hitler's victory would usher in "a new Dark Age made more sinister by perverted science." Bergen-Belsen proved that the new Dark Age was no mere figure of speech. For a moment it seemed as if the Allies had fought the war to save the Jews.

Epilogue

Sara Spier, her sister and brother, and their parents lived as a family in the Dutch town of Arnhem at the start of the war. She was fifteen when she went into hiding and her life underground hung by a thread. Forced to change addresses thirty-two times, Sara learned about instability, fear, and kindness. When she reentered society at eighteen, her parents and her brother had been deported and killed. Also in hiding, they had been betrayed by the host family's neighbors after an argument over clothespins. "They got into a quarrel. And then the neighbor said, 'Well, now I go to the police and tell you have Jews.' They didn't believe he would, but he did."[1]

Sara had no home after the war, no money, and no profession. "I couldn't go to university. I would have loved to. I had thought to study Dutch [literature] or medicine. But there I was: I had only two years of high school, I had no parents, and I could see that I was not going to be looked after. I had to look after myself from the very moment the war was over." Three weeks later, she took a nurse training position in a hospital, where she roomed and boarded, and got pocket money. When she went to introduce herself to the head nurse, she was told, "'You can come here, you can work like everybody else, but the war is over now, so no word about the war. . . . We won't speak about the war and you don't speak about your Jewish background. No stories.'"[2]

The head nurse had been in the resistance during the war. She had hidden Jews in that very hospital. But her message of denial was clear. She wanted, if not to forget the war, at least to ignore it. And she relegated Sara's Jewish identity and what she had experienced during the Holocaust years, if not to oblivion, at least to silence.

The postwar adaptation of survivors such as Sara is part of the history of the Holocaust, as is the absorption by western society of the catastrophe it had both permitted and endured. This complex story with its great local and national variations is beyond the scope of our book, however. Our object here is to trace the themes as they evolved, starting with the immediate postwar public silence about the persecution and murder of the Jews.

Public silence about the Holocaust was just one of many forms denial assumed after the war. As Jews, the survivors had no place in society. As human beings, they returned to naught. Survivors came home to find that their loved ones would never join them and that the Jewish community itself had been destroyed. Nothing they had left in their homes was to be found, and little that had been entrusted to friends and neighbors was recovered. It fell to the survivors to recreate a material and moral universe in which they could live once again. Among the first of the very practical problems they faced were administrative struggles and legal battles to regain their possessions. The financial loss to the Jewish communities was enormous, and the survivors attempted to recover their share in order to build again. The entire German-imposed structure which had legitimized every aspect of their material ruin (real estate, stocks and bonds, inheritances, bank account holdings, insurance policies, etc.) had to be dismantled, and the survivors struggled through this web to reclaim what had been theirs. It pitted them against their fellow countrymen who had profited by the enforced sales, the unclaimed accounts, the foregone insurance claims. For years survivors throughout the west of Europe fought with stock exchange officials, insurance companies, bank presidents.[3]

The significance of the Holocaust, the *enormity* of the Holocaust, was not acknowledged. This is not so surprising. The occupied populations had been barraged with antisemitic propaganda for a long time, and the Nazis themselves were Holocaust deniers. As we have seen, the Germans and their allies used a language of denial while involved with the actual business of murder.[4] Alerting his audience of SS leaders to the importance of what he was about to say that day in Posen in October 1943, Himmler noted that he wished to address "a really grave matter" hitherto surrounded by a "tactful" silence. "I am referring to the evacuation of the Jews, the annihilation of the Jewish people. . . . In our history, this is an unwritten and never-to-be-written page of glory."[5]

The Germans, as we know, did their best to keep it unwritten, to be opaque. They used code words for their murder system, calling deportation "resettlement" and "evacuation." Their words for murder were "special action" and "special measures." "Final solution" meant Judeocide, and "east" or "further east" meant killing centers. The SS at Auschwitz were instructed never to refer directly to gassing or to gas chambers. These words only occur by mistake; some forty of them survive in the correspondence and worksheets preserved in the Auschwitz Building Office archive. Perhaps the most important of these occurred in a letter the chief architect Karl Bischoff wrote on 29 January 1943 in which he referred to the gas chamber in the basement of crematorium 2 as a *Vergasungskeller* (gassing cellar). One architect of the Auschwitz Building Office was brought to trial in Vienna in 1972. Confronted with this letter, he remarked, "Bischoff had pointed out to me that the word 'gassing' should not appear. It is also possible that once such an order came from higher up. I can't remember that now. . . . I am surprised that Bischoff used the word 'gassing cellar' himself."[6] It is also surprising that this written record survived. In addition to the systematic attempt to avoid direct language, there was an equally systematic attempt to destroy such documentation as did exist when the Third Reich went up in flames.

Postwar denial, however, did not stem solely from negation: years of antisemitic propaganda and the wartime use of language. After the war, political movements throughout Europe advocated ideologies which, with high ideals, denied that the Jews had been singled out for murder. The newly elected Social Democratic governments in the west and the instituted Communist regimes in the east eschewed the nationalist and racist designations of Nazism and fascism. Their political theory insisted that all citizens were the same, were to be treated equally, and were to be considered as identical. In so doing, they failed to acknowledge, and indeed elided, the unique situation of the Jews during the war.

Down with the old, long live the new! the Social Democratic and Communist governments declared. The official story—east and west—was that the war had proved a fundamental rupture with the past. Europe would never return to that former world; it was gone forever. This ideology of a new beginning, a rebirth, allowed Europeans to avoid the question of accountability. Few were held responsible for national policies or programs of genocide or collusion in genocide. In each country a couple of figures were brought to court, but in general they were accused of high treason, not mass murder. The people who had benefited from their fellow countrymen's misfortunes, who had betrayed their neighbors, who had expropriated property; the bureaucrats who had maintained the national train systems and who had demanded payment for the Jews shipped on their lines; the industrialists who had used Jews as slave laborers, were rarely brought to trial. In short, the singular responsibility of each country toward its Jewish citizens was disregarded and the survivors' sensibilities dismissed. They were neither defended nor avenged.

Europeans had other concerns. In the immediate postwar period, they were preoccupied with the business of rebuilding their homes, businesses, country, and community. The cities had been bombed, the infrastructure shattered, and the financial system was in ruins. The population, which had been united under one flag before the war, had been riven apart by Nazism, fascism, and occupation. Resisters and collaborators had fought against each other for years while the great majority of people simply endured the hardships of war. There was no solidarity between these three factions. They had not experienced the war in the same way and there was no sympathy between them. It was the politicians' job to reconstruct their countries and to stitch their citizenry together. This was the predominant national project. The issue of the Jews, the iniquities perpetrated against them during the war, their current plight, and their uncertain future, was a low-priority problem. Surviving Jews were perceived to be marginal to society. Few in number, debilitated by their years of hardship, stripped of power and resources, they were not part of the mainstream.[7]

How very marginal the Jews were, and how little recognized and understood their unique predicament during the war, was reflected in the Nuremburg trials of 1946.[8] In a spectacular display of polite postwar denial, the particular assault Jewish civilians had endured was not on the agenda at Nuremburg. The concentration and extermination camps were an essential part of the case against the Nazis, but their central role in the Holocaust was irrelevant. For French prosecutors, the concentration camp empire was at the heart of a conspiracy against *civilization* itself—that very civilization France always defended so staunchly. National Socialism, Chief Prosecutor François de Menthon declared, was the negation of "all spiritual, rational, and moral values by which the nations have tried, for thousands of years, to improve human conditions." Its aim, he said, was to "plunge humanity back into barbarism, no longer the natural and spontaneous barbarism of primitive nations, but into a diabolical barbarism, conscious of itself and utilizing for its ends all material means put at the disposal of mankind by contemporary science."[9]

Most particularly, de Menthon accused the Nazis of "crimes against the human status." This, he explained, signified "all those faculties, the exercising and developing of which rightly constitute the meaning of human life."[10] The Nazis had assaulted the human status not only by decreeing whole groups—such as Slavs and Jews—to be of lesser value, but also by decreeing other groups—such as the Germans—to be of higher value. In his "everyone was a victim" argument, the Jews rated one sentence. "It is also known that racial discriminations were provoked against citizens of the occupied countries who were catalogued as Jews, measures particularly hateful, damaging to their personal rights and human dignity."[11] When the French prosecution presented six concentration camp survivors to give evidence about the German assault against civilization, they chose six gentiles. Not even the witness on the subject of atrocities at Auschwitz was a Jew: Marie Claude Vaillant Couturie, a gentile, had been arrested in 1942 for her resistance activities and deported to Auschwitz in 1943.

The Soviet chief prosecutor, Roman Rudenko, unlike his colleague de Menthon, described the Germans' atrocities against the Jews in detail, explaining the function of the *Einsatzgruppen,* the creation and liquidation of the ghettos, and the operation of the annihilation camps. At the same time, Rudenko agreed with de Menthon that the Jews were just one of many victim groups. There was nothing special about their lot. Rudenko, however, focused on his part of the world: all the inhabitants of eastern Europe were subjected to the same horrific misery. Indeed, the Jews came at the very end of the list. The Nazi

> New Order was a regime of terror by which, in the countries seized by the Hitlerites, all democratic institutions were abolished and all civil rights of the population were abrogated, while the countries themselves were plundered and rapaciously exploited. The population of these countries, and of

the Slav countries above others—especially Russians, Ukrainians, Bielorussians, Poles, Czechs, Serbians, Slovenes, Jews—were subjected to merciless persecution and mass extermination.[12]

The Americans and the British followed the Soviet model. German crimes against the Jews were framed within an equalizing structure. The American chief prosecutor, Robert H. Jackson, used the category "Persecution and Extermination of Jews and Christians."[13] The British chief prosecutor, Sir Hartley Shawcross, discussed the Holocaust in tandem with a lengthy discussion of the assault of many other peoples, especially the Slavs. "Genocide was not restricted to extermination of the Jewish people or the Gypsies," Sir Hartley told the court. "The technique varied from nation to nation, from people to people. The long-term aim was the same in all cases."[14] And even though the Kommandant of Auschwitz himself, Rudolf Höss, was arrested by the British, Sir Hartley did not bring him to the stand. Höss was called as a witness for the *defense*—the defense of Ernst Kaltenbrunner, the person who had taken the place of the assassinated Reinhard Heydrich as second in command to SS chief Heinrich Himmler.

The Nazis and the millions of people who collaborated with them had indeed targeted many groups for victimization. Given enough time, they would have subjected the Slav peoples to the machinery of death we call the Holocaust. With 10 million civilians and POWs killed by the end of the war, the Germans and their allies had made a beginning. Their ultimate intention, however, was not translated into a fully actualized program. On V-E Day, it was the Jews who had been wiped out, and Jewish culture in Europe which had been obliterated. That root of western society was eradicated. Sir Hartley grasped, if only briefly, the full measure of this iniquity. "There is one group to which the method of annihilation was applied on a scale so immense that it is my duty to refer separately to the evidence. I mean the extermination of the Jews. If there were no other crime against these men, this one alone, in which all of them were implicated, would suffice. History holds no parallel to these horrors."[15] Such statements were rare, however. In the 100-page preamble to the judgment explaining the nature of the crimes at issue, the murder of the Jews claimed but five pages.[16]

The establishment of the State of Israel in 1948 did not break the public silence about the Holocaust. Europeans, even those who had happily participated in the persecution of the Jews before 1945, were suddenly enthusiastic supporters of the new state because it provided a country for the Jews to build— an unwitting but nonetheless bizarre echo of Nazi support of Zionism in 1933. The survivors too could work toward the future of their own nation. Israel was a convenient counterpart to their own agenda and, by the way, an expedient national home—not for the Jews as individuals, but for people whose very presence remained a challenge to the Europeans' carefully constructed national histories of the war years and national self-perception as resistance heroes and charitable Christians.

Silence reigned in Israel too. Little sympathy was wasted on the "victims." Rather, the "martyrs and heroes" of the Jewish resistance were acknowledged and valorized. Yom ha-Shoah (Holocaust Remembrance Day), established by the Israeli parliament in 1951, was linked on the calendar to the Warsaw ghetto uprising. The new Israeli government faced hostile neighboring states, a weak economy, a country that wanted for nearly everything, and hundreds of thousands of traumatized fresh immigrants. They wanted the survivors to become strong, and to join the infant state in its mission. The government's goal was not to deal with the problems the survivors had brought with them, but to re-form and re-fashion them into future citizens.

The survivors understood. They recovered, gained weight, became healthy. They learned Hebrew, and abandoned the language, culture, and traditions of the world of their birth. Like Sara Spier in the Netherlands, they did not speak in public about what had happened to them in Europe. But it is not true that survivors of the Holocaust fell silent. What is true is that, as there was no public forum for their voice, they spoke to each other and at *Landsmanschaften* ([European] hometown fraternal organization) meetings. There were islands of speech, of articulated memory, but these islands were not in the public sphere.[17]

The trial of Adolf Eichmann exploded the silence barrier. Kidnapped by the Israelis from Argentina in 1960, Eichmann was brought to court in Jerusalem a year later. His trial focused attention on the Holocaust as never before. The highly public examination of one man—not a group or representatives of a system, but a single person—foregrounded the question of the psychological motivation of the bureaucratic murderer. And the highly visible witnesses for the prosecution were Jews. For the first time, survivors were prominent, present, and publicly vocal.[18]

The State of Israel became a voice for the murdered Jews of Europe. The victims of the Holocaust—the dead and the living—were embraced in the community of Israel.[19] The state, personified by Chief Prosecutor Gideon Hausner, spoke for the European Jews.

> As I stand before you, Judges of Israel, to lead the prosecution of Adolf Eichmann, I am not standing alone. With me are six million accusers. But they cannot rise to their feet and point an accusing finger towards him who sits in the dock and cry: "I accuse." For their ashes are piled up on the hills of Auschwitz and the fields of Treblinka, and are strewn in the forests of Poland. Their graves are scattered throughout the length and breadth of Europe. Their blood cries out, but their voice is not heard. Therefore I will be their spokesman and in their name I will unfold the awesome indictment.[20]

Hausner explained how the Holocaust was a unique crime in human history to date. Acknowledging earlier "wars of extermination," he noted that what was at issue here was a distinction with a difference. "Only in our generation has a nation attacked an entire defenseless and peaceful population, men and women, greybeards, children and infants, incarcerated them behind electrified fences, imprisoned them in concentration camps, and resolved to destroy them utterly." Hausner impressed upon his audience—which through the news media had grown to the entire western world—that this was "a new kind of murder." It involved "calculated decision and a painstaking planning; not through the evil design of an individual, but through a mighty criminal conspiracy involving thousands; not against one victim . . . but against an entire nation."[21]

The Eichmann trial affected the nation dramatically. Day after day, the proceedings were carried live on radio. School administrators canceled classes so that students might listen. People stood on line for seats in the courtroom. It was a pivotal moment. Hausner presented more than a hundred survivors as witnesses for the prosecution, men and women from every age, country, social background, and intellectual level: a true cross section of the nation. They could not testify about Eichmann's role or German criminal responsibility. But they—and only they—could describe how their daily lives had been shaped by the criminals and their crimes. Their experiences in the German-decreed ghettos, hunted by the *Einsatzgruppen,* in the camps, were essential to the court proceedings. The voices of the survivors and the suffering of the victims were acknowledged, honored, and legitimized. "Witnesses spoke Hebrew, Yiddish, German, Polish, English, more languages," Martha Gellhorn reported for the *Atlantic Monthly.*

> It was visible torture for all the witnesses to speak; one wandered in his head, screamed something wordless but terrifying to hear, fainted, remembering Auschwitz. The audience was tense, still, straining forward to listen, until now and again a voice would cry out in despair; then the police silently led the disturber from the hall. The glaring light—for the security of the prisoner, for the hidden television—hurt the eyes. The air conditioning was too cold, and yet one sweated. Every day was more than the mind and heart could bear; and the Trial was kept running, always on time, always under quiet control. No lawyers or judges anywhere else have been presented with such a task or so dominated it.[22]

In the Eichmann trial, in short, the Holocaust—the murder of the European Jews—for the first time was the central issue before the court.

The trial reframed the historical significance of the Holocaust not only in Israel but throughout the west. It was a turning point, and Holland took the lead.[23] By 1950, Dutch Jews and gentiles had agreed upon a mutually tolerable interpretation of the war years. "The persecution of the Jews in the Netherlands, even if it happened on Dutch soil, is not properly Dutch history," the Bergen-Belsen survivor Abel J. Herzberg maintained in his *Kroniek der Joden-vervolging, 1940–1945* (1950), the first systematic chronicle of the persecution of the Jews. "It did not arise from Dutch circumstances. One can even say with certainty that it could not have arisen from it. The *resistance* against the persecution of the Jews has been a Dutch affair."[24]

With the Eichmann trial, however, history closed in on the Netherlands. The received version of the past which had worked so well for a decade and a half began to fall apart. The trial, as well as time, the opportunity for reflection, and the advent of prosperity, led to a reinterpretation of the war years. In Louis de Jong's television series *Bezetting (Occupation)* the question of the Jews finally was raised—albeit in a limited context. Aired between 1960 and 1965, the twenty-one episodes became a national event. People who did not have a television went to those who did. The streets were empty.

Like its predecessors, *Bezetting* was a black-and-white vision, with occupiers and resisters, villains and heroes. The great mass of people who accommodated was left out and everyone could identify with the heroes. Even so, de Jong specifically included the persecution of the Jews. Echoing themes raised during the war by Victor Gollancz and Arthur Koestler, de Jong claimed that the mass murder of the Jews was not stopped because no one could imagine it. De Jong, a Jewish employee of the Dutch government-in-exile, had heard about the Holocaust from safety in London. He believed the news but he understood that most people could not. He did not bridge the question of responsibility; nevertheless, the cataclysm of the Judeocide was part of the history he told. "I feel a great need to speak some words to you as an introduction to what follows," de Jong began in the episode chronicling the early stages of the Shoah in Holland.

> As the result of the persecution of the Jews more than 100,000 of our fellow citizens were killed—men, women and children. I do not only want merely to mention these human losses—I want especially to point out that these losses occurred not as the result of a sudden explosion of a bomb, not as the result of death in military battle, but because all these struggling people were caught in the wheels of a merciless machine of destruction that, especially in the years 1942 and 1943, operated right through our own society. Young people who did not live through this period of fathomless horror ask us older people questions, often questions of conscience, which always converge on this one: How could this happen? It is a question with many answers. One of the answers is—and that I want to mention specifically first—that the imagination of most people (Jews and non-Jews) was unable to grasp in time that the National Socialists literally meant what they said when they spoke about the destruction of the Jews.[25]

Nearly twenty years after the war had ended, the murder of the Dutch Jews had become a central event in Dutch history. De Jong had written the Jews into the history of the Netherlands during the war. The disaster which had befallen them was part of the occupation of the nation. It was the historian and survivor Jacob Presser, however, who questioned the paradigm of suppression versus resistance, shaped the problem of responsibility, and precipitated the recognition of the dull gray of everyday collusion. Presser did not frame a historical context, he did not distinguish between different phases of persecution, and he treated the persecutors as a homogenous group. For him, the five-year oppression was a storm that had beaten the Jews senselessly, and he told the story of their death. His was the voice of lost neighbors, brothers, sisters, parents. "As I became more involved with the subject," Presser explained, "an understanding grew slowly of a special moral obligation . . . to be the voice of those who, fated to an eternal silence, would be heard only here and now, only for this one time. One time more on earth will their lamentation, their accusation resound. Nothing was left of their most pitiful possessions in their last hours, their ashes were scattered in the winds. They had no one in the world other than the historian who could hand down their message."[26]

Presser's *Ondergang* (*Going Under*, 1965) swept the country. From the beginning, it was seen as a monument. "The war is over, the liberation remembered, and there will be much joy, even perhaps at our war memorials. Only one thing was missing still: a memorial for the Jews who succumbed almost defenseless,"[27] the influential *Algemeen Handelsblad* (*General Business Journal*) observed. Presser's book filled that void. The politician Han Lammers urged that the book be subsidized so that everyone could afford to buy it. Only thus would it be possible to "make the monument, that Presser's book is, into a National Monument."[28]

There was no doubt that Presser's work was—and was accepted as—a monument. But was it a monument to Dutch Jews, or to Dutch failure? The Dutch began to search their souls. Letters to the editor filled the newspapers. One woman, B. Buitenrust Hettema, summarized the feelings of many that year: "We live. Many of those whom we are about to remember would also live today if we had a little bit more courage, a little bit more sense of responsibility, a little less cowardice, a little less love of ease."[29]

What Jacob Presser had done for the Dutch Jews, Georges Wellers did for the French with the publication first of a number of articles and then of his book, *L'Etoile Jaune à l'Heure de Vichy* (*The Yellow Star During the Vichy Era*, 1973), and Renzo de Felice did for the Italians with *Storia degli ebrei sotto il fascismo* (*The History of the Jews Under Fascism*, 1972). Both works were catalogued under the recently created U.S. Library of Congress subject heading "Holocaust—Jewish, 1939–1945." Established in 1968, the new classification reflected the way people had begun to think about the past, and the concomitant developments in the historical literature. These works, in turn, prompted broader perspectives. Each one of the Jewish victims had had neighbors. What had those neighbors done?

This very question was asked by young people involved in the 1968 student rebellions across the west, and even into Czechoslovakia and Poland. They were the generation born during or just after the war. They had been raised with stories of the German occupation in which resistance was considered the norm. Current scholarship revealed that few had been active in the resistance. In the eyes of many young people, the Holocaust represented the failure of bourgeois society. They focused on the role of non-German populations, of their parents and their peers, in the destruction of the Jews. Collaboration and collusion loomed large as the perspective moved away from the highways of history to the side streets, the streets where people actually lived. It was not history from above, but the story of those below—of ordinary people.

The official ideology of rupture and renewal, conceived in the immediate postwar years and preserved in the historiography of the war in the fifties and sixties, became suspect. Historians, novelists, and filmmakers questioned the idea that Nazism, and its vehicle, the German occupation of a large part of Europe, had been a decisive divide in European history. The focus shifted to the continuities from the 1930s through the 1960s. Accommodation was the norm, resistance the exception, and continuity was located in gray, everyday, tacit collusion. This was brilliantly illustrated by Marcel Ophüls in his film *Le Chagrin et la Pitié* (*The Sorrow and the Pity,* 1967) which traced the history of one French town, Clermont-Ferrand, during the occupation. Ophüls illuminated the constant of cowardly accommodation rather than the ideologically correct view of heroic rupture.

The Holocaust was well acknowledged by the 1980s. An all too rich body of denier literature also emerged, however, starting with the infamous Faurisson affair.[30] The catalyst for this scandal was a *L'Express* interview with Louis Darquier de Pellepoix. Living in comfortable exile in Spain, the former Vichy Commissioner General for Jewish Affairs alleged that the Holocaust had not occurred, that there had been no homicidal gas chambers in Auschwitz. "Only lice were gassed in Auschwitz," he declared.[31]

The Darquier interview provided Robert Faurisson, a French literary critic who had come to believe that the Holocaust never happened, with the opportunity he had been seeking for many years. Within days, he was published in the socialist newspaper *Le Matin.* The Darquier interview ought to convince the French that the Holocaust was fiction and the gas chambers fabrications, he asserted. "I hereby proclaim . . . that the massacres in so-called 'gas chambers' are a historical lie."[32]

The well-respected French newspaper *Le Monde* published (29 December 1978) a letter by Robert Faurisson entitled "Le problème des chambres de gaz, ou le rumeur d'Auschwitz" (The Problem of the Gas Chambers, or the Rumor of Auschwitz). "Nazism is dead, quite dead, and so is its Führer," Faurisson declared. "Today, only the truth remains. Let us dare to proclaim it: The nonexistence of the gas chambers is good news for pitiful humanity."[33] Worried, in advance, of the effect Fourisson's letter might have, the editors of *Le Monde*

asked Georges Wellers to write a letter of refutation. Both letters were published at the same time on the same page, thus creating the literary illusion that
the arguments were of equal significance and were equally valid. The publication of such language by the prestigious and influential *Le Monde* brought the
negationist denial of the gas chambers into public prominence for the first time.
Faurisson's coup had immediate reverberations outside France. An Italian
survivor of Auschwitz, the writer Primo Levi, responded in an interview in
Corriere della Sera.

> The operation has succeeded: it is not enough to read the horrors of Dar-
> quier de Pellepoix in *L'Express* last November, not enough to allow the mur-
> derers of those days space and voice in respectable magazines, so that they
> may dictate their truth with impunity: the truth that the millions of dead in
> the camps never died, that Genocide is a fable, that in Auschwitz they only
> used gas to kill lice. All that is obviously not enough. Obviously the time is
> ripe, and from his university chair Professor Faurisson comes to put the
> world at ease. Fascism and Nazism have been denigrated, slandered. We
> don't talk about Auschwitz any more: that was a sham. We talk about the lie
> of Auschwitz, the Jews are cheats, they always have been cheats, and liars,
> liars enough to concoct the gas chambers and the crematorium ovens all by
> themselves, *after the event.* . . . The trick succeeds. Black turns white. The
> dead are not dead, there is no murderer, there is no more guilt. There never
> was. It wasn't me who did something. That thing itself no longer exists.
>   No, Professor, life is not like that. The dead are truly dead. . . . If you deny
> the slaughter organized by your friends of that time, you must explain why,
> from 17 million in 1939, Jews were reduced to 11 million in 1945. You must
> deny the hundreds of thousands of widows and orphans, and you must deny
> us, the survivors. . . . [W]hat have the university authorities done in France,
> and the law? By letting you deny the dead, they have tolerated your killing
> them a second time.[34]

Back in France, thirty-seven prominent historians published a declaration
stating flatly that the question of whether such a mass murder was possible technically should not be raised—it was technically possible because it had occurred.
There is not, nor can there be, a debate over the existence of the gas chambers.[35]
Such a declaration did not settle the matter, of course. The Faurisson affair was
in full swing, and lurched forward until 1988, when Fred Leuchter from Massachusetts went to Auschwitz to "prove" that no gassings had occurred. He
published his good news findings in the *Leuchter Report,* hailed in denier circles
as a great breakthrough, and still very much in circulation fifteen years later.[36]
    Throughout the last decades of the twentieth century and into the twenty-
first, deniers of the Holocaust have continued their campaign to convince people—especially the college-aged—that there were no homicidal gas chambers

at Auschwitz and that there was no systematic attempt to annihilate Europe's
Jews. The Internet and strategic use of the alphabet have proved valuable tools:
students with little or no education about the Holocaust turn to search engines.
Choosing the first entries, they find themselves in denier web sites.

DENIERS OF the Holocaust are on the fringe, however. It may have taken fifty
years, but at the beginning of the twenty-first century, the western world has
come to acknowledge its own history. Every day, people read about contemporary issues rooted in the Holocaust that have come to the fore. The intense public interest in, and media coverage of, these events show no sign of abating. On
the contrary. The thorny question of "neutrality," well illustrated by the Swiss
gold controversy, has only begun to emerge. And what about the many shades
of culpability for collusion by big businesses—companies that profited from
"Aryanization," that profited from "unverifiable deaths," that profited from the
use of forced and slave laborers. The conundrum of identity and the secrets of
the past, foregrounded by the drama of former Secretary of State Madeleine
Albright's Jewish roots and the claims of heirs to paintings exhibited publicly in
major museums, continue to claim newspaper headlines.

Revelations about the Holocaust years awake passions throughout the western world. When a short book called *Neighbors* was published in 2000, describing how Poles turned on their Jewish neighbors in the town of Jedwabne in
1941, it triggered trenchant national debate.[37] Finally, thousands of Poles gathered in Jedwabne where, filmed by news programs worldwide, the Polish president asked Jews to forgive Polish crimes against Jews in Poland for centuries.
And Vatican leaders, realizing how Catholic doctrines have sown the seed for
modern antisemitism, finally have begun to tackle the church's fraught 2,000-
year-old relation to Judaism and Jews.

Indeed: the tentacles of the Holocaust reach deeply into the present and
nourish interest in the past. For early twenty-first-century war crimes trial
judges, adjudicating genocidal actions in Africa and the Balkans, Holocaust
atrocities served as a warning, a negative model.

In 1969, twenty-five years after the Nazis dismantled the gas chambers of
Auschwitz, the Jewish philosopher Emil Fackenheim observed that "the Nazi
Holocaust is totally present, contemporary, and nonanachronistic. The passage of time has brought it closer rather than moving it farther away."[38] His
assessment is echoed in the skylines of Washington, New York, Boston, Los
Angeles, Paris, Berlin, Vienna, and Jerusalem, changed by the erection of a
major museum, monument, or memorial to commemorate the Holocaust. Visibly in the center of the civic domain, these public buildings are expressions of
acceptance of the Holocaust as a pivotal event in the history of western civilization. They are expressions, too, of our continuing effort to understand its
significance.

The nomenclature of the SS ranks derived from the Free Corps of the period immediately after World War I, and consciously departed from army tradition, with its rigid social and functional distinctions between privates, non-commissioned officers, junior officers, senior officers, and general officers. In the SS, common membership in the organization was more important than functional difference in rank, and therefore all SS ranks from Corporal upward were designated as *Führer* (leader). The level of one's leadership was based on the size of the unit, which could be a *Rotte* (troop), *Schar* (group), *Sturm* (platoon), *Bann* (battalion), *Standarte* (regiment), *Brigade* (brigade), or *Gruppe* (division). Through the adjectives *unter-* (junior-), *ober-* (senior-), and *haupt-* (chief-), fine-tuning was obtained. The adjective *oberst-* (most senior-) was only used for the rank of SS-Oberstgruppenführer, right below the supreme rank of Reichsführer-SS.

SS-Schütze	Private
SS-Oberschütze	Private First Class
SS-Sturmmann	Acting Corporal
SS-Rottenführer	Corporal
SS-Unterscharführer	Sergeant
SS-Scharführer	Staff Sergeant
SS-Oberscharführer	Sergeant First Class
SS-Hauptscharführer	Master Sergeant
SS-Sturmscharführer	Sergeant Major
SS-Untersturmführer	Second Lieutenant
SS-Obersturmführer	First Lieutenant
SS-Hauptsturmführer	Captain
SS-Sturmbannführer	Major
SS-Obersturmbannführer	Lieutenant Colonel
SS-Standartenführer	Colonel
SS-Oberführer	[no equivalent]
SS-Brigadeführer	Brigadier General
SS-Gruppenführer	Major General
SS-Obergruppenführer	Lieutenant General
SS-Oberstgruppenführer	General
Reichsführer-SS	[no equivalent]

Notes

For the convience of the reader, all books translated into English are cited in the English edition. We have translated all other texts, interviews, and archive documents.

The names of survivors as they appear in the text are as they were at the time, with the insertion of women's married names, if used. The corresponding names in the notes are those in current use. Thus, for example, Hanna Kent-Sztarkman was born Hanna Sztarkman; Kent is her married name (read Hanna Kent, *née* Sztarkman). The current spelling of her name is Hannah Kent-Starkman, which is how it appears in the notes.

Note that page numbers have been given for the interview transcripts, although neither the tapes nor texts are held in a public repository. It is our hope that eventually they will be made available, and we have provided specific citations with that end in mind.

Introduction: DEATH'S GREAT CARNIVAL

1. See the Introduction, Miklós Radnóti, *The Complete Poetry,* trans. Emery George (Ann Arbor: Ardis, 1980).
2. See Zvi Erez, "Jews for Copper: Jewish-Hungarian Labor Service Companies in Bor," *Yad Vashem Studies,* vol. 28 (2000), 243–86.
3. Nathan Eck, "The March of Death from Serbia to Hungary (September, 1944) and the Slaughter of Cservenka," *Yad Vashem Studies,* vol. 2 (1958), 255–94.
4. Radnóti, *The Complete Poetry,* 277.
5. Ibid., 276.

Chapter One: JEWS, GENTILES, AND GERMANS

1. For more on this subject, see Elma Verhey, *Om het joodse kind* (Amsterdam: Nijgh & Van Ditmar, 1991), and Debórah Dwork, "Custody and Care of Jewish Children in the Postwar Netherlands: Ethnic Identity and Cultural Hegemony," in Peter Hayes, ed., *Lessons and Legacies,* Vol. III, *Memory, Memorialization, and Denial* (Evanston: Northwestern University Press, 1999), 109–37.
2. Verhey, *Om het joodse kind,* 23; Dwork, "Custody and Care of Jewish Children in the Postwar Netherlands," 113.
3. "De Joodsche Oorlogspleegkinderen?" *Trouw,* 13 June 1945, 1f.
4. "Diefstal van JOODSE KINDEREN," *Trouw,* 25 May, 1946.
5. See Debórah Dwork and Robert Jan van Pelt, "German Persecution and Dutch Accommodation: The Evolution of the Dutch National Consciousness of the Judeocide," in David Wyman, ed., *The World Reacts to the Holocaust* (Baltimore: Johns Hopkins University Press, 1996), 45–77.
6. On the shape of tradition, see David Gross, *The Past in Ruins: Tradition and the Critique of Modernity* (Amherst: University of Massachusetts Press, 1992), 8–19.
7. Matthew 16:18.
8. II Corinthians 3:6.
9. Hebrews 10:1.
10. Jeremiah 31:31–33.
11. Thomas Aquinas, *Summa contra Gentiles,* trans. James F. Anderson, 5 vols. (Notre Dame and London: University of Notre Dame Press, 1975), vol. 2, 137.
12. Dante Alighieri, *Monarchy,* trans. Prue Shaw (Cambridge: Cambridge University Press, 1996), 7.

13. See Jacob Katz, *Exclusiveness and Tolerance: Studies in Jewish-Gentile Relations in Medieval and Modern Times* (London: Oxford University Press, 1961), 24–47. See also Jacob Katz, *Tradition and Crisis: Jewish Society at the End of the Middle Ages* (New York: Schocken Books, 1971), 3–75, and H. H. Ben-Sasson, "The Middle Ages," in H. H. Ben Sasson, ed., *A History of the Jewish People* (Cambridge, MA: Harvard University Press, 1976), 385–723.

14. Ben-Sasson, "The Middle Ages," 561.

15. See David Nirenberg, *Communities of Violence: Persecution of Minorities in the Middle Ages* (Princeton: Princeton University Press, 1996).

16. Anne Brenon, *Les Cathares, vie et mort d'une église chrétienne* (Paris: Grancher, 1996).

17. See, for example, Gianfranco Poggi, *The Development of the Modern State* (Stanford: Stanford University Press, 1978); David Parker, *The Making of French Absolutism* (New York: St. Martin's Press, 1983); and Marc Raeff, *The Well-Ordered Police State* (New Haven: Yale University Press, 1983).

18. For a classic analysis of this, see Alexis de Tocqueville, *The Old Regime and the Revolution,* ed. François Furet and Françoise Mélono, trans. Alan S. Kahan (Chicago and London: University of Chicago Press, 1998), 196ff.

19. See, for example, Peter Gay, *The Party of Humanity* (New York: Alfred A. Knopf, 1964), 103–08.

20. Stanislaw de Clermont-Tonnerre, "Opinion," in *L'Assemblée Nationale Constituante: Motions, Discours et Rapports, la législation nouvelle.* Vol. 7 of *La Révolution Française et l'émancipation des Juifs* (Paris: EDHIS, 1968), 13.

21. On the Jewish enlightenment, see Michael A. Meyer, *The Origins of the Modern Jew: Jewish Identity and European Culture in Germany, 1794–1824* (Detroit: Wayne State University Press, 1967); also Jacob Katz, *Out of the Ghetto: The Social Background of Jewish Emancipation, 1770–1870* (Cambridge, MA: Harvard University Press, 1973).

22. See Patrick Girard, *La Révolution Française et les Juifs* (Paris: Laffont, 1989). For a good and concise account in the English language, see Paula E. Hyman, *The Jews of Modern France* (Berkeley: University of California Press, 1998), 17–35.

23. See Simon Schwarzfuchs, *Napoleon, the Jews and the Sanhedrin* (London, Boston, and Henley-on-Thames, UK: Routledge & Kegan Paul, 1979), and Franz Kobler, *Napoleon and the Jews* (New York: Schocken Books, 1976). The classic work on the topic is Robert Anchel, *Napoléon et les Juifs* (Paris: Presses Universitaires de France, 1928).

24. Schwarzfuchs, *Napoleon, the Jews and the Sanhedrin, 62.*

25. Kobler, *Napoleon and the Jews, 146.*

26. De Tocqueville, *The Old Regime and the Revolution, 98.*

27. For a penetrating analysis of the significance of the decapitation of Louis XVI as a universal fall from grace and the beginning of modern totalitarianism, see Albert Camus, *The Rebel,* trans. Anthony Bower (London: Hamish Hamilton, 1953), 89–93.

28. Ernest Renan, "What Is a Nation?" in Omar Dahbour and Micheline R. Ishay, eds., *The Nationalism Reader* (Atlantic Highlands, NJ: Humanities Press, 1995), 153.

29. See Francis Delaisi, *Political Myths and Economic Realities* (London: Noel Douglas, 1925).

30. Jules Michelet, *The People,* trans. John P. McKay (Urbana, Chicago, and London: University of Illinois Press, 1973), 204.

31. See Jacob Katz, "A State Within a State: History of an Anti-Semitic Slogan," in Jacob Katz, *Emancipation and Assimilation: Studies in Modern Jewish History* (Farnborough, UK: Gregg International Publishers, 1972), 47–76.

32. Fichte, "Beitrag zur Berichtigung der Urteile des Publikums über die französische Revolution," in Johann Gottlieb Fichte, *Schriften zur Revolution,* ed. Bernard Willms (Cologne and Opladen: Westdeutscher Verlag, 1967), 114–15.

33. For a solid overview of nineteenth-century antisemitism in Germany and Austria, see John Weiss, *Ideology of Death: Why the Holocaust Happened in Germany* (Chicago: Ivan R. Dee, 1996); also Jacob Katz, *From Prejudice to Destruction: Anti-Semitism, 1700–1933* (Cambridge, MA: Harvard University Press, 1980).

34. Michelet, *The People, 93.*

35. Heinrich von Treitschke, *History of Germany in the Nineteenth Century,* trans. Eden and Cedar Paul, 8 vols. (London: Jarrold & Sons, 1915), vol. 4, 556.

36. See Paul Lawrence Rose, *Revolutionary Antisemitism in Germany: From Kant to Wagner* (Princeton: Princeton University Press, 1990).

37. Letter to his mother, 26 May 1805, in Ludwig Börne, *Sämtliche Schriften,* ed. Inge and Peter Rippmann, 5 vols. (Düsseldorf: Joseph Melzer, 1977), vol. 4, 121.

38. See Orlando Figes, "Ludwig Börne and the Formation of a Radical Critique of Judaism," *Year Book of the Leo Baeck Institute,* vol. 29 (1984), 351–82.

39. See Julius Carlebach, *Karl Marx and the Radical Critique of Judaism* (London and Boston: Routledge & Kegan Paul, 1978).

40. Karl Marx, "On the Jewish Question," in Robert C. Tucker, ed., *The Marx-Engels Reader,* 2d edn. (New York and London: W. W. Norton, 1978), 48.

41. Ibid., 50.

42. Karl Marx and Friedrich Engels, "Manifesto of the Communist Party," in Tucker, ed., *The Marx-Engels Reader,* 500.

43. Wagner, "The Revolution," in Richard Wagner, *Richard Wagner's Prose Works,* trans. William Ashton Ellis, 8 vols. (London: Kegan Paul, Trench, Trübner & Co., 1899), vol. 8, 232f.

44. Ibid., 237f.

45. Wagner, "Judaism in Music," *Prose Works,* vol. 3, 81f.

46. On Marr, see Moshe Zimmermann, *Wilhelm Marr: The Patriarch of Anti-Semitism* (New York and Oxford: Oxford University Press, 1986).

47. Wagner, "What Is German?" *Prose Works,* vol. 4, 158.

48. Adolf Hitler, *Mein Kampf,* trans. Ralph Manheim (Boston: Houghton Mifflin, 1971), 57f.

49. Wagner, "What Is German?" *Prose Works,* vol. 4, 163. Italics in the original.

50. On the history of European racism, see George L. Mosse, *Toward the Final Solution: A History of European Racism* (New York: Howard Fertig, 1978); Léon Poliakov, *The Aryan Myth: A History of Racist and Nationalistic Ideas in Europe* (New York: Barnes & Noble, 1996); and Fritz Stern, *The Politics of Cultural Despair: A Study in the Rise of Germanic Ideology* (Berkeley: University of California Press, 1961).

51. Joseph Arthur Count de Gobineau, "Essay on the Inequality of the Human Races," in *Selected Political Writings,* ed. Michael D. Biddiss (New York: Harper & Row, 1970), 162f.

52. Renan, "What Is a Nation?" in Dahbour and Ishay, eds., *The Nationalism Reader,* 147.

53. Ibid., 149.

54. Ibid., 150.

55. Gobineau, "Essay on the Inequality of the Human Races," 68f.

56. Hitler, *Mein Kampf,* 296.

57. Ibid., 249.

58. Adolf Hitler, *Hitler's Secret Book,* introduction Telford Taylor, trans. Salvator Attanasio (New York: Grove Press, 1961), 28f.

59. Eugen Kretzer, *Joseph Arthur Graf von Gobineau: Sein Leben und sein Werk* (Leipzig: Hermann Seemann Nachfolger, 1902), 1.

60. Ibid., 71.

61. Ibid., 127.

62. Ibid., 128.

63. See, for example, Friedrich Nietzsche, *The Will to Power,* ed. Walter Kaufmann, trans. Walter Kaufmann and R. J. Hollingdale (New York: Random House, 1967), 97–162.

64. Ibid., 519.

65. Houston Stewart Chamberlain, *Foundations of the Nineteenth Century,* trans. John Lees, 2 vols. (London & New York: John Lane, 1912), vol. 1, 331.

66. See Jack Wertheimer, *Unwelcome Strangers: East European Jews in Imperial Germany* (New York and Oxford: Oxford University Press, 1987).

67. Heinrich von Treitschke, "Unsere Aussichten," *Preussische Jahrbücher,* vol. 44 (1879), 572–73.

68. Theodor Mommsen, *Auch ein Wort über unser Judenthum* (Berlin: Weidemann, 1880), 11.

69. For an overview of antisemitism in France before the Dreyfus Affair began, see Robert F. Byrnes, *Antisemitism in Modern France, Vol. 1, The Prologue to the Dreyfus Affair* (New Brunswick: Rutgers University Press, 1950).

70. See Eric Cahm, *The Dreyfus Affair in French Society and Politics* (London and New York: Longman, 1996).

71. Quoted in ibid., 10.

72. Bernard Lazare, *L'Affaire Dreyfus: Une erreur judiciaire* (Paris: Editions Allia, 1998), 6.

73. Emile Zola, "A Plea for the Jews," in *The Dreyfus Affair: J'accuse and Other Writings,* ed. Alain Pagès, trans. Eleanor Levieux (New Haven and London: Yale University Press, 1996), 4f.

74. Emile Zola, "Letter to the Young People," in *The Dreyfus Affair: J'accuse and Other Writings,* 33.

75. Ibid.

76. It was not until 7 September 1995, however, that the French army officially declared Dreyfus innocent.

77. Quoted in Alex Bein, "Theodor Herzl, a Biography," in Theodor Herzl, *The Jewish State* (New York: Dover Books, 1988), 34.

78. Ibid., 39f.

Chapter Two: THE GREAT WAR AND ITS TERRIBLE OUTCOME

1. Ralph H. Lutz, *Fall of the German Empire, Documents 1914–18,* 2 vols. (Stanford: Stanford University Press, 1932), vol. 1, 9. See also Peter Fritsche, *Germans into Nazis* (Cambridge: Harvard University Press, 1998), 13ff.

2. Adolf Hitler, *Mein Kampf*, trans. Ralph Manheim (Boston: Houghton Mifflin, 1943), 161.

3. Stefan Zweig, *The World of Yesterday* (London: Cassell & Co., 1943), 173f.

4. See Michael Geyer, "German Strategy in the Age of Machine Warfare, 1914–1945," in Peter Paret with Gordon A Craig and Felix Gilbert, eds., *Makers of Modern Strategy from Machiavelli to the Nuclear Age* (Princeton: Princeton University Press, 1986), 535ff.

5. Henri Barbusse, *Under Fire: The Story of a Squad (Le Feu)*, trans. Fitzwater Wray (New York: E. P. Dutton, 1917), 338f.

6. Quoted in Thomas Nevin, *Ernst Jünger and Germany: Into the Abyss, 1914–1945* (Durham, NC: Duke University Press, 1996), 65f.

7. See Roger Chickering, *Imperial Germany and the Great War, 1914–1918* (Cambridge: Cambridge University Press, 1998), 140ff.; Fritsche, *Germans into Nazis*, 66ff.; and Richard Bessel, *Germany After the First World War* (Oxford: Clarendon Press, 1993), 37ff.

8. Chickering, *Imperial Germany and the Great War*, 95ff.; Fritsche, *Germans into Nazis*, 36ff.

9. Jünger, "Die totale Mobilmachung," in Ernst Jünger, ed., *Krieg und Krieger* (Berlin: Junker und Dünnhaupt Verlag, 1930), 28.

10. Ibid., 29.

11. Karl Benno von Mechow, "Inneres Reich," *Das Innere Reich*, vol. 1 (1934), 5f.

12. A comprehensive, multi-author study of the changing relations between German Jews and Germans in and after the Great War is Werner E. Mosse, ed., *Deutsches Judentum in Krieg und Revolution 1916–1923* (Tübingen: J. C. B. Mohr, 1971).

13. Hitler, *Mein Kampf*, 193.

14. See Werner T. Angress, "The German Army's 'Judenzählung' of 1916: Genesis-Consequences-Significance," *Year Book of the Leo Baeck Institute*, vol. 23 (1978), 117–37; see also David Vital, *A People Apart: The Jews in Europe, 1789–1939* (Oxford and New York: Oxford University Press, 1999), 648ff.

15. Franz Oppenheimer, *Die Judenstatistik des preussischen Kriegsministeriums* (Munich: Verlag für Kulturpolitik, 1922), 48.

16. See Saul Friedländer, "Die politische Veränderungen der Kriegszeit und ihre Auswirkungen auf die Judenfrage," and Werner Jochmann, "Die Ausbreitung des Antisemitismus," in Mosse, ed., *Deutsches Judentum in Krieg und Revolution*, 27–65 and 409–510.

17. Oswald Spengler, *The Decline of the West*, trans. Charles Francis Atkinson, 2 vols. (New York: Alfred A. Knopf, 1970), vol. 2, 319.

18. The Jews argued otherwise. See David J. Engel, "Patriotism as a Shield: The Liberal Jewish Defence Against Antisemitism in Germany During the First World War," *Year Book of the Leo Baeck Institute*, vol. 31 (1986), 147–71.

19. Georg Hermann, "Weltabschied: Ein Essay," in *Unvorhanden und stumm, doch zu Menschen noch reden*, ed. Laureen Nussbaum (Mannheim: Persona Verlag, 1991), 237.

20. Ibid., 233f.

21. Ibid., 234.

22. Hitler, *Mein Kampf*, 169.

23. Quoted in A. J. Toynbee, *Turkey: A Past and a Future* (New York: George Doran, 1917), 15f.

24. Quoted in Vahakn N. Dadrian, "The Secret Young-Turk Ittihadist Conference and the Decision for the World War I Genocide of the Armenians," *Holocaust and Genocide Studies*, vol. 7 (1993), 181.

25. Quoted in Henry Morgenthau, *Ambassador Morgenthau's Story* (Garden City, NY: Doubleday, 1919), 295.

26. Quoted in Dadrian, "The Secret Young-Turk Ittihadist Conference and the Decision for the World War I Genocide of the Armenians," 196.

27. "The 10 Commandments of the Committee of Union and Progress," quoted in ibid., 175.

28. Morgenthau, *Ambassador Morgenthau's Story*, 351f.

29. Ibid., 309.

30. Ibid., 313f.

31. Ibid., 321f.

32. Rafael de Nogales, *Four Years Beneath the Crescent*, trans. Muna Lee (New York and London: Scribner's, 1926), 175f.

33. Ibid., 130f.

34. Ibid.

35. Quoted in Joseph Guttman, "The Beginnings of Genocide," *Turkish Armenocide, Documentary Series* (Philadelphia: Armenian Historical Research Association), vol. 2, 11.

36. Harry Stürmer, *Two Years in Constantinople*, trans. E. Allen (London: Hodder & Stoughton, 1917), 57.

37. Ibid., 80.

38. See the 684-page report of a commission chaired by Lord Bryce, presented to Parliament: *The Treatment of Armenians in the Ottoman Empire* (London, New York, and Toronto: Hodder & Stoughton, 1916).

39. William Colby Chester, "Turkey Reinterpreted," *Current History* (September 1922), 939–47.

40. Virginia Woolf, *Mrs. Dalloway,* ed. Claire Tomalin (Oxford: Oxford University Press, 1999), 157.

41. Quoted in Office of the United States Chief of Counsel for Prosecution of Axis Criminality, *Nazi Conspiracy and Aggression,* 9 vols. (Washington, DC: U.S. Government Printing Office, 1946), vol. 7, 753.

42. See Vital, *A People Apart,* 509ff.

43. "Appeal to the Russian People," quoted in Evgenii Semenov, *The Russian Government and the Massacres* (London: John Murray, 1907), 99ff.

44. For a classic history of the *Protocols,* see Norman Cohn, *Warrant for Genocide: The Myth of the Jewish World Conspiracy and the Protocols of the Elders of Zion* (London: Serif, 1996).

45. Quoted in Cohn, *Warrant for Genocide,* 126.

46. *The Jews in the Eastern War Zone* (New York: American Jewish Committee, 1916), 100; see also Vital, *A People Apart,* 653ff.

47. *The Jews in the Eastern War Zone,* 114–15.

48. Quoted in ibid., 82.

49. [Paul Nikolaus Cosmann], "Die Ostjuden," *Süddeutsche Monatshefte,* 13 (1915–16), 673; see also Julius Berger, "Deutsche Juden and polnische Juden," *Der Jude,* 1 (1916–17), 137–49.

50. See Steven E. Aschheim, *Brothers as Strangers: The East European Jew in German and German-Jewish Consciousness 1800–1923* (Madison: University of Wisconsin Press, 1982), 139ff.

51. Georg Fritz, *Die Ostjudenfrage: Zionismus und Grenzschluss* (Munich: J. F. Lehmanns, 1915).

52. Wolfgang Heinze, "Ostjüdische Einwanderung," *Preussische Jahrbücher,* 162 (1916), 98–117; Wolfgang Heinze, "Internationale jüdische Beziehungen," ibid., 169 (1917), 340–66; and ibid., 170 (1917), 65–81.

53. Cohn, *Warrant for Genocide,* 127.

54. For two contemporary accounts, see Elias Heifets, The *Slaughter of the Jews in the Ukraine in 1919* (New York: Thomas Seltzer, 1921), and Federation of Ukrainian Jews, *The Ukrainian Terror and the Jewish Peril* (London: Federation of Ukrainian Jews, 1921). See also N. Gergel, "The Pogroms in the Ukraine in 1918–1921," *YIVO Annual of Jewish Social Science,* vol. 6 (1951), 237–52; Peter Kenez, "Pogroms and White Ideology in the Russian Civil War," in John D. Klier and Shlomo Lambroza, eds., *Pogroms: Anti-Jewish Violence in Modern Jewish History* (Cambridge: Cambridge University Press, 1992), 293–313; and Vital, *A People Apart,* 653ff.

55. The journalist was J. E. Hodgson. Quoted in Kenez, "Pogroms and White Ideology in the Russian Civil War," 305.

56. Robert Cecil, *The Myth of the Master Race: Rosenberg and Nazi Ideology* (New York: Dodd, Mead, 1972), 17.

57. Alfred Rosenberg, "The Russian Jewish Revolution," in Barbara Miller Lane and Leila J. Rupp, eds., *Nazi Ideology Before 1933: A Documentation* (Manchester: University of Manchester Press, 1978), 56, italics in the original.

58. Alfred Rosenberg, "The Protocols of the Elders of Zion and Jewish World Policy," in Lane and Rupp, eds., *Nazi Ideology Before 1933,* 56.

59. Harry Rudolph Rudin, *Armistice 1918* (New Haven: Yale University Press, 1944), 144.

60. Geyer, "German Strategy in the Age of Machine Warfare, 1914–1945," 550f.; Jan Philipp Reemtsma, "The Concept of the War of Annihilation: Clausewitz, Ludendorff, Hitler," in Hannes Heer and Klaus Naumann, eds., *War of Extermination: The German Military in World War II, 1941–1944* (New York and Oxford: Berghahn, 2000), 25ff.

61. See A. J. Ryder, *The German Revolution of 1918* (Cambridge: Cambridge University Press, 1967).

62. See Bessel, *Germany After the First World War,* 69ff.

63. Thomas Mann, "Deutschland und die Demokratie," in *Essays,* ed. Hermann Kurzke and Stephan Stachorski, 6 vols. Frankfurt-am-Main: S. Fischer, 1993), vol. 2, 247f, italics in the original.

64. See Bessel, *Germany After the First World War,* 220ff.

65. Hitler, *Mein Kampf,* 240f.

66. Paul von Hindenburg, "The Stab in the Back," in Anton Kaes, Martin Jay, and Edward Dimendberg, eds., *The Weimar Republic Sourcebook* (Berkeley, Los Angeles, and New York: University of California Press, 1994), 15f.

67. Francesco Saverio Nitti, *The Decadence of Europe* (London: Unwin, 1922), 76.

68. David Lloyd George, *The Truth About the Peace Treaties,* 2 vols. (London: Victor Gollancz, 1938), vol. 1, 406.

69. Nitti, *The Decadence of Europe,* 95f.

70. Lloyd George, *The Truth About the Peace Treaties,* vol. 1, 406.

71. Institut zum Studium der Judenfrage, ed., *Die Juden in Deutschland* (Munich: Verlag Franz Eher Nachfolger, 1939), 111.

72. For a comprehensive study of the real and perceived role of Jews in the German revolution, see Werner T. Angress, "Juden im politischen Leben der Revolutionszeit," in Mosse, ed., *Deutsches Judentum in Krieg und Revolution 1916–1923* (Tübingen: J. C. B. Mohr [Paul Siebeck], 1971), 137–315.

73. Paul Breiner, "The Jew as Revolutionary: The Case of Gustav Landauer," *Year Book of the Leo Baeck Institute,* vol. 12 (1967), 75–84.

74. On the identification of the support of the liberal press for the peace treaty with Jewish interests, see Werner Becker, "Die Rolle der liberalen Presse," in Mosse, ed., *Deutsches Judentum in Krieg und Revolution,* 409–510.

75. See, inter alia, Ernst Jünger, "Die totale mobilmachung," in Jünger, ed., *Krieg und Krieger,* 28.

76. Hitler, *Mein Kampf,* 206.

77. Hermann Rauschning, *Hitler Speaks* (London: Thornton Butterworth, 1939), 235.

78. Adolf Hitler, *Hitler's Secret Book,* introduction Telford Taylor, trans. Salvator Attanasio (New York: Grove Press, 1961), 6f.

79. Hitler, *Mein Kampf,* 382.

80. Ibid., 65.

81. Ibid., 678f.

82. "The Program of the NSDAP," in Lane and Rupp, eds., *Nazi Ideology Before 1933,* 41.

83. See, for example, S. Steinberg, "Was wir estreben," *Zeitschrift des Vaterländischen Bundes jüdischer Frontsoldaten* (March 1922), quoted in Kaes, Jay, and Dimendberg, eds., *The Weimar Republic Sourcebook,* 258.

84. Hugo Bettauer, *The City Without Jews,* trans. Salomea Neumark Brainin (New York: Bloch, 1926), 13.

85. See Bruce F. Pauley, *From Prejudice to Persecution: A History of Austrian Anti-Semitism* (Chapel Hill: University of North Carolina Press, 1992), 102ff.

86. See George L. Mosse, *The Fascist Revolution: Toward a General Theory of Fascism* (New York: Howard Fertig, 1990), 13ff.

87. C. J. Lowe and F. Marzari, *Italian Foreign Policy, 1870–1940* (London and Boston: Routledge & Kegan Paul, 1975), 172f.

88. Benito Mussolini, *My Autobiography* (New York: Charles Scribner's Sons, 1928) 56.

89. Quoted in ibid., 66.

90. Ibid., 70.

91. Hilmar Stephen Raushenbush, *The March of Fascism* (New Haven: Yale University Press, 1939), 162–63.

92. Zweig, *The World of Yesterday,* 238f.

93. Clayton Sedgwick Cooper, *Understanding Italy* (London: John Long, 1923), 23.

94. Turati, "Rome or Moscow?" in Aúgusto Turati, *A Revolution and Its Leader,* foreword by Benito Mussolini (London: Alexander-Ouseley, 1930), 12.

95. Turati, "The New Order," in Turati, *A Revolution and Its Leader,* 72.

96. Mario Palmieri, *The Philosophy of Fascism* (Chicago: Dante Alighieri Society, 1936), 70f.

97. Mosse, *The Fascist Revolution,* 18ff.

98. Ibid., xvif.

99. Ibid., 31ff.

100. Zweig, *The World of Yesterday,* 238f.

101. See Harold J. Gordon, *Hitler and the Beer Hall Putsch* (Princeton: Princeton University Press, 1972).

102. For an account of the economic recovery after the inflation, see S. William Halperin, *Germany Tried Democracy: A Political History of the Reich from 1918 to 1933* (Hamden, CT, and London: Archon, 1963), 280ff.

103. Zweig, *The World of Yesterday,* 240.

104. Hans Ostwald, *Sittengeschichte der Inflation,* quoted in Kaes, Jay, and Dimendberg, eds., *The Weimar Sourcebook,* 78.

105. Halperin, *Germany Tried Democracy,* 347f.

Chapter Three: NATIONAL SOCIALIST PROMISE AND PRACTICE

1. Erich Eyck, *A History of the Weimar Republic,* 2 vols., trans. Harlan P. Hanson and Robert G. L. Waite (Cambridge, MA: Harvard University Press, 1962), vol. 2, 226ff.; S. William Halperin, *Germany Tried Democracy: A Political History of the Reich from 1918 to 1933* (Hamden, CT, and London: Archon, 1963), 403ff.

2. See David Schoenbaum, *Hitler's Social Revolution: Class and Status in Nazi Germany 1933–39* (Garden City, NY: Doubleday, 1966), 18, 29ff. Recently, Rainer Zitelman aptly summarized the Nazi program as the "politics of seduction"—Zitelman, *Hitler: The Politics of Seduction,* trans. Helmut Bögler (London: London House, 1999).

3. On the seductive quality of Nazi political ritual, see Karl Otten, *Geplante Illusionen* (Frankfurt-am-Main: Luchterhand, 1989); Simon Taylor, *Prelude to Genocide: Nazi Ideology and the Struggle for Power* (London: Gerald Duckworth, 1985), 174–93; on the rallies, see Hamilton T. Burden, *The Nuremberg Party Rallies: 1923–39* (London: Pall Mall Press, 1967); on the role of architecture within the politics of

seduction, see Dieter Bartetzko, *Zwischen Zucht und Ekstase: Zur Theatralik von NS-Architektur* (Berlin: Gebr. Mann, 1985).

4. Hitler, speech delivered in Munich, 27 February 1925, in Institut für Zeitgeschichte, ed., *Hitler, Reden, Schriften, Anordnungen: Februar 1925 bis Januar 1933*, 5 vols. (Munich: Saur, 1992–98), vol. 1, 21.

5. Hitler at Kumbach, 5 February 1928, quoted in Gordon W. Prange, ed., *Hitler's Words 1923–43* (Washington, DC: American Council on Public Affairs, 1944), 8; for the German text, see Institut für Zeitgeschichte, ed., *Hitler, Reden, Schriften, Anordnungen*, vol. 2/2, 662ff.

6. On Hitler's rhetoric on the centrality of struggle, see Detlef Grieswelle, *Propaganda der Friedlosigkeit: Eine Studie zu Hitler's Rhetorik, 1920–1933* (Stuttgart: Ferdinand Suhe, 1972), and Hans-Günther Zmarzlik, "Social Darwinism in Germany, Seen as a Historical Problem," in Hajo Holborn, ed., *Republic to Reich: The Making of the Nazi Revolution*, trans. Ralph Manheim (New York: Pantheon, 1972), 435–74.

7. Hermann Rauschning, *The Voice of Destruction* (New York: Putnam, 1940), 231f.

8. See, for example, R. T. Clark, *The Fall of the German Republic: A Political Study* (New York: Russell & Russell, 1964), 262ff.

9. See Theodor Eschenburg, "The Role of Personality in the Crisis of the Weimar Republic: Hindenburg, Brüning, Groener, Schleicher," in Holborn, ed., *Republic to Reich*, 23ff; Hans Mommsen, "Heinrich Brüning as Chancellor: The Failure of a Politically Isolated Strategy," in Hans Mommsen, *From Weimar to Auschwitz*, trans. Philip O'Connor (Princeton: Princeton University Press, 1991), 119–40.

10. Eyck, *A History of the Weimar Republic*, vol. 2, 253ff.

11. Ibid., 278ff.

12. Ibid., 299ff.

13. Hitler at the Industrie Klub in Düsseldorf, 27 January 1932, quoted in Norman H. Baynes, ed., *The Speeches of Adolf Hitler*, 2 vols. (Oxford: Royal Institute of International Affairs, 1942), vol. 1, 829; for the German text, see Institut für Zeitgeschichte, ed., *Hitler, Reden, Schriften, Anordnungen*, vol. 5/3, 110.

14. Flier published by the Hamburg chapter of the "Central-Verein deutscher Staatsbürger jüdischen Glaubens," quoted in Anton Kaes, Martin Jay, and Edward Dimendberg, eds., *The Weimar Republic Sourcebook* (Berkeley, Los Angeles, and London: University of California Press, 1994), 274. For a general overview of the Jewish response to antisemitism on the eve of the Nazi ascent to power, see Donald L. Niewyk, *The Jews in Weimar Germany* (Baton Rouge and London: Louisiana State University Press, 1980), 82ff.; for a comprehensive overview of the state of the German Jewish community in 1932, see Werner E. Mosse, ed., *Entscheidungsjahr 1932! Zur Judenfrage in der Endphase der Weimarer Republik* (Tübingen: J. C. B. Mohr [Paul Siebeck], 1965).

15. See Henry Ashby Turner, Jr., *Hitler's Thirty Days to Power: January 1933* (Reading, MA: Addison-Wesley, 1996).

16. Quoted in Ian Kershaw, *Hitler*, 2 vols. (Harmondsworth, UK: Penguin/Allen Lane, 1998–2000), vol. 1, 427.

17. The question of who caused the fire has been a matter of dispute for seventy years. The Nazis blamed it first on a Communist conspiracy, but were unable to prove this in court. They were able to convict the Dutch anarchist Marinus van der Lubbe, who was subsequently executed. Anti-Fascists believed from the very beginning that Göring was responsible. For a view which supports the belief that van der Lubbe set the fire, see Fritz Tobias, *The Reichstag Fire* (New York: G. P. Putnam's Sons, 1964); for the view that the Nazis were responsible, see *Braunbuch über Reichstagbrand und Hitler-Terror* (Basel: Universum, 1933), Internationale Komitee Luxemburg, *Der Reichstagbrand: Die Provokation des 20. Jahrhunderts* (Luxemburg: Der Freundenkreis, 1978), and, more recently, Alexander Bahar and Wilfried Kugel, *Der Reichstagbrand: Wie Geschichte gemacht wird* (Berlin: edition q, 2001). The last book makes a convincing case that the Nazis *did* set the fire. There is general agreement that the Nazis exploited the situation for whatever it was worth. See Gilbert Badia, *Feu au Reichstag: L'acte de naissance du régime Nazi* (Paris: Editions sociales, 1983), and Hans Mommsen, "The Reichstag Fire and Its Political Consequences," in Holborn, ed., *Republic to Reich*, 129–222.

18. "Verordnung des Reichspräsidenten zum Schutz von Volk und Staat," *Reichsgesetzblatt*, 28 February 1933, 83.

19. Quoted in Kershaw, *Hitler*, vol. 1, 460.

20. On the beginnings of the concentration camp system, see Martin Broszat, "The Concentration Camps 1933–45," in Helmut Krausnick, Hans Buchheim, Martin Broszat, and Hans-Adolf Jacobsen, eds., *Anatomy of the SS State*, trans. Richard Barry, Marion Jackson, and Dorothy Long (New York: Walker & Co., 1968), 397–420, and Debórah Dwork and Robert Jan van Pelt, *Auschwitz: 1270 to the Present* (New York: W. W. Norton, 1996), 100–04. The literature in German is vast. Klaus Drobisch and Guenther Wieland, *Das System der NS-Konzentrationslager, 1933–1939* (Berlin: Akademie, 1993), and Karin Orth, *Das System der nationalsozialistischen Konzentrationslager: Eine Politische Organisationsgeschichte* (Hamburg: Hamburger Edition, 1999), 23ff., deal with the system as a whole; and Hans-Günther Richardi, *Schule der Gewalt: Das Konzentrationslager Dachau, 1933–34* (Munich: Beck, 1983), provides an important

case study of Dachau. On early reports on the camps, see Claude Conter, "KZ-Literatur der 30er Jahre oder die Genese der KZ-Darstellung," in Claude Conter, ed., *Literatur und Holocaust* (Bamberg: Universität Bamberg, 1996), 24ff.

21. Hans Wendt, *Die Nationalversammlung von Potsdam* (Berlin: Mittler & Sohn, 1933), 1.

22. "Gesetz zur Behebung der Not von Volk und Reich," *Reichsgesetzblatt*, 25 (24 March 1933), 141.

23. Speech of Otto Wels for the Reichstag, 23 March 1933, quoted in Herbert Michaelis and Ernst Schraepler, eds., *Ursachen und Folgen: Vom deutschen Zusammenbruch 1918 bis 1945 bis zur staatlichen Neuordnung Deutschlands in der Gegenwart*, 26 vols. (Berlin: Dokumenten-Verlag Dr. Herbert Wendler & Co., n.d.), vol. 9, 146ff.

24. This quote and many that follow are taken from a unique collection of documents concerning the persecution of the Jews published in 1936 by Victor Gollancz in London, *The Yellow Spot: The Extermination of the Jews of Germany*. This compilation is described on the title page as documenting *The outlawing of half a million human beings: a collection of facts and documents relating to three years' persecution of German Jews derived chiefly from National Socialist sources, very carefully assembled by a group of investigators* (London: Victor Gollancz, 1936).

25. Quoted by Franz Borkenau, *The Communist International* (London: Faber & Faber, 1938), 376f.

26. Kershaw, *Hitler*, vol. 1, 472ff. See also Avraham Barkai, *From Boycott to Annihilation: The Economic Struggle of German Jews, 1933–1943*, trans. William Templer (Hanover, NH, and London: University Press of New England, 1989), 17ff.

27. Quoted in Max Domarus, *Hitler: Speeches and Proclamations, 1932–1945*, 4 vols. (Wauconda, IL: Bolchazy-Carducci, 1990–97), vol. 1, 299f.

28. Quoted in *The Yellow Spot*, 39.

29. Victor Klemperer, *I Will Bear Witness: A Diary of the Nazi Years, 1933–1941*, trans. Martin Chalmers (New York: Random House, 1998), 10.

30. Bertha Kahn-Rosenthal, oral history conducted by Debórah Dwork, New Haven, CT, 6 and 13 March 1992, transcript 20, 1–2, 20, 28.

31. Robert Weltsch, "Tragt ihn mit Stolz, den gelben Fleck!" in *JA-sagen zum Judentum* (Berlin: Verlag der "Jüdisches Rundschau," 1933), 24.

32. The literature on the Nazi assault on the German Jews between 1933 and 1939 is immense. See, inter alia: Karl A. Schleunes, *The Twisted Road to Auschwitz: Nazi Policy Toward German Jews 1933–1939* (Chicago: University of Illinois Press, 1970); David Bankier, ed., *Probing the Depths of German Antisemitism: German Society and the Persecution of the Jews, 1933–1941* (Jerusalem: Yad Vashem, 2000); Hermann Graml, *Antisemitism in the Third Reich*, trans. Tim Kirk (Oxford: Basil Blackwell, 1992); and John Weiss, *Ideology of Death: Why the Holocaust Happened in Germany* (Chicago: Ivan R. Dee, 1996).

33. Klemperer, *I Will Bear Witness*, 12.

34. Quoted in *The Yellow Spot*, 137f.

35. An attempt to create comprehensive anti-Jewish legislation in 1933 went nowhere. See Uwe D. Adam, "An Overall Plan for Anti-Jewish Legislation in the Third Reich?" *Yad Vashem Studies*, vol. 11 (1975), 33–55.

36. Klemperer, *I Will Bear Witness*, 15.

37. Michael Burleigh and Wolfgang Wippermann, *The Racial State: Germany 1933–1945* (Cambridge: Cambridge University Press, 1991), 136ff.

38. Quoted in Saul Friedländer, *Nazi Germany and the Jews*, Vol. 1, *The Years of Persecution* (New York: HarperCollins, 1997), 33.

39. See Sidney Pollard, *The Idea of Progress: History and Society* (Harmondsworth, UK: Penguin, 1971).

40. See Arthur Herman, *The Idea of Decline in Western History* (New York: The Free Press, 1997), 76ff., 221ff.

41. Friedrich Nietzsche, *On the Genealogy of Morals*, trans. Walter Kaufmann and R. J. Hollingdale (New York: Random House, 1967), 44.

42. Quoted in Herman, *The Idea of Decline in Western History*, 239.

43. Kurt Jakob Ball-Kadurie, *Das Leben der Juden in Deutschland in Jahre 1933: Ein Zeitbericht* (Frankfurt-am-Main: Europäische Verlagsanstalt, 1963), 212. See also Fred Grubel, Foreword, in Arnold Paucker ed., *Die Juden in Nationalsozialistischen Deutschland/The Jews in Nazi Germany 1933–1943* (Tübingen: J. C. B. Mohr [Paul Siebeck], 1986), xvi, and Leonard Baker, *Days of Sorrow and Pain: Leo Baeck and the Berlin Jews* (New York: Macmillan, 1978), 145ff.

44. Quoted in Kurt Jakob Ball-Kaduri, *Vor der Katastrophe: Juden in Deutschland* (Tel Aviv: Olamenu, 1967), 42.

45. The literature on the plight of the German Jews between 1933 and 1941 is rich and deep. Among the most important general works are Saul Friedländer, *Nazi Germany and the Jews*, Vol. 1, *The Years of Persecution*, and Marion A. Kaplan, *Between Dignity and Despair: Jewish Life in Nazi Germany* (New York and Oxford: Oxford University Press, 1998). Also Avraham Barkai, *From Boycott to Annihilation: The*

Economic Struggle of German Jews, 1933–1943, trans. William Templer; Werner Angress, *Between Fear and Hope: Jewish Youth in the Third Reich* (New York: Columbia University Press, 1988); and Frank Bajor, *The "Aryanization" of Jewish Businesses in Nazi Germany* (Oxford: Berghahn, 2001). Two important studies on the response of German Jews to Nazi persecution are Sidney M. Bolkosky, *The Distorted Image: German Jewish Perceptions of Germans and Germany, 1918–1935* (New York, Oxford, and Amsterdam: Elsevier, 1975), and John V. Dippel, *Bound upon a Wheel of Fire: Why So Many German Jews Made the Tragic Decision to Remain in Nazi Germany* (New York: Basic Books, 1996). Important anthologies include Wolfgang Benz, ed., *Die Juden in Deutschland 1933–1945* (Munich: C. H. Beck, 1988); Paucker, ed., *Die Juden in Nationalsozialistischen Deutschland/The Jews in Nazi Germany 1933–1943*; and five contributions in David Bankier, ed., *Probing the Depths of German Antisemitism: German Society and the Persecution of the Jews, 1933–1941.*

46. Quoted in Lucy S. Dawidowicz, *The War Against the Jews, 1933–1945* (New York: Holt, Rinehart & Winston, 1975), 174.

47. For Jewish emigration from Germany, see the chapter that follows.

48. Friedrich Katz, oral history conducted by Debórah Dwork, Chicago, 14 November 1987, transcript 3–4.

49. Ursula Herzberg-Lewinsky, oral history conducted by Debórah Dwork, Berlin, 18 and 20 July 1994, transcript 7f.

50. Studies on the SS include Hans Buchheim, "The SS—Instrument of Domination," in Krausnick, Buchheim, Broszat, and Jacobsen, eds., *Anatomy of the SS State*, 127–301; Gerald Reitlinger, *The SS: Alibi of a Nation, 1922–1945* (New York: Viking Press, 1957); Heinz Höhne, *The Order of the Death's Head: The Story of Hitler's SS*, trans. Richard Barry (London: Secker & Warburg, 1969); and Robert Lewis Koehl, *The Black Corps: The Structure and Power Struggles of the Nazi SS* (Madison: University of Wisconsin Press, 1983).

51. Adolf Hitler, *Mein Kampf*, trans. Ralph Manheim (Boston: Houghton Mifflin, 1943), Dedication, 687.

52. Taylor, *Prelude to Genocide*, 181.

53. Karl Lamprecht, *Deutsche Geschichte*, 9 vols. (Berlin: R. Gaertners Verlagsbuchhandlung, 1891), vol. 1, 135f.

54. Houston Stewart Chamberlain, *Foundations of the Nineteenth Century*, trans. John Lees, 2 vols. (London and New York: John Lane, 1912), vol. 1, 550.

55. Gunther d'Alquen, *Die SS: Geschichte, Aufgabe und Organisation der Schutzstaffeln der NSDAP* (Berlin: Junker und Dünnhaupt Verlag, 1939), 8.

56. Ibid.

57. The SS created an entire organization to ensure racial purity. See Michael H. Kater, *Das "Ahnenerbe" der SS, 1935–1945* (Stuttgart: Deutsche Verlags-Anstalt, 1974).

58. Ibid., 9.

59. Quoted in Reitlinger, *The SS: Alibi of a Nation*, 72.

60. D'Alquen, *Die SS*, 10.

61. Quoted in Gordon Craig, *Germany, 1866–1945* (New York: Oxford University Press, 1978), 589.

62. See Hermann Mau, "The 'Second Revolution'—June 30, 1934," in Holborn, ed., *Republic to Reich*, 223–48.

63. Quoted in Hans Buchheim, "The SS—Instrument of Domination," in Krausnick, Buchheim, Broszat, and Jacobsen, eds., *Anatomy of the SS State*, 130.

64. Winston Churchill, *Great Contemporaries* (London: Odhams Press, 1947), 203f.

65. Ibid., 209.

Chapter Four: THE THIRD REICH

1. Karl Richard Ganzer, *Das deutsche Führergesicht: 200 Bildnisse deutscher Kämpfer und Wegsucher aus zwei Jahrtausenden* (Munich: J. F. Lehmanns Verlag, 1935), 6ff.

2. Ibid., 234.

3. For a more substantial analysis of the Hitler myth, see Ian Kershaw, "The 'Hitler Myth': Image and Reality in the Third Reich," in David F. Crew, ed., *Nazism and German Society* (London and New York: Routledge, 1994), 197–215; also Richard Grunberger, *The Twelve-Year Reich: A Social History of Nazi Germany, 1933–1945* (New York: Holt, Rinehart & Winston, 1971), 72–89.

4. Quoted in Ian Kershaw, *Hitler*, 2 vols. (Harmondsworth, UK: Penguin/Allen Lane, 1998–2000), vol. 1, 529.

5. Martin Broszat, *The Hitler State: The Foundation and Development of the Internal Structure of the Third Reich*, trans. John W. Hiden (London and New York: Longman, 1981), 347.

6. Quoted in *The Yellow Spot: The Extermination of the Jews of Germany* (London: Victor Gollancz, 1936), 151f.

7. Ibid., 153.

8. See Volker Dahm, "Kulturelles und geistiges Leben," in Wolfgang Benz, ed., *Die Juden in Deutschland 1933–1945* (Munich: C. H. Beck, 1988), 75–267.

9. See, for example, Herbert Freeden, "A Jewish Theatre Under the Swastika," *Year Book of the Leo Baeck Institute,* vol. 1 (1956), 142–62.

10. Ralph Montrose (Rudolf Rosenberg), oral history conducted by Debórah Dwork, Cardiff, Wales, 22 July 1985, transcript 14.

11. Quoted in *The Yellow Spot,* 167f.

12. Hans Gaertner, "Problems of Jewish Schools in Germany During the Hitler Regime," *Year Book of the Leo Baeck Institute,* vol. 1 (1956), 123–41; Solomon Colodner, "Jewish Education Under National Socialism," *Yad Vashem Studies,* vol. 3 (1959), 161–86.

13. Lore Gang-Saalheimer, oral history conducted by Debórah Dwork, Cardiff, Wales, 22 July 1985, transcript 3, 9, 3.

14. Solomon Colodner, *Jewish Education in Germany Under the Nazis* (New York: Jewish Education Committee Press, 1964), 49, 65.

15. For more about the education of Jewish children and young adults in Nazi Germany, see, inter alia, Fritz Friedlander, "Trials and Tribulations of Jewish Education in Nazi Germany," *Year Book of the Leo Baeck Institute,* vol. 3 (1958), 187–201; Gaertner, "Problems of Jewish Schools in Germany During the Hitler Regime," 123–41; Max Grünewald, "Education and Culture of the German Jews Under Nazi Rule," *Jewish Review,* 5 (1948); Marion Kaplan, *Between Dignity and Despair: Jewish Life in Nazi Germany* (New York: Oxford University Press, 1998), 94–118; and Abraham Margaliot, "The Struggle for Survival of the Jewish Community in Germany in the Face of Oppression," and Joseph Walk, "Jewish Education Under the Nazis—An Example of Resistance to the Totalitarian Regime," both in *Jewish Resistance During the Holocaust, Proceedings of the Conference on Manifestations of Jewish Resistance* (Jerusalem: Yad Vashem, 1971), 100–11, 123–31.

16. Quoted in *The Yellow Spot,* 48.

17. Ibid., 56.

18. Ibid., 175.

19. Ibid., 227.

20. Ibid.

21. Quoted in Max Domarus, *Hitler: Speeches and Proclamations, 1932–1945,* 4 vols. (Wauconda, IL: Bolchazy-Carducci, 1990–97), vol. 2, 706.

22. Kaplan, *Between Dignity and Despair,* 248.

23. Quoted in J. Noakes and G. Pridham, *Nazism, 1919–1945,* 3 vols. (Exeter: University of Exeter Press, 1983–88), vol. 2, 538f.

24. Elke Fröhlich, ed., *Die Tagebücher von Joseph Goebbels: Samtliche Fragmente, Teil I,* 4 vols. (Munich: Saur, 1987), vol. 2, 540.

25. Quoted in *The Yellow Spot,* 21.

26. See Helmut Genschel, *Die Verdrängung der Juden aus der Wirtschaft im Dritten Reich* (Göttingen: Musterschmidt, 1966); Günter Plum, "Wirtschafts und Erwerbsleben," in Benz, ed., *Die Juden in Deutschland 1933–1945,* 314–412; and Frank Bajohr, "The Beneficiaries of 'Aryanization': Hamburg as a Case Study," *Yad Vashem Studies,* vol. 26 (1998), 173–202.

27. Quoted in *The Yellow Spot,* 113.

28. Ellen Eliel-Wallach, oral history conducted by Debórah Dwork, Amsterdam, 3 August 1987, transcript 1–2.

29. Ralph Montrose, oral history, transcript 2, 8.

30. Ibid., 2, 3, 11.

31. Ibid., 11, 15.

32. Quoted in *The Yellow Spot,* 24.

33. On the Nazi persecution of the Roma and Sinti, or "Gypsies," see Donald Kenrick and Grattan Puxon, *The Destiny of Europe's Gypsies* (London: Heinemann, 1972), 59–184; Joachim S. Hohmann, *Geschichte der Zigeunerverfolgung in Deutschland* (Frankfurt and New York: Campus, 1981); Henry H. Huttenbach, "The Romani Prajmos: The Nazi Genocide of Gypsies in Germany and Eastern Europe," in David Crowe and John Kolsti, eds., *The Gypsies of Eastern Europe* (Armonk, NY, and London: M. E. Sharpe, 1991), 31–49; Michael Burleigh and Wolfgang Wippermann, *The Racial State: Germany 1933–1945* (Cambridge: Cambridge University Press, 1991), 113–27; Yehuda Bauer, "Gypsies," in Yisrael Gutman and Michael Berenbaum, eds., *Anatomy of the Auschwitz Death Camp* (Bloomington and Indianapolis: Indiana University Press, 1994), 441–55; Guenther Lewy, *The Nazi Persecution of the Gypsies* (New York and Oxford: Oxford University Press, 2000); Michael Zimmermann, "The National Socialist 'Solution of the Gypsy Question,'" in Ulrich Herbert, ed., *National Socialist Extermination Policies: Contemporary German Perspectives and Controversies* (New York and Oxford: Berghahn Books, 2000), 186–209; and Martin Luchterhand, *Der Weg nach Birkenau: Entstehung und Verlauf der nationalsozialistischen Verfolgung der "Zigeuner"* (Lübeck: Schmidt-Römhild, 2000).

34. On Roma and Sinti in general, see Jean-Paul Clébert, *The Gypsies,* trans. Charles Duff (London: Vista Books, 1963), and Isabel Fonseca, *Bury Me Standing: The Gypsies and Their Journey* (London: Chatto & Windus, 1995).

35. Lewy, *The Nazi Persecution of the Gypsies,* 10ff.

36. Herbert F. Ziegler, *Nazi Germany's New Aristocracy: The SS Leadership, 1925–1939* (Princeton: Princeton University Press, 1989), 47.

37. Gunther d'Alquen, *Die SS: Geschichte, Aufgabe und Organisation der Schutzstaffeln der NSDAP* (Berlin: Junker und Dünnhaupt Verlag, 1939), 28f.

38. Quoted in Martin Broszat, "The Concentration Camps 1933–45," in Helmut Krausnick, Hans Buchheim, Martin Broszat, and Hans-Adolf Jacobsen, eds., *Anatomy of the SS State,* trans. Richard Barry, Marion Jackson, and Dorothy Long (New York: Walker & Co., 1968), 455.

39. Evan von Hase-Mihalik and Doris Kreuzkamp, *Du kriegst auch einen schönen Wohnwagen: Zwangslager für Sinto und Roma während des Nationalsozialismus in Frankfurt am Main* (Frankfurt-am-Main: Brandes & Apsel, 1990).

40. Lewy, *The Nazi Persecution of the Gypsies,* 42f.

41. See Joachim S. Hohmann, *Robert Ritter und die Erben der Kriminalbiologie: "Zigeunerforshung" im Nationalsozialismus und in Westdeutschland im Zeichen des Rassismus* (Frankfurt-am-Main: Peter Lang, 1991).

42. Quoted in Lewy, *The Nazi Persecution of the Gypsies,* 50f.

43. See Burleigh and Wippermann, *The Racial State: Germany 1933–1945,* 182–97; Hans-Georg Stümke, "From the 'People's Consciousness of Right and Wrong' to 'The Healthy Instincts of the Nation': The Persecution of Homosexuals in Nazi Germany," in Michael Burleigh, ed., *Confronting the Nazi Past* (London: Collin & Brown, 1996), 154–66; and Günter Grau, "Final Solution of the Homosexual Question? The Antihomosexual policies of the Nazis and the Social Consequences for Homosexual Men," and Rüdiger Lautmann, "The Pink Triangle: Homosexuals as 'Enemies of the State,'" both in Michael Berenbaum and Abraham J. Peck, eds., *The Holocaust and History: The Known, the Unknown, the Disputed, and the Reexamined* (Bloomington and Indianapolis: Indiana University Press, 1998), 338–44, 345–57. A monograph by John. C. Fout is eagerly awaited.

44. Alfred Rosenberg, *Der Kampf zwischen Schöpfung und Zerstörung: Kongressrede auf dem Reichsparteitag der Arbeit am 8. September 1937* (Munich: Zentralverlag der NSDAP/Franz Eher Nachf., 1937), 6.

45. Ibid., 7.

46. Ibid., 13.

47. Ibid., 15.

48. Hans Kerrl and Kurt Massmann, *Reichstagung in Nürnberg 1937: Der Parteitag der Arbeit* (Berlin: Vaterländischer Verlag C. A. Weller, 1937), 84.

49. Ibid.

50. On the political prehistory of the so-called Anschluss, see Bruce F. Pauley, *Hitler and the Forgotten Nazis: A History of Austrian National Socialism* (Chapel Hill and London: University of North Carolina Press, 1981), and Alfred D. Low, *The Anschluss Movement, 1931–1938, and the Great Powers* (Boulder, CO: East European Monographs/New York: Columbia University Press, 1985). On the events of March 1938, see Gordon Brook-Shepherd, *Anschluss: The Rape of Austria* (London: Macmillan, 1963); Evan Burr Bukey, *Hitler's Austria: Popular Sentiment in the Nazi Era 1938–1945* (Chapel Hill and London: University of North Carolina Press, 2000); and Walter Kleinadel, *"Gott schütze Österreich!" Der Anschluß 1938* (Vienna: Österreichischer Bundesverlag, 1988). For an interesting memoir by the last Austrian chancellor, see Kurt von Schuschnigg, *The Brutal Takeover* (London: Weidenfeld & Nicolson, 1969). For a useful collection of documents, see Dokumentationsarchiv des Österreichischer Widerstands, ed., *"Anschluß" 1938: Eine Dokumentation* (Vienna: Österreichischer Bundesverlag, 1988).

51. Stefan Zweig, *The World of Yesterday* (London: Cassell & Co., 1943), 215.

52. For a contemporary perspective, see Gerhard Schacher, *Central Europe and the Western World* (London: Allen & Unwin, 1936), 142ff.

53. George Eric Rowe Gedye, *The Fallen Bastions* (London: Victor Gollancz, 1939), 307.

54. Quoted in Domarus, *Hitler: Speeches and Proclamations, 1932–1945,* vol. 2, 1056.

55. Marianne Marco-Braun, oral history conducted by Debórah Dwork, Wimbledon, UK, 9 May 1987, transcript 3.

56. See Herbert Rosenkranz, "The Anschluss and the Tragedy of Austrian Jewry 1938–1945," in Josef Frankel, ed., *The Jews of Austria: Essays on Their Life, History, and Destruction* (London: Vallentine, Mitchell, 1967), 479–546.

57. Robert Kanfer, oral history conducted by Debórah Dwork, Vienna, 25 June 1990, transcript 12f.

58. Gedye, *The Fallen Bastions,* 31f.

59. Elisabeth Rosner-Jellinek, oral history conducted by Debórah Dwork, Vienna, 24 and 26 June 1990, transcript 35.

60. Robert Kanfer, oral history, transcript 6f.; also 19f. and 39f.

61. Robert Rosner, oral history conducted by Debórah Dwork, Vienna, 3 July 1990, transcript 34.

62. Marianne Marco-Braun, oral history, transcript 3f.

63. Gedye, *The Fallen Bastions,* 306.

64. Ibid., 357.

65. See Sybil Milton, "The Expulsion of Polish Jews from Germany, October 1938 to July 1939," *Year Book of the Leo Baeck Institute,* vol. 29 (1984), 169–99.

66. The November Pogrom commands an extensive literature. See, among others, Lionel Kochan, *Pogrom: 10 November 1938* (London: Andre Deutsch, 1957); Rita Thalmann and Emmanuel Feinemann, *Crystal Night: 9–10 November 1938,* trans. Gilles Cremonesi (London: Thames & Hudson, 1974); Anthony Read and David Fisher, *Kristallnacht: Unleashing the Holocaust* (London: Michael Joseph, 1989); Hans-Jürgen Döscher, *"Reichskristallnacht" Die Novemberpogrome 1938* (Frankfurt and Berlin: Ullstein, 1988); Peter Loewenberg, "The Kristallnacht as a Public Degradation Ritual," *Year Book of the Leo Baeck Institute,* vol. 32 (1987), 303–23; and Wolfgang Benz, "Der Novemberpogrom 1938," in Benz, ed., *Die Juden in Deutschland 1933–1945,* 499–544.

67. Lore Gang-Saalheimer, oral history, transcript 8ff.

68. Hilda Cohen-Rosenthal, oral history conducted by Debórah Dwork, Cardiff, Wales, 21 July 1985, transcript 8f.

69. Alfred Dellheim, oral history conducted by Debórah Dwork, Berlin, 19 and 22 July 1994, transcript 21f.

70. Ibid., 24.

Chapter Five: REFUGEES

1. Stefan Zweig, *The World of Yesterday* (London: Cassell & Co., 1943), 308.

2. Ibid., 309.

3. Ibid.

4. Franciscus de Victoria, "On the Indians Lately Discovered," in James Brown Scott, *The Spanish Origin of International Law: Francisco de Vitoria and His Law of Nations* (Oxford: Clarendon Press, 1934), Appendix A, xxxvi.

5. Ibid.

6. See, for example, Hugo Grotius, *The Law of War and Peace,* trans. Louise R. Loomis (New York: Walter J. Black, 1949), 85 ff.

7. For biblical sources, see, e.g., Deuteronomy 23: 15–16 and Isaiah 16: 3–4.

8. See Michael Marrus, *The Unwanted: European Refugees in the Twentieth Century* (New York and Oxford: Oxford University Press, 1985), 6ff.

9. The first treatise on international law that reflected the new reality of the nation-state was Emerich de Vattel, *The Law of Nations or Principles of the Law of Nature* (Dublin: Luke White, 1787). For his discussions on the significance of borders and the rights and duties of governments toward aliens, see 262ff. For his discussion on asylum, see 176f.

10. John Hope Simpson, *Refugees: Preliminary Report of a Survey* (London: Royal Institute of International Affairs, 1938), 99.

11. See John Hope Simpson, *The Refugee Problem: Report of a Survey* (London, New York, and Toronto: Oxford University Press, 1939).

12. Hope Simpson, *Refugees: Preliminary Report of a Survey,* 99f.

13. For qualifications, see Alexander B. Elkin, Appendix IX, "Conditions of Naturalization of Refugees in Various Countries," in Hope Simpson, *The Refugee Problem,* 599ff.

14. Hope Simpson, *The Refugee Problem,* 535.

15. For a description of the desperate situation of Romania's Jews, see Binjamin Segel, *Rumänien und seine Juden* (Berlin: Nibelungen Verlag, 1918).

16. Max Nordau, *Zionistische Schriften* (Berlin: Jüdischer Verlag, 1923), 109ff.

17. For the motivation of the English government to promise the Jews a national home in Palestine, see Mark Levene, *War, Jews, and the New Europe* (Oxford: Oxford University Press, 1992), 82ff., 143. For text of the Balfour Declaration, see Jewish Agency for Palestine, *Book of Documents* (New York: Jewish Agency for Palestine, 1947), 1.

18. Great Britain, Foreign Office, *The Constitutions of All Countries* (London: His Majesty's Stationery Office, 1938), 539ff.

19. See Vladimir Jabotinsky, *The War and the Jew* (New York: Dial Press, 1942), 190ff. Also Barukh Ben-Anat, "The Great Moment Found a Small Generation—The Nordau Plan 1919–1920," [Hebrew] in *Zionism,* vol. 19 (1995), 80–116.

20. Arthur Ruppin, "How Cheaply Can We Colonize?" and "Mass Immigration and Finance," both in Arthur Ruppin, *Three Decades of Palestine: Speeches and Papers on the Upbuilding of the Jewish National Home* (Jerusalem: Schocken Books, 1936), 96f., 110ff., 125.

21. David Ben-Gurion, *From Class to Nation* (1933), quoted in Shlomo Avineri, *The Making of Modern Zionism: The Intellectual Origins of the Jewish State* (New York: Basic Books, 1981), 200.

22. Arthur Koestler, *Arrow in the Blue* (London: Macmillan, 1969), 167.

23. Ibid., 244.

24. Kim (Joachim) Scharf, oral history conducted by Debórah Dwork, Stockholm 27 November 1995, transcript 3f.

25. Hannah Arendt, *The Origins of Totalitarianism* (New York: Meridian Books, 1958), 286.

26. Ibid., 289.

27. Dan Michman, "The Committee for Jewish Refugees in Holland (1933–1940)," *Yad Vashem Studies,* vol. 14 (1981), 205–32.

28. See Norman Bentwich, *The Refugees from Germany: April 1935 to December 1935* (London: Allen & Unwin, 1936), 37, 54.

29. Ibid., 174ff.; also Doron Niederland, "The Emigration of Jewish Academics and Professionals from Germany in the First Year of Nazi Rule," *Year Book of the Leo Baeck Institute,* vol. 33 (1988), 285–300. For a general overview of Jewish emigration after 1933, see Herbert A. Strauss, "Jewish Emigration from Germany—Nazi Policies and Jewish Responses," *Year Book of the Leo Baeck Institute,* vol. 25 (1980), 313–61; vol. 26 (1981), 343–409.

30. Quoted in Bentwich, *The Refugees from Germany,* 58.

31. See ibid., 72ff.; John I. Knudson, *A History of the League of Nations* (Atlanta: Turner E. Smith & Co., 1938), 258.

32. Quoted in Bentwich, *The Refugees from Germany,* 86.

33. Stephen M. Poppel, *Zionism in Germany, 1897–1933* (Philadelphia: Jewish Publication Society of America, 1977), 92f.

34. Quoted in Abraham Margaliot, "The Problem of Rescue of German Jewry During the Years 1933–1939; the Reasons for the Delay in Their Emigration from the Third Reich," in Yisrael Gutman and Efraim Zuroff, eds., *Rescue Attempts During the Holocaust: Proceedings of the Second Yad Vashem International Historical Conference* (Jerusalem: Yad Vashem, 1977), 255.

35. Johann von Leers, *14 Jahre Judenpolitik: Die Geschichte eines Rassenkampfes,* 2 vols. (Berlin: NS.-Druck und Verlag, 1933), vol. 2, 126.

36. On the Ha'avara Agreement, see Edwin Black, *The Transfer Agreement: The Dramatic Story of the Pact Between the Third Reich and Jewish Palestine* (New York: Macmillan, 1984).

37. Speech of 24 October, 1933, quoted in Norman H. Baynes, ed., *Hitler's Speeches, 1922–1939,* 2 vols. (Oxford: Royal Institute of International Affairs, 1942), vol. 1, 729.

38. See Heinz Höhne, *The Order of the Death's Head: The Story of Hitler's SS,* trans. Richard Barry (London: Secker & Warburg, 1969), 329ff.

39. "Ein Nazi fährt nach Palestina," *Der Angriff,* 9 October 1934, 4.

40. Quoted in Höhne, *The Order of the Death's Head,* 333.

41. Yfaat Weiss, "The Transfer Agreement and the Boycott Movement: A Jewish Dilemma on the Eve of the Holocaust," *Yad Vashem Studies,* vol. 26 (1998), 129–72.

42. Black, *The Transfer Agreement*; see also Curt D. Wormann, "German Jews in Israel: Their Cultural Situation Since 1933," *Year Book of the Leo Baeck Institute,* vol. 15 (1970), 73–103, and Mordechai Eliav, "German Jews' Share in the Building of the National Home in Palestine and the State of Israel," *Year Book of the Leo Baeck Institute,* vol. 30 (1985), 255–63.

43. See, for example, the vivid descriptions of the problems of adaptation in Martin Gumpert, "Immigrants by Conviction," *Survey Graphic,* vol. 30 (September 1941), 487; also Stefan Zweig, *The World of Yesterday,* 310.

44. Ernst L. Freud, ed., *The Letters of Sigmund Freud & Arnold Zweig,* trans. W. D. Robson-Scott (London: Hogarth Press, 1970), 56; also Wormann, "German Jews in Israel: Their Cultural Situation Since 1933," 87ff.

45. Freud, ed., *The Letters of Sigmund Freud & Arnold Zweig,* 108.

46. Ibid., 113.

47. Ibid., 122.

48. Abraham Margaliot, "The Problem of Rescue of German Jewry During the Years 1933–1939." in Yisrael Gutman and Efraim Zuroff, eds., *Rescue Attempts During the Holocaust* (Jerusalem: Yad Vashem, 1977), 255f.

49. Nahum Goldmann, *Community of Fate: Jews in the Modern World* (Jerusalem: Israel Universities Press, 1977), 45.

50. Ibid., 46.

51. Ibid., 44.

52. Ibid., 47.

53. Ibid.

54. On antisemitism in interwar Poland, see Ezra Mendelsohn, "Introduction: The Jews of Poland Between Two World Wars—Myth and Reality," Yisrael Gutman, "Political Antisemitism Between the Wars: An Overview," and Emanuel Melzer, "Antisemitism in the Last Years of the Second Polish Republic," all three in Yisrael Gutman, Ezra Mendelsohn, Jehuda Reinharz, and Chone Shmeruk, eds., *The Jews of Poland Between Two World Wars* (Hanover, NH, and London: University Press of New England, 1989), 1–6, 97–108, 126–37.

55. Alfred Döblin, *Journey to Poland,* trans. Joachim Neugroschel (New York: Pantheon Books, 1991), 151.

56. Ibid., 257.

57. See Celia S. Heller, *On the Edge of Destruction: Jews of Poland Between the Two Wars* (New York: Columbia University Press, 1977); Jerzy Tomaszewski, "The Civil Rights of Jews in Poland, 1918–1939," and Jerzy Holzer, "Polish Political Parties and Antisemitism," both in Anthony Polansky, Ezra Mendelsohn and Jerzy Tomaszewski, eds., *Jews in Independent Poland* (London and Washington, DC: Litman Library of Jewish Civilization, 1999), 115–28, 194–205; Edward D. Wynot, "The Polish Peasant Movement and the Jews, 1918–1939," in Gutman, Mendelsohn, Reinharz, and Shmeruk, eds., *The Jews of Poland Between Two World Wars,* 36–55; and Pawel Korzec, "Antisemitism in Poland," in Joshua Fishman, ed., *Studies on Polish Jewry 1919–1939* (New York: YIVO, 1974), 12–104.

58. Yaacov Shavit, *Jabotinksy and the Revisionist Movement, 1925–1948* (London: Frank Cass, 1988), 199f.

59. Chaim Weizmann, "The Jewish People and Palestine," in Meyer W. Weisgal, ed., *Chaim Weizmann: Statesman, Scientist, Builder of the Jewish Commonwealth* (New York: Dial Press, 1944), 306.

60. This short assessment of the economic condition of Polish Jewry can be found in Emil Lengyel, *The Cauldron Boils* (New York: Dial Press, 1932), 183.

61. See the American Committee on the Rights of Religious Minorities, *Roumania: Ten Years After* (Boston: Beacon Press, 1929).

62. See Nicholas Nagy-Talavera, *The Green Shirts and the Others: A History of Fascism in Hungary and Romania* (Stanford: Hoover Institution Press, 1970), and Z. Ornea, *The Romanian Extreme Right: The Nineteen Thirties,* trans. Eugenia Maria Popescu (Boulder, CO: East European Monographs, 1999).

63. See Alexander L. Easterman, *King Carol, Hitler and Lupescu* (London: Victor Gollancz, 1942), 101ff.; also Paul A. Shapiro, "Prelude to Dictatorship in Romania: The National Christian Party in Power, December 1937–February 1938," *Canadian-American Slavic Studies,* vol. 8 (1974), 45–88.

64. Radu Ioanid, "Romania," in David S. Wyman, ed., *The World Reacts to the Holocaust* (Baltimore and London: Johns Hopkins University Press, 1996), 230.

65. Shapiro, "Prelude to Dictatorship in Romania," 54ff.

66. Quoted in Easterman, *King Carol, Hitler and Lupescu,* 230.

67. Quoted in Karl A. Schleunes, *The Twisted Road to Auschwitz: Nazi Policy Toward the Jews* (Urbana and Chicago: University of Illinois Press, 1970), 203.

68. Ibid., 203ff.

69. Jochen von Lang with Claus Sibyll, eds., *Eichmann Interrogated: Transcripts from the Archives of the Israeli Police,* trans. Ralph Manheim (New York: Farrar, Straus & Giroux, 1983), 52, 56.

70. Elisabeth Rosner-Jellinek, oral history conducted by Debórah Dwork, Vienna, 24 and 26 June 1990, transcript 35.

71. Ibid., 32f.

72. Ibid., 128f.

73. Robert Rosner, oral history conducted by Debórah Dwork, Vienna, 3 July 1990, transcript 22.

74. Ibid., 24f.

75. Ibid., 25.

76. Ibid., 30.

77. Otto Suschny, oral history conducted by Debórah Dwork, Vienna, 18 July 1991, transcript 45.

78. Shalom Adler-Rudl, "The Evian Conference on the Refugee Question," *Year Book of the Leo Baeck Institute,* vol. 13 (1968), 235–73; Shlomo Z. Katz, "Public Opinion in Western Europe and the Evian Conference," *Yad Vashem Studies,* vol. 9 (1973), 105–32; Henry L. Feingold, *The Politics of Rescue: The Roosevelt Administration and the Holocaust, 1938–1945* (New York: Holocaust Library, 1970).

79. Quoted in Feingold, *The Politics of Rescue,* 23.

80. Quoted in Schleunes, *The Twisted Road to Auschwitz,* 209.

81. Great Britain, Foreign Office, *Palestine: Statement of Policy* (London: His Majesty's Stationery Office, 1939), 10f.

82. Ralph Montrose (Rudolf Rosenberg), oral history conducted by Debórah Dwork, Cardiff, Wales, 22 July 1985, transcript 10.

83. Ibid., 11f.

84. Ibid., 12f.

85. Lore Gang-Saalheimer, oral history conducted by Debórah Dwork, Cardiff, Wales, 21 July 1985, transcript 10f., 13.

86. Hilda Cohen-Rosenthal, oral history conducted by Debórah Dwork, Cardiff, Wales, 21 July 1985, transcript 2f., 5.

87. See Rebekka Göptert, *Der jüdische Kindertransport von Deutschland nach England* (Frankfurt-am-Main: Campus, 1997); Mark Jonathan Harris and Deborah Oppenheimer, *Into the Arms of Strangers: Stories of Kindertransport* (London: Bloomsbury, 2000).

88. Gerda Freistadt-Geiringer, oral history conducted by Debórah Dwork, Vienna, 10 and 15 July 1990, transcript 32.

89. Robert Rosner, oral history, transcript 33.

90. See John Hope Simpson *Refugees: A Review of the Situation Since September 1938* (London: Royal Institute of International Affairs, 1939), 24ff.

91. See Gordon Thomas and Max Morgan Witts, *The Voyage of the Damned* (Greenwich, CT: Fawcett, 1974). See too the master's thesis by Stefanie Fischer, "The *St. Louis* Fiasco: History and Myth," Center for Holocaust and Genocide Studies, Clark University, Worcester, MA.

92. Arthur Koestler, *Scum of the Earth* (London: Jonathan Cape, 1941), 90f.

93. Ellen Eliel-Wallach, oral history conducted by Debórah Dwork, Amsterdam, 3 August 1987, transcript 4f.

Chapter Six: GENTILE LIFE UNDER GERMAN OCCUPATION

1. Quoted in Wolfgang J. Mommsen, *Max Weber and German Politics, 1890–1920,* trans. Michael S. Steinberg (Chicago and London: University of Chicago Press, 1984), 312f.

2. William Harbutt Dawson, *Germany Under the Treaty* (New York: Longman, Green & Co., 1933), 382ff.

3. Johann Gottlieb Fichte, *Addresses to the German Nation,* ed. George A. Kelly, trans. R. F. Jones and G. H. Turnbull (New York: Harper & Row, 1968), 228.

4. See E. M. Butler, "Romantic 'Germanentum,'" in G. P. Gooch, ed., *The German Mind and Outlook* (London: Chapman & Hall, 1945), 100.

5. Quoted in Jeremy Noakes and Geoffrey Pridham, *Nazism 1919–1945,* 3 vols. (Exeter: Exeter University Publications, 1983–88), vol. 3, 681.

6. Hans Weigert, *Generals and Geographers: The Twilight of Geopolitics* (New York: Oxford University Press, 1942), 95.

7. Walther R. Darré, Preface, in Heinrich Bauer, *Geburt des Ostens: Drei Kämpfer um eine Idee* (Berlin: Frundsberg Verlag, 1933), 5.

8. Walther R. Darré, "The Farmers and the State," in Barbara Miller Lane and Leila J. Rupp, eds., *Nazi Ideology Before 1933: A Documentation* (Manchester: Manchester University Press, 1978), 133, italics in the original.

9. Kurt Trampler, *Am Volksboden und Grenze* (Heidelberg-Berlin: Kurt Vowinckel Verlag, 1935), 42.

10. Czecho-Slovakia consisted of the formerly Austrian-ruled Czech lands—comprising the Kingdom of Bohemia, the Duchy of (Austrian) Silesia, and the Margravate of Moravia—and the formerly Hungarian-ruled Slovak and Carpathian Rus regions.

11. See Radomir Luza, *The Transfer of the Sudeten Germans: A Study of Czech-German Relations, 1933–1962* (New York: New York University Press, 1964).

12. On Hitler's aims with the Czech lands, see Hermann Rauschning, *Hitler Speaks: A Series of Political Conversations with Adolf Hitler on His Real Aims* (London: Gerald Butterworth, 1939), 46.

13. Quoted in Max Domarus, *Hitler: Speeches and Proclamations, 1932–1945,* 4 vols. (Wauconda, IL: Bolchazy-Carducci, 1990–97), vol. 2, 1154.

14. Winston Churchill, *Blood, Sweat, and Tears* (New York: Putnam, 1941), 56, 66.

15. See Vojtech Mastny, *The Czechs Under Nazi Rule: The Failure of National Resistance* (New York and London: Columbia University Press, 1971), 20ff.

16. Quoted in ibid., 21.

17. Arnost Graumann, oral history conducted by Debórah Dwork, Cardiff, Wales, 23 July 1985, transcript 1.

18. Unpublished written statement by Arnost Graumann given to Debórah Dwork, 9.

19. Arnost Graumann, oral history, transcript 1f.

20. Ibid., 3.

21. Ibid., unpublished written statement, 9f.

22. Arnost Graumann, oral history, transcript 3.

23. See United States Department of State, *Documents on German Foreign Policy, 1918–1945,* Series D, 12 vols. (Washington, DC: U.S. Government Printing Office, 1949–62), vol. 4, 182.

24. Quoted in ibid., 194.

25. France, Ministry of Foreign Affairs, *Le Livre Jaune Français: Documents Diplomatiques, 1938–1939* (Paris: Impremerie Nationale, 1939), Document 45.

26. See *Documents on German Foreign Policy, 1918–1945,* vol. 4, 205.

27. See Heinrich Bodensieck, "Das Dritte Reich und die Lage der Juden in der Tschechoslowakei nach München," *Vierteljahreshefte für Zeitgeschichte,* vol. 9 (1961), 249–61. For a general overview of the history of the Czech Jews from 1938 to 1945, see Livia Rothkirchen, "The Jews of Bohemia and Moravia: 1938–1945," in Avigdor Dagan, ed., *The Jews of Czechoslovakia: Historical Studies and Surveys,* 3 vols. (Philadelphia: Jewish Publication Society of America, 1968–84), vol. 3, 3–74.

28. See Dierk O. Hoffman, "Czech Nationalists Occupy the German Landestheater/Ständetheater in Prague," in Sander L. Gilman and Jack Zipes, eds., *Yale Companion to Jewish Writing and Thought in German Culture, 1096–1996* (New Haven and London: Yale University Press, 1997), 390ff.

29. Livia Rothkirchen, "Czech Attitudes Towards the Jews During the Nazi Regime," *Yad Vashem Studies,* vol. 13 (1979), 303. The real impact of the 30,000 Jews would have been little, given that their German "vote" would have increased the German share by at best 1 percent.

30. Quoted in Livia Rothkirchen, "The Protectorate Government and the 'Jewish Question,' 1939–1941," *Yad Vashem Studies,* vol. 27 (1999), 335.

31. See *Documents on German Foreign Policy, 1918–1945,* vol. 4, 270.

32. Ibid., 283f.

33. Ibid., 284.

34. Ibid.

35. Ibid., 285. For a contemporary analysis of the absurdity of the Protectorate's constitution and its position in international law, see Eugene V. Erdely, *Germany's First European Protectorate: The Fate of the Czechs and Slovaks* (London: Robert Hale, 1941), 38ff.

36. See Mastny, *The Czechs Under Nazi Rule.*

37. Ibid., 340.

38. See John G. Lexa, "Anti-Jewish Laws and Regulations in the Protectorate of Bohemia and Moravia," in Dagan, ed., *The Jews of Czechoslovakia,* vol. 3, 75–103.

39. Quoted in Great Britain, Foreign Office, *The British War Blue Book: Documents Concerning German-Polish Relations and the Outbreak of Hostilities Between Great Britain and Germany on September 3, 1939* (New York: Farrar & Rinehart, 1939), 11f.

40. Quoted in ibid., 48.

41. See Geoffrey Robert, *The Unholy Alliance: Stalin's Pact with Hitler* (London: Tauris, 1989).

42. Count Galeazzo Ciano, *The Ciano Diaries 1939–1943,* ed. Hugh Gibson (Garden City, NY: Garden City Publishing, 1947), 580. This was Ciano's final entry in his diary. Dated 23 December 1943, it was written in cell 27 of the Verona jail, two weeks before his execution by the Italian puppet government of Salò.

43. General histories of World War II which we found useful were Peter Calvocoressi and Guy Wint, *Total War* (Harmondsworth, UK: Penguin, 1985); R. A. C. Parker, *Struggle for Survival: The History of the Second World War* (Oxford: Oxford University Press, 1989); and Gerhard L. Weinberg, *A World at Arms: A Global History of World War II* (Cambridge: Cambridge University Press, 1994).

44. Franz Lüdtke, *Ein Jahrtausend Krieg Zwischen Deutschland und Polen* (Stuttgart: Robert Lutz Nachfolger, 1941), 191.

45. Adolf Hitler, *My New Order,* ed. Raoul de Roussy de Sales (New York: Reynal & Hitchcock, 1941), 729.

46. Ibid., 737.

47. Ibid., 737f.

48. Quoted in Anthony Weymouth, *Journal of the War Years* (London: Littlebury & Co., 1948); see also David Nathan, "Failure of an Elderly Gentleman: Shaw and the Jews," in T. F. Evans, ed., *Shaw and Politics* (University Park, PA: Pennsylvania State University Press, 1991), 219–38.

49. See Eyal Benvenisti, *The International Law of Occupation* (Princeton: Princeton University Press, 1993).

50. See, for example, articles 41–48 of the "Oxford Manual" (1880). Dietrich Schindler and Jiri Toman, *The Laws of Armed Conflicts: A Collection of Conventions, Resolutions, and Other Documents* (Leiden: Sijthoff, 1977), 42f.

51. Quoted in Benvenisti, *The International Law of Occupation,* 27.

52. Quoted in Leon Friedman, ed., *The Law of War: A Documentary History,* 2 vols. (New York: Random House, 1972), vol. 1, 321.

53. Sharon Korman, *The Right of Conquest: The Acquisition of Territory by Force in International Law and Practice* (Oxford: Clarendon Press, 1996), 136ff.

54. Text in Harold William Temperley, ed., *A History of the Peace Conference of Paris,* 6 vols. (London: Oxford University Press, 1920–24), vol. 1, 437.

55. Noakes and Pridham, *Nazism 1919–1945,* vol. 3, 927.

56. See Helmut Krausnick, *Hitlers Einsatzgruppen: Die Truppen des Weltanschauungskrieges 1938–1942* (Frankfurt-am-Main: Fischer Taschenbuch Verlag, 1989), 26ff.; see also Hans Buchheim, "The SS—Instrument of Domination," in Helmut Krausnick, Hans Buchheim, Martin Broszat, and Hans-Adolf Jacobsen, eds., *Anatomy of the SS State,* trans. Richard Barry, Marian Jackson, and Dorothy Long (New York: Walker & Co., 1968), 177ff.

57. Quoted in Poland, Ministry of Information, *The Black Book of Poland* (New York: G. P. Putnam's Sons, 1942), 134.

58. "Erlass des Führers und Reichskanzlers zur Festigung deutschen Volkstums vom 7. Oktober 1939," ms., BA Koblenz, R 49–2, 3ff; translation from Robert Lewis Koehl, *RKFDV: German Resettlement and Population Policy, 1939–1945. A History of the Reich Commission for the Strengthening of Germandom* (Cambridge, MA: Harvard University Press, 1957), 247.

59. Hanns Johst, *Ruf des Reiches—Echo des Volkes: Eine Ostfahrt* (Munich: Franz Eher Nachfolger, 1940), 126f.

60. See Debórah Dwork and Robert Jan van Pelt, *Auschwitz: 1270 to the Present* (New York and London: W.W. Norton, 1996), 127–59; and Koehl, *RKFDV: German Resettlement and Population Policy, 1939–1945.*

61. Quoted in *The Black Book of Poland,* 104.

62. Ibid., 198f.

63. Quoted in Nuernberg Military Tribunals, "The RUSHA Case," *Trials of the War Criminals,* 15 vols. (Washington, DC: U.S. Government Printing Office, 1949–53), vol. 4, 762f.

64. See Richard C. Lukas, *The Forgotten Holocaust: The Poles Under German Occupation, 1939–1944,* 2d edn. (New York: Hippocrene, 1997); Jan Tomasz Gross, *Polish Society Under German Occupation: The Generalgouvernement* (Princeton: Princeton University Press, 1979); and Czeslaw Madajczyk, *Die Okkupationspolitik Nazideutschlands in Polen, 1939–1945,* trans. Berthold Puchert (Cologne: Pahl-Rugenstein, 1988). A critique of Madajczyk's tendency to minimize the tragedy of the Jews can be found in Shmuel Krakowski, "Policy of the Third Reich in Conquered Poland," *Yad Vashem Studies,* vol. 9 (1973), 225–46.

65. Noakes and Pridham, *Nazism 1919–1945,* vol. 3, 933.

66. Raphael Lemkin, *Axis Rule in Occupied Europe: Laws of Occupation, Analysis of Government, Proposals for Redress* (Washington, DC: Carnegie Endowment for International Peace, 1944), 79ff.

67. *The Black Book of Poland,* 21.

68. Ibid., 538f.

69. "The Jews Must Emigrate," *Naród,* 20 January 1942, quoted in Shmuel Krakowski, "Holocaust in the Polish Underground Press," *Yad Vashem Studies,* vol. 16 (1984), 265.

70. Quoted in Andrzej Bryk, "The Hidden Complex of the Polish Mind," in Antony Polonsky, ed., *My Brother's Keeper? Recent Polish Debates on the Holocaust* (London: Routledge, 1990), 166f.

71. *Szaniec,* 6 December 1940, quoted in Krakowski, "Holocaust in the Polish Underground Press," 262.

72. "Behind Ghetto Walls," *Wiadomosci Polskie,* 13 August 1942, quoted in Krakowski, "Holocaust in the Polish Underground Press," 249f.

73. Quoted in Bryk, "The Hidden Complex of the Polish Mind," 170.

74. Richard Petrow, *The Bitter Years: The Invasion and Occupation of Denmark and Norway, April 1940–May 1945* (New York: William Morrow, 1974), 45ff, 159ff.

75. Leni Yahil, *The Rescue of Danish Jewry: Test of a Democracy,* trans. Morris Gradel (Philadelphia: Jewish Publication Society of America, 1969), 42.

76. Petrow, *The Bitter Years,* 184ff.

77. See Hans Frederik Dahl, *Quisling: A Study in Treachery* (Cambridge: Cambridge University Press, 1999).

78. Petrow, *The Bitter Years,* 99ff.

79. Ibid., 114ff.

80. Bernhard Vollmer, "Die Niederlande als geschichtliche Raum," in Max Freiherr du Prel, ed., *Die Niederlande im Umbruch der Zeiten: Alte und neue Beziehungen zum Reich* (Würzburg: Konrad Triltsch, 1941), 3–26.

81. See Karl Lamprecht, *Deutsche Geschichte,* 10 vols. (Berlin: Weidmannsche Buchhandlung, 1913), vol. 3, 310–43; H. Witte, "Naar Oostland . . . ," in R. P. Oszwald, ed., *Deutsch-Niederländische Symphonie* (Wolfshagen-Scharbeutz: Westphal, 1937), 48–67; H. W. Van Etten, "Naar Oostland . . . ," in du Prel, ed., *Die Niederlande im Umbruch der Zeiten,* 179–84.

82. Konrad Kwiet, *Reichskommissariat Niederlande: Versuch und Scheitern nationalsozialistischer Neuordnung* (Stuttgart: Deutsche Verlags-Anstalt, 1968); Louis de Jong, *Het Koninkrijk der Nederlanden in de Tweede Wereldoorlog,* 14 vols. (The Hague: Martinus Nijhoff, 1969–91), vol. 4, 49ff.

83. Eugon Kogon, *The Theory and Practice of Hell* (New York: Berkley Books, 1984), 180–81.

84. Werrner Warmbrunn, *The Dutch Under German Occupation, 1940–1945* (Stanford: Stanford University Press, 1963), 106ff.; De Jong, *Het Koninkrijk der Nederlanden in de Tweede Wereldoorlog,* vol. 4, 861ff.

85. Warmbrunn, *The Dutch Under German Occupation, 1940–1945,* 112ff.

86. Joseph Goebbels, *The Goebbels Diaries, 1942–1943,* ed. Louis P. Lochner (Garden City, NY: Doubleday, 1948), 434.

87. See C. Hilbrink, *"In het belang van het Nederlandse volk . . ." Over de medewerking van de ambtelijke wereld aan de Duitse bezetting spolitiek 1940–1945* (The Hague: Sdu, 1995).

88. See Werner Warmbrunn, *The German Occupation of Belgium, 1940–1944* (New York: Peter Lang, 1993); Jacques Willequet, *La Belgique sous la botte: Résistances et collaborations 1940–1945* (Paris: Editions Universitaires, 1986).

89. See Dan Michman, ed., *Belgium and the Holocaust: Jews, Belgians, Germans* (Jerusalem: Yad Vashem, 1998).

90. See John Williams, *The Ides of May: The Defeat of France, May–June 1940* (London: Carlisle, 1968).

91. Quoted in Margaret Collins Weitz, *Sisters in the Resistance: How Women Fought to Free France, 1940–1945* (New York: John Wiley, 1995), 24.

92. Ian Ousby, *Occupation: The Ordeal of France, 1940–1944* (New York: St. Martin's Press, 1997), 19.

93. William L. Shirer, *20th Century Journey: A Memoir of a Life and the Times,* Vol. II, *The Nightmare Years* (Boston: Little, Brown, 1984), 532ff.

94. The literature on the collaborationism of Vichy is by now immense. Path-breaking was Robert O. Paxton, *Vichy France: Old Guard and New Order, 1940–1944* (New York: Alfred A. Knopf, 1972). In English, see also Robert Aron, *The Vichy Regime* (London: Pantheon Books, 1958); Bertram M. Gordon, *Collaborationism in France During the Second World War* (Ithaca and London: Cornell University Press, 1980); Richard Cobb, *French and Germans, Germans and French: A Personal Interpretation of France and Two Occupations* (Hanover, NH: University Press of New England, 1983); John F. Sweets, *Choices in Vichy France: The French Under Nazi Occupation* (New York and Oxford: Oxford University Press, 1988); Gerhard Hirschfeld and Patrick Marsh, eds., *Collaboration in France: Politics and Culture During the Nazi Occupation, 1940–1944* (Oxford: Oxford University Press, 1989); and Philippe Burrin, *France Under the Germans: Collaboration and Compromise* (New York: New Press, 1996).

95. Quoted in H. R. Kedward, *Occupied France: Collaboration, and Resistance, 1940–1944* (Oxford and New York: Basil Blackwell, 1985), 10.

96. Quoted in Ousby, *Occupation,* 268.

Chapter Seven: THE ASSAULT OF TOTAL WAR

1. See John Lukacs, *Five Days in London: May 1940* (New Haven and London: Yale University Pres, 1999).

2. Winston Churchill, *Blood, Sweat, and Tears* (New York: Putnam, 1941), 286.

3. Ibid., 314.

4. See Friedrich Naumann, *Central Europe* (London: P. S. King, 1916). For the impact of Naumann's vision, see Henry Cord Meyer, *Mitteleuropa in German Thought and Action, 1815–1945* (The Hague: Nijhoff, 1955)

5. See Joseph A. Mikus, *Slovakia: A Political History, 1918–1950* (Milwaukee: Marquette University Press, 1963), 66ff.; Jozef Lettrich, *History of Modern Slovakia* (New York: Frederick Praeger, 1955), 123ff.

6. See Ladislav Lipscher, "The Jews of Slovakia: 1939–1945," in Avigdor Dagan, ed., *The Jews of Czechoslovakia,* 3 vols. (Philadelphia: Jewish Publication Society of America, 1968–83), vol. 3, 165–261.

7. Ibid., vol. 3, 182.

8. See R. J. Crampton, *Eastern Europe in the Twentieth Century—And After,* 2d edn. (London and New York: Routledge, 1997), 31ff.

9. See Albert Kaas and Fedor de Lazarovics, *Bolshevism in Hungary: The Béla Kun Period* (London: Grant Richards, 1931).

10. Letter, R. W. Seton-Watson to J. Headlam-Morley, 28 May 1919, quoted in Nathaniel Katzburg, *Hungary and the Jews: Policy and Legislation 1920–1943* (Ramat-Gan, Israel: Bar-Ilan University Press, 1981), 35.

11. Quoted in ibid., 42f.

12. Biographies of Horthy written before 1940 tend to resemble medieval hagiographies. See, for example, Owen Rutter, *Regent of Hungary: The Authorized Lfe of Admiral Nicholas Horthy* (London: Rich & Cowan, 1939).

13. Thomas Sakmyster, *Hungary's Admiral on Horseback: Miklós Horthy, 1918–1944* (Boulder, CO: East European Monographs, 1994), 146ff.

14. Quoted in Randolph J. Braham, *The Politics of Genocide: The Holocaust in Hungary,* 2 vols. (New York: Columbia University Press, 1981), vol. 1, 41.

15. See Carlile Aylmer Macartney, *October Fifteenth: A History of Modern Hungary, 1929–1945,* 2 vols. (Edinburgh: Edinburgh University Press, 1957).

16. John Flournoy Montgomery, *Hungary, The Unwilling Satellite* (New York: Devin-Adair Co., 1947), 103.

17. Aladár Komlós, "The Tribulations of the Hungarian-Jewish Writer," in Andrew Handler, ed., *The Holocaust in Hungary: An Anthology of Jewish Response* (University, AL: University of Alabama Press, 1982), 37.

18. Quoted in Katzburg, *Hungary and the Jews,* 255.

19. Quoted in ibid., 96.

20. Quoted in Braham, *The Politics of Genocide,* vol. 1, 149.

21. Miklós Horthy, *Confidential Papers,* ed. Miklós Szinai and László Szücs (Budapest: Corvina Press, 1965), 150f.

22. Livia Rothkirchen, "Hungary—An Asylum for the Refugees of Europe," *Yad Vashem Studies,* vol. 7 (1968), 127–46.

23. Ibid., 131.

24. Quoted in Braham, *The Politics of Genocide,* vol. 1, 173.

25. Quoted in ibid., vol. 1, 173f.

26. Quoted in Katzburg, *Hungary and the Jews,* 218f.

27. Joseph Goebbels, *The Goebbels Diaries, 1942–1943,* ed. Louis P. Lochner (Garden City, NY: Doubleday, 1948), 95.

28. International Military Tribunal, *Trial of the Major War Criminals,* 41 vols. (Nuremberg: Secretariat of the International Military Tribunal, 1947–49), vol. 13, 259ff.

29. Quoted in Braham, *The Politics of Genocide,* vol. 1, 234.

30. Ibid., 241.

31. Quoted in Raul Hilberg, *Documents of Destruction* (Chicago: Quadrangle Books, 1971), 190. For Horthy's view, see Nicholas Horthy, *Memoirs* (New York: Robert Speller, 1957), 204ff.

32. Goebbels, *The Goebbels Diaries, 1942–1943,* 357.

33. Quoted in Katzburg, *Hungary and the Jews,* 223.

34. Quoted in Braham, *The Politics of Genocide,* vol. 1, 363.

35. Sakmyster, *Hungary's Admiral on Horseback,* 336.

36. See Paul Shapiro, "Prelude to Dictatorship in Romania: The National Christian Party in Power, December 1937–February 1938," *Canadian American Slavic Studies,* vol. 8 (1974), 45–88. See also Larry L. Watts, *Romanian Cassandra: Ion Antonescu and the Struggle for Reform, 1916–1941* (Boulder, CO: East European Monographs, 1993), 157ff., and Radu Ioanid, "Romania," in David S. Wyman, ed., *The World Reacts to the Holocaust* (Baltimore and London: Johns Hopkins University Press, 1996), 228ff.

37. Alexander L. Easterman, *King Carol, Hitler and Lupescu* (London: Victor Gollanz, 1942), 101.

38. Ibid., 103.

39. Radu Ioanid, *The Holocaust in Romania: The Destruction of Jews and Gypsies Under the Antonescu Regime, 1940–1944* (Chicago: Ivan R. Dee, 2000), 29ff.

40. See Ion Gheorghe, *Rumaniens Weg zum Satellitenstaat* (Heidelberg: Kurt Vowinckel, 1952); Andreas Hillgruber, *Hitler, König Carol und Marshall Antonescu: Die Deutsche-Rumanische Beziehungen 1938–1944* (Wiesbaden: Franz Steiner, 1954), 42ff.

41. Olivia Manning, *The Balkan Trilogy* (London: Arrow Books, 1997), 265.

42. Watts, *Romanian Cassandra,* 205 ff.

43. Max Domarus, *Hitler: Speeches and Proclamations 1932–1945,* 4 vols. (Wauconda, IL: Bolchazy-Carducci, 1997), vol. 3, 2068.

44. Count Galeazzo Ciano, *The Ciano Diaries 1939–1943,* ed. Hugh Gibson (Garden City, NY: Garden City Publishing, 1947), 288.

45. Ibid., 289.

46. See Watts, *Romanian Cassandra,* 261ff.

47. See Frederick B. Chary, *The Bulgarian Jews and the Final Solution, 1940–1944* (Pittsburgh: University of Pittsburgh Press, 1972), 27ff.

48. Quoted in Marshall Lee Miller, *Bulgaria During the Second World War* (Stanford: Stanford University Press, 1975), 31.

49. Quoted in Michael Bar-Zohar, *Beyond Hitler's Grasp: The Heroic Rescue of Bulgaria's Jews* (Holbrook, MA: Adams Media Corp., 1998), 25; also Chary, *The Bulgarian Jews and the Final Solution, 1940–1944,* 35ff.

50. Quoted in Bar-Zohar, *Beyond Hitler's Grasp,* 37.

51. Quoted in ibid., 32f.

52. Quoted in ibid., 34.

53. Quoted in Miller, *Bulgaria During the Second World War,* 55.

54. See Chary, *The Bulgarian Jews and the Final Solution,* 101ff. Cf. also Nissan Oren, "The Bulgarian Experience," *Yad Vashem Studies,* vol. 7 (1968), 83–106.

55. Fred Singleton, *Twentieth-Century Yugoslavia* (New York: Columbia University Press, 1976), 66ff.; John R. Lampe, *Yugoslavia as History: Twice There Was a Country* (Cambridge: Cambridge University Press, 1996), 126ff.

56. Lampe, *Yugoslavia as History,* 160ff.; Jill A Irvine, *The Croat Question* (Boulder, CO, and Oxford: Westview Press, 1993), 40ff. Also James J. Sadkovich, *Italian Support for Croatian Separatism* (New York: Garland, 1987).

57. See J. B. Hoptner, *Yugoslavia in Crisis, 1934–1941* (New York and London: Columbia University Press, 1962).

58. See Dragisa N. Ristic, *Yugoslavia's Revolution of 1941* (University Park, PA: Pennsylvania State University Press, 1966).

59. United States Department of State, *Documents on German Foreign Policy, 1918–1945,* Series D, 12 vols. (Washington, DC: U.S. Government Printing Office, 1949–62), vol. 12, 395.
60. The standard history of the German conquest of Yugoslavia and the events that followed is Ahmet Djon-lagic, Zarko Atanackovvic, and Duslan Plenca, *Yugoslavia in the Second World War,* trans. Lovett F. Edwards (Belgrade: Medjunarodna stampa Interpress, 1967). A superb new history is Jozo Tomasevich, *War and Revolution in Yugoslavia, 1941–1945* (Stanford: Stanford University Press, 2001); also Jozo Tomasevich, *The Chetniks* (Stanford: Stanford University Press, 1975).
61. *Documents on German Foreign Policy, 1918–1945,* vol. 12, 549.
62. Ladislaus Hory and Martin Broszat, *Die Kroatische Ustascha-Staat, 1941–1945* (Stuttgart: Deutsche Verlags-Anstalt, 1964).
63. See Edmond Paris, *Genocide in Satellite Croatia, 1941–1945,* trans. Lois Perkins (Chicago: Institute for Balkan Affairs, 1961). Also Vladimir Dedijer, *The Yugoslav Auschwitz and the Vatican: The Croatian Mas-sacre of the Serbs During World War II,* trans. Harvey L. Kendall (Buffalo: Prometheus, 1992).
64. Tomasevich, *The Chetniks,* 115ff.
65. Quoted in Dennis Reinharz, "Damnation of the Outsider: The Gypsies of Croatia and Serbia in the Balkan Holocaust, 1941–1945," in David Crowe and John Kolsti, eds., *The Gypsies of Eastern Europe* (Armonk, NY, and London: M. E. Sharpe, 1991), 89.
66. Phyllis Avty, *Tito: A Biography* (London: Longman, 1970), 165ff.
67. Curzio Malaparte, *Kaputt,* trans. Cesare Foligno (New York: E. P. Dutton, 1946), 266.
68. See MacGregor Knox, *Mussolini Unleashed 1939–1941: Politics and Strategy in Fascist Italy's Last War* (Cambridge: Cambridge University Press, 1982).
69. Ciano, *The Ciano Diaries 1939–1943,* 129.
70. Ibid., 235, 300.
71. Churchill, *Blood, Sweat, and Tears,* 442f.
72. See Mark Mazower, *Inside Hitler's Greece: The Experience of Occupation, 1941–44* (New Haven: Yale University Press, 1993).
73. Quoted in ibid., 44–46.
74. Two classic English-language histories of the German-Soviet War are Alan Clark, *Barbarossa: The Russian-German Conflict, 1941–1945* (New York: William Morrow, 1965), and Albert Seaton, *The Russo-German War, 1941–1945* (London: Arthur Barker, 1971).
75. See Alexander Dallin, *German Rule in Russia, 1941–1945* (New York: Macmillan, 1957), 67f.; Omer Bartov, *Hitler's Army: Soldiers, Nazis and War in the Third Reich* (New York and Oxford: Oxford University Press, 1991); and Gerd R. Ueberschär, "Hitlers Entschluß zum 'Lebensraum' Krieg im Osten: Programmatisches Ziel oder militärstrategisches Kalkul?" in Gerd R. Ueberschär and Wolfram Wette, eds., *Der deutsche Überfall auf die Sowjetunion: "Unternehmen Barbarossa" 1941* (Frankfurt-am-Main: S. Fischer, 1991), 13–44.
76. Franz Lüdtke, *Ein Jahrtausend Krieg zwischen Deutschland und Polen* (Stuttgart: Robert Lutz Nachfolger/Inhaber Rudolf Weisert, 1941), 7f.; see also Wolfram Wette, "Die propagandische Begleitmusik zum deutschen Überfall auf die Sowjetunion am 22. Juni 1941," in Ueberschär and Wette, eds., *Der deutsche Überfall auf die Sowjetunion,* 45–66.
77. See, for example, Peter Jahn, "'Russenfurcht' und Antibolschiwismus: Zur entstehung und Wirkung von Feindbildern," in Peter Jahn and Reinhard Rürup, eds., *Erobern und Vernichten: Der Krieg gegen die Sowjetunion, 1941–145* (Berlin: Argon, 1991), 47–64; Hans-Heinrich Wilhelm, "Motivation und 'Kriegsbild' deutscher Generale und Offiziere im Krieg gegen die Sowjetunion," in ibid., 153–82; Wolfram Wette, "Das Rußlandbild in der NS-Propaganda. Ein Problemaufriß," in Hans-Erich Volkmann, ed., *Das Rußlandbild im Dritten Reich* (Cologne: Böhlau, 1994), 55–78; Andreas Hillgruber, "Das Rußlandbild der führenden deutschen Militärs vor Beginn des Angriffs auf die Sowjetunion," in Volkmann, ed., *Das Rußlandbild im Dritten Reich,* 125–40; and Gerhard Hass, "Zum Rußlandbild der SS," in ibid., 201–24.
78. Charles Burdick and Hans-Adolf Jacobsen, eds., *The Halder War Diary, 1939–1942* (Novato, CA: Presidio, 1988), 346.
79. See, for example, Nuremberg Document 126-EC, "Report by the Economic Staff East, 23 May 1941," in International Military Tribunal, *Trial of the Major War Criminals,* 41 vols. (Nuremberg: Secretariat of the Tribunal, 1947–49), vol. 36, 145. On the German politics of hunger in the occupied Soviet Union, see Götz Aly and Susanne Heim, *Vordenker der Vernichtung: Auschwitz und die deutschen Pläne für eine neue europäische Ordnung* (Hamburg: Hoffmann und Campe, 1991), 365ff., and Götz Aly, *Final Solution: Nazi Population Policy and the Murder of the European Jews,* trans. Belinda Cooper and Allison Brown (London: Arnold, 1999), 185ff.
80. Malcom Muggeridge, ed., *Ciano's Diplomatic Papers,* trans. Stuart Hood (London: Odhams Press, 1948), 465.
81. On the administrative division of occupied Russia, see Dallin, *German Rule in Russia, 1941–1945,* 84–103; on Reichskommissariat Ostland, see ibid., 182–98; on Reichskommissariat Ukraine, see ibid., 146–67.

82. See Dallin, *German Rule in Russia, 1941–1945,* 409–27; Gerhard Hirschfeld, ed., *The Policies of Genocide: Jews and Soviet Prisoners of War in Nazi Germany* (London, Boston, and Sydney: Allen & Unwin/German Historical Institute, 1986); Christian Streit, *Keine Kamaraden: Die Wehrmacht und die sowjetischen Kriegsgefangenen 1941–1945* (Stuttgart: Deutsche Verlags-Anstalt, 1978); and Christian Streit, "Die Behandlung der sowjetischer Kriegsgefangenen und völkerrechtliche Problem des Krieges gegen die Sowjetunion," in Ueberschär and Wette, *Der deutsche Überfall auf die Soujetunion,* 159–84.

83. Quoted in Jürgen Förster, "The German Army and the Ideological War Against the Soviet Union," in Hirschfeld, ed., *The Policies of Genocide,* 20.

84. Dallin, *German Rule in Russia, 1941–1945,* 428–53.

85. See Alan S. Milward, *War, Economy and Society, 1939–1945* (London: Allen Lane, 1977), 221ff.; John H. E. Fried, *The Exploitation of Foreign Labour by Germany* (Montreal: International Labour Office, 1945); Edward L Homze, *Foreign Labor in Nazi Germany* (Princeton: Princeton University Press, 1967); H. Pfahlmann, *Fremdarbeiter und Kriegsgefangene in der deutschen Kriegswirtschaft, 1939–1945* (Darmstadt: Wehr un Wissen Verlagsgesellschaft, 1968); and Ulrich Herbert, "Zwangsarbeit in Deutschland: Sowjetische Zivilarbeiter und Kriegsgefangene 1941–1945," in Jahn and Rürup, eds., *Erobern und Vernichten,* 106–30.

86. See Dallin, *German Rule in Russia, 1941–1945,* 74ff., 209ff., 517ff.; John A. Armstrong, ed., *Soviet Partisans in World War II* (Madison: University of Wisconsin Press, 1964); and Matthew Cooper, *The Nazi War Against Soviet Partisans, 1941–1945* (New York: Stein & Day, 1979).

87. Quoted in Cooper, *The Nazi War Against Soviet Partisans,* 168.

88. See Sarah Neshamit, "Rescue in Lithuania During the Nazi Occupation, June 1941–August 1944," in Yisrael Gutman and Efraim Zuroff, eds., *Rescue Attempts During the Holocaust: Proceedings of the Second Yad Vashem International Historical Conference* (Jerusalem: Yad Vashem, 1977), 295f.

89. Yitzhak Arad, Shmuel Krakowski, and Shmuel Spector, eds., *The Einsatzgruppen Reports* (New York: Holocaust Library, 1989), 17. On the reliability of the assessment of the Operational Situation Reports concerning the attitudes of the various ethnic groups in the German-occupied Soviet Union, see Ronald Headland, *Messages of Murder: A Study of the Reports of the Einsatzgruppen of the Security Police and the Security Service, 1941–1943* (London and Toronto: Associated University Presses, 1992), 109ff.

90. Arad, Krakowski, and Spector, eds., *The Einsatzgruppen Reports,* 17.

91. See Andrew Ezergailis, *The Holocaust in Latvia, 1941–1944: The Missing Center* (Riga and Washington, DC: Historical Institute of Latvia and United States Holocaust Memorial Museum, 1996), 101ff.

92. Arad, Krakowski, and Spector, eds., *The Einsatzgruppen Reports,* 61.

93. Ibid., 31.

94. Ibid., 73.

95. Ibid., 131.

96. Ibid., 216.

97. Ibid., 68.

98. See Meir Michaelis, *Mussolini and the Jews: German-Italian Relations and the Jewish Question in Italy, 1922–1945* (Oxford: Oxford University Press, 1978); also his earlier "The Attitude of the Fascist Regime to the Jews of Italy," *Yad Vashem Studies,* vol. 4 (1960), 7–42.

99. Michaelis, *Mussolini and the Jews,* 28.

100. See Emil Ludwig, *Mussolinis Gespräche mit Emil Ludwig* (Berlin: Paul Zsolnay Verlag, 1932), 75f.

101. For the text of the *Race Manifesto,* see Renzo de Felici, *Storia degli ebrei italiani sotte il fascismo* (Turin: Einaudi, 1972), 541f.; see also U.S. edition, *The Jews in Fascist Italy: A History,* trans. Robert L. Miller (New York: Enigma Books, 2001), 690ff.

102. de Felice, *Storia degli ebrei sotto il fascismo,* 612.

103. *Civilitá Cattolica,* 29 July 1938, 373, quoted in Michaelis, *Mussolini and the Jews,* 153.

104. Quoted in ibid.

105. Laura Fermi, *Atoms in the Family* (Chicago: University of Chicago Press, 1954), 123.

106. Mariella Milano-Piperno, oral history conducted by Debórah Dwork, Rome, 6 June 1985, transcript 2.

107. De Felice, *Storia delgli ebrei sotto il facismo,* 415f.

108. Mariella Milano-Piperno, oral history, transcript 3.

109. Ibid., 3ff. See also the published memoirs: Fabio Della Seta, *L'Incendio del Tevere* (Trapani: Editore Celebes, 1969); Giorgio Piperno, "Fermenti di vita giovanile ebraica a Roma durante il periodo delle leggi razziali e dopo la liberazione della citta," in Daniel Carpi, Attilio Milano, and Umberto Nahon, eds., *Scritti in memoria di Enzo Sereni: Saggi sull'ebraismo romano* (Milan: Editrice Fondazione Sally Mayer, 1970), 293–313.

110. Galeazzo Ciano, *Ciano's Diary 1937–1938,* trans. Andreas Mayor (London: Methuen, 1952), 199.

111. Winston Churchill, *The Unrelenting Struggle* (Toronto: McClelland & Stewart, 1942), 95.

112. Goebbels, *The Goebbels Diaries,* 410f.

113. Ibid., 506.

114. Ibid., 467.

115. For the position of the Jews in the Italian Social Republic, see Liliana Picciotto Fargion, "The Anti-Jewish Policy of the Italian Social Republic," *Yad Vashem Studies,* vol. 17 (1986), 17–50.
116. Quoted in James D. Wilkinson, *The Intellectual Resistance in Europe* (Cambridge, MA: Harvard University Press, 1981), 215.
117. Quoted in Raul Hilberg, *The Destruction of the European Jews,* 3 vols. (New York and London: Holmes & Meier, 1985), vol. 2, 820.
118. Quoted in H.-A Jacobsen, *Der zweite Weltkrieg, Grundzüge der Politik und Strategie in Dokumenten* (Frankfurt-am-Main: S. Fischer, 1965), 180f.

Chapter Eight: JEWISH LIFE UNDER GERMAN OCCUPATION

1. Sara Grossman-Weil, oral history conducted by Debórah Dwork, Malverne, NY, 29 and 30 April 1987, transcript 6.
2. Ibid.
3. Ibid., 12.
4. Ibid.
5. Ibid., 13.
6. Ibid., 13–14f.
7. Mira Teeman, oral history conducted by Debórah Dwork, Stockholm, 6 September 1995, transcript 1.
8. Ibid.
9. Ibid., 9.
10. Ibid., 10, 12.
11. Ibid., 12.
12. "Selbsterlebte Geschichte in den Feldpostbriefen des Reichsinstituts für Geschichte des neuen Deutschlands 1939/40," in *Reich und Reichsfeinde I* (Hamburg: Hanseatische Verlagsanstalt, 1941), 14, 17.
13. "Polnische Juden auf 'Bienen' Jagd," *Illustrierter Beobachter* (vol. 14), 19 October 1939, 1152f.
14. Quoted in Christopher R. Browning, "Genocide and Public Health: German Doctors and Polish Jews, 1939–1941," *Holocaust and Genocide Studies,* vol. 3 (1988), 23.
15. Adam Czerniakow, *The Warsaw Diary of Adam Czerniakow,* trans. Stanislaw Staron and the staff of Yad Vashem, eds. Raul Hilberg, Stanislaw Staron, and Josef Kermisz (New York: Stein & Day, 1979), 90.
16. Quoted in Götz Aly, *Final Solution: Nazi Population Policy and the Murder of the European Jews,* trans. Belinda Cooper and Allison Brown (London: Edward Arnold, 1999), 17.
17. Quoted in Jeremy Noakes and Geoffrey Pridham, *Nazism 1919–1945,* 3 vols. (Exeter: Exeter University Publications, 1983–88), vol. 3, 927.
18. On the day-to-day routines of RSHA IV-B-4, see Yaacov Lozowick, "Malice in Action," *Yad Vashem Studies,* vol. 27 (1999), 287–330.
19. Quoted in Aly, *Final Solution,* 17.
20. Nuremberg Document 2278-PS, International Military Tribunal, *Trial of the Major War Criminals,* 41 vols. (Nuremberg: Secretariat of the International Military Tribunal, 1947–49), vol. 30, 95.; also Aly, *Final Solution,* 17.
21. "New Jewish State in Poland," *The Times,* 24 October 1939.
22. Quoted in Poland, Ministry of Information, *The Black Book of Poland* (New York: G. P. Putnam's Sons, 1942), 239f.
23. See Aly, *Final Solution,* 67f.
24. Czerniakow, *The Warsaw Diary of Adam Czerniakow,* 148.
25. Quoted in Aly, *Final Solution,* 88.
26. See United States Department of State, *Documents on German Foreign Policy, 1918–1945,* Series D, 12 vols. (Washington, DC: U.S. Government Printing Office, 1949–62), vol 5, 931, italics in the original.
27. Ibid.
28. Raul Hilberg, *The Destruction of the European Jews,* 3 vols. (New York and London: Holmes & Meier, 1985), vol. 2, 397f.
29. From a note made by Luther on 21 August 1942 about attempts to solve the Jewish Problem. Quoted in Kurt Pätzold, ed., *Verfolgung, Vetreibung, Vernichtung: Dokumente des faschistischen Antisemitismus* (Leipzig: Reclam, 1987), 350.
30. Czerniakow, *The Warsaw Diary of Adam Czerniakow,* 169.
31. Werner Präg and Wolfgang Jacobmeyer, eds., *Das Diensttagebuch des deutschen Generalgouverneurs in Polen, 1939–1945* (Stuttgart: Deutsche Verlags-Anstalt, 1975), 258.
32. Quoted in Aly, *Final Solution,* 3.
33. "Die Juden müssen arbeiten!" *Illustrierter Beobachter* (vol. 14), 12 October 1939, 1546f.
34. Quoted in *The Black Book of Poland,* 232.
35. Ibid., 233.

36. Quoted in Aly, *Final Solution,* 171.
37. Quoted in ibid., 175.
38. Hugh Trevor-Roper, ed., *Hitler's Table Talk, 1941–1944* (London: Phoenix Press, 2000), 87.
39. For a social history of Jewish life in Nazi Europe concentrating on the lives of children, see Debórah Dwork, *Children With A Star: Jewish Youth in Nazi Europe* (New Haven and London: Yale University Press, 1991).
40. The controversial role of the Jewish Councils in Nazi-occupied Europe has generated a large literature. Some, like Hilberg and Arendt, have interpreted the role of the *Judenräte* as (admittedly forced) collaborators of the Nazis; others have seen the Councils in more positive light. A few of the important studies and contributions to the debate (in English) include Hannah Arendt, *Eichmann in Jerusalem: A Report on the Banality of Evil* (New York: Viking Press, 1964); Jacob Robinson, *And the Crooked Shall Be Made Straight: The Eichmann Trial, the Jewish Catastrophe, and Hannah Arendt's Narrative* (New York: Macmillan, 1965); Nathan Eck, "Historical Research or Slander? (On R. Hilberg's Book)," *Yad Vashem Studies,* vol. 6 (1967), 385–429; Isaiah Trunk, *Judenrat: The Jewish Councils in Eastern Europe Under Nazi Occupation* (New York: Macmillan, 1972); Aharon Weiss, "Jewish Leadership in Occupied Poland—Postures and Attitudes," *Yad Vashem Studies,* vol. 12 (1977), 335–66; Shmuel Huppert, "King of the Ghetto—Mordecai Haim Rumkowski, the Elder of Lodz Ghetto," *Yad Vashem Studies,* vol. 15 (1983), 125–58; and Hilberg, *The Destruction of the European Jews,* vol. 3, 1037ff.
41. Hermann Erich Seifert, *Der Jude an der Ostgrenze* (Berlin: Eher, 1940), 82.
42. Hilberg, *The Destruction of the European Jews,* vol. 1, 215ff.
43. Dawid Sierakowiak, *The Diary of Dawid Sierakowiak,* ed. Alan Adelson (New York: Oxford University Press, 1996), 63, 70.
44. Halina Nelken, *And Yet, I Am Here!* (Amherst: University of Massachusetts Press, 1999), 59.
45. Chaim Kaplan, *Scroll of Agony: The Warsaw Diary of Chaim A. Kaplan,* trans. Abraham I. Katsch (New York: Collier Books, 1973), 78.
46. Ibid., 218–19.
47. Ibid., 219.
48. Yisrael Gutman, *The Jews of Warsaw, 1939–1943* (Bloomington: Indiana University Press, 1982), 48ff.
49. Aly, *Final Solution,* 50.
50. Quoted in ibid.; see also Gutman, *The Jews of Warsaw, 1939–1943,* 50f.
51. Czerniakow, *The Warsaw Diary of Adam Czerniakow,* 140; also Hilberg, *The Destruction of the European Jews,* vol. 1, 224f.
52. Browning, "Genocide and Public Health," 24; Gutman, *The Jews of Warsaw, 1939–1943,* 53f.
53. Quoted in Noakes and Pridham, *Nazism 1919–1945,* vol. 3, 1065.
54. Kaplan, *Scroll of Agony,* 225.
55. Nelken, *And Yet, I Am Here!,* 71–72, 78.
56. Hillel Seidman, *The Warsaw Ghetto Diaries,* trans. Yosef Israel (Southfield, MI: Targum, 1997), 227.
57. Ibid., 229f.
58. According to the historian Lucy Dawidowicz, approximately 330,000 Jews, or one-tenth of the Jewish population in Poland, became refugees. Lucy Dawidowicz, *The War Against the Jews* (New York: Bantam Books, 1986), 199–200.
59. Emmanuel Ringelblum, *Notes from the Warsaw Ghetto,* ed. Jacob Sloan (New York: Schocken Books, 1974), 82.
60. Peter-Heinz Seraphim, "Bevölkerungs- und wirtschaftspolitische Problem einer europäischen Gesamtlösung der Judenfrage," *Weltkampf,* vol. 1 (1941), 43ff.
61. Kaplan, *Scroll of Agony,* 50f, 230; also Gutman, *The Jews of Warsaw, 1939–1943,* 66ff.
62. Isaiah Trunk, "The Organizational Structure of the Jewish Councils in Eastern Europe," *Yad Vashem Studies,* vol. 7 (1968), 147–64; Hilberg, *The Destruction of the European Jews,* vol. 1, 230ff.; Gutman, *The Jews of Warsaw, 1939–1943,* 36ff.
63. Kaplan, *Scroll of Agony,* 231.
64. Hilberg, *The Destruction of the European Jews,* vol. 1, 255ff.; Gutman, *The Jews of Warsaw, 1939–1943,* 72ff.
65. Sierakowiak, *The Diary of Dawid Sierakowiak,* 77, 79, 81, 86f.
66. Gutman, *The Jews of Warsaw, 1939–1943,* 67ff.
67. Abraham Lewin, *A Cup of Tears: A Diary of the Warsaw Ghetto,* ed. Antony Polonsky (Oxford: Basil Blackwell, 1989), 77f.
68. Ibid., 131f.
69. In his diary entry for 5 September 1941, Czerniakow wrote: "At last permission was given today for opening the elementary schools," *The Warsaw Diary of Adam Czerniakow,* 277.
70. Janina Bauman, *Winter in the Morning: A Young Girl's Life in the Warsaw Ghetto and Beyond, 1939–1945* (London: Virago, 1986), 41.

71. Kaplan, *Scroll of Agony,* 86.

72. Trunk, *Judenrat,* 204.

73. Hannah Kent-Starkman, oral history conducted by Debórah Dwork, Stamford, CT, 13 December 1985, transcript 4.

74. Ibid., 7, 11.

75. Mira Teeman, oral history, transcript 13.

76. Esther Geizhals-Zucker, oral history conducted by Debórah Dwork, Bloomfield Hills, MI, 9 November 1985, transcript 2.

77. Avraham Tory, *Surviving the Holocaust: The Kovno Ghetto Diary,* ed. Martin Gilbert (Cambridge, MA: Harvard University Press, 1990). See entries of 21 April 1942 (78), 25 May 1942 (90), 6 July 1942 (104), and note to entry for 20 August 1942 (126).

78. Quoted in Tory, *Surviving the Holocaust,* 253f.

79. Ibid.

80. Ibid., 134, 140; see also Trunk, *Judenrat,* 206f.

81. Excerpt from Tamarah Lazerson's diary in Laurel Holliday, *Children in the Holocaust and World War II: Their Secret Diaries* (New York: Simon & Schuster, 1995), 128.

82. Ibid., 129.

83. Yitskhok Rudashevski, *The Diary of the Vilna Ghetto, June 1941–April 1943* (Kibbutz Lohamei-Haghettaot, Israel: Ghetto Fighters' House and Kibbutz Hameuchad Publishing House, 1973), 56, 65.

84. Czerniakow, *The Warsaw Diary of Adam Czerniakow,* 179, 295.

85. Ringelblum, *Notes from the Warsaw Ghetto,* 125.

86. Kaplan, *Scroll of Agony,* 321f.

87. Czerniakow, *The Warsaw Diary of Adam Czerniakow,* 358.

88. Joseph Kermish, "Emmanuel Ringelblum's Notes Hitherto Unpublished," *Yad Vashem Studies,* vol. 7 (1968), 176.

89. Ringelblum, *Notes from the Warsaw Ghetto,* 146.

90. Halina Nelken, *And Yet, I Am Here!,* 83.

91. Lucjan Dobroszycki, ed., *The Chronicle of the Lodz Ghetto, 1941–1944* (New Haven: Yale University Press, 1984), 83. The *Chronicle* was written surreptitiously by the Department of Archives, an official body in the Lodz ghetto. Shortly after the archives were founded, the ten to fifteen department members began their compilation. This was a clandestine activity, although it was not "formally" underground.

92. Ibid., 189.

93. Quoted in Yitzhak Arad, *Ghetto in Flames: The Struggle and Destruction of the Jews in Vilna in the Holocaust* (New York: Holocaust Library, 1982), 321f.

94. Seidman, *The Warsaw Ghetto Diaries,* 244f.

95. Lewin, *A Cup of Tears,* 80.

96. Joseph Walk, ed., *Das Sonderrecht für die Juden im NS-Staat* (Heidelberg and Karlsruhe: C. F. Müller Juristischer Verlag, 1981), 235.

97. Ibid., 254.

98. Ibid., 255.

99. Ibid., 283.

100. Quoted in Konrad Kwiet, "Nach dem Pogrom: Stufen der Ausgrenzung," in Wolfgang Benz, ed., *Die Juden in Deutschland 1933–1945* (Munich: Beck, 1988), 565.

101. Ibid., 581.

102. Hilma Ludomer-Geffen, oral history conducted by Debórah Dwork, Ann Arbor, MI, 29 November 1984, transcript 12.

103. Victor Klemperer, *I Will Bear Witness: A Diary of the Nazi Years, 1933–1945,* trans. Martin Chalmers, 2 vols (New York: Random House, 1998–99), vol. 1, 321.

104. Walk, ed., *Das Sonderrecht für die Juden im NS-Staat,* 319.

105. Klemperer, *I Will Bear Witness,* vol. 1, 323, 365.

106. Walk, ed., *Das Sonderrecht für die Juden im NS-Staat,* 343.

107. Quoted in Kwiet, "Nach dem Pogrom: Stufen der Ausgrenzung," 569.

108. Walk, ed., *Das Sonderrecht für die Juden im NS-Staat,* 255.

109. Ibid., 272.

110. Ibid.

111. Klemperer, *I Will Bear Witness,* vol. 1, 364.

112. Ibid., vol. 1, 433.

113. Gertrud Kolmar, *Briefe and die Schwester Hilde (1938–1943)* (Munich: Kösel Verlag, 1970), 108.

114. Klemperer, *I Will Bear Witness,* vol. 2, 127f.

115. On the Holocaust in the Netherlands, see (in English) Jacob Presser, *Ashes in the Wind: The Destruction of Dutch Jewry,* trans. Arnold Pomerans (Detroit: Wayne State University Press, 1988); Bob Moore, *Vic-*

tims and Survivors: The Nazi Persecution of the Jews in the Netherlands, 1940–1945 (London: Arnold, 1997); and Johannes C. H. Blom, "The Persecution of the Jews in the Netherlands: A Comparative Western European Perspective," *European History Quarterly,* vol. 19 (1989), 331–51. On the Holocaust in Belgium, see (in English) Dan Michman, ed., *Belgium and the Holocaust: Jews, Belgians, Germans* (Jerusalem: Yad Vashem, 1998).

116. The classic work on the policy of Vichy concerning the Jews is Michael R. Marrus and Robert O. Paxton, *Vichy France and the Jews* (New York: Schocken Books, 1983). See also Georges Wellers, *L'Etoile jaune à l'heure de Vichy* (Paris: Fayard, 1973), and Serge Klarsfeld, *Vichy-Auschwitz: Le rôle de Vichy dans la Solution Finale de la Question Juive en France, 1942* (Paris: Fayard, 1983).

117. Quoted in Marrus and Paxton, *Vichy France and the Jews,* 43.

118. Quoted in ibid., 53.

119. Arthur Koestler, *Scum of the Earth* (London: Jonathan Cape, 1941), 96.

120. Quoted in Noakes and Pridham, *Nazism 1919–1945,* vol. 3, 1079f.

121. Joseph Weill, *Contribution à l'histoire des camps d'internement dans l'anti-France* (Paris: Editions du Centre, 1946), 112f.

122. Marie Claus-Grindel, oral history conducted by Debórah Dwork, Paris, 2 June 1987, transcript 1–2.

123. Weill, *Contribution à l'histoire des camps d'internement,* 32f.

124. Ibid., 37–41.

125. Dwork, *Children With A Star,* 120f.; also Marrus and Paxton, *Vichy France and the Jews,* 172f, 176; Wellers, *L'Etoile jaune à l'heure de Vichy,* 100.

126. Elisabeth Hirsch, oral history conducted by Debórah Dwork, Neuilly-sur-Seine, France, 25 June 1987, transcript 14.

127. Privately published volume in honor of Ruth Lambert, by the Kibbutz Schluchot, doc. no. 10.

128. Centre Documentation Juive Contemporaine, Document CCXX-13, "Camp de Gurs, Noël 1940."

129. Vivette Samuel, "Journal d'une internée volontaire," *Evidences,* n.d., no. 14, p. 8.

130. Marrus and Paxton, *Vichy France and the Jews,* 3. See also Denis Peschanski, "The Statutes on Jews— October 3, 1940 and June 2, 1941," Pierre Laborie, "The Jewish Statutes in Vichy France and Public Opinion," and Renée Poznanski, "The Jews of France and the Statutes on Jews, 1940–1941," all three articles in *Yad Vashem Studies,* vol. 22 (1992), 65–88, 89–114, 115–46.

131. Quoted in Marrus and Paxton, *Vichy France and the Jews,* 87.

132. Quoted in ibid., 235.

133. Odette Bérujeau, in conversation with Debórah Dwork, Paris, France, June 1987; for a similar sentiment, see Janet Teissier du Cros, *Divided Loyalties,* ed. Janet Adam Smith (Edinburgh: Canongate, 1992), 234. On the German reaction to the introduction of the star, see Marlis G. Steinert, *Hitler's War and the Germans,* trans. Thomas E. J. de Witt (Athens, OH: Ohio University Press, 1977), 134ff.

Chapter Nine: IN THE SHADOW OF DEATH

1. Adam Czerniakow, *The Warsaw Diary of Adam Czerniakow,* trans. Stanislaw Staron and the staff of Yad Vashem, eds. Raul Hilberg, Stanislaw Staron, and Josef Kermisz (New York: Stein & Day, 1979), 396.

2. Yisrael Gutman, *The Jews of Warsaw, 1939–1943* (Bloomington: Indiana University Press, 1982), 66f.; Isaiah Trunk, *Judenrat: The Jewish Councils in Eastern Europe Under Nazi Occupation* (New York: Macmillan, 1972), 99ff. Kiryl Sosnowski has cited contemporary estimates that "the actual [ration] allowance covered, at the most, 10 per cent of basic requirements"—*The Tragedy of Children Under Nazi Rule* (Poznan: Western Press Agency, 1962), 113. See also Raul Hilberg, *The Destruction of the European Jews,* 3 vols. (New York and London: Holmes & Meier, 1985), vol. 1, 259ff., and Charles Roland, *Courage Under Siege* (New York: Oxford University Press, 1992).

3. Trunk, *Judenrat,* 135.

4. Henry (Heniek) Starkman, oral history conducted by Debórah Dwork, Bloomfield Hills, MI, 8 December 1984, 19 January 1985, transcript 20, 17, 18.

5. Ibid., 31f., 21.

6. Ibid., 19.

7. Hannah Kent-Starkman, oral history conducted by Debórah Dwork, Stamford, CT, 13 December 1985, transcript 11.

8. Adolf Berman, "Children in the Warsaw Ghetto," in Yisrael Gutman and Livia Rothkirchen, eds., *The Catastrophe of European Jewry: Antecedents, History, Reflections* (Jerusalem: Yad Vashem, 1976), 403.

9. Janina Bauman, *Winter in the Morning: A Young Girl's Life in the Warsaw Ghetto and Beyond, 1939–1945* (London: Virago, 1986), 41.

10. Emmanuel Ringelblum, *Notes from the Warsaw Ghetto,* ed. Jacob Sloan (New York: Schocken Books, 1974), 133.

11. Chaim Kaplan, *Scroll of Agony: The Warsaw Diary of Chaim A. Kaplan,* trans. Abraham I. Katsch (New York: Collier Books, 1973), 290.

12. Ringelblum, *Notes from the Warsaw Ghetto,* 234.

13. Ibid., 204f.

14. Sara Grossman-Weil, oral history conducted by Debórah Dwork, Malverne, NY, 29 and 30 April 1987, transcript 22, 25.

15. The findings are quoted in Roland, *Courage Under Siege,* 114f. The report was published in 1946 as Emil Apfelbaum, *Maladie de famine: Récherches cliniques sur la famine exécutées dans la ghetto de Varsovie en 1942* (Warsaw: American Joint Distribution Committee, 1946); see also Mordecai Lenski, "Problems of Disease in the Warsaw Ghetto," *Yad Vashem Studies,* vol. 3 (1959), 283–94.

16. Trunk, *Judenrat,* 147.

17. Dawid Sierakowiak, *The Diary of Dawid Sierakowiak,* ed. Alan Adelson (New York: Oxford University Press, 1996), 91.

18. Ringelblum, *Notes from the Warsaw Ghetto,* 189, 194ff.

19. Ibid., 218ff.

20. Kaplan, *Scroll of Agony,* 277.

21. Jan Karski, *Story of a Secret State* (Boston: Houghton Mifflin, 1944), 334.

22. SS-Hauptamt-Schulungsamt, *Der Kampf um die deutsche Ostgrenze* (Berlin: SS-Hauptamt, 1941), 41ff.

23. Guenther Lewy, *The Nazi Persecution of the Gypsies* (New York and Oxford: Oxford University Press, 2000), 112ff.

24. Lucjan Dobroszycki, ed., *The Chronicle of the Lodz Ghetto, 1941–1944* (New Haven: Yale University Press, 1984), 82.

25. Ibid., 86.

26. Ibid., 108.

27. Joseph Kermish, "Emmanuel Ringelblum's Notes Hitherto Unpublished," *Yad Vashem Studies,* vol. 7 (1968), 177f.

28. Kaplan, *Scroll of Agony,* 294.

29. Czerniakow, *The Warsaw Diary of Adam Czerniakow,* 368.

30. Werner Präg and Wolfgang Jacobmeyer, eds., *Das Diensttagebuch des deutschen Generalgouverneurs in Polen, 1939–1945* (Stuttgart: Deutsche Verlags-Anstalt, 1975), 466.

31. Curzio Malaparte, *Kaputt,* trans. Cesare Foligno (New York: E. P. Dutton, 1946), 98ff.

32. Avraham Tory, *Surviving the Holocaust: The Kovno Ghetto Diary* (Cambridge, MA: Harvard University Press, 1990), 43f.

33. Ibid., 44ff.

34. Ibid., 49ff.

35. Ibid., 56.

36. Ibid., 45.

37. Czerniakow, *The Warsaw Diary of Adam Czerniakow,* 23.

38. For a discussion of the survival through work strategy, see, inter alia, Yitzhak Arad, *Ghetto in Flames: The Struggle and Destruction of the Jews in Vilna in the Holocaust* (New York: Holocaust Library, 1982), 333ff., and Trunk, *Judenrat,* 75–99, 400–13.

39. Quoted in Trunk, *Judenrat,* 421.

40. Arad, *Ghetto in Flames,* 340.

41. Esther Geizhals-Zucker, oral history conducted by Debórah Dwork, Bloomfield Hills, MI, 9 November 1985, transcript 3.

42. Dobroszycki, ed., *Chronicle of the Lodz Ghetto,* 199.

43. Ibid., 211.

44. Ibid., 218.

45. Ibid., 226–28.

46. Ibid., 250–51.

47. Quoted in Trunk, *Judenrat,* 423.

48. Sara Grossman-Weil, oral history, transcript 21; see also the description by Josef Zelkowicz, "Days of Nightmare," in Lucy S. Dawidowicz, ed., *A Holocaust Reader* (New York: Behrman House, 1976), 298–316. Note the difference in tone between this account and his entry on the same subject in Dobroszycki, ed., *Chronicle of the Lodz Ghetto,* 250–55.

49. Sara Grossman-Weil, oral history, transcript 23.

50. Sierakowiak, *The Diary of Dawid Sierakowiak,* 226.

51. Abraham Lewin, *A Cup of Tears: A Diary of the Warsaw Ghetto,* ed. Antony Polonsky (Oxford: Basil Blackwell, 1989), 153f.

52. Hillel Seidman, *The Warsaw Ghetto Diaries,* trans. Yosef Israel (Southfield MI: Targum, 1997), 171f.

53. Sara Grossman-Weil, oral history, transcript 23.

54. Halina Nelken, *And Yet, I Am Here!* (Amherst: University of Massachusetts Press, 1999), 109f.
55. Dobroszycki, ed., *Chronicle of the Lodz Ghetto,* 255.
56. Siedman, *The Warsaw Ghetto Diaries,* 209f.
57. Dobroszycki, ed., *Chronicle of the Lodz Ghetto,* 255.
58. Seidman, *The Warsaw Ghetto Diaries,* 210.
59. Lewin, *A Cup of Tears,* 152, 178.
60. Dobroszycki, ed., *Chronicle of the Lodz Ghetto,* 342.
61. Nelken, *And Yet, I Am Here!* 110.
62. Dobroszycki, ed., *Chronicle of the Lodz Ghetto,* 289f.
63. Tory, *Surviving the Holocaust,* 65.
64. Trunk, *Judenrat,* 207.
65. Yitskhok Rudashevski, *The Diary of the Vilna Ghetto, June 1941–April 1943* (Kibbutz Lohamei-Haghettaot, Israel: Ghetto Fighters' House and Kibbutz Hameuchad Publishing House, 1973), 65f., 91.
66. Mania Salinger-Tenenbaum, oral history conducted by Debórah Dwork, Bloomfield, MI, 10 and 29 January, 7 March 1987, transcript 7f.
67. For a discussion of the role of the youth movements in the underground resistance, see Lester Eckman and Chaim Lazar, *The Jewish Resistance: The History of the Jewish Partisans in Lithuania and White Russia During the Nazi Occupation 1940–1945* (New York: Shengold Publishers, 1977), 62–69; Yisrael Gutman, "Essay: The Youth Movements in Eastern Europe as an Alternative Leadership," *Genocide and Holocaust Studies,* vol. 3 no. 1 (1988), 69–74; and Yisrael Gutman, "Youth Movements in the Underground and Ghetto Revolts," in Meier Grubsztein, ed., *Jewish Resistance During the Holocaust* (Jerusalem: Yad Vashem, 1971), 260–84.
68. See Reuben Ainsztein, *The Warsaw Ghetto Revolt* (New York: Holocaust Library, 1979); Joseph Kermish, "The Place of the Ghetto Revolts in the Struggle Against the Occupier," in Grubsztein, ed., *Jewish Resistance During the Holocaust,* 306–23; Yuri Suhl, ed., *They Fought Back: The Story of the Jewish Resistance in Nazi Europe* (New York: Crown Publishers, 1967); and Gutman, *The Jews of Warsaw, 1939–1943,* 336ff.
69. "The Last Act of the Great Tragedy," *Biuletyn Informacyjny,* 29 April 1943, quoted in Shmuel Krakowski, "Holocaust in the Polish Underground Press," *Yad Vashem Studies,* vol. 16 (1984), 257f.
70. Dobroszycki, ed., *Chronicle of the Lodz Ghetto,* 504, 509, 515f., 526.
71. Ibid., 526.
72. Sara Grossman-Weil, oral history, transcript 26f.
73. Ibid., 20.

Chapter Ten: TOWARD THE "FINAL SOLUTION"

1. Quoted in Jörg Wollenberg. "The Expropriation of the 'Rapacious' Capital," in Jörg Wollenberg, ed., *The German Public and the Persecution of the Jews, 1933–1945,* trans. Rado Pribic (Atlantic Highlands, NJ: Humanities Press, 1996), 123.
2. Quoted in Konrad Heiden, *The New Inquisition,* trans. Heinz Norden (New York: Starling Press/Alliance Book Corp., 1939), 145f.
3. Max Domarus, *Hitler: Speeches and Proclamations 1932–1945,* 4 vols. (Wauconda, IL: Bolchazy-Carducci, 1990–97), vol. 3, 1449.
4. Ibid.
5. Ernst Haeckel, *The History of Creation: Or the Development of the Earth and Its Inhabitants by the Action of Natural Causes,* trans. E. Ray Lankester, 2 vols. (New York: D. Appleton & Co., 1876), vol. 1, 170f.
6. Karl Binding and Alfred Hoche, *Die Freigabe der Vernichtung lebensunwertes Lebens: Ihr Mass und ihre Form* (Leipzig: Felix Meiner, 1920), 27ff.
7. Ibid., 100f.
8. Adolf Hitler, *Mein Kampf,* trans. Ralph Manheim (Boston: Houghton Mifflin; 1943), 255.
9. See Hans-Walter Schmuhl, *Rassenhygiene, Nationalsozialismus, Euthanasie: Von der Verhütung zur Vernichtung "lebensunwerten Lebens," 1890–1945* (Göttingen: Vandenhoeck & Ruprecht, 1987); Paul Klee, *"Euthanasie" im NS-Staat: Die "Vernichtung lebensunwertes Lebens"* (Frankfurt-am-Main: S. Fischer, 1983); Michael Burleigh and Wolfgang Wippermann, *The Racial State: Germany 1933–1945* (Cambridge: Cambridge University Press, 1991); and Henry Friedländer, *The Origins of Nazi Genocide: From Euthanasia to the Final Solution* (Chapel Hill and London: University of North Carolina Press, 1995).
10. "Zum Thema: Gnadentod," *Das Schwarze Korps,* vol. 3 no. 11 (1937), 9.
11. See Friedländer, *The Origins of Nazi Genocide,* 39ff.
12. Ibid., 46ff.
13. Christopher R. Browning, *Fateful Months: Essays on the Emergence of the Final Solution,* rev. edn. (New York and London: Holmes & Meier, 1991), 58ff.; Friedländer, *The Origins of Nazi Genocide,* 86ff.
14. Document 740, quoted in Jeremy Noakes and Geoffrey Pridham, *Nazism 1919–1945,* 3 vols. (Exeter:

Exeter University Publications, 1983–88), vol. 3, 1021; see also Friedländer, *The Origins of Nazi Genocide*, 67.

15. See Document 739, quoted in Noakes and Pridham, *Nazism 1919–1945*, vol. 3, 1019; see also Friedländer, *The Origins of Nazi Genocide*, 86ff.

16. Friedländer, *The Origins of Nazi Genocide*, 87f.

17. Klee, *"Euthanasie" im NS-Staat*, 207; Friedländer, *The Origins of Nazi Genocide*, 90ff.

18. Document 744, quoted in Noakes and Pridham, *Nazism 1919–1945*, vol. 3, 1025f.

19. Document 749, quoted in ibid., vol. 3, 1028; see also Friedländer, *The Origins of Nazi Genocide*, 101ff.

20. Browning, *Fateful Months*, 59; Friedländer, *The Origins of Nazi Genocide*, 136ff.

21. Document 762, quoted in Noakes and Pridham, *Nazism 1919–1945*, vol. 3, 1040.

22. Document 763, quoted in ibid., 1042.

23. Friedländer, *The Origins of Nazi Genocide*, 270ff.

24. Ibid., 143ff.

25. Quoted in Michael Burleigh and Wolfgang Wippermann, *The Racial State*, 164.

26. Minutes of the ministerial conference held at the Ministry of Propaganda, Berlin, 27 June 1941, in Willi A. Boelcke, ed., *The Secret Conferences of Dr. Goebbels: The Nazi Propaganda War, 1939–43*, trans. Eswald Oser (New York: E. P. Dutton, 1971), 176.

27. Ibid.

28. Herbert Backe, *Um die Nahrungs-Freiheit Europas* (Leipzig: Wilhelme Goldmann, 1942), 11.

29. See Dietrich Eichholtz, "Der Generalplan Ost: Über eine Ausgeburt imperialistischer Denkart und Politik (mit Dokumenten)," *Jahrbuch für Geschichte,* vol. 26 (1982), 217–74; Rolf-Dieter Müller, *Hitlers Ostkrieg und die deutsche Siedlungspolitik* (Frankfurt-am-Main: Fischer Taschenbuch Verlag, 1991); Bruno Wasser, *Himmlers Raumplanung im Osten: Der Generalplan Ost in Polen 1940–1944* (Basel, Berlin, and Boston: Birkhäuser Verlag, 1993); Mechtild Rössler and Sabine Schleiermacher, eds., *Der "Generalplan Ost": Hauptlinien der nationalsozialistischen Planungs- und Vernichtungspolitik* (Berlin: Akademie Verlag, 1993); and Czeslaw Madajczyk, ed., *Vom Generalplan Ost zum Generalsiedlungsplan* (Munich: Saur, 1994).

30. Erhard Wetzel, "Stellungnahme und gedanken zum Generalplan Ost des Reichsführers SS," *Vierteljahrshefte für Zeitgeschichte,* vol. 6 (1958), 297ff.

31. Dietrich Klagges, *Geschichtsunterricht als nationalpolitische Erziehung* (Frankfurt-am-Main: Moritz Diesterweg, 1937), 380.

32. On the Holocaust as a bureaucratic process, see Zygmunt Bauman, *Modernity and the Holocaust* (Ithaca: Cornell University Press, 1989); also Raul Hilberg, *The Destruction of the European Jews*, 3 vols. (New York and London: Holmes & Meier, 1985), vol. 1, 51ff., and Götz Aly and Susanne Heim, *Vordenker der Vernichtung: Auschwitz und die deutschen Pläne für eine neue europäische Ordnung* (Hamburg: Hoffmann und Campe, 1991).

33. I. C. Butnaru, *The Silent Holocaust: Romania and Its Jews* (Westport, CT: Greenwood Press, 1992), 65.

34. Radu Ioanid, *The Holocaust in Romania: The Destruction of Jews and Gypsies Under the Antonescu Regime, 1940–1944* (Chicago: Ivan R. Dee, 2000), 38ff.; Butnaru, *The Silent Holocaust*, 67f.

35. Hilberg, *The Destruction of the European Jews*, vol. 2, 764; Ioanid, *The Holocaust in Romania*, 52ff.

36. Ioanid, *The Holocaust in Romania*, 62ff.; Butnaru, *The Silent Holocaust*, 92ff.

37. Curzio Malaparte, *Kaputt*, trans. Cesare Foligno (New York: E. P. Dutton, 1946), 142.

38. Ibid., 143.

39. Jean Ancel, "The Romanian Way of Solving the 'Jewish Problem' in Bessarabia and Bukovina," *Yad Vashem Studies,* vol. 19 (1988), 187–232.

40. Quoted in Butnaru, *The Silent Holocaust*, 67f., 103.

41. Quoted in ibid., 67f. See also Jean Ancel, "Antonescu and the Jews," *Yad Vashem Studies,* vol. 23 (1993), 213–80.

42. Ioanid, *The Holocaust in Romania*, 195ff.

43. See David M. Crowe, *A History of the Gypsies of Eastern Europe and Russia* (New York: St. Martin's Press, 1994), 133ff.; also Ioanid, *The Holocaust in Romania*, 225ff.

44. Dalia Ofer, "Life in the Ghettos of Transnistria," *Yad Vashem Studies,* vol. 25 (1996), 229–74.

45. Quoted in Felicia (Steigman) Carmelly, *Shattered! 50 Years of Silence: History and Voices of the Tragedy in Romania and Transnistria* (Scarborough, Ontario: Abbeyfield, 1997), 263f.

46. Dora Litani, "The Destruction of the Jews of Odessa in the Light of Rumanian Documents," *Yad Vashem Studies,* vol. 6 (1967), 135–54; Ioanid, *The Holocaust in Romania*, 177ff.

47. Quoted in Butnaru, *The Silent Holocaust*, 127.

48. Ibid., 128f.

49. Ancel, "Antonescu and the Jews," 256ff.

50. Quoted in Butnaru, *The Silent Holocaust*, 103.

51. Letter, Franklin Mott Gunther, 4 November 1941, quoted in Jean Ancel, ed., *Documents Concerning the*

Fate of Romanian Jewry During the Holocaust, 12 vols. (New York: Beate Klarsfeld Foundation, 1985), vol. 3, 335.

52. Vlad Georgescu, *The Romanians: A History*, trans. Alexandra Bley-Vroman (Columbus, OH: Ohio State University Press, 1991), 218.

53. Andreas Hillgruber, *Hitler, König Carol und Marschall Antonescu: Die Deutsch-Rumänischen Beziehungen 1938–1944* (Wiesbaden: Franz Steiner, 1954), 241.

54. Ibid., 243.

55. See Ioanid, *The Holocaust in Romania*, 227ff.; Crowe, *A History of the Gypsies of Eastern Europe and Russia*, 133f.

56. Yitzhak Arad, "The Holocaust of Soviet Jewry in the Occupied Territories of the Soviet Union," *Yad Vashem Studies*, vol. 21 (1991), 1–48.

57. Christian Streit, "The German Army and the Policy of Genocide," in Gerhard Hirschfeld, ed., *The Politics of Genocide* (London, Boston, and Sydney: Allen & Unwin/German Historical Institute, 1986), 10.

58. Frans Pieter ten Kate, *De Duitse aanval op de Sovjet-Unie in 1941: Een krijgs-geschiedkundige studie*, 2 vols. (Groningen: Wolters-Noordhoff, 1968), vol. 1, 91f., 49, 70.

59. Quoted in Ernst Klee, Willi Dressen, and Volker Riess, *"The Good Old Days": The Holocaust as Seen by Its Perpetrators and Bystanders* (New York: Konecky & Konecky, 1991), 118.

60. The whole Jäger report can be found in Klee, Dressen, and Riess, *"The Good Old Days"*, 46–58.

61. Ibid., 54.

62. Ibid., 55.

63. Browning, *Fateful Months*, 59f.

64. Ibid., 64.

65. Wolfgang Diewerge, ed., *Deutsche Soldaten sehen die Sovjet-Union* (Berlin: Limpert, 1941), 38, 45.

66. See Hans-Heinrich Wilhelm, "The Holocaust in National-Socialist Rhetoric and Writings—Some Evidence Against the Thesis That Before 1945 Nothing Was Known about the 'Final Solution,'" *Yad Vashem Studies*, vol. 16 (1984), 95–128.

67. Raul Hilberg, ed., *Documents of Destruction: Germany and Jewry 1933–1945* (Chicago: Quadrangle Books, 1971), 87f.

68. Wladyslaw Bednarz, "Extermination Camp at Chelmno," in Central Commission for the Investigation of German Crimes in Poland, *German Crimes in Poland*, 2 vols. (Warsaw: Central Commission for the Investigation of German Crimes in Poland, 1946–47), vol. 1, 112f.

69. Shalom Kube, "The German Jews in the Minsk Ghetto," *Yad Vashem Studies*, vol. 17 (1986), 219–46.

70. Yitzhak Arad, Shmuel Krakowski, and Shmuel Spector, eds., *The Einsatzgruppen Reports* (New York: Holocaust Library, 1989), 269.

71. Hannes Heer, "Killing Fields: The Wehrmacht and the Holocaust in Belorussia, 1941–1942," in Hannes Heer and Klaus Naumann, *War of Extermination: The German Military in World War II, 1941–1945* (New York and Oxford: Berghahn Books, 2000), 68ff.

72. See Yitzhak Arad, "Alfred Rosenberg and the 'Final Solution' in the Occupied Soviet Territories," *Yad Vashem Studies*, vol. 13 (1979), 273ff.

73. Nuremberg Document 3665, quoted in Yitzhak Arad, Yisrael Gutman, and Abraham Margaliot, eds., *Documents on the Holocaust* (Jerusalem: Yad Vashem, 1981), 408f.

74. Nuremberg Document 3663 PS, in International Military Tribunal, *Trial of the Major War Criminals*, 46 vols. (Nuremberg: Secretariat of the International Military Tribunal, 1947–49), vol. 32, 436.

75. Nuremberg Document 3666 PS, in ibid., vol. 32, 437.

76. Elke Fröhlich, ed., *Die Tagebücher von Joseph Goebbels: Teil II, Diktate 1941–1945*, 15 vols. (Munich: Saur, 1996), vol. 2., 498f.

77. Letter, Göring to Heydrich, 31 July 1941, quoted in Lucy S. Dawidowicz, ed., *A Holocaust Reader* (New York: Behrman House, 1976), 72f.

78. Quoted in Noakes and Pridham, eds., *Nazism 1919–1945*, vol. 3, 1125f.

79. Werner Präg, and Wolfgang Jacobmeyer, *Das Diensttagebuch des deutschen Generalgouverneurs in Polen 1939–1945*, (Stuttgart: Deutsche Verlags-Anstalt, 1975), 457.

80. Ibid., 458f.

81. Debórah Dwork and Robert Jan van Pelt, *Auschwitz: 1270 to the Present* (New York: W. W. Norton & Co., 1996), 296ff.

82. Minutes of the Wannsee conference quoted in Dawidowicz, ed., *A Holocaust Reader*, 74. On the Wannsee conference, see Kurt Pätzold and Erika Schwarz, *Tagesordnung Judenmord: Die Wannsee-Konferenz am 20. Januar 1942* (Berlin: Metropol, 1992).

83. Quoted in Dawidowicz, ed., *A Holocaust Reader*, 78.

84. Ibid., 82.

85. Lewy, *The Nazi Persecution of the Gypsies*, 122ff.

86. Ibid., 196.

87. Max Domarus, *Hitler: Reden und Proklamationen 1932–1945,* 2 vols (Würzburg: Domarus Verlag, 1963), vol. 2, 1829.
88. Germany, Foreign Office, *Akten zur Deutschen Auswärtigen Politik, 1918–1945, Series E: 1941–1945,* 8 vols. (Göttingen: Vandenhoeck & Ruprecht, 1969–79), vol. 1, 403.

Chapter Eleven: HOLOCAUST

1. Curzio Malaparte, *Kaputt,* trans. Cesare Foligno (New York: E. P. Dutton, 1946), 144f.
2. Ibid.
3. Quoted in Ernst Klee, Willi Dressen, and Volker Riess, *"The Good Old Days": The Holocaust as Seen by Its Perpetrators and Bystanders* (New York: Konecky & Konecky, 1991), 205.
4. Ibid., 196ff.
5. Ibid., 201.
6. Lucy S. Dawidowicz, ed., *A Holocaust Reader* (New York: Behrman House, 1976), 133.
7. See Raul Hilberg, *The Destruction of the European Jews,* 3 vols. (New York and London: Holmes & Meier, 1985), vol. 2, 407ff.
8. Quoted in Jeremy Noakes and Geoffrey Pridham, *Nazism 1919–1945,* 3 vols. (Exeter: Exeter University Publications, 1983–88), vol. 3, 1147f.; on the relation between T4 and the Operation Reinhard camps, see Henry Friedländer, *The Origins of Nazi Genocide: From Euthanasia to Final Solution* (Chapel Hill and London: University of North Carolina Press, 1995), 284ff.
9. See Yitzhak Arad, *Belzec, Sobibor, Treblinka: The Operation Reinhard Death Camps* (Bloomington: Indiana University Press, 1987); also Hilberg, *The Destruction of the European Jews,* vol. 3, 875ff.
10. Arad, *Belzec, Sobibor, Treblinka,* 68ff.
11. Wilhelm Cornides, Diary, ms., Institute for Contemporary History, Munich, Document ED 81, printed in Raul Hilberg, ed., *Documents of Destruction: Germany and Jewry 1933–1945* (Chicago: Quadrangle Books, 1971), 209.
12. Ibid., 210f.
13. Ibid., 212.
14. Saul Friedländer, *Kurt Gerstein: The Ambiguity of Good* (New York: Alfred A. Knopf, 1969); Pierre Joffroy, *A Spy for God: The Ordeal of Kurt Gerstein* (London: Collins, 1971). There are two Gerstein reports. For the original publication of the first Gerstein Report, see Hans Rothfels, ed., "Augenzeugenbericht zu den Massenvergasungen," *Vierteljahreshefte für Zeitgeschichte,* vol. 1 (1953), 177–94; for the second, see Léon Poliakov, "Le Dossier Kurt Gerstein," *Le Monde Juif,* vol. 19 (January-March 1964), 1–16.
15. Quoted in Friedländer, *Kurt Gerstein,* 106.
16. Ibid., 107.
17. Arad, *Belzec, Sobibor, Treblinka,* Appendix A, 383ff.; Hilberg, *The Destruction of the European Jews,* vol. 3, 893.
18. Arad, *Belzec, Sobibor, Treblinka,* 30ff, 75ff, Appendix A, 390ff.; Hilberg, *The Destruction of the European Jews,* vol. 3, 893.
19. Arad, *Belzec, Sobibor, Treblinka,* 37ff, 81ff, Appendix A, 392ff.; Hilberg, *The Destruction of the European Jews,* vol. 3, 893. See also Gitta Sereny, *Into That Darkness: An Examination of Conscience* (New York: Vintage Books, 1983).
20. Arad, *Belzec, Sobibor, Treblinka,* 161; Hilberg, *The Destruction of the European Jews,* vol. 1, 947ff.
21. See Debórah Dwork and Robert Jan van Pelt, *Auschwitz: 1270 to the Present* (New York and London: W. W. Norton, 1996).
22. Pery Broad, "Reminiscences," in Rudolf Höss, Pery Broad, and Johann Paul Kremer, *KL Auschwitz Seen by the SS,* trans. Krystyna Michalik (Warsaw: Interpress Publishers, 1991), 119.
23. Dwork and van Pelt, *Auschwitz,* 177f.
24. Hugh Trevor-Roper, ed., *Hitler's Table Talk, 1941–1944* (London: Phoenix Press, 2000), 29.
25. Ibid., 409; see also Dwork and van Pelt, *Auschwitz,* 178f.
26. Rudolf Höss, *Death Dealer: The Memoirs of the SS Kommandant at Auschwitz,* ed. Steven Paskuly, trans. Andrew Pollinger (Buffalo: Prometheus Books, 1992), 29.
27. Irena Strzelecka, "Hospitals," in Yisrael Gutman and Michael Berenbaum, eds., *Anatomy of the Auschwitz Death Camp* (Bloomington and Indianapolis: Indiana University Press, 1994), 389.
28. Höss, *Death Dealer,* 28.
29. Dwork and van Pelt, *Auschwitz,* 292.
30. Wojciech Barz, "Die erste Vergasung," in H. G. Adler, H. Langbein, and Ella Lingens-Reiner, eds., *Auschwitz: Zeugnisse und Berichte* (Frankfurt-am-Main Athenäum, 1988), 17f.
31. Jean-Claude Pressac, with Robert Jan van Pelt, "The Machinery of Mass Murder at Auschwitz," in Gutman and Berenbaum, eds., *Anatomy of the Auschwitz Death Camp,* 209.

32. Danuta Czech, *Auschwitz Chronicle, 1939–1945,* trans. Barbara Harshav, Martha Humphreys, and Stephen Sheanir (New York: Henry Halt, 1990), 90.

33. Höss, *Death Dealer,* 156f.

34. See Pierre Vidal-Naquet, *The Jews: History, Memory, and the Present,* trans. David Ames Curtis (New York: Columbia University Press, 1996), 148f.

35. Peter Longerich, *Politik der Vernichtung: Eine Gesamtdarstellung der nationalsozialistischen Judenverfolgung* (Munich: Piper, 1998), 493ff, 513ff.

36. See, inter alia, Hilberg, *The Destruction of the European Jews,* vol. 2, 430ff.; Zdenek Lederer, *Ghetto Theresienstadt* (London: Goldston & Son, 1953), 8ff.; and H. G. Adler, *Theresienstadt, 1941–1945: Das Antlitz einer Zwangsgemeinschaft* (Tübingen: J. C. B. Mohr [Paul Siebeck], 1960).

37. Adler, *Theresienstadt,* 47–8. See also Adler's extended discussion of the statistics adduced on 37ff.

38. Ellen Eliel-Wallach, oral history conducted by Debórah Dwork, Amsterdam, 3 August 1987, transcript 23.

39. Lederer, *Ghetto Theresienstadt,* 52.

40. Ellen Eliel-Wallach, oral history, transcript 25.

41. Ibid., 25.

42. Irene Butter-Hasenberg, oral history conducted Debórah Dwork, Ann Arbor, MI, 10 October and 7 November 1986, 5 March and 16 April 1987, transcript 35.

43. Philip Mechanicus, *Waiting for Death* (London: Calder & Boyars, 1968), 111.

44. Unpublished diary of Otto Pollack, in the possession of his daughter, Helga Kinsky-Pollack, entry of 17 October 1944.

45. Ellen Eliel-Wallach, oral history, transcript 26.

46. Nuernberg Military Tribunals, *Trials of the War Criminals,* 15 vols. (Washington, DC: U.S. Government Printing Office, 1949–53), vol. 13, 164f.

47. Seminar on "Rescue and Resistance" taught by Marion Pritchard-van Binsbergen and Debórah Dwork, Center for Holocaust and Genocide Studies, Clark University, Worcester, MA, Spring 2000.

48. Ruth Andreas-Friedrich, *Berlin Underground, 1938–1945,* trans. Barrows Mussey (New York: Henry Holt, 1947), 88.

49. Ibid., 117.

50. Dawidowicz, ed., *A Holocaust Reader,* 133.

51. "The Corpse Factory," *The Times,* 17 April 1917.

52. Tony Kushner, *The Holocaust and the Liberal Imagination: A Social and Cultural History* (Oxford: Basil Blackwell, 1994), 56.

53. *Peoria Journal Transcript,* 9 March 1940, quoted in Deborah Lipstadt, *Beyond Belief: The American Press and the Coming of the Holocaust, 1933–1945* (New York: The Free Press, 1986), 137.

54. *Time,* 18 September 1939, quoted in Lipstadt, *Beyond Belief,* 137.

55. Jan Karski, *The Story of a Secret State* (Boston: Houghton Mifflin, 1944), esp. 339–52.

56. "Extermination of Polish Jewry: What Happened in the Warsaw Ghetto," *Polish Fortnightly Review,* no. 57 (1 December 1942), 3.

57. Quoted in Bernard Wasserstein, *Britain and the Jews of Europe 1939–1945* (Oxford: Clarendon Press, 1979), 172.

58. Ibid., 173.

59. Ibid., 309.

60. Ibid., 175.

61. Quoted in John Cornwell, *Hitler's Pope: The Secret History of Pius XII* (New York: Viking Press, 1999), 293.

62. See Appendix B: The First Korherr Report, attached to Georges Wellers, "The Number of Victims and the Korherr Report," in Serge Klarsfeld, ed., *The Holocaust and the Neo-Nazi Mythomania,* trans. Barbara Rucci (New York: Beate Klarsfeld Foundation, 1978), 177.

63. See letter, Rudolf Brandt to Richard Korherr, 10 April 1943, in Klarsfeld, ed., *The Holocaust and the Neo-Nazi Mythomania,* 194.

64. Appendix B in ibid., 206.

65. Ibid., italics indicate words underlined in the original.

66. Edmund Veesenmeyer, "Report on Hungary," in Jenö Lévai, ed., *Eichmann in Hungary: Documents* (New York: Howard Fertig, 1987), 58.

67. Ibid., 63.

68. Randolph J. Braham, *The Politics of Genocide: The Holocaust in Hungary,* 2 vols. (New York: Columbia University Press, 1981), vol., 391ff.

69. Dwork and van Pelt, *Auschwitz,* 337ff.

70. Rudolf Vrba with Alan Bestic, *I Cannot Forgive* (London: Sidgwick & Jackson, 1963), 197.

71. Ibid., 198.

72. Quoted in Martin Gilbert, *Auschwitz and the Allies* (London: Michael Joseph/Rainbird, 1981), 234.

73. Minutes of the session of the Council of Ministers, 29 March 1944, in Lévai, ed., *Eichmann in Hungary,* 66.

74. Braham, *The Politics of Genocide,* vol. 1, 418ff.

75. Letter, László Baky to the Minister of the Interior, in Lévai, ed., *Eichmann in Hungary,* 72.

76. Telegram, Veesenmeyer to the German Foreign Office, 23 April 1944, in ibid., 83.

77. Mária Ember, oral history conducted by Debórah Dwork, Paris, 28 May 1987, and subsequent conversations in Budapest, July 1987, transcript 3f.

78. Ibid., 5.

79. Ibid., 5f.; see also the discussion of the torture of Jews to compel them to surrender their valuables in Braham, *The Politics of Genocide,* vol. 1, 535, 572, 581f.

80. Mária Ember, oral history, transcript 6f.

81. Ibid., 7f.

82. András Garzó, oral history conducted by Debórah Dwork and Mária Ember (who interpreted from Hungarian to English and from English to Hungarian), Budapest, 16 and 18 July 1987, transcript 20f.

83. Mária Ember, oral history, transcript 9.

84. What they did not know, and what they could not know, was that conditions would be less harsh in Strasshof than in Auschwitz. Of the 21,000 Jews deported to Strasshof from Hungary, approximately 75 percent survived, including children. Lethal as was a 25 percent mortality rate, the comparable statistics for Hungarian Jews who were shipped to Auschwitz tell an even more bitter and bloody story. It was there that the vast majority were sent, and it was there that nearly all were killed. For older people and children up to the age of twelve or fourteen there was practically no hope at all, and for the rest only a very slim chance. See Braham, *Politics of Genocide,* vol. 2, 652, 674ff.

85. Alexander Ehrmann, oral history conducted by Debórah Dwork, West Bloomfield, MI, 15 November and 13 December 1986, 24 January 1987, transcript 34f.

86. Ibid., 37f.

87. Quoted in Gilbert, *Auschwitz and the Allies,* 251. Gilbert notes that the figure of 60,000 was a "telegraphic error." Lichtheim had the correct figure of 12,000 in his original message.

88. For the text of the eight-page summary, see Gilbert, *Auschwitz and the Allies,* 262ff.

89. Telegram, Leland Harrison to Secretary of State, 6 July 1944, containing a copy of Roswell McClelland's summary of the Vrba-Wetzler report to the War Refugee Board of the same date; in David S. Wyman, ed., *America and the Holocaust,* 13 vols. (New York and London: Garland, 1990), vol. 12, 71.

90. Ibid

91. Ibid., 74.

92. Daniel T. Brigham, "Two Death Camps Places of Horror," *The New York Times,* 6 July 1944, 6; see also "Czechs Report Massacre," *The New York Times,* 20 June 1944, 5.

93. Telegram, Veesenmeyer to German Foreign Office, 6 June 1944, in Lévai, ed., *Eichmann in Hungary,* 121.

94. Ibid

95. Braham, *The Politics of Genocide,* vol. 2, 762f.

96. German ultimatum to Horthy, 17 July 1944, in Lévai, ed., *Eichmann in Hungary,* 125.

Chapter Twelve: FROM WHENCE WOULD HELP COME?

1. Per Anger, *With Raoul Wallenberg in Budapest* (New York: Holocaust Library, 1981), 46.

2. On the War Refugee Board, see Henry L. Feingold, *The Politics of Rescue: The Roosevelt Administration and the Holocaust, 1938–1945* (New York: Holocaust Library, 1970), 248ff.; Saul S. Friedman, *No Haven for the Oppressed: United States Policy Toward Jewish Refugees, 1933–1945* (Detroit: Wayne State University Press, 1973), 215ff.; David S. Wyman, *The Abandonment of the Jews* (New York: Pantheon Books, 1984), 209ff.; and Monty Noam Penkower, *The Jews Were Expendable: Free World Diplomacy and the Holocaust* (Detroit: Wayne State University Press, 1988), 123ff.

3. On Wallenberg, see, inter alia: Per Anger, *With Raoul Wallenberg;* Jenö Levai, *Black Book on the Martyrdom of Hungarian Jewry* (Zurich: Central European Times, 1948), 381–82, 405–17; Jacques Derogy, *Le cas Wallenberg* (Paris: Editions Ramsay, 1980); John Bierman, *Righteous Gentile: The Story of Raoul Wallenberg, Missing Hero of the Holocaust* (New York: Viking Press, 1981); Frederick Werbell and Thurston Clarke, *Lost Hero: The Mystery of Raoul Wallenberg* (New York: McGraw-Hill, 1982); Kati Marton, *Wallenberg* (New York: Random House, 1982); Elenore Lester, *Wallenberg: The Man in the Iron Web* (Englewood Cliffs, NJ: Prentice-Hall, 1982); Elenore Lester, "Raoul Wallenberg: The Righteous Gentile from Sweden," in Randolph Braham and Bela Vago, eds., *The Holocaust in Hungary: Forty Years Later* (New York: Columbia University Press, 1985), 147–60; Robert Rozett, "Child Rescue in Budapest," *Holocaust and Genocide Studies,* vol. 2, no. 1 (1987), 49–59; George Barany, "The Current Stage of Research on Raoul Wallenberg," in Randolph L. Braham and Attila Pók, eds., *The Holocaust in Hungary: Fifty Years Later* (New York: Columbia University Press, 1997); and Paul L. Levine, *Indifference to Activism: Swedish Diplo-*

macy and the Holocaust, 1938–1944 (Uppsala: Uppsala University Library, 1998) 246f. See too an excellent master's thesis by Hans Ericsson, "A Chain of Rescue: Raoul Wallenberg in Budapest, 1944–1945" (2002), Center for Holocaust and Genocide Studies, Clark Univesity, Worcester, MA.

4. The fortitude and courage of Giorgio Perlasca, an Italian civilian who refused to return to German-ruled Italy and remained in Budapest to rescue Jews, is a special story. He worked with everybody, and is credited with having saved 3,500 Jews. See Enrico Deaglio, *La Banalita' del Bene: Storia di Giorgio Perlasca* (Milan: Feltrinelli, 1991).

5. Andrew Nagy, oral history conducted by Debórah Dwork, Ann Arbor, MI, 7 February 1986, transcript, 39f.

6. Norman Bentwich, *The Refugees from Germany: April 1935 to December 1935* (London: George Allen & Unwin, 1936), 86.

7. Chaim Weizmann, "The Jewish People and Palestine," in Meyer W. Weisgal, ed., *Chaim Weizmann: Statesman, Scientist, Builder of the Jewish Commonwealth* (New York: Dial Press, 1944), 306.

8. Ibid., 309.

9. John Hope Simpson, *Refugees: Preliminary Report of a Survey* (London: Royal Institute of International Affairs, 1938), 192.

10. Ibid., 193f.

11. Ibid., 195.

12. Ibid., 192f.

13. On the blockade, see W. N. Medlicott, *The Economic Blockade,* 2 vols. (London: His Majesty's Stationery Office, 1952–59).

14. Winston Churchill, *Blood, Sweat, and Tears* (New York: Putnam, 1941), 314.

15. See, inter alia, H. W. Koch, "The Spectre of a Separate Peace in the East: Russo-German 'Peace Feelers,' 1942–1944," *Journal of Contemporary History,* vol. 10 (1975), 531–49.

16. Quoted in Feingold, *The Politics of Rescue,* 207.

17. Quoted in Bernard Wasserstein, *Britain and the Jews of Europe, 1939–1945,* 2d edn. (London and New York: Leicester University Press, 1999), 219.

18. Great Britain, *Parliamentary Debates: House of Commons,* 5th series (London: His Majesty's Stationery Office, 1943), vol. 386, 31.

19. Victor Gollancz, *"Let My People Go": Some Practical Proposals for Dealing with Hitler's Massacre of the Jews and an Appeal to the British Public* (London: Victor Gollancz, 1943), 2f.

20. Jan Karski, *Story of a Secret State* (Boston: Houghton Mifflin, 1944), 326.

21. Ibid., 327.

22. On the Bermuda Conference, see Feingold, *The Politics of Rescue,* 167ff.; Friedman, *No Haven for the Oppressed,* 155ff.; Bernard Wasserstein, *Britain and the Jews of Europe 1939–1945* (Oxford: Clarendon Press, 1979), 188ff.; Irving Abella and Harold Troper, *None Is Too Many: Canada and the Jews of Europe 1933–1948* (New York: Random House, 1983), 126ff.; Wyman, *The Abandonment of the Jews,* 104ff.; and Penkower, *The Jews Were Expendable,* 98ff.

23. Quoted in Feingold, *The Politics of Rescue,* 198.

24. Ibid., 206.

25. Ibid.

26. Iza Erlich-Sznejerson, oral history, conducted by Debórah Dwork, New Haven, CT, 20 October, 2 November and 16 December 1993, 11 January 1994, transcript, part I, 67.

27. Ibid., part I, 82, 67.

28. For decades it was believed that Henryk Erlich had been killed by the Soviets. The family learned he had committed suicide only when the NKVD archives were opened after the fall of the Soviet Union—Iza Erlich-Sznejerson, oral history, transcript, part I, 8off.

29. Ibid., part I, 72.

30. Ibid., part II, 72f.

31. See, inter alia: David Kranzler, *Japanese, Nazis, and Jews: The Jewish Refugee Community of Shanghai, 1938–1945* (New York: Yeshiva University Press, 1976), 309–46; Zorach Warhaftig, *Refugee and Survivor: Rescue Efforts During the Holocaust* (Jerusalem: Yad Vashem, 1988), 91–190; Yukiko Sugihara, *Visas for Life,* trans. Hiroki Sugihara (San Francisco: Edu-Comm., 1995); Hillel Levine, *In Search of Sugihara* (New York: The Free Press, 1996); and Pamela Rotner Sakamoto, *Japanese Diplomats and Jewish Refugees* (Westport, CT: Praeger, 1998), 101–57.

32. Sugihara, *Visas for Life,* 10–19.

33. Iza Sznejerson, oral history, transcript, part II, 4.

34. His wife confirmed this frequently repeated account by refugees; see Sugihara, *Visas for Life,* 27.

35. See Manuel Franco, ed., *Spared Lives: The Actions of Three Portuguese Diplomats in World War II,* trans. Alexandra Andresen Leitao (Lisbon: Instituto Diplomatico-Ministerio dos Negócios Estrangeiros, 2000).

36. See, inter alia: Hugo Valentin, "Rescue Activities in Scandinavia," *YIVO Annual of Jewish Social Science,* vol. 8 (1953), 224–51; Harold Flender, *Rescue in Denmark* (New York: Holocaust Library, 1963); Leni Yahil, *The Rescue of Danish Jewry: Test of a Democracy,* trans. Morris Gradel (Philadelphia: Jewish Publication Society of America, 1969); Raul Hilberg, *The Destruction of the European Jews,* 3 vols. (New York: Holmes & Meier, 1985), vol. 2, 558–68; Tatiana Brustin-Berenstein, "The Historiographic Treatment of the Abortive Attempt to Deport the Danish Jews," *Yad Vashem Studies,* vol. 17 (1986), 181–218; Hans Kirchhoff, "*SS-Grupperführer* Werner Best and the Action Against the Danish Jews," *Yad Vashem Studies,* vol. 24 (1994), 195–222; Hans Kirchhoff, "Denmark: A Light in the Darkness of the Holocaust? A Reply to Gunnar Paulsson," *Journal of Contemporary History,* 30 (1995): 465–79; G. S. Paulsson, "The Bridge Over the Öresund: The Historiography on the Expulsion of the Jews from Nazi-Occupied Denmark," *Journal of Contemporary History,* 30 (1995), 171–75; Levine, *Indifference to Activism,* 229–45; and Hans Kirchhoff, "Denmark," in Walter Laqueur, ed., *The Holocaust Encyclopedia* (New Haven: Yale University Press, 2001), 145–48.

37. Quoted in Yehuda Bauer, *Jews for Sale? Nazi-Jewish Negotiations, 1933–1945* (New Haven and London: Yale University Press, 1994), 272.

38. On the Jews for trucks negotiations, see, inter alia: Jenö Levai, *Black Book on the Martyrdom of Hungarian Jewry* (Zurich: Central European Times, 1948), 270ff.; Alex Weissberg, *Advocate for the Dead: The Story of Joel Brand* (London: Andre Deutsch, 1958); André Biss, *A Million Jews to Save: Check to the Final Solution* (London: Hutchinson, 1973); Wasserstein, *Britain and the Jews of Europe,* 249ff.; Raul Hilberg, *The Destruction of the European Jews,* 3 vols. (New York and London: Holmes & Meier, 1985), vol. 2, 842ff.; and Bauer, *Jews for Sale?,* 145ff.

39. Gabor Czitrom, oral history conducted by Debórah Dwork, Paris, 30 June and 1 July 1987, transcript 14.

40. Ibid., 15.

41. Ibid., 20, 24.

42. See Bela Vago, "The Intelligence Aspects of the Joel Brand Mission," *Yad Vashem Studies,* vol. 10 (1974), 111–28.

43. Baven, *Jews for Sale,* 255f.

44. Braham, *Politics of Genocide,* vol. 2, 652, 674ff.

45. See, inter alia: Léon Poliakov and Jacques Sabille, *Jews Under Italian Occupation* (Paris: Centre de Documentation Juive Contemporaine, 1956); Renzo de Felice, *Storia degli ebrei italiani sotto il fascismo* (Turin: Einaudi, 1972), 392–402; Daniel Carpi, "The Rescue of the Jews in the Italian Zone of Occupied Croatia," in Yisrael Gutman and Efraim Zuroff, eds., *Rescue Attempts During the Holocaust* (Jerusalem: Yad Vashem, 1977), 468–506; Meir Michaelis, *Mussolini and the Jews: German Italian Relations and the Jewish Question in Italy, 1922–1945* (Oxford: Clarendon Press, 1978), 291–341; I. Herzer, K. Voigt, and J. Burgwyn, eds., *The Italian Refuge: Rescue of Jews During the Holocaust* (Washington, DC: Catholic University Press, 1989); and Jonathan Steinberg, *All or Nothing: The Axis and the Holocaust 1941–43* (London and New York: Routledge, 1990).

46. Quoted in Steinberg, *All or Nothing,* 53.

47. Ibid., 54.

48. Quoted in Carpi, "The Rescue of the Jews in the Italian Zone of Occupied Croatia," 495f.

49. See also Itzhak Garti, "The Living Conditions of Jewish Refugees from Yugoslavia Held as Civilian Prisoners of War in Fascist Italy up to the Fall of the Regime in July 1943," *Yad Vashem Studies,* vol. 25 (1996), 343–60.

50. Poliakov, *Jews Under Italian Occupation,* 148ff.; Carpi, "The Rescue of the Jews," 498ff.

51. Joseph Goebbels, *The Goebbels Diaries, 1942–1943,* ed. Louis P. Lochner (Garden City, NY: Doubleday, 1948), 241.

52. Quoted in Steinberg, *All or Nothing,* 93.

53. Ibid., 112.

54. Quoted in Asher Cohen, *Persécutations et sauvetages: Juifs et Français sous l'occupation et sous Vichy* (Paris: Cerf, 1993), 305.

55. For an analysis of these letters, see Cohen, *Persécutations et sauretages,* 305–08.

56. Margaret Ascher-Frydman, oral history conducted by Debórah Dwork, Paris, 5 June 1987, transcript 2.

57. Wladyslaw Bartoszewski, "On Both Sides of the Wall," in Wladyslaw Bartoszewski and Zofia Levin, eds., *Righteous Among Nations: How the Poles Helped the Jews, 1939–1945* (London: Earls Court Publications, 1969), lxxxiif.; also Philip Friedman, *Their Brothers' Keepers* (New York: Holocaust Library, 1978), 124.

58. Ewa Kurek-Lesik, "The Conditions of Admittance and the Social Background of Jewish Children Saved by Women's Religious Orders in Poland from 1939–1945," *Polin,* vol. 3 (1988), 244–75.

59. For a discussion of the role of the Catholic Church in general, and Pius XII in particular, see, inter alia: Leo Herbert Lehmann, *Vatican Policy in the Second World War* (New York: Agora, 1946); Daniel Carpi, "The Catholic Church and Italian Jewry Under Fascists," *Yad Vashem Studies,* vol. 4 (1960), 43–56; Carlo

Falconi, *Il silenzio di Pio XII* (Milan: Sugar Editore, 1965); Saul Friedlaender, *Pius XII and the Third Reich* (New York: Alfred A. Knopf, 1966); Meir Michaelis, *Mussolini and the Jews: German-Italian Relations and the Jewish Question in Italy* (Oxford: Clarendon Press, 1978); John F. Morley, *Vatican Diplomacy and the Jews During the Holocaust, 1939–1943* (New York: Ktav Publishing House, 1980); Michael Phayer, *The Catholic Church and the Holocaust, 1930–1965* (Bloomington: Indiana University Press, 2000); and Susan Zucotti, *Under His Very Windows: The Vatican and the Holocaust in Italy* (New Haven and London: Yale University Press, 2000).

60. The extent to which the Catholic institutions in Rome helped Jews during the occupation of that city has been the subject of some disagreement. Indeed, the specific question of the shelter and aid offered to the Jews of Rome during the nine-month occupation is a historical and historiographical chapter on its own. In 1961, the Jesuit priest Robert Leiber (who was a close associate of Pius XII) published the article, "Pio XII e gli Ebrei di Roma," in *La civilita cattolica* and *Stimmen der Zeit.* He adduced certain claims that reflected a great deal of help from the Church and its institutions. He maintained, for example, that over four thousand Jews were harbored by the Church during the occupation and that huge amounts of Vatican money were spent saving Jews. These distorted figures were subsequently repeated by excellent historians such as Guenter Lewy in his book, *The Catholic Church and Nazi Germany* (New York: McGraw-Hill, 1965), 301, and Renzo de Felice, *Storia degli ebrei italiani sotto il fascismo, 466–67.* Indeed, the latter work includes a short list from Leiber to provide an institutional breakdown of his earlier claim of some four thousand. In his book *The Pope's Jews* (London: Alcove Press, 1974), Sam Waagenaar challenged Leiber. On the basis of our research, we find Waagenaar's refutation convincing. Pope Pius XII did nothing. Many convents and monasteries helped—but not to the extent that Pius's close associate Robert Leiber claimed.

61. For the history of the Jews of Rome during the German occupation, see especially Giacomo Debenedetti, *16 ottobre 1943* (Rome: OET, 1945), and Robert Katz, *Black Sabbath* (New York: Macmillan, 1969). See also R. P. Capano, *La resistenza in Roma* (Naples: Gaetano Macchiaroli Editore, 1963); Alberto Giovannetti, *Roma città aperta* (Milan: Editrice Ancora, 1962); and Pinchas Lapide, *Three Popes and the Jews* (New York: Hawthorn Books, 1967).

62. Emma Fiorentino-Alatri, oral history conducted by Debórah Dwork, Rome, 2 June 1985, transcript 5.

63. Ibid.

64. Ibid., 7.

65. Sergio Tagliacozzo, oral history conducted by Debórah Dwork, Rome, June [n.d.] 1985, transcript 7.

66. See, inter alia: Centre de Documentation Juive Contemporaine, *L'Activité des organisations juives en France* (Paris: Editions du Centre, 1947); René Nodot, *Les Enfants ne partiront pas!* (Lyon: Nouvelle Lyonnaise, 1970); David Diamant, *Les Juifs dans la resistance française, 1940–1944—Avec armes ou sans armes* (Paris: Le Pavillon, 1971); Hillel Kieval, "Legality and Resistance in Vichy France: The Rescue of Jewish Children," *Proceedings of the American Philosophical Society,* vol. 124, no. 5 (1980), 355, 358–59; Anny Latour, *The Jewish Resistance in France* (New York: Holocaust Library, 1981); Lucien Lazare, *La Résistance juive en France* (Paris: Editions Stock, 1987), 208–11; and Lucien Lazare, *L'abbé Glasberg* (Paris: Cerf, 1990).

67. Georges Garel, "Travail clandestin de l'OSE. Témoignage de M. Georges Garel, Directeur-Général de l'Union O.S.E. à Paris," n.d., ms., Centre de Documentation Juive Contemporaine (CDJC), Document CCXVIII-104, 1f.

68. Lily Garel-Taget, oral history conducted by Debórah Dwork, Paris, 19 June 1987, transcript 4.

69. Ibid.

70. Elisabeth Hirsch, oral history conducted by Debórah Dwork, Neuilly-sur-Seine, France, 25 June 1987, transcript 24.

71. Garel, "Travail clandestin de l'OSE," 2.

72. See testimony of Magda Trocmé on this point in Pierre Sauvage's documentary film *Weapons of the Spirit* (1989). On the question of motivation, see Philip Hallie, *Lest Innocent Blood Be Shed* (New York: Harper & Row, 1980).

73. In her doctoral dissertation, Christine van der Zanden has widened the lens to explore rescue activities throughout the plateau Vivarais-Lignon. She has focused less on motivation for rescue and more sharply on process: precisely how the initiative unfolded, and how it was managed day to day. She also has focused on the Jews who found shelter on the plateau. "The Plateau of Hospitality: Jewish Refugee Life on the Plateau Vivarais-Lignon," Ph.D. diss., Center for Holocaust and Genocide Studies, Clark University, Worcester, MA. See too Philippe Boegner, *"Ici on a aimé les juifs"* (Paris: J.-C. Lattes, 1982); Pierre Bolle, *Le Plateau Vivarais-Lignon: Acceuil et Résistance* (Le Chambon-sur-Lignon, France: Société d'histoire de la montagne, 1992); Marc Donadille, "Le Coteau Fleuri at le Chambon-sur-Lignon," in Jeanne Merle d'Aubigne and Vilette Mouchons, eds., *God's Underground* (St. Louis: Bethany Press, 1970); Hallie, *Lest Innocent Blood be Shed;* Carol Rittner and Sondra Myers, *The Courage to Care* (New York: New York University Press, 1986), 97–119; Pierre Sauvage, "A Most Persistent Haven: Le Chambon-sur-

Lignon," *Moment* (October 1983); and Sabine Zeitoun, *Ces enfants qu'il fallait sauver* (Paris: Albin Michel, 1989), 211–44.

74. Naomi Lévi, oral history conducted by Debórah Dwork, Paris, 22 May 1987, transcript 5ff.

75. Cirlène Liberman-Zinger, oral history conducted by Debórah Dwork, Paris, 23 May 1987, transcript 4–5.

Chapter Thirteen: RESCUE

1. Centre de Documentation Juive Contemporaine (CDJC), *L'Activité des organisations juives en France* (Paris: Editions du Centre, 1947), 157ff.; also Georges Garel, "Travail clandestin de l'OSE. Témoignage de M. Georges Garel, Directeur-Général de l'Union O.S.E. à Paris," n.d., ms., CDJC, Document CCXVIII-104, 3ff.

2. CDJC, *L'Activité des organisations juives,* 141f; also Garel, "Travail clandestin de l'OSE," Document CCXVIII-104, 8f.; "Exposé sur le circuit Garel," ms., CDJC, Document CCXVI-12a; "La situation actuelle du judaisme en France," ms., July 1941, CDJC, Document CCLXVI-16, 25. According to this report, 1,000–1,200 children were evacuated by OSE-Nord from the occupied zone to the south.

3. "Exposé sur le circuit Garel," ms., CDJC, Document CCXVI-12a, 1.

4. Ibid., 1f. According to a statement by the American Joint Distribution Committee, OSE was responsible for smuggling two thousand children into Switzerland. "American Joint Distribution Committee," ms., CDJC Document CCCLXVI-14, 5.; also Bruno-Georges Loinger, oral history conducted by Debórah Dwork, Paris, 25 June 1987, transcript 1ff.

5. "Exposé sur le circuit Garel," Document CCXVI-12a, 1f.; Garel, "Travail clandestin de l'OSE," Document CCXVIII-104, 3ff.

6. Irene Tomaszewski and Tecia Werbowski, *Zegota: The Council for Aid to Jews in Occupied Poland, 1942–1945* (Montreal: Price-Patterson, 1999), 55ff.

7. See Nahum Bogner, "The Convent Children: The Rescue of Jewish Children in Polish Convents During the Holocaust," *Yad Vashem Studies,* vol. 27 (1999), 235–86.

8. See Wladyslaw Bartoszewski, "On Both Sides of the Wall," and Irena Sendler, "People Who Helped Jews," both in Wladyslaw Bartoszewski and Zofia Lewin, eds., *Righteous Among Nations: How Poles Helped the Jews, 1939–1945* (London: Earls Court Publications, 1969), xliv–lii and 41–62 (see also the section, "Under the Wings of 'Zegota,'" 41–108); Kazimierz Iranek-Osmecki, *He Who Saves One Life* (New York: Crown Publishers, 1971), 139–51, 224–26, 234–37, 315–16; Yisrael Gutman, "The Attitude of the Poles to the Mass Deportations of Jews from the Warsaw Ghetto in the Summer of 1942," and Joseph Kermish, "The Activities of the Council for the Aid to Jews ('Zegota') in Occupied Poland," both in Yisrael Gutman and Efraim Zuroff, eds., *Rescue Attempts During the Holocaust* (Jerusalem: Yad Vashem, 1977), 413–14, 367–98 (see also the debate, 451–63); Philip Friedman, *Their Brothers' Keepers* (New York: Holocaust Library, 1978), 118–21; Yisrael Gutman and Shmuel Krakowski, *Unequal Victims: Poles and Jews During World War II* (New York: Holocaust Library, 1986), 252–99; Teresa Prekerowa, "The Relief Council for Jews in Poland, 1942–1945," in Chimen Abramsky, Maciej Jachimczyk, and Antony Polonsky, eds., *The Jews in Poland* (London: Basil Blackwell, 1986), 161–76; and Tomaszewski and Werbowski, *Zegota,* 59–65.

9. Marianne Marco-Braun, oral history conducted by Debórah Dwork, London, 9 May 1987, transcript 8ff.

10. Ida Groenewegen van Wyck-Roose, Cor Grootendorst, and Truus Grootendorst-Vermeer, oral histories conducted by Debórah Dwork, Nieuw Vennep, the Netherlands, 1 July 1986, transcript 3.

11. Ibid., 4.

12. Virrie Cohen, oral history conducted by Debórah Dwork, Amsterdam, 19 June 1986, transcript 1f.; Anita van Ommeren and Ageeth Scherphuis, "De Crèche, 1942–1943," *Vrij Nederland,* 18 January 1986, 2–21; Jacob Presser, *The Destruction of the Dutch Jews* (New York: Dutton & Co., 1969), 281–82.

13. Groenewegen, Grootendorst, and Grootendorst, oral histories, transcript 8; Semmy Riekerk-Glasoog, oral history conducted by Debórah Dwork, Amsterdam, 4 July 1986, transcript 19.

14. Semmy Riekerk-Glasoog, oral history, transcript 20. Of the five people at that original meeting, only Semmy Riekerk-Glasoog is still living. Jaap Musch was caught by the Germans on 7 September 1944 and shot on the spot for his underground activities. Theo Woortman was arrested on 19 July 1944 in Amsterdam and sent to Amersfoort. On 4 September he was deported to Bergen-Belsen, where he died on 12 March 1945. Gerard Musch and Dick Groenewegen were arrested in Amsterdam's central railway station on 9 May 1944. Both were deported, Dick to Burscheid (via Amersfoort) and Gerard to Sachsenhausen (via Vught). Both survived and died of natural causes much later (Musch in 1979 and Groenewegen in 1985). For a history of the N.V., see the journalist Max Arian's personal and historical account, "Het grote kinderspel," in *De Groene Amsterdammer,* 4 May 1983, 5ff.; and his interview with Semmy Riekerk in the same issue, 10ff. See also Bert-Jan Flim, *Omdat Hun Hart Sprak: Geschiendenis van de Georganiseered Hulp aan Joodse Kinderen in Nederland, 1942–1945* (The Hague: Kok Kampen, 1996), 230ff., 330ff.

15. Rebecca van Delft, letter to Debórah Dwork, Graft-de Rijp, the Netherlands, 16 June 1986.
16. Ibid.
17. Jooske Koppen-de Neve, oral history conducted by Debórah Dwork, Amerongen, the Netherlands, 7 August 1987, transcript 9, 3f.
18. Virrie Cohen, oral history, transcript 2f.
19. Marion Pritchard-van Binsbergen, oral history conducted by Debórah Dwork, New Haven, CT, 6 June and 31 July 1994; Wellfleet, MA., 2 and 3 August 1994; Vershire, VT, 24 October 1994, transcript, part I, 48.
20. Ibid., part II, 49.
21. Ibid., part II, 65ff.
22. Ibid., part I, 8, 70, 62, 74; see too the documentary film, *Courage to Care,* and Gay Block and Malka Drucker, *Rescuers: Portraits of Moral Courage in the Holocaust* (New York: TV Books), 59–68.
23. Marion Pritchard-van Binsbergen, oral history conducted by Debórah Dwork, Worcester, MA, 20 August 2001, tape.
24. Marion Pritchard-van Binsbergen, oral history, transcript, part I, 81ff.
25. Sara Spier, oral history conducted by Debórah Dwork, Amsterdam, 20 June 1984, transcript 5.
26. Emmanuel Ringelblum, *Polish-Jewish Relations During the Second World War* (New York: Howard Fertig, 1976), 226.
27. Ibid., 229.
28. Marion Pritchard-van Binsbergen, oral history, transcript, part II, 44f.
29. Yona Nadelman-Kuntsler, oral history conducted by Debórah Dwork, London, 7, 11, and 12 July 1985, transcript 55f, 60f.
30. Salvador Bloemgarten, oral history conducted by Debórah Dwork and Robert Jan van Pelt, Amsterdam, 18 June 1986, transcript 11.
31. Martin Koby, oral history conducted by Debórah Dwork, Ann Arbor, MI, 11 and 25 November 1987, transcript 49.
32. Herta Montrose-Heymans, oral history conducted by Debórah Dwork, Cardiff, Wales, 21 July 1985, transcript 11, 14.
33. Paul Sved, oral history conducted by Debórah Dwork, London, 14 May 1987, transcript 3.
34. Victor Gollancz, *"Let My People Go": Some Practical Proposals for Dealing with Hitler's Massacre of the Jews and an Appeal to the British Public* (London: Victor Gollancz, 1943), 8.
35. Quoted in Ian Hamilton, *Koestler: A Biography* (London: Secker & Warburg, 1982), 77.
36. Ruth Andreas-Friedrich, *Berlin Underground 1938–1945,* trans. Barrows Mussey (New York: Henry Holt & Co., 1947), 116ff.

Chapter Fourteen: THE CONCENTRATION CAMP WORLD

1. The vast bibliography on the German concentration camps spans many languages. This selection focuses on some of the important books in English. Early classics in the literature are Eugen Kogon, *The Theory and Practice of Hell: The German Concentration Camps and the System Behind Them,* trans. Heinz Norden (New York: Farrar, Strauss & Co, 1950); David Rousset, *The Other Kingdom,* trans. Ramon Guthrie (New York: Reynal & Hitchcock, 1947); and in a literary vein, Tadeusz Borowski, *This Way for the Gas, Ladies and Gentlemen,* trans. Barbara Vedder (New York: Viking Press, 1967), and Primo Levi, *Survival in Auschwitz,* trans. Stuart Woolf (New York: Touchstone, 1996). An important early political interpretation is Hannah Arendt, "The Image of Hell," in Hannah Arendt, *Essay in Understanding, 1930–1954,* ed. Jerome Kohn (New York, San Diego, and London: Harcourt Brace & Co., 1994), 197–205. A good introduction to the scope and history of the concentration camps is provided by Konnilyn G. Feig, *Hitler's Death Camps: The Sanity of Madness* (New York and London: Holmes & Meier, 1981), and Martin Broszat, "The Concentration Camps, 1933–45," in Helmut Krausnick, Hans Buchheim, Martin Broszat, and Hans-Adolf Jacobsen, eds. *Anatomy of the SS State,* trans. Richard Barry, Marian Jackson, and Dorothy Long (New York: Walker & Co., 1968), 397–504. For more recent studies on the concentration camp system, see Klaus Drobisch and Guenther Wieland, *Das System der NS-Konsentrationslager, 1933–1939* (Berlin: Akademie, 1993); Karin Orth, *Das System der nationalsozialischen Konsentrationslager: Eine Politische Organisationsgeschichte* (Hamburg: Hamburger Edition, 1999). A very useful collection of articles is Yisrael Gutman and Avital Saf, eds., *The Nazi Concentration Camps; Structure and Aims—The Image of the Prisoner—The Jews in the Camps* (Jerusalem: Yad Vashem, 1984). On the history of the largest camp, see Debórah Dwork and Robert Jan van Pelt, *Auschwitz: 1270 to the Present* (New York and London: W. W. Norton, 1996).
2. See Dwork and van Pelt, *Auschwitz,* 100ff.; also Broszat, "The Concentration Camps, 1933–45," 397ff.; Falk Pringel, "The Concentration Camps as Part of the National-Socialist System of Domination," in

Gutman and Saf, eds., *The Nazi Concentration Camps,* 7ff.; and Aharon Weiss, "Categories of Camps," in ibid., 117ff.

3. Leni Yahil, "Jews in Concentration Camps in Germany Prior to World War II," in Gutman and Saf, eds., *The Nazi Concentration Camps,* 69–100.

4. David A. Hackett, ed., *The Buchenwald Report* (Boulder, CO, and Oxford: Westview Press, 1995), 169f.

5. Broszat, "The Concentration Camps," 458.

6. Hackett, ed., *The Buchenwald Report,* 247f.

7. By the end of war, some Jews could have ended up in more than twenty different types of camps. These included *Durchgangslager* (DuLag or transit camps), *Firmenlager* or *Judenlager* (Fl or company camp for Jewish forced laborers), *Judenarbeitslager* (*JAL* or labor camp for Jews), *Judenaufangslager* (*JauL,* or reception camp for Jews), *Konzentrationslager* (*KL* or concentration camp), *Lager für Ausländische Juden* (*LAJ* or camp for foreign Jews), *Restgetto* (*RG,* or residual ghetto), *Sammellager* (*SaL* or assembly camp), *Schutzhaftlager* (*SchHL* or protective custody camp), *Straflager* (*SL* or punishment camp), *Zwangarbeitslager* (*ZAL* or forced labor camp); see Martin Weinmann with Anne Kaiser and Ursula Krause-Schmitt, *Das national-sozialistische Lagersystem* (Frankfurt-am-Main: Zweitausendeins, 1990); also Aharon Weiss, "Categories of Camps," in Gutman and Saf, eds., *The Nazi Concentration Camps,* 115–32.

8. For a collection of excellent oral histories of surviving *Sonderkommandos,* see Gideon Greif, *Wir weinten tränenlos: Augenzeugenberichte der jüdischen "Sonderkommandos" in Auschwitz* (Cologne, Weimar, and Vienna: Böhlau, 1995); an important memoir is Filip Müller, *Auschwitz Inferno: The Testimony of a Sonderkommando,* with Helmut Freitag, trans. Susanne Flatauer (London: Routledge & Kegan Paul, 1979). See also the very important reflections on the fate of the *Sonderkommandos* in Primo Levi, *The Drowned and the Saved,* trans. Raymond Rosenthal (New York: Summit Books, 1988), 50ff.

9. Gradowski was forced into the *Sonderkommando,* and he was one of the leaders in their revolt. Expecting to die, he buried his journal in an aluminum canteen. He had calculated correctly. The uprising failed, and the Germans crushed his skull. His journal and an accompanying letter were uncovered when the Russians liberated the camp in 1945—Nathan Cohen, "Diaries of the Sonderkommandos in Auschwitz: Coping with Fate and Reality," *Yad Vashem Studies,* vol. 20 (1990), 276ff.

10. Salmen Gradowski, "Diary," in Jadwiga Bezwinska and Danuta Czech, eds., *Amidst a Nightmare of Crime: Manuscripts of Members of Sonderkommando,* trans. Krystyna Michalik (Oswiecim: State Museum at Oswiecim, 1973), 81.

11. Ibid., 82f.

12. Ibid., 95, 98.

13. Ibid., 99f.

14. Ibid., 104f.

15. On the history of Auschwitz, see Yisrael Gutman and Michael Berenbaum, eds., *Anatomy of the Auschwitz Death Camp* (Bloomington and Indianapolis: Indiana University Press, 1994); Danuta Czech, *Auschwitz Chronicle: 1939–1945,* trans. Barbara Harshav, Martha Humphreys, and Stephen Shearier (New York: Henry Hold & Co., 1990); and Dwork and van Pelt, *Auschwitz: 1270 to the Present.* Important sources are Rudolf Höss, *Death Dealer: The Memoirs of the SS Kommandant at Auschwitz,* ed. Steven Paskuly, trans. Andrew Pollinger (Buffalo: Prometheus Books, 1992) and H. G. Adler, H. Langbein, and Ella Lingens-Reiner, eds., *Auschwitz: Zeugnisse and Berichte* (Frankfurt-am-Main: Athenäum Verlag, 1988).

16. Sara Grossman-Weil, oral history conducted by Debórah Dwork, Malverne, NY, 29–30 April 1987, transcript 27.

17. Ibid., 28.

18. Ibid.

19. Sara and the other women admitted that they were not tattooed. In the summer of 1944, those Jews who arrived in Auschwitz for selection only, and who were destined from the very beginning for labor elsewhere, were not registered in the camp, and therefore not given a number.

20. Sara Grossman-Weil, oral history, transcript 29.

21. Ibid., 29–30.

22. Ibid., 30–31.

23. See Livia Rothkirchen, "The 'Final Solution' in Its Last Stages," *Yad Vashem Studies,* vol. 8 (1970), 7ff.

24. See Marek Orski, "The Jewish Subsidiary of the Stutthof Concentration Camp (Konzentrationslager Stutthof) at Brusy-Dziemiany (1944–1945)," *Yad Vashem Studies,* vol. 22 (1992), 273–86.

25. Alexander Ehrmann, oral history conducted by Debórah Dwork, 15 November and 13 December 1986, 24 January 1987, transcript, part II, 4f.

26. Ibid., part II, 8f.

27. Henry Starkman, oral history conducted by Debórah Dwork, 8 December 1984, 19 January 1985, West Bloomfield, MI, transcript 54.

28. Ibid, 55f.

29. Ibid., 56ff.
30. Ibid., 59f.
31. Ibid., 67ff.
32. Ibid., 75f.
33. Helga Kinsky-Pollack, oral history conducted by Debórah Dwork, 15 August 1989, Vienna, transcript 40, 37.
34. Ellen Eliel-Wallach, oral history conducted by Debórah Dwork, Amsterdam, 3 August 1987, transcript 30.
35. Mira Teeman, oral history conducted by Debórah Dwork, Stockholm, 6 September 1995, transcript 27, 30.
36. Ibid., 30.
37. Thomas Krause, *Plattenhaus Poppenbüttel,* Geschichte des KZ-Aussenlagers Hamburg-Sasel (Hamburg-Porträt Nr.25) (Hamburg: Museum für Hamburgische Geschichte, 1990), 167; 325. See also Hermann Kaienburg, *Das Konzentrationslager Neuengamme, 1938–1945* (Bonn: Dietz, 1997).
38. Mira Teeman, oral history, transcript 31.
39. Ibid., 31f.
40. Ibid., 32f.
41. Ibid., 33ff.
42. See Shmuel Krakowski, "The Death Marches in the Period of the Evacuation of the Camps," in Gutman and Saf, eds., *The Nazi Concentration Camps,* 475–89; Daniel Blatman, "The Death Marches, January-May 1945: Who Was Responsible for What?" *Yad Vashem Studies,* vol. 28 (2000), 203–42.
43. The basic source of information on Bergen-Belsen is the record of the Belsen trial held in the fall of 1945 in the German city of Lüneburg, and hence also known as the Lüneburg trial; see Raymond Phillips, ed., *Trial of Josef Kramer and Forty-Four Others (The Belsen Trial)* (London, Edinburgh, and Glasgow: William Hodge & Co., 1949); also Eberhard Kolb, "Bergen-Belsen, 1943–1945," in Gutman and Saf, eds., *The Nazi Concentration Camps,* 331–42.
44. Hannah Kent-Starkman, oral history conducted by Debórah Dwork, Stamford, CT, 13 December 1985, 15 July 1995, transcript 30f.
45. Ibid., 33f.
46. Ibid., 35f.
47. Henry Starkman, oral history, transcript 69ff.
48. Ibid., 70.
49. Alexander Ehrmann, oral history, transcript, part II, 11ff.
50. Sara Grossman-Weil, oral history, transcript 34.
51. Ibid.
52. Ibid, 34f.
53. See Jon Bridgman, *The End of the Holocaust: The Liberation of the Camps* (Portland, OR: Areopagitica Press, 1990), and Joanne Reilly, *Belsen: The Liberation of a Concentration Camp* (London and New York: Routledge, 1998); also Norbert Frei, "'Wir waren blind, ungläubig und langsam' Buchenwald, Dachau und die amerikanischen Medien im Frühjahr 1945," *Vierteljahreshefte für Zeitgeschichte,* vol. 35 (1987), 385–401; Harold Marcuse, *Legacies of Dachau: The Uses and Abuses of a Concentration Camp, 1933–2001* (Cambridge: Cambridge University Press, 2001), 52ff.
54. Quoted in Desmond Hawkins, ed., *War Report: D-Day to VE-Day* (London: BBC Books, 1994), 318.

Epilogue

1. Sara Spier, oral history conducted by Debórah Dwork, Amsterdam, 27 June 1984, transcript 4.
2. Ibid., 31.
3. See David S. Wyman, ed., *The World Reacts to the Holocaust* (Baltimore and London: Johns Hopkins University Press, 1996).
4. On the use of words as camouflage, see Nachman Blumenthal, "On the Nazi Vocabulary," *Yad Vashem Studies,* vol. 1 (1957), 59ff.;Shaul Esh, "Words and Their Meaning: 25 Examples of Nazi-Idiom," *Yad Vashem Studies,* vol. 4 (1960), 154ff.
5. Lucy S. Dawidowicz, ed., *A Holocaust Reader* (New York: Behrman House, 1976), 133.
6. Quoted in Robert Jan van Pelt, *The Case for Auschwitz: Evidence from the Irving Trial* (Bloomington and Indianapolis: Indiana University Press, 2002), 297.
7. On the reconstruction of war-torn societies in Europe, see David W. Ellwood, *Rebuilding Europe: Western Europe, America and Postwar Reconstruction* (London and New York: Longman, 1992).
8. Michael R. Marrus, "The Holocaust at Nuremberg," *Yad Vashem Studies,* vol. 26 (1998), 5–42.
9. International Military Tribunal, *Trial of the Major War Criminals,* 41 vols. (Nuremberg: Secretariat of the Tribunal, 1947–49), vol. 5, 373.

10. Ibid., vol. 5, 407.

11. Ibid., vol. 5, 412.

12. Ibid., vol. 7, 153.

13. Ibid., vol. 19, 404.

14. Ibid., vol. 19, 497.

15. Ibid., vol. 19, 501.

16. Ibid., vol. 1, 247ff.

17. See Dalia Ofer, "Israel," in Wyman, ed., *The World Reacts to the Holocaust,* 864ff.

18. Ibid., 873ff.

19. See also Marion Muskat, "The Concept 'Crime Against the Jewish People' in the Light of International Law," *Yad Vashem Studies,* vol. 5 (1963), 237–54.

20. State of Israel, Ministry of Justice, *The Trial of Adolf Eichmann: Record of Proceedings in the District Court of Jerusalem,* 5 vols. (Jerusalem: Trust for the Publication of the Eichmann Trial, 1992), vol. 1, 62.

21. Ibid.

22. Martha Gellhorn, "Eichmann and the Private Conscience," *Atlantic Monthly,* vol. 209 (February 1962), 54.

23. See Debórah Dwork and Robert Jan van Pelt, "The Netherlands," in Wyman, ed., *The World Reacts to the Holocaust,* 61ff.

24. Abel J. Herzberg, *Kroniek der Jodenvervolging, 1940–1945* (Amsterdam: Meulenhoff, 1985), 9.

25. Louis de Jong, *De Bezetting: Tekst en beeldmateriaal van de uitzendingen van de Nederlandse Televisie-Stichting over het Koninkrijk der Nederlanden in de Tweede Wereldoorlog, 1940–1945* (Amsterdam: Querido, 1966), 353.

26. Jacob Presser, *Ondergang: De Vervolging en Verdelging van het Nederlandse Jodendom 1940–1945,* 2 vols. (The Hague: Staatsuitgeverij/Martinus Nijhoff, 1965), vol. 1, viii.

27. "Monument," *Algemeen Handelsblad,* 24 April 1965.

28. Han Lammers in *De Groene Amsterdammer,* 24 April 1965.

29. B. Buitenrust Hettema, "Waarom Presser niet?" *Nieuwe Rotterdamse Courant,* 4 May 1965.

30. See van Pelt, *The Case for Auschwitz,* 23ff.

31. Quoted in Gill Seidel, *The Holocaust Denial: Antisemitism, Racism and the New Right* (Leeds: Beyond the Pale Collective, 1986), 99.

32. Quoted in Ibid., 101.

33. Letter, Faurisson to *Le Monde,* 29 December 1978, quoted in Robert Faurisson, *Mémoire en défense contre ceux qui m'accusent de falsifier l'histoire/La question des chambres à gaz,* preface by Noam Chomsky (Paris: La Vieille Taupe, 1980), 73.

34. Primo Levi, *Corriere della Sera,* 3 January 1979, quoted in Myriam Anissimov, *Primo Levi: Tragedy of an Optimist,* trans. Steve Cox (Woodstock, NY: Overlook Press, 1999), 331f.

35. Van Pelt, *The Case for Auschwitz,* 29.

36. Ibid., 42ff.

37. Jan Tomasz Gross, *Neighbors: The Destruction of the Jewish Community in Jedwabne, Poland* (Princeton: Princeton University Press, 2001).

38. Emil Fackenheim, *The Jewish Return into History* (New York: Schocken Books, 1978), 106.

Index